CLASSICAL SOCIOLOGICAL THEORY

CLASSICAL SOCIOLOGICAL THEORY

George Ritzer
University of Maryland

McGRAW-HILL, INC.

New York   St. Louis   San Francisco   Auckland   Bogotá
Caracas   Lisbon   London   Madrid   Mexico   Milan   Montreal
New Delhi   Paris   San Juan   Singapore   Sydney   Tokyo   Toronto

This book was set in Palatino by Arcata Graphics/Kingsport.
The editors were Phillip A. Butcher and Ira C. Roberts;
the production supervisor was Denise L. Puryear.
The cover was designed by Rafael Hernandez.
R. R. Donnelley & Sons Company was printer and binder.

CLASSICAL SOCIOLOGICAL THEORY

ISBN 0-07-052972-8

4 5 6 7 8 9 0   DOC DOC   9 0 9 8 7 6 5 4 3

Library of Congress Cataloging-in-Publication Data

Ritzer, George.
    Classical sociological theory / George Ritzer.
        p.   cm.
    Includes bibliographical references and index.
    ISBN 0-07-052972-8
    1. Sociology—History.   2. Sociology—Methodology—History.
3. Sociologists—Biography.
HM19.R48   1992
301′.01—dc20   91-19189

PERMISSIONS ACKNOWLEDGMENTS

Text

Chapter 3: Excerpts from Auguste Comte, *A General View of Positivism,* tr. by J. H. Bridges. New York: Robert Speller & Sons, Publishers, Inc., 1957. Used by permission of the publisher.

Chapter 5: Excerpts from Karl Marx, *The Economic and Philosophic Manuscripts of 1844,* ed. by Dirk K. Struik. © 1964 by International Publishers Co., Inc. Excerpts from Karl Marx, *Capital,* vol. 1. © 1967 by International Publishers Co., Inc. Both used by permission of the publisher.

Chapter 7: Excerpts from Max Weber, *Economy and Society,* 2 vols., ed. by Guenther Roth and Claus Wittich, tr. by the editors and others. Copyright © 1978 The Regents of the University of California. Used by permission of The University of California Press.

Chapter 8: Excerpts from Georg Simmel, *The Philosophy of Money,* ed. and tr. by Tom Bottomore and David Frisby. London: Routledge and Kegan Paul. Copyright 1907, 1978. Used by permission of Routledge.

Chapter 9: Excerpts from George Herbert Mead, *Mind, Self, and Society,* ed. and introduced by Charles W. Morris. Copyright 1934 by The University of Chicago. Copyright 1962 by Charles W. Morris.

Excerpts from Leonard S. Cottrell, Jr., "George Herbert Mead: The Legacy of Social Behaviorism," in Robert K. Merton and Matilda White Riley, eds., *Sociological Traditions from Generation to Generation: Glimpses of the American Experience.* © 1980. Used by permission of Ablex Publishing Corp., Norwood, NJ.

Chapter 10: Excerpts from Alfred Schutz, *Collected Papers I: The Problem of Social Reality,* ed. and introduced by Maurice Natanson with a preface by H. L. Van Breda. The Hague: Martinus Nijhoff, 1962, 1973, 1990. Copyright 1962 by Martinus Nijhoff, The Hague, Netherlands. All rights reserved, including the right to translate or to reproduce this book or parts thereof in any form.

Chapter 11: Excerpts reprinted with permission of The Free Press, a Division of Macmillan, Inc. from THE SOCIAL SYSTEM by Talcott Parsons. Copyright © 1951, renewed 1979 by Talcott Parsons. Excerpts from Robert K. Merton, "Remembering the Young Talcott Parsons," *American Sociologist,* 15 (1980). Used by permission of The American Sociological Association.

Figures

Figures 11.1 and 11.3 reprinted by permission of the publishers from THE AMERICAN UNIVERSITY by Talcott Parsons and Gerald Platt, Cambridge, MA: Harvard University Press, Copyright © 1973 by the President and Fellows of Harvard College.

Figure 11.2 from Talcott Parsons, SOCIETIES: Evolutionary and Comparative Perspectives, © 1966. Adapted by permission of Prentice Hall, Englewood Cliffs, New Jersey.

Photos

Page   6:   Culver Pictures
Page 29:   National Library of Medicine
Page 46:   Courtesy, University of Chicago
Page 52:   Courtesy, American Sociological Association
Page 60:   Courtesy, Howard Press
Page 84:   Culver Pictures
Page 110:   Culver Pictures
Page 148:   The Granger Collection, New York
Page 184:   The Bettmann Archive
Page 214:   The Granger Collection, New York
Page 262:   The Granger Collection, New York
Page 294:   Courtesy, University of Chicago
Page 318:   Courtesy, Estate of Alfred Schutz
Page 342:   The Granger Collection, New York

ABOUT THE AUTHOR

GEORGE RITZER is Professor of Sociology at the University of Maryland. His major areas of interest are sociological theory and the sociology of work. He has served as Chair of the American Sociological Association's sections on Theoretical Sociology (1989–1990) and Organizations and Occupations (1980–1981). Professor Ritzer has been Distinguished Scholar-Teacher at the University of Maryland and has been awarded a Teaching Excellence award. He has held a Fulbright-Hays Fellowship and been Scholar-in-Residence at the Netherlands Institute for Advanced Study and the Swedish Collegium for Advanced Study in the Social Sciences.

In 1992 McGraw-Hill will publish the third editions of Professor Ritzer's basic texts in sociological theory—*Sociological Theory* and *Contemporary Sociological Theory*—that have been adopted in many countries, as well as throughout the United States and Canada, in undergraduate and graduate courses in social theory.

Dr. Ritzer's main theoretical interests lie in metatheory as well as in the theory of rationalization. In metatheory, his most recent book is *Metatheorizing in Sociology* (Lexington Books, 1991). Earlier books on this topic include *Sociology: A Multiple Paradigm Science* (1975, 1980) and *Toward an Integrated Sociological Paradigm* (1981). He has written a number of essays on rationalization as well as the soon-to-be published *The McDonaldization of Society* (Pine Forge Press, 1993).

TO MOTHER
with Appreciation
and Love

CONTENTS

LIST OF BIOGRAPHICAL SKETCHES

PREFACE

*T*HIS first edition of a text in classical sociological theory has its roots in the earlier editions of my book, *Sociological Theory,* that covered both classical and contemporary theory. Many of the users of that text taught classical sociological theory and thus were able to use only about half of the chapters. They wanted a text that focused on classical theory. This book responds to that need.

The base of this book is six revised and updated chapters, as well as the Appendix, from *Sociological Theory.* This book opens with the two chapters on the history of sociological theory, includes core chapters on Karl Marx, Emile Durkheim, Max Weber, and Georg Simmel, and closes with the Appendix on sociological metatheorizing as well as the metatheoretical schema used as a mode of analysis throughout the text.

Five chapters have been added to that core to produce a full-fledged analysis of classical sociological theory. Following the two introductory historical chapters are chapters devoted to the early figures in sociological theory—Auguste Comte and Herbert Spencer. The text then moves on to the chapters devoted to Marx, Durkheim, Weber, and Simmel. I was then confronted with the decision of whether to deal in depth with other early theorists (some notable possibilities were Pareto, Cooley, and Tocqueville), or to insert into the classical tradition more recent theorists. I opted to proceed in the latter direction and the text, therefore, closes with chapters devoted to the ideas of George Herbert Mead, Alfred Schutz, and Talcott Parsons. In my view, as time moves on, these thinkers are clearly becoming part of the classical tradition. Furthermore, their theories resemble those of the other classical theorists in terms of their scope and ambition. Finally, they are included, like the other theorists covered in this text, because of their continuing relevance to sociological theory. Thus, while this is a book about classical theory, it covers the work of thinkers whose ideas in varying ways, and to varying degrees, continue to be relevant to contemporary sociological theory.

I would like to thank several of my graduate students for their help in the preparation of this book—Pam Gindoff, Terri LeMoyne, Shanyang Zhao, and particularly Jie Yang. Ira Roberts, Editing Supervisor, on this project for McGraw-Hill, was invaluable in the final production of this book. I would also like to thank Phil Butcher, Executive Editor at McGraw-Hill, for his out-standing support in the writing of this book, as well as in a number of other continuing projects. My son, Jeremy Ritzer, created a marvelous index.

Finally, I must acknowledge the following reviewers for their many helpful comments and suggestions: Robert Antonio, University of Kansas; John Bald-win, University of California, Santa Barbara; Deirdre Boden, Washington Uni-versity; Ira Cohen, Rutgers University; Paul Colomy, University of Denver; Karen Cook, University of Washington; James Farganis, Vassar College; Gary Fine, University of Georgia; Robert A. Jones, University of Illinois; Stephen Kalberg, Harvard University; Frank J. Lechner, Emory University; Donald N. Levine, University of Chicago; Whitney Pope, Indiana University; George Psa-thas, Boston University; Steven Seidman, SUNY at Albany; and Jonathan H. Turner, University of California, Riverside.

George Ritzer

CLASSICAL SOCIOLOGICAL THEORY

CHAPTER 1

A HISTORICAL SKETCH OF SOCIOLOGICAL THEORY: THE EARLY YEARS

*T*HIS book is designed as an introduction to the work of the classical sociological theorists, and we begin with one-sentence statements that get to the essence of the theories to be covered in these pages:

- We are evolving in the direction of a world dominated by science. (*Auguste Comte*)
- The world is moving in the direction of increasing order and harmony. (*Herbert Spencer*)
- Capitalism is based on the exploitation of the workers by the capitalists. (*Karl Marx*)
- The modern world offers less moral cohesion than earlier societies. (*Emile Durkheim*)
- The modern world is an iron cage of rational systems from which there is no escape. (*Max Weber*)
- The city spawns a particular type of person. (*Georg Simmel*)
- People's minds and their conceptions of themselves are shaped by their social experiences. (*George Herbert Mead*)

• In their social relationships, people often rely on tried and true "recipes" for how to handle such relationships. (*Alfred Schutz*)

• Society is an integrated system of social structures and functions. (*Talcott Parsons*)

This book is devoted to helping the reader to better understand these theoretical ideas, as well as the larger theories from which they are drawn, within the context of the lifework of the nine classical theorists listed above.

INTRODUCTION

By *classical* sociological theory we mean theories of great scope and ambition that either were created during sociology's classical age in Europe (roughly the early 1800s through the early 1900s) or had their roots in that period and culture. The theories of Comte, Spencer, Marx, Durkheim, Weber, and Simmel were produced during the classical age in France, England, and Germany. The theories of Mead, Schutz, and Parsons were largely produced later and mainly in the United States, but they had their sources in the classical age and in European intellectual traditions.

The work of these nine theorists is discussed in this book for two basic reasons. First, in all cases their work was important in its time and played a central role in the development of sociology in general and sociological theory in particular. Second, their ideas continue to be relevant to, and read by, contemporary sociologists, although this is less true of the work of Comte and Spencer (who are of more historical significance) than it is of the others.

This book does not deal with all sociological theory but rather with classical theory. However, in order to better understand the ideas of the nine classical theorists to be discussed in depth throughout this book, we begin with two chapters that offer an overview of the entire history of sociological theory.[1] Chapter 1 deals with the early years of sociological theory, while Chapter 2 brings that history up to the present day and to the most recent developments in sociological theory. Taken together, these two chapters offer the context within which the work of the nine classical theorists is to be understood. The two introductory chapters are animated by the belief that it is important to understand not only the historical sources of classical theories but also their later impact. More generally, the reader should have a broad sense of sociological theory before turning to a detailed discussion of the classical theorists. The remainder of the body of this book (Chapters 3 through 11) deals with the ideas of the major classical theorists mentioned above. Thus, the ideas of the major classical theorists will be discussed twice. They will be introduced very briefly in either the first or second chapter in their historical context, and they will be discussed in great depth in the chapter devoted to each of the theorists.

---

[1] There is also an elaborate metatheoretical approach and schema that inform these two chapters as well as the rest of the book. These are outlined in the Appendix.

Why focus on these nine theorists and not the innumerable others whose names and ideas will arise in the course of these first two chapters? The simplest answer to this question is that space limitations make it impossible to deal with all classical theorists. Beyond that, many theorists are not given full-chapter treatment because their theories do not *belong to, or have centrally important roots in, the classical age.* Furthermore, to be discussed in depth, theories must meet a series of other criteria. That is, to be included, theories must have a *wide range* of application, must deal with *centrally important social issues,* and must have stood up well under the *test of time* (that is, they must continue to be read and to be influential).[2] Thus, a number of theorists who are briefly discussed in this chapter (for example, Louis DeBonald and Gaetano Mosca) will not be discussed in detail later because their ideas do not meet one or more of the criteria listed above, especially the fact that their theories have not stood the test of time. A number of the more contemporary theorists discussed in Chapter 2 (for example, Erving Goffman and Harold Garfinkel) are not discussed further later in the book because they are associated more with the contemporary era than with classical sociological theory.

Our focus is on the important classical theoretical work of *sociologists,* as well as on work done by those who are often associated with other fields (for example, Karl Marx and his association with the field of economics) but which has come to be *defined as important in sociology.* To put it succinctly, this is a book about the "big ideas" in the history of sociology, ideas that deal with major social issues and are far-reaching in their scope.

Presenting a history of sociological theory is an enormous task, but because we devote only the first two chapters to it, what we offer is a highly selective historical sketch.[3] The idea is to provide the reader with a scaffolding which should help in putting the later detailed discussions of classical theorists in a larger context. As the reader proceeds through the later chapters, it might prove useful to return to these two overview chapters and place the discussions in that context. (It would be especially useful to glance back occasionally to Figures 1.1 and 2.1, which are schematic representations of the histories covered in those chapters.)

One cannot really establish the precise date when sociological theory began. People have been thinking about, and developing theories of, social life since early in history. But we will not go back to the early historic times of the Greeks or Romans or even to the Middle Ages. This is not because people in those epochs did not have sociologically relevant ideas, but because the return

---

[2] These four criteria constitute our definition of (classical) *sociological theory.* Such a definition stands in contrast to the formal, "scientific" definitions that are often used in theory texts of this type. A scientific definition might be that a theory is a set of interrelated propositions that allow for the systematization of knowledge, explanation, and prediction of social life and the generation of new research hypotheses (Faia, 1986). Although such a definition has a number of attractions, it simply does not fit many of the idea systems to be discussed in this book. In other words, most classical (and contemporary) theories fall short on one or more of the formal components of theory, but they are nonetheless considered theories by most sociologists.

[3] For a much more detailed historical sketch see, for example, Szacki (1979).

FIGURE 1.1 Sociological Theory: The Early Years

FRANCE

Enlightenment Montesquieu (1689–1755) Rousseau (1712–1778)	*Conservative Reaction* de Bonald (1754–1840) de Maistre (1753–1821)	Saint-Simon (1760–1825)	Comte (1798–1857)	Durkheim (1858–1917)

GERMANY

Kant (1724–1804) Hegel (1770–1831) *Young Hegelians*
Feuerbach
(1804–1872) Marx (1818–1883) *Economic Determinists*
Kautsky
(1854–1938) *Hegelian Marxists*
Lukács
(1885–1971)

German Historicism
Dilthey (1833–1911) Weber
(1864–1920)

Nietzsche (1844–1900) Simmel
(1858–1918)

ITALY

Pareto (1848–1923) Mosca (1858–1941)

GREAT BRITAIN

Political Economy
Smith (1723–1790) Ricardo (1772–1823) *Evolutionary Theory*
Spencer (1820–1903)

SOCIAL FORCES

- Political revolutions
- Industrial Revolution and the rise of capitalism
- Rise of socialism
- Urbanization
- Religious change
- Growth of science

FIGURE 1.1 Sociological Theory: The Early Years

on our investment in time would be small; we would spend a lot of time getting very few ideas that are relevant to modern sociology. In any case, none of the thinkers associated with those eras thought of themselves, and few are now thought of, as sociologists. (For discussion of one exception, see the biographical sketch of Ibn-Khaldun.) It is only in the 1800s that we begin to find thinkers who can be clearly identified as sociologists. These are the sociological thinkers we shall be interested in, and we begin by examining the main social and intellectual forces that shaped their ideas.

SOCIAL FORCES IN THE DEVELOPMENT OF SOCIOLOGICAL THEORY

All intellectual fields are profoundly shaped by their social settings. This is particularly true of sociology, which is not only derived from that setting but takes the social setting as its basic subject matter. We will focus briefly on a few of the most important social conditions of the nineteenth and early twentieth centuries, conditions that were of the utmost significance in the development of sociology. We also will take the occasion to begin introducing the major figures in the history of sociological theory.

Political Revolutions

The long series of political revolutions ushered in by the French Revolution in 1789 and carrying over through the nineteenth century was the most immediate factor in the rise of sociological theorizing. The impact of these revolutions on many societies was enormous, and many positive changes resulted. However, what attracted the attention of many early theorists was not the positive consequences, but the negative effects of such changes. These writers were particularly disturbed by the resulting chaos and disorder, especially in France. They were united in a desire to restore order to society. Some of the more extreme thinkers of this period literally wanted a return to the peaceful and relatively orderly days of the Middle Ages. The more sophisticated thinkers recognized that social change had made such a return impossible. Thus they sought instead to find new bases of order in societies that had been overturned by the political revolutions of the eighteenth and nineteenth centuries. This interest in the issue of social order was one of the major concerns of classical sociological theorists, especially Comte, Durkheim, and Parsons.

The Industrial Revolution and the Rise of Capitalism

At least as important as political revolution in the shaping of sociological theory was the Industrial Revolution, which swept through many Western societies, mainly in the nineteenth and early twentieth centuries. The Industrial Revolution was not a single event but many interrelated developments that culminated in the transformation of the Western world from a largely agricultural to an overwhelmingly industrial system. Large numbers of people left farms and agricultural work for the industrial occupations offered in the burgeoning factories. The factories themselves were transformed by a long series of technological improvements. Large economic bureaucracies arose to provide the many services needed by industry and the emerging capitalist economic system. In this economy, the ideal was a free marketplace where the many products of an industrial system could be exchanged. Within this system, a few profited greatly while the majority worked long hours for low wages. A reaction against the industrial system and against capitalism in general followed and led to the labor movement as well as to various radical movements aimed at overthrowing the capitalist system.

The Industrial Revolution, capitalism, and the reaction against them all involved an enormous upheaval in Western society, an upheaval that affected sociologists greatly. Four major figures in the early history of sociological theory—Karl Marx, Max Weber, Emile Durkheim, and Georg Simmel—were preoccupied, as were many lesser thinkers, with these changes and the problems

---

ABDEL RAHMAN IBN-KHALDUN: A Biographical Sketch

There is a tendency to think of sociology as exclusively a comparatively modern, Western phenomenon. In fact, however, scholars were doing sociology long ago and in other parts of the world. One example is Abdel Rahman Ibn-Khaldun.

Ibn-Khaldun was born in Tunis, North Africa, on May 27, 1332 (Faghirzadeh, 1982). Born to an educated family, Ibn-Khaldun was schooled in the Koran (the Muslim holy book), mathematics, and history. In his lifetime, he served a variety of sultans in Tunis, Morocco, Spain, and Algeria as ambassador, chamberlain, and member of the scholar's council. He also spent two years in prison in Morocco for his belief that state rulers were not divine leaders. After approximately two decades of political activity, Ibn-Khaldun returned to North Africa, where he undertook an intensive five-year period of study and writing. Works produced during this period increased his fame and led to a lectureship at the center of Islamic study, Al-Azhar Mosque University in Cairo. In his well-attended lectures on society and sociology, Ibn-Khaldun stressed the importance of linking sociological thought and historical observation.

By the time he died in 1406, Ibn-Khaldun had produced a corpus of work that had many ideas in common with contemporary sociology. He was committed to the scientific study of society, empirical research, and the search for causes of social phenomena. He devoted considerable attention to various social institutions (for example, politics, economy) and their interrelationships. He was interested in comparing primitive and modern societies. Ibn-Khaldun did not have a dramatic impact on classical sociology, but as scholars in general, and Islamic scholars in particular, rediscover his work, he may come to be seen as being of greater historical significance.

they created for society as a whole. They spent their lives studying these problems, and in many cases they endeavored to develop programs that would help solve them.

The Rise of Socialism

One set of changes aimed at coping with the excesses of the industrial system and capitalism can be combined under the heading "socialism." Although some sociologists favored socialism as a solution to industrial problems, most were personally and intellectually opposed to it. On the one side, Karl Marx was an active supporter of the overthrow of the capitalist system and its replacement by a socialist system. Although he did not develop a theory of socialism per se, he spent a great deal of time criticizing various aspects of capitalist society. In addition, he engaged in a variety of political activities that he hoped would help bring about the rise of socialist societies.

However, Marx was atypical in the early years of sociological theory. Most of the early theorists, such as Weber and Durkheim, were opposed to socialism (at least as it was envisioned by Marx). Although they recognized the problems within capitalist society, they sought social reform within capitalism rather than the social revolution argued for by Marx. They feared socialism more than they did capitalism. This fear played a far greater role in shaping sociological theory than did Marx's support of the socialist alternative to capitalism. In fact, as we will see, in many cases sociological theory developed in reaction *against* Marxian and, more generally, socialist theory.

Urbanization

Partly as a result of the Industrial Revolution, large numbers of people in the nineteenth and twentieth centuries were uprooted from their rural homes and moved to urban settings. This massive migration was caused, in large part, by the jobs created by the industrial system in the urban areas. But it presented many difficulties for those people who had to adjust to urban life. In addition, the expansion of the cities produced a seemingly endless list of urban problems—overcrowding, pollution, noise, traffic, and so forth. The nature of urban life and its problems attracted the attention of many early sociologists, especially Max Weber and Georg Simmel. In fact, the first major school of American sociology, the Chicago school, was in large part defined by its concern for the city and its interest in using Chicago as a laboratory in which to study urbanization and its problems.

Religious Change

Social changes brought on by political revolutions, the Industrial Revolution, and urbanization had a profound effect on religiosity. Many early sociologists came from religious backgrounds and were actively, and in some cases professionally, involved in religion (Hinkle and Hinkle, 1954). They brought to sociology the same objectives as they had in their religious lives. They wished to improve people's lives (Vidich and Lyman, 1985). For some (such as Comte), sociology was transformed into a religion. For others, their sociological theories bore an unmistakable religious imprint. Durkheim wrote one of his major works on religion. Morality played a key role not only in Durkheim's sociology but also in the work of Talcott Parsons. A large portion of Weber's work also was devoted to the religions of the world. Marx, too, had an interest in religiosity, but his orientation was far more critical. Spencer also discussed religion ("ecclesiastical institutions") as a significant component of society.

The Growth of Science

As sociological theory was being developed, there was an increasing emphasis on science, not only in colleges and universities but in society as a whole. The technological products of science were permeating every sector in life, and science was acquiring enormous prestige. Those associated with the most successful sciences (physics, biology, and chemistry) were accorded honored places in society. Sociologists (especially Comte, Durkheim, Spencer, Mead, and Schutz) from the beginning were preoccupied with science, and many wanted to model sociology after the successful physical and biological sciences. However, a debate soon developed between those who wholeheartedly accepted the scientific model and those (such as Weber) who thought that distinctive characteristics of social life made a wholesale adoption of a scientific model difficult and unwise. The issue of the relationship between sociology and science is debated to this day, although even a glimpse at the major journals in the field indicates the predominance of those who favor sociology as a science.

These are just a few of the major social factors that played key roles in the early years of sociological theory. The impact of these factors will become clear as we discuss the various theorists throughout the body of the book.

Although social factors are important, the primary focus of this chapter is the intellectual forces that played a central role in shaping sociological theory. In the real world, of course, intellectual factors cannot be separated from social forces. For example, in the discussion of the Enlightenment that follows, we will find that that movement was intimately related to, and in many cases provided the intellectual basis for, the social changes discussed above.

INTELLECTUAL FORCES AND THE RISE OF SOCIOLOGICAL THEORY

The many intellectual forces that shaped the development of classical social theories are discussed within the national context where their influence was primarily felt. We begin with the Enlightenment and its influences on the development of sociological theory in France.

The Enlightenment and the Founding of Sociology in France

It is the view of many observers that the Enlightenment constitutes a critical development in terms of the later evolution of sociology (Hawthorn, 1976; Nisbet, 1967; Seidman, 1983; Zeitlin, 1981, 1990). The Enlightenment was a period of remarkable intellectual development and change in philosophical thought.[4] A number of long-standing ideas and beliefs—many of which related to social life—were overthrown and replaced during the Enlightenment. The most prominent thinkers associated with the Enlightenment were the French philosophers Charles Montesquieu (1689–1755) and Jean Jacques Rousseau (1712–1778). The influence of the Enlightenment on sociological theory, however, was more indirect and negative than it was direct and positive. As Irving Zeitlin puts it, "Early sociology developed as a reaction to the Enlightenment" (1981:10).

The thinkers associated with the Enlightenment were influenced, above all, by two intellectual currents—seventeenth-century philosophy and science.

Seventeenth-century philosophy was associated with the work of thinkers such as René Descartes, Thomas Hobbes, and John Locke. The emphasis was on producing grand, general, and very abstract systems of ideas that made rational sense. The later thinkers associated with the Enlightenment did not reject the idea that systems of ideas should be general and should make rational sense, but they did make greater efforts to derive their ideas from the real world and to test them there. In other words, they wanted to combine empirical research with reason (Seidman, 1983:36–37). The model for this was science, especially Newtonian physics. At this point, we see the emergence of the application of the scientific method to social issues. At another level, not only did Enlightenment thinkers want their ideas to be, at least in part, derived from the real world, but they also wanted them to be useful to the social world, especially in the critical analysis of that world.

Overall, the Enlightenment was characterized by the belief that people could comprehend and control the universe by means of reason and empirical research. The view was that because the physical world was dominated by natural laws, it was likely that the social world was, too. Thus it was up to the philosopher, using reason and research, to discover these social laws. Once they understood how the social world worked, the Enlightenment thinkers had a practical goal—the creation of a "better," more rational world.

With an emphasis on reason, the Enlightenment philosophers were inclined

---

[4] This section is based on the work of Irving Zeitlin (1981, 1990). Although Zeitlin's analysis is presented here for its coherence, it has a number of limitations: there are better analyses of the Enlightenment, there are many other factors involved in shaping the development of sociology, and Zeitlin tends to overstate his case in places (for example, on the impact of Marx). But on the whole, Zeitlin provides us with a useful starting point, given our objectives in this chapter.

to reject beliefs in traditional authority. When these thinkers examined traditional values and institutions, they often found them to be irrational—that is, contrary to human nature and inhibitive of human growth and development. The mission of the practical and change-oriented philosophers of the Enlightenment was to overcome these irrational systems.

Conservative Reaction to the Enlightenment   The theorist who was most directly and positively influenced by Enlightenment thinking was Karl Marx, but he formed his early theoretical ideas in Germany. On the surface, we might think that French classical sociological theory, like Marx's theory, was directly and positively influenced by the Enlightenment. After all, didn't French sociology become rational, empirical, scientific, and change-oriented? The answer is that it did, but not before it was also shaped by a set of ideas that was developed in reaction to the Enlightenment. In Seidman's view, "The ideology of the counter-Enlightenment represented a virtual inversion of Enlightenment liberalism. In place of modernist premises, we can detect in the Enlightenment critics a strong anti-modernist sentiment" (1983:51). As we will see, sociology in general, and French sociology in particular, has from the beginning been an uncomfortable mix of Enlightenment and counter-Enlightenment ideas.

The most extreme form of opposition to Enlightenment ideas was French Catholic counterrevolutionary philosophy, as represented by the ideas of Louis de Bonald (1754–1840) and Joseph de Maistre (1753–1821). These men were reacting against not only the Enlightenment but also the French Revolution, which they saw partly as a product of the kind of thinking characteristic of the Enlightenment. De Bonald, for example, was disturbed by the revolutionary changes and yearned for a return to the peace and harmony of the Middle Ages. In this view, God was the source of society; therefore, reason, which was so important to the Enlightenment philosophers, was seen as inferior to traditional religious beliefs. Furthermore, it was believed that because God had created society, people should not tamper with it and should not try to change a holy creation. By extension, de Bonald opposed anything that undermined such traditional institutions as patriarchy, the monogamous family, the monarchy, and the Catholic Church. To call de Bonald's position conservative is to understate the case.

Although de Bonald represented a rather extreme form of the conservative reaction, his work constitutes a useful introduction to its general premises. The conservatives turned away from what they considered to be the "naive" rationalism of the Enlightenment. They not only recognized the irrational aspects of social life but also assigned them positive value. Thus they regarded such phenomena as tradition, imagination, emotionalism, and religion as useful and necessary components of social life. In that they disliked upheaval and sought to retain the existing order, they deplored developments such as the French Revolution and the Industrial Revolution, which they saw as disruptive forces. The conservatives tended to emphasize social order, an emphasis that became one of the central themes of the work of several, classical, sociological theorists.

Zeitlin (1981) has outlined ten major propositions that he sees as emerging from the conservative reaction and providing the basis for the development of classical French sociological theory.

1 Whereas Enlightenment thinkers tended to emphasize the individual, the conservative reaction led to a major sociological interest in, and emphasis on, society and other large-scale phenomena. Society was viewed as something more than simply an aggregate of individuals. Society was seen as having an existence of its own with its own laws of development and deep roots in the past.

2 Society was the most important unit of analysis; it was seen as more important than the individual. It was society that produced the individual, primarily through the process of socialization.

3 The individual was not even seen as the most basic element within society. A society consisted of such component parts as roles, positions, relationships, structures, and institutions. The individuals were seen as doing little more than filling these units within society.

4 The parts of society were seen as interrelated and interdependent. Indeed, these interrelationships were a major basis of society. This view led to a conservative political orientation. That is, because the parts were held to be interrelated, it followed that tampering with one part could well lead to the undermining of other parts and, ultimately, of the system as a whole. This meant that changes in the social system should be made with extreme care.

5 Change was seen as a threat not only to society and its components but also to the individuals in society. The various components of society were seen as satisfying people's needs. When institutions were disrupted, people were likely to suffer, and their suffering was likely to lead to social disorder.

6 The general tendency was to see the various large-scale components of society as useful for both society and the individuals in it. As a result, there was little desire to look for the negative effects of existing social structures and social institutions.

7 Small units, such as the family, the neighborhood, and religious and occupational groups, also were seen as essential to individuals and society. They provided the intimate, face-to-face environments that people needed in order to survive in modern societies.

8 There was a tendency to see various modern social changes, such as industrialization, urbanization, and bureaucratization, as having disorganizing effects. These changes were viewed with fear and anxiety, and there was an emphasis on developing ways of dealing with their disruptive effects.

9 While most of these feared changes were leading to a more rational

society, the conservative reaction led to an emphasis on the importance of nonrational factors (ritual, ceremony, and worship, for example) in social life.

10 Finally, the conservatives supported the existence of a hierarchical system in society. It was seen as important to society that there be a differential system of status and reward.

These ten propositions, derived from the conservative reaction to the Enlightenment, should be seen as the immediate intellectual basis of the development of sociological theory in France. Many of these ideas made their way into early sociological thought, although some of the Enlightenment ideas (empiricism, for example) were also influential.

Although we have emphasized the discontinuities between the Enlightenment and the counter-Enlightenment, Seidman makes the point that there also are continuities and linkages. First, the counter-Enlightenment carried on the scientific tradition developed in the Enlightenment. Second, it picked up the Enlightenment emphasis on collectivities (as opposed to individuals) and greatly extended it. Third, both had an interest in the problems of the modern world, especially its negative effects on individuals.

We turn now to the actual founding of sociology as a distinctive discipline—specifically, to the work of three French thinkers, Claude Saint-Simon, Auguste Comte, and especially Emile Durkheim.

Claude Henri Saint-Simon (1760–1825) Saint-Simon was older than Auguste Comte, and in fact Comte, in his early years, served as Saint-Simon's secretary and disciple. There is a very strong similarity between the ideas of these two thinkers, and yet a bitter debate developed between them that led to their eventual split (Thompson, 1975). Because Comte is generally considered to be more important to the founding of sociology, we need say only a few words about Saint-Simon's thinking.

The most interesting aspect of Saint-Simon was his significance to the development of *both* conservative sociological theory (like Comte's) and Marxian theory, which was in many ways the opposite of conservative theory. On the conservative side, Saint-Simon wanted to preserve society as it was, but he did not seek a return to life as it had been in the Middle Ages, as did de Bonald and de Maistre. In addition, he was a *positivist* (Durkheim, 1928/1962:142), which meant that he believed that the study of social phenomena should employ the same scientific techniques as were used in the natural sciences. On the radical side, Saint-Simon saw the need for socialist reforms, especially the centralized planning of the economic system. But Saint-Simon did not go nearly as far as Marx did later. Although he, like Marx, saw the capitalists superseding the feudal nobility, he felt it inconceivable that the working class would come to replace the capitalists. Many of Saint-Simon's ideas are found in Comte's work, and we now turn to a brief examination of it.

Auguste Comte (1798–1857)   Comte (see Chapter 3) was the first to use the term *sociology*. He had an enormous influence on later sociological theorists (especially Herbert Spencer and Emile Durkheim). And he believed that the study of sociology should be scientific, just as many classical theorists did and most contemporary sociologists do (Lenzer, 1975).

Comte's work can be seen, at least in part, as a reaction against the French Revolution and the Enlightenment, which he saw as the main cause of that revolution (1830/1842/1855). He was greatly disturbed by the anarchy that pervaded society and was critical of those French thinkers who had spawned both the Enlightenment and the revolution. He developed his scientific view, "positivism," or "positive philosophy," to combat what he considered to be the negative and destructive philosophy of the Enlightenment. Comte was in line with, and influenced by, the French counterrevolutionary Catholics (especially de Bonald and de Maistre). However, his work can be set apart from theirs on at least two grounds. First, he did not think it possible to return to the Middle Ages; advances of science and industry made that impossible. Second, he developed a much more sophisticated theoretical system than his predecessors, one that was adequate to shape a good portion of early sociology.

Comte developed *social physics*, or what in 1822 he called *sociology*, to combat the negative philosophies and the anarchy that in his view pervaded French society. The use of the term *social physics* made it clear that Comte sought to model sociology after the "hard sciences." This new science, which in his view would ultimately become *the* dominant science, was to be concerned with both social statics (existing social structures) and social dynamics (social change). Although both involved the search for laws of social life, he felt that social dynamics was more important than social statics. This focus on change reflected his interest in social reform, particularly of the ills created by the French Revolution and the Enlightenment. Comte did not urge revolutionary change, because he felt the natural evolution of society would make things better. Reforms were needed only to assist the process a bit.

This leads us to the cornerstone of Comte's approach—his evolutionary theory, or the *law of the three stages*. The theory proposes that there are three intellectual stages through which the world has gone throughout its history. According to Comte, not only does the world go through this process, but groups, societies, sciences, individuals, and even minds go through the same three stages. The *theological* stage is the first, and it characterized the world prior to 1300. During this period, the major idea system emphasized the belief that supernatural powers, religious figures, modeled after humankind, were at the root of everything. In particular, the social and physical world was seen as produced by God. The second stage is the *metaphysical* stage, which occurred roughly between 1300 and 1800. This era was characterized by the belief that abstract forces like "nature," rather than personalized gods, explain virtually everything. Finally, in 1800 the world entered the *positivistic* stage, characterized by belief in science. People now tended to give up the search for absolute causes (God or nature) and concentrated instead on observation of the social and physical world in the search for the laws governing them.

It is clear that in his theory of the world Comte focused on intellectual factors. Indeed, he argued that intellectual disorder was the cause of social disorder. The disorder stemmed from earlier idea systems (theological and metaphysical) that continued to exist in the positivistic (scientific) age. Only when positivism gained total control would social upheavals cease. Because this was an evolutionary process, there was no need to foment social upheaval and revolution. Positivism would come, although perhaps not as quickly as some would like. Here Comte's social reformism and his sociology coincide. Sociology could expedite the arrival of positivism and hence bring order to the social world. Above all, Comte did not want to seem to be espousing revolution. There was, in his view, enough disorder in the world. In any case, from Comte's point of view, it was intellectual change that was needed, so there was little reason for social and political revolution.

We have already encountered several of Comte's positions that were to be of great significance to the development of classical sociology—his basic conservatism, reformism, and scientism, and his evolutionary view of the world. Several other aspects of his work deserve mention because they also were to play a major role in the development of sociological theory. For example, his sociology does *not* focus on the individual but rather takes as its basic unit of analysis larger entities such as the family. He also urged that we look at *both* social structure and social change. Of great importance to later sociological theory, especially the work of Spencer and Parsons, is Comte's stress on the systematic character of society—the links among and between the various components of society. He also accorded great importance to the role of consensus in society. He saw little merit in the idea that society is characterized by inevitable conflict between workers and capitalists. In addition, Comte emphasized the need to engage in abstract theorizing and to go out and do sociological research. He urged that sociologists use observation, experimentation, and comparative historical analysis. Finally, Comte was an elitist; he believed that sociology ultimately would become the dominant scientific force in the world because of its distinctive ability to interpret social laws and to develop reforms aimed at patching up problems within the system.

Comte was in the forefront of the development of positivistic sociology (Bryant, 1985; Halfpenny, 1982). To Jonathan Turner, Comte's positivism emphasized that "the social universe is amenable to the development of abstract laws that can be tested through the careful collection of data," and "these abstract laws will denote the basic and generic properties of the social universe and they will specify their 'natural relations' " (1985a:24). As we will see, a number of classical theorists (especially Spencer and Durkheim) shared Comte's interest in the discovery of the laws of social life.

Even though Comte lacked a solid academic base on which to build a school of Comtian sociological theory, he nevertheless laid a basis for the development of a significant stream of sociological theory. But his long-term signifi-cance is dwarfed by that of his successor in French sociology and the inheritor of a number of its ideas, Emile Durkheim.

Emile Durkheim (1858–1917)   Although for Durkheim, as for Comte, the Enlightenment was a negative influence, it also had a number of positive effects on his work (for example, the emphasis on science and social reform-ism). However, Durkheim is best seen as the inheritor of the conservative tradition, especially as it was manifested in Comte's work. But whereas Comte had remained outside of academia, Durkheim developed an increasingly solid academic base as his career progressed. Durkheim legitimized sociology in France, and his work ultimately became a dominant force in the development of sociology in general and of sociological theory in particular.

Durkheim was politically liberal, but he took a more conservative position intellectually. Like Comte and the Catholic counterrevolutionaries, Durkheim feared and hated social disorder. His work was informed by the disorders produced by the general social changes discussed earlier in this chapter, as well as by others (such as industrial strikes, disruption of the ruling class, church-state discord, the rise of political anti-Semitism) more specific to the France of Durkheim's time (Karady, 1983). In fact, most of his work was devoted to the study of social order. His view was that social disorders were *not* a necessary part of the modern world and could be reduced by social reforms. Whereas Marx saw the problems of the modern world as inherent in society, Durkheim (along with most other classical theorists) did not. As a result, Marx's ideas on the need for social revolution stood in sharp contrast to the reformism of Durkheim and the others. As classical sociological theory developed, it was the Durkheimian interest in order and reform that came to dominate, while the Marxian position was eclipsed.

In two books published in the late 1800s, Durkheim developed a distinctive conception of the subject matter of sociology and then tested it in an empirical study. In *The Rules of Sociological Method* (1895/1964), Durkheim argued that it is the special task of sociology to study what he called *social facts*. He conceived of social facts as forces (Takla and Pope, 1985) and structures that are external to, and coercive of, the individual. The study of these large-scale structures and forces—for example, institutionalized law and shared moral beliefs—and their impact on people became the concern of many later sociological theorists (Parsons, for example). Durkheim was not content simply to define the subject matter of sociology; he sought through sociological research to demonstrate the utility of such a focus. He chose as his subject suicide. In a book entitled *Suicide* (1897/1951), Durkheim reasoned that if he could link such an individ-ual behavior as suicide to social causes (social facts), he would have made a persuasive case for the importance of the discipline of sociology. But Durk-heim did not examine why individual *A* or *B* committed suicide; rather he was interested in the causes of differences in suicide rates among groups, regions, countries, and different categories of people (for example, married and single). His basic argument was that it was the nature of, and changes in, social facts that led to differences in suicide rates. For example, a war or an economic depression would create a collective mood of depression that would in turn lead to increases in suicide rates. As we will see in Chapter 6, on Durkheim, there is much more to be said on this subject, but the key point for our purposes here is that Durkheim developed a distinctive view of sociology and sought to demonstrate its usefulness in a scientific study of suicide.

In *The Rules of Sociological Method*, Durkheim differentiated between two types of social facts—material and nonmaterial. Although he dealt with both in the course of his work, his main focus was on *nonmaterial social facts* (for example, culture, social institutions) rather than *material social facts* (for example, bureaucracy, law). This concern for nonmaterial social facts was already clear in his earliest major work, *The Division of Labor in Society* (1893/1964). His focus there was a comparative analysis of what held society together in the primitive and modern cases. He concluded that earlier societies were held together primarily by nonmaterial social facts, specifically, a strongly held common morality, or what he called a strong "collective conscience." However, because of the complexities of modern society, there had been a decline in the strength of the collective conscience. The primary bond in the modern world was an intricate division of labor, which tied people to others in dependency relationships. However, Durkheim felt that the modern division of labor brought with it several "pathologies"; it was, in other words, an inadequate method of holding society together. Given his conservative sociology, Durkheim did not feel that revolution was needed to solve these problems. Rather, he suggested a variety of reforms that could "patch up" the modern system and keep it functioning. Although he recognized that there was no going back to the age when a powerful collective conscience predominated, he did feel that the common morality could be strengthened in modern society and that people thereby could cope better with the pathologies that they were experiencing.

In his later work, nonmaterial social facts occupied an even more central position. In fact, he came to focus on perhaps the ultimate form of a nonmaterial social fact—religion—in his last major work, *The Elementary Forms of Religious Life* (1912/1965). In this work, Durkheim examined primitive society in order to find the roots of religion. He believed that he would be better able to find those roots in the comparative simplicity of primitive society than in the complexity of the modern world. What he found, he felt, was that the source of religion was society itself. Society comes to define certain things as religious and others as profane. Specifically, in the case he studied, the clan was the source of a primitive kind of religion, *totemism*, in which things like plants and animals are deified. Totemism, in turn, was seen as a specific type of nonmaterial social fact, a form of the collective conscience. In the end, Durkheim came to argue that society and religion (or, more generally, the collective conscience) were one and the same. Religion was the way society expressed itself in the form of a nonmaterial social fact. In a sense, then, Durkheim came to deify society and its major products. Clearly, in deifying society, Durkheim took a highly conservative stance: one would not want to overturn a deity *or* its societal source. Because he identified society with God, Durkheim was not inclined to urge social revolution. Instead, he was a social reformer seeking ways of improving the functioning of society. In these and other ways, Durkheim was clearly in line with French conservative sociology. The fact that he avoided many of its excesses helped make him the most significant figure in French sociology.

These books and other important works helped carve out a distinctive domain for sociology in the academic world of turn of the century France, and they earned Durkheim the leading position in that growing field. In 1898, Durkheim set up a scholarly journal devoted to sociology, *L'année sociologique* (Besnard, 1983b). It became a powerful force in the development and spread of sociological ideas. Durkheim was intent on fostering the growth of sociology, and he used his journal as a focal point for the development of a group of disciples. They would later extend his ideas and carry them to many other locales and into the study of other aspects of the social world (for example, sociology of law and sociology of the city) (Besnard, 1983a:1). By 1910, Durkheim had established a strong center of sociology in France, and the academic institutionalization of sociology was well under way in that nation. (For an overview of more recent developments in French sociology, see Lemert [1981].)

The Development of German Sociology

Whereas the early history of French sociology is a fairly coherent story of the progression from the Enlightenment and the French Revolution to the conservative reaction and to the increasingly important sociological ideas of Saint-Simon, Comte, and Durkheim, German sociology was fragmented from the beginning. A split developed between Marx (and his supporters), who remained on the edge of sociology, and the early giants of mainstream German sociology, Max Weber and Georg Simmel.[5] However, although Marxian theory itself was deemed unacceptable, its ideas found their way in a variety of positive and negative ways into mainstream German sociology. Our discussion here is divided between Marxian and non-Marxian theory in Germany.

The Roots and Nature of the Theories of Karl Marx (1818–1883)   The dominant intellectual influence on Karl Marx was the German philosopher G. W. F. Hegel (1770–1831). Marx's education at the University of Berlin was shaped by Hegel's ideas as well as by the split that developed among Hegel's followers after his death. The "Old Hegelians" continued to subscribe to the master's ideas, while the "Young Hegelians," although still working in the Hegelian tradition, were critical of many facets of his philosophical system. Among the Young Hegelians was Ludwig Feuerbach (1804–1872), who tried to revise Hegel's ideas. Marx was influenced by both Hegel's ideas and Feuer-

---

[5] For an argument against this and the view of continuity between Marxian and mainstream sociology, see Seidman (1983).

bach's revisions, but he extended and combined the two philosophies in a novel and insightful way.

Two concepts represent the essence of Hegel's philosophy—the dialectic and idealism (Hegel, 1807/1967, 1821/1967). The very complicated idea of the dialectic will be discussed in Chapter 5, on Marx, but a few introductory remarks are needed at this point. The *dialectic* is both a way of thinking and an image of the world. On the one hand, it is a way of thinking that stresses the importance of processes, relations, dynamics, conflicts, and contradictions—a dynamic rather than a static way of thinking about the world. On the other hand, it is a view that the *world* is made up not of static structures but of processes, relationships, dynamics, conflicts, and contradictions. Although the dialectic is generally associated with Hegel, it certainly predates him in philosophy. Marx, trained in the Hegelian tradition, accepted the significance of the dialectic. However, he was critical of some aspects of the way Hegel used it. For example, Hegel tended to apply the dialectic only to ideas, whereas Marx felt that it applied as well to more material aspects of life, for example, the economy.

Hegel is also associated with the philosophy of *idealism*, which emphasizes the importance of the mind and mental products rather than the material world. It is the social definition of the physical and material worlds that matters most, not those worlds themselves. In its extreme form, idealism asserts that *only* the mind and psychological constructs exist. Some idealists believed that their mental processes would remain the same even if the physical and social worlds no longer existed. Idealists emphasize not only mental processes but also the ideas produced by these processes. Hegel paid a great deal of attention to the development of such ideas, especially to what he referred to as the "spirit" of society.

In fact, Hegel offered a kind of evolutionary theory of the world in idealistic terms. At first, people were endowed only with the ability to acquire a sensory understanding of the world around them. They could understand things like the sight, smell, and feel of the social and physical world. Later, people developed the ability to be conscious of, to understand, themselves. With self-knowledge and self-understanding, people began to understand that they could become more than they were. In terms of Hegel's dialectical approach, a contradiction developed between what people were and what they felt that they could be. The resolution of this contradiction lay in the development of an individual's awareness of his or her place in the larger spirit of society. Individuals come to realize that their ultimate fulfillment lies in the development and the expansion of the spirit of society as a whole. Thus, individuals in Hegel's scheme evolve from an understanding of things to an understanding of self to an understanding of their place in the larger scheme of things.

Hegel, then, offered a general theory of the evolution of the world. It is a subjective theory in which change is held to occur at the level of consciousness. However, that change occurs largely beyond the control of actors. Actors are reduced to little more than vessels swept along by the inevitable evolution of consciousness.

Ludwig Feuerbach was an important bridge between Hegel and Marx. As a Young Hegelian, Feuerbach was critical of Hegel for, among other things, his excessive emphasis on consciousness and the spirit of society. Feuerbach's adoption of a materialist philosophy led him to argue that what was needed was to move from Hegel's subjective idealism to a focus not on ideas but on the material reality of real human beings. In his critique of Hegel, Feuerbach focused on religion. To Feuerbach, God is simply a projection by people of their human essence onto an impersonal force. People set God over and above themselves, with the result that they become alienated from God and project a series of positive characteristics onto God (that He is perfect, almighty, and holy), while they reduce themselves to being imperfect, powerless, and sinful. Feuerbach argued that this kind of religion must be overcome and that its defeat could be aided by a materialist philosophy in which people (not religion) became their own highest object, ends in themselves. Real people, not abstract ideas like religion, are deified by a materialist philosophy.

Marx was simultaneously influenced by, and critical of, *both* Hegel and Feuerbach. Marx, following Feuerbach, was critical of Hegel's adherence to an idealist philosophy. Marx took this position not only because of his adoption of a materialist orientation but also because of his interest in practical activities. Social facts like wealth and the state are treated by Hegel as ideas rather than as real, material entities. Even when he examined a seemingly material process like labor, Hegel was looking only at abstract mental labor. This is very different from Marx's interest in the labor of real, sentient people. Thus Hegel was looking at the wrong issues as far as Marx was concerned. In addition, Marx felt that Hegel's idealism led to a very conservative political orientation. To Hegel, the process of evolution was occurring beyond the control of people and their activities. In any case, in that people seemed to be moving toward greater consciousness of the world as it could be, there seemed no need for any revolutionary change; the process was already moving in the "desired" direction. Whatever problems did exist lay in consciousness, and the answer therefore seemed to lie in changing thinking.

Marx took a very different position, arguing that the problems of modern life can be traced to real, material sources (for example, the structures of capitalism) and that the solutions, therefore, can be found *only* in the overturning of those structures by the collective action of large numbers of people (Marx and Engels, 1845/1956:254). Whereas Hegel "stood the world on its head" (that is, focused on consciousness, not the real material world), Marx firmly embedded his dialectic in a material base.

Marx applauded Feuerbach's critique of Hegel on a number of counts (for example, its materialism and its rejection of the abstractness of Hegel's theory), but he was far from fully satisfied with Feuerbach's own position. For one thing, Feuerbach focused on the religious world, whereas Marx believed that it was the entire social world, and the economy in particular, that had to be analyzed. Although Marx accepted Feuerbach's materialism, he felt that Feuerbach had gone too far in focusing one-sidedly, nondialectically, on the material world. Feuerbach failed to include the most important of Hegel's contributions, the dialectic, in his materialist orientation, particularly the relationship between people and the material world. Finally, Marx argued that Feuerbach, like most philosophers, failed to emphasize praxis—practical activity—in particular, revolutionary activity. As Marx put it, "The philosophers have only *interpreted* the world, in various ways; the point, however, is to *change* it" (cited in Tucker, 1970:109).

Marx extracted what he considered to be the two most important elements from these two thinkers—Hegel's dialectic and Feuerbach's materialism—and fused them into his own distinctive orientation, *dialectical materialism*, which focuses on dialectical relationships within the material world.

Marx's materialism and his consequent focus on the economic sector led him rather naturally to the work of a group of *political economists* (for example, Adam Smith and David Ricardo). Marx was very attracted to a number of their positions. He lauded their basic premise that labor was the source of all wealth. This ultimately led Marx to his *labor theory of value*, in which he argued that the profit of the capitalist was based on the exploitation of the laborer. Capitalists performed the rather simple trick of paying the workers less than they deserved, because they received less pay than the value of what they actually produced in a work period. This *surplus value*, which was retained and reinvested by the capitalist, was the basis of the entire capitalist system. The capitalist system grew by continually increasing the level of exploitation of the workers (and therefore the amount of surplus value) and investing the profits for the expansion of the system.

Marx also was affected by the political economists' depiction of the horrors of the capitalist system and the exploitation of the workers. However, whereas they depicted the evils of capitalism, Marx criticized the political economists for seeing these evils as inevitable components of capitalism. Marx deplored their general acceptance of capitalism and the way they urged people to work for economic success within it. He also was critical of the political economists for failing to see the inherent conflict between capitalists and laborers and for denying the need for a radical change in the economic order. Such conservative economics was hard for Marx to accept, given his commitment to a radical change from capitalism to socialism.

Marx was not a sociologist and did not consider himself to be one. Although his work is too broad to be encompassed by the term *sociology*, there is a sociological theory to be found in Marx's work. From the beginning, there were those who were heavily influenced by Marx, and there has been a continuous strand of Marxian sociology, primarily in Europe. But for the majority of early sociologists, his work was a negative force, something against which to shape their sociology. Until very recently, sociological theory, especially in America, has been characterized by either hostility to or ignorance of Marxian theory. This has, as we will see in Chapter 2, changed dramatically in the last two decades, but the negative reaction to Marx's work was a major force in the shaping of much of sociological theory (Gurney, 1981).

The basic reason for this rejection of Marx was ideological. Many of the early sociological theorists were inheritors of the conservative reaction to the disruptions of the Enlightenment and the French Revolution. Marx's radical ideas and the radical social changes he foretold and sought to bring to life were clearly feared and hated by such thinkers. Marx was dismissed as an ideologist. It was argued that he was not a serious sociological theorist. However, ideology per se could not have been the real reason for the rejection of Marx, because the work of Comte, Durkheim, and other conservative thinkers was also heavily ideological. It was the nature of the ideology, not the existence of ideology as such, that put off many sociological theorists. They were ready and eager to buy conservative ideology wrapped in a cloak of sociological theory, but not the radical ideology offered by Marx and his followers.

There were, of course, other reasons why Marx was not accepted by many early theorists. He seemed to be more an economist than a sociologist. Although the early sociologists would certainly admit the importance of the economy, they would also argue that it was only one of a number of components of social life.

Another reason for the early rejection of Marx was the nature of his interests. Whereas the early sociologists were reacting to the disorder created by the Enlightenment, the French Revolution, and later the Industrial Revolution, Marx was not upset by these disorders—or by disorder in general. Rather, what interested and concerned Marx most was the oppressiveness of the capitalist system that was emerging out of the Industrial Revolution. Marx wanted to develop a theory that explained this oppressiveness and that would help overthrow that system. Marx's interest was in revolution, which stood in contrast to the conservative concern for reform and orderly change.

Another difference worth noting is the difference in philosophical roots between Marxian and conservative sociological theory. Most of the conservative theorists were heavily influenced by the philosophy of Immanuel Kant. Among other things, this led them to think in linear, cause-and-effect terms. That is, they tended to argue that a change in A (say, the change in ideas during the Enlightenment) leads to a change in B (say, the political changes of the French Revolution). In contrast, Marx was most heavily influenced, as we have seen, by Hegel, who thought in dialectical rather than cause-and-effect terms. Among other things, the dialectic attunes us to the ongoing reciprocal effects of social forces. Thus, a dialectician would reconceptualize the example discussed above as a continual, ongoing interplay of ideas and politics. It is admittedly difficult to get a feel for the complicated differences between Kantian and Hegelian philosophy, but the crucial point for our purposes is that these basic philosophical differences were an important source of the negative reaction of early sociological theorists to Marxian theory.

Many volumes have been written about the substance of Marx's theory, and we devote Chapter 5 to it. Marx published most of his major works in the middle third of the nineteenth century. Not only is there a great deal of his work, but it is a difficult body of work, not easy to summarize.

To oversimplify enormously, Marx offered a theory of capitalist society based on his image of the basic nature of human beings. Marx believed that people are basically productive; that is, in order to survive, people need to work in, and with, nature. In so doing, they produce the food, clothing, tools, shelter, and other necessities that permit them to live. Their productivity is a perfectly natural way by which they express basic creative impulses. Furthermore, these impulses are expressed in concert with other people; in other words, people are inherently social. They need to work together to produce what they need to survive.

Throughout history this natural process has been subverted, at first by the mean conditions of primitive society and later by a variety of structural arrangements erected by societies in the course of history. In various ways, these structures interfered with the natural productive process. However, it is in capitalist society that this breakdown is most acute; the breakdown in the natural productive process reaches its culmination in capitalism.

Basically capitalism is a structure (or, more accurately, a series of structures) that erects barriers between an individual and the production process, the products of that process, and other people; ultimately, it even divides the individual himself or herself. This is the basic meaning of the concept of *alienation*: it is the breakdown of the natural interconnection between people and between people and what they produce. Alienation occurs because capitalism has evolved into a two-class system in which a few capitalists own the production process, the products, and the labor time of those who work for them. Instead of naturally producing for themselves, people produce unnaturally in capitalist society for a small group of capitalists. Intellectually, Marx was very concerned with the structures of capitalism and their oppressive impact on actors. Politically, he was led to an interest in emancipating people from the oppressive structures of capitalism.

Marx actually spent very little time dreaming about what a utopian socialist state would look like. He was more concerned with helping to bring about the demise of capitalism. He believed that the contradictions and conflicts within capitalism would lead dialectically to its ultimate collapse, but he did not think that the process was inevitable. People had to act at the appropriate times and in the appropriate ways for socialism to come into being. The capitalists have great resources at their disposal to forestall the coming of socialism, but they could be overcome by the concerted action of a class-conscious proletariat. What would the proletariat create in the process? What is socialism? Most basically, it is a society in which, for the first time, people could approach Marx's ideal image of productivity. With the aid of modern technology, people could interact harmoniously with nature and other people to create what they needed to survive. To put it another way, in socialist society, people would no longer be alienated.

The Roots and Nature of the Theories of Max Weber (1864–1920) and Georg Simmel (1858–1918)   Although Marx and his followers in the late nineteenth and early twentieth centuries remained outside of mainstream German sociology, to a considerable extent early German sociology can be seen as developing in opposition to Marxian theory. In the view of some, this explains a large part of the theory of the early giant of German sociology, Max Weber. Albert Salomon, for example, claimed that Weberian theory developed "in a long and intense debate with the ghost of Marx" (1945:596). This is probably an exaggeration, but in many ways Marxian theory did play a negative role in Weberian theory. In other ways, however, Weber was working *within* the Marxian tradition, trying to "round out" Marx's theory. Also, there were many inputs into Weberian theory other than Marxian theory (Burger, 1976). We can clarify a good deal about the sources of German sociology by outlining each of these views of the relationship between Marx and Weber (Antonio and Glassman, 1985; Schroeter, 1985). It should be borne in mind that Weber was not intimately familiar with Marx's work (much of it was not published until after Weber's death) and that Weber was reacting more to the work of the Marxists than to Marx's work itself (Antonio, 1985:29; B. Turner, 1981:19–20).

Weber *did* tend to view Marx and the Marxists of his day as economic determinists who offered single-cause theories of social life. That is, Marxian theory was seen as tracing all historical developments to economic bases and viewing all contemporaneous structures as erected on an economic base. Although this is not true of Marx's own theory (as we will see in Chapter 5), it was the position of many later Marxists.

One of the examples of economic determinism that seemed to rankle Weber most was the view that ideas are simply the reflections of material (especially economic) interests, that material interests determine ideology. From this point of view, Weber was supposed to have "turned Marx on his head" (much as Marx had inverted Hegel). Instead of focusing on economic factors and their effect on ideas, Weber devoted much of his attention to ideas and their effect on the economy. Rather than seeing ideas as simple reflections of economic factors, Weber saw them as fairly autonomous forces capable of profoundly affecting the economic world. Weber certainly devoted a lot of attention to ideas, particularly systems of religious ideas, and he was especially concerned with the impact of religious ideas on the economy. In *The Protestant Ethic and the Spirit of Capitalism* (1904–1905/1958), he was concerned with Protestantism, mainly as a system of ideas, and its impact on the rise of another system of ideas, the "spirit of capitalism," and ultimately on a capitalist economic system. Weber had a similar interest in other world religions, looking at how their nature might have obstructed the development of capitalism in their respective societies. On the basis of this kind of work, some scholars came to the conclusion that Weber developed his ideas in opposition to those of Marx.

A second view of Weber's relationship to Marx, as mentioned earlier, is that he did not so much oppose Marx as try to round out his theoretical perspective. Here Weber is seen as working more within the Marxian tradition than in opposition to it. His work on religion, interpreted from this point of view, was simply an effort to show that not only do material factors affect ideas but ideas themselves affect material structures. This interpretation of Weber's work obviously places it much closer to, in fact in line with, Marxian theory.

A good example of the view that Weber was engaged in a process of rounding out Marxian theory is in the area of stratification theory. In this work on stratification, Marx focused on social *class*, the economic dimension of stratification. Although Weber accepted the importance of this factor, he argued that other dimensions of stratification were also important. He argued that the notion of social stratification should be extended to include stratification on the basis of prestige (*status*) and *power*. The inclusion of these other dimensions does not constitute a refutation of Marx but is simply an extension of his ideas.

Both of the views outlined above accept the importance of Marxian theory for Weber. There are elements of truth in both positions; at some points Weber *was* working in opposition to Marx, while at other points he *was* extending Marx's ideas. However, a third view of this issue may best characterize the relationship between Marx and Weber. In this view, Marx is simply seen as only one of many influences on Weber's thought.

We can identify a number of sources of Weberian theory, including German historians, philosophers, economists, and political theorists. Among those who influenced Weber, the philosopher Immanuel Kant (1724–1804) stands out above all the others. But we must not overlook the impact of Friedrich Nietzsche (1844–1900)—especially his emphasis on the hero—on Weber's work on the need for individuals to stand up to the impact of bureaucracies and other structures of modern society.

The influence of Immanuel Kant on Weber and on German sociology generally shows that German sociology and Marxism grew from different philosophical roots. As we have seen, it was Hegel, not Kant, who was the important philosophical influence on Marxian theory. Whereas Hegel's philosophy led Marx and the Marxists to look for relations, conflicts, and contradictions, Kantian philosophy led at least some German sociologists to take a more static perspective. To Kant the world was a buzzing confusion of events that could never be known directly. The world could only be known through thought processes that filter, select, and categorize these events. The content of the real world was differentiated by Kant from the forms through which that content can be comprehended. The emphasis on these forms gave the work of those sociologists within the Kantian tradition a more static quality than that of the Marxists within the Hegelian tradition.

German sociology emerged in a complex interplay with Marxian theory and a variety of other intellectual currents. The foremost exponents of early German sociology were Max Weber and Georg Simmel.

Whereas Karl Marx offered basically a theory of capitalism, Weber's work was fundamentally a theory of the process of rationalization (Brubaker, 1984; Kalberg, 1980, 1990). Weber was interested in the general issue of why institutions in the Western world had grown progressively more rational while powerful barriers seemed to prevent a similar development in the rest of the world.

Although rationality is used in many different ways in Weber's work, what interests us here is a process involving one of four types identified by Kalberg (1980, 1990; see also Brubaker, 1984; Levine, 1981a), *formal rationality*. Formal rationality involves, as was usually the case with Weber, a concern for the actor making choices of means and ends. However, in this case, that choice is made in reference to universally applied rules, regulations, and laws. These, in turn, are derived from various large-scale structures, especially bureaucracies and the economy. Weber developed his theories in the context of a large number of comparative historical studies of the West, China, India, and many other regions of the world. In these studies, he sought to delineate the factors that helped bring about or impede the development of rationalization.

Weber saw the bureaucracy (and the historical process of bureaucratization) as the classic example of rationalization, but rationalization is perhaps best illustrated today by the fast-food restaurant (Luxenberg, 1985; Ritzer, 1983, forthcoming a). The fast-food restaurant is a formally rational system in which people (both workers and customers) are led to seek the most rational means to ends. The drive-through window, for example, is a rational means by which workers can dispense, and customers can obtain, food quickly and efficiently. Speed and efficiency are dictated by the fast-food restaurants and the rules and regulations by which they operate.

Weber embedded his discussion of the process of bureaucratization in a broader discussion of the political institution. He differentiated among three types of authority systems—traditional, charismatic, and rational-legal. Only in the modern Western world can a rational-legal authority system develop, and only within that system does one find the full-scale development of the modern bureaucracy. The rest of the world remains dominated by traditional or charismatic authority systems, which generally impede the development of a rational-legal authority system and modern bureaucracies. Briefly, *traditional* authority stems from a long-lasting system of beliefs. An example would be a leader who comes to power because his or her family or clan has always provided the group's leadership. A *charismatic* leader derives his or her authority from extraordinary abilities or characteristics, or more likely simply from the *belief* on the part of followers that the leader has such traits. Although these two types of authority are of historical importance, Weber believed that the trend in the West, and ultimately in the rest of the world, is toward systems of *rational-legal* authority. In such systems, authority is derived from rules legally and rationally enacted. Thus, the president of the United States derives his authority ultimately from the laws of society. The evolution of rational-legal authority, with its accompanying bureaucracies, is only one part of Weber's general argument on the rationalization of the Western world.

Weber also did detailed and sophisticated analyses of the rationalization of such phenomena as religion, law, the city, and even music. But we can illustrate Weber's mode of thinking with one other example—the rationalization of the economic institution. This discussion is couched in Weber's broader analysis of the relationship between religion and capitalism. In a wide-ranging historical study, Weber sought to understand why a rational economic system (capitalism) had developed in the West and why it had failed to develop in the rest of the world. Weber accorded a central role to religion in this process. At one level, he was engaged in a dialogue with the Marxists in an effort to show that, contrary to what many Marxists of the day believed, religion was not merely an epiphenomenon. Instead, it had played a key role in the rise of capitalism in the West and in its failure to develop elsewhere in the world. Weber argued that it was a distinctively rational religious system (Calvinism) that played the central role in the rise of capitalism in the West. In contrast, in the other parts of the world that he studied, Weber found more irrational religious systems (for example, Confucianism, Taoism, Hinduism), which helped to inhibit the development of a rational economic system. However, in the end, one gets the feeling that these religions provided only temporary barriers, for the economic systems—indeed, the entire social structure—of these societies ultimately would become rationalized.

There is a great deal more to Weberian theory than this. For example, his work on rationalization has much more historical detail and innumerable theoretical insights. Beyond that, although rationalization lies at the heart of Weberian theory, it is far from all there is to the theory. But this is not the place to go into that rich body of material. Instead, let us return to the development of sociological theory. A key issue in that development is: Why did Weber's theory prove more attractive to later sociological theorists than Marxian theory?

One reason is that Weber proved to be more acceptable politically. Instead of espousing Marxian radicalism, Weber was more of a liberal on some issues and a conservative on others (for example, the role of the state). Although he was a severe critic of many aspects of modern capitalist society and came to many of the same critical conclusions as did Marx, he was not one to propose radical solutions to problems. In fact, he felt that the radical reforms offered by many Marxists and other socialists would do more harm than good.

Later sociological theorists, especially Americans, saw their society under attack by Marxian theory. Largely conservative in orientation, they cast about for theoretical alternatives to Marxism. One of those who proved attractive was Max Weber. (Durkheim and Vilfredo Pareto were others.) After all, rationalization affected not only capitalist but also socialist societies. Indeed, from Weber's point of view, rationalization constituted an even greater problem in socialist than in capitalist societies.

Also in Weber's favor was the form in which he presented his judgments. He spent most of his life doing detailed historical studies, and his political conclusions were often made within the context of his research. Thus they usually sounded very scientific and academic. Marx, although he did much serious research, also wrote a good deal of explicitly polemical material. Even his more academic work is laced with acid political judgments. For example, in *Capital* (1867/1967), he described capitalists as "vampires" and "werewolves." Weber's more academic style helped make him more acceptable to later sociologists.

Another reason for the greater acceptability of Weber was that he operated in a philosophical tradition that also helped shape the work of later sociologists. That is, Weber operated in the Kantian tradition, which meant, among other things, that he tended to think in cause-and-effect terms. This kind of thinking was more acceptable to later sociologists, who were largely unfamiliar and uncomfortable with the dialectical logic that informed Marx's work.

Finally, Weber appeared to offer a much better rounded approach to the social world than Marx. Whereas Marx appeared to be almost totally preoccupied with the economy, Weber was interested in a wide range of social phenomena. This diversity of focus seemed to give later sociologists more to work with than the apparently more single-minded concerns of Marx.

Weber produced most of his major works in the late 1800s and early 1900s. Early in his career, Weber was identified more as a historian who was concerned with sociological issues, but in the early 1900s his focus grew more and more sociological. Indeed, he became the dominant sociologist of his time in Germany. In 1910, he founded (with, among others, Georg Simmel, whom we discuss below) the German Sociological Society. His home in Heidelberg was an intellectual center not only for sociologists but for scholars from many fields. Although his work was broadly influential in Germany, it was to become even more influential in the United States, especially after Talcott Parsons introduced Weber's ideas (and those of other European theorists, especially Durkheim) to a large American audience. Although Marx's ideas did not have a significant positive effect on American sociological theorists until the 1960s, Weber was already highly influential by the late 1930s.

Georg Simmel was Weber's contemporary and a cofounder of the German Sociological Society. As with Marx and Weber, we will devote a chapter to Simmel (Chapter 8); here we place him within the historical development of sociological theory.

Simmel was a somewhat atypical sociological theorist (Frisby, 1981; Levine, Carter, and Gorman, 1976a, 1976b). For one thing, he had an immediate and profound effect on the development of American sociological theory, whereas Marx and Weber were largely ignored for a number of years. Simmel's work helped shape the development of one of the early centers of American sociology—the University of Chicago—and its major theory, symbolic interactionism. The Chicago school and symbolic interactionism came, as we will see, to dominate American sociology in the 1920s and early 1930s (Bulmer, 1984). Simmel's ideas were influential at Chicago mainly because the dominant figures in the early years of Chicago, Albion Small and Robert Park, had been exposed to Simmel's theories in Berlin in the late 1800s. Park attended Simmel's lectures in 1899 and 1900, and Small carried on an extensive correspondence with Simmel during the 1890s. They were instrumental in bringing Simmel's ideas to students and faculty at Chicago, in translating some of his work, and in bringing it to the attention of a large-scale American audience (Frisby, 1984:29).

Another atypical aspect of Simmel's work is his "level" of analysis, or at least that level for which he became best known in America. Whereas Weber and Marx were preoccupied with large-scale issues like the rationalization of society and a capitalist economy, Simmel was best known for his work on smaller-scale issues, especially individual action and interaction. He became famous early for his thinking, derived from Kantian philosophy, on *forms* of interaction (for example, conflict) and *types* of interactants (for example, the stranger). Basically, Simmel saw that understanding interaction among people was one of the major tasks of sociology. However, it was impossible to study the massive number of interactions in social life without some conceptual tools. This is where forms of interaction and types of interactants came in. Simmel felt that he could isolate a limited number of forms of interaction that could be found in a large number of social settings. Thus equipped, one could analyze and understand these different interaction settings. The development of a limited number of types of interactants could be similarly useful in explaining interaction settings. This work had a profound effect on symbolic interactionism, which, as the name suggests, was focally concerned with interaction. One of the ironies, however, is that Simmel also was concerned with large-scale issues similar to those that obsessed Marx and Weber. However, this work was much less influential than his work on interaction, although there are contemporary signs of a growing interest in the large-scale aspects of Simmel's sociology.

It was partly Simmel's style in his work on interaction that made him accessible to early American sociological theorists. Although he wrote heavy tomes like Weber and Marx, he also wrote a set of deceptively simple essays on such interesting topics as poverty, the prostitute, the miser and the spendthrift, and the stranger. The brevity of such essays and the high interest level of the material made the dissemination of Simmel's ideas much easier. Unfortunately, the essays had the negative effect of obscuring Simmel's more massive works (for example, *Philosophy of Money*, translated in 1978), which were potentially as significant to sociology. Nevertheless, it was partly through the short and clever essays that Simmel had a much more significant effect on early American sociological theory than either Marx or Weber.

We should not leave Simmel without saying something about *Philosophy of Money*, because its English translation has made Simmel's work attractive to a whole new set of theorists interested in culture and society. Although this macro orientation is clearer in *Philosophy of Money*, it always existed in Simmel's work. For example, it is clear in his famous work on the dyad and the triad. Simmel thought that some crucial sociological developments take place when a two-person group (or *dyad*) is transformed into a *triad* by the addition of a third party. Social possibilities emerge that simply could not exist in a dyad. For example, in a triad, one of the members can become an arbitrator or mediator of the differences between the other two. More important, two of the members can band together and dominate the other member. This represents on a small scale what can happen with the emergence of large-scale structures that become separate from individuals and begin to dominate them.

This theme lies at the base of *Philosophy of Money*. Simmel was primarily

---

SIGMUND FREUD: A Biographical Sketch

Another leading figure in German social science in the late 1800s and early 1900s was Sigmund Freud. Although he was not a sociologist, Freud influenced the work of many sociologists and continues to be of relevance to sociologists (Carveth, 1982).

Sigmund Freud was born in the Austro-Hungarian city of Freiberg on May 6, 1856 (Puner, 1947). In 1859, his family moved to Vienna, and in 1873, Freud entered the medical school at the University of Vienna. Freud was more interested in science than medicine and took a position in a physiology laboratory. He completed his degree in medicine, and after leaving the laboratory in 1882, he worked in a hospital and then set up a private medical practice with a specialty in nervous diseases.

Freud at first used hypnosis in an effort to deal with a type of neurosis known as *hysteria*. He had learned the technique in Paris from Jean Martin Charcot in 1885. Later he adopted a technique, pioneered by a fellow Viennese physician, Joseph Breuer, in which hysterical symptoms disappeared when the patient talked through the circumstances in which the symptoms first arose. By 1895, Freud had published a book with Breuer with a series of revolutionary implications: that the causes of neuroses like hysteria were psychological (not, as had been believed, physiological) and that the therapy involved talking through the original causes. Thus was born the practical and theoretical field of *psychoanalysis*. Freud began to part company with Breuer as he came to see sexual factors, or more generally the *libido*, at the root of neuroses. Over the next several years, Freud refined his therapeutic techniques and wrote a great deal about his new ideas.

By 1902, Freud began to gather a number of disciples around him, and they met weekly at his house. By 1903 or 1904, others (like Carl Jung) began to use Freud's ideas in their psychiatric practices. In 1908, the first Psychoanalytic Congress was held, and the next year a periodical for disseminating psychoanalytic knowledge was formed. As quickly as it had formed, the new field of psychoanalysis became splintered as Freud broke with people like Jung and they went off to develop their own ideas and found their own groups. World War I slowed the development of psychoanalysis, but it expanded and developed greatly in the 1920s. With the rise of Nazism, the center of psychoanalysis shifted to the United States, where it remains to this day. But Freud remained in Vienna until the Nazis took over in 1938, despite the fact that he was Jewish and the Nazis had burned his books as early as 1933. On June 4, 1938, only after a ransom had been paid and President Roosevelt had interceded, Sigmund Freud left Vienna. Freud had suffered from cancer of the jaw since 1923, and he died in London on September 23, 1939.

concerned with the emergence in the modern world of a money economy that becomes separate from the individual and predominant. This theme, in turn, is part of an even broader and more pervasive one in Simmel's work, the domination of the culture as a whole over the individual. As Simmel saw it, in the modern world, the larger culture and all its various components (including the money economy) expand, and as they expand, the importance of the individual decreases. Thus, for example, as the industrial technology associated with a modern economy expands and grows more sophisticated, the skills and abilities of the individual worker grow progressively less important. In the end, the worker is confronted with an industrial machine over which he or she can exert little, if any, control. More generally, Simmel thought that in the modern world, the expansion of the larger culture leads to the growing insignificance of the individual.

Although sociologists have become increasingly attuned to the broader implications of Simmel's work, his early influence was primarily through his studies of small-scale social phenomena, such as the forms of interaction and types of interactants.

The Origins of British Sociology

We have been examining the development of sociology in France (Comte, Durkheim) and Germany (Marx, Weber, and Simmel). We turn now to the parallel development of sociology in England. As we will see, Continental ideas had their impact on early British sociology, but more important were native influences.

Political Economy, Ameliorism, and Social Evolution Philip Abrams (1968) contended that British sociology was shaped in the nineteenth century by three often conflicting sources—political economy, ameliorism, and social evolution.[6] Thus when the Sociological Society of London was founded in 1903, there were strong differences over the definition of *sociology*. However, there were few who doubted the view that sociology could be a science. It was the differences that gave British sociology its distinctive character, and we will look at each of them briefly.

We have already touched on *political economy*, which was a theory of industrial and capitalist society traceable in part to the work of Adam Smith (1723–1790).[7] As we saw, political economy had a profound effect on Karl Marx. Marx studied political economy closely, and he was critical of it. But that was not the direction taken by British economists and sociologists. They tended to accept Smith's idea that there was an "invisible hand" that shaped the market

---

[6] For more recent developments in British sociology, see Abrams et al (1981).

[7] Smith is usually included as a leading member of the Scottish Enlightenment (Chitnis, 1976) and as one of the Scottish Moralists (Schneider, 1967:xi), who were seeking to establish the basis for sociology.

for labor and goods. The market was seen as an independent reality that stood above individuals and controlled their behavior. The British sociologists, like the political economists and unlike Marx, saw the market as a positive force, as a source of order, harmony, and integration in society. Because they saw the market, and more generally society, in a positive light, the task of the sociologists was not to criticize society but simply to gather data on the laws by which it operated. The goal was to provide the government with the facts it needed to understand the way the system worked and to direct its workings wisely.

The emphasis was on facts, but which facts? Whereas Marx, Weber, Durkheim, and Comte looked to the structures of society for their basic facts, the British thinkers tended to focus on the individuals who made up those structures. In dealing with large-scale structures, they tended to collect individual-level data and then combine them to form a collective portrait. In the mid-1800s it was the statisticians who dominated British social science, and this kind of data collection was deemed to be the major task of sociology. The objective was the accumulation of "pure" facts without theorizing or philosophizing. As Kent (1981:187) argues, these empirical sociologists were detached from the concerns of social theorists. Instead of general theorizing, the "emphasis settled on the business of producing more exact indicators, better methods of classification and data collection, improved life tables, higher levels of comparability between discrete bodies of data, and the like" (Abrams, 1968:18).

It was almost in spite of themselves that these statistically oriented sociologists came to see some limitations in their approach. A few sociologists began to feel the need for broader theorizing. To them, a problem such as poverty pointed to failings in the market system as well as in the society as a whole. But most, focused as they were on individuals, did not question the larger system; they turned instead to more detailed field studies and to the development of more complicated and more exact statistical techniques. To them, the source of the problem had to lie in inadequate research methods, *not* in the system as a whole. As Philip Abrams noted, "Focusing persistently on the distribution of individual circumstances, the statisticians found it hard to break through to a perception of poverty as a product of social structure. . . . They did not and probably could not achieve the concept of structural victimization" (1968:27). In addition to their theoretical and methodological commitments to the study of individuals, the statisticians worked too closely with government policy makers to arrive at the conclusion that the larger political and economic system was the problem.

Related to, but separable from, political economy was the second defining characteristic of British sociology—*ameliorism*, or a desire to solve social problems by reforming individuals. Although British scholars began to recognize that there were problems in society (for example, poverty), they still believed in that society and wanted to preserve it. They desired to forestall violence and revolution and to reform the system so that it could continue essentially as it was. Above all, they wanted to prevent the coming of a socialist society. Thus, like French sociology and some branches of German sociology, British sociology was conservatively oriented.

Because the British sociologists could not, or would not, trace the source of problems such as poverty to the society as a whole, the source had to lie within the individuals themselves. This was an early form of what William Ryan (1971) later called "blaming the victim." Much attention was devoted to a long series of individual problems—"ignorance, spiritual destitution, impurity, bad sanitation, pauperism, crime, and intemperance—above all intemperance" (Abrams, 1968:39). Clearly, there was a tendency to look for a simple cause for all social ills, and the one that suggested itself before all others was alcoholism. What made this perfect to the ameliorist was that this was an individual pathology, not a social pathology. The ameliorists lacked a theory of social structure, a theory of the social causes of such individual problems.

But a stronger sense of social structure was lurking below the surface of British sociology, and it burst through in the latter part of the nineteenth century with the growth of interest in *social evolution*. One important influence was the work of Auguste Comte, part of which had been translated into English in the 1850s. Although Comte's work did not inspire immediate interest, by the last quarter of the century, a number of thinkers had been attracted to it and to its concern for the larger structures of society, its scientific (positivistic) orientation, its comparative orientation, and its evolutionary theory. However, a number of British thinkers sharpened their own conception of the world in opposition to some of the excesses of Comtian theory (for example, the tendency to elevate sociology to the status of a religion).

In Abrams's view, the real importance of Comte lay in his providing one of the bases on which opposition could be mounted against the "oppressive genius of Herbert Spencer" (Abrams, 1968:58). In both a positive and a negative sense, Spencer was a dominant figure in British sociological theory, especially evolutionary theory.

Herbert Spencer (1820–1903) In attempting to understand Spencer's ideas (see Chapter 4), it is useful to compare and contrast them with Comtian theory. Spencer is often categorized with Comte in terms of their influence on the development of sociological theory, but there are some important differences between them. For example, it is less easy to categorize Spencer as a conservative. In fact, in his early years, Spencer is better seen as a political liberal, and he retained elements of liberalism throughout his life. However, it is also true that Spencer grew more conservative during the course of his life and that his basic influence, as was true of Comte, was conservative.

One of his liberal views, which coexisted rather uncomfortably with his conservatism, was his acceptance of a laissez-faire doctrine: he felt that the state should not intervene in individual affairs, except in the rather passive function of protecting people. This meant that Spencer, unlike Comte, was not interested in social reforms; he wanted social life to evolve free of external control.

This difference points to Spencer as a *Social Darwinist* (G. Jones, 1980). As such, he held the evolutionary view that the world was growing progressively better. Therefore, it should be left alone; outside interference could only worsen the situation. He adopted the view that social institutions, like plants and animals, adapted progressively and positively to their social environment. He also accepted the Darwinian view that a process of natural selection, "survival of the fittest," occurred in the social world. (Interestingly, it was Spencer who coined the phrase "survival of the fittest" several years *before* Charles Darwin's work on natural selection.) That is, if unimpeded by external intervention, people who were "fit" would survive and proliferate whereas the "unfit" would eventually die out. Another difference was that Spencer emphasized the individual, whereas Comte focused on larger units such as the family.

Although there are important differences between Comte and Spencer, their shared orientations, or at least the similar ways in which they were interpreted, proved to be more important than their differences for the development of sociological theory.

Comte and Spencer shared with Durkheim and others a commitment to a science of sociology, which was a very attractive perspective to early theorists. Another influence of Spencer's work, shared with both Comte and Durkheim, was his tendency to see society as an *organism*. In this, Spencer borrowed his perspective and concepts from biology. He was concerned with the overall structure of society, the interrelationship of the *parts* of society, and the *functions* of the parts for each other as well as for the system as a whole.

Most important, Spencer, like Comte, had an evolutionary conception of historical development. However, Spencer was critical of Comte's evolutionary theory on several grounds. Specifically, he rejected Comte's law of the three stages. He argued that Comte was content to deal with evolution in the realm of ideas, in terms of intellectual development. Spencer, however, sought to develop an evolutionary theory in the real, material world.

Although Spencer is best remembered as an evolutionary theorist, his theory is highly complex, takes varied forms, and is often unclear and ambiguous (Haines, 1988; Perrin, 1976). However, it is possible to identify at least two major evolutionary perspectives in Spencer's work.

The first of these theories relates primarily to the increasing *size* of society. Society grows through both the multiplication of individuals and the union of groups (compounding). The increasing size of society brings with it larger and more differentiated social structures, as well as the increasing differentiation of the functions they perform. In addition to their growth in terms of size, societies evolve through compounding, that is, by unifying more and more adjoining groups. Thus, Spencer talks of the evolutionary movement from simple to compound, doubly-compound, and trebly-compound societies.

Spencer also offers a theory of evolution from *militant* to *industrial* societies. Earlier, militant societies are defined by being structured for offensive and defensive warfare. While Spencer was critical of warfare, he felt that in an earlier stage it was functional in bringing societies together (through, for example, military conquest) and in creating the larger aggregates of people necessary for the development of industrial society. However, with the emergence of industrial society, warfare ceases to be functional and serves to impede further evolution. Industrial society is based on friendship, altruism, elaborate specialization, recognition for achievements rather than the characteristics one is born with, and voluntary cooperation among highly disciplined individuals. Such a society is held together by voluntary contractual relations and, more important, by a strong common morality. The government's role is restricted and focuses only on what people ought not to do. Obviously, modern industrial societies are less warlike than their militant predecessors. Although Spencer sees a general evolution in the direction of industrial societies, he also recognizes that it is possible that there will be periodic regressions to warfare and more militant societies.

In his ethical and political writings, Spencer offered other ideas on the evolution of society. For one thing, he saw society as progressing toward an ideal, or perfect, moral state. For another, he argued that the fittest societies survive, while unfit societies should be permitted to die off. The result of this process is adaptive upgrading for the world as a whole.

Thus Spencer offered a rich and complicated set of ideas on social evolution. As we will see, his ideas first enjoyed great success, then were rejected for many years, and recently have been revived with the rise of neoevolutionary sociological theories (Buttel, 1990).

The Reaction against Spencer in Britain   Despite his emphasis on the individual, Spencer was best known for his large-scale theory of social evolution. In this, he stood in stark contrast to the sociology that preceded him in Britain. However, the reaction against Spencer was based more on the threat that his idea of survival of the fittest posed to the ameliorism so dear to most early British sociologists. Although Spencer later repudiated some of his more outrageous ideas, he *did* argue for a survival-of-the-fittest philosophy and against government intervention and social reform. He did say things like:

> Fostering the good-for-nothing at the expense of the good, is an extreme cruelty. It is a deliberate stirring-up of miseries for future generations. There is no greater curse to posterity than that of bequeathing to them an increasing population of imbeciles and idlers and criminals. . . . The whole effort of nature is to get rid of such, to clear the world of them, and make room for better. . . . If they are not sufficiently complete to live, they die, and it is best they should die.

> (Spencer, cited in Abrams, 1968:74)

Such sentiments were clearly at odds with the ameliorative orientation of the British reformer-sociologists.

Key Figures in Italian Sociology

We can close this sketch of early, primarily conservative, European sociological theory with brief mention of two Italian sociologists, Vilfredo Pareto (1848–1923) and Gaetano Mosca (1858–1941). These two sociologists were influential in their time, but their contemporary relevance is minimal. Few people read Mosca today. There was a brief outburst of interest in Pareto's (1935) work in the 1930s, when the major American theorist, Talcott Parsons, devoted as much attention to him as he gave to Weber and Durkheim. However, in recent years, except for a few of his major concepts, Pareto also has receded in importance and contemporary relevance.

Zeitlin argued that Pareto developed his "major ideas as a refutation of Marx" (1981:171). In fact, Pareto was rejecting not only Marx but also a good portion of Enlightenment philosophy. For example, whereas the Enlightenment philosophers emphasized rationality, Pareto emphasized the role of non-rational factors such as human instincts. This emphasis also was tied to his rejection of Marxian theory. That is, because nonrational, instinctual factors were so important *and* so unchanging, it was unrealistic to hope to achieve dramatic social changes with an economic revolution.

Pareto also developed a theory of social change that stood in stark contrast to Marxian theory. Whereas Marx's theory focused on the role of the masses, Pareto offered an elite theory of social change, which held that society inevitably is dominated by a small elite that operates on the basis of enlightened self-interest. It rules over the masses of people, who are dominated by non-rational forces. Because they lack rational capacities, the masses, in Pareto's system, were unlikely to be a revolutionary force. Social change occurs when the elite begins to degenerate and is replaced by a new elite derived from the nongoverning elite or higher elements of the masses. Once the new elite is in power, the process begins anew. Thus, we have a cyclical theory of social change instead of the directional theories offered by Marx, Comte, Spencer, and others. In addition, Pareto's theory of change largely ignores the plight of the masses. Elites come and go, but the lot of the masses remains the same.

This theory, however, was not Pareto's lasting contribution to sociology. That lay in his scientific conception of sociology and the social world: "My wish is to construct a system of sociology on the model of celestial mechanics [astronomy], physics, chemistry" (cited in Hook, 1965:57). Briefly, Pareto conceived of society as a system in equilibrium, a whole consisting of interdependent parts. A change in one part was seen as leading to changes in other parts of the system. Pareto's systemic conception of society was the most important reason Parsons devoted so much attention to Pareto's work in his 1937 book, *The Structure of Social Action*, and it was Pareto's most important influence on Parsons's thinking. Fused with similar views held by those who had an organic image of society (Comte, Durkheim, and Spencer, for example), Pareto's theory played a central role in the development of Parsons's theory and, more generally, in structural functionalism.

Although few modern sociologists now read Pareto's work (one exception is Powers, 1986), virtually none ever read Mosca's. But his work also can be seen as a rejection of the Enlightenment and of Marxism. The important point is that Mosca, like Pareto, offered an elite theory of social change that stands in opposition to the Marxian perspective.

Turn of the Century Developments in European Marxism

While many nineteenth-century sociologists were developing their theories in opposition to Marx, there was a simultaneous effort by a number of Marxists to clarify and extend Marxian theory. Between roughly 1875 and 1925, there was little overlap between Marxism and sociology. (Weber is an exception to this.) The two schools of thought were developing in parallel fashion with little or no interchange between them.

After the death of Marx, Marxian theory was first dominated by those who saw in his theory scientific and economic determinism. Wallerstein calls this the era of "orthodox Marxism" (1986:1301). Friedrich Engels, Marx's benefactor and collaborator, lived on after Marx's death and can be seen as the first exponent of such a perspective. Basically, this view was that Marx's scientific theory had uncovered the economic laws that ruled the capitalist world. Such laws pointed to the inevitable collapse of the capitalist system. Early Marxian thinkers, like Karl Kautsky, sought to gain a better understanding of the operation of these laws. There were several problems with this perspective. For one thing, it seemed to rule out political action, a cornerstone of Marx's position. That is, there seemed no need for individuals, especially workers, to do anything. In that the system was inevitably crumbling, all they had to do was sit back and wait for its demise. On a theoretical level, deterministic Marxism seemed to rule out the dialectical relationship between individuals and larger social structures.

These problems led to a reaction among Marxian theorists and to the development of "Hegelian Marxism" in the early 1900s. The Hegelian Marxists refused to reduce Marxism to a scientific theory that ignored individual thought and action. They are labeled *Hegelian Marxists* because they sought to combine Hegel's interest in consciousness (which some, including the author of this text, view Marx as sharing) with the determinists' interest in the economic structures of society. The Hegelian theorists were significant for both theoretical and practical reasons. Theoretically, they reinstated the importance of the individual, consciousness, and the relationship between thought and action. Practically, they emphasized the importance of individual action in bringing about a social revolution.

The major exponent of this point of view was George Lukács (Fischer, 1984). According to Martin Jay, Lukács was "the founding father of Western Marxism" and the author of *Class and Class Consciousness*, which is "generally acknowledged as the charter document of Hegelian Marxism" (1984:84). Lukács had begun in the early 1900s to integrate Marxism with sociology (in particular, Weberian and Simmelian theory). This integration was soon to accelerate with the development of critical theory in the 1920s and 1930s.

SUMMARY

This chapter sketches the early history of sociological theory in two parts. The first, and much briefer, section deals with the various social forces involved in the development of sociological theory. Although there were many such influences, we focus on how political revolution, the Industrial Revolution and the rise of capitalism, socialism, urbanization, religious change, and the growth of science affected sociological theory. The second part of the chapter examines the influence of intellectual forces on the rise of sociological theory in various countries. We begin with France and the role played by the Enlightenment, stressing the conservative and romantic reaction to it. It is out of this interplay that French sociological theory developed. In this context, we examine the major figures in the early years of French sociology—Claude Henri Saint-Simon, Auguste Comte, and Emile Durkheim.

Next we turn to Germany and the role played by Karl Marx in the development of sociology in that country. We discuss the parallel development of Marxian theory and sociological theory and the ways in which Marxian theory influenced sociology, both positively and negatively. We begin with the roots of Marxian theory in Hegelianism, materialism, and political economy. Marx's theory itself is touched upon briefly. The discussion then shifts to the roots of German sociology. Max Weber's work is examined in order to show the diverse sources of German sociology. Also discussed are some of the reasons that Weber's theory proved more acceptable to later sociologists than did Marx's ideas. This section closes with a brief discussion of Georg Simmel's work.

The rise of sociological theory in Britain is considered next. The major sources of British sociology were political economy, ameliorism, and social evolution. In this context, we touch on the work of Herbert Spencer as well as on some of the controversy that surrounded it.

This chapter closes with a brief discussion of Italian sociological theory, especially the work of Vilfredo Pareto, and the turn of the century developments in European Marxian theory, primarily economic determinism and Hegelian Marxism.

This concludes our review of the early history of sociological theory. In this chapter, we have already discussed, in historical context, the work of six theorists who will later receive full-chapter treatment—Comte, Spencer, Marx, Durkheim, Weber, and Simmel. We will also touch on these theorists in the next chapter in terms of their influence on later sociological theory. Chapter 2 will also include a brief discussion, within the historical context of more recent theoretical developments, of the work of the other three theorists defined here as classical thinkers and treated in depth later in the book—Mead, Schutz, and Parsons.

A HISTORICAL SKETCH OF SOCIOLOGICAL THEORY: THE LATER YEARS

*I*N Chapter 1 we discussed the development of sociological theory, largely in nineteenth-century Europe. In this chapter, we focus on late nineteenth- and twentieth-century developments, with particular attention to developments in the United States. Figure 2.1 shows the important intellectual influences on this development as well as the major theories and theorists.

EARLY AMERICAN SOCIOLOGICAL THEORY

It is difficult to give a precise date for the founding of sociology in the United States. There was a course in social problems taught at Oberlin as early as

1858; Comte's term *sociology* was used by George Fitzhugh in 1854; and William Graham Sumner taught social science courses at Yale beginning in 1873. During the 1880s, courses specifically bearing the title "Sociology" began to appear. The first department with *sociology* in its title was founded at the University of Kansas in 1889. In 1892, Albion Small moved to the University of Chicago and set up the new department of sociology. The Chicago department became the first important center of American sociology in general and of sociological theory in particular (Matthews, 1977).

The Politics of Early American Sociology

A major study of the politics of early American sociological theory (Schwendinger and Schwendinger, 1974) argued that the early sociologists are best described as political liberals and not, as was true of most early European theorists, as conservatives. The liberalism characteristic of early American sociology had basically two elements. First, it operated with a belief in the freedom and welfare of the individual. In this, it was far more influenced by Spencer's orientation than by Comte's more collective position. Second, many sociologists associated with this orientation adopted an evolutionary view of social progress (W. Fine, 1979). However, they split over how best to bring about this progress. Some argued that steps should be taken by the government to aid social reform, while others pushed a laissez-faire doctrine, arguing that the various components of society should be left to solve their own problems.

Liberalism, taken to its extreme, comes very close to conservatism. The belief in social progress—in reform or a laissez-faire doctrine—and the belief in the importance of the individual both lead to positions supportive of the system as a whole. The overriding belief is that the social system works or can be reformed to work. There is little criticism of the system as a whole; in the American case this means, in particular, that there is little questioning of capitalism. Instead of imminent class struggle, the early sociologists saw a future of class harmony and class cooperation. Ultimately this meant that early American sociological theory helped to rationalize exploitation, domestic and international imperialism, and social inequality (Schwendinger and Schwendinger, 1974). In the end, the political liberalism of the early sociologists had enormously conservative implications.

Social Change, Intellectual Currents, and Early American Sociology

In their analyses of the founding of American sociological theory, Roscoe Hinkle (1980) and Ellsworth Fuhrman (1980) outline several basic contexts from which that body of theory emerged. Of utmost importance are the social changes that occurred in American society after the Civil War (Bramson, 1961). In Chapter 1, we discussed an array of factors involved in the development of European sociological theory; several of these factors (such as industriali-

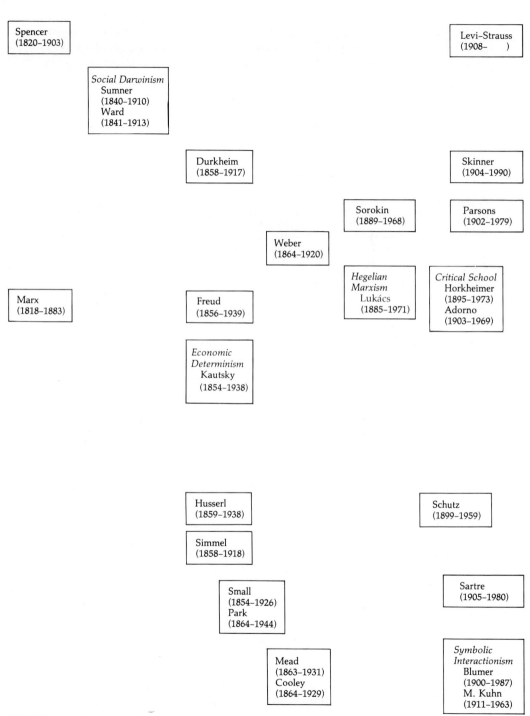

FIGURE 2.1   Sociological Theory: The Later Years

Structuralism	*Poststructuralism* Foucault (1926–1984)

Network Theory

Homans
(1910–1989)

Exchange Theory
Blau
(1918–   )
Emerson
(1925–1982)

Structural Functionalism
Merton
(1910–   )

Neofunctionalism
Alexander
(1947–   )

Radical Sociology
Mills
(1916–1962)

Conflict Theory
Dahrendorf
(1929–   )

Structural Marxism
Althusser
(1918–1990)

*Feminist
Sociological Theory*

Economic Marxism
Sweezy
(1910–   )
Braverman
(1920–1976)

Habermas
(1929–   )

*Micro–Macro and
Agency–Structure
Integration Theory*

*Metatheorizing
in Sociology*

Historical Marxism
Wallerstein
(1930–   )

*Synthetic
Theory*

*Phenomenological
Sociology*
Berger
(1929–   )
Luckmann
(1927–   )

Ethnomethodology
Garfinkel
(1929–   )

Existential Sociology

Goffman
(1922–1982)

zation and urbanization) were also intimately involved in the development of theory in America. In Fuhrman's view, the early American sociologists saw the positive possibilities of industrialization, but they were also well aware of its dangers. Although these early sociologists were attracted to the ideas about dealing with the dangers of industrialization generated by the labor movement and socialist groups, they were not in favor of radically overhauling society.

Arthur Vidich and Stanford Lyman (1985) have recently made a strong case for the influence of Christianity, especially Protestantism, on the founding of American sociology. In their view, American sociologists retained the Prostestant interest in saving the world and merely substituted one language (science) for another (religion). They argue: "From 1854, when the first works in sociology appeared in the United States, until the outbreak of World War I, sociology was a moral and intellectual reponse to the problems of American life and thought, institutions, and creeds" (Vidich and Lyman, 1985:1). Sociologists sought to define, study, and help solve these social problems. While the clergyman worked within religion to help improve it and people's lot within it, the sociologist did the same within society. Given their religious roots, and the religious parallels, the vast majority of sociologists did not challenge the basic legitimacy of society.

Another major factor in the founding of American sociology discussed by both Hinkle and Fuhrman is the simultaneous emergence in America, in the late 1800s, of both academic professions (including sociology) and the modern university system. In Europe, in contrast, the university system was already well established *before* the emergence of sociology. Although sociology had a difficult time becoming established in Europe, it found the going easier in the more fluid setting of the new American university system.

Still another factor was the impact of established European theory on American sociological theory. European theorists largely created sociological theory, and the Americans were able to rely on this groundwork. The Europeans most important to the Americans were Spencer and Comte. Simmel was of some importance in the early years, but the influence of Durkheim, Weber, and Marx was not to have a dramatic effect for a number of years. As an illustration of the impact of early European theory on American sociology, the history of the ideas of Herbert Spencer is interesting and informative.

Herbert Spencer's Influence on Sociology   Why were Spencer's ideas so much more influential in the early years of American sociology than those of Comte, Durkheim, Marx, and Weber? Hofstadter (1959) offered several explanations. To take the easiest first, Spencer wrote in English, while the others did not. In addition, Spencer did not write very technically, thereby making his work broadly accessible. Indeed, some have argued that the lack of technicality is traceable to Spencer's *not* being a very sophisticated scholar. But there are other, more important reasons for Spencer's broad appeal. He offered a scientific orientation that was attractive to an audience becoming enamored of science and its technological products. He offered a comprehensive theory that seemed to deal with the entire sweep of human history. The breadth of his ideas, as well as the voluminous work he produced, allowed his theory to be many different things to many different people. Finally, and perhaps most important, his theory was soothing and reassuring to a society undergoing the wrenching process of industrialization—society was, according to Spencer, steadily moving in the direction of greater and greater progress.

Spencer's most famous American disciple was William Graham Sumner, who accepted and expanded upon many of Spencer's Social Darwinist ideas. Spencer also influenced other early American sociologists, among them Lester Ward, Charles Horton Cooley, E. A. Ross, and Robert Park.

But by the 1930s, Spencer was in eclipse in the intellectual world in general, as well as in sociology. His Social Darwinist, laissez-faire ideas seemed ridiculous in the light of massive social problems, a world war, and a major economic depression. In 1937 Talcott Parsons announced Spencer's intellectual death for sociology when he echoed historian Crane Brinton's words of a few years earlier, "Who now reads Spencer?" Today Spencer is of little more than historical interest, but his ideas *were* important in shaping early American sociological theory. Let us look briefly at the work of two American theorists who were influenced, at least in part, by Spencer's work.

William Graham Sumner (1840–1910)   It is convenient to start a discussion of early American sociological theorists with William Graham Sumner, because he was the person who taught the first course in the United States that could be called sociology. Sumner contended that he had begun teaching sociology "years before any such attempt was made at any other university in the world" (Curtis, 1981:63).

Sumner was the major exponent of Social Darwinism in the United States, although he appeared to change his view late in life (N. Smith, 1979). The following exchange between Sumner and one of his students illustrates his "liberal" views on the need for individual freedom and his position against government interference:

> "Professor, don't you believe in any government aid to industries?"
> "No! It's root, hog, or die."
> "Yes, but hasn't the hog got a right to root?"
> "There are no rights. The world owes nobody a living."
> "You believe then, Professor, in only one system, the contract-competitive system?"
> "That's the only sound economic system. All others are fallacies."
> "Well, suppose some professor of political economy came along and took your job away from you. Wouldn't you be sore?"
> "Any other professor is welcome to try. If he gets my job, it is my fault. My business is to teach the subject so well that no one can take the job away from me."
>
> (Phelps, cited in Hofstadter, 1959:54)

Sumner basically adopted a survival-of-the-fittest approach to the social world. Like Spencer, he saw people struggling against their environment, and the fittest were those who would be successful. Thus Sumner was a supporter of human aggressiveness and competitiveness. Those who succeeded deserved it, and those who did not succeed deserved to fail. Again like Spencer, Sumner was opposed to efforts, especially government efforts, to aid those who had failed. In his view such intervention operated against the natural selection that, among people as among lower animals, allowed the fit to survive and the unfit to perish. As Sumner put it, "If we do not like the survival of the fittest, we have only one possible alternative, and that is survival of the unfittest" (Curtis, 1981:84). This theoretical system fit in well with the development of capitalism because it provided theoretical legitimacy for the existence of great differences in wealth and power.

Sumner is of little more than historical interest for two main reasons. First, his orientation and Social Darwinis90m in general have come to be regarded as little more than a crude legitimation of competitive capitalism and the status quo. Second, he failed to build a solid enough base at Yale to build a school of sociology with many disciples. That kind of success was to occur some years later at the University of Chicago (Heyl and Heyl, 1976). In spite of success in his time, "Sumner is remembered by few today" (Curtis, 1981:146).

Lester F. Ward (1841–1913)   Another sociologist of note in his time but of little lasting significance is Lester Ward. He had an unusual career in that he spent most of it as a paleontologist working for the federal government. During that time, Ward read Spencer and Comte and developed a strong interest in sociology. He published a number of works in the late 1800s and early 1900s in which he expounded his sociological theory. As a result of the notoriety that this work achieved, Ward was elected the first president of the American Sociological Society in 1906. It was only then that he took his first academic position, at Brown University, a position that he held until his death.

Ward, like Sumner, was influenced by the ideas of Herbert Spencer. He accepted the idea that people had evolved from lower forms to their present status. He believed that early society was characterized by its simplicity and its moral poverty, whereas modern society was more complex, happier, and offered greater freedom. One task of sociology, *pure sociology*, was to study the basic laws of social change and social structure. But Ward was not content simply to have sociology study social life. He believed that sociology should have a practical side; there should also be an *applied sociology*. This involved the conscious use of scientific knowledge to attain a better society. Thus, Ward was not an extreme Social Darwinist; he believed in the need for and importance of social reform.

Although of historical significance, Sumner and Ward have not been of long-term significance to sociological theory. We turn now, however, to some theorists, especially Mead, and to a school, the Chicago school, that came to dominate sociology in America. The Chicago school was unusual in the history of sociology in that it was one of the few (the Durkheimian school in Paris was another) "collective intellectual enterprises of an intergrated kind" in the history of sociology (Bulmer, 1984:1). The tradition begun at the University of Chicago is of continuing importance to sociology and its theoretical (and empirical) status.

The Chicago School[1]

The department of sociology at the University of Chicago was founded in 1892 by Albion Small. Small's intellectual work is of less contemporary significance than the key role he played in the institutionalization of sociology in the United States (Faris, 1970; Matthews, 1977). He was instrumental in creating a department at Chicago that was to become the center of the discipline in the United States for many years. Small collaborated on the first textbook in sociology in 1894. In 1895 he founded the *American Journal of Sociology*, a journal that to this day is a dominant force in the discipline. In 1905, Small cofounded the American Sociological Society, *the* major professional association of American sociologists to this date (Rhoades, 1981). (The embarrassment caused by the initials of the American Sociological Society, A.S.S., led to a name change in 1959 to the American Sociological Association—A.S.A.)

Early Chicago Sociology The early Chicago department had several distinctive characteristics. For one thing, it had a strong connection with religion (Vidich and Lyman, 1985). Some members were ministers themselves, and others were sons of ministers. Small, for example, believed that "the ultimate goal of sociology must be essentially Christian" (Matthews, 1977:95). This opinion led to a view that sociology must be interested in social reform, and this was combined with a belief that sociology should be scientific.[2] Scientific sociology with an objective of social amelioration was to be practiced in the burgeoning city of Chicago, which was beset by the positive *and* negative effects of urbanization and industrialization.

We might note here the contributions of one of the earliest members of the Chicago sociology department, W. I. Thomas (1863–1947). In 1895, Thomas became a fellow at the Chicago department, where he wrote his dissertation in 1896. Thomas's lasting significance was in his emphasis on the need to do scientific research on sociological issues (Lodge, 1986). Although he championed this position for many years, its major statement came in 1918 with the publication of *The Polish Peasant in Europe and America*, which he coauthored with Florian Znaniecki. Martin Bulmer sees it as a "landmark" study because it moved sociology away from "abstract theory and library research and

---

[1] See Bulmer (1985) for a discussion of what defines a school and why we can speak of the "Chicago school." Tiryakian (1979, 1986) also deals with schools in general, and the Chicago school in particular, and emphasizes the role played by charismatic leaders as well as methodological innovations. See also Amsterdamska (1985).

[2] As we will see, however, the Chicago school's conception of science was to become too "soft," at least in the eyes of the positivists who later came to dominate sociology.

ROBERT PARK: A Biographical Sketch

Robert Park did not follow the typical career route of an academic sociologist—college, graduate school, professorship. Instead, he led a varied career before he became a sociologist late in life. Despite his late start, Park had a profound effect on sociology in general and on theory in particular. Park's varied experiences gave him an unusual orientation to life, and this view helped to shape the Chicago school, symbolic interactionism, and, ultimately, a good portion of sociology.

Park was born in Harveyville, Pennsylvania, on February 14, 1864 (Matthews, 1977). As a student at the University of Michigan, he was exposed to a number of great thinkers, such as John Dewey. Although he was excited by ideas, Park felt a strong need to work in the real world. As Park said, "I made up my mind to go in for experience for its own sake, to gather into my soul . . . 'all the joys and sorrows of the world' " (1927/1973:253). Upon graduation, he began a career as a journalist, which gave him this real-world opportunity. He particularly liked to explore ("hunting down gambling houses and opium dens" [Park, 1927/1973:254]). He wrote about city life in vivid detail. He would go into the field, observe and analyze, and finally write up his observations. In fact, he was already doing essentially the kind of research ("scientific reporting") that came to be one of the hallmarks of Chicago sociology—that is, urban ethnology using participant observation techniques.

Although the accurate description of social life remained one of his passions, Park grew dissatisfied with newspaper work, because it did not fulfill his familial or, more important, his intellectual needs. Furthermore, it did not seem to contribute to the improvement of the world, and Park had a deep interest in social reform. In 1898, at age thirty-four, Park left newspaper work and enrolled in the philosophy department at Harvard. He remained there for a year

toward the study of the empirical world utilizing a theoretical framework" (1984:45). Norbert Wiley sees *The Polish Peasant* as crucial to the founding of sociology in the sense of "clarifying the unique intellectual space into which this discipline alone could see and explore" (1986:20). The book was the product of eight years of research in both Europe and the United States and was primarily a study of social disorganization among Polish migrants. The data were of little lasting importance. However, the methodology was significant. It involved a variety of data sources, including autobiographical material, paid writings, family letters, newspaper files, public documents, and institutional letters.

Although *The Polish Peasant* was primarily a macrosociological study of social institutions, over the course of his career, Thomas gravitated toward a microscopic, social-psychological orientation. He is best known for his social-psychological statement: "If men define situations as real, they are real in their consequences" (Thomas and Thomas, 1928:572). The emphasis was on the importance of what people think and how this affects what they do. This but then decided to move to Germany, at that time the heart of the world's intellectual life. In Berlin he encountered Georg Simmel, whose work was to have a profound influence on Park's sociology. In fact, Simmel's lectures were the *only* formal sociological training that Park received. As Park said, "I got most of my knowledge about society and human nature from my own observations" (1927/1973:257). In 1904, Park completed his doctoral dissertation at the University of Heidelberg. Characteristically, he was dissatisfied with his dissertation: "All I had to show was that little book and I was ashamed of it" (Matthews, 1977:57). He refused a summer teaching job at the University of Chicago and turned away from academe as he had earlier turned away from newspaper work.

His need to contribute to social betterment led him to become secretary and chief publicity officer for the Congo Reform Association, which was set up to help alleviate the brutality and exploitation then taking place in the Belgian Congo. During this period, he met Booker T. Washington, and he was attracted to the cause of improving the lot of black Americans. He became Washington's secretary and played a key role in the activities of the Tuskegee Institute. In 1912 he met W. I. Thomas, the Chicago sociologist, who was lecturing at Tuskegee. Thomas invited him to give a course on "the Negro in America" to a small group of graduate students at Chicago, and Park did so in 1914. It was successful, and he gave it again the next year to an audience twice as large. At this time, he joined the American Sociological Society, and only a decade later he became its president. Park gradually worked his way into a full-time appointment at Chicago, although he did not get a full professorship until 1923, when he was fifty-nine years old. Over the approximately two decades that he was affiliated with the University of Chicago, he played a key role in shaping the intellectual orientation of the sociology department.

Park remained peripatetic even after his retirement from Chicago in the early 1930s. He taught courses and oversaw research at Fisk University until he was nearly eighty years old. He traveled extensively. He died on February 7, 1944, one week before his eightieth birthday.

microscopic, social-psychological focus stood in contrast to the macroscopic, social-structural and -cultural perspectives of such European scholars as Marx, Weber, and Durkheim. It was to become one of the defining characteristics of Chicago's theoretical product—symbolic interactionism (Rock, 1979:5).

Another figure of significance at Chicago was Robert Park (1864–1944). Park had come to Chicago as a part-time instructor in 1914 and quickly worked his way into a central role in the department. As was true of Small, Park's long-term significance was not simply in his intellectual contributions. His importance for the development of sociology lay in several areas. First, he became the dominant figure in the Chicago department, which, in turn, dominated sociology into the 1930s. Second, Park had studied in Europe and was instrumental in bringing Continental thinkers to the attention of Chicago sociologists. Of particular theoretical importance, Park had taken courses with Simmel, and Simmel's ideas, particularly his focus on action and interaction, were instrumental in the development of the Chicago school's theoretical orientation (Rock, 1979:36–48). Third, prior to becoming a sociologist, Park had been a reporter, and this experience gave him a sense of the importance of urban problems and of the need to go out into the field to collect data through personal observation. Out of this emerged the Chicago school's substantive interest in urban ecology. Fourth, Park played a key role in guiding graduate students and helping develop "a cumulative program of graduate research" (Bulmer, 1984:13). Finally, in 1921, Park and Ernest W. Burgess published the first truly important sociology textbook, *An Introduction to the Science of Sociology*. It was to be an influential book for many years and was particularly notable for its commitments to science, to research, and to the study of a wide range of social phenomena.

Beginning in the late 1920s and early 1930s, Park began to spend less and less time in Chicago. Finally, his lifelong interest in race relations (he had been secretary to Booker T. Washington before becoming a sociologist) led him to take a position at Fisk University (a black university) in 1934. Although the decline of the Chicago department was not caused solely or even chiefly by Park's departure, its status began to wane in the 1930s. But before we can deal with the decline of Chicago sociology and the rise of other departments and theories, we need to return to the early days of the school and the two figures whose work was to be of the most lasting theoretical significance— Charles Horton Cooley and, most important, George Herbert Mead.

Charles Horton Cooley (1864–1929) The association of Cooley with the Chicago school is interesting in that he spent his career at the University of Michigan, not the University of Chicago. But Cooley's theoretical perspective was in line with the theory of symbolic interactionism that was to become Chicago's most important product.

Cooley received his Ph.D. from the University of Michigan in 1894. He had developed a strong interest in sociology, but there was as yet no department of sociology at Michigan. As a result, the questions for his Ph.D. examination came from Columbia University, where sociology had been taught since 1889 under the leadership of Franklin Giddings. Cooley began his teaching career at Michigan in 1892 before completion of his doctorate, and he remained there throughout his career.

Although Cooley had a wide range of views, he is mainly remembered today for his insights into the social-psychological aspects of social life. His work in this area is in line with that of George Herbert Mead, although Mead was to have a deeper and more lasting effect on sociology than Cooley. Cooley had an interest in consciousness, but he refused (as did Mead) to separate consciousness from the social context. This is best exemplified by a concept of his that survives to this day—the *looking-glass self*. By this concept, Cooley understood that people possess consciousness and that it is shaped in continuing social interaction.

A second basic concept that illustrates Cooley's social-psychological interests, and which is also of continuing interest and importance, is that of the primary group. *Primary groups* are intimate, face-to-face groups that play a key role in linking the actor to the larger society. Especially crucial are the primary groups of the young—mainly the family and the peer group. Within these groups, the individual grows into a social being. It is basically within the primary group that the looking-glass self emerges and that the ego-centered child learns to take others into account and, thereby, to become a contributing member of society.

Both Cooley and Mead rejected a *behavioristic* view of human beings, the view that people blindly and unconsciously respond to external stimuli. On the positive side, they believed that people had consciousness, a self, and that it was the responsibility of the sociologist to study this aspect of social reality. Cooley urged sociologists to try to put themselves in the place of the actors they were studying, to use the method of *sympathetic introspection*, in order to analyze consciousness. By analyzing what they as actors might do in various circumstances, sociologists could understand the meanings and motives that are at the base of social behavior. The method of sympathetic introspection seemed to many to be very unscientific. In this area, among others, Mead's work represents an advance over Cooley's. Nevertheless, there is a great deal of similarity in the interests of the two men, not the least of which is their shared view that sociology should focus on such social-psychological phenomena as consciousness, action, and interaction.

George Herbert Mead (1863–1931)   *The* most important thinker associated with the Chicago school and symbolic interactionism was not a sociologist but a philosopher, George Herbert Mead.[3] Mead started teaching philosophy at the University of Chicago in 1894, and he taught there until his death in 1931. He is something of a paradox, given his central importance in the history of sociological theory, both because he taught philosophy, not sociology, and because he published comparatively little during his lifetime. The paradox is, in part, resolved by two facts. First, Mead taught courses in social psychology in the philosophy department, and they were taken by many graduate students in sociology. His ideas had a profound effect on a number of them. These students combined Mead's ideas with those they were getting in the sociology department from people like Park and Thomas. Although there was no theory known as symbolic interactionism at the time, it was created by students out of these various inputs. Thus Mead had a deep, personal impact on the people who were later to develop symbolic interactionism. Second, these students put together their notes on Mead's courses and published a posthumous volume under his name. The work, *Mind, Self and Society* (Mead, 1934/1962), moved his ideas from the realm of oral to that of written tradition. Widely read to this day, this volume forms the main intellectual pillar of symbolic interactionism.

We deal with Mead's ideas in Chapter 9, but it is necessary at this point to underscore a few points in order to situate him historically. Mead's ideas need to be seen in the context of psychological behaviorism. Mead was quite impressed with this orientation and accepted many of its tenets. He adopted

---

[3] For a dissenting view on this, see Lewis and Smith (1980).

its focus on the actor and his behavior. He regarded as sensible the behaviorists' concern with the rewards and costs involved in the behaviors of the actors. What troubled Mead was that behaviorism did not seem to go far enough. That is, it excluded consciousness from serious consideration, arguing that it was not amenable to scientific study. Mead vehemently disagreed and sought to extend the principles of behaviorism to an analysis of the "mind." In so doing, Mead enunciated a focus similar to that of Cooley. But whereas Cooley's position seemed unscientific, Mead promised a more scientific conception of consciousness by extending the highly scientific principles and methods of psychological behaviorism.

Mead offered American sociology a social-psychological theory that stood in stark contrast to the primarily societal theories offered by most of the major European theorists—Marx, Weber, Durkheim, Comte, and Spencer. The only exception was Simmel. Thus symbolic interactionism was developed, in large part, out of Simmel's interest in action and interaction and Mead's interest in consciousness. However, such a focus led to a weakness in Mead's work, as well as in symbolic interactionism in general, at the societal and cultural levels.

The Waning of Chicago Sociology   Chicago sociology reached its peak in the 1920s, but by the 1930s, with the death of Mead and the departure of Park, the department began to lose its position of central importance in American sociology. Fred Matthews (1977; see also Bulmer, 1984) pinpoints several reasons for the decline of Chicago sociology, two of which seem of utmost importance.

First, the discipline had grown increasingly preoccupied with being scientific—that is, using sophisticated methods and employing statistical analysis. However, the Chicago school was viewed as emphasizing descriptive, ethnographic studies, often focusing on their subjects' personal orientations (in Thomas's terms, their "definitions of the situation"). Park came progressively to despise statistics (he called it "parlor magic") because it seemed to prohibit the analysis of subjectivity, of the idiosyncratic, and of the peculiar. The fact that important work in quantitative methods was done at Chicago (Bulmer, 1984:151–189) tended to be ignored in the face of its overwhelming association with qualitative methods. Second, more and more individuals outside of Chicago grew increasingly resentful of Chicago's dominance of both the American Sociological Society and the *American Journal of Sociology*. The Eastern Sociological Society was founded in 1930, and eastern sociologists became more vocal about the dominance of the Midwest in general and Chicago in particular (Wiley, 1979:63). By 1935, the revolt against Chicago led to a non-Chicago secretary of the association and the establishment of a new official journal, the *American Sociological Review* (Lengermann, 1979). According to Wiley, "the Chicago school had fallen like a mighty oak" (1979:63). This signaled the growth of other power centers, most notably Harvard and the Ivy League in general. Symbolic interactionism was largely an indeterminate, oral tradition and as such eventually lost ground to more explicit and codified theoretical systems like the structural functionalism associated with the Ivy League (Rock, 1979:12).

SOCIOLOGICAL THEORY TO MID-CENTURY

The Rise of Harvard, the Ivy League, and Structural Functionalism

We can trace the rise of sociology at Harvard from the arrival of Pitirim Sorokin in 1930. When Sorokin arrived at Harvard, there was no sociology department, but by the end of his first year one had been organized, and he had been appointed its head. Although Sorokin was a sociological theorist, and he continued to publish into the 1960s, his work is surprisingly little cited today. His theorizing has not stood the test of time very well. Sorokin's long-term significance may well have been in the creation of the Harvard sociology department and the hiring of Talcott Parsons (who had been an instructor of economics at Harvard) for the position of instructor of sociology. Parsons became *the* dominant figure in American sociology for introducing European theorists to an American audience, for his own sociological theories, and for his many students who themselves became major sociological theorists.

Pitirim Sorokin (1889–1968) Sorokin wrote an enormous amount and developed a theory that, if anything, surpassed Parsons's in scope and complexity. The most complete statement of this theory is contained in the four-volume *Social and Cultural Dynamics* published between 1937 and 1941. In it, Sorokin drew on a wide range of empirical data to develop a general theory of social and cultural change. In contrast to those who sought to develop evolutionary theories of social change, Sorokin developed a cyclical theory. He saw societies as oscillating among three different types of mentalities—sensate, ideational, and idealistic. Societies dominated by *sensatism* emphasize the role of the senses in comprehending reality; those dominated by a more transcendental and highly religious way of understanding reality are *ideational*; and *idealistic* societies are transitional types balancing sensatism and religiosity.

The motor of social change is to be found in the internal logic of each of these sytems. That is, they are pressed internally to extend their mode of thinking to its logical extreme. Thus a sensate society ultimately becomes so sensual that it provides the groundwork for its own demise. As sensatism reaches its logical end point, people turn to ideational systems as a refuge. But once such a system has gained ascendancy, it too is pushed to its end point, with the result that society becomes excessively religious. The stage is then set for the rise of an idealistic culture and, ultimately, for the cycle to repeat itself. Sorokin not only developed an elaborate theory of social change, but he also marshaled detailed evidence from art, philosophy, politics, and so forth to support his theory. It was clearly an impressive accomplishment.

PITIRIM A. SOROKIN: A Biographical Sketch

Pitirim Sorokin was born in a remote village in Russia on January 21, 1889. In his teenage years, and while a seminary student, Sorokin was arrested for revolutionary activities and spent four months in prison. Eventually, Sorokin made his way to St. Petersburg University and interspersed diligent studies, teaching responsibilities, and revolutionary activities that once again landed him in prison briefly. Sorokin's dissertation was scheduled to be defended in March 1917, but before his examination could take place, the Russian Revolution was under way. Sorokin was not able to earn his doctorate until 1922. Active in the revolution, but opposed to the Bolsheviks, Sorokin took a position in Kerensky's provisional government. But when the Bolsheviks emerged victorious, Sorokin once again found himself in prison, this time at the hands of the Bolsheviks. Eventually, under direct orders from Lenin, Sorokin was freed and allowed to return to the university and pick up where he had left off. However, his work was censored, and he was harassed by the secret police. Sorokin finally was allowed to leave Russia, and, after a stay in Czechoslovakia, he arrived in the United States in October 1923.

At first, Sorokin gave lectures at various universities but eventually obtained a position at the University of Minnesota. He soon became a full professor. Sorokin already had published several books in Russia, and he continued to turn them out at a prodigious rate in the United States. Of his productivity at Minnesota, Sorokin said, "I knew it exceeded the lifetime productivity of the average sociologist" (1963:224). Books such as *Social Mobility* and *Contemporary Sociological Theories* gave him a national reputation, and by 1929 he was offered (and accepted) the first chair at Harvard University in sociology. The position was placed in the department of economics because there was not yet a sociology department at Harvard.

Soon after his arrival at Harvard, a separate department of sociology was created, and Sorokin was named as its first chairman. In that position, Sorokin helped build the most important sociology department in the United States. During this period, Sorokin also completed what would become his best-known work, *Social and Cultural Dynamics* (1937–1941).

Pitirim Sorokin has been described as "the Peck's bad boy and devil's advocate of American sociology" (Williams, 1980b:100). Blessed with an enormous ego, Sorokin seemed

There is much more to Sorokin's theorizing, but this introduction should give the reader a feeling for the breadth of his work. It is difficult to explain why Sorokin has fallen out of favor in sociological theory. Perhaps it is the result of one of the things that Sorokin loved to attack, and in fact wrote a book about, *Fads and Foibles in Modern Sociology and Related Sciences* (1956). It may be that Sorokin will be rediscovered by a future generation of sociological theorists. At the moment, his work remains outside the mainstream of modern sociological theorizing.

Talcott Parsons (1902–1979) Although he published some early essays, Parsons's major contribution in the early years was in his influence on gradcritical of almost everyone and everything. As a result, Sorokin and his work were the subject of much critical analysis. All of this is clear in an excerpt from a letter he wrote to the editor of the *American Journal of Sociology:*

> The strongly disparaging character of the reviews is a good omen for my books because of a high correlation between the damning of my books . . . and their subsequent career. The more strongly they have been damned (and practically all my books were damned by your reviewers), the more significant and successful were my damned works.
>
> (Sorokin, 1963:229)

One of Sorokin's more interesting and long-running feuds was with Talcott Parsons. Parsons had been appointed at Harvard as an instructor of sociology when Sorokin was chairman of the department. Under Sorokin's leadership, Parsons made very slow career progress at Harvard. Eventually, however, he emerged as the dominant sociologist at Harvard and in the United States. The conflict between Sorokin and Parsons was heightened by the extensive overlap between their theories. Despite the similarities, Parsons's work attracted a far wider and far more enduring audience than did Sorokin's. As the years went by, Sorokin developed a rather interesting attitude toward Parsons's work, which was reflected in several of his books. On the one hand, he was inclined to criticize Parsons for stealing many of his best ideas. On the other hand, he was severely critical of Parsonsian theory. Another tension in their relationship was over graduate students. One of the great achievements of the early Harvard department was its ability to attract talented graduate students like Robert Merton. Although these students were influenced by the ideas of both men, Parsons's influence proved more enduring than Sorokin's. Parsons replaced Sorokin as chairman of the sociology department and transformed it into the Department of Social Relations. Of that, Sorokin said:

> So I am not responsible for whatever has happened to the department since, either for its merging with abnormal and social psychology and cultural anthropology to form a "Department of Social Relations," or for the drowning of sociology in an eclectic mass of the odds and ends of these disciplines. . . . The Department of Social Relations . . . has hardly produced as many distinguished sociologists as the Department of Sociology did . . . under my chairmanship.
>
> (Sorokin, 1963:251)

Sorokin was eventually isolated in the Harvard department, relegated to a "desolate looking" office, and reduced to putting a mimeographed statement under the doors of departmental offices claiming that Parsons had stolen his ideas (Coser, 1977:490).

Sorokin died on February 11, 1968.

uate students who themselves were to become notable sociological theorists. The most famous was Robert Merton, who received his Ph.D. in 1936 and soon became a major theorist and the heart of Parsonsian-style theorizing at Columbia University. In the same year (1936), Kingsley Davis received his Ph.D., and he, along with Wilbert Moore (who received his Harvard degree in 1940), wrote one of the central works in structural-functional theory, the theory that was to become the major product of Parsons and the Parsonsians. But Parsons's influence was not restricted to the 1930s. Remarkably, he produced graduate students of great influence well into the 1960s.

The pivotal year for Parsons and for American sociological theory was 1937, the year in which he published *The Structure of Social Action*. This book was of significance to sociological theory in America for four main reasons. First, it served to introduce grand European theorizing to a large American audience. The bulk of the book was devoted to Durkheim, Weber, and Pareto. His interpretations of these theorists shaped their images in American sociology for many years.

Second, Parsons devoted almost no attention to Marx, although he emphasized the work of Durkheim and Weber and even Pareto. As a result, Marxian theory was to continue to be largely excluded from legitimate sociology.

Third, *The Structure of Social Action* made the case for sociological theorizing as a legitimate and significant sociological activity. The theorizing that has taken place in the United States since then owes a deep debt to Parsons's work.

Finally, Parsons argued for specific sociological theories that were to have a profound influence on sociology. At first, Parsons was thought of, and thought of himself, as an action theorist. He seemed to focus on actors and their thoughts and actions. But by the close of his 1937 work and increasingly in his later work Parsons sounded more like a structural-functional theorist focusing on large-scale social and cultural systems. Although Parsons argued that there was no contradiction between these theories, he became best known as a structural functionalist, and he was the primary exponent of this theory, which gained dominance within sociology and maintained that position until recent years. Parsons's theoretical strength, and that of structural functionalism, lay in delineating the relationships among large-scale social structures and institutions (see Chapter 11).

Parsons's major statements on his structural-functional theory came in the early 1950s in several works, most notably *The Social System* (1951). In that work and others, Parsons tended to concentrate on the structures of society and their relationship to each other. These structures were seen as mutually supportive and tending toward a dynamic equilibrium. The emphasis was on how order was maintained among the various elements of society. Change was seen as an orderly process, and Parsons (1966, 1971) ultimately came to adopt a neoevolutionary view of social change. Parsons was concerned not only with the social system per se but also with its relationship to the other *action systems,* especially the cultural and personality systems. But his basic view on intersystemic relations was essentially the same as his view of intrasystemic relations, that is, that they were defined by cohesion, consensus, and order. In other words, the various *social structures* performed a variety of positive *functions* for each other.

It is clear, then, why Parsons came to be defined primarily as a *structural functionalist.* As his fame grew, so did the strength of structural-functional theory in the United States. His work lay at the core of this theory, but his students and disciples also concentrated on extending both the theory and its dominance in the United States.

Although Parsons played a number of important and positive roles in the history of sociological theory in the United States, his work also had a number of negative consequences. First, he offered interpretations of European theorists that seemed to reflect his own theoretical orientation more than theirs. Many American sociologists were initially exposed to erroneous interpretations of the European masters. Second, as was pointed out above, early in his career Parsons largely ignored Marx, with the result that Marx's ideas continued for many years on the periphery of sociology. Third, his own theory as it developed over the years had a number of serious weaknesses. However, Parsons's preeminence in American sociology served for many years to mute or overwhelm the critics. Not until much later did the weaknesses of Parsons's theory, and more generally of structural functionalism, receive a full airing.

But we are getting too far ahead of the story, and we need to return to the early 1930s and other developments at Harvard. We can gain a good deal of insight into the development of the Harvard department by looking at it through an account of its other major figure—George Homans.

George Homans **(1910–1989)**   A wealthy Bostonian, George Homans received his bachelor's degree from Harvard in 1932 (Homans, 1962, 1984). As a result of the Great Depression, he was unemployed but certainly not penniless. In the fall of 1932, L. J. Henderson, a physiologist, was offering a course in the theories of Vilfredo Pareto, and Homans was invited to attend and accepted. (Parsons also attended the Pareto seminars.) Homans's description of why he was drawn to and taken with Pareto says much about why American sociological theory was so highly conservative, so anti-Marxist:

> I took to Pareto because he made clear to me what I was already prepared to believe. I do not know all the reasons why I was ready for him, but I can give one. Someone has said that much modern sociology is an effort to answer the arguments of the revolutionaries. As a Republican Bostonian who had not rejected his comparatively wealthy family, I felt during the thirties that I was under personal attack, above all from the Marxists. I was ready to believe Pareto because he provided me with a defense.
>
> (Homans, 1962:4)

Homans's exposure to Pareto led to a book, *An Introduction to Pareto* (coauthored with Charles Curtis), published in 1934. The publication of this book made Homans a sociologist even though Pareto's work was virtually the only sociology he had read up to that point.

In 1934 Homans was named a junior fellow at Harvard, a program started to avoid the problems associated with the Ph.D. program. In fact, Homans never did earn a Ph.D. even though he became one of the major sociological figures of his day. Homans was a junior fellow until 1939, and in those years he absorbed more and more sociology. In 1939 Homans was affiliated with the sociology department, but the connection was broken by the war.

By the time Homans had returned from the war, the Department of Social Relations had been founded by Parsons at Harvard, and Homans joined it. Although Homans respected some aspects of Parsons's work, he was highly critical of his style of theorizing. A long-run exchange began between the two men that later manifested itself publicly in the pages of many books and journals. Basically, Homans argued that Parsons's theory was not a theory at all but rather a vast system of intellectual categories into which most aspects of the social world fit. Further, Homans believed that theory should be built from the ground up on the basis of careful observations of the social world. Parsons's theory, however, started on the general theoretical level and worked its way down to the empirical level.

In his own work, Homans amassed a large number of empirical observations over the years, but it was only in the 1950s that he hit upon a satisfactory theoretical approach with which to analyze these data. That theory was psychological behaviorism, as it was best expressed in the ideas of his colleague at Harvard, the psychologist B. F. Skinner. On the basis of this perspective, Homans developed his exchange theory. We will pick up the story of this theoretical development later in the chapter. The crucial point here is that Harvard and its major theoretical product, structural functionalism, became preeminent in sociology in the late 1930s, replacing the Chicago school and symbolic interactionism.

The Chicago School in Decline

We left the Chicago department in the mid-1930s on the wane with the death of Mead, the departure of Park, the revolt of eastern sociologists, and the founding of the *American Sociological Review*. But the Chicago school did not disappear. Into the early 1950s it continued to be an important force in sociology. Important Ph.D.s were still produced there, such as Anselm Strauss and Arnold Rose. Major figures remained at Chicago, such as Everett Hughes (Faught, 1980), who was of central importance to the development of the sociology of occupations.

However, the central figure in the Chicago department in this era was Herbert Blumer (1900–1987) (*Symbolic Interaction*, 1988). He was a major exponent of the theoretical approach developed at Chicago out of the work of Mead, Cooley, Simmel, Park, Thomas, and others. In fact, it was Blumer who coined the phrase *symbolic interactionism* in 1937. Blumer played a key role in keeping this tradition alive through his teaching at Chicago. He also wrote a number of essays that were instrumental in keeping symbolic interactionism vital into the 1950s. Blumer was also important because of the organizational positions he held in sociology. From 1930 to 1935, he was the secretary-treasurer of the American Sociological Society, and in 1956 he became its president. More important, he held institutional positions that affected the nature of what was published in sociology. Between 1941 and 1952, he was editor of the *American Journal of Sociology* and was instrumental in keeping it one of the major outlets for work in the Chicago tradition in general and symbolic interactionism in particular.

While the East Coast universities were coming under the sway of structural functionalism, the Midwest remained (and to this day remains) a stronghold of symbolic interactionism. In the 1940s, major symbolic interactionists fanned out across the Midwest—Arnold Rose was at Minnesota, Robert Habenstein at Missouri, Gregory Stone at Michigan State, and, most important, Manford Kuhn (1911–1963) at Iowa.

There developed a split between Blumer at Chicago and Kuhn at Iowa; in fact, people began to talk of the differences between the Chicago and the Iowa schools of symbolic interactionism. Basically, the split occurred over the issue of science and methodology. Kuhn accepted the symbolic-interactionist focus on actors and their thoughts and actions, but he argued that they should be studied more scientifically—for example, by using questionnaires. Blumer was in favor of "softer" methods such as sympathetic introspection and participant observation.

Despite this flurry of activity, the Chicago school was in decline, especially given the movement of Blumer in 1952 from Chicago to the University of California at Berkeley. The University of Chicago continued to have a strong sociology department, of course, but it had less and less in common with the Chicago tradition. Although the Chicago school was moribund, symbolic interactionism still had vitality with its major exponents being dispersed across the country.

Developments in Marxian Theory

From the early 1900s to the 1930s, Marxian theory had continued to develop largely independently of mainstream sociological theory. At least partially, the exception to this was the emergence of the critical, or Frankfurt, school out of the earlier Hegelian Marxism.

The idea of a Frankfurt school for the development of Marxian theory was the product of Felix J. Weil. The Institute of Social Research was officially founded in Frankfurt, Germany, on February 3, 1923 (Bottomore, 1984; Jay, 1973, 1986). Over the years, a number of the most famous thinkers in Marxian theory were associated with the critical school—Max Horkheimer, Theodor Adorno, Erich Fromm, Herbert Marcuse, and, more recently, Jurgen Habermas.

The institute functioned in Germany until 1934, but by then things were growing increasingly uncomfortable under the Nazi regime. The Nazis had little use for the Marxian ideas that dominated the institute, and their hostility was heightened because many of those associated with the institute were Jewish. In 1934 Horkheimer, as head of the institute, came to New York to discuss its status with the president of Columbia University. Much to Horkheimer's surprise, he was invited to affiliate the institute with the university, and he was even offered a building on campus. And so *a* center of Marxian theory moved to *the* center of the capitalist world. The institute stayed there until the end of the war, but after the war, pressure mounted to return it to Germany. In 1949, Horkheimer did return to Germany, and he brought the institute with him. Although the institute itself moved to Germany, many of the figures associated with it took independent career directions.

It is important to underscore a few of the most important aspects of critical theory. In its early years, those associated with the institute tended to be fairly traditional Marxists devoting a good portion of their attention to the economic domain. But around 1930, a major change took place as this group of thinkers began to shift its attention from the economy to the cultural system, which it came to see as the major force in modern capitalist society. This was consistent with, but an extension of, the position taken earlier by Hegelian Marxists like Georg Lukács. To help them understand the cultural domain, the critical theorists were attracted to the work of Max Weber (Greisman and Ritzer, 1981). The effort to combine Marx with Weber gave the critical school some of its distinctive orientations and served to make it more legitimate in later years to sociologists who began to grow interested in Marxian theory.

A second major step taken by at least some members of the critical school was to employ the rigorous social-scientific techniques developed by American sociologists to research issues of interest to Marxists. This, like the adoption of Weberian theory, made the critical school more acceptable to mainstream sociologists.

Third, critical theorists made an effort to integrate individually oriented Freudian theory with the societal- and cultural-level insights of Marx and Weber. This seemed to many sociologists to represent a more inclusive theory than that offered by either Marx or Weber alone. If nothing else, the effort to combine such disparate theories proved stimulating to sociologists and many other intellectuals.

The critical school has done much useful work since the 1920s, and a significant amount of it is of relevance to sociologists. However, the critical school had to await the late 1960s before it was "discovered" by large numbers of American theorists.

SOCIOLOGICAL THEORY FROM MID-CENTURY

Structural Functionalism: Peak and Decline

The 1940s and 1950s were paradoxically the years of greatest dominance and the beginnings of the decline of structural functionalism. In these years, Parsons produced his major statements that clearly reflected his shift from action theory to structural functionalism. Parsons's students had fanned out across the country and occupied dominant positions in many of the major sociology departments (for example, Columbia and Cornell). These students were producing works of their own that were widely recognized contributions to structural-functional theory. For example, in 1945 Kingsley Davis and Wilbert Moore published an essay analyzing social stratification from a structural-functional perspective. It was one of the clearest statements ever made of the structural-functional view. In it, they argued that stratification was a structure that was functionally necessary for the existence of society. In other words, in ideological terms they came down on the side of inequality.

In 1949 Merton (1949/1968) published an essay that became *the* program statement of structural functionalism. In it, Merton carefully sought to delineate the essential elements of the theory and to extend it in some new directions. He made it clear that structural functionalism should deal not only with positive functions but also with negative consequences (dysfunctions). Moreover, it should focus on the net balance of functions and dysfunctions or whether a structure is overall more functional or more dysfunctional.

However, just as it was gaining theoretical hegemony, structural functionalism came under attack, and the attacks mounted until they reached a crescendo in the 1960s and 1970s. The Davis-Moore structural-functional theory of stratification was attacked from the start, and the criticisms persist to this day. Beyond that, a series of more general criticisms received even wider recognition in the discipline. There was an attack by C. Wright Mills on Parsons in 1959, and other major criticisms were mounted by David Lockwood (1956), Alvin Gouldner (1959/1967, 1970), and Irving Horowitz (1962/1967). In the 1950s, these attacks were seen as little more than "guerrilla raids," but as sociology moved into the 1960s, the dominance of structural functionalism was clearly in jeopardy.[4]

George Huaco (1986) linked the rise and decline of structural functionalism to the position of American society in the world order. As America rose to world dominance after 1945, structural functionalism achieved hegemony within sociology. Structural functionalism supported America's dominant position in the world in two ways. First, the structural-functional view that "every pattern has consequences which contribute to the preservation and survival of the larger system" was "nothing less than a celebration of the United States and its world hegemony" (Huaco, 1986:52). Second, the structural-functional emphasis on equilibrium (the best social change is no change) meshed well with the interests of the United States, then "the wealthiest and most powerful empire in the world." The decline of U.S. world dominance in the 1970s coincided with structural functionalism's loss of its preeminent position in sociological theory.

Radical Sociology in America: C. Wright Mills

As we have seen, although Marxian theory was largely ignored or reviled by mainstream American sociologists, there were exceptions, the most notable of which is C. Wright Mills (1916–1962). Although Mills's own lasting theoretical contributions are few, he is notable for his almost single-handed effort to keep a Marxian tradition alive in sociological theory. Modern Marxian sociologists have far outstripped Mills in theoretical sophistication, but they owe him a

---

[4]In spite of this, Patricia Wilner (1985) reports a continuing focus on "consensus" articles in the *American Sociological Review* between 1936 and 1982. However, it should be added that although structural functionalism is sometimes called consensus theory, a focus on consensus does *not* mean that one is necessarily using structural-functional theory.

C. WRIGHT MILLS: A Biographical Sketch

C. Wright Mills was born on August 28, 1916, in Waco, Texas. He came from a conventional middle-class background; his father was an insurance broker and his mother a housewife. He attended the University of Texas and by 1939 had obtained both a bachelor's and a master's degree. He was quite an unusual student who, by the time he left Texas, already had published articles in the two major sociology journals. Mills did his doctoral work at, and received a Ph.D. from, the University of Wisconsin (Scimecca, 1977). He took his first job at the University of Maryland but spent the bulk of his career, from 1945 until his death, at Columbia University.

Mills was a man in a hurry (Horowitz, 1983). By the time he died at forty-five from his fourth heart attack, Mills had made a number of important contributions to sociology.

One of the most striking things about C. Wright Mills was his combativeness; he seemed to be constantly at war. He had a tumultuous personal life, characterized by many affairs, three marriages, and a child from each marriage. He had an equally tumultuous professional life. He seemed to have fought with and against everyone and everything. As a graduate student at Wisconsin, he took on a number of his professors. Later, in one of his early essays, he engaged in a thinly disguised critique of the ex-chairman of the Wisconsin department. He called the senior theorist at Wisconsin, Howard Becker, a "real fool" (Horowitz, 1983). He eventually came into conflict with his coauthor, Hans Gerth, who called Mills "an excellent operator, whippersnapper, promising young man on the make, and Texas cowboy á la ride and shoot" (Horowitz, 1983:72). As a professor at Columbia, Mills was isolated and estranged from his colleagues. Said one of his Columbia colleagues:

> There was no estrangement between Wright and me. We began estranged. Indeed, at the memorial services or meeting that was organized at Columbia University at his death, I seemed to be the only person who could not say: 'I used to be his friend, but we became somewhat distant.' It was rather the reverse.
>
> (cited in Horowitz, 1983:83)

Mills was an outsider and he knew it: "I am an outlander, not only regionally, but down deep and for good" (Horowitz, 1983:84). In *The Sociological Imagination* (1959), Mills not only challenged the dominant theorist of his day, Talcott Parsons, but also the dominant methodologist, Paul Lazarsfeld, who also happened to be a colleague at Columbia.

Mills, of course, was not only at odds with people; he was also at odds with American society and challenged it on a variety of fronts. But perhaps most telling is the fact that when Mills visited the Soviet Union and was honored as a major critic of American society, he took the occasion to attack the censorship in the Soviet Union with a toast to an early Soviet leader who had been purged and murdered by the Stalinists: "to the day when the complete works of Leon Trotsky are published in the Soviet Union!" (Tilman, 1984:8)

C. Wright Mills died in Nyack, New York, on March 20, 1962.

deep debt nonetheless for the personal and professional activities that helped set the stage for their own work (Alt, 1985–1986). Mills was not a Marxist, and he did not read Marx until the mid-1950s. Even then he was restricted to the few available English translations, because he could not read German. As Mills had published most of his major works by then, his work was not informed by a very sophisticated Marxian theory.

Mills published two major works that reflected his radical politics as well as his weaknesses in Marxian theory. The first was *White Collar* (1951), an acid critique of the status of a growing occupational category, white-collar workers. The second was *The Power Elite* (1956), a book that sought to show how America was dominated by a small group of businessmen, politicians, and military leaders. Sandwiched in between was his most theoretically sophisticated work, *Character and Social Structure* (1953), coauthored with Hans Gerth. Ironically, considering Mills's major role in the history of Marxian sociological theory, this book was stronger in Weberian and Freudian theory than Marxian theory. Despite this, the book is a major theoretical contribution, though it is not widely read today—possibly because it did not seem to fit well with Mills's best-known radical works. In fact, it was heavily influenced by Hans Gerth, who had a keen interest in Weberian theory.

In the 1950s, Mills's interest moved more in the direction of Marxism and in the problems of the Third World. This interest resulted in a book on the communist revolution in Cuba, *Listen, Yankee: The Revolution in Cuba* (1960) and *The Marxists* (1962). Mills's radicalism put him on the periphery of American sociology. He was the object of much criticism, and he, in turn, became a severe critic of sociology. The critical attitude culminated in *The Sociological Imagination* (1959). Of particular note is Mills's severe criticism of Talcott Parsons and his practice of grand theory. In fact, many sociologists were more familiar with Mills's critique than they were with the details of Parsons's work.

Mills died in 1962, an outcast in sociology. However, before the decade was out, both radical sociology and Marxian theory were to begin to make important inroads into the discipline.

The Development of Conflict Theory

Another precursor to a true union of Marxism and sociological theory was the development of a conflict-theory alternative to structural functionalism. As we have just seen, structural functionalism had no sooner gained leadership in sociological theory than it came under increasing attack. The attack was multifaceted: structural functionalism was accused of such things as being politically conservative, unable to deal with social change because of its focus on static structures, and incapable of adequately analyzing social conflict.

One of the results of this criticism was an effort on the part of a number of sociologists to overcome the problems of structural functionalism by integrating a concern for structure with an interest in conflict. This work constituted the development of *conflict theory* as an alternative to structural-functional theory. Unfortunately, it often seemed little more than a mirror image of structural functionalism with little intellectual integrity of its own.

The first effort of note was Lewis Coser's (1956) book on the functions of social conflict. This work clearly tried to deal with social conflict from within the framework of a structural-functional view of the world. Although it is useful to look at the functions of conflict, there is much more to the study of conflict than an analysis of its positive functions.

Other people sought to reconcile the differences between structural functionalism and conflict theory (Coleman, 1971; Himes, 1966; van den Berghe, 1963). Although these efforts had some utility, the authors were generally guilty of papering over the major differences between the two theoretical alternatives (A. Frank, 1966/1974).

The biggest problem with most of conflict theory was that it lacked what it needed most—a sound basis in Marxian theory. After all, Marxian theory was well developed outside of sociology and should have provided a base on which to develop a sophisticated sociological theory of conflict. The one exception here is the work of Ralf Dahrendorf (born 1929).

Dahrendorf is a European scholar who is well versed in Marxian theory. He sought to embed his conflict theory in the Marxian tradition. However, in the end his conflict theory looked more like a mirror image of structural functionalism than a Marxian theory of conflict. Dahrendorf's major work, *Class and Class Conflict in Industrial Society* (1959), was the most influential piece in conflict theory, but that was largely because it sounded so much like structural functionalism that it was palatable to mainstream sociologists. That is, Dahrendorf operated at the same level of analysis as the structural functionalists (structures and institutions) and looked at many of the same issues. (In other words, they are part of the same paradigm; see Appendix.) He recognized that although aspects of the social system could fit together rather neatly, there also could be considerable conflict and tension among them.

In the end, conflict theory should be seen as little more than a transitional development in the history of sociological theory. It failed because it did not go far enough in the direction of Marxian theory. It was still too early in the 1950s and 1960s for American sociology to accept a full-fledged Marxian approach. But conflict theory was helpful in setting the stage for the beginning of that acceptance by the late 1960s.

We should note the contribution to conflict theory by Randall Collins (1975, 1990). On the one hand, Collins's effort suffers from the same weakness as the other works in the conflict tradition: it is relatively impoverished in terms of Marxian theory. However, Collins did point up another weakness in the conflict tradition, and he attempted to overcome it. The problem is that conflict theory generally focuses on social structures; it has little or nothing to say about actors and their thoughts and actions. Collins, schooled in the phenomenological-ethnomethodological tradition (see below), attempted to move conflict theory in this direction.

The Birth of Exchange Theory

Another important theoretical development begun in the 1950s was the rise of exchange theory. The major figure in this development is George Homans, a sociologist whom we left earlier just as he was being drawn to B. F. Skinner's psychological behaviorism. Skinner's behaviorism is the major source of Homans's, and sociology's, exchange theory.

Dissatisfied with Parsons's deductive strategy of developing theory, Homans was casting about for a workable alternative for handling sociological theory inductively. Further, Homans wanted to stay away from the cultural and structural foci of Parsonsian theory and wanted to concentrate instead on people and their behavior. With this in mind, Homans turned to the work of his colleague at Harvard, B. F. Skinner. At first, Homans did not see how Skinner's propositions, developed to help explain the behavior of pigeons, might be useful for understanding human social behavior. But as Homans looked further at data from sociological studies of small groups and anthropological studies of primitive societies, he began to see that Skinner's behaviorism was applicable and that it provided a theoretical alternative to Parsonsian-style structural functionalism. This led to an article entitled "Social Behavior as Exchange" in 1958 and in 1961 to a full-scale, book-length statement of Homans's theoretical position, *Social Behavior: Its Elementary Forms*. These works represented the birth of exchange theory as an important perspective in sociology. Since then exchange theory has attracted a good deal of attention, both positive and negative.

Homans's basic view was that the heart of sociology lies in the study of individual behavior and interaction. He was little interested in consciousness or in the various kinds of large-scale structures and institutions that were of concern to most sociologists. His main interest was rather in the reinforcement patterns, the history of rewards and costs, that lead people to do what they do. Basically, Homans argued that people continue to do what they have found to be rewarding in the past. Conversely, they cease doing what has proved to be costly in the past. In order to understand behavior, we need to understand an individual's history of rewards and costs. Thus, the focus of sociology should not be on consciousness or on social structures and institutions but on patterns of reinforcement.

As its name suggests, exchange theory is concerned not only with individual behavior but also with interaction between people involving an exchange of rewards and costs. The premise is that interactions are likely to continue when there is an exchange of rewards. Conversely, interactions that are costly to one or both parties are much less likely to continue.

Another major statement in exchange theory is Peter Blau's *Exchange and Power in Social Life*, published in 1964. Blau basically adopted Homans's perspective, but there was an important difference. Whereas Homans was content to deal mainly with elementary forms of social behavior, Blau wanted to integrate this with exchange at the structural and cultural levels, beginning with exchanges among actors, but quickly moving on to the larger structures that emerge out of this exchange. He ended by dealing with exchanges among large-scale structures. This is very different from the exchange theory envisioned by Homans. In some senses, it represents a return to the kind of Parsonian-style theorizing that Homans found so objectionable. Nevertheless, the effort to deal with both small- and large-scale exchange in an integrated way proved a useful theoretical step.

While he was eclipsed for many years by Homans and Blau, Richard Emerson (1981) has recently emerged as a central figure in exchange theory. He is particularly noted for his effort to develop a more integrated macro-micro approach to exchange theory. In sum, exchange theory has now developed into a significant strand of sociological theory, and it continues to attract new adherents and to take new directions (Cook, O'Brien, and Kollock, 1990; see also below).

Dramaturgical Analysis: The Work of Erving Goffman

Erving Goffman (1922–1982) is often thought of as the last major thinker associated with the original Chicago school. He received his Ph.D. from Chicago in 1953, one year after Herbert Blumer (who had been Goffman's teacher) had left Chicago for Berkeley. Soon after, Goffman joined Blumer at Berkeley, where they were able to develop something of a center of symbolic interactionism. However, it never became anything like Chicago had been. Blumer was past his organizational prime, and Goffman did not become a focus of graduate-student work. After 1952 the fortunes of symbolic interactionism declined, although it continues to be a prominent sociological theory.

In spite of the decline of symbolic interactionism in general, Goffman carved out a strong and distinctive place for himself in contemporary sociological theory. Between the 1950s and the 1970s, Goffman published a series of books and essays that gave birth to dramaturgical analysis as a variant of symbolic interactionism. Although Goffman shifted his attention in his later years, he remained best known for his *dramaturgical theory.*

Goffman's best-known statement of dramaturgical theory, *Presentation of Self in Everyday Life,* was published in 1959. (Over the next fifteen years Goffman published several books and a number of essays that expanded upon his dramaturgical view of the world.) To put it simply, Goffman saw much in common between theatrical performances and the kinds of "acts" we all put on in our day-to-day actions and interactions. Interaction is seen as very fragile, maintained by social performances. Poor performances or disruptions are seen as great threats to social interaction just as they are to theatrical performances.

Goffman went quite far in his analogy between the stage and social interaction. In all social interaction there is a *front region,* which is the parallel of the stage front in a theatrical performance. Actors on the stage and in social life are both seen as being interested in appearances, wearing costumes, and using props. Furthermore, in both there is a *back region,* a place to which the actors can retire to prepare themselves for their performance. Backstage, or offstage in theater terms, the actors can shed their roles and be themselves.

Dramaturgical analysis is clearly consistent with its symbolic-interactionist roots. It has a focus on actors, action, and interaction. Working in the same arena as traditional symbolic interactionism, Goffman found a brilliant metaphor in the theater to shed new light on small-scale social processes.

Goffman's work is widely read today and acknowledged for its originality and its profusion of insights (R. Collins, 1986; Ditton, 1980). Although he is viewed as an important theorist, not everyone accepts that view. There are several reasons for this. First, he is seen as having been interested in rather esoteric topics rather than the truly essential aspects of social life. Second, he was a micro theorist in an era in which the great rewards have gone to macro theorists. As Randall Collins says, "The more we look at this [Goffman's] work . . . the more he emerges as the leading figure in the microsociology of our times" (1981c:6). Third, he attracted few students who were able to build theoretically upon his insights; indeed, some believe that it is impossible to build upon Goffman's work. It is seen as little more than a series of idiosyncratic bursts of brilliant insight. Finally, little theoretical work has been done by others in the dramaturgical tradition (one exception is Lyman and Scott [1970].)

The one area in which Goffman's work has proved fruitful is in empirical research utilizing his dramaturgical approach. In recent years a number of works employing his dramaturgical approach have appeared, including Snow, Zurcher, and Peters's (1984) study of victory celebrations of crowds at football games as dramaturgical performances, Haas and Shaffir's (1982) dramaturgical analysis of the medical profession, Zurcher's (1985) look at war games, and Kitahara's (1986) study of the dramaturgical devices used by Commodore Perry to open Japan to the West.

It is difficult to predict the future of dramaturgical analysis, although it has been dimmed because Goffman himself later moved in structural directions in his work.

The Development of the "Creative" Sociologies

The 1960s and 1970s witnessed a boom (Ritzer, 1985) in several theoretical perspectives that Monica Morris (1977) lumped together under the heading of "creative" sociology. Included under this heading are phenomenological sociology, ethnomethodology, and existential sociology.

Phenomenological Sociology and the Work of Alfred Schutz (1899–1959) The philosophy of phenomenology, with its focus on consciousness, has a long history, but the effort to develop a sociological variant of phenomenology can be traced to the publication of Alfred Schutz's *The Phenomenology of the Social World* in Germany in 1932. However, it was not translated into

English until 1967, with the result that it has only recently had a dramatic effect on American sociological theory. Schutz arrived in the United States in 1939 after fleeing the Nazis in Austria. Shortly after, he took a position at the New School for Social Research in New York, from which he was able to influence the development of phenomenological, and later ethnomethodological, sociology in the United States.

As we will see in Chapter 10, Schutz took the phenomenological philosophy of Edmund Husserl, which was aimed inward toward an understanding of the transcendental ego, and turned it outward toward a concern for intersubjectivity. Schutz was focally concerned with the way in which people grasp the consciousness of others while they live within their own stream of consciousness. Schutz also used intersubjectivity in a larger sense to mean a concern with the social world, especially the social nature of knowledge.

Much of Schutz's work focuses on an aspect of the social world called the *life-world*, or the world of everyday life. This is an intersubjective world in which people both create social reality and are constrained by the preexisting social and cultural structures created by our predecessors. While much of the life-world is shared, there are also private (biographically articulated) aspects of that world. Within the life-world, Schutz differentiated between intimate face-to-face relationships ("we-relations") and distant and impersonal relationships ("they-relations"). While face-to-face relations are of great importance in the life-world, it is far easier for the sociologist to study more impersonal relations scientifically. Although Schutz turned away from consciousness and to the intersubjective life-world, he did offer insights into consciousness, especially in his thoughts on meaning and people's motives.

Overall, Schutz was concerned with the dialectical relationship between the way people construct social reality and the obdurate social and cultural reality that they inherit from those who preceded them in the social world.

The mid-1960s were crucial in the development of phenomenological sociology. Not only was Alfred Schutz's major work translated and his collected essays published, but Peter Berger and Thomas Luckmann collaborated to publish a book, *The Social Construction of Reality* (1967), that became one of the most widely read theory books of the time. It made at least two important contributions. First, it constituted an introduction to Schutz's ideas that was written in such a way as to make it available to a large American audience. Second, it presented an effort to integrate Schutz's ideas with those of mainstream sociology. Since 1967 phenomenology has grown in popularity in sociology.

Ethnomethodology   Although we will see that there are important differences between them, this theoretical perspective is, in the eyes of many people, hard to distinguish from phenomenology. Indeed, the creator of this perspective, Harold Garfinkel, was a student of Alfred Schutz at the New School. Garfinkel had an interesting intellectual background. He was a student of Parsons in the late 1940s and fused Parsons's orientation with that of Schutz, whom he was exposed to a few years later. After he received his Ph.D. from Harvard in 1952, Garfinkel arrived in 1954 (Sharrock and Anderson, 1986) at the University of California at Los Angeles (Heritage, 1984), and it was there that ethnomethodology was developed by Garfinkel and his graduate students. Geographically, ethnomethodology was the first distinctive theoretical product of the West Coast, and it has remained centered there to this day (although there is now a large group of British ethnomethodologists). In part, this is a result of the desire of the ethnomethodologists to remain together, but it is at least equally the result of opposition to this perspective by most mainstream sociologists.

Garfinkel became the focal point for a group of students and faculty members at UCLA interested in his approach. A series of seminars was held at UCLA beginning in the early 1950s. Over the years a number of major ethnomethodologists emerged from this milieu.

Ethnomethodology began to receive a wide national audience with the publication in 1967 of Garfinkel's *Studies in Ethnomethodology*. Although written in a difficult and obscure style, the book elicited a lot of interest. Coming at the same time as the translation of Schutz's *The Phenomenology of the Social World* and the publication of Berger and Luckmann's *The Social Construction of Reality*, it seemed to indicate that "subjective" or "creative" sociology was coming of age.

Basically, *ethnomethodology* is the study of "the body of common-sense knowledge and the range of procedures and considerations [the methods] by means of which the ordinary members of society make sense of, find their way about in, and act on the circumstances in which they find themselves" (Heritage, 1984:4). Writers in this tradition are heavily tilted in the direction of the study of everyday life at the individual level. While phenomenological sociologists tend to focus on what people think, ethnomethodologists are more concerned with what people actually do. Thus, ethnomethodologists devote a lot of attention to the detailed study of conversations. Such micro-level concerns stand in stark contrast to the interest of many mainstream sociologists in such large-scale objective phenomena as bureaucracies, capitalism, the division of labor, and the social system. Ethnomethodologists might be interested in these structures as contexts of everyday life; they are not interested in such structures as phenomena in themselves.

Although the works of ethnomethodologists had links to earlier sociological perspectives such as symbolic interactionism and dramaturgical analysis, there was clearly something threatening here to the mainstream sociologists who were still in control of the discipline. In fact, both phenomenology and, more important, ethnomethodology have been subjected to some brutal attacks by mainstream sociologists. Here are two examples. The first is from a review of Garfinkel's *Studies in Ethnomethodology* by James Coleman:

> Garfinkel simply fails to generate any insights at all from the approach. . . .
>
> Perhaps the program would be more fertile in the hands of someone more carefully observant but it is strangely sterile here. . . .

. . . this chapter appears to be not only an ethnomethodological disaster in itself but also evidence of the more general inadequacies of ethnomethodology. . . .

. . . this chapter is another major disaster, combining the rigidities of the most mathematically enraptured technicians with the technical confusions and errors of the soft clinician and without the insights or the technical competence of the creative and trained sociologist.

Once again, Garfinkel elaborates very greatly points which are so commonplace that they would appear banal if stated in straightforward English. As it is, there is an extraordinarily high ratio of reading time to information transfer, so that the banality is not directly apparent upon a casual reading.

(Coleman, 1968:126–130)

The second example is Lewis Coser's 1975 presidential address to the American Sociological Association. Coser saw few redeeming qualities in ethnomethodology and subjected it to a savage attack, engaging in a great deal of name-calling, labeling ethnomethodology "trivial," "a massive cop-out," "an orgy of subjectivism," and a "self-indulgent enterprise." The bitterness of these and other attacks is an indication of the success of both ethnomethodology and phenomenology and the degree to which they represent a threat to the establishment in sociology.

Existential Sociology   Of the three creative sociologies, existential sociology is the least important, at least at the moment. It shares with the other approaches an interest in actors and their thoughts and actions. *Existential sociology* focuses on the complexities of individual life and on the ways actors attempt to deal with those complexities. It has a particular interest in individual feelings, sentiments, and the self. Although it shares a number of intellectual roots with phenomenology and ethnomethodology, existential sociology also tries to separate itself from them (see Fontana, 1980, 1984). It sees itself as more involved in the real world than either of the other creative sociologies. It also has a number of distinctive sources, such as the work of Jean-Paul Sartre (Craib, 1976). Although existential sociology has made some headway in the discipline (for example, Douglas and Johnson, 1977; Hayim, 1980; Kotarba and Fontana, 1984; Manning, 1973; Tiryakian, 1965), it remains on the periphery. But when its influence is combined with that of ethnomethodology and phenomenology, we can see that the creative sociologies are making inroads in sociology despite substantial opposition from many sociologists.

In the last few pages, we have dealt with an array of micro theories— exchange theory, phenomenological sociology, ethnomethodology, and existential sociology. Although the last three theories share a sense of a thoughtful and creative actor, such a view is not held by exchange theorists. Nevertheless, all four theories have a micro orientation to actors and their actions and behavior. In the 1970s, such theories grew in strength in sociology and threatened to replace more macro-oriented theories (such as structural functionalism, conflict theory, neo-Marxian theories) as the dominant theories in sociology (Knorr-Cetina, 1981; Ritzer, 1985).

Systems Theory

One of the more interesting developments in sociology was the meteoric rise and equally meteoric fall of systems theory. Systems theory more or less burst on the scene in the 1960s, culminating in the publication of Walter Buckley's *Sociology and Modern Systems Theory* in 1967. Systems theory is derived from the hard sciences, where both organic and mechanical entities are viewed in systems terms. *Systems theory* views society as a huge system composed of a number of interrelated parts. It is necessary to examine the relationship among the parts as well as the relationship between the system and other social systems. Concern is also focused on the inputs into the social system, the way the inputs are processed by society, and the outputs that are produced.

Systems theory seemed quite attractive to sociologists in the 1960s. Structural functionalism was under attack, and systems theory seemed a likely successor. After all, Parsons had entitled his 1951 book *The Social System* and had talked in terms that were close to systems theory. Furthermore, systems theory, with its roots in the hard sciences, was very attractive to sociologists interested in furthering scientific sociology. But systems theory was a bright prospect that never blossomed. Little was done with it either theoretically or empirically. Only eleven years after Buckley's book was published, Robert Lilienfeld (1978) published a blistering attack on systems theory for its failures, its scientific pretensions, and its implicit conservative ideology. In recent years systems theory has enjoyed a modest rebirth in the work of Archer (1988) and Bailey (1990).

The Ascendancy of Marxian Sociology

The late 1960s also were the point at which Marxian theory finally began to make significant inroads into American sociological theory (Jay, 1984). There are a number of reasons for this. First, the dominant theory (structural functionalism) was under attack for a number of things, including being too conservative. Second, Mills's radical sociology and conflict theory, although not representing sophisticated Marxian theory, had laid the groundwork for an American theory that was true to the Marxian tradition. Third, the 1960s was the era of black protests, the reawakening of the women's movement, the student movement, and the anti–Vietnam War movement. Many of the young sociologists trained in this atmosphere were attracted to radical ideas. At first, this interest was manifest in what was called in those days "radical sociology" (Colfax and Roach, 1971). This was useful as far as it went, but like Mills's work, it was rather weak on the details of Marxian theory.

It is hard to single out one work as essential to the development of Marxian sociology in America, but one that did play an important role was Henri Lefebvre's *The Sociology of Marx* (1968). It was important for its essential argument, which was that although Marx was not a sociologist, there was a sociology in Marx. Since that time an increasing number of sociologists have turned to Marx's original work, as well as that of many Marxists, for insights that would be useful in the development of a Marxian sociology. At first this simply meant that American theorists were finally reading Marx seriously, but we now see many significant pieces of Marxian scholarship by American sociologists.

American theorists have been particularly attracted to the work of the critical school, especially because of its fusion of Marxian and Weberian theory. Many of the works have been translated into English, and a number of American scholars have made careers for themselves by writing books about the critical school for an American audience (for example, Jay, 1973, 1986).

Along with an increase in interest has come institutional support for such an orientation. Several journals devote considerable attention to Marxian sociological theory, including *Theory and Society, Telos,* and *Marxist Studies.* A section on Marxist sociology was created in the American Sociological Association in 1977. Not only is the first generation of critical theorists now well known in America, but second-generation thinkers, especially Jurgen Habermas, have received wide recognition.

Of greatest importance is the development of significant pieces of American sociology done from a Marxian point of view. One very significant strand is a group of sociologists doing historical sociology from a Marxian perspective (for example, Skocpol, 1979; Wallerstein, 1974, 1980, 1989). Another is a group analyzing the economic realm from a sociological perspective (for example, Baran and Sweezy, 1966; Braverman, 1974; Burawoy, 1979). Still others are doing fairly traditional empirical sociology, but work that is informed by a strong sense of Marxian theory (Kohn, 1976, for example).

The Challenge of Feminist Theory

Beginning in the late 1970s, precisely at the moment that Marxian sociology gained significant acceptance from American sociologists, a new theoretical outsider issued a challenge to established sociological theories—and even to Marxian sociology itself. This latest brand of radical social thought is contemporary feminist theory.

In Western societies, one can trace the record of critical feminist writings back almost 400 years (Donovan, 1985; Rossi, 1974; Spender, 1982) and there has been an organized political movement by and for women for more than 150 years (Banner, 1984; Carden, 1974; Chafetz and Dworkin, 1986; Deckard, 1979; Giddings, 1984; Kandal, 1988; O'Neill, 1971; Ryan, 1990). In America in 1920, that movement finally won the right for women to vote, fifty-five years after that right had been constitutionally extended to black men. Exhausted and to a degree satiated by victory, the American women's movement over the next thirty years weakened in both size and vigor, only to spring back to life, fully reawakened, in the 1960s. Three factors helped create this new wave of feminist activism: the general climate of critical thinking that characterized the period; the anger of women activists who flocked to the antiwar, civil rights, and student movements only to encounter the sexist attitudes of the liberal and radical men in those movements (Densimore, 1973; Evans, 1980; Morgan, 1970; Shreve, 1989; Snitow, et al., 1983); and women's experience of prejudice and discrimination as they moved in ever larger numbers into wage work and higher education (Bookman and Morgen, 1988; Garland, 1988; Lengermann and Wallace, 1985; MacKinnon, 1979). For these reasons, particularly the last, the women's movement in this new second phase continued to expand during the 1970s and into the 1980s, even though the activism of many other 1960s movements faded. Moreover during these years activism by and for women became an international phenomenon.

A major feature of this international women's movement has been an explosively growing new literature on women that makes visible all aspects of women's hitherto unconsidered lives and experiences. This literature, which is popularly referred to as *women's studies* or the *new scholarship on women*, is the work of an international and interdisciplinary community of writers, located both within and outside universities and writing for both the general public and specialized academic audiences. In what must be one of the more impressive examples of sustained intellectual work in recent times, feminist scholars have launched a probing, multifaceted critique that makes visible the complexity of the system that subordinates women.

Feminist theory is the theoretical strand running through this literature: sometimes implicit in writings on such substantive issues as work (Daniels, 1988; Kanter, 1977; Rollins, 1985) or rape (Sanday, 1990; Scully, 1990) or popular culture (Radway, 1984); sometimes centrally and explicitly presented, as in the analyses of motherhood by Adrienne Rich (1976), Nancy Chodorow (1978), and Jessica Benjamin (1988); and as the new scholarship on women has achieved critical mass, with increasing frequency the sole, systematic effort of a piece of writing. Of this recent spate of wholly theoretical writing, certain statements have been particularly salient to sociology because they are directed to sociologists by people well versed in sociological theory (Chafetz, 1984; P. Collins, 1990; Cook and Fonow, 1986; Hartsock, 1983; Lengermann and Niebrugge-Brantley, 1990; Smith, 1979, 1987, 1990; Stacey and Thorne, 1986; Wallace, 1989). Journals that bring feminist theory to the attention of sociologists include *Signs, Feminist Studies, Sociological Inquiry,* and *Gender and Society,* as does the professional association Sociologists for Women in Society (S.W.S.) and the National Women's Studies Association (NWSA).

Feminist theory looks at the world from the vantage point of a hitherto unrecognized and invisible minority, women, with an eye to discovering the significant but unacknowledged ways in which the activities of that minority help to create our world. This viewpoint dramatically reworks our understanding of social life. From this base, feminist theorists have begun to challenge sociological theory.

Those issuing this challenge argue that sociologists have persistently refused to incorporate the insights of the new scholarship on women into their discipline's understanding of the social world. Instead, feminist sociologists have been segregated from the mainstream, and feminism's comprehensive theory of social organization has been reduced to a single research variable, sex, and a simple social role pattern, gender (Farnham, 1987; Smith, 1990; Stacey and Thorne, 1985; Wallace, 1989; Yeatman, 1987). To date these charges seem valid. Reasons for sociology's avoidance of feminist theory may include deep antifeminist prejudices, suspicion of the scientific credentials of a theory so closely associated with political activism, and caution born of half recognition of the profoundly radical implications of feminist theory for sociological theory and method. Yet it should also be remembered that it took some time for Marxian theory to "arrive" in sociology and that a significant body of explicitly theoretical feminist writings is a very recent event in academic life. These writings have begun, however, to assume a critical mass. They offer an exciting new and important theory of social life. And those whose experiences and perceptions make them a receptive audience for this theory—women in general and both women and men affected by feminism in particular—are an important constituency in the sociological community. For all these reasons, implications of feminist theory are moving increasingly into the mainstream of the discipline.

Structuralism and Poststructuralism

One development that we have said little about up to this point is the increase in interest in *structuralism* (Lemert, 1990). Usually traced to France (and often called *French structuralism* [Clark and Clark, 1982; Kurzweil, 1980]), structuralism has now become an international phenomenon. Although its roots lie outside sociology, structuralism clearly has made its way into sociology. The problem is that structuralism in sociology still is so undeveloped that it is difficult to define it with any precision. The problem is exacerbated by structuralism's more or less simultaneous development in a number of fields; it is difficult to find one single coherent statement of structuralism. Indeed, there are significant differences among the various branches of structuralism.

We can get a preliminary feeling for structuralism by delineating the basic differences that exist among those who support a structuralist perspective. There are those who focus on what they call the "deep structures of the mind." It is their view that these unconscious structures lead people to think and act as they do. The work of the psychoanalyst Sigmund Freud might be seen as an example of this orientation. Then there are structuralists who focus on the invisible larger structures of society and see them as determinants of the actions of people as well as of society in general. Marx is sometimes thought of as someone who practiced such a brand of structuralism, with his focus on the unseen economic structure of capitalist society. Still another group sees structures as the models they construct of the social world. Finally, a number of structuralists are concerned with the dialectical relationship between individuals and social structures. They see a link between the structures of the mind and the structures of society. The anthropologist Claude Lévi-Strauss is most often associated with this view.

The problem with structural sociology at the moment is that it remains largely a melange of ideas derived from various fields, including linguistics (Saussure), anthropology (Lévi-Strauss), psychology (Freud, Lacan), and Marxism (Althusser). Until these ideas are put together in a coherent fashion, structuralism will remain marginal to sociology. However, the developments in related fields have been so significant and so attractive to those in sociology that a structural theory in sociology is likely to attract more attention in coming years.

As structuralism grows within sociology, outside of sociology a movement is developing beyond the early premises of structuralism: *poststructuralism* (Lemert, 1990). The major representative of poststructuralism is Michel Foucault. In his early work, Foucault focused on structures, but he later moved beyond structures to focus on power and the linkage between knowledge and power. More generally, poststructuralists accept the importance of structure but go beyond it to encompass a wide range of other concerns.

SOCIOLOGICAL THEORY IN THE 1990s

While many of the developments discussed in the preceding pages are still important in the 1990s, in this section we will deal with four broad movements that promise to be of utmost importance in this decade, as well as decades to come—the interest in micro-macro integration, agency-structure integration, theoretical syntheses, and metatheorizing in sociology.

Micro-Macro Integration

A good deal of the most recent work in American sociological theory has been concerned with the linkage between micro and macro theories and levels of analysis. In fact, I have argued (Ritzer, 1990a) that micro-macro linkage emerged as the central problematic in American sociological theory in the 1980s and it continues to be of focal concern in the 1990s.

There are a number of recent examples of efforts to link micro-macro levels of analysis and/or theories. In my own work (Ritzer, 1979; 1981a), I have sought to develop an integrated sociological paradigm that integrates micro and macro levels in both their objective and subjective forms. Thus, in my view, there are four major levels of social analysis that must be dealt with in an integrated manner—macro-subjectivity, macro-objectivity, micro-subjectivity, and micro-objectivity. Jeffrey Alexander (1982–83) has created a "multidimensional sociology" which deals, at least in part, with a model of levels of analysis that closely resembles the model developed by Ritzer. Alexander (1987) develops his model based on the problem of order, which is seen as having individual (micro) and collective (macro) levels, and the problem of action, which is viewed as possessing materialist (objective) and idealist (subjective) levels. Out of these two continuua, Alexander develops four major levels of analysis—collective-idealist, collective-materialist, individual-idealist, individual-materialist. While the overall model developed by Alexander is strikingly similar to Ritzer's, Alexander accords priority to the collective-idealist level, while Ritzer insists that we be concerned with the dialectical relationship among all levels. Still another kindred approach is developed by Norbert Wiley (1988) who also delineates four very similar major levels of analysis—self or individual, interaction, social structure, and culture. However, while both Ritzer and Alexander focus on both objective and subjective levels, Wiley's are purely subjective. James Coleman (1986) has concentrated on the micro-to-macro problem, while Allen Liska (1990) has extended Coleman's approach to deal with the macro-to-micro problem as well. Coleman (1990) has recently extended his micro-to-macro model and developed a much more elaborate theory of the micro-macro relationship based on a rational choice approach derived from economics.

There are many other efforts at micro-macro integration. There is much work to be done on this issue, and it promises to be a significant area of concern in American sociological theory for some time to come.

Agency-Structure Integration

Paralleling the growth in interest in the United States in micro-macro integration, has been a concern in Europe for agency-structure integration. Just as I saw the micro-macro issue as the central problem in American theory, Margaret Archer (1988) sees the agency-structure topic as the basic concern in European social theory. While there are many similarities between the micro-macro and agency-structure literatures, there are also substantial differences between them. For example, while agents are usually micro-level actors, collectivities like labor unions can also be agents. And while structures are usually macro-level phenomena, we also find structures at the micro-level. Thus, we must be careful in equating these two bodies of work and much care needs to be taken in trying to interrelate them.

There are four major efforts underway in contemporary European social theory that can be included under the heading of agency-structure integration. The first is Anthony Giddens's (1984) structuration theory. The key to Giddens's approach is that he sees agency and structure as a "duality." That is, they cannot be separated from one another: agency is implicated in structure and structure is involved in agency. Giddens refuses to see structure as simply constraining (as, for example, does Durkheim), but sees structure as both constraining *and* enabling. Margaret Archer (1982) rejects the idea that agency and structure can be viewed as a duality, but rather sees them as a dualism.

That is, agency and structure can and should be separated. In distinguishing them, we become better able to analyze their relationship to one another. Archer (1988) is also notable for extending the structure-agency literature to a concern for the relationship between culture and agency.

While both Giddens and Archer are British, the third major contemporary figure involved in the agency-structure literature is Pierre Bourdieu (1977) from France. In Bourdieu's work, the agency-structure issue translates into a concern for the relationship between habitus and field. Habitus is an internalized mental, or cognitive, structure, through which people deal with the social world. The habitus both produces, and is produced by, the society. The field is a network of relations among objective positions. The structure of the field serves to constrain agents, be they individuals or collectivities. Overall, Bourdieu is concerned with the relationship between habitus and field. While the field conditions the habitus, the habitus constitutes the field. Thus, there is a dialectical relationship between habitus and field.

The final major theorist of the agency-structure linkage is the German, Jurgen Habermas. We have already mentioned Habermas as a significant contemporary contributor to critical theory. In his more recent work, Habermas (1987) has dealt with the agency-structure issue under the heading of "the colonization of the life-world." The life-world is a micro-world where people interact and communicate. The system has its roots in the life-world, but it ultimately comes to develop its own structural characteristics. As these structures grow in independence and power, they come to exert more and more control over the life-world. In the modern world, the system has come to "colonize" the life-world, that is, to exert control over it.

There is much more to agency-structure integration than the work of Giddens, Archer, Bourdieu and Habermas. However, they are the major representatives of this contemporary genre of sociological theory.

Theoretical Syntheses

The movements toward micro-macro and agency-structure integration began in the 1980s and both continue to be strong in the 1990s. They set the stage for the broader movement toward theoretical syntheses which began at about the beginning of the 1990s. What is involved here is a wide-ranging effort to synthesize two or more different theories (for example, structural functionalism and symbolic interactionism). Such efforts have always occurred in the history of sociological theory. However, there are two distinctive aspects of the new synthetic work in sociological theory. First, it is very widespread and not restricted to isolated attempts at synthesis. Secondly, the goal is generally a relatively narrow synthesis of theoretical ideas, and not the development of a grand synthetic theory that overarches all of sociological theory.

These synthetic works are occurring within and among many of the theories discussed in this chapter as well as in and among some theories that we have yet to mention.

Within structural functionalism, we have seen the rise of neofunctionalism

(Alexander, 1985a; Alexander and Colomy, 1985; Alexander and Colomy, 1990; Colomy, 1990). Neofunctionalism seeks to overcome many of the limitations of structural functionalism by integrating into it ideas derived from a wide range of other theories. Alexander and Colomy see this as a dramatic reconstruction of structural functionalism so that a new name, neofunctionalism, is required to differentiate this new theoretical approach from its ancestor.

Symbolic interactionism is undergoing a dramatic transformation as it has, in Fine's terms, "cobbled a new theory from the shards of other theoretical approaches" (1990:136–137). Thus symbolic interactionists are borrowing ideas from phenomenological sociology, feminist theory, and exchange theory, among others. In addition, major figures in the history of symbolic interactionism such as Mead and Blumer are being redefined as being more synthetic and integrative theorists.

Exchange theory has long had integrative and synthetic works like Blau's *Exchange and Power in Social Life* (1964). In recent years increasing attention is being devoted to the work of Richard Emerson (1972a; 1972b) and that of his disciples, especially Karen Cook (1987a). Emerson began with the principles of behaviorism, but ultimately sought to relate them to social structure and social exchange relationships. More recently, Cook, O'Brien and Kollock (1990) have come to define exchange theory in inherently integrative terms and to synthesize it with ideas derived from other theories such as symbolic interactionism and network theory.

A relatively new, and inherently synthetic development in sociological theory is the rise of postmodernist social theory (Baudrillard, 1983; Harvey, 1989; Lyotard, 1984; Kellner, 1990a, 1990b). This theory is premised on the idea that we have moved in recent years from a modern to a postmodern society. While modern society was highly rational and rigid, postmodern society is viewed as more irrational and more flexible. A new, postmodernist theory has arisen to analyze this new type of society. Postmodernist theory is inherently integrative drawing upon ideas from a wide range of disciplines—philosophy, cultural theory, and social theory, among others. Moreover, postmodernists reject the idea of the development of a single grand overarching theory, or as they call it, a "metadiscourse." Rather, postmodernists argue for far narrower and specific synthetic efforts of the kind being undertaken in sociological theory in the 1990s.

Post-Marxist theory encompasses three synthetic theoretical developments. The first is analytic Marxism which involves the efforts to bring "state-of-the-art" methods of analytical philosophy and social science to bear on traditional Marxian concerns. Thus, for example, a number of theorists (Roemer, 1986; Elster, 1985) are using the ideas of rational choice theory to analyze Marxian issues. Others (for example, Wright, 1985) are employing mainstream sociological methods to analyze such issues as class. The second is a set of postmodern Marxists (for example, Laclau and Mouffe, 1986; Jameson, 1984; Harvey, 1989) who are borrowing ideas from postmodernist theory and synthesizing them with aspects of traditional Marxian theory. Finally, there is the work of Bowles and Gintis (1986) which seeks to integrate Marxian and liberal theory.

Metatheorizing in Sociology

Metatheorizing may be defined very broadly as the systematic study of the underlying structure of sociological theory (Ritzer, 1990c, 1990d, forthcoming b, forthcoming c). It may be distinguished from theorizing even though most theorists have done metatheorizing and most metatheorists have also theorized. While metatheorists take theory as their subject of study, theorists think about the social world. There has been a considerable increase in metatheoretical work (Fuhrman and Snizek, 1990), and there is every sign that such work will continue to grow in the future.

Metatheoretical work has been part of sociology since the inception of the field. Most of the early theorists did metatheoretical studies of their intellectual ancestors. Particularly notable are Marx's studies of Hegel, the Young Hegelians, the political economists, and the utopian socialists. Parsons's *The Structure of Social Action* (1937, 1949) is described by him as an "empirical" study of the work of his theoretical ancestors. In the 1950s Paul Furfey (1953/1965) offered the first, albeit significantly flawed, systematic effort to define metatheoretical work. Alvin Gouldner's attempt in *The Coming Crisis of Western Sociology* (1970) to define a sociology of sociological theory is an important, although also flawed, precursor to contemporary metatheorizing. A specific set of works (Friedrichs, 1970; Ritzer 1975a), based on Thomas Kuhn's (1962, 1970) concept of a paradigm, also played a key role in the development of metatheoretical work in sociology.

Metatheorizing in sociology is coming of age in the 1990s (see Appendix) and it promises to play a central role in clarifying extant sociological theories as well as in helping in the development of new integrative and synthetic theories.

SUMMARY

This chapter picks up where Chapter 1 left off and deals with the history of sociological theory since the beginning of the twentieth century. We begin with the early history of American sociological theory, which was characterized by its liberalism, by its interest in Social Darwinism, and consequently by the influence of Herbert Spencer. In this context, the work of the two early sociological theorists, Sumner and Ward, is discussed. However, they did not leave a lasting imprint on American sociological theory. In contrast, the Chicago school, as embodied in the work of people like Small, Park, Thomas, Cooley, and, especially Mead, did leave a strong mark on sociological theory, especially on symbolic interactionism.

While the Chicago school was still predominant, a different form of sociological theory began to develop at Harvard. Pitirim Sorokin played a key role in the founding of sociology at Harvard, but it was Talcott Parsons who was to lead Harvard to a position of preeminence in American theory, replacing Chicago's symbolic interactionism. Parsons was important not only for legitimizing "grand theory" in the United States and for introducing European theorists to an American audience but also for his role in the development of action theory and, more important, structural functionalism. In the 1940s and 1950s, structural functionalism was furthered by the disintegration of the Chicago school that began in the 1930s and was largely complete by the 1950s.

The major development in Marxian theory in the early years of the twentieth century was the creation of the Frankfurt, or critical, school. This Hegelianized form of Marxism also showed the influence of sociologists like Weber and of the psychoanalyst Sigmund Freud. Marxism did not gain a widespread following among sociologists in the early part of the century.

Structural functionalism's dominance within American theory in mid-century was rather short-lived. Although traceable to a much earlier date, phenomenological sociology, especially the work of Alfred Schutz, began to attract significant attention in the 1960s. Marxian theory was still largely excluded from American theory, but C. Wright Mills kept a radical tradition alive in America in the 1940s and 1950s. Mills also was one of the leaders of the attacks on structural functionalism, attacks that mounted in intensity in the 1950s and 1960s. In light of some of these attacks, a conflict-theory alternative to structural functionalism emerged in this period. Although influenced by Marxian theory, conflict theory suffered from an inadequate integration of Marxism. Still another alternative born in the 1950s was exchange theory, and it continues to attract a small but steady number of followers. Although symbolic interactionism was in eclipse, the work of Erving Goffman on dramaturgical analysis in this period kept it from being moribund.

Important developments took place in the "creative sociologies" in the 1960s and 1970s. Phenomenological sociology, ethnomethodology, and existential sociology continue to attract a great deal of attention in sociology. At the same time, Marxian sociology came into its own, and its several varieties continue to cause a great deal of excitement in sociological theory. While creative sociology and Marxian theory have been on the rise, systems theory gained popularity in the 1960s only to encounter a dramatic drop in popularity in the 1970s. Among the most important recent developments in sociological theory are feminist theory, structuralism, and poststructuralism.

Four developments are most striking about sociological theory in the 1980s and 1990s. First, is the rise in interest in the United States in the micro-macro link. Second, is the parallel increase in attention in Europe to the relationship between agency and structure. Third, there is the growth, especially in the 1990s, of a wide range of synthetic efforts. Finally, there is the increase in interest in metatheoretical work, or the systematic study of sociological theory.

From the point of view of the remainder of this book, this chapter has played two major roles. First, it demonstrated that the classical theorists introduced in Chapter 1—Comte, Spencer, Marx, Durkheim, Weber, and Simmel— influenced the later development of sociological theory in a variety of direct and indirect ways. Second, it allowed us to introduce, within their historical context, the other classical theorists who will be discussed in detail later in this book—Mead, Schutz, and Parsons.

AUGUSTE COMTE

ALFRED North Whitehead said: "A science which hesitates to forget its founders is lost" (1917/1974:115). Practitioners in an advanced science like physics *have* forgotten the field's founders, or at least they have relegated them to works on the history of the field. A student in physics does not ordinarily read about the work of Isaac Newton but rather about the contemporary state of knowledge on the issues that Newton, and other classic physicists, first addressed. The state of knowledge in contemporary physics has far outstripped that of Newton; hence there is no need for a student to learn about his ideas. Newton's still useful ideas have long since been integrated into the knowledge base of physics. According to Whitehead, physics is *not* lost; it has (largely) forgotten Isaac Newton and the other important figures in the early history of the field.

Why then are students in sociology being asked to read about the work of an early nineteenth-century thinker like Auguste Comte (1798–1857), as well as the other theorists to be discussed in this volume? The fact is that the majority of Comte's ideas ought to be forgotten. Thus, while we will discuss those of Comte's ideas that are worth remembering, we will also focus on the weaknesses and problems in his work; in other words, we will examine why much of it is best forgotten. In addition to offering us some useful ideas, the examination of Comte's work will yield a number of negative lessons on what *not* to do in sociological theory. Another reason for examining Comte's ideas is that while most of them are no longer important today, they were important in their time and influenced the work of a number of major sociological theorists. Overall, we will see that sociological theory *has* progressed far beyond many of the ideas of Comte. Sociology may not yet be in the position of physics, able to forget all its founders as people, but it has certainly progressed far enough to forget at least some of their ideas.

Another quotation from Whitehead clearly applies to Comte: "It is characteristic of a science in its earlier stages . . . to be both ambitiously profound in its aims and trivial in its handling of detail" (1917/1974:116). We will see that the useful derivatives from Comte's work relate to his broad, often outrageous, objectives; the details of his work are not only trivial but in many cases downright ludicrous.

However, while there is comparatively little to learn from Comte, the same cannot be said about the other theorists discussed in this book. They all had many things to say that continue to be relevant to contemporary sociological theory. The positive derivatives from the work of classic thinkers like Marx, Durkheim, Weber, Simmel, Schutz, Parsons, and, to a lesser extent, Spencer far exceed the negative lessons of their work.

COMTE'S PROFOUND AMBITIONS

Positivism: The Search for Invariant Laws

Comte is remembered to this day in sociology for his championing of *positivism* (Halfpenny, 1982; J. Turner, 1985a, 1990a). While this term has a multitude of meanings, it is usually used to mean the search for invariant laws of both the natural and the social world. In Comte's version of positivism these laws can be derived from doing research on the social world and/or from theorizing about that world. Research is needed to uncover these laws, but in Comte's view the facts derived from research are of secondary importance to sound speculation. Thus Comte's positivism involves empirical research, but that research is subordinated to theory.

Comte's thinking is premised on the idea that there is a real world (for example, biological, sociological) out there and that it is the task of the scientist to discover and report on it. Because of this view, Comte is what we would now call a *realist*. Here is the way Comte puts the issue: "Positive philosophers . . . approach the questions with the simple aim of ascertaining the true state of things, and reproducing it with all possible accuracy in their theories" (1830–42/1855:385). Later, Comte argued that positivist philosophy (or any philosophy) "can only be valid insofar as it is an exact and complete representation of the relations naturally existing" (1851/1957:8–9). (This is sometimes called the "copy theory" of truth.)

There are two basic ways of getting at the real world that exists out there—doing research and theorizing. As we saw above, while Comte recognized the importance of research, he emphasized the need for theory and speculation.

While there are many contemporary sociologists who think of themselves as positivists, positivism has come under severe attack in recent years. Considerable work in the philosophy of science has cast doubt on whether positivism fits the natural sciences, and this tends to raise even greater doubts about the possibility of positivistic sociology. Some sociologists (interpretationalists) never accepted a positivist approach, and others who did have either totally abandoned it or adopted a modified positivist perspective (for example, R. Collins, 1989a). Positivism has not disappeared from sociology, but it seems clear that sociology now finds itself in a postpositivist age (Shweder and Fiske, 1986).

Comte's interest in positivism is intimately related to his interest in sociology. By his own account, Comte (1851/1968:ix) "discovered" sociology in 1822, and his claim is generally accepted by most historians of sociology. Consistent with his commitment to positivism, he defined *sociology* as a positivistic science. In fact, in defining *sociology*, Comte related it to one of the most positivistic sciences, physics: "Sociology . . . is the term I may be allowed to invent to designate social physics" (1830–42/1855:444).

Comte (1830–42/1855) developed a hierarchy of the positivistic sciences— mathematics, astronomy, physics, biology (physiology), chemistry, and at the pinnacle (at least in his early work)—sociology.[1] (It is interesting to note that Comte leaves no place for psychology, which would seem to be reduced to a series of biological instincts.) This hierarchy descends from the sciences that are the most general, abstract, and remote from people to those that are the most complex, concrete, and interesting to people (Heilbron, 1990). Sociology builds upon the knowledge and procedures of the sciences that stand beneath it, but in Comte's view sociology is "the most difficult and important subject of all" (1851/1968:31). Given his high estimation of sociology, it is easy to see why Comte has long been esteemed by sociologists. And given the fact that as a positivist, Comte viewed theorizing as the ultimate activity, it is clear why he has had such high status among theorists.

Comte explicitly identified three basic methods for sociology—three basic ways of doing social research in order to gain empirical knowledge of the real social world. The first is *observation*, but Comte is quick to reject isolated, atheoretical observations of the social world. Without theory we would not know what to look for in the social world and we would not understand the significance of what we find. Observations should be directed by some theory, and when made, they should be connected to some law. The second of Comte's methods is the *experiment*, but this method is better suited to the other sciences than it is to sociology. It is obviously virtually impossible to interfere with, and to attempt to control, social phenomena. The one possible exception would be a natural experiment in which the consequences of something that happens in one setting (for example, a tornado) are observed and compared to the conditions in settings in which such an event did not occur. Finally, there is *comparison,* which Comte divides into three subtypes. First, we can compare humans to lower animal societies. Second, we can compare societies in different parts of the world. Third, we can compare the different stages of

---

[1] In his later work, Comte added a seventh science that ranked above sociology—morals. We will have more to say about this later.

societies over time. Comte found this last subtype particularly important; in fact, he labeled it the "chief scientific device" of sociology (1830–42/55:481). It is so important that we separate it from the other comparative methods and accord it independent status as Comte's fourth major methodology—*historical research*. In fact, John Stuart Mill sees this as one of Comte's most important contributions in placing the "necessity of historical studies as the foundation of sociological speculation" (1961:86). In his own work, Comte used the historical method almost exclusively, although, as we will see, there are very real questions about how well he actually used this methodology.

Although Comte wrote about research, he most often engaged in speculation or theorizing in order to get at the invariant laws of the social world. He did not derive these laws inductively from observations of the social world; rather, he deduced them from his general theory of human nature. (A critic might ask questions like: How did Comte derive his theory of human nature? Where did he get it from? How can we ascertain whether or not it is true?) In this way Comte (1891/1973:302–304) created a number of general positivistic laws, laws which he applied to the social world.

Law of the Three Stages

Comte's most famous law is the *law of the three stages*. Comte identified three basic stages and proceeded to argue that the human mind, people through the maturation process, all branches of knowledge, and the history of the world (and even, as we will see later, his own mental illness) *all* pass successively through these three stages. Each stage involves the search by human beings for an explanation of the things around them.

1. The Theological Stage   Comte saw the theological stage as the first step and the necessary point of departure for the other two stages. In this stage, the human mind is searching for the essential nature of things, particularly their origin (where do they come from?) and their purpose (why do they exist?). What this comes down to is the search for absolute knowledge. It is assumed that all phenomena are created, regulated, and given their purposes by supernatural forces or beings (gods). While Comte includes *fetishism* (the worship of an object such as a tree) and *polytheism* (the worship of many gods) in the theological stage, the ultimate development in this stage is *monotheism*, or the worship of a single divinity which explains everything.

2. The Metaphysical Stage   This is the least important of the three stages to Comte. It is a transitional stage between the preceding theological stage and the ensuing positivistic stage. It exists because Comte believes that an immediate jump from the theological to the positivistic stage is too abrupt for people to handle. In the metaphysical stage, abstract forces replace supernatural beings as the explanation for the original causes and purposes of things in the world. For example, mysterious forces such as "nature" are invoked to explain why things are the way they are ("it was an act of nature"). Mill gives as an example of a metaphysical perspective Aristotle's contention that the "rise of water in a pump is attributed to nature's horror of a vacuum" (1961:11). Or to take a more social example, we could say that an event occurred because it was the "will of the people." While numerous entities can be seen as causes in the metaphysical stage, its ultimate point is reached when one great entity (for example, nature) is seen as the cause of everything.

3. The Positivist Stage This, of course, is the final and most important stage in Comte's system. At this point people give up their vain search for original causes or purposes. All we can know are phenomena and the relations among them, not their essential nature or their ultimate causes. People drop such nonscientific ideas as supernatural beings and mysterious forces. Instead, they look for the invariable natural laws that govern *all* phenomena. Examinations of single phenomena are oriented toward linking them to some general fact. The search for these laws involves both doing empirical research and theorizing. Comte differentiated between concrete and abstract laws. Concrete laws must come inductively from empirical research, while abstract laws must be derived deductively from theory. Comte was much more interested in creating abstract laws than in creating concrete ones. While positivism can be characterized by many different laws, he sees it ultimately gravitating toward a smaller and smaller number of general abstract laws.

While Comte recognized an inevitable succession through these three stages, he also acknowledged that at any given point in time all three might be operant. What he envisioned in the future of the world was a time when the positivistic stage would be complete and we would see the elimination of theological or metaphysical thinking.

Comte applied the law of the three stages in a number of different arenas. He saw people going through the three stages and viewed the child as a theologian, the adolescent as a metaphysician, and the adult as a positivist.[2] He also saw all the sciences in his hierarchy going through each of these stages. (Because it was a new science in Comte's time, sociology had not yet gone through the positivistic stage. Comte devoted much of his life to the development of positivistic sociology.) And he saw the history of the world in these terms. The early history of the world was the theological stage; the world next went through the metaphysical stage; and during Comte's lifetime the world was entering the last, or positivistic, stage. He believed that in the positivistic stage people would come to better understand the invariant laws that dominate them and would be able to adapt to these laws "with fewer difficulties and with greater speed" (Comte, 1852/1968:383). These laws would

---

[2] Comte came to associate the history of the world with these life stages—infancy (theological), adolescence (metaphysical), and maturity (positivist).

AUGUSTE COMTE: A Biographical Sketch

Auguste Comte was born in Montpellier, France, on January 19, 1798. Although a precocious student, Comte never received a college-level degree, and this had a negative effect on his teaching career. In 1818 he became secretary (and "adopted son" [Manuel, 1962:251]) to Claude Henri Saint-Simon, a philosopher forty years Comte's senior. They worked together for several years, but in 1824 they had a falling out because Comte believed that Saint-Simon was not giving him adequate credit for his contributions. Comte later wrote of his relationship with Saint-Simon as "the morbid lesson of his early youth with a depraved juggler" (Durkheim, 1928/1962:144). Despite his later hostility to Saint-Simon, Comte often acknowledged his great debt to him: "I certainly owe a great deal intellectually to Saint-Simon . . . he contributed powerfully to launching me in the philosophic direction that I clearly created for myself today and which I will follow without hesitation all my life" (Durkheim, 1928/1962:144).

In 1826, Comte concocted a scheme by which he would present a series of seventy-two public lectures on his philosophy of life. The course drew a distinguished audience, but it was halted after only three lectures when Comte suffered a nervous breakdown. He continued to suffer from mental problems and once in 1827 tried to commit suicide by throwing himself into the Seine River.

Although he could not get a regular position at the Ecole Polytechnique, Comte did get a minor position as lecturer there in 1832. In 1837, Comte was given the additional post of admissions examiner, and this, for the first time, gave him an adequate income. During this period, Comte worked on the six-volume work for which he is best known, *Cours de Philosophie Positive*, which was finally published in 1842. He outlined his view that sociology was the ultimate science. He attacked the Ecole Polytechnique in that work, and the result was that in 1844 his lectureship there was not renewed. By 1851 he had completed the four-volume *Système de Politique Positive*, which had a more practical intent of offering a grand plan for the reorganization of society.

Comte had a series of bizarre ideas. For example, he believed in "cerebral hygiene"; that is, Comte avoided reading the work of other people, with the result that he became hopelessly out of touch with intellectual developments. Comte also came to fancy himself as the high priest of a new religion of humanity; he believed in a world that eventually would be led by sociologist-priests. In spite of such outrageous ideas, Comte developed a considerable following in France as well as in other countries.

Auguste Comte died on September 5, 1857.

also guide people in making choices that can expedite the emergence, but not alter the course, of inevitable social developments.

Positivism: The Search for Order and Progress

While Comte used the term *positivism* in the sense of a science committed to the search for invariant laws, he also used it in another way—as the opposite of the negativism that, in his view, dominated the social world of his day. More specifically, that negativity was the moral and political disorder and chaos that occurred in France, and throughout Western Europe, in the wake of the French Revolution of 1789 (Levy-Bruhl, 1903/1973). Among the symptoms of this malaise were intellectual anarchy, political corruption, and incompetence of political leaders. Comte's positive philosophy was designed to counter the negative philosophy and its symptoms that he found all around him.

But while Comte placed great blame on the French Revolution, he found the major source of the disorder in his ideas on the Law of the Three Stages. "The great political and moral crisis that societies are now undergoing is shown by a rigid analysis to arise out of intellectual anarchy" (Comte, 1830–42/1855:36). That intellectual anarchy is traced by Comte to the coexistence during his lifetime of all three "incompatible" philosophies—theological, metaphysical, and positivistic. Not only did all three exist at one time, but none of them at that point was very strong. Theology and metaphysics were in decay, in a "state of imbecility," and positivsm as it relates to the social world (sociology) was as yet unformed. The conflict among, and weaknesses of, these three intellectual schemes allowed a wide variety of "subversive schemes" to grow progressively more dangerous. The answer to this intellectual chaos clearly lay in the emergence of any one of them as preeminent, and given Comte's law, the one that was destined to emerge supreme was positivism. Positivism had already become preeminent within the sciences (except sociology) and had brought order to each, where previously there was chaos. All that was needed was for positivism to bring social phenomena within its domain. Furthermore, Comte saw this as the way to end the revolutionary crisis that was tormenting France and the rest of Western Europe.

Comte also put this issue in terms of two of his great concerns—order and progress. From his point of view, theology offered a system of order, but without progress; it was a stagnant system. Metaphysics offered progress without order; he associated it with the anarchy of his day, in which things were changing in a dizzying and disorderly way. Because of the coexistence of theology and metaphysics (as well as positivism), Comte's time was marked by *disorder* and a *lack* of progress. Positivism was the only system which offered both order *and* progress. On the one hand, positivism would bring order through the restraint of intellectual and social disorder. On the other hand, it would bring progress through an increase in knowledge and through perfection of the relationship among the parts of the social system so that society would move nearer, although never fully attain, its determinate end (the gradual expansion of human powers). Thus, positivism is the only stage in the history of humankind that offers us both order *and* progress.

Comte sees order and progress in dialectical terms, and in this sense he offers a perspective close to that of Marx (see Chapter 5). This means that Comte refuses to see order and progress as separate entities but views them as mutually defining and interpenetrating. "Progress may be regarded simply as the development of Order; for the order of nature necessarily contains within itself the germ of all positive progress. . . . Progress then is in its essence identical with Order, and may be looked upon as Order made manifest" (Comte, 1851/1957:116).

It is interesting and important to underscore the fact that in Comte's view the crisis of his time was a *crisis of ideas* and that this crisis could be resolved only by the emergence of a preeminent idea (positivism). In fact, Comte often described positivism as a "spirit." In this sense, Comte is an idealist: "Ideas govern the world" (1830–42/1855:36). In this, rather than being in accord with Marx, he stands in stark contrast to Marx (a materialist). Marx saw the capitalist crisis as stemming from the material conflict between capitalists and the proletariat, and he believed that its solution lay in a material revolution in which the economic system of capitalism would be overthrown and replaced by a communist system. Marx scoffed at the idea that he was dealing with a crisis of ideas that could be solved in the ideational realm. In this, Marx was distancing himself from the idealism of Hegel; Comte, in contrast, had adopted a viewpoint that resembled, at least in a few respects, Hegelian idealism.

COMTE'S SOCIOLOGY

We turn now more directly to Comte's sociology, or his thoughts about the social world. Here we begin with another of Comte's lasting contributions—his distinction between *social statics* and *social dynamics*. While we do not use those terms today, the basic distinction remains important in the differentiation between social structure and social change. (By the way, Comte believed that all sciences, not just sociology, are divided into statics and dynamics.)

Social Statics

Comte defines the sociological study of social statics as "the investigation of the laws of action and reaction of the different parts of the social system" (1830–42/55:457). Contrary to what one might think, the laws of the ways in which parts of the social system interact (social statics) are *not* derived from empirical study. Rather, they are "deduced from the laws of human nature" (Comte, 1852/1968:344–345). Here, again, we see Comte's preference for theory over empirical research.

In his social statics, Comte was anticipating many of the ideas of later structural functionalists (see Chapter 11, on Parsons). Deriving his thoughts from biology, Comte developed a perspective on the parts (or *structures*) of society, the way in which they *function*, and their (functional) relationship to the larger social system. Comte also saw the parts and the whole of the social system in a state of harmony. The idea of harmony was later transformed by structural functionalists into the concept of equilibrium. Methodologically, Comte recommended that since we know about the whole, we start with it and then proceed to the parts. (Later structural functionalists also came to grant priority to the whole [the "social system"] over the parts [the "subsystems"].) For these and many other reasons Comte is often seen as a forerunner of structural functionalism.

Comte argues that "in Social Statics we must neglect all questions of time, and conceive the organism of society in its fullness. . . . Our ideal" (1852/1968:249). In other words, to use a concept developed by Weber (see Chapter 7), *social statics* describes an "ideal typical" society. The system of social statics conceived by Comte never really existed; it was an idealized model of the social world at a given point in time. In order to construct such a model, the sociologist must, at least for the purposes of analysis, hold time still.

At a manifest level, Comte is doing a *macro*sociology of social statics (and dynamics), since he is looking at the interrelationship among the parts and the whole of the social system. Indeed, Comte explicitly defined *sociology* as the macro-level study of "collective existence" (1891/1973:172).

The Individual in Comte's Theory   However, Comte's isolated thoughts on micro-level individuals are important not only for understanding his social statics but also for comprehending many other aspects of his work. For example, the individual is a major source of energy in his social system. It is the preponderance of affect or emotion in individuals that gives energy and direction to people's intellectual activities. It is the products of those intellectual activities that lead to changes in the larger social system.

More important for understanding his social statics, as well as his overall view of the world, is the fact that Comte sees the individual as imperfect, dominated by "lower" forms of egoism rather than "higher," more social forms of altruism. In fact, Comte sees this dominance of egoism as rooted in the brain, which is viewed as having both egoistic and altruistic regions. Egoism is seen as having higher energy, thereby helping to ensure the "natural feebleness" of altruism (Comte, 1852/1968:139). Putting egoism and altruism in slightly different terms, Comte argues: "Self-love . . . when left to itself is far stronger than Social Sympathy" (1851/1957:24–25). To Comte (1852/1968:122), the chief problem of human life is the need for altruism to dominate egoism. He sees all the social sciences as being concerned with this problem and with the development of various solutions to it.

Thus, left to themselves, people will, in Comte's view, act in a selfish manner. If we are to hope to be able to create a "better" world, the selfish motives of individuals must be controlled so that the altruistic impulses will emerge. Since egoism cannot be controlled from within the individual, the controls must come from outside the individual, from society. "The higher impulses within us are brought under the influence of a powerful stimulus from without. By its means they are enabled to control our discordant impulses" (Comte, 1851/1957:25–26). Thus Comte, like Durkheim (see Chapter 6), his successor within French sociology, saw people as a problem (egoism was a central concern to both) that could be handled only through external control over people's negative impulses. In terms almost identical to those later used by Durkheim, Comte argues that "true liberty is nothing else than a rational submission to the . . . laws of nature" (1830–42/1855:435). Without such external controls,

> our intellectual faculties, after wasting themselves in wild extravagancies, would sink rapidly into incurable sloth; our nobler feelings would be unable to prevent the ascendancy of the lower instincts; and our active powers would abandon themselves to purposeless agitation. . . . Our propensities are so heterogeneous and so deficient in elevation, that there would be no fixity or consistency in our conduct . . . without them [external restrictions] all its [reason's] deliberations would be confused and purposeless.
>
> (Comte, 1851/1957:29–30)

Thus Comte concludes: "This need of conforming our Acts and our Thoughts to a Necessity without us, far from hampering the real development of our nature, forms the first general condition of progress towards perfection in man" (1852/1968:26).

Not only does Comte have a highly negative view of people and their innate propensity to egoism, but he also has a very limited view of the creative capacities of individuals. "We are powerless to create: all that we can do in bettering our condition is to modify an order in which we can produce no radical change" (Comte, 1851/1957:30). Thus, Comte's actors are not only egoistic but also weak and powerless. In a very real sense, people do not create the social world; rather, the social world creates people, at least those animated by the nobler altruistic motives.

Comte addresses this issue in another way, in terms of the relationship between what he calls the "subjective" and "objective" principles. The subjective principle involves "the subordination of the intellect to the heart," while the objective principle entails "the immutable Necessity of the external world . . . actually existing without us"[3] (Comte, 1851/1957:26–27). Given the preceding discussion, it should be clear why Comte argues that the subjective principle must be subordinated to the objective principle. The "heart" (especially its egoism), which dominates the intellect, must be subordinated to external societal constraints so that another aspect of the "heart," altruism, can emerge triumphant.

Comte had other, more specific things to say about the individual. For example, he distinguished among four basic categories of instincts—nutrition, sex, destruction and construction, and pride and vanity (Comte, 1854/1968:249–252). Clearly, all but the constructive instinct are in need of external control. While Comte does attribute other, more positive instincts to people (attachment to others, veneration of predecessors), it is the instincts in need

---

[3] It is this kind of viewpoint that leads us, once again, to think of Comte as a social realist; there is a real world out there.

of external control that define to a great degree his thoughts on the larger society. Larger social structures like the family and society are needed to restrain individual egoism and to help bring forth individual altruism.

Collective Phenomena In spite of his clear ideas on the individual, Comte's sociology overtly begins at a more macro level with the family, which Comte labels the "fundamental institution." The family, *not* the individual, is the building block of Comte's sociology, as he explains: "As every system must be composed of elements of the same nature with itself, the scientific spirit forbids us to regard society as composed of individuals. The true social unit is certainly the family" (1830–42/1855:502). Comte clearly believes that individuals constitute a different "level" of analysis than families (and society), which are, after all, "nothing but our smallest society" (1852/1968:161). These "smaller societies" form the natural building blocks of the larger society. Methodologically, Comte argues that "a system can only be formed out of units similar to itself and differing only in magnitude" (1852/1968:153). Individuals constitute different (microscopic) units and (macroscopic) society cannot be formed out of them. Families are similar, albeit smaller, macroscopic units, and therefore they *can* be the basis of the larger society. In fact, Comte traces a progression whereby out of families tribes emerge and from tribes come nations. The family is "the true germ of the various characteristics of the social organism" (Comte, 1830–42/1855:502). The family not only is the building block of society but also serves to integrate the individual and society, since it is through the family that people learn to be social; the family is the "school" of society. Thus, it is the family that must play a crucial role in the control of egoistic impulses and the emergence of individual altruism. Furthermore, if we are ever to improve society significantly, a change in the family will be the fundamental basis of any such alteration. Since the family is such a pivotal institution, a change in it will have profound effects on both individuals and the larger society.

While the family is the most basic and most pivotal institution, the most important institution to Comte is religion, "the universal basis of all society" (1852/1968:7). Doing a kind of structural-functional analysis, Comte identifies two major functions of religion. First, it serves to regulate individual life, once again primarily by subduing egoism and elevating altruism. Second, it has the more macroscopic function of fostering social relationships among people, thereby providing the basis for the emergence of large-scale social structures.

Another important social institution to Comte is language. Language is profoundly social; it is what allows people to interact with one another. Thus, language helps promote unity among people. It connects people not only with their contemporaries but also with their predecessors (we can read their ideas) and their successors (they can read our ideas). Language is also crucial to religion in that it permits the formation, transmission, and application of religious ideas.

Another element of society that serves to hold people together is the division of labor[4] (a view very much like that of Durkheim; see Chapter 6). Social solidarity is enhanced in a system in which individuals are dependent upon others. Society should have a division of labor so that people can occupy the positions for which they qualify on the basis of their abilities and training. Conversely, society should not force people into positions for which they are either underqualified or overqualified (Durkheim calls this the "forced division of labor"). While Comte argues for the need for a division of labor, he is very concerned here, as he is elsewhere, about the dangers of excess specialization in work in general and in intellectual work in particular. He worries about the tendency in society toward overspecialization and argues that the government should intervene to emphasize the good of the whole.

The government, in Comte's view, is based on force. While force can hold society together, if the use of force gets out of hand, the government will be more of a destructive than an integrative factor in society. To prevent this from occurring, the government needs to be regulated by a "broader and higher society. . . . This is the mission of true Religion" (Comte, 1852/1968:249). Comte clearly did not have a high regard for government, and he felt that religion was needed "to repress or to remedy the evils to which all governments are prone" (1852/1968:252).

Social Dynamics

While Comte does have other things to say about social statics, he devoted more attention to social dynamics. He felt that less was known about social statics than social dynamics. Furthermore, the topic of social dynamics was, in his opinion, more interesting and of far greater importance than social statics. However, one may question these contentions. How is it that Comte knew more about the history of the world than he did about the nature of his own society? Why is the past (and future) more interesting than the present? In response to these questions, and contrary to Comte, it can be clearly argued that we always know more about the present than the past (or certainly the future) and that the here-and-now is far more interesting and far more important than the past (or future). Nevertheless, it is on the basis of his beliefs on these issues that Comte abbreviates his discussion of social statics and moves on to the study of social dynamics.

The goal of Comte's social dynamics is to study the laws of succession of social phenomena. Society is always changing, but the change is ordered and subject to social laws. There is an evolutionary process in which society is progressing in a steady fashion to its final harmonious destiny under the laws of positivism: "We are always becoming more intelligent, more active, and more loving" (Comte, 1853/1968:60). Alternatively, Comte labels *social dynamics* the "theory of the Natural Progress of Human Society" (1830–42/1855:515).

---

[4] Or what Comte calls the "division of employments."

Overall, Comte sees us evolving toward our "noblest dispositions," toward the dominance of altruism over egoism. Comte also offers a somewhat more specific view of this future state toward which we are evolving:

> The individual life, ruled by personal instincts; the domestic, by sympathetic instincts; and the social, by the special development of intellectual influences, prepare for the states of human existence which are to follow: and that which ensues is, first, personal morality, which subjects the preservation of the individual to a wise discipline; next, domestic morality, which subordinates selfishness to sympathy; and lastly, social morality, which directs all individual tendencies by enlightened reason, always having the general economy in view, so as to bring into concurrence all the faculties of human nature, according to their appropriate laws."

(Comte, 1830–42/1855:515)

In his view, society invariably follows this law of progressive development; only its speed from one time period, or one society, to another may vary.

Because invariant laws are controlling this process of change, there is relatively little that people can do to affect the overall direction of the process. Nevertheless, people can make a difference by acting "upon the intensity and secondary operation of phenomena, but without affecting their nature or their filiation" (Comte, 1830–42/1855:470). People can modify (for example, speed up) only what is in accord with existing tendencies; that is, people are able to bring about only things that would have happened in any event. It is the fact that people can affect the development of society, if only marginally, that led Comte to his ideas on changing society and his thoughts on the relationship between theory and practice. We will have much more to say about this issue later in this chapter. However, it should be pointed out here that the idea that people can have only a minimal impact did not prevent Comte from developing grandiose plans for the future, positivistic society.

Comte's theory of the evolution of society is based on his theory of the evolution of the mind through the three stages described above. He contends that he himself has "tested" this law by means of all the major methods—observation, experiment, comparison, historical research—and found it "as fully demonstrated as any other law admitted into any other department of natural philosophy" (Comte, 1830–42/1855:522).

Having derived this social law theoretically (from the laws of human nature), he turns to a "study" of the history of the world to see whether the "data" support his abstract theory. However, Comte's use of the words *study* and *data* is misleading, since his methods did not incorporate the criteria that we usually associate with a research study and the data derived from it. For one thing, if Comte's findings contradicted the basic laws of human nature, he would conclude that the research was wrong rather than question the theory (Mill, 1961:85). Comte did no systematic study of the history of the world (how could one systematically study such a vast body of material?), and he did not produce data about that history (he merely provided a series of broad generalizations about vast periods of history). In other words, Comte did not do a research study in the positivistic sense of the term. In fact, Comte acknowledges this by saying that all he is offering is an abstract history; science is not yet ready for a concrete history of the world.

As he had in other areas of his work, Comte offered a dialectical sense of the history of the world. What this meant, in particular, was that he saw the roots of each succeeding stage in history in its prior stage or stages. In addition, each stage prepared the ground for the next stage or stages. In other words, each stage in history is dialectically related to past and future stages. A similar viewpoint is offered by Marx (see Chapter 5), who sees capitalism as being dialectically related to previous economic systems (for example, feudalism) as well as to the future communist society. Although on this point, and on several others, Comte's ideas resemble those of Marx, the reader should bear in mind that the differences between the two thinkers far exceed their similarities. This will be clearest when we discuss Comte's conservative views about the future of the world, which are diametrically opposed to Marx's radical communist society.

Never humble, Comte *began* his analysis of social dynamics by asserting, "My principle of social development . . . affords a *perfect* interpretation of the past of human society—at least in its principal phases" (1830–42/1855:541; italics added). Similarly, at the close of the historical discussion briefly outlined below, Comte concluded, "The laws originally deduced from an abstract examination of human nature have been demonstrated to be real laws, *explaining the entire course of the destinies of the human race*" (1853/1968:535; italics added).

Comte limited his study to Western Europe (and the "white race") because it had evolved the most and because it was, in his view, the "elite" of humanity. We need not go into great detail here about his historical theory because it is of little lasting significance. Furthermore, because it is more central to Comte's underlying theory, we will focus on the changing nature of ideas rather than on more material transformations (for example, Comte sees society as evolving from the warfare characteristic of the theological stage to industry, which was to dominate the positivist stage). Comte begins with the theological stage, which he traces to antiquity. He divides the theological stage into three succeeding periods—fetishistic, polytheistic, and monotheistic. In the early fetishistic stage, people personify external objects (for example, a tree), give them lives like their own, and then deify those objects. Much later, polytheism in Egypt, Greece, and Rome developed. Finally, Comte analyzes the rise of monotheism, especially Roman Catholicism, in the Middle Ages. Although all of these are part of the theological stage, Comte is careful to show that they also possess the germs of the positivism that was to emerge at a much later point in history.

Comte sees the fourteenth century as a crucial turning point as theology began a long period of enfeeblement and decline. More specifically, Catholicism was undermined and eventually replaced by Protestantism, which Comte sees as nothing more than a growing protest against the old social order's intellectual basis (theology). This, for Comte, represents the beginning of the negativity that he sought to counteract with his positivism, a negativity which did not begin to be systematized into a doctrine until the mid-seventeenth century. Protestantism laid the groundwork for this negativity by encouraging unlimited free inquiry. This change in ideas, the development of a negative philosophy, led to a corresponding negativity in the social world and to the social crisis that obsessed Comte. This negative doctrine was developed by French thinkers like Voltaire (1694–1778) and Jean Jacques Rousseau (1712–1778), whom Comte did not see as systematic thinkers; as a result, he believed they were incapable of producing coherent speculations. Nevertheless, these incoherent theories gained a following among the masses because they appeared at a time when theology was greatly weakened and positivism was not yet ready to take its place. Most generally, this entire period was the transitional period, the metaphysical stage, between theology and positivism.

Comte, himself, was writing during what he believed to be the close of the metaphysical stage: "We find ourselves therefore living at a period of confusion, without any general view of the past, or sound appreciation of the future, to enlighten us for the crisis prepared by the whole progress yet achieved" (Comte, 1830–42/1855:738–739). Negativity had far outstripped positivity, and there was, as yet, no available intellectual means to reorganize society. Everywhere Comte turned there was crisis—art was "adrift," science was suffering from overspecialization, and philosophy had fallen into "nothingness." Overall, Comte describes "the philosophical anarchy of our time" (1830–42/1855:738). This philosophical anarchy prepared the way for social revolution, especially the French Revolution, which while negative in many senses was salutary in that it paved the way for the positivistic reorganization of society. As a social event it demonstrated "the powerlessness of critical principles to do anything but destroy" (Comte, 1830–42/1855:739).

Not only was France the site of the major political revolution, but it was to take the lead in the reorganization of Western Europe. It had the most advanced negative ideas and developments, *and* it had gone furthest in positive directions. In terms of the latter, its industrial activity was most "elevated," its art was most advanced, it was "foremost" in science, and it was closer to the new, positive philosophy (and, of course, his eminence, Auguste Comte, lived there). While Comte saw signs during this period of the development of positivism, he recognized that in the short run metaphysics (and the metaphysical stage) had won out. He described the effort in France to develop a constitutional government as being based on metaphysical principles, and he felt that at a philosophical level Rousseau's "retrograde" philosophy had won out. He felt that Rousseau sought to emulate older societies, in which people were freer and more natural, rather than provide a basis for modern society. While this negative development held sway for a half-century in France, Comte also saw within it positive developments in industry, art, science, and philosophy.

Comte saw this period as dominated by a focus on the individual and the metaphysical notion of individual rights. Concern for the individual only led to disorder; in its place, Comte, as we have seen, urged a focus on collective phenomena like the family and society. In addition, a focus on individual rights furthered the tendency toward disorder and chaos; Comte sought a society based on what he viewed as the positive idea of *duties* rather than on individual rights. The idea of duties was seen as a positive notion both because it was more scientific (for example, more "precise") and because it had a "calming" influence on people's egoism as well as on the rampant negativity of the day. Instead of focusing on their individual rights, people were urged to concentrate on their duties to the larger society. This emphasis on duties would enable society to control individual egoism and to better bring out the altruism innate in people. These new duties were to help form the basis of a new spiritual authority that would help regenerate society and morality. This new spiritual authority was, of course, positivism.

THEORY AND PRACTICE

The above, in broad outline, is Comte's theory of social dynamics. Yet Comte (like Marx) wanted to do more than theorize. He wanted his theoretical ideas to lead to practical social changes; he explicitly and self-consciously sought the "connection between theory and practice" (Comte, 1851/1968:46). To this end, Comte sees two objectives for positivism. The first, covered in the preceding sections, is to generalize scientific conceptions—in other words, to advance the science of humanity. The second, covered in this section, is to systematize the art and practice of life (Comte, 1851/1957:3). Thus, positivism is *both* a scientific philosophy and a political practice; the two "can never be dissevered" (Comte, 1851/1968:1).

One of the first political questions addressed by Comte is: Which social groups are likely to support the new doctrine of positivism? It was assumed by Comte that many philosophers would be ardent supporters of this new set of ideas, but philosophers are limited in terms of their ability to implement their ideas. What of the groups of people who are more actively engaged in the social world?

Comte begins by excluding the upper classes because they are in the thrall of metaphysical theories, are too self-seeking, occupy positions too overly specialized to understand the total situation, are too aristocratic, are absorbed in fighting over remnants of the old system, and are blinded by their educational experiences. Overall, he sees the wealthy as more likely than other social groups to be characterized by "avarice, ambition, or vanity" (Comte, 1851/1957:144). Comte also did not expect too much help from the middle classes because they are too busily involved in trying to move into the upper classes. Comte did expect help from three groups—in addition to the philosophers, who would supply the intellect, the working class would bring the needed action and women would provide the required feeling. The philosophers, especially those attracted to positivistic ideas, would be involved, but the major agents of political change would be women and members of the working class: "It is among women, therefore, and among the working classes that the heartiest supporters of the new doctrine will be found" (Comte, 1851/ 1957:4). Both groups are generally excluded from government positions and thus will be more likely to see the need for political change. Furthermore, discrimination against them in the educational system ("the present worthless methods of instruction by words and entities" [Comte, 1851/1957:142]) is less likely to blind them to the need for such change. Comte also sees both women and the working class as possessing "strong social instincts" and "the largest stock of good sense and good feeling" (1851/1957:142).

In Comte's view, the members of the working class are better able to think during the workday because their jobs are not as fully absorbing as those of people in the higher social classes. Presumably this means that the working class has more time and energy to reflect on the benefits of positivism than do the upper classes. Not only is the working class superior intellectually, at least in the sense discussed above, but it is superior morally. Comte offers a highly romanticized view of the morality of the working class: "The life of the workman . . . is far more favourable to the development of the nobler instincts" (1851/1957:144–145). More specifically, Comte attributes a long series of traits to members of the working class, including more affectionate ties at home; the "highest and most genuine types of friendship"; "sincere and simple respect for superiors"; experience with life's miseries, which stimulates them to nobler sympathies; and a greater likelihood of engaging in "prompt and unostentatious self-sacrifice at the call of a great public necessity" (Comte, 1851/1957:145–146).

Comte sees the spread of communism among the working classes in his day as evidence that the trend toward social revolution is focusing in on moral issues. But Comte reinterprets communism as a moral rather than an economic movement so that it fits into his scheme. He argues that communism must be separated from the "numerous extravagant schemes" (presumably Saint-Simon's socialism or Marx's call for a communist revolution) that were being discussed at the time (Comte, 1851/1957:167). To Comte, communism was "a simple assertion of the paramount importance of Social Feeling" (1851/ 1957:169). To show how far he is willing to water down the idea of communism, Comte argues that "the word *Republican* expresses the meaning as well, and without the same danger" (1851/1957:169). Clearly, this is a very different meaning of the term *communism* than the one used by Marx (see Chapter 5) and most other thinkers who have employed the term.

Comte sees positivism as *the* alternative to communism: positivism is the "only doctrine which can preserve Western Europe from some serious attempt to bring Communism into practical operaton" (1851/1957:170). Comte offers a number of contrasts between positivism and communism. First, positivism focuses on moral responses rather than on political responses and economic issues. (Here Comte clearly recognizes that communism, at least as it was being practiced in his time, was an economic and political, rather than a moral, system). Second, communism seeks to suppress individuality, whereas posi-

MP.
Leaders.

tivism seeks both individuality and cooperation among independent individuals. Third, communism seeks the elimination of the leaders of industry, whereas positivism sees them as essential. (Thus, while the leaders of industry cannot play a role in the positivist revolution, they do play, as we will see later, a central role, along with bankers, in Comte's vision of the revamped positivist society.) Fourth, communism seeks to eliminate inheritance, while positivism sees inheritance as important because it provides for historical continuity from generation to generation. In spite of his rejection of communism, Comte sees it as important as another, largely negative, force providing the groundwork for the emergence of positivism.

Comte's interest in the working class as a revolutionary force is not unusual, but his attraction to women as such a group is. Comte had some extraordinary views about women. His major position was that women brought to politics the needed subordination of intellect to social feeling. And Comte came to believe that feeling was preeminent, far more important than intellect or action: feeling is "the predominating principle, the motive power of our being, the only basis on which the various parts of our natures can be brought into unity" (1851/1957:227). Women are "the best representatives of the fundamental principle on which Positivism rests, the victory of social over selfish affections" (Comte, 1851/1957:232). Comte sometimes gushes with his admiration for women in general (as he did more specifically for his beloved "Saint" Clotilde)[5]: "Morally . . . she merits always our loving veneration, as the purest and simplest impersonation of Humanity, who can never be adequately represented in any masculine form" (1851/1957:234). Or even more strongly, "Woman is the spontaneous priestess of Humanity" (Comte, 1851/1957:253). (Of course, this means that men in general, and Comte in particular, are the priests of humanity.) Nevertheless, in spite of his admiration for women, it is men who are superior practically and intellectually. On the intellectual issue Comte contends; "Women's minds no doubt are less capable than ours of generalizing very widely, or of carrying on long processes of deduction . . . less capable than men of abstract intellectual exertion" (1851/1957:250). Because of their intellectual and practical superiority, it is men who are to take command in the actual implementation of positivism.

On the one hand, Comte clearly admired the moral and affectual aspects of women, and as a result, he was willing to accord them a key revolutionary role. On the other hand, he felt that men excelled in intellect and action, and he tended to demean the intellectual and active capacities of women.

In terms of implementing their role in the positivist revolution, women were supposed to alter the educational process within the family and to form "salons" to disseminate positivistic ideas. In spite of his veneration of women, Comte did not believe in equality: "Equality in the position of the two sexes is contrary to their nature" (1851/1957:275). He defends this view on the basis

[5] In fact, Comte thanks Clotilde for helping him come to understand the importance of affection.

of the fact that positivism has *discovered* the following "axiom": "Man should provide for Woman" (Comte, 1851/1957:276). More practically, positivism will institute a new doctrine: "Worship of Woman, publicly and privately" (Comte, 1851/1957:283).

Comte's focus on women, and his emphasis on their capacity for feeling, represented a general change in perspective from his earlier positions. As we saw above, Comte emphasized order in social statics and progress in social dynamics. To order and progress he now added the importance of feeling (love), which he associated with women. As a result he came to proclaim the "positivist motto, *Love, Order, Progress*" (Comte, 1851/1957:7). Positivism was no longer important just intellectually but morally as well. Similarly, Comte added the emotional element to his previous commitment to thought and action by arguing that positive philosophy represented a comprehensive perspective encompassing "Thoughts, Feelings, and Actions" (1851/1957:8).

But Comte went further than simply according feeling equal status with thought and action; he gave feeling the preeminent place in his system. Feeling was to direct the intellect as well as practical activity. In particular, Comte argued that "individual happiness and public welfare are far more dependent upon the heart than upon the intellect" (1851/1957:15). It is this kind of viewpoint that led the champion of positivist intellectual life to the anti-intellectualism that is one of the problems we will discuss later in this chapter.

The emphasis on feeling and love led Comte in his later work to add the science of morality (the study of sentiment) to his list of sciences. "Morals is the most *eminent* of the Sciences" (Comte, 1853/1968:41). Morality was a science which in his system exceeds even sociology. "The field of Morals is at once more *special*, more *complex*, and more *noble* than that of Sociology" (Comte, 1853/1968:40). Not only was morality the most important science, but it was also crucial in giving direction to political changes. In Comte's terms, morality is "the ultimate object of all Philosophy, and the starting point of all Polity" (1851/1957:101). In other words, morality lies at the center of the relationship between theory and practice. Comte sees a natural morality in the world, and it is the task of the positivist to discover its laws. It is these underlying laws of morality that guide our intellectual thoughts and our political actions. Comte concludes, "It is henceforth a fundamental doctrine of Positivism, a doctrine of as great political as philosophical importance, that the Heart preponderates over the Intellect" (1851/1957:18).

Having added morality to the list of his major concerns, Comte returns to his law of the three stages to look at each stage from the point of view of thoughts, feelings, and actions. He sees the theological stage as being dominated by feeling and imagination, with only slight restraint from reason. Theology operated on a purely subjective level, with the result that it was out of touch with the objectivity of practice in the real world. "Theology asserted all phenomena to be under the dominion of Wills more or less arbitrary," but in the real world people were, of course, led by "invariable laws" (Comte, 1851/1957:10). The transitional metaphysical stage continued to be dominated by feeling, was muddled in its thoughts, and was even less able to deal with the practical world. However, positivism finally offered the unity and harmony of thought, feeling, and action. The ideas of positivism are derived from the practical world; they are certainly a monumental intellectual achievement; and positivism also came to comprehend the moral sphere. Only when positivism incorporates morality "can the claims of theology be finally set aside" (Comte, 1851/1957:13). Among other things, morality (feeling) is important for giving direction to thought and action. For example, without the direction of morality, positivism is prone to be too specialized and to deal with "useless or insolvable questions" (Comte, 1851/1957:21). Under the guidance of morality, positivism comes to focus on the broadest, most important, most pressing, and most solvable problems of the day.

With morality added to positivism, it is but a short step for Comte to declare positivism a religion: "Thus Positivism becomes, in the true sense of the word, a Religion; the only religion which is real and complete; destined therefore to replace all imperfect and provisional systems resting on the primitive basis of Theology" (1851/1957:365). And this means that Comte and his principal followers become priests of humanity, with far greater influence than any other previous priesthood. In fact, Comte, with customary humility, declared himself the "founder of the Religion of Humanity" (1853/1968:x). The object of worship in the new religion of positivism is not a god or gods but humanity, or what Comte later referred to as the "Great Being," that is, "the whole constituted by the beings [including animals], past, future, and present, which co-operate willingly in perfecting the order of the world" (1854/1968:27). The Great Being lies at the base of the positivist religion: "The Positive Religion inspires all the servants of the Great Being with a sacred zeal to represent that Being as fully as possible" (Comte, 1852/1968:65).

COMTE'S PLANS FOR THE FUTURE

Given Comte's exaggerated conception of positivism, as well as of his own position in it, it should come as little surprise that he ultimately conceived a grand visionary plan for the future of the world. It is here that we find most of Comte's most outrageous and ridiculous ideas. (Some would say that by this point in his life Comte was embittered and perhaps somewhat insane. It might be that one should take his earlier theories more seriously than his later vision of the future.) Standley calls Comte's vision of the future a "Memorable Fancy" (1981:158). We do not want to go into too much detail, so we will merely suggest the lengths to which Comte went in proposing ways of implementing his positivistic ideas.

For example, he suggested a new positivistic calendar which was to be composed of thirteen months, each divided into twenty-eight days. He created a large number of public holidays to reaffirm positivism, its basic principles, and its secular heroes. He even got into the question of the design of new positivistic temples. He specified the number of priests and vicars required in each temple. Forty-two of the vicars were to be chosen as the priests of human-ity, and from that group the high priest ("the Pontiff") of positivism was to be chosen (as opposed to the Catholic pontiff, who resided in Italy, the posi-tivist pontiff was normally supposed to reside in Paris). (Comte saw himself as the current pontiff and worried over the fact that there was no clear suc-cessor on the horizon.) All these religious figures were to be freed of material cares and therefore were to be supported by the bankers! Comte even specified incomes for religious figures—240 pounds for vicars, 480 pounds for priests, and 2400 pounds for the high priest. Given Comte's views on the positive influence of women, all the priests were to be married so that "they may be under the full influence of affection" (Comte, 1854/1968:224). However, in spite of his high esteem for women, they were not permitted to serve as priests, vicars, or the pontiff. These positions were reserved for men.

While he did not see them as revolutionary forces, Comte eventually accorded members of the upper class, such as bankers and industrialists, cen-tral roles in the new positivist society. It was specified that Western Europe was to have "two thousand bankers, a hundred thousand merchants, two hundred thousand manufacturers, and four hundred thousand agriculturists" (Comte, 1854/1968:269). Merchants, manufacturers, and industrialists were to be apportioned an adequate number of members of the proletariat. Bankers would be both the centers of the commercial world and the suppliers of required funds to the positivist priesthood. Furthermore, from those bankers who are most distinguished for "breadth of thought and generosity of feeling" would be derived the supreme triumvirate (bankers representing merchants, manufacturers, and agriculturalists), which was to handle governmental func-tions (Comte, 1854/1968:301). However, overseeing and directing the opera-tion of this government would be the pontiff and his priests, armed with the religion of positivism.

Turning to other matters, Comte urged the adoption of a positivist library of 100 titles (already specified by him). Additional reading was to be dis-couraged because it hampered meditation. This, too, is reflective of Comte's growing anti-intellectualism (see below).

Given Comte's negative views on individual passion, he urged chastity within the positivist family. He felt that positivism would "discredit and repress the most troublesome of the egoistic instincts [sex!]" (Comte, 1854/1968:251). To deal with the problem of sex, Comte espoused virgin birth. While he did not yet know how virgin birth was to be accomplished (could he have anticipated artificial insemination?), he seemed confident that others would be able to solve the problem eventually. He also favored eugenics, in which only the "higher types" of people (women) would be allowed to repro-duce. Such a plan "would improve the human race" (Comte, 1854/1968:244). He said that we should devote "the same attention to the propagation of our species as to that of the more important domestic animals" (Comte, 1891/1973:222).

The positive family was to be composed of a husband, a wife, ordinarily three children, *and* the husband's parents. The latter were included to bring the wisdom of the past into the family of the present. The mother of the husband, possessing not only the wisdom of advanced age but also the feeling inherent in the female sex, would become the "goddess" of the positivist family.

The above are just a few of the myriad of highly detailed proposals Comte put forth on the basis of his positivist theory. He is careful to point to a division of labor in the development of these guidelines. The positivist philosopher is to come up with the ideas, but he is not to intervene himself in the social world. Such interventions are left to the politician, guided, of course, by the positivist priesthood.

COMTE: A CRITICAL ASSESSMENT

From the above discussion of a few of Comte's largely ludicrous ideas about the future, the reader might conclude that Comte ought to be dismissed out of hand. In fact, it might even be asked once again why a chapter on Comte is included in this book. Thus, we will begin this concluding section with an overview of Comte's most important contributions to sociology. Later we will turn to the far more numerous weaknesses in Comte's work; weaknesses which lead us to conclude that it is safe for the science of sociology to forget much of Comte's work and get on with its own development, which has forged far ahead of Comte's ideas.

Positive Contributions

First, of course, Comte was the first thinker to use the term *sociology*; he can be seen as the "founder" of sociology. While it is certainly the case that thinkers throughout the course of human history have dealt with sociological issues, Comte was the first to make such a focus explicit and to give it a name.

Second, Comte defined *sociology* as a positivistic science. While this is, as we will see later, a mixed blessing, the fact is that the majority of contemporary sociologists continue to see sociology as a positivistic science. They believe that there are invariant laws of the social world and that it is their task to discover those laws. Many search for such laws empirically, while others (for example, J. Turner, 1985a) follow Comte's model and go about the search for such laws theoretically. Much of contemporary empirical sociology, and a significant segment of sociological theory, continues to accept Comte's positivistic model of sociology.

Third, Comte articulated three major methods for sociology—experiment, observation, and comparison (the historical comparative method is sufficiently important to be distinguished as a fourth methodology)—which continue to be widely used in sociology. While Comte's work is badly dated in most respects, it is surprisingly contemporary in terms of its methodological pronouncements. For example, there has been a substantial resurgence of interest in historical studies in contemporary sociology (for example, Mann, 1986; Wallerstein, 1989).

Fourth, Comte differentiated in sociology between social statics and social dynamics. This continues to be an important differentiation in sociology, but the concepts are now called *social structure* and *social change*. Sociologists continue to focus on society as it is presently constituted as well as on its changing nature.

Fifth, although again a mixed blessing, Comte defined *sociology* in macroscopic terms as the study of collective phenomena. This was to take clearer form in the work of Durkheim, who defined *sociology* as the study of social facts (see Chapter 6). More specifically, many of Comte's ideas played a key role in the development of a major contemporary sociological theory—structural functionalism (see Chapter 11).

Sixth, Comte stated clearly his basic ideas about the domination of human nature, if left on its own, by egoism. Because he is clear about such basic views, the reader gets a sound understanding of where Comte's thoughts on the larger structures of society come from. Basically, those larger structures are needed to control individual egoism and to permit the emergence of individual altruism.

Seventh, Comte offered a dialectical view of macro structures. He saw con- *CONNECT* *ED* temporary macro structures as being the product of past structures and as possessing the seeds of future structures. This gave his work a strong sense of historical continuity. His dynamic, dialectical view of social structure is superior to positions taken by many later, even contemporary, theorists of social structure who have tended to adopt static, ahistorical perspectives.

Eighth, Comte was not content with simply developing abstract theory but was interested in integrating theory and practice. While this ambition was *PRACT* marred by some of his ludicrous ideas for the future society, the integration *CHANGE* of theory and practice remains a cherished objective among contemporary sociologists. In fact, there is a growing interest in what is now called *applied sociology*, and the American Sociological Association now has a section on sociological practice.

Basic Weaknesses in Comte's Theory

While Comte made some lasting contributions to sociology, the fact is that the contemporary student of sociology has relatively little to gain from reading Comte's work. All his positive contributions have been integrated into contemporary sociology and further developed and refined. Thus, the positive derivatives from Comte's work can be acquired more directly from a reading of the contemporary literature in sociology and sociological theory. Furthermore, many of the specifics of Comte's work have not withstood the test of time, and even many of his generalities have little to offer to the modern student of sociology. Most important, Comte's work is marred by a series of problems, although we can learn a good deal by examining some of Comte's most glaring mistakes.

We can begin the discussion of Comte's specific weaknesses with a quotation from one of his severest critics, Isaiah Berlin:

> His grotesque pedantry, the unreadable dullness of his writing, his vanity, his eccentricity, his solemnity, the pathos of his private life, his insane dogmatism, his authoritarianism, his philosophical fallacies . . . [his] obstinate craving for unity and symmetry at the expense of experience . . . with his fanatically tidy world of human beings joyfully engaged in fulfilling their functions, each within his own rigorously defined province, in the rationally ordered, totally unalterable hierarchy of the perfect society.
>
> (Berlin, 1954:4–5, 22)

One is hard-pressed to think of a more damning critique of any social theorist, yet the fact is that much of it is warranted. The issue here is: Where and how did Comte go wrong in his social theorizing?

First, I would argue that Comte's theory was overly influenced by the trials and tribulations of his own life. For example, very much ignored in his lifetime, Comte became increasingly grandiose in his theoretical and practical ambitions. For another, his largely unfulfilled relationships with women, especially his beloved Clotilde, led him to a series of outrageous ideas about women and their role in society. This problem was amplified by a sexism that led him to accord feelings to women, while men were given intellectual capacities and political and economic power. Then we must add the fact that Comte was deeply troubled psychologically; one often feels, especially in regard to the later works, that one is reading the rantings of a lunatic. While it is obviously difficult to keep one's psychological disturbances out of one's theorizing, it is clear from Comte's case that theorists need to be vigilant to the dangers of allowing their personal experiences to affect the way they develop theories about how the social world operates.

Second, Comte seemed to increasingly fall out of touch with the real world. After *Positive Philosophy*, his theories were characterized by a spinning out of the internal logic of his own ideas. One of the causes of this is the fact that despite his claims, Comte actually did no real empirical research. His idea of doing empirical research was to offer gross generalities about the historical stages, and the evolution, of the world. Comte's looseness about data analysis is reflected in the following statement: "Verification of this theory may be found *more or less distinctly* in every period of history" (1851/1957:240; italics added). Had Comte been a better data analyst, and had he been more generally in touch with the historical and contemporary worlds, his theories might not have become so outrageous.

Third, Comte also grew progressively out of touch with the intellectual work of his time. Indeed, he is famous for practicing cerebral hygiene rather early in his life. He systematically avoided reading newspapers, periodicals, and books (except for a few favorite poems) and thereby sought to keep the ideas of others from interfering with his own theorizing. In effect, Comte was increasingly anti-intellectual. This ultimately became manifest in his substantive work, in which he urged such things as the abolition of the university and the withdrawal of economic support for science and scientific societies. It is also manifest in his positivist reading list of 100 books. Presumably, this limited list meant that all other books did not need to be read and could be safely burned. Comte's anti-intellectualism is also found in other aspects of his substantive work. For example, in making the case that strong affect helps lead to important scientific findings, Comte downgrades the importance of rigorous scientific work: "Doubtless, the method of pure science leads up to it also; but only by a long and toilsome process, which exhausts the power of thought, and leaves little energy for following out the new results to which this great principle gives rise" (1851/1957:243). The clear lesson of Comte's errors is that a theorist must remain in touch with *both* the empirical and the intellectual worlds.

Fourth, he failed as a positivist, both in his empirical and in his theoretical work. As to his empirical work, we have seen that he did woefully little of it and that the work he did was really little more than a series of gross generalizations about the course of world history. There was certainly little or no induction from data derived from the real world. Regarding his theoretical work, it is hard to even think of many of his bizarre generalizations about the social world as sociological laws. Even if we take Comte's word that these were, in fact, laws, it remains the case that few, if any, social thinkers have confirmed the existence of these invariant laws. While Comte argued that his laws should be reflections of what actually transpired in the social world, the fact is that he most often seemed to impose his vision on the world.

Fifth, while Comte is credited with creating sociology, there is very little actual sociology in his work. His sketchy overviews of vast sweeps of history hardly qualify as historical sociology. His admittedly weak statements on a few elements of social statics contributed little or nothing to our understanding of social structure. Thus, little, if any, of Comte's substantive sociology survives to this day. John Stuart Mill was quite right when he argued, "Comte has not, in our opinion, created sociology . . . he has, for the first time, made the creation possible" (1961:123–124). Comte's lasting legacy is that he created some domains—sociology, positivist sociology, social statics, social dynamics—which his successors have filled in with some genuine substantive sociology.

Sixth, it can be argued that Comte really made no original contributions.[6] Mill clearly minimizes Comte's contribution in this domain: "The philosophy called Positive is not a recent invention of M. Comte, but a simple adherence to the traditions of all the great scientific minds whose discoveries have made

---

[6] Heilbron (1990:155) disagrees arguing that Comte's original contribution lies in his *"historical and differential theory of science."* (This theory is discussed early in this chapter.)

the human race what it is" (1961:8–9; see also, Heilbron, 1990). Mill also argues that Comte was well aware of his lack of originality: "M. Comte claims no originality for his conception of human knowledge" (1961:6). Comte readily acknowledged his debt to such renowned positivists as Bacon, Descartes, and Galileo. A similar point could be made about Comte's contribution to sociology. Comte clearly recognized important forerunners in sociology, such as Charles de Montesquieu (1689–1755) and Giambatista Vico (1668–1774). While he may have invented the term *sociology*, he certainly did not create the practice of sociology.

Seventh, whatever sociology Comte did have to offer was distorted by a primitive organicism, in which he saw strong similarities between the workings of the human and the social body. For example, Comte argues that composite groups like social classes and cities are "the counterpart of animal tissues and organs in the organisation of the Great Being" (1852/1968:153). Later, he contends that the family is the social counterpart of cells in an organism. Furthermore, Comte sees an analogy between social disorder and disease in organisms. Just as medicine deals with physical diseases, it "is left for Positivism to put an end to this long disease [social anarchy]" (Comte, 1852/1968:375). This kind of organicism has long been eliminated from sociology.

Eighth, Comte tended to develop theoretical ways of thinking and theoretical tools that he then imposed on whatever issue he happened to be analyzing. For example, Comte seemed to be fond of things that came in threes, and many of his theoretical ideas had three components. In terms of theoretical tools, he was not content to apply his law of the three stages to social history; he also applied it to the history of sciences, the history of the mind, and the development of individuals from infancy through adulthood. A particularly bizarre example of this tendency to apply the law of the three stages to anything and everything is Comte's application of it to his own mental illness:

> I will confine myself to recording here the valuable phenomena I was able to observe in the case of my own cerebral malady in 1826. . . . The complete course . . . enabled me to verify twice over my then recently discovered Law of the Three Stages; for while I passed through those stages, first *inversely*, then *directly*, the order of their succession never varied.
>
> During the three months in which the medical treatment aggravated my malady, I descended gradually from positivism to fetishism, halting first at monotheism, and then longer at polytheism. In the following five months . . . I reascended slowly from fetishism to polytheism, and from that to monotheism, whence I speedily returned to my previous positivism . . . thus furnishing me with a decisive confirmation of my fundamental Law of the Three Stages.
>
> (Comte, 1853/1968:62–63)

Ninth, Comte's "outrageous," "colossal" self-conceit (Mill, 1961) led him to make a series of ridiculous blunders. On the one hand, his never powerful theoretical system grew progressively weak as he increasingly subordinated the intellect to feeling. One manifestation of this is his unrealistic and highly romanticized view of the working class and women as agents of the positivist revolution. This decline in intellect is also manifest in his practice of cerebral hygiene as well as in his limiting of the number of positive books. On the other hand, and more important, his oversized ego led him to suggest a series of social changes, many of which, as we have seen, are ludicrous.

Tenth, Comte seemed to sacrifice much of what he stood for in his later turn toward positivist religion. In the framing of this religion, Comte seemed to be most influenced by the structure of Catholicism. In fact, T. H. Huxley called Comte's system "Catholicism minus Christianity" (cited in Standley, 1981:103). Comte acknowledged his debt to Catholicism when he argued that positivism is "more coherent, as well as more progressive, than the noble but premature attempt of medieval Catholicism" (1851/1957:3). His positivist religion mirrored Catholicism with its priests, vicars, and even its pontiff. Clearly, positivist religion has had no lasting impact, and it certainly served to subvert Comte's scientific pretensions.

Finally, there is the issue of the totalitarian implications of Comte's plans for the future. For one thing, these were highly detailed plans in which Comte personally sought to dictate what the various agents in his system would do. For another, his plans even extended to specific institutions such as the family. Particularly notable here are his ideas on the application of the principles of animal husbandry to humans. Ultimately, of course, his plans encompassed religion, with his notion of a supreme pontiff who would rule over the positivist empire.

SUMMARY

This is not an unbiased presentation of Comte's ideas. It is clear that contemporary sociology has moved far beyond Comtian theory, and this chapter underscores that point. While there are a number of useful derivatives from Comte's theory, the main point is that there are innumerable weaknesses in that theory which make it largely irrelevant to a contemporary student of sociology. Focusing on the needs of such a student, this chapter is concerned with the limited number of positive derivatives from Comte's theories and, more important, the negative lessons that can be of utility to the modern sociologist.

On the positive side, Comte offers us a positivist perspective, and many contemporary sociologists continue to accept the idea of the search for invariant social laws. Comte has also given us the term *sociology*, and his focus within that field on social statics and social dynamics remains a viable distinction. His basic methods of social research—observations, experimentation, comparison, and historical research—remain major methods of social research. Within his work on social statics, he made a number of contributions (a focus on structures, functions, equilibrium) that were important in the development of the contemporary theory of structural functionalism. Also within social statics, it is to Comte's credit that he laid out a detailed view of human nature on which he then erected his macrosociological theory. At the macro level, Comte offers a dialectical sense of structural relations, and his social realism anticipates that of Durkheim and many other later theorists. His work on social dynamics was relevant to later evolutionary theorists. Finally, Comte was not content to simply speculate, but was interested in linking theory and practice.

While the above are important accomplishments, there are far more things to be critical of in Comte's work. He allowed his theoretical work to be distorted by his personal experiences. He lost touch with both the social and intellectual worlds. His empirical and theoretical work was lacking, given his own positivistic standard. There is really little substantive sociology in his work, and that which he offers is distorted by a primitive organicism. There is little in his work that was new at the time. Comte tended to impose his theoretical schemes on anything and everything, no matter how good the fit. His oversized ego led him to a number of outrageous theoretical blunders as well as many ludicrous suggestions for reforming the social world. His reform proposals were further undermined by his increasing preoccupation with positivism as a religion and his role as the pontiff of this new religion. Finally, his blueprint for the future positivist society had many totalitarian implications.

All things considered, Comte belongs to the early history of sociological theory. Some of his ideas (especially in *Positive Philosphy*) continue to be relevant, but the modern student of sociology is safe in not rereading most of his work, especially his later statements on his plans for the future. This will not be true for most of the theorists covered in this book, but we turn now to the ideas of Herbert Spencer in an effort to see whether much of his work, like Comte's, can be safely ignored by contemporary sociologists. It will be shown that there are many more theoretical ideas of contemporary relevance in Spencerian theory than in Comtian theory.

HERBERT SPENCER

*I*N the theoretical ideas of Herbert Spencer (1820–1903) we see a considerable advance over those of Auguste Comte. Not only was Spencer's work important in the development of sociological theory, but many of his theoretical ideas stand up well from the vantage point of contemporary sociological theory. In spite of this, Jonathan Turner (1985b), who is strongly in sympathy with many of Spencer's ideas, has pointed out that modern sociological theorists have been disinclined to take Spencer seriously, relegating him, like Comte, to the "dustbin" of history. (Actually, in superheated terms, Turner argues that contemporary social theorists have been inclined to "spit on the grave of Spencer" [1985b:71].) This negativity is, to a large extent, traceable to Spencer's highly conservative libertarian (*not* liberal) politics and to his belief in a sociologial version of survival of the fittest. While I do not fully share Turner's enthusiasm for Spencer, there is much of merit in Spencer's work. It will be demonstrated that a number of Spencer's theoretical ideas continue to be important and relevant to sociological theory. However, there are also serious problems with Spencer's theory which lead to the conclusion that while it represents an advance over Comtian theory, it is not quite up to the standard of the other major early theorists—Marx, Durkheim, Weber, and Simmel—to be discussed in the ensuing four chapters.

SPENCER AND COMTE

A useful starting point for this discussion is the relationship between Spencer's ideas and those of Auguste Comte. While the lives of Spencer and Comte overlapped, the two men were separated by the English Channel (Spencer was British, while Comte was French) and there was a substantial difference in their ages (Comte was twenty-two years old when Spencer was born, and the latter lived for forty-six years after Comte's death and into the twentieth century). Thus, Comte had completed most of his work before Spencer published his first book, *Social Statics,* in 1850. However, almost as soon as Spencer had published *Social Statics,* comparisons began to be made between his theories and those of Comte. There are a number of seeming similarities between the work of the two men, but Spencer most often felt the need to distinguish his theories from those of Comte.

Spencer commented on Comte's work in various places and even felt compelled to write an essay entitled "Reasons for Dissenting from the Philosophy of M. Comte" (1864/1883/1968). Spencer began with great, if only obligatory, praise for Comte's work: "In working out this conception [of positivism] he has shown remarkable breadth of view, great originality, immense fertility of thought, unusual powers of generalization" (1864/1883/1968:118). In spite of such an encomium, Spencer was mainly concerned with positioning himself as one of Comte's "antagonists" and with distinguishing his own ideas from those of Comte because their work is "so utterly different in nature" (Spencer, 1904a:414).

Spencer did acknowledge his terminological debt to Comte by admitting, "I also adopt his word, Sociology" (1864/1883/1968:130). Both derived the terms *structure* and *function* largely from biology, and they tended to use them in similar ways. In utilizing these terms, and the perspective they imply, both Spencer and Comte played key historic roles in the development of structural functionalism. However, regarding another set of terms, *social statics* and *social dynamics,* there are important differences between the two men. While Spencer uses these terms, he denies that they are drawn from or resemble Comte's identical terms. In his autobiography, Spencer contends that when *Social Statics* (1850/1954) was published, he "knew nothing more of Auguste Comte, than that he was a French philosopher" (1904a:414). For Comte, these terms refer to all types of societies, while Spencer relates them specifically to his future ideal society. Spencer defines *social statics* as dealing with "the equilibrium of a perfect society" and *social dynamics* as relating to "the forces by which society is advanced toward perfection" (1850/1954:367). Thus, for Spencer the terms *social statics* and *social dynamics* are normative, while for Comte they are descriptive.

Spencer classifies himself, like Comte, as a positivist interested in the discovery of the invariant laws of the social world, but he hastens to add that positivism was not invented by Comte. While Spencer sees himself as a positivist, he does not accept Comte's version of positivism, especially Comte's sense of a positivist religion. Spencer, like Comte, dealt with a wide range of sciences, but unlike Comte, he argued that "the sciences cannot be rightly placed in any linear order whatever" (1883:185). Rather, Spencer viewed the sciences as being interconnected and interdependent. Another major distinction made by Spencer was between Comte's subjectivity (his concern with ideas) and Spencer's objectivity (his concern with things):

> What is Comte's professed aim? To give a coherent account of the progress of *human conceptions*. What is my aim? To give a coherent account of the progress of the *external world*. Comte proposes to describe the necessary, and the actual, filiation of *ideas*. I propose to describe the necessary, and actual, filiation of *things*. Comte professes to interpret the genesis of *our knowledge of nature*. My aim is to interpret, as far as it is possible, the genesis of the *phenomena which constitute nature*. The one end is *subjective*, the other is *objective*.

(Spencer, 1904b:570)

Thus, although both Spencer and Comte were concerned with the evolution of the world, Comte was mainly interested in the evolution of ideas, while Spencer focused on structural (and functional) evolution.

Finally, there are powerful political differences between Spencer and Comte. As we saw in the last chapter, Comte wanted to construct a society, even a world, dominated by a positivistic religion of humanity and led by the high priests of positivism. Spencer countered that Comte's faith that "the 'Religion of Humanity' will be the religion of the future is a belief countenanced neither by induction nor by deduction" (1873/1961:283). In addition, Spencer had little regard for centralized control, which he felt would do far more harm than good. Thus, Spencer's ideal is a society in which the government is reduced to a minimum and individuals are allowed maximum freedom. We will return to Spencer's political ideas later in the chapter, but suffice it to say that they are radically different from Comte's politics. Spencer was led to muse on how "profoundly opposed" were Comte's and his "avowed or implied ideals of human life and human progress" (1904a:414).

Comte believed that individuals could be taught morality, largely through the positivist religion, but Spencer ridiculed the idea that morality could be taught in any fashion and by any means. Spencer believed that moral ideas emerge from individual action. In arriving at this conclusion, Spencer used here, as he did in many other places in his work, a survival-of-the-fittest perspective. In this specific case, the requirements of an orderly life will force people to act on the basis of their higher moral sentiments and repress their lower sentiments; in other words, people will be rewarded for moral behavior and penalized for immoral behavior. To put it another way, moral actions are likely to survive, while immoral actions are not. Spencer concludes that this "natural selection" of moral actions "alone is national education" (1873/ 1961:340).

In sum, while Spencer and Comte shared concerns with sociology, structures and functions, social statics and social dynamics, positivism, the rela-

HERBERT SPENCER: A Biographical Sketch

Herbert Spencer was born in Derby, England, on April 27, 1820. He was not schooled in the arts and humanities, but rather in technical and utilitarian matters. In 1837 he began work as a civil engineer for a railway, an occupation he held until 1846. During this period, Spencer continued to study on his own and began to publish scientific and political works.

In 1848 Spencer was appointed an editor of *The Economist,* and his intellectual ideas began to solidify. By 1850, he had completed his first major work, *Social Statics.* During the writing of this work, Spencer first began to experience insomnia, and over the years his mental and physical problems mounted. He was to suffer a series of nervous breakdowns throughout the rest of his life.

In 1853 Spencer received an inheritance that allowed him to quit his job and live for the rest of his life as a gentleman scholar. He never earned a university degree or held an academic position. As he grew more isolated, and physical and mental illness mounted, Spencer's productivity as a scholar increased. Eventually, Spencer began to achieve not only fame within England but also an international reputation. As Richard Hofstadter put it: "In the three decades after the Civil War it was impossible to be active in any field of intellectual work without mastering Spencer" (1959:33). Among his supporters was the important industrialist Andrew Carnegie, who wrote the following to Spencer during the latter's fatal illness of 1903:

> Dear Master Teacher . . . you come to me every day in thought, and the everlasting "why" intrudes— Why lies he? Why must he go? . . . The world jogs on unconscious of its greatest mind. . . . But it will wake some day to its teachings and decree Spencer's place is with the greatest.
> (cited in Peel, 1971:2)

tionships among the sciences, the evolution of the world, the future ideal society, and morality, there are profound differences in their views on most of these topics as well as in their overall theories. Given this relationship—or, more accurately, this lack of a strong relationship—we turn to a discussion of Spencer's sociological theory.

GENERAL THEORETICAL PRINCIPLES

Spencer's thoughts on the social world are based on a series of general theoretical principles. He begins by arguing that in the early history of humankind religion and science were unified in their efforts to analyze and understand the world (Spencer, 1902/1958). Gradually, the two begin to separate, with religion coming to focus on the unknowable and science on that which can be known. However, this differentiation is far from complete, even in the modern era, so that religion and science continue to overlap and to conflict. In fact, Spencer sees his own work as involving elements of science (intelligence) and religion (morals).

But that was not to be Spencer's fate.

One of Spencer's most interesting characteristics, one that was ultimately to be the cause of his intellectual undoing, was his unwillingness to read the work of other people. In this, he resembled another early giant of sociology, Auguste Comte, who practiced "cerebral hygiene." Of the need to read the works of others, Spencer said: "All my life I have been a thinker and not a reader, being able to say with Hobbes that 'if I had read as much as other men I would have known as little' (Wiltshire, 1978:67). A friend asked Spencer's opinion of a book, and "his reply was that on looking into the book he saw that its fundamental assumption was erroneous, and therefore did not care to read it" (Wiltshire, 1978:67). One author wrote of Spencer's "incomprehensible way of absorbing knowledge through the powers of his skin . . . he never seemed to read books" (Wiltshire, 1978:67).

If he didn't read the work of other scholars, where, then, did Spencer's ideas and insights come from? According to Spencer, they emerged involuntarily and intuitively from his mind. He said that his ideas emerged "little by little, in unobtrusive ways, without conscious intention or appreciable effort," (Wiltshire, 1978:66). Such intuition was deemed by Spencer to be far more effective than careful study and thought: "A solution reached in the way described is more likely to be true than one reached in the pursuance of a determined effort [which] causes perversion of thought" (Wiltshire, 1978:66).

Spencer suffered because of his unwillingness to seriously read the works of other people. In fact, if he read other work, it was often only to find confirmation for his own, independently created ideas. He ignored those ideas that did not agree with his. Thus, his contemporary, Charles Darwin, said of Spencer: "If he had trained himself to observe more, even at the expense of . . . some loss of thinking power, he would have been a wonderful man" (Wiltshire, 1978:70). Spencer's disregard for the rules of scholarship led him to a series of outrageous ideas and unsubstantiated assertions about the evolution of the world. For these reasons, sociologists in the twentieth century came to reject Spencer's work and to substitute for it careful scholarship and empirical research.

Spencer died on December 8, 1903.

Spencer's main concern was with the knowable world and was therefore much more scientific than it was religious. (This is another contrast to Comte, whose later work became far more religious than scientific.) Science could never know the ultimate nature of things, but it could strive for the highest possible degree of knowledge. Before we can get to his thoughts on science, we first need to deal with his philosophy, which Spencer sees as transcending the sciences in the search for the complete unification of knowledge, for "truths which unify concrete phenomena belonging to all divisions of Nature" (1902/1958:277). In this section we will discuss Spencer's "general philosophy," in which he deals with "universal truths" for all the world, while later we will analyze his "special philosophies" and the narrower, but still universal, truths of specific areas, especially those relating to the *social* world. In emphasizing the overarching character of philosophy, Spencer rejects the positivistic idea that the goal of science is the reduction of an array of complex laws to a simple law and accepts, instead, the goal of knowledge integrated from a range of specific scientific fields.

Spencer articulates a series of general truths about the world, including the facts that matter is indestructible, there is continuity of motion and persistence of force, the relations among forces persist, and matter and motion are continually redistributed. By a process of *deduction* from these general laws, Spencer articulates a series of ideas that constitute his general *evolutionary theory*.

Spencer believes that all inorganic, organic, and superorganic (societal) phenomena undergo evolution and devolution, or dissolution. That is, phenomena undergo a process of evolution whereby matter becomes integrated and motion tends to dissipate. Phenomena also undergo a process of devolution in which motion increases and matter moves toward disintegration. Having deduced these general principles of evolution and dissolution from his overarching principles, Spencer then turns to specific areas in order to show that his theory of evolution (and devolution) holds inductively, that is, that "all orders *do* exhibit a progressive integration of Matter and concomitant loss of Motion" (1902/1958:308).

The combination of induction and deduction leads Spencer to his "final" evolutionary formula:

> Evolution is an integration of matter and concomitant dissipation of motion; during which the matter passes from an indefinite, incoherent homogeneity to a definite, coherent, heterogeneity; and during which the retained motion undergoes a parallel transformation.

(Spencer, 1902/1958:394)

Let us decompose this general perspective and examine each of the major elements of Spencer's evolutionary theory.

First, evolution involves progressive change from a less coherent to a more coherent form; in other words, it involves increasing *integration*. Second accompanying increasing integration is the movement from homogeneity to more and more heterogeneity; in other words, evolution involves increasing *differentiation*. Third, there is a movement from confusion to order, from indeterminacy to determined order, "an increase in the distinctness with which these parts are marked off from one another" (Spencer, 1902/1958:361); in other words, evolution involves movement from the *indefinite to the definite*. (In Chapter 11 we will see that Parsons developed a similar evolutionary theory in his later work.)

Thus, the three key elements of evolution are increasing integration, heterogeneity, and definiteness. More specifically, Spencer is concerned with these elements, and his general theory of evolution, as they apply to both *structures* and *functions*. At the most general level, Spencer associates structures with "matter" and sees them growing more integrated, heterogeneous, and definite. Functions are linked to "retained motion," and they, too, are seen as growing increasingly integrated, heterogeneous, and definite. We will have occasion to deal with Spencer's more concrete thoughts on the evolution of functions and structures in his work on society.

Having outlined his general theory of evolution, Spencer turns to the issue of the reasons for the occurrence of evolution. First, Spencer argues that homogeneous phenomena are inherently unstable: "the absolutely homogeneous must lose its equilibrium; and the relatively homogeneous must lapse into the relatively less homogeneous" (1902/1958:426). One reason for this instability is the fact that the different parts of a homogeneous system are constantly subjected to different forces, thereby tending to differentiate them from one another. Changes in one part of the once homogeneous system will inevitably result in changes in other parts, leading, in turn, to greater multiformity. A second factor in sequence, but not in importance, is the multiplication of effects. In Spencer's view, the multiplication of effects proceeds in a geometric manner. In other words, a small change in a once homogeneous system has increasingly ramifying effects. Thus, over time, the once homogeneous system grows increasingly heterogeneous. Third, Spencer discusses the effects of segregation on evolution. A sector becomes segregated from the others because of a likeness among its components, which are different from the components of other sectors. This serves to maintain differences among the sectors, and this, in turn, furthers the multiplication of effects when one sector is exposed to, and incorporates, the distinguishing characteristics of other sectors.

Given that evolution is an inevitable process, the issue becomes: Where is evolution headed? While en route to their end state, phenomena move through a series of transitional states that can be described as "moving equilibria," while the end state of the process is a new equilibrium. It could be argued that we are moving to "a state of quiescence," and it could then be asked: "Are we not manifestly progressing toward omnipresent death" through the dissipation of moving forces? (Spencer, 1902/1958:508). Spencer responds negatively to this question, arguing that we are moving toward universal life through new stages in the evolutionary process. He does however posit an end state of the evolutionary process: "Evolution can end only in the establishment of the greatest perfection and the most complete happiness" (Spencer, 1902/1958:511). Spencer obviously has great faith in the evolutionary process, and its ultimate state of perfection gives him a standard by which he can assess all other steps in the evolutionary process.

In spite of his faith in evolution, Spencer recognizes, in a dialectical fashion, that the process of dissolution complements the evolutionary process and periodically leads to its undoing. The dissolution process is likely to occur when evolution has ended and the evolved phenomenon has begun to decay.

Evolution constitutes the focus of Spencer's work in a variety of realms, but our concern is with the evolution of human societies in terms of their growth and with the evolution of structures and functions. Following Spencer, we will look at the evolution of society in general as well as that of a number of specific social institutions. Spencer's rationale for devoting so much attention to the evolution of society and its institutions is his view that a fully adequate understanding of human social relations requires an understanding of their evolution (as well as their cycles and dissolution).

SOCIOLOGY

Defining the Science of Sociology

Given Spencer's focus on evolution, he defines "the study of Sociology as the study of Evolution in its most complex form" (1873/1961:350). To put it another way, sociology is "the natural history of societies" or more specifically, "an order among those structural and functional changes which societies pass through" (Spencer, 1873/1961:63–64). However, Spencer does not restrict sociology to historical societies but also accepts the study of the ways in which *contemporary* organizations and institutions "are severally related to other phenomena of their respective times—the political institutions, the class-distinctions, the family arrangements, the modes of distribution and degrees of intercourse between localities, the amounts of knowledge, the religious beliefs, the morals, the sentiments, the customs, the ideas" (1873/1961:120). But while Spencer sanctions the need for contemporaneous research, he feels that the true meaning of his work is found only when it is placed in a historical, evolutionary context. However, whether sociological research focuses on historical or contemporary issues, it is clear that Spencer's sociology concentrates largely on macro-level social phenomena (social aggregates)—societies, social structures, social institutions—as well as the functions of each.[1]

Spencer (1873/1961:115) shares with Comte the view that sociology should deal with social questions in the same scientific manner in which we address issues in the natural sciences. Furthermore, Spencer, like Comte, sees sociology, especially in its evolutionary concerns, as the most complex of sciences.

While Spencer sees sociology as a (complex) science, he recognizes that it is not an exact science, but he rhetorically wonders how many sciences are exact sciences? To be a science, in Spencer's view, requires only that there be generalizations (laws) and interpretations based on those generalizations. Sociology seeks laws of social phenomena in the same way that the natural sciences seek the laws of natural phenomena. "Either society has laws or it has not. If it has not, there can be no order, no certainty, no system in its phenomena. If it has, then are they like the other laws of the universe—sure, inflexible, ever active, and having no exceptions" (Spencer, 1850/1954:40). Although sociology and other sciences seek to make predictions about the future on the basis of laws, in most cases all sciences must be satisfied with only the most general predictions.

In endeavoring to lay the groundwork for his kind of scientific sociology, Spencer confronted the problem that many other early sociologists faced—the need to legitimize the field. For example, he felt compelled to argue that laypeople lack the capacity to grasp the complex issues of concern to sociologists: One needs to be a trained sociologist in order to comprehend them. Because in their everyday lives they deal with the same issues that are of concern to

[1] In his work, though, Spencer does offer some insightful micro accounts, especially of rituals in his discussion of ceremonies (see pages 128–130).

sociologists, laypeople in Spencer's day and to this day as well, are convinced, erroneously, that they can do as good a job of social analysis as trained sociologists. Spencer also confronted the misplaced confidence of laypeople in their views and their hostility to sociologists by arguing that the incapacity of the layperson "is accompanied by extreme confidence of judgment on sociological questions, and a ridicule of those who, after long disicpline, begin to perceive what there is to be understood, and how difficult is the right understanding of it" (1873/1961:115). As a result of these lay attitudes, Spencer sees many barriers to sociology's receiving the recognition it deserves. These include the fact that few laypeople will be able to grasp the complexity of sociology's subject matter, an unconsciousness on the part of laypeople that there are any such complex phenomena, their misplaced confidence, and the fact that the minds of most laypeople are not adaptable and flexible enough to accept the new perspective offered by sociology.

Spencer felt that sociologists, in contrast to laypeople, require disciplined habits of thought and that those habits are to be derived from a careful study of other sciences. This need to study other sciences is buttressed by an argument similar to one made by Comte, that is, that the science of sociology encompasses the phenomena of concern in all other sciences. Spencer gave particular importance to the need for sociologists to be familiar with the fields of biology and psychology.

Spencer saw three basic linkages between biology and sociology. First, he believed that all social actions are determined by the actions of individuals and that those actions conform to the basic laws of life in general. Thus, to understand social actions, the sociologist must know the basic laws of life, and it is biology that helps us comprehend those laws. Second, there are powerful analogies between sociology and biology. That is, society as a whole, like the living body, is characterized by, among other things, growth, structure, and function. Thus an understanding of the biology of the living organism, which after all is far easier to study than the social organism, offers many keys to understanding society. Spencer concludes, "There can be no rational apprehension of the truths of Sociology until there has been reached a rational apprehension of the truths of Biology" (1873/1961:305). Third, a kind of natural progression and linkage exist between the two fields, since humans are the "terminal" problem for biology and the starting point for sociology.

A more specific similarity between biology and sociology is the operation of the survival-of-the-fittest process in both living and social organisms. Spencer felt that survival of the fittest occurs in both the biological and the social realms and that the lessons of biology from the natural world are that there should be no interference with this process in the social world.

Spencer also devoted considerable attention to psychology as another major base for sociology. He adopted the general position that "psychological truths underlie sociological truths" (Spencer, 1873/1961:348). As he saw it, psychology is the study of intelligence, feeling, and action. He believes that one of the great lessons of psychology is that feeling, *not* intelligence, is linked to action. This leads Spencer to emphasize sentiments and to downgrade the importance of intelligence and cognition in his sociological analyses (see the preceding chapter, on Comte, for a similar view). While people throughout history have been dominated by sentiments and desires, this was especially true in primitive societies. Primitive people were inherently impulsive, and because they were "not much habituated to associated life," they were "habituated to that uncontrolled following of immediate desires" (Spencer, 1908a:64). In contrast, people in the modern world, while still dominated by feelings, emotions, and desires, are better able to control them because they are more habituated to collective life. Thus, Spencer is led to argue that primitive people are characterized by greater selfishness and that there is more altruism in the modern world. This general orientation leads Spencer to focus substantively on collective phenomena, and politically this emphasis on the importance of feelings is one of the factors causing him to oppose conscious and intelligent change of society.

While Spencer embeds his sociology in a set of assumptions about the psychological characteristics of individuals, he does *not* accept the idea that these characteristics are fixed. Rather, psychological characteristics change with the changes in society as well as with those in the larger environment.

From his study of psychology, and more generally from his basic philosophical orientation, Spencer comes to the "methodological individualist" conclusion that the units of society are individuals and that individuals are the source of social phenomena. Everything in society is derived from the motives of individuals, the combined similar motives of many individuals, or the conflict between those with one set of motives and others with another set. However, while Spencer bases his sociology on such psychological principles, he does not spend much time analyzing the ways in which these psychological phenomena lead to the development of society and its various institutions. Rather, Spencer assumes that individuals are the units, and the base, of society and institutions, and then he proceeds to the macro level to study the evolution of society and its institutions. This lack of concern (with a few exceptions; see below on ceremonial institutions) for how macro-level phenomena (society and institutions) emerge from micro-level units (individuals and their motives) is a serious weakness in Spencer's sociological theory.

Sociological Methods

Within the context of Spencer's definition of sociology as a science, he addressed a range of methodological problems. Spencer attempts to show "how greatly the advance of Sociology is hindered by the nature of its subject-matter" (1873/1961:66). He believes that sociology confronts several difficulties that differentiate it from natural sciences. To begin with, there are objective difficulties that involve the intrinsic nature of the facts that sociologists must analyze. For example, social phenomena are not directly perceptible. Unlike natural phenomena, they cannot be studied and measured with such instruments as clocks, thermometers, scales, and microscopes. (Of course, modern sociology has demonstrated that at least some social phenomena *can* be studied and measured with instruments [for example, audiotapes and video-tapes].) Another methodological difficulty for sociologists, in Spencer's view, is that they, unlike psychologists, cannot utilize introspection as a method; social facts cannot be studied through introspection, while this method can be used to study psychological facts. (Again, at least some modern sociologists [for example, phenomenologists] do use introspection as a method.)

The facts of concern to sociologists not only are different from those found in the natural sciences and psychology but also are far more complex and difficult to study. Sociologists inevitably deal with an enormous range of highly dispersed details. It is often difficult to gain a sense of what is happening, because things occur over a wide geographic area and over long periods of time. Thus, for example, Spencer contends that the increasing division of labor is very difficult to study and was underway for quite some time before its development was recognized.

Another objective difficulty facing sociology is the untrustworthiness of its data, derived from *both* past and present societies. For one thing, the data are often distorted by the subjective states of the witnesses to the events under study, but sociologists must rely on the reports of such witnesses for their data. For another, the sociological observer is often misled by superficial and trivial facts and fails to see what is truly important. Spencer offers a number of cautions to sociologists: "In every case we have to beware of the many modes in which evidence may be vitiated- have to estimate its worth when it has been discounted in various ways; and have to take care that our conclusions do not depend on any particular class of acts gathered from any particular place or time" (1873/1961:103). While Spencer recognizes that the objective difficulties are formidable, he still feels that sociology can deal scientifically with general classes of facts, although not with specific facts.

Sociologists must also confront the reality that they are the human observers of humanly created phenomena. As human beings, sociologists use modes of observation and reasoning in their daily lives, and such habits may not be useful in, or may even be impediments to, sociological study. Sociologists must be wary of assessing others on the basis of their own standards. They are likely to experience difficulties in their own society, and those difficulties are greatly magnified when sociologists examine other societies.

Sociologists also have a very different relationship to the facts they observe than do natural scientists. Sociologists' emotions may affect their judgments of social phenomena or lead them to make judgments without sufficient evidence. Spencer argues that "minds thus swayed by disproportionate hates and admirations, cannot frame those balanced conclusions respecting social phenomena which alone constitute Social Science" (1873/1961:144). In this context, Spencer deals with a number of specific emotional biases.

First, there is what Spencer calls an *educational bias*. He traces this to the fact that we live in a society that combines elements of both militant and industrial societies (see below). The result is that we are taught a tangle of ideas derived from both systems, and this causes the sociologist to misinterpret social phenomena. The sociologist must not be biased against either militant or industrial society and must be able to study both impartially and to recognize that both have been necessary historically. For example, as we will discuss later, Spencer, in spite of his biases against warfare, is able to see that war is functional for militant societies.

Second, there is the *bias of patriotism* (and antipatriotism). As Spencer argues: "'Our country, right or wrong,' . . . Whoever entertains such a sentiment has not that equilibrium of feeling required for dealing scientifically with social phenomena" (1873/1961:185). Sociologists must emancipate themselves from the bias of patriotism, but Spencer recognizes that such emancipation is not easy to accomplish. However, he holds out hope for the future, since he believes that the triumph of industrial society, the resulting increase in harmonious sentiments, and the decrease in hostility to societies different from our own will lead to a decline in patriotic bias and an increased capacity to be objective about our society and others, both historically and contemporaneously.

Third, there is *class bias*, found in the upper and lower classes, among employers and the employed, which Spencer regards as the most serious of the biases in sociological work. Since all sociologists come from a given class, they are likely to reflect this bias in their work. Once again, however, Spencer holds out hope for the future, in which greater societal harmony will lead to less class antagonism and to the increased ability of sociologists to come to more balanced conclusions about social phenomena. However, Spencer goes further and uses the argument about class bias to underscore his conservative orientation: "The class-bias obscures the truth, otherwise not easy to see, that the existing type of industrial organization, like the existing type of political organization, is about as good as existing human nature allows. The evils there are in it are nothing but the evils brought round on men by their own imperfections" (1873/1961:229). Spencer's conservatism, and its implications for his sociology, will be touched upon throughout this chapter.

Fourth, Spencer discusses *political bias*. The current government, its laws, and its political parties, among other political phenomena, serve to bias sociologists in their work. Not only are sociologists prone to view things the way the current political system sees them, but they are led to examine visible political forms and ignore less visible political phenomena (for example, "national character"). Furthermore, the existing political system tends to obscure the unanticipated effects of legal and other political changes. For example, the government will attune observers to acknowledge the anticipated benefits of political changes and to ignore their unanticipated evils.

Finally, Spencer looks at *theological bias*. For example, the sociologist may be led to assess things relative to the creed of a given religion rather than to the way they relate to human welfare in general. While Spencer foresees no end to religion, he does see it undergoing the evolutionary trend described above, and this will serve to mitigate theology as a source of bias in the future.

In seeking to exclude these and other biases from sociological research, Spencer is articulating a "value-free" position for the discipline (see Chapter 7, on Weber, for a more complex view of this issue). He argues, for example, that

> in pursuing our sociological inquiries . . . we must, as much as possible, exclude whatever emotions the facts are calculated to excite . . . trustworthy interpretations of social arrangements imply an almost passionless consciousness. Though feeling cannot and ought not to be excluded from the mind when otherwise contemplating them, yet it ought to be excluded when contemplating them as natural phenomena to be understood in their causes and effects.
>
> (Spencer, 1908b:230,232)

In his own work Spencer employed what has come to be called the *comparative-historical* method. That is, he engaged mainly in the comparative study of the different stages of societies over time as well as of various kinds of contemporary societies. His goal in this research was always to seek out, inductively, support (or, presumably, lack of support) for the theories derived deductively from his most general orientation. He was also interested in developing empirical generalizations based on his comparative, especially evolutionary, studies.

We must not close this section without mentioning the fifteen volumes of data on various societies (for example, ancient Mexicans, ancient Romans) commissioned by Spencer but put together by others in accord with a category system developed by Spencer (J. Turner, 1985b:95–104). While these volumes have been little read or used by sociologists, and while they are almost impossible to find today, they reflect Spencer's commitment to empirical research of the comparative-historical variety in order to create a base whereby he and others could inductively support, or fail to support, theories derived deductively.

THE EVOLUTION OF SOCIETY

Spencer employs his evolutionary theory in his massive three-volume work, *The Principles of Sociology* (1908a, 1908b, 1908c). (Much of this work had been published in serial form in magazines in the late 1800s.) In this more specific focus on the evolution of society and its major institutions, Spencer employs the three general dimensions outlined above—increasing *integration* (increasing size and coalescence of masses of people), *heterogeneity,* and *definiteness* (clearly demarcated social institutions). In addition, he employs a fourth dimension, the *increasing coherence* of social groups (modern civilized nations hold together far longer than early wandering groups of people). Thus, he offers the following statement as his general formula of social evolution: "There is progress toward greater size, coherence, multiformity and definiteness" (Spencer, 1908a:597).

Before we go any further, it is important to make it clear that in spite of appearances, Spencer does *not* adopt an inevitable, unilinear view of social evolution. That is, evolution does not have to occur, and it does *not* always move in a single direction. Societies are constantly changing in light of changes in their environs, but these changes are not necessarily evolutionary. "Only now and then does the environing change initiate in the organism a new complication, and so produce a somewhat higher structure" (Spencer, 1908a:95–96). It is possible at any given moment for there to be no change, dissolution, *or* evolution. Not only is evolution not inevitable, but when it does occur, it does not take the form of a simple unilinear pattern; the stages do not necessarily occur in serial order.

Before getting to the actual evolution of society, we need a definition of *society*. Spencer discusses the issue of *nominalism* (society is nothing more than its component parts) versus *realism* (society is a distinct and separable entity) and comes down on the side of realism because of the "permanence of the relations among component parts which constitutes the individuality of a whole" (1908a:447). "Thus we consistently regard society as an entity, because, though formed of discrete units, a certain concreteness in the aggregate of them is implied by the general persistence of the arrangements among them throughout the area occupied" (Spencer, 1908a:448). Thus, Spencer considers society a "thing," but it is unlike any other thing except for parallel principles in the way the component parts are arranged.

It should be pointed out here that there is an uncomfortable fit between Spencer's social realism and his previously discussed methodological individualism. Methodological individualism generally leads to, and is more comfortable with, a nominalist position on society. Conversely, methodological individualism generally rules out a realist orientation to society. Spencer holds to both without telling us much about how he is able to adopt two such discordant perspectives or how they are linked to one another. In other words, how do individuals create a "real" society? Spencer begins with assumptions about individuals, imposes the existence of society, and then ends (as we will see later) with a series of concerns about the negative impact of society on individuals.

Spencer sees societies as being like organic bodies (but unlike inorganic bodies) in that both are characterized by permanent relations among the component parts. Spencer's *organicism* led him to see a number of parallelisms between society and organic entities. Among other similarities, both increase in size and are subject to structural and functional differentiation. Furthermore, both are characterized by an increasing division of labor, the development of interrelated differentiations that make still other differentiations possible. The component parts of both society and an organism are interconnected and in need of each other. In addition, if the whole of society or an organism dies, parts can live on; conversely, the whole can live on even if parts die (for example, society continues even after individuals die).

One issue here is whether Spencer believed that society is an organism or that there are simply important analogies between the two. While at times Spencer discussed society as an organism, his avowed position was that there are merely important parallels between the two and that one could improve one's understanding of society by better understanding the parallelisms.

In a more concrete sense, Spencer (1908b) sees society as a gathering of people forming a group in which there is cooperation to seek common ends. Cooperation in society implies some form of organization. In Spencer's view, there are two basic types of cooperation. The first is the division of labor, which is a spontaneously and unconsciously developed system that directly serves the interests of individuals and indirectly those of society. Here we have a situation in which individuals consciously pursue their private ends and the unconsciously evolving organization is *not* coercive. The second cooperative system is the one for defense and government, that is, the political organization, which is a consciously and purposefully created system that directly serves the interests of society and indirectly those of the individual. The political system involves the conscious pursuit of public ends, and this consciously evolving organization is coercive in regard to individuals.

The first element in Spencer's work on the evolution of society is society's growth in size. In his view, societies, similar to living organisms, "begin as germs" (Spencer, 1908a:463). "Superorganic" (social) phenomena, like organisms, grow through both the multiplication of individuals and the union ("compounding") of groups (for example, tribes), both of which may go on simultaneously.

The increase in the size of society is accompanied by an increase in *structure*. Spencer defines a *structure* as "an organization" (1908c:3). Greater size requires more differentiation, a greater unlikeness of parts. In fact, Spencer argues that "to reach great size [society] must acquire great complexity" (1908a:471). More generally, he contends that "all social structures result from specializations of a relatively homogeneous mass" (Spencer, 1908c:181). The first differentiation is the emergence of one or more people claiming and/or exercising authority. This is followed soon after by the division between the *regulative* and the *sustaining* structures of society. We will have more to say about these structures later, but at this early stage the regulative structure is associated with military activities while economic activities that maintain the group are linked to the sustaining structures. At first, this differentiation is closely linked to the division of labor among the sexes, with men handling the regulative structure (the military) and women the sustaining structures. As society evolves, each of these structures undergoes further differentation; for example, the regulative agency acquires a system of kings, local rulers, petty chiefs, and so on. Then there are differentiations of social classes as the military, the priestly, and the slave classes emerge. Further differentiations occur *within* each social class; in the priestly class, for example, sorcerers, priests, diviners, and exorcists develop. Overall, society moves toward increasing structural differentiation and complexity.

The increasing differentiation of structures is accompanied by increasingly differentiated functions. A *function* is "the need subserved" by a structure (Spencer, 1908c:3). Spencer argues that "changes of structures cannot occur without changes of functions" (1908a:485). More generally, he contends that one cannot truly understand structures without a clear conception of their functions, or the needs served by the structures. In a relatively undifferentiated state, the various parts of society can perform each other's functions. Thus, in a primitive society the male warriors could raise food and the females could fight if it became necessary. However, as society grows increasingly complex structurally, it is more and more difficult for highly specialized parts to perform each other's functions. Evolution brings functional progress along with structural progress: "With advance of organization, every part, more limited in its office, performs its office [that is, function] better; the means of exchanging benefits becomes greater; each aids all, and all aid each with increasing efficiency; and the total activity we call life, individual or national, augments" (Spencer, 1908a:489).

Having argued that societies evolve both structurally and functionally, Spencer returns to the sustaining and regulative systems mentioned above and adds a third, the *distributing* system. In the discussion of these three systems, Spencer makes great use of analogies between social systems and organisms. In both social systems and organisms the sustaining system is concerned with the *internal* matters needed to keep them alive. In the living body the sustaining system takes the form of the alimentary organs, while in the social system it adopts the form of the various elements of the industrial system. *External* matters for both social systems and organisms are handled by the regulative system. The regulative system takes the form of the neuromuscular system in organisms and the government-military apparatus in social systems. Both are concerned with warfare with other systems and conflicts with the environment. Finally, the distributive system links the sustaining and regulative organs and systems. Here Spencer sees an analogy between blood vessels (in organisms) and roads (in social systems), "channels which carry, in the one case blood-corpuscles and serum, and in the other case men and commodities" (1908a:510). In addition to describing each of these structures and the functions they perform, Spencer also demonstrates how each is undergoing a process of evolution.

Simple and Compounded Societies

On the basis of what he claims are inductions from the evolution of past and present societies, Spencer develops two different systems for classifying societies. The first, or primary, method is based on the increasing number of members of the aggregate as well as the degree to which that aggregate is *compounded*, or added to, by combining with other aggregates through such means as conquest or peaceful merger. While, as we saw above, Spencer has argued in general against a simple unilinear theory of evolution, the latter is just what he seems to offer here: "The stages of compounding and recompounding *have to be passed through in succession*. No tribe becomes a nation by simple growth; and no great society is formed by the direct union of the smallest societies" (1908a:555; italics added).

Spencer identifies four types of societies on the basis of their degree of compounding. First, there are *simple* societies, which constitute single working entities that are not connected with any other entities. These are relatively homogeneous and uncivilized societies that have not gone through a compounding process. Second, we find *compound* societies, in which there is some increase in heterogeneity. For example, here we may find the emergence of a supreme chief who rules over the chiefs of several simple groups. Obviously, since there are now several groups, some compounding has occurred either by conquest or peaceful means. We also find in compound societies, as a result of increasing heterogeneity, an increase in the division of economic labor and in organization. Third, there are *doubly-compound* societies, formed on the basis of the recompounding of compound groups. Here we find still more heterogeneity and further advances in civilization. Thus, in the political realm we find even more developed and stable governments. Spencer describes many other advances in these societies, such as the development of an ecclesiastical hierarchy, a more complex division of economic labor, law emerging from custom, more towns and roads, and more advanced knowledge and arts. Finally, there are the *trebly-compound* societies, or the great nations of the world, which are even more advanced in the areas just mentioned as well as in many others. Included in this category are both older societies, like the Roman Empire, and modern nations.

Militant and Industrial Societies

Spencer offers a secondary system of classifying societies, although this one became better known than his primary system of classifying societies by their degree of compounding. This is his famous distinction between *militant* and *industrial* societies and the character of societies as they oscillate between the two. Militant societies tend to be dominated by the regulative system, while industrial societies are characterized by their more highly developed sustaining systems. These are ideal types, as Spencer recognizes: "During social evolution there has habitually been a mingling of the two" (1908b:568). Spencer sees a long-term evolutionary trend from militant to industrial societies, although here he is more careful to be clear that this trend is *not* unilinear. Spencer also briefly mentions the possibility of a future, "higher" type of society characterized by intellectual and esthetic concerns (Perrin, 1976), but he has little to say of a substantive nature about the possibility of this third type of society.

Spencer goes into much more detail about militant societies than industrial societies, and what he says about them is much clearer, because militant societies had long been in existence whereas industrial societies were still emerging in his day.

Militant societies are characterized by highly structured organizations for offensive and defensive warfare. In effect, the army and the nation are one:

"The army is the nation mobilized while the nation is the quiescent army, and which, therefore, acquires a common structure to army and nation" (Spencer, 1908a:557). The militant society is dominated by its regulative system, with centralized and despotic government control, unlimited political control over personal conduct, and a rigidly controlled, disciplined, and regimented population. The cooperation that exists in society is a result of compulsion. The individual exists for the good of the collectivity: "Under the militant type the individual is owned by the state. While preservation of the society is the primary end, preservation of each member is a secondary end" (Spencer, 1908b:572). There is a rigid status hierarchy, and individual positions are fixed as to rank, occupation, and locality. Industry, such as it is, exists largely to fill the needs of the government-military.

While he is critical of warfare, and hopes for a future society in which warfare is reduced or eliminated, Spencer believes that war is useful in militant societies in producing social aggregation (by, for example, military conquest). It is also useful in laying the groundwork for industrial society: "Without war large aggregates of men cannot be formed, and . . . without large aggregates of men there cannot be a developed industrial state" (Spencer, 1873/1961:176). This attitude toward warfare is also linked to Spencer's views on survival of the fittest: "We must recognize the truth that the struggles for existence between societies have been instrumental to their evolution" (1908b:241). However, with the development of industrial society, war becomes more dysfunctional than functional, as it serves to block industrial growth, consumes needed people and materials, draws off intellectual resources, and fosters antisocial attitudes and behaviors in a society that values harmony.

As is his normal pattern, Spencer arrives at the characteristics of the militant society deductively and then demonstrates that they are supported by induction from actual militant societies. However, he is forced to deviate from his usual pattern in the case of industrial societies because their characteristics are not fully emergent and continue to be hidden by the militant characteristics of society. Therefore, in his depiction of industrial societies Spencer is forced to rely even more heavily on the deductive method, although he does find some support in data derived from societies with industrial characteristics.

The industrial society is dominated by the sustaining system, and its industrial system is more developed and diverse. The regulative control that continues to exist tends to be negative (people shall *not* do certain things) rather than positive (people must do certain things). There is no need for despotic control, and the government tends to be democratic, with representatives of the people exercising power. The control that remains tends to be much more decentralized. There is voluntary cooperation among people, and the collectivity exists to serve the welfare of the people. Individuality is protected and permitted to flourish. The military system is subordinated to the needs of the industrial system. Control is exercised by contracts voluntarily entered into by individuals. Harmony, rather than conflict and warfare, characterizes industrial societies. While militant societies are forced to be economically autonomous because of the hostility of and toward their neighbors, industrial societies are much more interdependent economically. While militant societies tend to be rather inflexible, industrial societies are much more changeable and adaptable.

The above, of course, are ideal types that vary greatly from one setting to another. Spencer made clear the ideal-typical character of his depiction of a militant society: "Having contemplated the society *ideally* organized for war, we shall be prepared to recognize in real societies the characteristics which war has brought about" (1908b:569; italics added). Spencer details a number of factors that contribute to variation within each of these types, including racial composition, the nature of the immediately preceding society, the habitat, and surrounding societies. Spencer also discusses "hybrid societies," which are only partially militant or industrial, although he contends that hybrid societies are likely to be more like militant societies than industrial societies. In fact, he describes the society in which he lived as such a transitional hybrid—semimilitant and semi-industrial (Spencer, 1908c:551). Finally, while there is a general evolutionary trend toward industrial societies, Spencer recognizes that regression to more militant societies is possible. For example, an international conflict can cause an industrial society to grow more militant, engaging in more aggressive external acts and developing a more repressive internal government. While Spencer sees a continual threat of rebarbarization, he hopes for some sort of federation of the nations of the world that would forbid wars among member nations. Thus, in his militant-industrial categorization system Spencer does *not* offer a unilinear view of the evolution of society.

Having dealt with the evolution of society as a whole, Spencer turns to the evolution of a variety of social institutions, and we will deal with each of them below. In general, Spencer takes as his objective the description of a society's "*institutions,* regulative and operative, and the ways in which *structures* and *functions* have gradually established themselves" (1873/1961:52; italics added).

THE EVOLUTION OF SOCIETAL INSTITUTIONS

Domestic Institutions

Spencer sees family (or domestic) institutions performing several important functions. First, they help to preserve the social aggregates (for example, societies) in which they occur. Different family structures exist in different societies, and that type of family which survives in any given society is viewed by Spencer as "relatively appropriate" for that society (1908a:610). (We encounter here, again, the conservative implications of Spencer's structural-functional orientation, since he seems to be offering a defense of any family structure that exists at a given point in time.) Second, a function of families is to provide society with the maximum possible number of healthy offspring raised to maturity. Third, as family structures evolve, they further more, and burden less, the interests of parents. Parents receive the advantages of longer periods before reproduction, a decreased number of offspring, an increased pleasure in child care, and a longer life span after reproduction and child rearing are completed. The last years of the parents' lives bring pleasure to both the parents and their offspring. This last phase in the evolution of the family brings biological and sociological advantages, and it is also the highest stage in an ethical sense.

In primitive (or simple) societies the family as we know it does not exist since life is unsettled and indefinite. The relations between the sexes are unregulated by larger institutions and systems of ideas. Spencer, reflecting his Victorian biases, describes a number of "repugnant practices" in primitive societies, such as the lending of wives and incest. He describes an evolution from this "repugnant" base, but it is not a uniform, unilinear process. For example, he finds a number of "civilized" domestic customs among the primitives and some "uncivilized" domestic customs in more advanced societies. "Nevertheless, on contemplating the facts in their *ensemble,* we see that progress towards higher social types is joined with progress towards higher types of domestic institutions" (Spencer, 1908a:621–622). Spencer, in spite of his caveats, proceeds to trace the history of "successively higher forms of family structure" (1908a:622). In other words, there is a progression to more evolved family forms in terms of greater coherence, multiformity, and definiteness.

Spencer looks at this evolution from the vantage point of the various types of relations between men and women, husbands and wives. In the most primitive state he finds *promiscuity* predominant. However, in his view this incoherent and indefinite domestic form (if it can even be called that) must give way to other types of relationships between husband and wife: "As, however, under ordinary conditions the rearing of more numerous and stronger offspring must have been favoured by more regular sexual relations, there must, on the average, have been a tendency for the societies most characterized by promiscuity to disappear before those less characterized by it" (Spencer, 1908a:652). We encounter again Spencer's tendency to use the survival-of-the-fittest perspective. The irregularity of promiscuity is not suitable for the constant production of large numbers of offspring, and thus it must die out and be replaced by more regular relations between husbands and wives, which are better able to perform this function.

The next evolutionary stage is characterized by *polyandry,* in which one woman is related to several men. This constitutes an advance over promiscuity and itself undergoes a process of evolution (for example, from the case in which a woman is married to several unrelated husbands to one in which the several husbands are brothers). While polyandry may be well adapted to certain settings and may work well within them, in most settings it does not work well in terms of social preservation, the rearing of offspring, and the welfare of adults. "Other things equal, this *inferior* family-type has yielded to *superior* family-types; both because of its inferior fertility, and because of the smaller family-cohesion, and consequently smaller social cohesion, resulting from it" (Spencer, 1908a:663; italics added).

The next evolutionary stage is *polygyny,* in which one husband has a plurality of wives. Spencer sees this as an advance over both promiscuity and polyandry because of the more definite relationships between husbands and wives. Further, it functions better in the sense of better fulfilling social needs by reducing the mortality of children and women. Furthermore, it fills the needs of society by contributing to social cohesion through more widely ramifying family connections. It has done this, for example, by furthering that political stability which results from an established succession of rulers in the same family line and by making possible a more developed form of ancestor worship. Such collective worship is a source of societal cohesion. However, in the end, Spencer sees polygyny as being adaptive for only "low stages of social evolution . . . it repeats within the household the barbarism characterizing the life outside the household" (1908a:678). In other words, it seems suited only to the militant stage.

Finally, there is *monogamy,* which, again from the vantage point of Spencer's Victorian England, where it was the norm, is the most advanced form of domesticity. While monogamy is found in the most primitive societies, it grows increasingly common as societies evolve. Among other things, it is the most evolved family system in terms of definiteness and the strength of the links among family members. In Spencer's view, monogamy better serves the interests of offspring, parents, and the larger society than do other types of relations. The monogamous family is best suited to the industrial-type society.

Spencer links the evolution of the family toward monogamy with improvements in the status of women and children. Women tend to be treated cruelly in militant societies, but their status increases and their treatment improves with the shift toward industrial societies and monogamy. Part of this is traceable to the increasing altruism of industrial societies, which benefits all social relationships, and part of it to the shift from the low status of women, associated with polygyny, to their higher status, associated with monogamy. There is a similar improvement in the situation of children. In early societies children are more often treated badly, and because of the need for (male) warriors, female children are treated more poorly than their male counterparts. In industrial societies there is more recognition of the rights of children and more equality in the treatment of male and female children.

In his analysis of the evolution of the family, Spencer relies mainly on a series of inductions made from empirical evidence. However, he argues that the conclusions derived from induction are in accord with his overall theory of evolution. Within the family we see movement from the "small, incoherent, and indefinite . . . to [the] most coherent, most definite, most complex" (Spencer, 1908a:757–758). More contemporary families function better than their predecessors in providing for the welfare of the species, offspring, parents, and society.

Finally, Spencer looks to the future of the family and makes it clear that he does not adopt a unilinear theory of evolution: "We must beware of supposing that developed societies [and families] will become universal" (1908a:763). "Inferior" types of societies and families will survive in "inferior" settings to which they are well adapted. He expects that the militant societies, and their attendant less developed family types, will continue to survive in some areas of the world. However, within industrial societies Spencer does adopt a unilinear view with regard to the family: "The monogamic form of the sexual relation is manifestly the ultimate form; and any changes to be anticipated must be in the direction of completion and extension of it" (1908a:764). Along with the triumph of the monogamous family will come a number of positive benefits, such as the extinguishing of promiscuity, the suppression of bigamy and adultery, a decrease in domestic dissension, an increase in altruism, and greater solicitude of children by parents and of aged parents by their children. Spencer also anticipates greater equality of the sexes in domestic life, "but it seems improbable that absolute equality with men will be reached" (1908a:768).

Ceremonial Institutions

Next Spencer turns to ceremonial institutions as structures which regulate people's lives. Actually, as Jonathan Turner (1985b:116) points out, ceremonies are preinstitutional or subinstitutional. On the one hand, they form the base of later, full-fledged religious and political institutions. On the other hand, they mainly involve more micro-level interactions among people that are the basis of later, more macro-level social institutions. (This is one of the few areas in which Spencer works at the micro level.)

In the most primitive societies ceremonies function to exert social, political, and religious control over people. But over time these forms of control differentiate, become autonomous, exert control by themselves, and develop independent ceremonies. Primitive tribes may lack political and religious regulation, but they do have an early form of social regulation through ceremonies themselves. While most social functions have correspondingly large structures, the functions of ceremonial control have minuscule correlative structures. As society evolves, large-scale political and religious structures emerge to perform these functions. But at the same time, ceremonial control grows less important as these structures exert more definite and detailed control. Indeed, ceremonies, which are based largely on fear, work best in militant societies and erode with the passage to the more peaceful and harmonious industrial society.

Spencer takes pains to point out that the evolution of ceremonies is not a result of individual choice or deliberate action but rather has a "natural genesis." That is, ceremonies evolve gradually. They flow naturally from the emotional characteristics of individuals. Since they develop naturally and are the products of emotions, not intellect, they should not be altered as a result of cognitive thought and conscious human action.

Spencer begins by identifying a number of components of ceremonial rule and describing how they change over time.

Trophies give their possessors status and power, but since the winning of trophies is linked to militancy, the practice diminishes with industrialism and "complete industrialism necessitates entire cessation of it"(Spencer, 1908b:51). *Mutilations,* or the cutting off of parts of the body, are also associated with militancy and also tend to disappear with the increase of industrialism. *Presents*, originally spontaneous gifts to authorities, are more likely in militant societies because of the fear of those in power. Rather than disappearing, presents become more mandatory with the development of industrialism. Presents once given to rulers eventually become political revenue, and those given to gods eventually become ecclesiastical revenue.

Unlike the ceremonies discussed above, *visits* are not usually found in simple societies. They tend to appear in compound societies in the form of visits to the chief or king. But they are associated even more with the structure of society than with size alone. That is, visits represent manifestations of obedience in militant societies and tend to become less imperative with increasing industrialism. In addition to becoming less likely as a form of obedience, visits also tend to move away from being exclusively paid to the most powerful leaders and toward being paid to less and less powerful leaders. Eventually, visits take the form of propitiations among equals. This shift from appeasement of elites to propitiation of equals is manifest in other ceremonies as well.

Obeisances are demonstrations of subjection to a master. Initially, an obeisance may take the form of prostrating oneself before a king, but later it moves to descending to one knee and still later to kissing the king's hand. Such forms of obeisance are more likely in militant societies (because of fear of the king) and are likely to decline with the movement toward industrialism. Obeisances, like visits, change over time and come to take forms such as shaking hands among equals. *Forms of address* are similar to obeisances and state in words what obeisances do in acts. They, too, are more likely in militant societies and are also likely to come to be employed by equals.

Titles, or descriptive names of honor, originate in militant societies, with those accorded titles being military leaders. In fact, even the word *God* is rooted in words expressing superiority. Titles tend to evolve during the militant period and to dissolve with the coming of industrialism:

> It is indisputable, then, that serving first to commemorate the triumphs of savages over their foes, titles have expanded, multiplied and differentiated, as conquests have formed large societies by consolidation and reconsolidation of small ones; and that, belonging to the social type generated by habitual war, they tend to lose their uses and their values, in proportion as this type is replaced by one fitted for carrying on the pursuits of peace.

> (Spencer, 1908b:178)

To be rich in militant societies implies that one is victorious in warfare. With the spoils of war, one is able to construct the highest and most ornate homes. However, with the evolution to industrialism, wealth and the signs of it are no longer directly traceable to being a military leader. It even becomes harder to distinguish members of the industrial elite from their subordinates because the latter emulate their superiors in the external signs of wealth. This is like the situation in *fashion:* rather than not doing what the leaders do, subordinates demonstrate respect by copying what the leaders do and wear. Fashion, therefore, tends to accompany industrial, not militant, society, since it tends toward a system of greater equality. This trend toward greater equalization and individuality tends to weaken ceremonies in general.

Much of the preceding discussion relates changing ceremonies to the evolution from militant to industrial societies. Spencer also relates this change to the simple, compound, doubly-compound and trebly-compound growth of military (but not industrial) societies. With increasing size, there are great increases in the number of ceremonies and the degree to which they regulate all actions of life. Ceremonies take on increasingly heterogeneous forms. They also increase in definiteness, "ending . . . in fixed forms prescribed in all their details, which must not under penalty be departed from. And in sundry places . . . [they are] consolidated into coherent codes set forth in books" (Spencer, 1908b:217). Thus, ceremonies tend to evolve with the increasing size of militant societies, but this tendency is reversed when we move from militant to industrial societies. Ceremonies decline with industrialism, and when Spencer peers into the future, he anticipates further declines in ceremonies.

Political Institutions

"The political organization is to be understood as that part of social organization which constantly carries on directive and restraining functions for public ends" (Spencer, 1908b:247). Before getting to the evolution of political organizations, we must discuss the source of political power in early societies. In Spencer's view, the sole source of political power in such societies is the feeling of the community. Furthermore, political organizations (as well as ceremonial and ecclesiastical organizations) "are at once the products of aggregate feeling, derive their powers from it, and are restrained by it" (Spencer, 1908b:325). Not only did public opinion control political authority in early society, but it continues to do so to a large extent in contemporary society. This, of course, tends to downgrade the importance of any specific political system, since all political systems derive their power from the collective feeling of the community.

There are small primitive societies without political organizations. However, as tribes grow in size, they tend to begin to develop a rudimentary political organization, as exemplified by the emergence of a chief and later a chief who rules over a series of minor chieftains. Such early political organizations are functional in a variety of ways, such as the removal of antagonisms that impede cooperation, the maintenance of order, the enablement of a more elaborate division of labor, and the formation of still larger aggregates. However, these political organizations can also be dysfunctional by being tyran-nical, demanding excessive taxes, and exercising excessive retraints on people. In addition, as the political system grows, it can become an impediment to the further growth of society by resisting needed efforts to reorganize society and absorbing resources needed for the growth of society. Thus, there is a dialectical relationship here—political organizations are needed for growth, but they can also serve to impede growth. Overall, however, Spencer believes that the political organization is advantageous. It is a gradually and uncon-sciously evolved system that secures for individuals benefits they could not have achieved if they acted singly.

After growth, Spencer deals with integration in the evolution of the political system. Political integration, like all evolutionary integration, occurs when the elements of society are subjected to like forces. These forces may be external to society (for example, climate) or internal to society (for example, racial composition), but the general rule is that a common set of such forces serves to transform what was at first an incoherent political system into one which is increasingly integrated. Then there is the increasing differentiation of the political organization. The primitive, homogeneous political system tends to break down, as all homogeneous systems must. Over time, an increasingly differentiated political system evolves.

In addition to discussing the evolution of the political organization in gen-eral terms, Spencer deals with the evolution of a number of specific elements of that system, such as political heads, consultative bodies, representative bod-ies, ministries, local governing agencies, military systems, the judiciary, the executive, laws, and revenue. Needless to say, he finds confirmation within each for his general theory of evolution. Let us look at just a few examples:

• The despotic leader is instrumental, at least in militant societies, in advancing civilization. The despot is particularly useful in engaging in warfare that compounds societies, consolidating smaller and weaker societies into larger and more powerful ones. However, with the transition to peaceful and voluntary industrial societies, despotism ceases to be a functional form of political leadership.

• There are early manifestations of representative bodies, such as the selec-tion of leaders by lot, but it is with the transition to industrial societies and their voluntary cooperation that the election of representatives and the for-mation of representative bodies become common.

• Ministries are initially formed out of the ruler's aides, and they are, at first, "vague and irregular" (Spencer, 1908b:445). With evolution, ministries grow in size and number, become better defined, develop increasingly differ-entiated offices (structures) and functions, grow more integrated with the var-ious offices forming an incorporated body, and come increasingly to represent the public will rather than that of the leader.

• In early, militant societies, the military coincides with the political and economic institutions, but with evolution the military becomes a separate, differentiated entity. The military itself becomes an increasingly structured, unified, and coherent organization with increasingly centralized command.

• The judicial system is at first undifferentiated from the military, with the combined system handling both internal and external aggression. Over time, the judicial system comes to be separated and itself becomes a centralized and heterogeneous organization.

• Revenue for the government is at first very irregular and indefinite, but over time it grows more regular and definite in the form of taxation. War is the main reason for new taxes or the increasing of old taxes, and even in modern society, where war is less common, war or the threat of war is very often the source of tax increases.

Spencer closes with some thoughts on the political future. He is careful to make it clear that there is no single political future and that there will be variations from one society to another. While the same evolutionary principles that dominated in the past will continue to dominate in the future, and while industrial societies are less prone to warfare than militant societies, one cannot predict whether or not nations will make war on one another. Spencer depicts a future political regime which is the logical extreme of the industrial-type political structure, but the "possibility of a high social state, political as well as general, fundamentally depends on the cessation of war" (1908b:663). War, as we have seen, has ceased to be functional: "From war has been gained all that it had to give" (Spencer, 1908b:664). Nevertheless, wars will continue to occur, and their frequency will affect the likelihood of the emergence of Spencer's ideal political regime.

Looking at future ideal structures first, Spencer depicts an elective headship and a representative legislature responsive to the general will. Government will grow less centralized, allowing for more local and individual control. Turning to functions, he sees less need to protect members from outsiders and therefore greater attention to protecting individuals from one another. This will help contribute to more equitable relationships among members of society Political activity will be more restricted, and there will be limitations on political functions. The limitations on political structures and functions will allow for more individual freedom.

Ecclesiastical Institutions

As he does with all other institutions, Spencer looks at religion from his familiar evolutionary perspective: "Ecclesiastical institutions illustrate very clearly the general law of evolution" (1908c:150). In spite of their general adherence to this law, the progress of ecclesiastical institutions, like all others, is "irregular."

Spencer sees ecclesiastical institutions as structures,[2] and he inquires, in his

---

[2] This is more than a little confusing, since modern sociologists distinguish between largely subjective institutions and largely objective structures (Blau, 1960).

normal pattern, about where they come from and what needs (functions) they perform. On the first issue, Spencer makes it clear that religion is not innate in "human nature," since there are primitive societies in which no religion is found. In primitive societies in which he finds the roots of religion, he traces the phenomena to efforts to appease ghosts.

In primitive, and therefore militant, societies, medicine men predominate over priests because they are the ones who deal antagonistically with ghosts; thus, they are best fitted to the overriding hostility of a militant society. Internally and externally, primitive societies are dominated by *enmity* rather than *amity*. In the long run, however, priests are destined to win out over medicine men for a variety of reasons, but most important because amity will win out over enmity, altruism over selfishness, and industrial societies over militant ones.

At first, the priestly function is vaguely diffused throughout society. However, as a result of the law of the instability of the homogeneous, differentiation begins to occur, and one member of the group, usually the eldest male descendant, emerges as the first differentiated quasi priest. Over time, this differentiation tends to become more fixed and definite.

Spencer believes that both ecclesiastical and political institutions are derived from the same human sentiments of reverence. As a result, in primitive societies there is little distinction between the sacred and secular worlds ("originally Church and State are undistinguished" [Spencer, 1908c:125]). Thus, one person tends to be the ruler-priest. The early chief was likely to be both the best warrior *and* the priest; consequently, the chief performed *both* military and sacerdotal functions. Thus, the early priests were militant, often engaging in brutal and savage military actions. Over time, however, the priests' linkage to warfare grew more and more distant.

Differentiation is likely to occur as the two structures divide and there emerges an independent priest who intervenes with the supernatural not merely on behalf of himself or his family but for a range of unrelated persons. Once differentiated, ecclesiastical institutions grow by the subordination of other religious institutions (as a result, for example, of the conquest of neighboring societies and their religious institutions).

Ecclesiastical institutions do not evolve in isolation from the changing nature of other social institutions, especially the polity: "The component institutions of each society habitually exhibit kindred traits of structure. Where the political organization is but little developed, there is but little development of the ecclesiastical organization; while along with a centralized coercive civil rule there goes a religious rule no less centralized and coercive" (Spencer, 1908c:81). In primitive, unsettled societies with similarly disorganized institutions, the religious institutions tend to be similarly unsettled. However, once society grows more settled, the ecclesiastical institutions tend to become more distinct and more developed.

Once ecclesiastical institutions become distinguished from political institutions, a struggle for supremacy begins between them. At first, religion has a series of advantages in this struggle. For example, as a representative of the deity, religion gives authority to the ruler; it has influence with the feared (and revered) supernatural beings; it can grant or refuse to grant forgiveness for sins; its representatives are the cultured class, and they have accumulated substantial property. As a result, spiritual power is at first predominant over temporal power.

However, in the long term, temporal power gains ascendacy over spiritual power. This change is related to the rise of industrialism. Among other things, this means that voluntary cooperation with the state is substituted for the compulsory cooperation required by religion. The general resistance to authority in industrialism translates into a resistance to church authority. As philosophy and science advance, the increasing belief in and knowledge of natural causes replaces the religious emphasis on supernatural causation. Finally, the more general diffusion of knowledge reduces the significance and power of priestly knowledge.

While the transition to industrialism implies a decline in the importance of religion, Spencer sees religion as functional even in modern industrial socie-ties. He argues that ecclesiastical institutions "have been indispensable com-ponents of social structures from the beginning down to the present time: groups in which they did not arise having failed to develop" (Spencer, 1908c:148). Among the many functions of religion are serving as a force of cohesion, acting as a check on warfare within society, promoting the conser-vation and continuity of social arrangements, functioning as a supplementary regulative system to the regulation imposed by the political system, and pro-viding obedient individuals through both coercion by the church and self-restraint by the members. Thus, Spencer, again taking a conservative position, applauds ecclesiastical institutions for their resistance to change and their abil-ity to hold individuals and the social aggregate together, as well as for linking both to their past. As he puts it, "Ecclesiasticism stands for the principle of social continuity. *Above all other agencies* it is that which conduces to cohesion; not only between the coexisting parts of a nation, but also between its present generation and its past generations" (Spencer, 1908c:105; italics added).

Professional Institutions

One of the distinctive aspects of Spencer's sociology is the amount of attention he devoted to the professions, a subject that became a traditional (Ritzer and Walczak, 1986) and continuing (Abbott, 1988) concern of sociologists. The pro-fessions represent for Spencer a paradigm case of his overarching perspective: "No group of institutions illustrates with greater clearness the process of social evolution; and none shows more undeniably how social evolution conforms to the law of evolution at large" (1908c:317).

Spencer begins his discussion of the professions by arguing that groups provide a variety of functions for society, including the preservation of society from destruction by its enemies, the regulation of life, and the sustaining of life. Beyond these specific functions, "there is the augmentation of life; and this function it is which the professions in general subserve" (Spencer, 1908c: 180). Thus, the professions constitute a structure whose function is the *augmentation of life*. Physicians physically increase the life span, while a range of other professionals, such as composers, poets, artists, scientists, and teachers, expand upon and improve the quality of life.

Spencer traces the roots of the professions to the homogeneous political-ecclesiastical agency, but when this agency subdivides, he sees religion as the main source of the professions. The obvious reason for this is the existence of professional priests; more indirect is the connection between religion and later lawyers and teachers, which stems from the fact that the early priests are characterized by their intellectual capacity, knowledge, and power. Priests were "able to devote time and energy to that intellectual labour and discipline which are required for professional occupations as distinguished from other occupations" (Spencer, 1908c:184).

Physicians can be traced to the early medicine men, who believed diseases were the result of supernatural causes and who thus employed supernatural cures. As part of the primitive militant societies, medicine men dealt with diseases antagonistically. As a result, Spencer sees priests as a more important source of physicians, since priests attempted to deal with the supernatural sympathetically rather than antagonistically. The priest tended to see diseases as being of divine origin. Thus, the cause of epilepsy was believed to be possession by the devil, and the cure lay in exorcism. Eventually, both physicians and surgeons differentiated from the priesthood, with the early physicians continuing to be similar to the priests in dealing with physical evils supernaturally inflicted, while the surgeons came to focus on more naturally caused (and cured) physical injuries.

Over time an increasing division of labor occurs among physicians (and surgeons) as they come to focus on highly specific parts of the body or illnesses. With this increasing differentiation comes an increase in integration through, among other things, professional associations, common educational experiences, and a centralized system of licensing.

Spencer proceeds to analyses of the evolution of a wide range of specific occupations that he, sometimes questionably,[3] considers professions. For example, he details the differentiation of law from the ecclesiastical institution and then examines the process of specialization within law itself. In the end, Spencer, in his typically conservative manner, concludes that all the specific professions, as well as the professions in general, are indispensable to society.

Industrial Institutions

Industry is the final institution that Spencer examines from an evolutionary perspective. A central aspect of the industrial structure is the division of labor

---

[3] For example, most contemporary sociologists would not agree with Spencer's categorization of orators or biographers as professions.

and the functions it performs. The *division of labor* is defined as "that special-ization of functions which directly or indirectly concerns the fulfillment of material wants, and the making of material aids to mental wants" (Spencer, 1908c:340). Spencer's first concern is to find the root causes of the division of labor.

He begins by examining a number of physio-psychological causes, such as differences in the natural aptitudes of individuals, social classes, and males and females. In terms of the role of gender differences in the division of labor, Spencer places much of the blame on males in "rude" (that is, primitive) societies and on their ability "to force on the females the least desirable occu-pations . . . to the women is deputed all drudgery not beyond their strength" (1908c:345). However, Spencer is most concerned with the inhumane way males deal with females in militant societies, but he comforts himself with the belief that such treatment becomes more humane with the evolution to indus-trial society. However, even though the treatment of females is more humane, a division of labor continues to exist between the sexes: "The men do the heavy, outdoor work, and the women the light, indoor work" (Spencer, 1908c:344–345). Many contemporary sociologists would be critical of this divi-sion, but Spencer reserves his criticisms for earlier, less humane systems.

Spencer sees other causes of the division of labor, such as the character of the physical environment, divisions within the same locale, divisions between locales, and differences between the productive and distributive sectors of society. Whatever the causes, evolution brings with it an ever-increasing divi-sion of labor.

The next issue is the evolution from simple acquisition of that which is needed for survival (for example, by hunting and gathering) to the production of needed commodities. Production itself goes through an evolution from the use of human power to the use of animal power and ultimately machine power. The early development of production is inhibited by the early militant societies. While such societies are conducive to some production (for example, guns), "in most respects the destroying activities have been antagonistic to the productive activities" (Spencer, 1908c:366). Thus, chronic warfare tends to destroy nascent industrial organizations and to be hostile to occupations that are not related to warfare. The progress of industry is intimately related to the decline of militancy.

Another barrier to industrial development is, interestingly, human nature. In order for industrial evolution to continue, "human nature has to be re-moulded" (Spencer, 1908c:362). As we have seen, Spencer argues that human nature is not set but evolves as society evolves. Thus, the primitive character of human nature tends to inhibit industrial development. But industry does advance, albeit slowly at first because of the limitations of human nature. Changes in society like the advance of industry tend to expand human nature, permitting further industrial progress. Thus, "production increases as the desires multiply and become stronger" (Spencer, 1908c:364). There is, then, a dialectic between the advances of industry and of human nature, with advances in each furthering the other.

A necessary concomitant of the increasing division of labor and the expansion of production is the expansion of the distributive system needed to transport goods from one setting to another. Here we see the evolutionary differentiation of distributors from producers. Over time, there is expansion in the complexity of the system of distribution. Along with the evolution of the distributive system comes the need for the evolution of the system of exchange, ending in the development of paper money, which makes distribution and production easier.

Another element of the industrial system is the means of regulating labor. Initially, the regulation of labor is fused in a combined industrial-political-ecclesiastical organization. Over time, industrial control tends to differentiate, with the result that "the control of industrial activity has gradually become independent of Church and State" (Spencer, 1908c:420). Spencer traces the history of the regulation of labor from paternal regulation (father controls production) through patriarchal regulation (father and grandfather control production; ultimately a step toward communal control) and communal regulation (at first on the basis of blood ties, but expanding to the larger group) to regulation by guilds and trade unions. The latter often begin as militant organizations and continue to be militant in Spencer's day because their militancy is required in that transitional phase in order to keep opposing forces (for example, harsh employers) in check. However, they also give workers an experience of cooperation, and Spencer believes that their cooperative aspect will increase and their militant characteristics will decline as we move further away from militant societies and toward industrial societies.

Spencer also deals with slavery and serfdom as early forms of control over labor that are associated with militant societies. These inefficient and compulsory systems decline as society moves toward the voluntary cooperation of industrial society. It is free labor on the basis of contracts that fits best in the modern, industrial society.

In looking to the future of industrial systems, Spencer is not sympathetic to socialism, which he sees as fitting better in a militant society than in an industrial society characterized by voluntary cooperation (we will have more to say about his views on socialism shortly). Spencer is more concerned with the growing power of the state than he is with the expansion of socialism. He sees a trend toward state regulation of industry, and as a result, "the present voluntary industrial organization will have its place entirely usurped by a compulsory industrial organization" (Spencer, 1908c:605). He fears that ultimately there "will be established a state in which no man can do what he likes but every man must do what he is told" (Spencer, 1908c:605). In fact, he sees "statism" as standing in opposition to "individualism" (Spencer, 1892/1965). Thus, Spencer fears an evolutionary retrogression with restraint coming to replace the historic movement toward greater individual freedom.

ETHICS AND POLITICS

In his earliest book, *Social Statics* (1850/1954), and in much later books, especially his two-volume *The Principles of Ethics* (1897/1978), Spencer articulated a rather consistent ethical and political position that informs, and is informed by, his substantive work. He subtitled *Social Statics* "The conditions essential to human happiness specified, and the first of them developed," while he described *The Principles of Ethics* as a set of "rules of right conduct on a scientific basis" (Spencer, 1897/1978:xiv). We will briefly examine in this section Spencer's ethical and political ideas. A key issue is whether these ideas greatly enhanced or fatally injured his sociology.

Spencer's moral and political ideas are derived, to a large extent, from his methodological individualism. As we have seen throughout this chapter, Spencer focused on macro-level phenomena, but he did so with the view that the base of these phenomena was individual "units." This specific view of the social world is deduced, like many others, from his general principles: "As a multitude is but an assemblage of units, and as the characteristics of a multitude result from the properties of its units, so social phenomena are consequences of the natures of individual men" (Spencer, 1902/1958:8). Or, more strongly, "The properties of the units determine the properties of the aggregate" (Spencer, 1873/1961:41).[4] The characteristics of people in an associated state are derived from the inherent properties of individuals: "No phenomenon can be presented by a corporate body but what there is a preexisting capacity in its individual members for producing" (Spencer, 1850/1954:17). Just as macro-level phenomena are derived from individuals, so too is the moral law of society: "The right ruling of humanity in its state of *multitude* is to be found in humanity in its state of *unitude*" (Spencer, 1850/1954:18). Spencer believes that individuals are endowed with a moral sense that dictates their actions and ultimately the structure and functioning of society.

While individuals are the proximate cause of social morality, the more distant cause is God. The things that people come to view as moral are in line with divine rule. Spencer castigates those who "doubt the foresight and efficiency of the Divine arrangements" (1850/1954:47). He further argues that "human happiness is the divine will" (Spencer, 1850/1954:67). Thus, society is seen as evolving toward an increasing state of perfection and happiness.

Another factor in this evolution to a perfect moral state is that evil, in his view, progressively disappears. To explain this disappearance, Spencer once again employs the survival-of-the-fittest argument.[5] As he sees it, evil is a result of nonadaptation to external conditions, or "unfitness to the conditions of existence" (Spencer, 1850/1954:59). However, such nonadaptation is con-

---

[4] While we see here (and have seen elsewhere) that individual units lie at the base of aggregates, Spencer also recognizes a dialectic in which changes in the aggregate in turn alter the units. Spencer specifies a number of superorganic products that serve to modify the individual, including material "appliances" (for example, the steam engine), language, knowledge, science, customs and laws, esthetic products (literature), and so on.

[5] By the way, Spencer (1897/1978) later makes it clear that his ideas on evolution are *not* indebted to Charles Darwin, whose book *On the Origin of the Species* appeared in 1859, almost a decade *after* Spencer had published *Social Statics*. However, in the Preface to the fourth edition of *First Principles* (1902/1958), Spencer did admit to altering some of his ideas as a result of Darwin's influence.

stantly diminishing and must ultimately disappear. More generally, Spencer argues that "all excess and all deficiency must disappear; that is, all unfitness must disappear; that is, all imperfection must disappear" (1850/1954:59). As a result of the survival-of-the-fittest argument applied to evil, Spencer concludes that "the ultimate development of the ideal man is logically certain" (1850/1954:59).

Turning the argument around, Spencer contends that human happiness comes from the satisfaction of desires and that gratification can come only from an exercise of human faculties. Thus, people must be free to exercise their faculties; that is, they must have liberty. Spencer invokes God on the side of this viewpoint as well: "God intends he [the human] should have that liberty. Therefore he has a right to that liberty" (1850/1954:69). He also embeds this argument in his methodological individualism by contending that people are endowed with "an *instinct of personal rights*" (Spencer, 1850/1954:86). Furthermore, this liberty must not be the right of just a few; since everyone has these faculties, all individuals have the right to exercise them freely.

However, there are limits on personal liberty, most importantly in the fact that an individual, in exercising his or her liberty, cannot be allowed to infringe on the liberty of others. However, since individuals are not endowed with the capacity to prevent their actions from infringing on the rights of others, society is needed to perform this function. This leads to Spencer's libertarian political position that there is a role for the state but it is a highly limited one. In his view the state must protect the liberty of individuals, but "it ought to do nothing more than protect" (Spencer, 1850/1954:264–265). Because he does see this limited role for the state, Spencer rejects the label "laissez-faire theorist" that some affixed to him.

Of course, such a libertarian position fits well with Spencer's views on evolution and survival of the fittest. Other than protecting individual liberty, the state is to get out of the way and allow the "law" and dynamics of evolution to work themselves out. Here is one of the ways in which Spencer describes that law:

> The well-being of existing humanity and the unfolding of it into this ultimate perfection are both secured by that same beneficent, though severe, discipline to which animate creation at large is subject: a discipline which is pitiless in the working out of good: a felicity-pursuing law which never swerves for the avoidance of partial and temporary suffering. The poverty of the incapable, the distresses that come upon the imprudent, the starvation of the idle, and those shoulderings aside of the weak by the strong, which leaves so many "in shallows and in miseries," are the decrees of a large, far-seeing benevolence.

(Spencer, 1850/1954:288–289)

Thus, Spencer does not look upon such "harsh realities" as hunger and disease as evil; rather, they "are seen to be full of the highest benificence—the same benificence which brings to early graves the children of diseased parents and singles out the low-spirited, the intemperate, and the debilitated as the victims of an epidemic" (Spencer, 1850/1954:289). Similarly, and more harshly, "Society is constantly excreting its unhealthy, imbecile slow, vacillating, faithless members" (Spencer, 1850/1954:289). To put it more directly, those who are not healthy, not smart, not steadfast, and not believers in the divine should, and will, for the benefit of the larger society, die, as long as the natural process of evolution is left to operate in accord with its basic laws.

Thus we return to Spencer's libertarian politics. The state, as well as private philanthropists, is enjoined from preventing misery because to do so would cause greater misery for future generations. That is, if the unfit are allowed to survive, they will produce only similarly unfit offspring and that will only increase the magnitude of the problem for societies of the future. Those individuals, both in and out of the government, who think of themselves as doing good are in fact doing great harm to society. Interference by the state (and other agencies) serves only to encourage the multiplication of the unfit, to discourage the multiplication of the fit, and to stop the "purifying" process of natural evolution. Those who interfere "bequeath to posterity a continually increasing curse" (Spencer, 1850/1954:290).

Specifically, Spencer opposes state-administered charity (or any charity, for that matter) and state-run education. He even opposes government involvement in sanitation matters, such as garbage removal. Throughout his work Spencer often returns to the theme of the evils of state intervention.

In the end, the government is to refrain from intervention not only because such interference hampers the natural process of evolution but also because it curtails individual rights: "For a government to take from a ctiizen more property than is needful for the efficient defense of that citizen's rights is to infringe his rights" (Spencer, 1850/1954:333). What Spencer seeks is a "society organized upon the same [evolutionary] system as an individual being" (1850/1954:403).

In his autobiography, Spencer railed against the distortion of his libertarian position ("genuine liberalism") by the "modern perversion of it which, while giving them nominal liberties in the shape of votes . . . is busily decreasing their liberties, both by the multiplication of restraints and commands, and by taking away larger parts of their incomes to be spent not as they individually like, but as public officials like" (1904a:487–488). Elsewhere, Spencer described the contrast in this way: "Liberalism habitually stood for individual freedom *versus* State-coercion" (1892/1965:5).

In response to the critics of the above position, Spencer (1873/1961) expressed shock at being seen as an enemy of the poor and other unfortunate members of society. He depicts himself as more humane than that. He argues that he is not for inaction but rather for the use of "fit means" to deal with the problems of the unfortunate. Of course, one wonders about the credibility of such a position in light of views like his concern that "the diligent and provident labourer had to pay that the good-for-nothings might not suffer" (Spencer, 1892/1965:113). Obviously, Spencer had little regard for those on the public dole and wished that those who worked hard should not have to pay for the poor, with the result, presumably, that the poor would be permitted to suffer and ultimately die.

Obviously, if Spencer is opposed to state intervention, he would certainly be opposed to any radical (for example, socialist, communist) alteration of society. He believes that sociology, with its focus on the long history of unintentional evolutionary changes, will help disabuse us of the notion that "social evils admit of radical cures" (Spencer, 1873/1961:19). Societies arise by slow evolution, not by human manufacture and certainly not by human demolition and remanufacture. Spencer's fears about the controls exercised by the capitalist state were nothing in comparison to his fears about socialistic control, which he equated with slavery and tyranny. As a result of this view, Spencer associates socialism with militant societies and argues that it will "cease to be normal as fast as the society becomes predominantly industrial in its type" (1908c:577).

Spencer differentiates his own ideal society from that of socialists and communists by arguing that he is not in favor of giving people equal shares of things but rather of giving "each an opportunity of acquiring the objects he desires" (Spencer, 1850/1954:118). Spencer sees socialism as standing in opposition to the selfishness which he feels is an inherent part of human nature. It is unrealistic to expect that selfish people will voluntarily surrender their excess productivity to others; selfish people cannot produce an unselfish system. Relatedly, as we saw earlier in this chapter, Spencer views people as being endowed with an "instinct for personal rights," and one of those rights, which he sees as an element of human nature, is a desire for property. Therefore, socialism stands in opposition to this element of human nature and, as a result, cannot survive.

Spencer's opposition to socialism and communism is also related to his opposition to any abrupt or revolutionary change. This follows from his oft-stated view that evolution is, and must be, a gradual process. Not only does abrupt change violate evolution, but it also would lead to a radically altered society that would be out of harmony with human nature, which changes glacially.

The moral and political views outlined above, as well as many others, led many sociologists, as Jonathan Turner (1985b) argues, to dismiss Spencer's theoretical perspective. That is, contemporary, often liberal or radical, sociological theorists tend to reject the kind of conservative morality and politics preached by Spencer. Their rejection of his morality and politics led to a rejection of his sociological theory. I agree with Turner that this is not a good reason to reject a theory. That is, one should not reject a theory merely because one opposes the morals or politics of its creator. However, there is another reason to question Spencer's theory, and that is on the basis of the feeling that his scientific sociology is shaped and distorted by his moral and political views. From my perspective, there is a very suspicious fit between Spencer's "scientific" sociology and his moral and political views. In fact, it could be argued that Spencer's claim to being scientific is vitiated by the fact that his work is biased by his moral and political biases. (Of course, similar things could be said about Marx, Weber, Simmel, and many other classical theorists.) Spencer cautioned sociologists about being biased in their work, but it seems clear that Spencer's sociological theory is weakened by his own biases. Thus it is not Spencer's specific morality or politics that leads us to question his work but rather the fact that they biased and distorted his theory.

That being said, we should not lose sight of the fact that there is much more of merit in Spencer's sociological theory than he is usually given credit for today. His meritorious ideas have been analyzed and underscored throughout this chapter.

SUMMARY

Herbert Spencer has a much more powerful theory, and his work has far more contemporary significance, than that of the other significant figure in the "pre-history" of sociological theory, Auguste Comte. Their theories have some similarities (for example, positivism) but far more differences (for example, Comte's faith in a positivist religion and Spencer's opposition to any centralized system of control).

Spencer offers a series of general principles from which he deduces an evolutionary theory involving increasing integration, heterogeneity, and definiteness of both structures and functions. Indeed, sociology, for Spencer, is the study of the evolution of societies. While Spencer sought to legitimize sociology as a science, he also felt that sociology is linked to, and should draw upon, other sciences such as biology (especially the idea of survival of the fittest) and psychology (especially the importance of sentiments). In part from his concern with psychology, Spencer developed his methodological-individualist approach to the study of society.

Spencer addresses a number of the methodological difficulties confronting sociology as a science. He is especially concerned with various biases the sociologist must overcome—educational, patriotic, class, political, and theological. In seeking to exclude these biases, Spencer articulates a "value-free" position for sociology. In much of his substantive work, Spencer employs the comparative-historical method.

The evolution of society occupies a central place in Spencer's sociology. In his analysis of societal evolution, Spencer employs the three general aspects of evolution mentioned above—increasing integration (increasing size and coalescence of masses of people), heterogeneity, and definiteness (here, clearly demarcated institutions)—as well as a fourth aspect—the increasing coherence of social groups. In his evolutionary social theory, Spencer, traces, among other things, the movement from simple to compounded societies and from militant to industrial societies.

In addition to dealing with the overall evolution of society, Spencer also deals in considerable detail with the evolution of a number of social institutions—domestic, ceremonial, political, ecclesiastical, professional, and industrial. In each case, he employs the elements of his general theory of evolution, and he pays special attention to the evolution of structures and functions in these institutions, as well as in the larger society.

Spencer also articulates a series of ethical and political ideals. Consistent with his methodological individualism, Spencer argues that people must be free to exercise their abilities; they must have liberty. The only role for the state is the protection of individual liberty. Such a laissez-faire political perspective fits well with Spencer's ideas on evolution and survival of the fittest. Given his perspective on the gradual evolution of society, Spencer also rejects the idea of any radical solution (for example, communism) to society's problems.

KARL MARX

*T*HERE has long been an uneasy and often bizarre relationship between sociological theory and the work of Karl Marx (1818–1883). In some sectors of the world, at least until the recent (apparent) end of the "cold war," sociological theory was virtually identical with Marxian and neo-Marxian theory, and in others (most notably the United States) Marx had been virtually ignored (at least until recently) as a significant sociological thinker. In Eastern Europe Marx's influence was, at least until recently, overwhelming, with sociological theory largely reduced to various forms of traditional and neo-Marxian thinking. In Western Europe Marx's influence has been highly variable. Among some Western European sociologists, Marx has had a profound positive influence; others have fashioned their sociological theory specifically *against* Marxian theory. In the United States sociological theorists prior to the 1960s (with a few exceptions, like C. Wright Mills) tended to ignore, be ignorant of, or even be hostile to Marx's ideas. For example, in the book that revived grand theory in the United States, Talcott Parsons (1937, 1949) dismissed Marx's work in a few pages but spent hundreds of pages on the work of Emile Durk-heim, Max Weber, and the marginally significant Vilfredo Pareto. Most American theorists dismissed Marx as an ideologist who had little to contrib-ute to the development of *scientific* sociological theory. However, in the 1960s young American sociologists—at least partly because of their personal expe-riences in the civil-rights, anti-Vietnam War, and student-rights movements—began to give serious attention to Marx as a sociological theorist. Reflecting this change was a book by Henri Lefebvre (1968) in which he argued that, although Marx was not simply a sociologist, there is a sociology in Marx's work. Since the late 1960s, a serious effort has been made to integrate Marxian and neo-Marxian theory into American sociological theory, while in the rest of the world Marx's influence has continued strong and even grown in strength in some areas. Although resistance to Marx remains among some American sociologists, many thinkers now are willing to accord Marx his rightful place among the giants of sociological thought.

With the recent failure of communist societies and their turn to a more capitalistically oriented economy, it is necessary to address what this means for the role of Marxian theory within sociology. On the surface it appears that these changes suggest that we will see a substantial decline in interest in Marx-ian theory among sociologists. In fact, this *is* likely to occur, especially as a result of the fact that new theorists are less likely to turn to Marx for answers to the problems of modern capitalistic societies. However, the retreat from Marxian sociological theory is likely to be limited for several reasons.

First, most sociologists who have adopted a Marxian perspective have a deep and long-term commitment to it that is not likely to be greatly modified by changes in societies that were very remote from Marx's principles and ideals. Second, and relatedly, many of Marx's ideas have been integrated into various sociological perspectives (see, for example, the integrated paradigm discussed in the Appendix), and they will not be excised merely because of failures in the communist bloc. Third, and most important, it is the thesis of this chapter that it is Marx's *sociological* theory, not his economic theory, that is of greatest importance. As we will see, Marx offered an abstract, coherent, and greatly satisfying sociological theory that can be used to analyze *any* soci-ety, not just capitalistic societies and their economic systems. Since that so-ciological theory was uninvolved in the creation of communist societies, and in fact was contradicted by them, it is unscathed by recent developments in the communist world. Sociologists will continue to be attracted to the scope and elegance of Marx's sociological theory.

Many students (and some academicians), both pro- and anti-Marx, might be surprised to find Marx mentioned as one of the major theorists in the history of the discipline. Students trained in an anti-Marxian tradition or influ-enced by a similarly oriented mass media are socialized to believe that Marx was a bloodthirsty radical whose ideological commitments prohibited him from producing a serious scientific theory. It is crucial to sound scholarship that this myth be dispelled, and there are two bases on which it can be attacked. Similarly, it must be demonstrated to pro-Marxian students that it is legitimate to consider Marx a sociologist.

Two basic arguments can be made to those anti-Marxists who reject Marx as a sociologist because of his ideological orientation. First, although it is true that Marx's approach is heavily influenced by his ideology, it is important to recognize that *all* sociological theorists have an ideological bias. This is as true for Comte, Spencer, Durkheim, Weber, and Simmel as it is for Marx. There is no such thing as a "value-free" sociological theory. In theorizing about social phenomena, sociologists find it impossible to be completely neutral, and this remains true whether or not they are willing to recognize it or to admit it. Thus it *is* true that Marx's sociological theory is ideological, but that is no reason to dismiss it, because this is also true of *all* other sociological theories. The *major* difference between Marx and other sociological theorists is that Marx made no effort to conceal the ideological character of his work; indeed, as we will see, it is built into the very structure of his theorizing.

Second, it is important to point out that although Marx was avowedly ideological in his theorizing, the widely shared view of Marx as a blood-crazed fanatic is not admissible. As we will see throughout this chapter, Marx was a humanist who was deeply hurt by the suffering and exploitation that he witnessed among the working class under capitalism. His humanism led him to call for a revolution that would overturn the economic system, which was exploitative of the vast majority of people, and that would lead to the creation of a more humane socialist society. Although he called for revolution, Marx did *not* believe that the change *had* to be bloody. It was possible for the transition to socialism to occur peacefully, and given Marx's humanistic proclivities, this would clearly have been the most desirable course of action to him.

Although these points might ease some of the doubts among readers with an anti-Marxian bias, they will not satisfy those who begin with a pro-Marxian orientation. Such students might object that to label Marx a "sociologist" is much too restrictive. In their view, Marx defies simple categorization, because he was also a philosopher, a revolutionary, a pamphleteer, a journalist, a political scientist, a dialectician, and so forth. It is true that Marx is a highly complex thinker whose work is attractive to people in a wide range of endeavors, but among the many labels that fit Marx *is* that of sociologist. We can deal with those elements of Marx's thought that are relevant to sociology as long as we recognize that he is also many other things to many other people.

There is another debate that must be addressed at this point, this one among various interpreters of Marx's work. There are a number of schools of neo-Marxian theory, and many of their differences stem from varying interpretations of Marx's theory. For example, some stress Marx's early work on human potential and see the rest of it as derived from, and consistent with, his earlier work (see, for example, Ollman, 1976; Wallimann, 1981; Wartenberg, 1982). Others stress Marx's later work on the structures of society, especially the economic structures, and see that work as separable, and even different, from his early, largely philosophical work on human nature (see

Althusser, 1969; Gandy, 1979; McMurty, 1978). This chapter is based on the premise that there is no discontinuity or contradiction between Marx's early work on human potential and his later work on the structures of capitalist society. After a general introduction to Marx's mode of thinking (the dialectic), we will look at Marx's work on human potential and then show its relationship to his later work on the larger structures of society.

THE DIALECTIC

Marx adopted the dialectical mode of logic from Hegel. However, whereas Hegel focused on a dialectic of ideas, Marx tried to embed his dialectical approach in the material world. This is a crucial transformation because it allowed Marx to move the dialectic out of the realm of philosophy and into the realm of what some consider a science of social relations as they exist in the material world. It is this focus on material social relationships that makes Marx's work most relevant to sociology, even though the dialectical approach is very different from the mode of thinking used by most sociologists (Ball, 1979; Friedrichs, 1972a, 1972b; Ollman, 1976; Schneider, 1971).

Two basic features of dialectical analysis contrast sharply with most sociological thinking. First, the dialectical method of analysis does not see a simple, one-way, cause-and-effect relationship among the various parts of the social world. For the dialectical thinker, social influences never simply flow in one direction as they do for cause-and-effect thinkers. To the dialectician one factor may have an effect on another, but it is just as likely that the latter will have a simultaneous effect on the former. For example, the increasing exploitation of the proletariat by the capitalist may cause the workers to become increasingly dissatisfied and more militant, but the increasing militancy of the proletariat might well cause the capitalists to react by becoming even more exploitative in order to crush the resistance of the workers. This kind of thinking does not mean that the dialectician never considers causal relationships in the social world. It does mean that when dialectical thinkers talk about causality, they are always attuned to reciprocal relationships among social factors as well as to the dialectical totality of social life in which they are embedded.

The second feature of dialectical analysis is even more at odds with most contemporary sociological thinking. In dialectical analysis, especially as Marx developed it, social values are not separable from social facts. Most sociologists believe that their values can and must be separated from their study of facts about the social world. The dialectical thinker believes that not only is it impossible to keep values out of the study of the social world but it is also undesirable because it produces a dispassionate, inhuman sociology that has little to offer to people in search of answers to the problems they confront. Facts and values are inevitably intertwined, with the result that the study of social phenomena is value laden. Thus to Marx, it was impossible, and even if possible, undesirable, to be dispassionate in his analysis of the two major

KARL MARX: A Biographical Sketch

Karl Marx was born in Trier, Prussia, on May 5, 1818. His father, a lawyer, provided the family with a fairly typical middle-class existence. Both parents were from rabbinical families, but for business reasons the father had converted to Lutheranism.

In 1841 Marx received his doctorate in philosophy from the University of Berlin, a school heavily influenced by Hegel and the Young Hegelians, supportive, yet critical, of their master. Marx's doctorate was a dry philosophical treatise that bore little resemblance to his later, more radical and more pragmatic work. After graduation he became a writer for a liberal-radical newspaper and within ten months had become its editor-in-chief. However, because of its political positions, the paper was closed shortly thereafter by the government. The early essays published in this period began to reflect a number of the positions that would guide Marx throughout his life. They were liberally sprinkled with democratic principles, humanism, and idealism. He rejected the abstractness of Hegelian philosophy, the naive dreaming of utopian communists, and those activists who were urging what he considered to be premature political action. In rejecting these activists, Marx laid the groundwork for his own life's work:

> Practical attempts, even by the masses, can be answered with a cannon as soon as they become dangerous, but ideas that have overcome our intellect and conquered our conviction, ideas to which reason has riveted our conscience, are chains from which one cannot break loose without breaking one's heart; they are demons that one can only overcome by submitting to them.
>
> (Marx, 1842/1977:20)

Marx married in 1843 and soon thereafter left Germany for the more liberal atmosphere of Paris. There he continued to grapple with the ideas of Hegel and the Young Hegelians, but he also encountered two new sets of ideas—French socialism and English political economy. It was the unique way in which he combined Hegelianism, socialism, and political economy that shaped his intellectual orientation. Also of great importance at this point was meeting the man who was to become his lifelong friend, benefactor, and collaborator— Friedrich Engels (Carver, 1983). The son of a textile manufacturer, Engels had become a socialist critical of the conditions facing the working class. Much of Marx's compassion for the misery of the working class came from his exposure to Engels and his ideas. In 1844 Engels and Marx had a lengthy conversation in a famous café in Paris and laid the groundwork for a lifelong association. Of that conversation Engels said, "Our complete agreement in all theoretical fields became obvious . . . and our joint work dates from that time" (McLellan, 1973:131). During this period Marx produced academic works (many unpublished in his lifetime) that were mainly concerned with sorting out his link to the Hegelian tradition (for example, *The Holy Family* and *The German Ideology*), but he also produced

classes within capitalism—the bourgeoisie (also called "capitalists") and the proletariat (the workers). In *Capital* (1867/1967), for example, Marx talked about the capitalists as werewolves and vampires who suck the blood out of the workers, and he was very sympathetic to the plight of the proletariat. But Marx's emotional involvement in what he was studying did not mean that

The Economic and Philosophic Manuscripts of 1844, which better integrated all of the intellectual traditions in which he was immersed and which foreshadowed his increasing preoccupation with the economic domain.

While Marx and Engels shared a theoretical orientation, there were many differences between the two men. Marx tended to be a highly abstract thinker, a disorderly intellectual, and very oriented to his family. Engels was a practical thinker, a neat and tidy businessman, and a womanizer. In spite of their differences, Marx and Engels forged a close union in which they collaborated on books and articles and worked together in radical organizations, and Engels even helped support Marx throughout the rest of his life so that Marx could devote himself to his intellectual and political endeavors.

In spite of the close association of the names of Marx and Engels, Engels made it clear that he was the junior partner:

> Marx could very well have done without me. What Marx accomplished I would not have achieved. Marx stood higher, saw farther, and took a wider and quicker view than the rest of us. Marx was a genius.
>
> (Engels, cited in McLellan, 1973:131–132)

In fact, many believe that Engels failed to understand many of the subtleties of Marx's work. After Marx's death, Engels became the leading spokesperson for Marxian theory and in various ways distorted and oversimplified it.

Because some of his writings had upset the Prussian government, the French government (at the request of the Prussians) expelled Marx in 1845, and he moved to Brussels. His radicalism was growing, and he had become an active member of the international revolutionary movement. He also associated with the Communist League and was asked to write a document (with Engels) expounding its aims and beliefs. The result was the *Communist Manifesto* of 1848, a work that was characterized by ringing political slogans (for example, "Working men of all countries, unite!").

In 1849 Marx moved to London, and, in light of the failure of the political revolutions of 1848, he began to withdraw from active revolutionary activity and to move into serious and detailed research on the workings of the capitalist system. In 1852, he began his famous studies in the British Museum of the working conditions in capitalism. These studies ultimately resulted in the three volumes of *Capital,* the first of which was published in 1867; the other two were published posthumously. He lived in poverty during these years, barely managing to survive on a small income from his writings and the support of Engels. In 1863 Marx became reinvolved in political activity by joining the *International,* an international movement of workers. He soon gained dominance within the movement and devoted a number of years to it. He began to gain fame both as leader of the *International* and as the author of *Capital.* But the disintegration of the *International* by 1876, the failure of various revolutionary movements, and personal illness took their toll on Marx. His wife died in 1881, a daughter in 1882, and Marx himself on March 14, 1883.

his observations were inaccurate. It could even be argued that Marx's passionate views on these issues gave him unparalleled insight into the nature of capitalist society. A less passionate student might have delved less deeply into the dynamics of the system. In fact, research into the work of scientists indicates that the idea of a dispassionate scientist is largely a myth and that the very best scientists are the ones who are most passionate about, and committed to, their ideas (Mitroff, 1974).

Both of the above characteristics of the dialectic reflect Marx's view that there are no hard and fast dividing lines between phenomena in the social world. Marx believed that the various components of the social world blended gradually and imperceptibly into one another. Thus, to take two of Marx's major concerns, he would argue that the capitalists and the proletariat are not clearly separated but gradually blend into one another. This means that there are a large number of people who either exist in the interstices between the two classes or move from one class to another (the successful worker who becomes a capitalist; the capitalist who fails and drops into the working class).

Dialectical thinkers also take a *relational* view of the social world (Ollman, 1976). They focus on the relations within and among various aspects of the social world. Thus, in examining a bureaucracy, they look at the various social relationships that go into its construction. Relationships between individuals, between groups of people, and between various subunits within the organization (for example, the personnel department and the engineering department) all would come under the intense scrutiny of the dialectical thinker. In addition, a dialectician never would concentrate on one social unit in isolation from other social units. Thus, the relationship between a given bureaucracy and various other social units in the social world would be of chief concern to the dialectician.

Dialecticians are interested not only in the relationships of social phenomena in the *contemporary* world but also in the relationship of those contemporary realities to both *past* (Bauman, 1976:81) and *future* social phenomena. This has two distinct implications for a dialectical sociology. First, it means that dialectical sociologists are concerned with studying the historical roots of the contemporary world as Marx (1857–58/1964) did in his study of the sources of modern capitalism. In fact, dialectical thinkers are very critical of modern sociology for its failure to do much historical research. A good example of Marx's thinking in this regard is found in the following famous quotation from "The Eighteenth Brumaire of Louis Bonaparte":

> Men make their own history, but they do not make it just as they please; they do not make it under circumstances chosen by themselves, but under circumstances directly encounterd from the past. The tradition of all the dead generations weighs like a nightmare on the brain of the living.
>
> (Marx, 1852/1963:15)

Second, dialectical thinkers are attuned to the future directions of society. This interest in the future is one of the main reasons that dialectical sociology is inherently political. It has an image of the future world, and it is interested in encouraging practical activities that would bring that world into existence. In trying to grasp the nature of this future world, dialecticians believe that much is to be learned from a careful study of the contemporary world. It is their view that social change is a coming to be of what potentially is, that the sources of the future exist in the present. To take an example from Marx, the proletariat of modern capitalism, which does not own the means of production, is a model of what all people will be like in socialist society. There is to be no private ownership of the means of production in socialism. This does not mean that people will not own clothes, television sets, and cars, but rather that one class will not own and dominate the industrial and corporate structure as it does in contemporary capitalism.

But in saying that the dialectical thinker believes that the future is the coming to be of what potentially is, we do *not* imply the deterministic view that the future course of the world is preset and unchangeable. The basic nature of the dialectic militates against a deterministic orientation. Because social phenomena are constantly acting and reacting, the social world defies a simple, deterministic model. The future *may* be based on some contemporary model, but not inevitably. Marxists hoped and believed that the future was to be found in socialism, but the proletariat could not simply wait passively for it to arrive. They had to work for it, and there were no ironclad guarantees that it would occur.

This disinclination to think deterministically is what makes the best-known model of the dialectic—thesis, antithesis, synthesis—a gross distortion. This simple model implies that a social phenomenon will inevitably spawn an opposing form and that the clash between these two will inevitably lead to a new, synthetic social form. *But in the real world, there are no inevitabilities.* Furthermore, social phenomena are not easily divided into simple thesis, antithesis, and synthesis categories. The dialectician is interested in the study of real relationships rather than grand abstractions. It is this disinclination to deal in grand abstractions that led Marx away from Hegel and would lead him today to reject such a great oversimplification of the dialectic as thesis, antithesis, synthesis. Marx analyzed the conflict between the capitalists and the proletariat, and although he foresaw a revolution and, ultimately, a new type of society, he did not see this as an inevitable process. The proletariat would have to work and fight for socialism if it were to occur. But even if the workers did strive for it, they were not assured that it would come to pass. Actions of the capitalists have made the working class more satisfied with their lot, and this has militated against the occurrence of a working-class revolt.

What is perhaps best known about the dialectic is its concern with *conflict* and *contradiction* (Elster, 1985). This leads to a number of by-products, including a concern for the process of change as well as a political program. But what is of importance here is that the dialectic leads to an interest in the conflicts and contradictions among various levels of social reality, rather than to the more traditional sociological interest in the ways that these various levels mesh rather neatly into a cohesive whole. Although Marx was aware of how the ideologies of the capitalists mesh with their objective interests, he wanted to concentrate on issues like the conflict between the large-scale structures created by capitalists and the interests of the proletariat.

Perhaps the ultimate contradiction within capitalism for Marx exists in the relationship between the bourgeoisie and the proletariat. In Marx's terms, the bourgeoisie produces the proletariat, and in producing and expanding that class the capitalists are producing their own gravediggers. The capitalist produces the proletariat by forcing workers to sell their labor-time for very low wages. As capitalism expands, the number of workers exploited, and the degree of exploitation, increases. The escalating level of exploitation leads to more and more resistance on the part of the proletariat. Resistance begets more exploitation and oppression, and the likely result is a confrontation between the two classes, a confrontation that the proletariat, in Marx's view, is likely to win.

Despite the importance to Marx of the future communist society, he spent surprisingly little time depicting what this world would be like. In fact, he was critical of those utopian socialists who wrote book after book on their dreamlike images of future society. To Marx, the most important task was the critical analysis of contemporary capitalist society. He believed that such criticism would help bring down capitalism and create the conditions for the rise of a new socialist world. There would be time to construct communist society once capitalism was overcome.

Dialectical thinkers in general are also interested (as Marx was) in the structures of society and the actors within society, as well as with the dialectical relationship between actors and social structures. But the dialectical method is even more complex than this, because, as we have already seen, the dialectician considers past, present, and future circumstances, and this applies to both actors and structures. Figure 5.1 is a simplified schematic representation of this enormously complex and sophisticated perspective.

Marx made it abundantly clear throughout his work that he was working with a model like Figure 5.1. He was attuned to the ongoing interplay among the major levels of social analysis. For example, Marx and Engels said, "Circumstances make men *just as much* as men make circumstances" (1845–46/ 1970:59; italics added). Lefebvre was therefore quite accurate when he argued

FIGURE 5.1   Schematic Representation of a Sociologically Relevant Dialectic

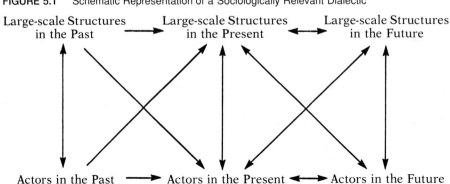

that the heart of Marx's thought lies in the relationship between people and the large-scale structures they create (1968:8) (On the one hand, these large-scale structures help people to fulfill themselves; on the other, they represent a grave threat to humanity)

Despite his general commitment to the dialectic, in particular the dialectical relationship between large-scale structures and actors, Marx came to focus more and more of his attention on the structures of capitalist society. In part, this is traceable to Marx's political interests, which led him to examine and criticize the structures of capitalism in order to help bring about revolutionary change. By so doing, the transition to socialism could be expedited. A good portion of this chapter will be devoted to a discussion of Marx's analysis of the structures of capitalism. But before we can analyze these, we need to begin with Marx's thoughts on the more microscopic aspects of social reality. Marx built his critical analysis of the structure of capitalist society on his premises about actors, action, and interaction.

HUMAN POTENTIAL

The basis of much of Marx's thinking lies in his ideas on the potential of human beings (or what he called *species-being*). He believed that until his time in history, people had not even begun to approach what they ultimately could become. The nature of societies prior to capitalism had been too harsh to allow people to realize their potentialities. They were too busy trying merely to get enough food, shelter, and protection to develop their higher capacities. Although capitalism solved some of these problems, it was too oppressive an environment to allow most people to develop their human potential. It was Marx's hope and belief that communism would provide the kind of environment in which people could begin to express that potential fully. Thus Marx could not describe human potential in any detail, because it had yet to be allowed to develop to its fullest and to express itself adequately. Marx's critique of capitalist society was based in part on what he felt humans could become once they were freed from the shackles of capitalism and allowed to express themselves in the unfettered environment of communism.

Powers and Needs

AFFECTED BY SOCIAL SETTINGS

The bases of Marx's conception of human potential were his ideas on the powers and needs of people (Heller, 1976; Ollman, 1976). *Powers* may be defined as the faculties, abilities, and capacities of people. In the Marxian system, human powers are not simply what they are now, but also what they were historically and what they can be in the future under changed social circumstances) *Needs* are the desires people feel for things that are usually not immediately available. Needs, like powers, are greatly affected by the social settings in which people exist. Even the most microscopic notions of human powers and needs cannot be discussed without taking into account the larger setting of society as a whole.

It is necessary to differentiate between natural powers and needs and species powers and needs. In brief, _natural_ powers and needs are those shared with other animals, whereas _species_ powers and needs are those that are uniquely human. Natural powers and needs per se are of little interest to us because, as Bertell Ollman argued, "natural" man is "_not yet_ a man but still an animal" (1976:80). However, all natural powers and needs can be expressed in distinctly human ways. Sex, for example, is a behavior common to human beings and all other animals, but when it is expressed in peculiarly human ways, it moves into the category of species powers and needs.

Consciousness

The heart of the notion of human potential lies in Marx's view that people differ from animals in their possession of consciousness as well as in their ability to link this consciousness to their actions. The emphasis on consciousness is directly related to Marx's ties to Hegelian philosophy and its interest in the phenomenon. Although borrowing from Hegel here, Marx was critical of Hegel for discussing consciousness as if it existed independently of people rather than _focusing on the consciousness of real, sentient people_. The following is the famous quotation from Marx in which he acknowledged his ties to Hegel and laid out his basic point of departure from Hegel's orientation:

> Hegel makes man _the man of self-consciousness_ instead of making self-consciousness the _self-consciousness of man_, of real man, man living in a real objective world and determined by that world. He stands the world _on its head_ and can therefore dissolve _in the head_ all the limitations which naturally remain in existence for _evil sensuousness_, for _real_ man.
>
> (Marx and Engels, 1845/1956:254)

Thus, Marx was opposed to Hegel not only on intellectual grounds but also because his ephemeral image of self-consciousness was a barrier to the kind of political action that to Marx was imperative.

Marx went further than arguing simply in general terms that people are distinguished from other animals by their consciousness. According to Ollman (1976), Marx believed the following mental capacities set humans apart from other animals:

1 While animals just "do," people can set themselves off mentally from whatever they are doing.
2 Since they have a distinctive form of consciousness, human actors are able to choose to act or not to act. Furthermore, they are capable of choosing what kind of action to undertake.
3 The minds of human beings enable them to plan beforehand what their action is going to be.

4 Human beings possess both physical and mental flexibility.

5 Human beings are capable of giving close attention to what they are doing over a long period of time.

6 The nature of the human mind leads people to be highly social.

Consciousness is a characteristic of people, and it is shaped out of human action and interaction: "Consciousness is, therefore, from the very beginning a social product, and remains so as long as men exist at all" (Marx and Engels, 1845–46/1970:51). Out of people's activities, social relationships, and the production of material life comes an expansion of consciousness:

> Not only do the objective conditions change in the act of production . . . but the producers change, too, in that they bring out new qualities in themselves, develop themselves in production, transform themselves, develop new powers and ideas, new modes of intercourse, new needs and new language.
>
> (Marx, 1857–58/1974:494)

It is not just consciousness or self-consciousness that differentiates human beings from other animals but also the relationship of that mental capacity to the peculiar kinds of activities of which people are capable. Human beings are capable of *activity* of a distinctive kind, quality, and pace. It is the ability to control activities through consciousness that distinguishes people from animals. Marx is perfectly explicit on this point:

> The animal is immediately one with its life activity. . . . Man makes his life activity itself the object of his will and of his consciousness.
>
> (Marx, 1932/1964:113)

> A spider conducts operations that resemble those of a weaver, and a bee puts to shame many an architect in the construction of her cells. But what distinguishes the worst architect from the best of bees is this, that the architect raises his structure in imagination before he erects it in reality. At the end of every labor-process we get a result that already existed in imagination of the laborer at its commencement.
>
> (Marx, 1867/1967:178)

McMurty (1978) argues that to Marx the special property of human nature is its creative intelligence, the ability to raise a structure in one's imagination and then to erect that structure in reality. To Marx, at the most abstract level, consciousness and its ability to direct activity were the distinctive characteristics of human beings, at least potentially.

But the problem with this conception of human potential is that it is highly abstract, and Marx had to bring it down to the level of the real world. People, their consciousness, and their activities cannot exist in isolation; they must be related to the natural world. People require objectives for their thoughts and actions, and the most important of these objectives are other people and nature. Humans must act on something, and what they act on mainly, with all their creative powers and in interaction with other people, is nature. We can differentiate three components of the relationship between human beings and nature—perception, orientation, and appropriation.

3 COMPONENTS OF REL BTWN H.B + NATURE

Perception is the immediate contact that people have with nature through their senses. But a mass of unorganized perceptions is likely to leave actors quite disoriented. What is needed is a process of *orientation* that organizes, patterns, and imposes a framework on the various perceptions of the world. Once the world has been perceived and the perceptions organized, the stage is set for *appropriation,* in which actors use their creative powers on nature in order to satisfy their needs. The conscious, creative capacity of human beings only makes sense in Marx's view when it is seen in relationship to the perception, orientation, and appropriation of nature. Not only does the nature of people's powers and needs shape the form of perception, orientation, and appropriation, but the form that they take in a particular social setting affects, in turn, the nature of these powers and needs. This reinforces the idea that for Marx human nature was not carved in stone but was very much affected by the nature of the social setting.

Following Marx, we may differentiate three basic epochs in the relationship between human potential and the processes of perception, orientation, and appropriation—primitive society, capitalism, and communism.

In *primitive society* people used natural resources to produce the things that they needed (for example, boats and shelters). Because relatively few things were produced—and those rather inefficiently—we can say that people developed their capacities to only a slight degree. Because powers were expressed to only this slight degree, the needs of people remained at a minimal level in primitive society (Ollman, 1976:91). In earliest times, people were busy desperately trying to survive and, as a result, were able to develop and express only a limited number of needs: "In lowest stages of production . . . few human needs have yet been produced and thus few to be satisfied" (Marx, 1857–58/1974:398). The ability of people to think, their consciousness, was limited and amounted to little more than animal, "sheep-like," consciousness (Marx and Engels, 1845–46/1970:51).

Capitalism was viewed by Marx as an epoch in which the creative capacity of most human beings as it is expressed in the act of appropriation is virtually eliminated. Instead, most people are reduced to wanting to make enough money to be able to *own* the commodities they desire. Thus the goal becomes ownership rather than the expression of human potentialities. In comparing primitive society to capitalism, Marx noted, "The ancients provide a narrow satisfaction, whereas the modern world leaves us unsatisfied, or, where it appears to be satisfied with itself, it is *vulgar* and *mean*" (1857–58/1964:85).

Communism, however, was viewed as an era in which the structural forces leading to this distortion of human nature are overthrown, and people are allowed to express their human potential in ways never before possible. The meanness of primitive life permitted only a minimal expression of that potential, and the structures of capitalism (for example, division of labor, private property, and money), while freeing people from the limitations of primitive society, represent barriers to the expression of many species powers and needs. But capitalism was seen by Marx as an important stage, because it developed the *organizational* and *technological* forms that a communist society could use, although in radically different ways, to free individuals further from the kinds of limitations encountered in primitive society. They could then express their human capacities in new and unprecedented ways. To Marx, communism is an epoch in which human beings are able to "bring their species powers out of themselves" (1932/1964:151; Barbalet, 1983:47, 55). With a slightly different emphasis, Ollman contended that "communism is the time of full, personal appropriation" (1976:93).

Activity

[handwritten: APPROP. OBJECTS FR. NATURE METHODS→ PURPOSEFUL ENDEVORS]

Activity now can be viewed as the means by which people appropriate objects from nature. In discussing activity, we are moving out of the subjective realm of consciousness and touching on the objective realm. But because Marx's work, to its credit, is a dialectically related whole, it is virtually impossible to talk about one aspect of social reality without at least touching on the others.

It is important to note that Marx's use of activity is virtually indistinguishable from his concepts of work and creativity. Marx was most prone to use the idea of work but in a way that is much different from common usage. Ollman defined the Marxian notion of work as "conscious, purposive activity in the productive process" (1976:98). By this definition, then, work is an expression of people's distinctive abilities. In fact, work is not restricted to economic activities but encompasses all productive activities that use the creative capacities of the actor. Work, in turn, also serves to allow greater development of people's powers and needs. *[handwritten margin note: create capac. of actors]*

Although Marx did not clearly differentiate among activity, work, and creativity, he tended to use different terms at different stages in his career. However, what is important here is that each of these terms highlights a different aspect of people's relationship to nature. *Activity* refers to the motions involved in purposeful endeavors; *work* refers to the process of material production; and *creativity* refers to the ability of people to make unique products (Ollman, 1976:102). In capitalism, work tends to be separated from activity and creativity; in communism, we are likely, in Marx's view, to find a situation where as far as possible work and activity fully involve the creative capacity of human beings.

Objectification In the activity involved in appropriating the natural world, people, according to Marx, always engage in the process of *objectification*, which means that they produce objects (food, clothes, and shelters). The process of objectification was important to Marx for several reasons. First, it reaffirmed his materialist orientation, his interest in the real world of real actors. He was not merely concerned with work in the abstract or objectification in the realm of consciousness, as was Hegel, but with objectification in the real world. Second, Marx saw objectification as the true arena in which people express their human capacities. Human potential is actualized in the objectification of products.

This process of objectification is normal and expressive of human potential if it involves certain characteristics (Israel, 1971:39). First, the activity must involve the consciousness of the actors. Second, the actors must be able to express their capabilities in a comprehensive manner. Third, they must be able to express their inherently social character in the process of objectification. Fourth, the process of objectification must not merely be a means to some other end (that is, the earning of money). In its most general sense, this means that objectification must involve the creative capacities of individuals.

— WORK, ACTIVITY + CREATIVITY

Labor In the context of this image of truly human objectification Marx discusses work in capitalist society. For this type of society, Marx usually did not use the interrelated concepts of work, activity, and creativity. Pointedly, he was most likely to refer to *labor*. In one sense, as is clear from the following quotations, Marx used the idea of labor as an equivalent to these other concepts:

> Labor is a creator of use-value, . . . a necessary condition, independent of all forms of society, for the existence of the human race.
>
> (Marx, 1867/1967:42–43)

> Labor is . . . a process in which both man and Nature participate, and in which man of his own accord starts, regulates, and controls the material re-actions between himself and Nature. He opposes himself to Nature as one of her own forces, setting in motion arms and legs, head and hands, the natural forces of his body, in order to appropriate Nature's productions in a form adapted to his own wants. By this acting on the external world and changing it, he at the same time changes his own nature. He develops his slumbering powers and compels them to act in obedience to his sway.
>
> (Marx, 1867/1967:177)

CAP = MEANS TO AN END, $

There seems little doubt that Marx is using *labor* here to mean work, activity, and creativity. Clearly implied is appropriation, objectification, and the full expression of human potential. However, as will be made clear throughout this chapter, Marx saw labor in capitalist society as taking on some distinct and perverted forms. Instead of being an end in itself, an expression of human capabilities, labor in capitalism is reduced to a means to an end—earning money (Marx, 1932/1964:173). In capitalism, labor is *not* the equivalent of work, activity, and creativity.

Sociability

Another aspect of Marx's image of human potential is the idea that people are inherently *social*. Marx and Engels talked of "the need, the necessity, of intercourse with other men" (1845–46/1970:51). Elsewhere Marx wrote, "Man is in the most literal sense of the word a *zoon politikon,* not only a social animal,

[handwritten: PEOPLE NEED NATURE + OTHER PEOPLE = HUMANESS]

but an animal which can develop into an individual only in society" (1857–58/1964:84).

At one level, as we have already seen, this means that all other truly human capabilities make no sense in isolation; they must be related to *both* the natural and the social worlds. In Marx's view, people cannot express their humanness without nature and without other people. At another level, sociability is an integral part of human nature. That is, to Marx people are inherently social. They need to relate to other people both for the sake of relating and in order to be able to appropriate nature adequately (Mészáros, 1970:149).

Unanticipated Consequences

Finally, a little-discussed aspect of Marx's image of human nature is directly related to the development of capitalism. It addresses the issue of how people, endowed with at least potentially positive human characteristics, are able to produce a structure of capitalism that serves to distort their essential nature. This is the notion of *unanticipated consequences* (Elster, 1985:3). Although we most often associate this idea with the work of Max Weber, it seems clear that Marx too had a conception of unanticipated consequences: "Here, then, is the dialectical worm: while we are highly successful in bringing about the immediate results of our conscious intentions, we still too often fail to anticipate and forestall the undesired remoter consequences of those results themselves" (cited in Venable, 1945:76).

[handwritten margin note: INH + BUT PROD CAPI ☹]

At the most general level, we can argue that capitalism was the unanticipated consequence of a large number of actions. People did not intend to create a structure that distorted humanity, but that is just what they did. It is also necessary to point out that the idea of unanticipated consequences, like other aspects of Marx's image of human nature, is tied to the social context. Although it is an integral part of past and present society, Marx probably would have argued (had he addressed the issue) that unanticipated consequences need not be a characteristic of society. That is, communism need not be subverted by unanticipated consequences. Yet the concept of unanticipated consequences is very useful in thinking about capitalist society. For example, capitalists believe that their actions are furthering their interests as well as the interests of the captialist system as a whole. But as Marx believed, many of the actions of capitalists create the conditions for the system's ultimate collapse. To take only one very broad example, capitalists believe that it is in their interest as well as in the interest of the system itself to extract every last ounce of productivity from the worker. Although in the short run this may create greater profits, in the long run, in Marx's view, it creates the class that will eventually destroy the capitalist system—the proletariat.

ALIENATION

Up to this point, we have been discussing a number of components of Marx's work at the microscopic level—human potential (species-being), powers, needs, self-consciousness and consciousness, activity, work, creativity, labor (perception, orientation, appropriation), objectification, sociability, and unanticipated consequences. This discussion has been derived mainly from Marx's early work. Marx rarely allowed himself the luxury later in his life of such philosophical analyses, for it was then that he wrote about the nature of capitalist society. In his early works, Marx called the distortions of human nature caused by the structure of capitalist society *alienation.* Although he shied away from this heavily philosophical term later in his work, it remained, in a different guise, one of his main concerns. As Barbalet says, "In *Capital* Marx seldom uses the term—although he clearly employs the concept—'alienation'" (1983:95). For in the end Marx was a humanist, and even as he explored the structure of capitalist society, he never lost sight of its impact on the actor (Wartenberg, 1982).

Although it is the actor who feels alienated in capitalist society, Marx's basic analytic concern was with the structures of capitalism that cause this alienation. Thus, contrary to the view of many interpreters who argue that he takes a social-psychological approach, Marx basically offered a theory of alienation rooted in social structure. It is social structure that acts to break down the natural interconnections that characterize human nature in an ideal sense. Of crucial significance here is the two-class system in which the capitalists employ the workers (and thereby own their labor-time) and own the *means of production* (tools and raw materials) as well as the ultimate products. In order to survive and to have access to tools and nature, workers are forced to sell their labor-time to capitalists. Although the workers then use the tools and apply them to nature in order to manufacture products, the natural interrelationships are shattered.

Components of Alienation

Alienation can be seen as having four basic components. First, the workers in capitalist society are alienated from their *productive activity*. In such a society they do not work for themselves in order to satisfy their own needs. Instead, they work for capitalists, who pay them a subsistence wage in return for the right to use the workers in any way they see fit. Both workers and capitalists come to believe that the payment of a wage means that the productive activity belongs to the capitalist. Because productive activity belongs to the capitalists, and because they decide what is to be done with it, we can say that workers are alienated from that activity. Instead of being a process that is satisfying in and of itself, productive activity in capitalism is reduced, Marx argued, to an often boring and stultifying means to the fulfillment of the only end that really matters in capitalism—earning enough money to survive.

Second, the workers are alienated not only from productive activities but also from the object of those activities—the *product*. The product of their labor does not belong to the workers, to be used by them in order to satisfy basic needs. Instead, the product, like the process that resulted in its production, belongs to the capitalists, who may use it in any way they wish. This usually means that the capitalists sell it for a profit. Not only do workers not have control over the product, but they do not even have a very good sense, in many cases, of what they are producing. They often perform highly specialized tasks and as a result have little sense of their role in the total production process. For example, automobile assembly-line workers who tighten a few bolts on an engine assembly may have little feel for their role in the production of the engine, let alone for their contribution to the production of the entire car. Assembly lines often are so long and involve so many steps that individuals are reduced to insignificant roles in the overall process. Playing such small roles in the process, workers often come to feel that it is the assembly line—rather than the people who work on it—that produces the final product. Third, the workers in capitalism are alienated from their *fellow workers*. Marx's assumption was that people basically need and want to work cooperatively in order to appropriate from nature what they require to survive. But in capitalism this natural cooperation is disrupted, and people, often strangers, are forced to work side by side for the capitalist. Even if the workers on the assembly line, for example, are close friends, the nature of the technology makes for a great deal of isolation. Here is the way one worker describes his social situation on the assembly line:

> You can work next to a guy for months without even knowing his name. One thing, you're too busy to talk. Can't hear. . . . You have to holler in his ear. They got these little guys coming around in white shirts and if they see you runnin' your mouth, they say, "This guy needs more work." Man, he's got no time to talk.
> (Terkel, 1974:165)

But this social situation is worse than simple isolation; the workers are often forced into outright competition, and sometimes conflict, with one another. In order to extract maximum productivity and to prevent the development of cooperative relationships, the capitalist pits one worker against another to see who can produce more, work more quickly, or please the boss more. The ones who succeed are given a few extra rewards; those who fail are discarded. In either case, considerable hostility is generated among the workers toward their peers. This is useful to the capitalists because it tends to deflect hostility that otherwise would be aimed at them. The isolation and the interpersonal hostility tend to make workers in capitalism alienated from fellow workers. Finally, and most generally, workers in capitalist society are alienated from their own *human potential*. Individuals perform less and less like human beings as they are reduced in their work to animals, beasts of burden, or inhuman machines. Consciousness is numbed and, ultimately, destroyed as relations with other humans and with nature are progressively severed. The result is a mass of people who are unable to express their essential human qualities, a mass of alienated workers.

Distortions Resulting from Alienation

Alienation, then, is the structurally imposed breakdown of the natural and total interconnectedness that is, to Marx, an essential part of life, at least in an ideal sense. Communism implies a reestablishment of the interconnections that have been broken in capitalism. Alienation, then, can be seen as the opposite of what people can be potentially (Barbalet, 1983:53). As Elster puts it, "Marx's discussion of alienation only makes sense against the background of a normative view of what constitutes the good life for man . . . a life of all-sided creative activity" (1985:51). As a result of alienation, work in capitalism is reduced to mere labor in which the individual "does not affirm himself but denies himself, does not feel content but unhappy, does not develop freely his physical and mental energy but mortifies his body and ruins his mind" (Marx, 1932/1964:110). Labor in capitalism is therefore very different from genuine human activity.

One of Marx's most beautiful examples of the perversion of humanity by capitalism is found in his discussion of *money*. Ideally, to Marx, people can be no more or less than they actually are, but in capitalism money can bestow on people powers and abilities that they do not actually possess. The following is Marx's penetrating statement on this point:

> That which is for me through the medium of *money*—that for which I can pay (i.e., which money can buy)—that am *I*, the possessor of the money. The extent of the power of money is the extent of my power. Money's properties are my properties and essential powers—the properties and powers of its possessor. Thus, what I *am* and *am capable* of is by no means determined by my individuality. I *am* ugly, but I can buy for myself the most *beautiful* of women. Therefore I am not *ugly*, for the effect of *ugliness*—its deterrent power—is nullified by money. I, as an individual, am *lame*, but money furnishes me with twenty-four feet. Therefore I am not lame. I am bad, dishonest, unscrupulous, stupid; but money is honored, and hence its possessor. Money is the supreme good; therefore its possessor is good. Money, besides, saves me the trouble of being dishonest: I am therefore presumed honest. I am *stupid*, but money is the *real mind* of all things and how then should its possessor be stupid? Besides, he can buy talented people for himself, and is he who has power over the talented not more talented than the talented? Do not I, who thanks to money am capable of *all* that the human heart longs for, possess all human capacities? Does not money, therefore, transform all my incapacities into their contrary?
>
> (Marx, 1932/1964:167)

Although money is capable of buying virtually anything in capitalism, it cannot perform that function in a truly human world. In such a world one can, for example, "exchange love only for love" (Marx, 1932/1964:119). Wealth is only a veneer that when stripped away leaves nothing but "the universality of needs, capacities, enjoyments, productive powers, etc., of individuals, produced in universal exchange. . . . What, if not the full development of human control over the forces of nature—those of his own nature—

as well as those of so-called 'nature'? What, if not the absolute elaboration of his creative dispositions?" (Marx, 1857–58/1964:84–85).

The list of distortions caused by capitalist society is lengthy. First, the structure of manufacturing turns workers into "crippled monstrosities" by forcing them to work on minute details rather than allowing them to use all their capabilities (Marx, 1867/1967:360). Similarly, the natural interrelationship between head and hand is broken in capitalism so that only a few people are allowed to do headwork; most others do handwork that is devoid of mental components (Marx, 1867/1967:508). Then there is the monotony of doing the same specialized task over and over again. Engels underscored this problem: "Nothing is more terrible than being constrained to do alone one thing every day from morning to night against one's will . . . in such unbroken monotony, that this alone must make his work a torture . . . if he has the least human feeling left" (Venable, 1945:137). Then there is the point that human beings are no longer creative but are oriented solely toward owning and possessing objects. To Marx, private property makes people so "stupid and one-sided" that they feel that an object is only theirs when they possess it, that is, when it is "eaten, drunk, worn, inhabited," and so forth. For all these reasons, work in capitalism largely ceases to be an expression of human potential. In fact, in many ways it is the opposite. With human functions so highly alienating, a person is no longer able to satisfy human powers and needs and is forced to concentrate on natural powers and needs.

NO creativity only owning + possess P.P.

> As a result, therefore, man (the worker) only feels himself freely active in his animal functions—eating, drinking, procreating, or at most in his dwelling and in dressing-up, etc.; and in his human functions he no longer feels himself to be anything but an animal. What is animal becomes human and what is human becomes animal.
>
> (Marx, 1932/1964:111)

Perhaps this is the height of unanticipated consequences. People have produced a society that allows them to feel comfortable only when they function like animals.

Marx argued that capitalism is an inverted world, in which those who rightfully should be on top are relegated to the bottom, and those who deserve to be on the bottom rise to the pinnacle of society. Thus the people who Marx believed should be most important to society—the producers (the proletariat)—are near the bottom, scraping by on a subsistence wage and dominated by the capitalists. The capitalists, who produce nothing of their own but simply live off the labor of others, are the dominant force in society. Also inverted is the sense of what is real in society. For example, it is people who set prices, but they fail to see their essential role in this process. Rather, it appears as if it is the unreal "market" that sets prices. Finally, the reality of life in capitalism is hidden while illusion is seen as fact. For example, from Marx's perspective, the capitalists exploit the proletariat, but the dominant belief is that the abilities of the capitalist lead to success for the worker. We shall return to this

CAP. INVERTED WORLD

theme later in a discussion of ideology in capitalism, but the key point is that in many ways, capitalism is an inverted and distorted social system.

Emancipation

Marx's critique of capitalist society is not an end in itself, of course, but an effort to help bring about the changes needed to create a society in which human potential can be adequately expressed. We can say that the goal of Marx's sociology lies in the ultimate emancipation of humanity from the enslavement of capitalist society (Mészáros, 1970:200). As Marx put it: "Human emancipation will only be complete when the real, individual man . . . has become a *species-being*" (cited in Bender, 1970:66). Vernon Venable catches the essence of the problem and the need for reform quite well:

> Hence human activity ought to be aimed . . . at their collective rescue from the pitiable, fragmentary, self-divided, craft-idiotic, class-enslaved state in which they find themselves. It should aim, in short, at the transformation of human nature. It should make man dignified, integrated, complete and free, so that the resources and potentialities that reside in him . . . may develop, expand, and find fruitful expression.
>
> (Venable, 1945:151–152)

Thus Marx's work on human potential led him both to a critique of capitalist society and to a political program oriented to overcoming the structures of capitalism so that people can express their essential humanity (Mészáros, 1970).

The transition to socialist society and emancipation is brought about through concrete action, or *praxis*. At one level, this concept means that we must not be content with philosophizing about capitalism but rather must develop a critical intellectual stance that will help bring about the action needed to revolutionize society. This concept also is construed to mean that capitalism can be transformed only through concrete action. Thus the proletariat must act to bring about the transition to socialism; they cannot sit back and wait for it to collapse because of internal contradictions. Marx's usage of praxis was both political and theoretical.

The communist society that would be created by praxis "does not rule over the individuals and is nothing in itself beyond the concrete individuals in their social relation to each other" (Gould, 1978:166). This would serve to eliminate alienation ("the human condition in the pre-communist stage" [Barbalet, 1983:53]) and reunite people with their products, productive activities, other people, and themselves. The goal of emancipation is *species-being.* Another way of saying this is that the goal of emancipation is communism,[1] which is "the first real emergence, the actual realization for man of man's essence and of

---

[1] According to Berki, communism is "the *only thing* that is important about Marx's thought" (1983:1).

his essence as something real" (Marx, 1932/1964:187). In Avineri's view, "Marx's postulate about the ultimate possibility of human self-emancipation must be related to his philosophical premise about the initial creation of the world by man" (1968:65). In other words, we cannot understand communism without understanding species-being.

THE STRUCTURES OF CAPITALIST SOCIETY

We have spent many pages analyzing Marx's thoughts on actors, mental processes, and action, much of which is embodied in his work on human potential and its distortion (alienation) by the structure of society, in particular the structure of capitalist society. It is time now to turn to Marx's work on those large-scale structures that are the cause of alienation in capitalist society.

The first issue to be addressed is whether Marx thought of these social structures as "things," that is, as hardened structures. Another way of putting this is to ask whether Marx adopted the position taken by Durkheim (1895/1964) that social facts should be treated as if they were "things." Marx's views on large-scale social structures were shaped by his dialectical approach, especially his tendency to focus on social relations (Ollman, 1976). Marx thought of social structures as being composed of a large number of continuing social relationships. This dynamic, or dialectical, perspective stands in sharp contrast to the view of many neo-Durkheimians, who overlook Durkheim's warning to simply *treat* social facts as things and who regard them as things *in fact*. Although he held a dynamic view of social structures, Marx did regard the set of relationships in capitalism as external to, and coercive of, actors. This is not to say that this set of relationships is inevitable or eternal, but they certainly have achieved objective reality in capitalism, and they must be overthrown in order to move on to communism. We can see how this meshed with Marx's political commitments, because this more relational view makes social structures much more changeable than would a view of them as things.

Commodities

The basis of all of Marx's work on social structures, and the place in which that work is most clearly tied to his views on human potential, is in his analysis of *commodities*. As Georg Lukács put it, "The problem of commodities is . . . the central, *structural* problem of capitalist society" (1922/1968:83).

Marx's conception of commodity was rooted in his materialist orientation, with its focus on the productive activities of actors. As we saw earlier, it was Marx's view that in their interactions with nature and with other actors, people always produce the objects that they need in order to survive; objectification is a necessary and universal aspect of human life. These objects are produced for use by oneself or by others in the immediate environment—they are *use values*. The objects are the products of human labor and cannot achieve an independent existence because they are controlled by the actors. However, in capitalism this process of objectification takes on a new and dangerous form. Instead of producing for themselves or their immediate associates, the actors produce for someone else (the capitalist). The products, instead of being used immediately, are exchanged in the open market for money (*exchange values*). While people produce objects in capitalism, their role in producing commodities, and their control over them, becomes mystified. At first they are led to believe that these objects and the market for them have an independent existence, and then this belief turns into reality as the objects and their market *do* become real, independent phenomena. The commodity becomes an independent, almost mystical external reality (Marx, 1867/1967:35).

Fetishism of Commodities   With the development of commodities comes the process Marx labeled the *fetishism of commodities*. The basis of this process is the labor that gives commodities their value. The fetishism of commodities involves the process by which actors forget that it is their labor that gives the commodities their value. They come to believe that value arises from the natural properties of the things themselves or that the impersonal operation of the market gives commodities value. Thus the *market* takes on a function in the eyes of the actors that in Marx's view *only* actors could perform—the production of value. In Marx's terms, "A definite social relation between men . . . assumes, in their eyes, the fantastic form of a relation between things" (1867/1967:72). Granting reality to commodities and the market, the individual in capitalism progressively loses control over them.

> A commodity is therefore a mysterious thing, simply because in it the social character of men's labor appears to them as an objective character stamped upon the product of that labor: because the relations of the producers to the sum total of their own labor is presented to them as a social relation, existing not between themselves, but between the products of their labor.
>
> (Marx, 1867/1967:72)

The beauty of Marx's discussion of commodities and their fetishism is that it takes us from the level of the individual actor and action to the level of large-scale social structures. That is, people endowed with creative minds interact with other people and nature to produce objects, but this natural process results in something grotesque in capitalism. The fetishism of commodities imparts to them and to the marketplace an independent objective reality that is external to, and coercive of, the actor.

Reification   The concepts of commodities and fetishism of commodities would appear to be of limited sociological use. The concepts seem to be restricted to the economic realm—that is, to the end result of productive activity. Yet productive activity can—indeed must—be looked at more broadly if we are to grasp the whole of Marx's meaning as well as its application to sociology. We need to understand that people produce not only economic objects (food, clothing, shelters) but also social relationships and, ultimately, social structures. Looked at in this way, the fetishism of commodities is translated into the broader concept of reification (Lukács, 1922/1968). *Reification* can be thought of as the process of coming to believe that humanly created social forms are natural, universal, and absolute and, as a result, that those social forms do in fact acquire those characteristics. The concept of reification implies that people believe that social structures are beyond their control and unchangeable. This belief often comes to be a self-fulfilling prophecy. Then the structures actually *do* acquire the character people endowed them with. By using this concept, we can see that people reify not only commodities but also the whole range of social structures.

We can find the groundwork for a broader concept of reification in Marx's own discussion of labor. Basically, Marx argued that, as a *social* phenomenon, labor becomes a commodity under the peculiar circumstances of capitalism: "Labor-power can appear in the market as a commodity, only if, and so far as, its possessor, the individual whose labor-power it is, offers it for sale, or sells it, as a commodity" (1867/1967:168). Once we admit the possibility of one social phenomenon (labor) becoming reified, it becomes possible for a wide range of other social phenomena to take on the same characteristic (Lefebvre, 1968:16). Just as people reify commodities and other economic phenomena (for example, the division of labor [Rattansi, 1982; Walliman, 1981]), they also reify religious (Barbalet, 1983:147), political, and organizational structures. Marx made this point in reference to the state: "And out of this very contradiction between the individual and . . . the community the latter takes an independent form as the *State,* divorced from the real interests of individual and community" (cited in Bender, 1970:176).

Marx had a few things to say about the range of reified social structures, but he focused primarily on the structural components of the economy. It is these economic structures that Marx saw as causing alienation by breaking down the natural interconnectedness of people and nature.

Capital

The most general economic structural element in Marx's work is *capital,* or the capitalist system. As an independent structure, capital (through the actors who operate in its behalf, the bourgeoisie) exploits the workers, who were and are responsible for its creation. Marx talked of the power of capital appearing "as a power endowed by Nature—a productive power that is immanent in Capital" (1867/1967:333). Thus people tend to reify capital by believing that it is natural for the capitalist system to be external to, and coercive of, them. Workers are exploited by a system that they have *forgotten* they *produced* through their labor and have the capacity to change. "By means of its conversion into an automaton, the instrument of labor confronts the laborer, during the labor-process, in the shape of capital, of dead labor, that dominates, and pumps

AUTOMATION

away, living labor-power" (Marx, 1867/1967:423). This is what led Marx to conclude that capitalism is an inverted world.

Before we get to a discussion of some of Marx's economic ideas, and later to a case study of Marx's economics, the reader should be reminded that this is a book in sociological, not economic, theory. Thus, the economic ideas are introduced in order to illustrate underlying and more basic sociological ideas.

Circulation of Commodities Marx discussed not only the character of capital in general but also the character of more specific components of the capitalist system. For example, Marx examined the circulation of commodities, which he considered "the starting-point of capital" (1867/1967:146). Marx discussed two types of circulation of commodities. Both represent the sum total of patterned economic relationships that are external to, and coercive of, the actor. One of these types of circulation—Money-Commodities-Money (M-C-M)—is characteristic of capital; the other—Commodities-Money-Commodities (C-M-C)—is not.

In the simple circulation of commodities, the circuit C-M-C predominates. An example of C-M-C would be the fisherman who sells his catch and then uses the money to buy bread. In a society characterized by the simple circulation of commodities, exchange is accomplished by "the conversion of the commodity into money, and the reconversion of the money into a commodity" (Marx, 1867/1967:105). This circuit, however, does not exist in isolation; it is inextricably interrelated to similar circuits involving other commodities. This type of exchange process "develops a whole network of social relations spontaneous in their growth and entirely beyond the control of the actors" (Marx, 1867/1967:112).

The simple circulation of commodities that is characterized by the circuit C-M-C can be considered the second historical type of circulation of commodities. Barter is the first historical form. Both of these circuits eventually lead to the circulation of commodities under capitalism, which is characterized by the circuit M-C-M.

In the capitalist circuit, referred to by Marx as "buying in order to sell" (1867/1967:147), the individual actor buys a commodity with money and in turn exchanges it for money. Here our hypothetical fisherman buys new nets with his profits in order to increase his future profits. This circuit, similar to the circuit under the simple circulation of commodities, is characterized by two antithetical yet complementary phases. At one and the same time, one person's purchase is another's sale. The circulation of commodities under capitalism begins with a purchase (new nets) and ends with a sale (a larger catch of fish). Furthermore, the end of this circuit is not the consumption of the use value, as it is in the simple circulation of commodities. The end is money in an expanded form, money that is qualitatively identical to that at the beginning of the circuit but quantitatively different (Marx, 1867/1967:150).

The importance of the M-C-M circuit, from our point of view, is that it is an even more abstract process than C-M-C. The "real" commodity declines in significance, with the result that the essence of capital is reduced ultimately to the "unreal" circulation of money. This greater abstractness makes reification easier, with the result that the system is even more likely to become external to, and coercive of, actors.

Private Property

HuM PoT = PP

Marx also analyzed the process by which *private property* becomes reified in capitalism. In his view, of course, private property, like the other structural components of capitalism, is derived from the labor of workers. "*Private property* is thus the product, the result, the necessary consequence, of *alienated labor*, of the external relation of the worker to nature and to himself" (Marx, 1932/1964:117). But workers lose sight of, and ultimately control over, this fact. Instead of controlling private property, the workers are controlled by it. As with all other structural components of Marx's work, his conception of private property was directly related to his early work on human potential and action as well as to his political goals. In relating private property to his earlier work, Marx made it clear that not only is private property the product of alienated labor but, once in existence, it in turn exacerbates alienation by imposing itself between people and the production process. If people are to realize their human potential, they must overthrow private property as well as all the other structural components of capitalist society: "The positive transcendence of *private property*, as the appropriation of *human* life, is therefore the positive transcendence of all estrangement—that is to say, the return of man from religion, family, state, etc., to his *human*, i.e., social existence" (Marx, 1932/1964:136).

Division of Labor

The division of labor is another structural component of capitalism that comes under Marx's scrutiny. Marx and Engels traced the origins of the modern division of labor to the early family, "where wife and children are the slaves of the husband" (1845–46/1970:52). Although Marx was obviously critical of these early forms of the division of labor, he was most critical of its particularly pernicious form within capitalism.

Marx's most basic view of the division of labor is set forth in his distinction between the owners of the means of production and those who must sell their labor-time to the owners in order to survive. More specifically, Marx was interested in the tendency to structure work so that people are forced to specialize in ever more minute tasks. Such specialization prevents actors from realizing and expressing their human potential (Marx, 1867/1967:350).

Marx offered a number of criticisms of the division of labor in capitalism (Venable, 1945). First, the existence of the division of labor artificially separates the individual from the community as a whole. Indeed, people come to focus almost totally on their own slots and ignore, or even fight against, the interest of the whole community. Second, the labor process is broken down so that

1 SEP IND PR COMM-

[handwritten margin notes: "2/ SEG MENT PHYS TASKS", "3/ POWERS OF IND - SIMPLY A TOOL IN PROD PROC", "4/ SMALL CONTR"]

functions that ideally would be integrated are separated. For example, intellectual functions are separated from manual tasks; work and enjoyment are separated; and the act of production is radically separated from the act of consumption. Third, the powers of the individual are reduced to simply another tool in the production process. Fourth, each person makes only a small contribution to the final product. The worker is disassociated from that product and everything that happens to it after it is produced. More generally, workers as a class lose control over *all* the things that they produce as well as the market for them. Finally, the narrow specialization has the effect on man of "stunting him, dehumanizing him, reducing him to a mere fragment of a man, a crippled monstrosity, an appendage to a machine" (Venable, 1945:124).

These criticisms of the structure of the division of labor led Marx to an inevitable political conclusion—that a society must be created in which people are *not* narrowly specialized:

> In communist society, where nobody has one exclusive sphere of activity but each can become accomplished in any branch he wishes, society regulates the general production and thus makes it possible for me to do one thing today and another tomorrow, to hunt in the morning, fish in the afternoon, rear cattle in the evening, criticize after dinner, just as I have a mind without ever becoming hunter, fisherman, shepherd or critic.
>
> (Marx and Engels, 1845–46/1970:53)

Although Marx probably never believed that such a society was totally possible, it does reflect his interest in eliminating the destructive effects of specialization. Marx was not saying that everyone can or will become good at everything. His point was that the division of labor has artificially prevented people, particularly the proletariat, from developing their abilities to the fullest. As David McLellan makes clear, Marx did not believe "that each should do the work of Raphael, but that anyone in whom there is a potential Raphael should be able to develop without hindrance. The exclusive concentration of artistic talent in particular individuals, and its suppression in the broad mass . . . is a consequence of division of labor" (1971:218). Thus in communism people will not all become, in Marx's view, poets or artists or lawyers, but the artificial barriers preventing people from developing to their fullest will be eliminated. Foremost among these barriers, and one that must be eliminated, is the division of labor.

Social Class

One other aspect of Marx's interest in social structure was social class (primarily the bourgeoisie and the proletariat). Although Marx actually spent very little time analyzing social class as a concept, it is clear that he viewed social classes as structures that are external to, and coercive of, people.

Although Marx himself offered us only hints, Ollman's interpretation of

social
class
Rel which take on
ind - existance

Marx is quite explicit about social class. Ollman emphasized that *social classes* are "reified social relations" or "the relations between men [that] have taken on an independent existence" (1976:204–205). He also linked the emergence of social classes to the previously discussed emergence of commodities in capitalism. "*Class and commodity are brothers under the skin*" (Ollman, 1976:205; italics added). Social classes arise out of the acts of production; people come to reify classes, and as a result these classes come to have a life of their own that constrains the actor. Marx did not make this explicit, but it makes sense, given the general thrust of his arguments.

In this section, we have examined Marx's views on large-scale social structures. We saw that he tended to view them relationally rather than as real, material structures. Nevertheless, they are external and coercive forces to Marx. All his views on such structures were rooted in his conception of commodities and the fetishism of commodities. Moving beyond the purely economic realm, Marx adopted the same view about social structures. But the bulk of Marx's work concerns the structures of the economy in capitalism—commodities, capital, private property, the division of labor, and social class. All these evolve out of the thoughts and actions of actors, and once in existence, they constrain the very processes that created them. Most of Marx's political attention was devoted to the question of how these structures could be overcome so that a communist society might be created.

CULTURAL ASPECTS OF CAPITALIST SOCIETY

Marx focused on the large-scale structures of capitalist society and their alienating impact on human beings. He did not have a great deal to say about the cultural domain, but a careful analysis indicates that he was not insensitive to the importance of this aspect of social reality. Marx's materialism led him away from a concern with culture, and it could be said that at times Marx went too far in his rejection of this domain, which he associated with the weaknesses of Hegelian philosophy. For example, in *The Critique of Political Economy* Marx wrote:

> The totality of these relations of production constitutes the *economic structure* of society, the *real foundation*, on which arises a legal and political superstructure and to which correspond definite forms of *social consciousness*. The mode of production of *material life conditions* the general processes of social, political, and intellectual life. It is not the consciousness of men that determines their existence, but their social existence that determines their consciousness.
>
> (Marx, 1859/1970:20–21; italics added)

Marx might be thought of here as talking about consciousness in a cultural sense (that is, talking about norms, values, or in Hegel's terms, spirit, or *Geist*) and not in the sense of mental processes and the social construction of reality. Given this interpretation, Marx seemed to be relegating the cultural level to the status of an "epiphenomenon" determined by social and economic structures. This seems to be confirmed when, slightly later in the same work, Marx appeared to reduce all social change to change of the material base on which is erected the cultural superstructure:

> Then begins an era of social revolution. The changes in the *economic foundation* lead sooner or later to the transformation of the whole immense *superstructure*. In studying such transformations it is always necessary to distinguish between the *material* transformation of the economic conditions of production, which can be determined with the precision of natural science, and the *legal, political, religious, artistic* or *philosophic—in short, ideological forms* in which men become *conscious* of this conflict and fight it out. *Just as one does not judge an individual by what he thinks about himself, so one cannot judge such a period of transformation by its consciousness, but on the contrary, this consciousness must be explained from the contradictions of material life.*
>
> (Marx, 1859/1970:21; italics added)

It is even clearer here that Marx was talking about the cultural level ("the legal, political, religious, artistic, philosophic—in short, ideological forms"). He even differentiated between individual consciousness and the consciousness of a "period." We must applaud Marx for this awareness and this clear differentiation, but we also must be highly critical of his tendency to reduce the cultural domain to an epiphenomenon, if that is in fact what he did.

However, contrary to these words from the preface to *The Critique of Political Economy*—which is, unfortunately, one of Marx's most simplistic statements— we are led by the thrust of his entire work and by his commitment to the dialectic to dismiss such deterministic statements. A commitment to the dialectic means a commitment to studying the interrelationships among phenomena; it is inherently antideterministic. It could be argued that the nature of capitalism led to the preeminence of the structural level, with the result that the other levels are under its sway. Although this is true to Marx's characterization of capitalism, he still did not simply dismiss the cultural level; he had a number of things to offer here, particularly in his discussions of class consciousness and false consciousness as well as ideology.

Class Consciousness and False Consciousness

The ideas of class consciousness and false consciousness are intimately related in Marx's work. Both refer to idea systems shared by social classes. In capitalism both capitalists and workers have incorrect assessments of how the system works and of their role and interest in it (*false consciousness*). In the evolution toward communism, there is the possibility that the proletariat will develop an accurate conception of how capitalism works and how it affects them (*class consciousness*).

What is characteristic of capitalism, for *both* the proletariat and the bourgeoisie, is false consciousness. We are not surprised to learn that workers have false consciousness, but it is sometimes startling to think of capitalists in this

BOTH—F.C.

way. After all, they are presumably exploiting the system, and the proletariat, to their advantage. Georg Lukács (1922/1968), one of the foremost interpreters of Marx, pointed to a number of elements of the false consciousness of the bourgeoisie. The bourgeoisie is unaware of its own history and the role it played in the formation of capitalism. More important, it is unaware of the contradictions that exist within capitalism as well as of the role it is playing in contributing to those burgeoning contradictions. The bourgeoisie, like the proletariat, is unaware of the consequences of its actions. Its idea systems contain delusions about its control over the capitalist system. The fact is that its actions are contributing to the ultimate demise of the system that it believes it is serving to buttress. The proletariat's thought system is at least as deluded as the bourgeoisie's.

HISTORY — CONTRA- DICTIONS — CONSER- UENCE

There is, however, a crucial difference here between the two classes. The bourgeoisie can never transform its false consciousness into true class consciousness; this is possible only for the proletariat. In Marx's view, the proletariat occupies this privileged position because as the propertyless class, it is the model for the future propertyless society. At the height of capitalism, the proletariat "is already a class in opposition to capital, but not yet a class for itself" (McLellan, 1971:155). It is not adequate for the proletariat to be a "class in itself"; it must become a "class for itself." If the proletariat is to take on its historic role in capitalism, "it must become a class not only 'as against capital' but also 'for itself'; that is to say, the class struggle must be raised from the level of economic necessity to the level of conscious aim and effective class consciousness" (Lukács, 1922/1968:76).

In talking about class (and false) consciousness, Marx was talking not about individual consciousness but about the consciousness of the class as a whole. Furthermore, the concepts of class consciousness and false consciousness are not, in Marx's hands, static but are rather dynamic idea systems that make sense only in terms of social change and development. False consciousness describes the situation throughout the capitalist epoch, whereas class consciousness is the condition that awaits the proletariat and that can help bring about the change from capitalist to communist society.

NOT IND CLASS

Ideology

INO/EXT TO/COERSIUE OF ACTE

The other major cultural dimension of Marx's analysis is ideology. An _ideology_ can be defined as an integrated system of ideas that is external to, and coercive of, people (Lefebvre, 1968). Although Marx often talked of ideologies in the same way as he talked about class and false consciousness—that is, as mere reflections of the material base—it is clear that ideologies, too, take on an independent existence in his system. Some analysts make much of the apparent determinism of passages like the following, but it is the author's view that Marx was only offering one side of his multifaceted analysis here:

> The _ideas_ [italics added] of the ruling class are in every epoch the ruling ideas, i.e., the class which is the ruling _material_ force of society, is at the same time, its ruling

OR Ruling class

intellectual force. The class, which has the means of material production at its disposal, has control at the same time over the means of mental production, so that
thereby, generally speaking, the ideas of those who lack the means of mental production are subject to it. *The ruling ideas are nothing more than the ideal expression of
the dominant material relationships* [italics added], the dominant material relationships
grasped as ideas.

(Marx and Engels, 1845–46/1970:64)

At least three basic interrelated ideas are involved in Marx's conceptualization of ideologies. First, they certainly do represent the interests of the ruling
class, but that is not to say that these ideas do not have a reciprocal impact
on material interests. Second, they constitute an "inverted, truncated reflection
of reality" (Lefebvre, 1968:64). Third, ideologies have an independent existence that is coercive of people. Lefebvre caught the essential point for us here
in discussing the effect of ideologies on members of the oppressed class: "It
is the role of ideologies to secure the assent of the oppressed and exploited.
Ideologies represent the latter to themselves in such a way as to wrest from
them, in addition to material wealth, their spiritual acceptance of this situation, even their support" (1968:76).

An ideological system functions to alter the thoughts and actions of members of the oppressed class. In this way, ideologies serve to foster the exploitation of the proletariat. Of course, ideologies do not function in a vacuum;
they operate through agents who carry out their dictates. Thus ideologies
affect the actions of agents of the ruling class, who, in turn, affect the thoughts
and actions of the proletariat.

MARX'S ECONOMICS: A CASE STUDY

This chapter is devoted to an analysis of Marx's sociology, but of course it is
his economics for which he is far better known. Although we have touched
on a number of aspects of Marx's economics, we have not dealt with it in a
coherent fashion. In this closing section, we will look at Marx's economics,
not as economics per se, but rather as an exemplification of his sociological
theory (Mazlish, 1984).[2] There is much more to Marxian economics, but this
is the most relevant way to deal with it in a book devoted to sociological
theory.

A starting point for Marxian economics is in the concepts, previously
touched on, of use value and exchange value. People have always created use
values; that is, they have always produced things that directly satisfy their
wants. A *use value* is defined qualitatively; that is, something either is or is
not useful. An *exchange value*, however, is defined quantitatively, not quali-

---

[2] *One* way of looking at Marx's economic theory (for example, the labor theory of value) is as
a specific application of his more general sociological theory. This stands in contrast to G. Cohen's
(1978) work, in which his overriding concern is the underlying *economic* theory in Marx's work.
Although Cohen sees the "economic" and the "social" as being interchangeable in Marx's work,
he clearly implies that Marx's economic theory is the more general.

tatively. It is defined by the amount of labor needed to appropriate useful qualities. Whereas use values are produced to satisfy one's own needs, exchange values are produced to be exchanged for values of another use. Whereas the production of use values is a natural human expression, the existence of exchange values sets in motion a process by which humanity is distorted. The entire edifice of capitalism, including commodities, the market, money, and so forth, is erected on the base of exchange values.

To Marx, the basic source of any value was the amount of socially necessary labor-time needed to produce an article under the normal conditions of production and with the average degree of skill and intensity of the time. This is the well-known *labor theory of value.* Although it is clear that labor lies at the base of use value, this fact grows progressively less clear as we move to exchange values, commodities, the market, and capitalism. To put it another way, "The determination of the magnitude of value by labor-time is therefore a secret, hidden under the apparent fluctuations in relative values of commodities" (Marx, 1867/1967:75). Labor, as the source of all value, is a secret in capitalism that allows the capitalists to exploit the workers.

According to Peter Worsley, Marx "put at the heart of his sociology—as no other sociology does—the theme of exploitation" (1982:115). The capitalists pay the workers *less* than the value the workers produce and keep the rest for themselves. The workers are not aware of this exploitation, and, often, neither are the capitalists. The capitalists believe that this extra value is derived from their own cleverness, their capital investment, their manipulation of the market, and so on. Marx stated that "so long as trade is good, the capitalist is too much absorbed in money grubbing to take notice of this gratuitous gift of labor" (1867/1967:207). In sum, Marx said:

> The capitalist does not know that the normal pace of labor also includes a definite quantity of unpaid labor, and that this very unpaid labor is the normal source of his gain, the category, surplus labor-time, does not exist at all for him, since it is included in the normal working-day, which he thinks he has paid for in wages.
> (Marx, 1867/1967:550)

This leads us to Marx's central concept of *surplus value.* This is defined as the difference between the value of the product and the value of the elements consumed in the formation of that product. Although means of production (raw materials and tools, the value of which comes from the labor involved in extracting or producing them) are consumed in the production process, it is labor that is the real source of surplus value. "The rate of surplus-value is therefore an exact expression for the degree of exploitation of labor-power by capital, or of the laborer by the capitalist" (Marx, 1867/1967:218). This points to one of Marx's more colorful metaphors: "Capital is dead labor, that, vampire-like, only lives by sucking living labor, and lives the more, the more labor it sucks" (1867/1967:233).

The surplus derived from this process is used by the capitalists to pay for such things as rent to landowners and interest to banks. But the most important derivation from it is profit. The capitalists can use this profit for private consumption, but that would not lead to the expansion of capitalism. Rather they expand their enterprise by converting it into a base for the creation of still more surplus value.

The desire for more profit and more surplus value for expansion pushes capitalism toward what Marx called the *general law of capitalist accumulation.* The capitalists seek to exploit workers as much as possible: "The constant tendency of capital is to force the cost of labor back towards . . . zero" (Marx, 1867/1967:600). Marx basically argued that the structure and the ethos of capitalism push the capitalists in the direction of the accumulation of more and more capital. In order to do this, given Marx's view that labor is the source of value, the capitalists are led to intensify the exploitation of the proletariat. Ultimately, however, increased exploitation yields fewer and fewer gains; an upper limit of exploitation is reached. In addition, as this limit is approached, the government is forced to place restrictions on the actions of capitalists (for example, laws limiting the length of the workday). As a result, the capitalists must look for other devices, and a major one is the substitution of machines for people. This substitution is made relatively easy, because the capitalists already have reduced the workers to laboring machines performing a series of simple operations. As mechanization proceeds, more and more people are put out of work and fall from the proletariat to the "industrial reserve army." At the same time, heightening competition and the burgeoning costs of technology lead to a progressive decline in the number of capitalists. In the end, Marx foresaw a situation in which society would be characterized by a tiny number of exploitative capitalists and a huge mass of proletarians and members of the industrial reserve army. In these extreme circumstances, capitalism would be most vulnerable to revolution. As Marx put it, the expropriation of the masses by the capitalists would be replaced by "the expropriation of a few usurpers by the mass of people" (1867/1967:764). The capitalists, of course, seek to forestall their demise. For example, they sponsor colonial adventures with the objective of shifting at least some of the burden of exploitation from the home front to the colonies. However, in Marx's view these efforts are ultimately doomed to failure, and the capitalists will face rebellion at home and abroad.

The key point about the general law of capitalist accumulation is the degree to which actors, both capitalist and proletarian, are impelled by the structure and ethos of capitalism to do what they do. Marx usually did not blame individual capitalists for their actions; he saw these actions as largely determined by the logic of the capitalist system. This is consistent with his view that actors in capitalism generally are devoid of creative independence. However, the developmental process inherent in capitalism provides the conditions necessary for the ultimate reemergence of such creative action and, with it, the overthrow of the capitalist system.

Now that we have discussed Marx's economic ideas in some detail, the reader should remember that we are not interested in those economic ideas per se; rather, we are interested in them for what they tell us about Marx's more basic sociological theory.

SUMMARY

Despite his overwhelming importance to sociology in both a positive and a negative sense, Karl Marx's work rarely has received its due in historical analyses of the development of sociological theory. It is one of the goals of this book to accord Marx his proper place in that history.

The chapter begins with a discussion of the dialectical approach that Marx derived from Hegel and that shapes all of Marx's work. An interest in the dialectic leads into complex philosophical issues, but our discussion concentrates on those elements of the dialectic that are most relevant to Marx's sociology and to sociological theory in general. The dialectic is contrasted with the causal logic that dominates much of sociological thinking. Among other things, the dialectic emphasizes that there are no simple cause-and-effect relationships among elements of the social world; there is no clear dividing line between fact and value; and there are no hard-and-fast dividing lines among phenomena in the social world. Further, the dialectic stresses that we should focus on social relationships; we should be oriented not only to the present but also to the past and future; we should resist the idea that there are social inevitabilities; and we should be concerned with conflicts and contradictions within the social world. Despite his political orientation toward the creation of a communist society, Marx devoted his attention to dialectical *and* critical analyses of capitalist society. It was his hope that such criticism would help bring about the overthrow of capitalist society and the coming of socialism.

In analyzing the substance of Marx's work, we begin with an analysis of the potential of human beings. This is Marx's image of human nature, but it is a human nature that is greatly affected by its social setting. Marx saw capitalism as a setting that distorts humanity, whereas communism would be a setting in which humanness would be allowed to express itself. Marx's actors are endowed with consciousness and creativity, which are expressed in various types of actions and interactions. Of utmost importance here is the need to interact with other people and with nature in order to produce the objects that people need to survive. It is significant that this natural process is subverted as a result of the unanticipated consequences of capitalism.

The distortions of humans caused by the structures of capitalism fall within the bounds of Marx's famous concept of *alienation.* People are naturally connected with their productive activity, their products, their fellow workers, and, ultimately, with themselves, with their inherent nature as human beings. But all these connections are severed by the structures of capitalism. On a political level, this led Marx to an interest in emancipating people from the oppressive structures of capitalism. On an intellectual level, it led him to examine the nature of the structures of capitalism and their oppressive impact on actors.

We examine various aspects of the structure of capitalist society. We discuss the central role played by commodities in capitalism and the way they are created by the process known as the *fetishism of commodities.* In effect, people endow commodities, and the market for them, with a life of their own. This concept is later expanded (by Lukács) to the idea of reification; that is, people make fetishes not only of commodities but also of many other structural components of capitalist society. In this context, we look at capital as the most general reified structure in capitalist society. Also, we examine a number of reified components in capitalist society, including private property, the division of labor, and social class.

Although Marx, especially in his later work, was particularly concerned with the structures of capitalism, he did have some things to say about the cultural aspects of capitalist society, especially class consciousness, false consciousness, and ideology.

We close the chapter with a discussion of Marxian economics as an illustration of Marx's overall sociological theory. Although for various reasons people have tended to ignore it, there is a very powerful sociological theory in Marx's work.

EMILE DURKHEIM

*E*MILE Durkheim's theoretical orientation, unlike that of many other major sociological thinkers, contains little ambiguity. He was deeply concerned with the impact of the large-scale structures of society, and society itself, on the thoughts and actions of individuals. He was most influential in shaping structural-functional theory, with its emphasis on social structure and culture. In light of this, our objective in this chapter is to describe Durkheim's theoretical perspective, with particular (but not exclusive) attention to its macrosociological concerns.

The development and use of the concept of a social fact lies at the heart of Durkheim's sociology. We will have a great deal to say about this concept in this chapter, but a brief introduction to it is needed at this point. In modern terms, *social facts* are the social structures and cultural norms and values that are external to, and coercive of, actors. Thus readers of this text, as students, are constrained by such social structures as the university bureaucracy as well

as the norms and values of American society, which place such great importance on getting a college education. Similar social facts constrain people in
all areas of social life.

To understand why Durkheim developed the concept of social fact and
what it means, we need to examine at least a few aspects of the intellectual
context in which he lived.

In Durkheim's (1900/1973:3) view, sociology was born in France in the
nineteenth century. He recognized its roots in the ancient philosophers (Plato,
Aristotle) and more proximate sources in French philosophers such as Montesquieu and Condorcet. For example, Durkheim noted, "It is Montesquieu
who first laid down the fundamental principles of social science" (1893/
1960:61). However, in Durkheim's view, Montesquieu (and Condorcet) did not
go far enough: "They limited themselves to offering ingenious or novel views
on social facts rather than seeking to create an entirely new discipline" (1900/
1973:6). Durkheim (1928/1962:142) gave Saint-Simon credit for first formulat-
ing the notion of a science of the social world, but Saint-Simon's ideas were
seen as scattered and imperfect. Those ideas were, in Durkheim's view, per-
fected by Comte, "the first to make a coherent and methodical effort to establish the positive science of societies" (1900/1973:10).

Although, as we saw in Chapter 3, the term *sociology* had been coined some
years earlier by Comte, there was no field of sociology per se in late nineteenth-century France. There were no schools, departments, or even professors
of sociology. There were a few thinkers who were dealing with ideas that
were in one way or another sociological, but there was as yet no disciplinary
"home" for sociology. Indeed, there was strong opposition from existing disciplines to the founding of such a field. The most significant opposition came
from psychology and philosophy, two fields that claimed already to cover the
domain sought by sociology. The dilemma for Durkheim, given his aspirations
for sociology, was how to create for it a separate and identifiable niche.

To separate it from philosophy, Durkheim argued that sociology should be
oriented toward empirical research. This seems simple enough, but the situation was complicated by Durkheim's belief that sociology was also threatened
by a philosophical school *within* sociology itself. In his view, the two other
major figures of the epoch who thought of themselves as sociologists, Comte
and Spencer, were far more interested in philosophizing, in abstract theorizing, than they were in studying the social world empirically. If the field were
to continue in the direction set by Comte and Spencer, Durkheim felt, it would
become nothing more than a branch of philosophy. As a result, he found it
necessary to attack both Comte and Spencer (Durkheim, 1895/1964:19–20). He
accused both of substituting preconceived ideas of social phenomena for the
actual study of the phenomena in the real world. Thus Comte was said to be
guilty of assuming theoretically that the social world was evolving in the
direction of an increasingly perfect society, rather than engaging in the hard,
rigorous, and basic work of actually studying the changing nature of various
societies. Similarly, Spencer was accused of assuming harmony in society
rather than studying whether harmony actually existed.

SOCIAL FACTS

In order to help sociology move away from philosophy and to give it a clear and separate identity, Durkheim argued that the distinctive subject matter of sociology should be the study of social facts. The concept of social fact has several components, but crucial in separating sociology from philosophy is the idea that *social facts are to be treated as things.* In that they are to be treated as *things,* social facts are to be studied empirically, *not* philosophically. Durkheim believed that ideas can be known introspectively (philosophically), but *things* "cannot be conceived by purely mental activity"; they require for their conception "data from outside the mind" (1895/1964:xliii). This empirical study of social facts as things sets Durkheimian sociology apart from the largely introspective theorizing of Comte and Spencer.

Although treating social facts as things countered the threat from philosophy (at least as far as Durkheim was concerned), it was only part of the answer to the problem of dealing with the threat coming from psychology. Like Durkheimian sociology, psychology was already highly empirical. To differentiate sociology from psychology, Durkheim argued that social facts were *external to,* and *coercive of,* the actor. Sociology was to be the study of social facts, whereas psychology was relegated the study of psychological facts. To Durkheim, psychological facts were basically inherited phenomena. Although this certainly does not describe psychology today (and was not a very accurate description of the subject matter of psychology even then), it did allow Durkheim to draw a clear differentiation between the two fields. Psychological facts are clearly internal (inherited), and social facts are external and coercive. As we will soon see, this differentiation is not so neat as Durkheim would have liked us to believe. Nevertheless, by defining a social fact as a *thing* that is *external to, and coercive of, the actor,* Durkheim seems to have done a reasonably good job (at least for that historical era) of attaining his objective of separating sociology from both philosophy and psychology. However, it should be noted that to do this, Durkheim took an "extremist" position (Karady, 1983:79–80), especially in limiting sociology to the study of social facts. This position was to limit at least some branches of sociology to the present day.

We know that a social fact is a thing and that it is external and coercive, but what else is a social fact? Actually, Durkheim differentiated between two broad types of social facts—material and nonmaterial. *Material social facts* are the clearer of the two because they are real, material entities, but they are also of lesser significance in Durkheim's work. As Durkheim put it, "The social fact is sometimes materialized so far as to become an element of the external world" (1897/1951:313). Architecture and the law would be two examples of what he meant by material social facts. We will encounter other examples in this chapter.

But the bulk of Durkheim's work, and the heart of his sociology, lies in the study of nonmaterial social facts. Durkheim said: "Not all social consciousness achieves . . . externalization and materialization" (1897/1951:315). What sociologists now call *norms* and *values,* or more generally culture (see Alexander, 1988), are good examples of what Durkheim meant by *nonmaterial social facts.*

But this idea creates a problem: How can nonmaterial social facts like norms and values be external to the actor? Where could they be found except in the minds of actors? And if they are in the minds of actors, then are they not internal rather than external?

To clarify this issue, we must refine Durkheim's argument by contending that while material social facts are clearly external and coercive, nonmaterial social facts are not so clear-cut. (For a similar distinction, see Takla and Pope [1985:82].) To at least some extent, they are found in the minds of actors. The best way to conceptualize nonmaterial social facts is to think of them as external to, and coercive of, psychological facts. In this way we can see that both psychological facts and *some* social facts exist within and between consciousness. Durkheim made this clear in a number of places. At one point he said of social facts, "Individual minds, forming groups by mingling and fusing, give birth to a being, *psychological if you will*, but constituting a psychic individuality of a new sort" (Durkheim, 1895/1964:103; italics added). At another point, Durkheim said, "This does not mean that they [nonmaterial social facts] are not also mental after a fashion, since they all consist of ways to thinking or behaving" (1895/1964:xlix). Thus it is best to think of nonmaterial social facts, at least in part, as mental phenomena, but mental phenomena that are external to, and coercive of, another aspect of the mental process—psychological facts. This confounds Durkheim's differentiation between sociology and psychology somewhat, but it does serve to make the differentiation more realistic and as a result more defensible. Sociology *is* concerned with mental phenomena, but they are usually of a different order from the mental concerns of psychology. Durkheim thus was arguing that sociologists are interested in norms and values, whereas psychologists are concerned with such things as human instincts.

Social facts, then, play a central role in the sociology of Emile Durkheim. A useful way of extracting the most important social facts from his work, and for analyzing his thoughts on the relationships among these phenomena, is to begin with Durkheim's efforts to organize them into *levels* of social reality. He began at the level of material social facts, not because it was the most important level to him, but because its elements often take causal priority in his theorizing. They affect nonmaterial social facts, which are the real focus of his work. (Although we will focus here on both types of social facts, we will have some things to say later about Durkheim's thoughts on the more microscopic aspects of social reality.)

The major levels of social reality (Lukes, 1972:9–10) in Durkheim's work can be depicted as follows:

A. Material Social Facts
  1. Society
  2. Structural components of society (for example, church and state)
  3. Morphological components of society (for example, population distribution, channels of communication, and housing arrangements)

B. Nonmaterial Social Facts
1. Morality
2. Collective conscience
3. Collective representations
4. Social currents

The levels within the two categories are listed in terms of descending order of generality.

It is his focus on macro-level social facts that is one of the reasons why Durkheim played a central role in the development of structural functionalism, which has a similar, macro-level orientation (see Chapter 11, on Parsons). More specifically, drawing on biology and using an organismic analogy, Durkheim saw society as composed of "organs" (social facts), or social structures, that had a variety of functions for society. Durkheim urged that we distinguish functions, or the ends served by various structures, from the factors that caused them to come into existence. Durkheim was interested in studying both the causes of social structures and the functions they perform, although he wanted to carefully differentiate between these two topics of study.

We can trace the logic of Durkheim's theory in his analysis of the development of the modern world. This is most clearly shown in one of his most important works, *The Division of Labor in Society* (Durkheim, 1893/1964).

THE DIVISION OF LABOR IN SOCIETY

Durkheim based his analysis in *The Division of Labor in Society* on his conception of two ideal types of society. The more primitive type, characterized by *mechanical solidarity*, has a relatively undifferentiated social structure, with little or no division of labor. The more modern type, characterized by *organic solidarity*, has a much greater and more refined division of labor. To Durkheim the *division of labor in society* is a material social fact that involves the degree to which tasks or responsibilities are specialized. People in primitive societies tend to occupy very general positions in which they perform a wide variety of tasks and handle a large number of responsibilities. In other words, a primitive person tended to be a jack-of-all-trades. In contrast, those who live in more modern societies occupy more specialized positions and have a much narrower range of tasks and responsibilities. For example, being a mother-housewife in primitive societies is a much less specialized position than it is in a modern society. Laundry services, diaper services, home delivery, and labor-saving devices (dishwashers, microwave ovens, Cuisinarts, and so forth) perform a number of tasks that were formerly the responsibility of the mother-housewife.

The changes in the division of labor have had enormous implications for the structure of society, and some of the more important implications are reflected in the differences between the two types of solidarity—mechanical

EMILE DURKHEIM: A Biographical Sketch

Emile Durkheim was born on April 15, 1858, in Epinal, France. He was descended from a long line of rabbis and himself studied to be a rabbi, but by the time he was in his teens, he had rejected his heritage and become an agnostic. From that time on, his lifelong interest in religion was academic rather than theological. He was dissatisfied not only with his religious training but also with his general education and its emphasis on literary and esthetic matters. He longed for schooling in scientific methods and in the moral principles needed to guide social life. He rejected a traditional academic career in philosophy and sought instead to acquire the scientific training needed to contribute to the moral guidance of society. Although he was interested in scientific sociology, there was no field of sociology at that time, so between 1882 and 1887 he taught philosophy in a number of provincial schools in the Paris area.

His appetite for science was whetted further by a trip to Germany, where he was exposed to the scientific psychology being pioneered by Wilhelm Wundt. In the years immediately after his visit to Germany, Durkheim published a good deal, basing his work, in part, on his experiences there. These publications helped him gain a position in the department of philosophy at the University of Bordeaux in 1887. There Durkheim offered the first course in social science in a French university. This was a particularly impressive accomplishment, because only a decade earlier, a furor had erupted in a French university by the mention of Auguste Comte in a student dissertation. Durkheim's main responsibility, however, was the teaching of courses in education to schoolteachers, and his most important course was in the area of moral education. His goal was to communicate a moral system to the educators, who he hoped would then pass it on to young people in an effort to help reverse the moral degeneration he saw around him in French society.

The years that followed were characterized by a series of personal successes for Durkheim. In 1893 he published his French doctoral thesis, *The Division of Labor in Society,* as well as his Latin thesis on Montesquieu. His major methodological statement, *The Rules of Sociological Method,* appeared in 1895, followed (in 1897) by his empirical application of those methods in the study *Suicide.* By 1896 he had become a full professor at Bordeaux. In 1902 he was summoned to the famous French university, the Sorbonne, and in 1906 he was named professor of the science of education, a title that was changed in 1913 to professor of the science of education *and sociology.* The other of his most famous works, *The Elementary Forms of Religious Life,* was published in 1912.

Durkheim is most often thought of today as a political conservative, and his influence within sociology certainly has been a conservative one. But in his time, he was considered a liberal, and this was exemplified by the active public role he played in the defense of Alfred Dreyfus, the Jewish army captain whose court-martial for treason was felt by many to be anti-Semitic.

and organic. In addressing the issue of solidarity, Durkheim was interested in what holds society together. A society characterized by mechanical solidarity is unified because all people are generalists. The bond among people is that they are all engaged in similar activities and have similar responsibilities. In contrast, a society characterized by organic solidarity is held together by the

Durkheim was deeply offended by the Dreyfus affair, particularly its anti-Semitism. But Durkheim did not attribute this anti-Semitism to racism among the French people. Characteristically, he saw it as a symptom of the moral sickness confronting French society as a whole. He said:

> When society undergoes suffering, it feels the need to find someone whom it can hold responsible for its sickness, on whom it can avenge its misfortunes: and those against whom public opinion already discriminates are naturally designated for this role. These are the pariahs who serve as expiatory victims. What confirms me in this interpretation is the way in which the result of Dreyfus's trial was greeted in 1894. There was a surge of joy in the boulevards. People celebrated as a triumph what should have been a cause for public mourning. At least they knew whom to blame for the economic troubles and moral distress in which they lived. The trouble came from the Jews. The charge had been officially proved. By this very fact alone, things already seemed to be getting better and people felt consoled.
>
> (Lukes, 1972:345)

Thus, Durkheim's interest in the Dreyfus affair stemmed from his deep and lifelong interest in morality and the moral crisis confronting modern society.

To Durkheim, the answer to the Dreyfus affair and crises like it lay in ending the moral disorder in society. Because that could not be done quickly or easily, Durkheim suggested more specific actions such as severe repression of those who incite hatred of others and government efforts to show the public how it is being misled. He urged people to "have the courage to proclaim aloud what they think, and to unite together in order to achieve victory in the struggle against public madness" (Lukes, 1972:347).

Durkheim's (1928/1962) interest in socialism is also taken as evidence against the idea that he was a conservative, but his kind of socialism was very different from the kind that interested Marx and his followers. In fact, Durkheim labeled Marxism as a set of "disputable and out-of-date hypotheses" (Lukes, 1972:323). To Durkheim, socialism represented a movement aimed at the moral regeneration of society through scientific morality, and he was not interested in short-term political methods or the economic aspects of socialism. He did not see the proletariat as the salvation of society, and he was greatly opposed to agitation or violence. Socialism for Durkheim was very different from what we usually think of as socialism; it simply represented a system in which the moral principles discovered by scientific sociology were to be applied.

Durkheim, as we will see throughout this book, had a profound influence on the development of sociology, but his influence was not restricted to it. Much of his impact on other fields came through the journal *L'année sociologique,* which he founded in 1898. An intellectual circle arose around the journal with Durkheim at its center. Through it, he and his ideas influenced such fields as anthropology, history, linguistics, and—somewhat ironically, considering his early attacks on the field—psychology.

Durkheim died on November 15, 1917, a celebrated figure in French intellectual circles, but it was not until over twenty years later, with the publication of Talcott Parsons's *The Structure of Social Action* (1937), that his work became a significant influence on American sociology.

differences among people, by the fact that they have different tasks and responsibilities. Because people in modern society perform a relatively narrow range of tasks, they need many other people in order to survive. The primitive family headed by father-hunter and mother-food gatherer is practically self-sufficient, but the modern family, in order to make it through the week, needs the grocer, baker, butcher, auto mechanic, teacher, police officer, and so forth. These people, in turn, need the kinds of services that others provide in order to live in the modern world. Modern society, in Durkheim's view, is thus held together by the specialization of people and their need for the services of many others. Furthermore, Durkheim was concerned not only with the specialization of individuals but also that of groups, structures, and institutions. One final difference between mechanical and organic solidarity is worth mentioning. Because people in societies characterized by mechanical solidarity are more likely to be similar to one another in terms of what they do, there is a greater likelihood of competition among them. In contrast, in societies with organic solidarity differentiation allows people to cooperate more and to all be supported by the same resource base.

Dynamic Density

The division of labor was a material social fact to Durkheim because it is the pattern of interaction in the social world. Another, and closely related, material social fact is the major causal factor in Durkheim's theory of the transition from mechanical to organic solidarity—*dynamic density*. This concept refers to the number of people in a society and the amount of interaction that occurs among them. Neither population increase nor an increase in interaction, when taken separately, is a significant factor in societal change. An increase in numbers of people *and* an increase in the interaction among them (which is dynamic density) lead to the change from mechanical to organic solidarity because together they bring about more competition for scarce resources and a more intense struggle for survival among the various parallel and similar components of primitive society. Because individuals, groups, families, tribes, and so forth perform virtually identical functions, they are likely to clash over these functions, especially if resources are scarce. The rise of the division of labor allows people and the social structures they create to complement, rather than conflict with, one another, and this, in turn, makes peaceful coexistence more likely. Furthermore, the increasing division of labor makes for greater efficiency, with the result that resources increase and more and more people can survive peacefully.

Although Durkheim was interested in explaining how the division of labor and dynamic density lead to different types of social solidarity, he was primarily interested in the impact of these material changes on, and the nature of, nonmaterial social facts in both mechanically and organically solidified societies. However, because of his image of what a *science* of sociology should be, Durkheim felt that it was impossible to study nonmaterial social facts directly. Direct consideration of nonmaterial social facts was, for him, more philosophical than sociological. In order to study nonmaterial social facts scientifically, the sociologist would have to seek and examine material social facts that reflect the nature of, and changes in, nonmaterial social facts. In *The Division of Labor in Society* it is law, and the differences between law in societies with mechanical solidarity and law in societies with organic solidarity, that plays this role.

Law

Durkheim argued that a society with mechanical solidarity is characterized by *repressive law.* Because people are very similar in this type of society, and because they tend to believe very strongly in a common morality, any offense against their shared value system is likely to be of significance to most individuals. Because most people feel the offense and believe deeply in the common morality, an offender is likely to be severely punished for any action that is considered an offense against the collective moral system. The theft of a pig must lead to the cutting off of the offender's hands; blaspheming against God or gods might well result in the removal of one's tongue. Because people are so involved in the moral system, an offense against it is likely to be met with swift, severe punishment.

In contrast, a society with organic solidarity is characterized by *restitutive law.* Instead of being severely punished for even seemingly minor offenses against the collective morality, individuals in this more modern type of society are likely simply to be asked to comply with the law or to repay—make restitution to—those who have been harmed by their actions. Although some repressive law continues to exist in a society with organic solidarity (for example, the death penalty), restitutive law is more characteristic. There is little or no powerful and coercive common morality; the vast majority of people do not react emotionally to a breach of the law. The monitoring of repressive law is largely in the hands of the masses in a society with mechanical solidarity, but the maintenance of restitutive law is primarily the responsibility of specialized agencies (for example, the police and the courts). This is consistent with the increased division of labor in a society with organic solidarity.

Changes in a material social fact like the law are, in Durkheim's theoretical system, merely reflections of changes in the more crucial elements of his sociology—nonmaterial social facts such as morality, collective conscience, collective representations, social currents, and, most questionably from a modern sociological perspective, the group mind. (All these concepts will be discussed below.)

At the most general and all-inclusive level, Durkheim was a sociologist of morality. Indeed, Ernest Wallwork (1972:182) argued that Durkheim's sociology is merely a by-product of his concern with moral issues. That is, Durkheim's interest in the moral problems of his day led him as a sociologist to devote most of his attention to the moral elements of social life. At its most basic level, Durkheim's great concern was with the declining strength of the common morality in the modern world. In Durkheim's view, people were in danger of a "pathological" loosening of moral bonds. These moral bonds were important to Durkheim, for without them the individual would be enslaved by ever-expanding and insatiable passions. People would be impelled by their passions into a mad search for gratification, but each new gratification would lead only to more and more needs. Durkheim held the seemingly paradoxical view that the individual needs morality and external control in order to be free. This is a curious definition of freedom, but it is the position that Durkheim took.

Anomie

Many of the problems that occupied Durkheim stem from his concern with the decline of the common morality. In the concept of *anomie*, Durkheim best manifested his concern with the problems of a weakened common morality (Hilbert, 1986). Individuals are said to be confronted with anomie when they are not faced with sufficient moral constraint, that is, when they do not have a clear concept of what is and what is not proper and acceptable behavior.

The central "pathology" in modern society was, in Durkheim's view, the *anomic* division of labor. By thinking of anomie as a pathology, Durkheim manifested his belief that the problems of the modern world can be "cured." Durkheim believed that the structural division of labor in modern society is a source of cohesion that compensates for the declining strength of the collective morality. However, the thrust of his argument is that the division of labor cannot entirely make up for the loosening of the common morality, with the result that anomie is a pathology associated with the rise of organic solidarity. Individuals can become isolated and be cut adrift in their highly specialized activities. They can more easily cease to feel a common bond with those who work and live around them. But it is important to remember that this is viewed by Durkheim as an abnormal situation, because only in unusual circumstances does the modern division of labor reduce people to isolated and meaningless tasks and positions. The concept of anomie can be found not only in *The Division of Labor* but also in *Suicide* (Durkheim, 1897/1951) as one of the major types of suicide. Anomic suicide occurs because of the decline in collective morality and the lack of sufficient external regulation of the individual to restrain his or her passions.

Collective Conscience

Durkheim attempted to deal with his interest in common morality in various ways and with different concepts. In his early efforts to deal with this issue, Durkheim developed the idea of the *collective conscience*, which he characterized in *The Division of Labor in Society* in the following way:

> The totality of beliefs and sentiments common to average citizens of the same society forms a determinate system which has its own life; one may call it the *collective* or *common conscience*. . . . It is, thus, an entirely different thing from particular consciences, although it can be realized only through them.
>
> (Durkheim, 1893/1964:79–80)

Several points are worth underscoring in this definition, given our interest in the collective conscience as an example of a nonmaterial social fact. First, it is clear that Durkheim thought of the collective conscience as occurring throughout a given society when he wrote of the "totality" of people's beliefs and sentiments. Second, Durkheim clearly conceived of the collective conscience as being an independent, determinate cultural system. Although he held such views of the collective conscience, Durkheim also wrote of its being "realized" through individual consciousness. (That Durkheim did *not* conceive of the collective conscience as totally independent of individual consciousness will be important when we examine the charge that Durkheim holds a group-mind concept.)

The concept of the collective conscience allows us to return to Durkheim's analysis, in *The Division of Labor*, of material social facts and their relationship to changes in the common morality. The logic of his argument is that the increasing division of labor (brought on by the increasing dynamic density) is causing a diminution of the collective conscience. The collective conscience is of much less significance in a society with organic solidarity than it is in a society with mechanical solidarity. People in modern society are more likely to be held together by the division of labor and the resulting need for the functions performed by others than they are by a shared and powerful collective conscience. Anthony Giddens (1972; see also Pope and Johnson, 1983) performed a useful service by pointing out that the collective conscience in the two types of society can be differentiated on four dimensions—volume, intensity, rigidity, and content. *Volume* refers to the number of people enveloped by the collective conscience; *intensity* to how deeply the individuals feel about it; *rigidity* to how clearly it is defined; and *content* to the form that the collective conscience takes in the two polar types of society. In a society characterized by mechanical solidarity, the collective conscience covers virtually the entire society and all its members; it is believed in with great intensity (as reflected, for one thing, by the use of repressive sanctions when it is violated); it is extremely rigid; and its content is highly religious in character. In a society with organic solidarity, the collective conscience is much more limited in its domain and in the number of people enveloped by it; it is adhered to with much less intensity (as reflected in the substitution of restitutive for repressive laws); it is not very rigid; and its content is best described by the phrase "moral individualism," or the elevation of the importance of the individual to a moral precept.

Collective Representations

The idea of the collective conscience, while useful to Durkheim, clearly is very broad and amorphous. Durkheim's dissatisfaction with the character of the concept of the collective conscience led him to abandon it progressively in his later work in favor of the much more specific concept of collective representations. *Collective representations* may be seen as specific states, or substrata, of the collective conscience (Lukes, 1972). In contemporary terms, we may think of collective representations as the norms and values of specific collectivities such as the family, occupation, state, and educational and religious institutions. The concept of collective representations can be used both broadly and specifically, but the critical point is that it allowed Durkheim to conceptualize nonmaterial social facts in a narrower way than the all-encompassing notion of the collective conscience. Despite their greater specificity, collective representations are *not* reducible to the level of individual consciousness: *"Representations collectives* result from the substratum of associated individuals . . . but they have *sui generis* characteristics" (Durkheim, cited in Lukes, 1972:7). The Latin term *sui generis* means unique. When Durkheim used this term to refer to the structure of collective representations, he was saying that their unique character is not reducible to individual consciousness. This places them squarely within the realm of nonmaterial social facts. They transcend the individual because they do not depend on any particular individual for their existence. They are also independent of individuals in the sense that their temporal span is greater than the lifetime of any individual. Collective representations are a central component of Durkheim's system of nonmaterial social facts.

SUICIDE AND SOCIAL CURRENTS

Durkheim offered an even more specific (and more dynamic) and less crystallized concept that is also a nonmaterial social fact—*social currents*. These were defined by Durkheim as nonmaterial social facts "which have the same objectivity and the same ascendancy over the individual" as the social facts discussed above, but "without such crystallized form" (1895/1964:4). He gave as examples "the great movements of enthusiasm, indignation, and pity in a crowd" (Durkheim, 1895/1964:4). Although social currents are less concrete than other social facts, they are nevertheless social facts, as Durkheim made clear when he said, "They come to each one of us from without and can carry us away in spite of ourselves" (1895/1964:4).

Durkheim explicated the idea of social currents in *The Rules of Sociological Method* (1895/1964), but he used it as his major explanatory variable in an empirical study that became a model for the development of American empirical research (Selvin, 1958). In fact, the research reported in *Suicide* (1897/1951) can be seen as an effort to use the ideas developed in *The Rules* in an empirical study of a specific social phenomenon—suicide. In *Suicide* he demonstrated that social facts, in particular social currents, are external to, and coercive of, the individual. Durkheim chose to study suicide because it is a relatively concrete and specific phenomenon. There were relatively good data available on suicide, and above all it is generally considered to be one of the most private and personal of acts. Durkheim believed that if he could show that sociology had a role to play in explaining such a seemingly individualistic act as suicide, it would be relatively easy to extend sociology's domain to phenomena that are much more readily seen as open to sociological analysis. Finally, Durkheim chose to study suicide because if the intellectual community could be convinced of his case in the study of this phenomenon, then sociology would have a reasonable chance of gaining recognition in the academic world.

As a sociologist, Durkheim was not concerned with studying why any specific individual committed suicide. That was to be left to the psychologist. Instead, Durkheim was interested in explaining differences in suicide *rates*, that is, he was interested in why one group had a higher rate of suicide than another. Durkheim tended to assume that biological, psychological, and social-psychological factors remain essentially constant from one group to another or from one time period to another. If there is variation in suicide rates from one group to another or from one time period to another, Durkheim assumed that the difference would be due to variations in sociological factors, in particular, social currents.

Committed as he was to empirical research, Durkheim was not content simply to dismiss other possible causes of differences in suicide rates; instead he tested them empirically. He began *Suicide* with a series of alternative ideas about the causes of suicide. Among these are individual psychopathology, race, heredity, and climate. Although Durkheim marshaled a wide range of facts to reject each of these as crucial to differences in suicide rates, his clearest argument, and the one that was most consistent with his overall perspective, was on the relevance of racial factors to the differences. One of the reasons that race was rejected is that suicide rates varied among groups *within* the same race. If race were a significant cause of differences in suicide rates, then we would assume that it would have a similar impact on the various subgroups. Another piece of evidence against race as a significant cause of variations in rates is the change in rates for a given race when it moves from one society to another. If race were a relevant social fact, it should have the same effect in different societies. Although Durkheim's argument is not powerful here, and is even weaker on the other factors that he rejected, this does give us a feel for the nature of Durkheim's approach to the problem of empirically dismissing what he considered extraneous factors so that he could get to what he thought of as the most important causal variables.

In addition to rejecting the factors discussed above, Durkheim examined and rejected the imitation theory associated with the early French social psychologist Gabriel Tarde (1843–1904). The theory of imitation argues that people commit suicide (and engage in a wide range of other actions) because they are imitating the actions of others who have committed suicide. This social-psychological approach to sociological thinking is foreign to Durkheim's focus on social facts. As a result, Durkheim took pains to reject it. For example, Durkheim reasoned that if imitation were truly important, we should find that the nations that border on a country with a high suicide rate would themselves have high rates. He looked at the data on the significance of this geographical factor and concluded that no such relationship existed. Durkheim admitted that some individual suicides may be the result of imitation, but it is such a minor factor that it has no significant effect on the overall suicide rate. In the end, Durkheim rejected imitation as a significant factor because of his view that one social fact could only be the cause of another social fact. Because imitation is a social-psychological variable, it cannot, in his system, serve as a significant cause of differences in social suicide rates. As Durkheim put it, "The social suicide-rate can be explained only sociologically" (1897/1951:299).

To Durkheim, the critical factors in changes in suicide rates were to be found in differences at the level of social facts. Of course, there are two types of social facts—material and nonmaterial. As usual, material social facts occupy the position of causal priority but not of causal primacy. For example, Durkheim looked at the significance of dynamic density for differences in suicide rates but found that its effect is only indirect. But differences in dynamic density (and other material social facts) do have an effect on differences in nonmaterial social facts, and these differences have a direct effect on suicide rates. Durkheim was making two related arguments. On the one hand, he was arguing that different collectivities have different collective consciences and collective representations. These, in turn, produce different social currents, which have differential effects on suicide rates. One way to study suicide is to compare different societies or other types of collectivities. On the other hand, Durkheim was arguing that changes in the collective conscience lead to changes in social currents, which, in turn, lead to changes in suicide rates. This leads to the historical study of changes in suicide rates within a given collectivity. In either case, cross-culturally or historically, the logic of the argument is essentially the same: differences or changes in the collective conscience lead to differences or changes in social currents, and these, in turn, lead to differences or changes in suicide rates. In other words, changes in suicide rates are due to changes in social facts, primarily social currents. Durkheim was quite clear on the crucial role played by social currents in the etiology of suicide:

> Each social group has a collective inclination for the act, quite its own, and the source of all individual inclination rather than their result. It is made up of *currents of egoism, altruism or anomy* running through . . . society. . . . These tendencies of the whole social body, by affecting individuals, cause them to commit suicide.
>
>   (Durkheim, 1897/1951:299–300; italics added)

The Four Types of Suicide

Durkheim's theory of suicide, and the structure of his sociological reasoning, can be seen more clearly if we examine each of his four types of suicide—egoistic, altruistic, anomic, and fatalistic. Durkheim linked each of the types of suicide to the degree of integration into, or regulation by, society. *Integration* refers to the degree to which collective sentiments are shared. Altruistic suicide is associated with a high degree of integration and egoistic suicide with a low degree of integration. *Regulation* refers to the degree of external constraint on people. Fatalistic suicide is associated with high regulation, anomic suicide with low regulation. Whitney Pope (1976:12–13) offered a very useful summary of the four types of suicide discussed by Durkheim. He did this by interrelating high and low degrees of integration and regulation in the following way:

Integration	Low	⟶	Egoistic suicide _—weak c.c._
	High	⟶	Altruistic suicide
Regulation	Low	⟶	Anomic suicide
	High	⟶	Fatalistic suicide

Egoistic Suicide   High rates of _egoistic suicide_ are likely to be found in those societies, collectivities, or groups in which the individual is not well integrated into the larger social unit. This lack of integration leads to a sense of meaninglessness among individuals. Societies with a strong collective conscience and the protective, enveloping social currents that flow from it are likely to prevent the widespread occurrence of egoistic suicide by, among other things, providing people with a sense of the broader meaning of their lives. When these social currents are weak, individuals are able rather easily to surmount the collective conscience and do as they wish. In large-scale social units with a weak collective conscience, individuals are left to pursue their private interests in whatever way they wish. Such unrestrained egoism is likely to lead to considerable personal dissatisfaction, because all needs cannot be fulfilled, and those that are fulfilled simply lead to the generation of more and more needs and, ultimately, to dissatisfaction—and, for some, to suicide (Breault, 1986). However, strongly integrated families, religious groups, and polities act as agents of a strong collective conscience and discourage suicide. Here is the way Durkheim puts it in terms of religious groups:

> Religion protects man against the desire for self-destruction. . . . What constitutes religion is the existence of a certain number of beliefs and practices common to all the faithful, traditional and thus obligatory. The more numerous and strong these collective states of mind are, the stronger the integration of the religious community, also the _greater its preservative_ value.
>
> (Durkheim, 1897/1951:170; italics added)

The disintegration of society produces distinctive social currents, and these are the principal causes of differences in suicide rates. For example, Durkheim talked of societal disintegration leading to "currents of depression and disillusionment" (1897/1951:214). The moral disintegration of society predisposes the individual to commit suicide, but the currents of depression must also be there to produce differences in rates of egoistic suicide. Interestingly, Durkheim was here reaffirming the importance of social forces, even in the case of egoistic suicide, where the individual might be thought to be free of social constraints. Actors are _never_ free of the force of the collectivity: "However individualized a man may be, there is always something collective remaining—the very depression and melancholy resulting from this same exaggerated individualism. He effects communion through sadness when he no longer has anything else with which to achieve it" (Durkheim, 1897/1951:214). The case of egoistic suicide indicates that in even the most individualistic, most private of acts, social facts are the key determinant.

Altruistic Suicide   The second type of suicide discussed by Durkheim is altruistic suicide. Whereas egoistic suicide is more likely to occur when social integration is too weak, *altruistic suicide* is more likely when "social integration is too strong" (Durkheim, 1897/1951:217). The individual is literally forced into committing suicide.

One notorious example of altruistic suicide was the mass suicide of the followers of the Reverend Jim Jones in Jonestown, Guyana. They knowingly took a poisoned drink and in some cases had their children drink it as well. They were clearly committing suicide because they were pushed, either force-fully or gently, into giving their lives for the tightly integrated society of Jones's fanatical followers. More generally, those who commit altruistic sui-cide do so because they feel that it is their duty to do so.

As was the case with egoistic suicide, the degree of integration (in this case, a high degree) is not the direct cause of altruistic suicide. Rather, different degrees of integration produce different social currents, and these different currents affect suicide rates. As with egoistic suicide, Durkheim saw melan-choly social currents as the cause of high rates of altruistic suicide. Whereas higher rates of egoistic suicide stem from "incurable weariness and sad depression," the increased likelihood of altruistic suicide "springs from hope, for it depends on the belief in beautiful perspectives beyond this life" (Durk-heim, 1897/1951:225).

Anomic Suicide   The final major form of suicide discussed by Durkheim is *anomic suicide,* which is more likely to occur when the regulative powers of society are disrupted. Such disruptions are likely to leave individuals dissat-isfied because there is little control over their passions (see below), which are free to run wild in an insatiable race for gratification. Rates of anomic suicide are likely to rise whether the nature of the disruption is positive (for example, an economic boom) or negative (an economic depression). Either type of dis-ruption renders the collectivity temporarily incapable of exercising its author-ity over individuals. Such changes put people in new situations in which the old norms no longer apply but new ones have yet to develop. Periods of disruption unleash currents of anomie—moods of rootlessness and normless-ness—and these currents lead to an increase in rates of anomic suicide. This is relatively easy to envisage in the case of a depression. The closing of a factory due to an economic depression may lead to the loss of a job, with the result that the individual is cut adrift from the regulative effect that both the company and the job may have had. Being cut off from these structures or others (for example, family, religion, and state) can leave the individual highly vulnerable to the effects of currents of anomie. Somewhat more difficult to imagine is the effect of an economic boom. In this case, it might be argued that sudden success leads individuals away from the traditional structures in which they are embedded. Economic success may lead individuals to quit their jobs, move to a new community, perhaps even find a new spouse. All these changes disrupt the regulative effect of extant structures and leave the individual in boom periods vulnerable to anomic social currents.

The increases in rates of anomic suicide during periods of deregulation of social life are consistent with Durkheim's views on the pernicious effect of individual passions when freed of external constraint. People thus freed will become slaves to their passions and as a result, in Durkheim's view, commit a wide range of destructive acts, including killing themselves in greater numbers than they ordinarily would.

Fatalistic Suicide   There is a little mentioned fourth type of suicide—fatalistic—that Durkheim discussed only in a footnote in *Suicide*. Whereas anomic suicide is more likely to occur in situations in which regulation is too weak, *fatalistic suicide* is more likely to occur when regulation is excessive. Durkheim described those who are more likely to commit fatalistic suicide as "persons with futures pitilessly blocked and passions violently choked by oppressive discipline" (1897/1951:276). The classic example is the slave who takes his own life because of the hopelessness associated with the oppressive regulation of his every action. Too much regulation—oppression—unleashes currents of melancholy that, in turn, cause a rise in the rate of fatalistic suicide.

A Group Mind?

Given the emphasis on norms, values, and culture in contemporary sociology, we have little difficulty accepting Durkheim's interest in nonmaterial social facts. It is true that the concept of social currents does cause us a few problems. Particularly troublesome is the idea of a set of independent social currents "coursing" through the social world as if they are somehow suspended in a social void. This problem has led many to accuse Durkheim of having a group-mind orientation (Catlin, 1964:xxii–xxiii; see also Pope, 1976:192–194). Those who accuse Durkheim of having such a perspective argue that he accorded nonmaterial social facts an autonomous existence, separate from actors. But cultural phenomena cannot float by themselves in a social void, and Durkheim was well aware of this.[1]

As a specific component of the supposed group mind, the notion of social currents can be defended as an unfortunately named, but otherwise now widely accepted, part of the cultural world. In more contemporary terms, social currents can be viewed as sets of meanings that are shared intersubjectively by members of a collectivity. As such, they cannot be found in the mind

---

[1] Some Durkheimians would argue that Durkheim did offer, in many places, ideas that reflect a belief in something like a group mind.

of any given individual, but they are mentally shared by the set of actors in the collectivity. To take one of Durkheim's examples, a social current of "languorous melancholy" cannot be deduced from any one individual, but it can be derived from the mood of a significant segment of the total population. These collective "moods," or social currents, vary from one collectivity to another, with the result that there is variation in the rates of certain behaviors, including suicide. Similarly, as these collective "moods" change, the rates of suicide also may change (Douglas, 1967:42).

In defense of Durkheim at a more general level, it must be argued that Durkheim had a very modern conception of nonmaterial social facts that encompasses what we now call norms, values, culture, and a variety of shared social-psychological phenomena. Such a conception is not susceptible to the group-mind charge, but its defense is complicated, because in order to lay out a separate domain for sociology, Durkheim often made some highly exaggerated claims about social facts. As we saw earlier in this chapter, Durkheim often talked as if social facts were rigidly separated from psychological facts, and such a separation would be supportive of the group-mind argument. However, in other places Durkheim admitted that this was an artificial dichotomy; in other words, nonmaterial social facts are firmly anchored in the mental processes of individuals (1893/1964:350; see also Lukes, 1972:16).

Durkheim put to rest once and for all the group-mind thesis:

> Either the *collective conscience* floats like a void, a kind of indescribable absolute, or else it is connected to the rest of the world by a substratum upon which, consequently, it is dependent. Moreover, what can this substratum be made up of, if it is not the members of society as they are combined socially?
>
> (Durkheim, cited in Giddens, 1972:159)

It seems that Durkheim, outside of some outrageous arguments made to justify a niche for the fledgling sociology, offered an eminently reasonable position on nonmaterial social facts. Durkheim began with an interest in this level, retained it throughout his career, and, if anything, grew even more interested in it in his later years. This increasing concern can best be seen in *The Elementary Forms of Religious Life*, published in 1912.

RELIGION

As we have seen, Durkheim felt the need to focus on material manifestations of nonmaterial social facts (for example, law in *The Division of Labor* and suicide rates in *Suicide*). But in *The Elementary Forms of Religious Life*, Durkheim felt comfortable enough to address nonmaterial social facts, in particular religion, more directly.[2] Religion is, in fact, the ultimate nonmaterial social fact, and an examination of it allowed him to shed new light on this entire aspect of his theoretical system. Religion has what Durkheim calls a "dynamogenic"

---

[2] Alexander (1988:11) argues that it is this work that forms the basis of renewed contemporary interest in cultural studies. Collins (1988b:108) sees it as his "most important book."

quality; that is, it has the capacity not only to dominate individuals but also to elevate them above their ordinary abilities and capacities (R. Jones, 1986).

Although the research reported in *The Elementary Forms* is not Durkheim's own, he felt it necessary, given his commitment to empirical science, to embed his thinking on religion in published data. The major sources of his data were studies of a primitive Australian tribe, the Arunta. Durkheim felt it important to study religion within such a primitive setting for several reasons. For one thing, he believed that it is much easier to gain insight into the essential nature of religion in a primitive setting than in more modern society. Religious forms in primitive society could be "shown in all their nudity," and it would require "only the slightest effort to lay them open" (Durkheim, 1912/1965:18). Second, primitive religions' ideological systems are less well developed than those of modern religions, with the result that there is less obfuscation. As Durkheim put it, "That which is accessory or secondary . . . has not yet come to hide the principal elements. All is reduced to that which is indispensable, to that without which there could be no religion" (1912/1965:18). Third, whereas religion in modern society takes diverse forms, in primitive society there is "intellectual and moral conformity" (Durkheim, 1912/1965:18). As a result, religion can be studied in primitive society in its most pristine form. Finally, although Durkheim studied primitive religion, it was not because of his interest in that religious form per se. Rather, he studied it in order "to lead to an understanding of the religious nature of man, that is to say, to show us an essential and permanent aspect of humanity" (Durkheim, 1912/1965:13). More specifically, Durkheim examined primitive religion to shed light on religion in modern society.

Given the uniform and ubiquitous character of religion in primitive societies, we may equate that religion with the collective conscience. That is, religion in primitive society is an all-encompassing collective morality. But as society develops and grows more specialized, religion comes to occupy an increasingly narrow domain. Instead of being the collective conscience in modern society, religion becomes simply one of a number of collective representations. Although it expresses some collective sentiments, other institutions (for example, law and science) come to express other aspects of the collective morality. Although Durkheim recognized that religion per se comes to occupy an ever narrower domain, he also contended that most, if not all, of the various collective representations of modern society have their origin in the all-encompassing religion of primitive society.

Sacred and Profane

The ultimate question for Durkheim was the source of modern religion. Because specialization and the ideological smoke screen make it impossible to study directly the roots of religion in modern society, Durkheim addressed the issue in the context of primitive society. The question is: Where does primitive (and modern) religion come from? Operating from his basic methodological position that only one social fact can cause another social fact, Durkheim concluded that society is the source of all religion. Society (through individuals) creates religion by defining certain phenomena as sacred and others as profane. Those aspects of social reality that are defined as *sacred*—that is, that are set apart and deemed forbidden—form the essence of religion. The rest are defined as *profane*—the everyday, the commonplace, the utilitarian, the mundane aspects of life. The sacred brings out an attitude of reverence, respect, mystery, awe, and honor. The respect accorded to certain phenomena transforms them from the profane to the sacred.

The differentiation between the sacred and the profane, and the elevation of some aspects of social life to the sacred level, are necessary but not sufficient conditions for the development of religion. Three other conditions are needed. First, there must be the development of a set of religious beliefs. These *beliefs* are "the representations which express the nature of sacred things and the relations which they sustain, either with each other or with profane things" (Durkheim, 1912/1965:56). Second, a set of religious *rites* is necessary. These are "the rules of conduct which prescribe how a man should comport himself in the presence of these sacred objects" (Durkheim, 1912/1965:56). Finally, a religion requires a *church*, or a single overarching moral community. The interrelationships among the sacred, beliefs, rites, and church led Durkheim to the following definition of a religion: "*A religion is a unified system of beliefs and practices which unite into one single moral community called a Church, all those who adhere to them*" (1912/1965:62).

Totemism

Durkheim's view that society is the source of religion shaped his examination of totemism among the Australian Arunta. *Totemism* is a religious system in which certain things, particularly animals and plants, come to be regarded as sacred and as emblems of the clan. Durkheim viewed totemism as the simplest, most primitive form of religion. It is paralleled by a similarly primitive form of social organization, the *clan*. If Durkheim could have shown that the clan is the source of totemism, he could have demonstrated his argument that society is at the root of religion. Here is the way that Durkheim made this argument:

> A religion so closely connected to a social system surpassing all others in simplicity may well be regarded as the most elementary religion we can possibly know. If we succeed in discovering the origins of the beliefs which we have just analyzed, we shall very probably discover at the same time the causes leading to the rise of the religious sentiment in humanity.
>
> (Durkheim, 1912/1965:195)

Although a clan may have a large number of totems, Durkheim was not inclined to view these as a series of separate, fragmentary beliefs about specific animals or plants. Instead, he tended to view them as an interrelated set of ideas that give the clan a more or less complete representation of the world. The plant or animal is not the source of totemism; it merely represents that source. The totems are the material representations of the immaterial force that is at their base. And that immaterial force is none other than the now familiar collective conscience of society:

> Totemism is the religion, not of such and such animals or men or images, but of an anonymous and impersonal force, found in each of these beings but not to be confounded with any of them. . . . Individuals die, generations pass and are replaced by others; but this force always remains actual, living and the same. It animates the generations of today as it animated those of yesterday and as it will those of tomorrow.
>
> (Durkheim, 1912/1965:217)

Totemism, and more generally religion, is derived from the collective morality and becomes itself an impersonal force. It is not simply a series of mythical animals, plants, personalities, spirits, or gods.

everything comes from society

Collective Effervescence

The collective conscience is the source of religion, but where does the collective conscience itself come from? In Durkheim's view, it comes from only one source—society. In the primitive case examined by Durkheim, this meant that the clan is the ultimate source of religion. Durkheim was quite explicit on this point: "Religious force is nothing other than the collective and anonymous force of the clan" (1912/1965:253). Although we may agree that the clan is the source of totemism, the question remains: How does the clan create totemism? The answer lies in a central but little discussed component of Durkheim's conceptual arsenal—*collective effervescence*.

HIST MOVE = CHANGE IN STRUCT.

The notion of collective effervescence is not well spelled out in any of Durkheim's works, including *The Elementary Forms of Religious Life*. He seemed to have in mind, in a general sense, the great moments in history when a collectivity is able to achieve a new and heightened level of collective exaltation that in turn can lead to great changes in the structure of society. The Reformation and the Renaissance would be examples of historical periods when collective effervescence had a marked effect on the structure of society. Durkheim also argued that it is out of collective effervescence that religion arises: "It is in the midst of these effervescent social environments and out of this effervescence itself that the religious idea seems to be born" (1912/1965:250). During periods of collective effervescence, the clan members create totemism.

In sum, totemism is the symbolic representation of the collective conscience, and the collective conscience, in turn, is derived from society. Therefore, society is the source of the collective conscience, religion, the concept of God, and ultimately everything that is sacred (as opposed to profane). In a very real sense, then, we can argue that the sacred (and ultimately God, as something sacred) and society are one and the same. This is fairly clear-cut in primitive society. It remains true today, even though the relationship is greatly obscured by the complexities of modern society.

SOCIAL REFORMISM

We have now worked our way through most of Durkheim's most important types of nonmaterial social facts—morality, collective conscience, collective representations, social currents, and religion. These concepts were at the center of Durkheim's thinking from the beginning of his career. Earlier we touched on the significance of material social facts in Durkheim's work, but it is clear that they were not nearly as important to him as nonmaterial social facts. They occupy the role of either causal priorities to nonmaterial social facts (for example, dynamic density in the *The Division of Labor*) or objective indices of nonmaterial social facts (for example, law in *The Division of Labor*). There is still another significant part that material social facts play in Durkheim's system— as structural solutions to the moral problems of our times.

Durkheim was a social reformer who saw problems in modern society as temporary aberrations and not as inherent difficulties (Fenton, 1984:45). In taking this position, he stood in opposition to both the conservatives and the radicals of his day. Conservatives like Louis de Bonald and Joseph de Maistre saw no hope in modern society and sought instead a return to a more primitive type of existence. Radicals like the Marxists of Durkheim's time agreed that the world could not be reformed, but they hoped that a revolution would bring into existence socialism and communism. In contrast, Durkheim, following up on his analogy between social and biological processes, argued that the problems of the day were "pathologies" that could be "cured" by the "social physician" who recognized the moral nature of the modern world's problems and undertook structural reforms to alleviate them. For example, in *The Division of Labor*, Durkheim talked of three abnormal, or pathological, forms of the division of labor. These are caused by temporary or transient forces and are not inherent in modern society. The pathologies Durkheim described are anomie, inequality in the structure of the work world (the wrong people in the wrong positions), and inadequate organization (incoherence) in the work world.

Durkheim was a reformist, not a radical or a revolutionary. Thus, when he devoted a book to socialism, it was to study it as a social fact, not to outline a revolutionary doctrine (Durkheim, 1928/1962). He was quite explicit about his political position in discussing his interest in the study of social facts:

> Our reasoning is not at all revolutionary. We are even, in a sense, essentially conservative, since we deal with social facts as such, recognize their flexibility, but conceive them as deterministic rather than arbitrary. How much more dangerous is the doctrine which sees in social phenomena only the results of unrestrained

manipulation, which can in an instant, by a simple dialectical artifice, be completely upset.

(Durkheim, 1895/1964:xxxviii–xxxix)[3]

More specific to a communist revolution, Durkheim said:

Let us suppose that by a miracle the whole system of property is entirely transformed overnight and that on the collectivist formula the means of production are taken out of the hands of the individual and made over absolutely to collective ownership. All the problems around us that we are debating today will still persist in their entirety.

(Durkheim, 1957:30)

Occupational Associations

OWNERS, MANAGER, WORKERS

The major reform that Durkheim proposed for social pathologies was the development of occupational associations. In looking at the organizations of his time, Durkheim did not believe that there was a basic conflict of interest among the various types of people found within them—owners, managers, and workers. In this, of course, he was taking a position diametrically opposed to that of Marx, who saw an essential conflict of interest between the owners and the workers. Durkheim believed that such a clash was occurring at that time because the various people involved lacked a common morality and that the lack of morality was traceable to the lack of an integrative structure. He suggested that the structure needed to provide this integrative morality was the occupational association, which would encompass "all the agents of the same industry united and organized into a single group" (Durkheim, 1893/1964:5). Such an organization was deemed to be different from, and superior to, such organizations as labor unions and employer associations, which in Durkheim's view served only to intensify the differences between owners, managers, and workers. Involved in a common organization, people in these categories would recognize their common interests as well as their common need for an integrative moral system. That moral system, with its derived rules and laws, would serve to counteract the tendency toward atomization in modern society as well as help stop the decline in significance of collective morality.

Cult of the Individual

In the end, structural reform was subordinated in Durkheim's mind to changes in the collective morality. He believed that the essential problems of modern society were moral in nature and that the only real solution lay in reinforcing the strength of the collective morality. Although Durkheim rec-

---

[3] Not only was Durkheim treating us to his own conservative politics, but he also was attacking the revolutionary theories of Marx and Marx's followers.

NORMS

ognized that there was no returning to the powerful collective conscience of societies characterized by mechanical solidarity, he felt that a modern, although weakened, version of it was emerging. He labeled the modern form of the collective conscience the *cult of the individual*. This was a curious concept for Durkheim, because it seems to fuse the seemingly antagonistic forces of morality and individualism. Embedded in this concept is the idea that individualism is becoming the moral system of modern society. Elevated to the status of a moral system, individualism was acceptable to Durkheim. What he continued to oppose was egoism, because this is individualism without a collective base; it is rampant hedonism. Presumably, by following a morality of individualism, the actor would be able to keep his or her passions in check. Ironically, paradoxically, and ultimately a bit unsatisfactorily, Durkheim proposed the cult of the individual as the solution to modern egoism. It appears that Durkheim came to recognize that there was no stemming the tide of individualism in modern society, so rather than continue to fight it, he made the best of a bad situation (judged by his moral principles) by elevating at least some forms of individualism to the level of a moral system. One of the many problems with this view is the virtual impossibility of differentiating in real life between actions based on moral individualism and those based on egoism. However, Durkheim might argue that it is possible to distinguish between people guided by a morality which requires them to give due recognition to the inherent dignity, rights, and freedom of the individual and people who are simply acting to promote their own egotistically defined self-interest.

this is OK when moral

THE ACTOR IN DURKHEIM'S THOUGHT

The bulk of this chapter is devoted to Durkheim's concern with social facts. However, Durkheim had insights into the microscopic aspects of social reality, and we will deal with some of them here. The reader should keep in mind that much of what Durkheim offered at this level was derived from his overriding interest in social facts and cannot really be separated from it.

Durkheim's often overly zealous arguments for sociology and against psychology have led many to argue that he had little to offer on the human actor and the nature of action (Lukes, 1972:228). Many contend that Durkheim had little to say about individual consciousness (Nisbet, 1974:32; Pope, 1975:368, 374), because he did not feel that it was amenable to scientific analysis. As Robert Nisbet put it:

> We cannot go to internal states of mind. . . . Consciousness, though real enough, will not serve the austere tests of scientific method. If we are to study mere phenomena in an objective fashion, we must substitute for the internal fact of consciousness an external index which symbolizes it and study the former in light of the latter.
>
> (Nisbet, 1974:52; see also Pope, 1976:10–11)

Although there is some truth to this claim, it grossly exaggerates the reality to be found in Durkheim's work. Although Durkheim may have made statements against the study of consciousness, he did deal with it in a variety of places and ways. Nevertheless, it is true that he treated the actor, and the actor's mental processes, as secondary factors, or more commonly as dependent variables to be explained by the independent and focal factors—social facts.

Durkheim was critical of dealing with consciousness, but he demonstrated his awareness of the significance of mental processes and even integrated them directly into his work. Although he made a similar point in several places (for example, Durkheim, 1897/1951:315), the following is Durkheim's clearest statement of his interest in mental processes:

> In general, we hold that sociology has not completely achieved its task so long as it has not penetrated into the mind . . . of the individual in order to relate the institutions it seeks to explain to their psychological conditions. . . . Man is for us less a point of departure than a point of arrival.
>
> (Durkheim, cited in Lukes, 1972:498–499)

It appears that Durkheim focused on "external" facts—suicide rates, laws, and so forth—because they are open to scientific analysis, but he did not deem such a macroscopic focus sufficient in itself. The ultimate goal was to integrate an understanding of mental processes into his theoretical system. This is manifest, for example, in his work on suicide, in which social causes are linked to subjective states. Even though he never quite achieved an adequate integration, he did address the issue of consciousness in several different ways.

Assumptions about Human Nature

We may gain insight into Durkheim's views on consciousness by examining his assumptions about human nature. Despite having made a number of crucial assumptions about human nature, Durkheim denied that he had done so. He argued that he did *not* begin by postulating a certain conception of human nature in order to deduce a sociology from it. Instead, he said that it was from sociology that he sought an increasing understanding of human nature. However, Durkheim may have been less than honest with us, and perhaps even with himself.

Durkheim did in fact identify a number of components of human nature. At a basic level, he accepted the existence of biological drives. But of greater significance to sociology, he acknowledged the importance of social feelings, including "love, affection, sympathetic concern, and associated phenomena" (Wallwork, 1972:28). Durkheim viewed people as naturally social, for "if men were not naturally inclined toward their fellows, the whole fabric of society, its customs and institutions, would never arise" (Wallwork, 1972:29–30). However, these sentiments did not play an active role in his sociology, and he therefore relegated them to psychology. Another of Durkheim's basic assumptions, which received only scant attention from him, is the idea that people are able to think: "Men differ from animals, Durkheim contends, precisely because images and ideas intervene between innate inclinations and behavior" (Wallwork, 1972:30).

Whereas the preceding are of marginal significance to his work, another of Durkheim's assumptions about human nature—one that we have already encountered—may be viewed as the basis of his entire sociology. That assumption is that people are endowed with a variety of egoistic drives that, if unbridled, constitute a threat to themselves as well as to society. To Durkheim, people possess an array of passions. If these passions are unrestrained, they multiply to the point where the individual is enslaved by them. This led Durkheim to his curious (on the surface) definition of *freedom* as external control over passions. People are free when their passions are constrained by external forces, and the most general and most important of these forces is the common morality. It can be argued that Durkheim's entire theoretical edifice, especially his emphasis on collective morality, was erected on this basic assumption about people's passions. As Durkheim put it, "Passion individualizes, yet it also enslaves. Our sensations are essentially individual; yet we are more personal the more we are freed from our senses and able to think and act with concepts" (1912/1965:307–308). This same issue is manifest in the differentiation Durkheim (1914/1973) made between body and soul and the eternal conflict between them. The body represents the passions; the soul stands for civilization's common morality. "They mutually contradict and deny each other" (Durkheim, 1914/1973:152). Clearly, Durkheim wished this conflict to be resolved in the direction of the soul rather than of the body: "It is civilization that has made man what he is; it is what distinguishes him from the animal: man is man only because he is civilized" (1914/1973:149).

For Durkheim, freedom came from without rather than from within. This requires a collective conscience to constrain the passions. "Morality begins with disinterest, with attachment to something other than ourselves" (Durkheim, 1914/1973:151). But freedom, or autonomy, has another sense in Durkheim's work. That is, freedom is also derived from the internalization of a common morality that emphasizes the significance and independence of the individual (Lukes, 1972:115, 131). However, in both senses freedom is a characteristic of society, not of individuals. Here, as elsewhere, we see the degree to which Durkheim emphasized nonmaterial social facts (in this case "moral individualism") over mental processes.

We can also include *individual representations* within Durkheim's assumptions about human nature. Whereas collective representations are created by the interaction of people, individual representations are formed by the interaction of brain cells. Individual representations were relegated to psychology, as were many other aspects of Durkheim's thoughts on consciousness. This is the portion of the mental process that Durkheim was unwilling to explore, and it is on this that he is most vulnerable to attack. George Homans (1969), for example, argued that Durkheim exhibited a very limited conception of psychology by confining it to the study of instincts. The psychology of today goes far beyond the study of instincts and encompasses a number of social phenomena that Durkheim would have seen as part of sociology. Homans concluded that "sociology is surely not a corollary of the kind of psychology Durkheim had in mind" (1969:18). However, it is much harder, if not impossible, in Homans's view, to clearly separate sociology from the psychology of today.

INT = EDUC + SOCIAL.

Socialization and Moral Education

Given his views on innate human passions and the need to constrain them by common morality, it should come as no surprise that Durkheim was very much interested in the *internalization* of social morals through education and, more generally, through socialization. Social morality exists primarily at the cultural level, but it is also internalized by the individual. In Durkheim's words, common morality "penetrates us" and "forms part of us" (Lukes, 1972:131).

Durkheim was not primarily concerned with the issue of internalization but rather with how it bore upon the cultural and structural problems of his day (Pope, 1976:195). He did not specify how the common morality was internalized. He was much more concerned with what seemed to be a lessening of the power of this internalization of morality in contemporary society. The essence of the matter for Durkheim was the decline in the degree to which social facts exercise constraint upon consciousness. As Robert Nisbet put it, "Durkheim would never really abandon the idea that the Western society he knew was undergoing a major crisis and that the crisis consisted at bottom in a pathological loosening of moral authority upon the lives of individuals" (1974:192). Durkheim put it this way: "History records no crisis as serious as that in which European societies have been involved for more than a century. Collective discipline in its traditional form has lost its authority" (1973:101). Durkheim's interest in anomie in both *Suicide* and *The Division of Labor in Society* can be seen as a manifestation of this concern.

Much of Durkheim's work on education, and socialization in general, can be seen in light of this concern for moral decay and possible reforms to halt the spread of it. *Education* and *socialization* were defined by Durkheim as the processes by which the individual learns the ways of a given group or society—acquires the physical, intellectual, and, most important to Durkheim, moral tools needed to function in society (Durkheim, 1922/1956:71). Moral education has three important aspects (Wallwork, 1972).

First, its goal is to provide individuals with the *discipline* they need to restrain the passions that threaten to engulf them:

> The totality of moral regulations really forms about each person an imaginary wall, at the foot of which a multitude of human passions simply die without being able to go further. For the same reason—that they are contained—it becomes possible to

Handwritten margin notes: MORAL EDUCATION — Restrain passions DISCIPLINE — Autonomy Real, that will, any goal, given DEVOTION TO Sc. Moral

satisfy them. But if at any point this barrier weakens, human forces—until now restrained—pour tumultuously through the open breach; once loosed, they find no limits where they can or must stop.

(Durkheim, 1973:42)

More specifically, on the education of children, Durkheim says that only through discipline "and by means of it alone are we able to teach the child to rein in his desires, to set limits to his appetites of all kinds, to limit, and through limitation, to define the goals of his activity. This limitation is the condition of happiness and of moral health" (1973:43–44).

Second, individuals are provided with a sense of autonomy, but it is a characteristically atypical kind of autonomy in which "the child understands the reasons why the rules prescribing certain forms of behavior should be 'freely desired,' that is to say, 'willingly accepted' by virtue of 'enlightened assent' " (Wallwork, 1972:127).

Finally, the process of socialization aims at developing a sense of devotion to society and to its moral system. These aspects of moral education are efforts to combat the pathological loosening of the grip of collective morality on the individual in modern society.

At the most general level, Durkheim was concerned with the way in which collective morality constrains people both externally and internally. In one sense, nonmaterial social facts stand outside people and shape their thoughts (and actions). Of course, social facts cannot act on their own but only through their agents. Of greater importance, however, is the degree to which individuals constrain themselves by internalizing social morality. As Durkheim put it, "The collective force is not entirely outside of us; it does not act upon us wholly from without; but rather, since society cannot exist except in and through individual consciousness, this force must also penetrate us and organize itself within us" (1912/1965:240). In addition to making clear the process of internalization, the preceding quotation also shows once again that Durkheim rejected the idea of a group mind, for he stated that collective forces can exist only in individual consciousness. Ernest Wallwork did an excellent job of clarifying the importance of the internalization of morality in Durkheim's system: *Collective forces /in INDIVIDUALS*

A normal mind, Durkheim observes, cannot consider moral maxims without considering them as obligatory. Moral rules have an "imperative character"; they "exercise a sort of ascendancy over the will which feels constrained to conform to them." This constraint is not to be confused with physical force or compulsion; the will is not forced to conform to the norms it entertains even if these norms are enforced by public opinion. Moral "constraint does not consist in an exterior and mechanical pressure; it has a more intimate and psychological character." But this intimate, psychological sense of obligation is, nevertheless, none other than the authority of public opinion which penetrates, like the air we breathe, into the deepest recesses of our being.

(Wallwork, 1972:38)

Durkheim offered a specific example of internal constraint in his study on religion:

> If [an individual] acts in a certain way towards the totemic beings, it is not only because the forces resident in them are physically redoubtable, but because he feels himself morally obliged to act thus; he has the feeling that he is obeying an imperative, that he is fulfilling a duty.
>
> (Durkheim, 1912/1965:218)

These concerns with internalization, socialization, and education all can be seen in the context of the constraining effect of collective morality on the actor. Whether the constraint is external or internal, it still comes down to collective morality controlling the thoughts and actions of individuals.

Durkheim's limited thoughts on consciousness led many people to assume that his ideal actor is one who is almost wholly controlled from without—a total conformist. Although there is much to recommend this view—and some modern sociologists in following Durkheim seem to have adopted this position—Durkheim himself did not subscribe to such an extreme view of the actor: "Conformity must not be pushed to the point where it completely subjugates the intellect. Thus it does not follow from a belief in the need for discipline that it must be blind and slavish" (cited in Giddens, 1972:113). Durkheim does see a role for individuals: they are all not simply mirror images of collective ideas; there is individuality. Each of us has unique temperaments, habits, and so forth. "Each of us puts his own mark on them [collective ideas]; and this accounts for the fact that each person has his own particular way of thinking . . . about the rules of common morality" (Durkheim, 1914/1973:161; see also Durkheim 1913–14/1983:91–92). Although Durkheim left open the possibility of individuality, the thrust of his work is in the direction of outlining external constraints on actors and, furthermore, the desirability of such constraint.

CONSCIOUSNES IS DET·BY
S·F· -DCP·

Dependent Variables

In Durkheim's works, consciousness most often occupies the position of a dependent variable, determined by various material and especially nonmaterial social facts.

> Durkheim viewed sociologically relevant subjective states as the product of social causes. They "are like prolongations . . . inside individuals" . . . of the social causes on which they depend. They may enter sociological explanations as effects, but never as causes. Appeal to subjective states as causal agents, according to Durkheim, threatened the legitimacy of sociology's claim to scientific status by reducing it to psychology.
>
> (Pope, Cohen, and Hazelrigg, 1975:419)

Although we will discuss several such dependent variables, it should be made clear that Durkheim usually dealt with them in only a vague and cursory way. In *Suicide,* for example, Durkheim was quite uncertain about how social currents affect individual consciousness and how changed consciousness, in turn, leads to a heightened likelihood of suicide (Pope, 1976:191). The same criticism applies to every other treatment by Durkheim of consciousness.

In *The Division of Labor,* consciousness was dealt with indirectly, but it is clear that it is a dependent variable. That is, the sense of the argument is that changes at the cultural and societal levels lead to changes in the processes of individual consciousness. In a society with mechanical solidarity, individual consciousness is limited and highly constrained by a powerful collective conscience. In a society with organic solidarity, individual potentialities expand, as does individual freedom. But again, although this sense of consciousness as a dependent variable is there, it was left largely implicit by Durkheim. In *Suicide,* however, the status of consciousness as a dependent variable is much clearer. Schematically, the main independent variable is collective morality, and the ultimate dependent variable is suicide rates, but intervening is another set of dependent variables that can only be mental states. Steven Lukes, in the following statement about "weak points" in the individual, implied the mental level: "The currents impinge from the outside on suicide-prone individuals at their 'weak points' " (1972:214).

Lukes (1972:216–217) went further on this issue and argued that there is a social-psychological theory beneath the "aggressively sociologistic language" found in *Suicide.* One part of that theory is the belief that individuals need to be attached to social goals. Another aspect is that individuals cannot become so committed to such goals that they lose all personal autonomy. Finally, as we have discussed before, there was Durkheim's belief that individuals possess passions and that they can be contented and free only if these passions are restrained from without.

We find in *Suicide* specific conscious states associated with each of the three main types of suicide:

> These subjective states, themselves effects of given social conditions, impel the individual to suicide. . . . The egoistic suicide is characterized by a general depression in the form either of melancholic languor or Epicurean indifference. . . . Anomic suicide is accompanied by anger, disappointment, irritation, and exasperated weariness . . . while the altruistic suicide may experience a calm feeling of duty, the mystic's enthusiasm, or peaceful courage.
>
> (Pope, 1976:197)

Durkheim perceived well-defined states of consciousness accompanying each form of suicide. It is clear that these were peripheral interests for him, as he maintained a consistently large-scale focus. Even such an ardent supporter as Nisbet wished that Durkheim had given more attention to individual consciousness: "Admittedly, one might wish that Durkheim had given more attention to the specific mechanisms by which collective representations in society are translated, in distinctly human, often creative ways, into the individual representations that reflect man's relationship to society" (1974:115). Lukes made the same point: "[Durkheim's] exclusive concentration on the society end of the schema, on the impact of social conditions on individuals rather than the way individuals perceive, interpret, and respond to social conditions, led him to leave inexplicit and unexamined the social-psychological assumptions on which his theories rested" (1972:35).

Mental Categories   We can find a specific example of this tendency to accord priority to the level of society in Durkheim and Marcel Mauss's[4] work on the impact of the structure of society on the form of individual thought. Basically, Durkheim (and Mauss) argued that the form society takes affects the form that thought patterns take. Contesting those who believe that mental categories shape the social world, their view was that the social world shapes mental categories: "Far from it being the case . . . that the social relations of men are based on logical relations between things, in reality it is the former which have provided the prototype for the latter" (Durkheim and Mauss, 1903/1963:82). Although specific large-scale structures (for example, family structure and economic and political systems) play a role in shaping logical categories, Durkheim and Mauss devoted most of their attention to the effect of society as a whole:

> Society was not simply a model which classificatory thought followed; it was its own divisions which served as divisions for the system of classification. The first logical categories were social categories; the first classes of things were classes of men. . . . It was because men were grouped, and thought of themselves in the form of groups, that in their ideas they grouped other things, and in the beginning the two modes of grouping were merged to the point of being indistinct.
> (Durkheim and Mauss, 1903/1963:82–83)

Durkheim's emphasis on large-scale phenomena is well illustrated by this discussion of the impact of society on logical categories. However, Durkheim did not analyze the corresponding process—the way in which the operation of mental categories, in turn, shapes the structures of society.

To create a more adequate sociology, Durkheim had to do more with consciousness than treat it as an unexplored dependent variable. An almost total focus on large-scale phenomena leaves out important elements of an adequate sociological model. Lukes made some telling points in his discussion of *Suicide*. He argued, quite rightly, that an adequate explanation of suicide cannot stop with an examination of social currents. In his view, "Explaining suicide—and explaining suicide rates—*must* involve explaining why people commit it" (Lukes, 1972.221, italics added). Durkheim also was wrong in assuming that consciousness is not open to scientific inquiry and explanation. Such inquiry can and must be undertaken if we are to go beyond partial theories of social life. Nothing is solved by simply acknowledging the existence of consciousness and refusing to examine it. Durkheim's commitment to a narrow view of science led him astray, as did his tendency toward making radically sociologistic statements that rule out recourse to consciousness:

---

[4] Marcel Mauss, Durkheim's nephew and a scholar of some note, coauthored the material on mental categories with Durkheim.

He need only have claimed that "social" facts cannot be wholly explained in terms of "individual" facts; instead he claimed that they can only be explained in terms of social facts. . . . It would have been enough to have claimed that no social phenomenon, indeed few human activities, can either be identified or satisfactorily explained without reference, explicit or implicit, to social factors.

(Lukes, 1972:20)

Durkheim also failed to give consciousness an active role in the social process. People are in general controlled by social forces in his system; they do not actively control those systems. This led Wallwork to contend that "the principal weakness . . . is Durkheim's failure to consider *active* moral judgment" (1972:65; italics added). Durkheim gave too little independence to actors (Pope and Cohen, 1978:1364). Actors can reject some, most, or perhaps even all of the moral principles to which they are exposed. When Durkheim did talk of autonomy, it was in terms of the acceptance of moral norms of autonomy. Individuals seem capable of accepting moral constraint and of controlling themselves only through the internalization of such norms. But as Wallwork pointed out, autonomy has a much more active component: "Autonomy also involves willful exploration, spontaneous initiative, competent mastery, and creative self-actualization. . . . The child must also be encouraged to exercise his own will, initiative, and creativity" (1972:148).

Indeed, research into cognitive processes, in part done by Jean Piaget, who was working in the Durkheimian tradition, indicates that individual creativity is an important component of social life. In summarizing the work of Piaget, Lawrence Kohlberg (who did research on the cognitive elements in moral development), and others, Wallwork said:

In addition to cultural conditioning, the cognitive activity of the subject is necessary to constitute the experience. Piaget and Kohlberg conclude from their studies that the distinctive phenomenological character of moral experience is always as much a product of the cognitive construction of the subject as it is an accommodation to cultural conditioning by the subject.

(Wallwork, 1972:67)

In other words, a more complete sociology requires a more creative actor and deeper insight into the creative processes.

We have seen that, contrary to the view of many, Durkheim did have a variety of things to say about mental processes. However, the peripheral character of mental processes in his theoretical system makes his insights vague and amorphous. More damning is the fact that the thrust of his work leads to a passive image of the actor, although an active actor is, in this author's view, an essential component of a fully adequate sociological theory.

INDIVIDUAL ACTION AND INTERACTION

Durkheim was weakest in his work on individual action and interaction. Implied in his system are various changes at this level resulting from changes at the level of large-scale social phenomena, but they are not detailed. For example, it seems clear that the nature of action and interaction is quite different in societies with mechanical rather than organic solidarity. The individual in a society with mechanical solidarity is likely to be enraged at a violation of the collective conscience and to act quickly and aggressively toward the violator. In contrast, an individual in a society with organic solidarity is more likely to take a more measured approach, such as calling the police or suing in the courts.[5] Similarly, in *Suicide* the assumption behind the study of changes in suicide rates is that the nature of individual action and interaction changes as a result of alterations in social currents. Suicide rates are used as cumulative measures of changes at the individual level, but the nature of these changes is not explored, at least not in any detail. Similar points could be made about Durkheim's other works, but the critical point is that individual action and interaction are largely unanalyzed in Durkheim's work.

SUMMARY

Emile Durkheim offered a more coherent theory than any of the other classical sociological theorists. He articulated a rather clear theoretical orientation and used it in a variety of specific works. Supporters would say that the clarity of Durkheim's thinking stems from this coherence, whereas detractors might contend that the clarity is the result of the comparative simplicity of his theory. Whatever the case, it is certainly easier to convey the essence of Durkheim's thinking than that of the other classical theorists.

The heart of Durkheim's theory lies in his concept of social fact. Durkheim differentiated between two basic types of social facts—material and nonmaterial. Although they often occupied a place of causal priority in his theorizing, material social facts (for example, division of labor, dynamic density, and law) were not the most important large-scale forces in Durkheim's theoretical system. The most important focus for Durkheim was on nonmaterial social facts. He dealt with a number of them, including collective conscience, collective representations, and social currents.

Durkheim's study of suicide is a good illustration of the significance of nonmaterial social facts in his work. In his basic causal model, changes in nonmaterial social facts ultimately cause differences in suicide rates. Durkheim differentiated among four types of suicide—egoistic, altruistic, anomic, and fatalistic—and showed how each is affected by different changes in social currents. The study of suicide was taken by Durkheim and his supporters as evidence that sociology has a legitimate place in the social sciences. After all, it was argued, if sociology could explain so individualistic an act as suicide, then it certainly could be used to explain other, less individual aspects of social life.

---

[5] Although in some cases (for example, an assault on one's baby), people in both types of society are likely to react violently. Thus, to some degree, differences between the two societies are dependent on the nature of the crime.

Given his focus on nonmaterial social facts and some unfortunate statements made in an effort to define a distinctive domain for sociology, Durkheim is sometimes accused of having a metaphysical, "group-mind" orientation. Despite some seemingly indefensible statements, Durkheim did not believe in a group mind and, in fact, had a very modern conception of culture.

In his later work, Durkheim focused on another aspect of culture, religion. In his analysis of primitive religion, Durkheim sought to show the roots of religion in the social structure of society. It is society that defines certain things as sacred and others as profane. Durkheim demonstrated the social sources of religion in his analysis of primitive totemism and its roots in the social structure of the clan. Furthermore, totemism was seen as a specific form of the collective conscience as manifested in a primitive society. Its source, as well as the source of all collective products, lies in the process of collective effervescence. In the end, Durkheim argued that religion and society are one and the same, two manifestations of the same general process.

Because he identified society with God, and because he deified society, Durkheim did not urge social revolution. Instead, he should be seen as a social reformer interested in improving the functioning of society. Whereas Marx saw irreconcilable differences between capitalists and workers, Durkheim believed that these groups could be united in occupational associations. He urged that these associations be set up to restore some collective morality to the modern world and to cope with some of the curable pathologies of the modern division of labor. But in the end, such narrow, structural reforms could not really cope with the broader cultural problems that plague the modern world. Here Durkheim invested some hope in the curious modern system of collective morality that he labeled the "cult of the individual."

Durkheim had comparatively little to say about micro-level phenomena, but this is not to say he had nothing to offer here. He had useful insights into human nature, socialization, and moral education. But micro-level phenomena are most often treated in his work as dependent variables determined by large-scale changes. Although Durkheim dealt with all major levels of social reality, he focused on the large-scale forces and their causal impact on the individual level.

CHAPTER 7

MAX WEBER

METHODOLOGY
    History and Sociology
    Verstehen
    Causality
    Ideal Types
    Values

SUBSTANTIVE SOCIOLOGY
    What Is Sociology?
    Social Action
    Class, Status, and Party
    Structures of Authority
    Rationalization
    Religion and the Rise of Capitalism

*M*AX Weber (1864–1920) is probably the best-known and most influential figure in sociological theory (R. Collins, 1985; Scaff, 1989; Sica, 1988).[1] Weber was a prolific writer and a complicated thinker, and this, while it contributed to his fame, makes it difficult to summarize his work in a single chapter. Not only do we have to deal with the enormous amount of work produced by Weber, but we also need to consider the even larger body of work produced by his numerous critics and analysts. To make matters even more difficult, Weber is known not only for his general theoretical approach but also for the number of specific ideas that in themselves have generated a considerable amount of analysis and critique. For example, a large part of the work in the sociology of organizations is traceable to his work on bureaucracies. Similarly, his ideas on the relationship between Protestantism and capitalism have been extraordinarily controversial. The bulk, diversity, and complexity of Weber's work make it difficult enough to summarize, but the problem is exacerbated by Weber's inconsistency and his occasional failure to say precisely what he meant. Thus, although Weber's work is provocative and rich in insight, it defies simple summary and analysis.

Weber's work is so varied and subject to so many interpretations that it has influenced a wide array of sociological theories. It certainly had an influence on structural functionalism, especially through the work of Talcott Parsons. It

---

[1] For a time, his position was threatened by the increase in interest in the work of Karl Marx who was already much better known to those in other fields and to the general public. But with the demise of world communism, Weber's position of preeminence seems secure once again.

MAX WEBER: A Biographical Sketch

Max Weber was born in Erfurt, Germany, on April 21, 1864, into a decidedly middle-class family. Important differences between his parents had a profound effect upon both his intellectual orientation and his psychological development. His father was a bureaucrat who rose to a relatively important political position. He was clearly a part of the political establishment and as a result eschewed any activity or idealism that would require personal sacrifice or threaten his position within the system. In addition, the senior Weber was a man who enjoyed earthly pleasures, and in this and many other ways he stood in sharp contrast to his wife. Max Weber's mother was a devout Calvinist, a woman who sought to lead an ascetic life largely devoid of the pleasures craved by her husband. Her concerns were more otherworldly; she was disturbed by the imperfections that were signs that she was not destined for salvation. These deep differences between the parents led to marital tension, and both the differences and the tension had an immense impact on Weber.

Because it was impossible to emulate both parents, Weber was presented with a clear choice as a child (Marianne Weber, 1975:62). He first seemed to opt for his father's orientation to life, but later he drew closer to his mother's approach. Whatever the choice, the tension produced by the need to choose between such polar opposites negatively affected Max Weber's psyche.

At age eighteen, Max Weber left home for a short time to attend the Unversity of Heidelberg. Weber had already demonstrated intellectual precocity, but on a social level he entered Heidelberg shy and underdeveloped. However, that quickly changed after he gravitated toward his father's way of life and joined his father's old dueling fraternity. There he developed socially, at least in part because of the huge quantities of beer he consumed with his peers. In addition, he proudly displayed the dueling scars that were the trademarks of such fraternities. Weber not only manifested his identity with his father's way of life in these ways but also chose, at least for the time being, his father's career—the law.

After three terms, Weber left Heidelberg for military service, and in 1884 he returned to Berlin and to his parents' home to take courses at the University of Berlin. He remained there for most of the next eight years as he completed his studies, earned his Ph.D., became a lawyer, and started teaching at the University of Berlin. In the process, his interests shifted more toward his lifelong concerns—economics, history, and sociology. During his eight years

has also come to be seen as important to the conflict tradition (R. Collins, 1975, 1990) and to critical theory, which was shaped almost as much by Weber's ideas as it was by Marx's orientation, as well as that of Jurgen Habermas, major inheritor of the critical-theory tradition. Symbolic interactionists have been affected by Weber's ideas on *verstehen*, as well as by other of Weber's ideas. Alfred Schutz, whom we will consider in Chapter 10, was powerfully affected by Weber's work on meanings and motives, and he, in turn, played a crucial role in the development of both phenomenology and ethnomethodology. Weber was and is a widely influential theorist.

We begin this chapter with a discussion of Weber's (1903–17/1949) ideas on the methodology of the social sciences, because a clear understanding of in Berlin, Weber was financially dependent on his father, a circumstance he progressively grew to dislike. At the same time, he moved closer to his mother's values, and his antipathy to his father increased. He adopted an ascetic life and plunged deeply into his work. For example, during one semester as a student, his work habits were described as follows: "He continues the rigid work discipline, regulates his life by the clock, divides the daily routine into exact sections for the various subjects, saves in his way, by feeding himself evenings in his room with a pound of raw chopped beef and four fried eggs" (Mitzman, 1970:48; Marianne Weber, 1975:105). Thus Weber, following his mother, had become ascetic and diligent, a compulsive worker—in contemporary terms a "workaholic."

This compulsion for work led in 1896 to a position as professor of economics at Heidelberg. But in 1897, with Weber's academic career blossoming, his father died following a violent argument between them. Shortly thereafter Weber began to manifest symptoms that were to culminate in a nervous breakdown. Often unable to sleep or to work, Weber spent the next six or seven years in near-total collapse. After a long hiatus, some of his powers began to return in 1903, but it was not until 1904, when he delivered (in the United States) his first lecture in six and one-half years, that Weber was able to begin to return to active academic life. In 1904 and 1905, he published one of his best-known works, *The Protestant Ethic and the Spirit of Capitalism.* In this work, Weber announced the ascendance of his mother's religion on an academic level. Weber devoted much of his time to the study of religion, though he was not personally religious.

Although he continued to be plagued by psychological problems, after 1904 Weber was able to function, indeed to produce some of his most important work. In these years, Weber published his studies of the world's religions in world-historical perspective (for example, China, India, and ancient Judaism). At the time of his death (June 14, 1920), he was working on his most important work, *Economy and Society.* Although this book was published, and subsequently translated into many languages, it was unfinished.

In addition to producing voluminous writings in this period, Weber undertook a number of other activities. He helped found the German Sociological Society in 1910. His home became a center for a wide range of intellectuals, including sociologists such as Georg Simmel and Robert Michels and the philosopher and literary critic Georg Lukács (Scaff, 1989:186–222). In addition, Weber was active politically and wrote essays on the issues of the day.

There was a tension in Weber's life and, more important, in his work, between the bureaucratic mind, as represented by his father, and his mother's religiosity. This unresolved tension permeates Weber's work as it permeated his personal life.

these ideas is necessary in dealing with Weber's substantive and theoretical ideas. Weber was opposed to pure abstract theorizing. Instead, his theoretical ideas are embedded in his empirical, usually historical, research. Weber's methodology shaped his research, and the combination of the two lies at the base of his theoretical orientation.

METHODOLOGY

History and Sociology

Weber tended to deemphasize methodological issues, viewing them as "the precondition of fruitful intellectual work" (1903–17/1949:115; see also Marianne Weber, 1975:309). Weber focused on substantive work: "Only by laying bare and solving *substantive problems* can sciences be established and their methods developed. On the other hand, purely epistemological and methodological reflections have never played the crucial role in such developments" (1903–17/1949:116). It is important to examine Weber's methodological orientations, in spite of their secondary role in his work, not only because they help us better understand his substantive sociology, but also because many of them are important in sociological methodology today.

To deal with Weber's methodology, we first must clarify his thinking on the relationship between history and sociology. Even though Weber was a student of, and took his first academic job in, law, his early career was dominated by an interest in history. In fact, his doctoral dissertations were historical studies of the Middle Ages and of Rome. In his later years, however, he identified more and more with sociology. It has been argued that it was in 1909, the year Weber started writing his massive *Economy and Society*, that he began to devote himself fully to sociology (R. Frank, 1976:13).

As Weber moved more in the direction of the relatively new field of sociology, he sought to clarify its relationship to the established field of history. Although Weber felt that each field needed the other, his view was that the task of sociology was to provide a needed "service" to history (Roth, 1976:307). In Weber's words, sociology performed only a "preliminary, quite modest task" (cited in R. Frank, 1976:21). Weber explained the difference between sociology and history: "Sociology seeks to formulate type concepts and generalized uniformities of empirical processes. This distinguishes it from history, which is oriented to the causal analysis and explanation of individual actions, structures, and personalities possessing cultural significance" (1921/1968:19). Despite this seemingly clear-cut differentiation, in his own work Weber was able to combine the two. His sociology was oriented to the development of clear concepts so that he could perform a causal analysis of historical phenomena. Weber defined his ideal procedure as "the sure imputation of individual concrete events occurring in historical reality *to concrete, historically* given causes through the study of precise empirical data which have been selected from specific points of view" (1903–17/1949:69). We can think of Weber as a historical sociologist.

Weber's thinking on sociology was profoundly shaped by a series of intellectual debates (*Methodenstreit*) raging in Germany during his time. The most important of these was over the issue of the relationship between history and science. At the poles in this debate were those (the positivists) who thought that history was composed of general (*nomothetic*) laws and those (the subjectivists) who reduced history to idiosyncratic (*idiographic*) actions and events. (The positivists thought that history could be like a natural science; the subjectivists saw the two as radically different.) For example, a nomothetic thinker would generalize about social revolutions, whereas an idiographic analyst would focus on the specific events leading up to the American Revolution. Weber rejected both extremes and in the process developed a distinctive way of dealing with historical sociology. In Weber's view, history is composed of unique empirical events; there can be no generalizations at the empirical level. Sociologists must, therefore, separate the empirical world from the conceptual universe that they construct. The concepts never completely capture the empirical world, but they can be used as heuristic tools for gaining a better understanding of reality. With these concepts, sociologists can develop generalizations, but these generalizations are not history and must not be confused with empirical reality.

Although Weber was clearly in favor of generalizing, he also rejected those historians who sought to reduce history to a simple set of laws: "For the knowledge of historical phenomena in their concreteness, the most general laws, because they are devoid of content, are also the least valuable" (1903–17/1949:80). For example, he rejected one historian (Wilhelm Roscher) who took as his task the search for the laws of the historical evolution of a people and who believed that all peoples went through a typical sequence of stages (Weber, 1903–06/1975). As Weber put it, "The reduction of empirical reality . . . to 'laws' is meaningless" (1903–17/1949:80). In other terms: "A systematic science of culture . . . would be senseless in itself" (Weber, 1903–17/1949:84). This view is reflected in various specific historical studies. For example, in his study of ancient civilizations, Weber admitted that, although in some respects earlier times were precursors of things to come, "the long and continuous history of Mediterranean-European civilization does not show either closed cycles or linear progress. Sometimes phenomena of ancient civilizations have disappeared entirely and then come to light again in an entirely new context" (1896–1906/1976:366).

In rejecting these opposing views of German historical scholarship, Weber fashioned his own perspective, which constituted a fusion of the two orientations. Weber felt that history (that is, historical sociology) was appropriately concerned with both individuality *and* generality. The unification was accomplished through the development and utilization of general concepts (what we later will call "ideal types") in the study of particular individuals, events, or societies. These general concepts are to be used "to identify and define the individuality of each development, the characteristics which made the one conclude in a manner so different from that of the other. Thus done, one can then determine the causes which led to the differences" (Weber, 1896–1906/1976:385). In doing this kind of causal analysis, Weber rejected, at least at a conscious level, the idea of searching for a single causal agent throughout history.[2] He instead used his conceptual arsenal to rank the various factors involved in a given historical case in terms of their causal significance (Roth, 1971).

Weber's views on historical sociology were shaped in part by the availability of, and his commitment to the study of, empirical historical data. His

---

[2] Ironically, Weber did seem (as we will see later in this chapter) to argue in his substantive work that there was such a causal agent in society—rationalization.

was the first generation of scholars to have available reliable data on historical phenomena from many parts of the world (MacCrae, 1974). Weber was more inclined to immerse himself in these historical data than he was to dream up abstract generalizations about the basic thrust of history. Although this led him to some important insights, it also created serious problems in understanding his work; he often got so involved in historical detail that he lost sight of the basic reasons for the historical study. In addition, the sweep of his historical studies encompassed so many epochs and so many societies that he could do little more than make rough generalizations (Roth, 1971). Despite these problems, Weber's commitment to the scientific study of empirical phenomena made him attractive to the developing discipline of sociology in the United States.

In sum, Weber believed that history was composed of an inexhaustible array of specific phenomena. To study these phenomena, it was necessary to develop a variety of concepts designed to be useful for research on the real world. As a general rule, although Weber (as we will see) did not adhere to it strictly and neither do most sociologists and historians, the task of sociology was to develop these concepts, which history was to use in causal analyses of specific historical phenomena. In this way, Weber sought to combine the specific and the general in an effort to develop a science that did justice to the complex nature of social life.

Verstehen

Weber felt that sociologists had an advantage over natural scientists. That advantage resided in the sociologist's ability to *understand* social phenomena, whereas the natural scientist could not gain a similar understanding of the behavior of an atom or a chemical compound. The German word for understanding is *verstehen*. Weber's special use of the term *verstehen* in his historical research is one of his best-known, and most controversial, contributions to the methodology of contemporary sociology. As we clarify what Weber meant by *verstehen*, we will also underscore some of the problems involved in his conceptualization of it. The controversy surrounding the concept of *verstehen*, and some of the problems involved in interpreting what Weber meant, grows out of a general problem with Weber's methodological thoughts. As Thomas Burger (1976; see also Hekman, 1983:26) argued, Weber was neither very sophisticated nor very consistent in his methodological pronouncements. He tended to be careless and imprecise because he felt that he was simply repeating ideas that were well known in his day among German historians. Furthermore, as pointed out above, Weber did not think too highly of methodological reflections.

Weber's thoughts on *verstehen* were relatively common among German historians of his day and were derived from a field known as *hermeneutics* (Mueller-Vollmer, 1985). Hermeneutics was a special approach to the understanding and interpretation of published writings. Its goal was to understand the thinking of the author as well as the basic structure of the text. Weber and others (for example, Wilhelm Dilthey) sought to extend this idea from the understanding of texts to the understanding of social life:

> Once we have realized that the historical method is nothing more or less than the classical method of interpretation applied to overt action instead of to texts, a method aiming at indentifying a human design, a "meaning" behind observable events, we shall have no difficulty in accepting that it can be just as well applied to human interaction as to individual actors. From this point of view all history is interaction, which has to be interpreted in terms of the rival plans of various actors.
>
> (Lachman, 1971:20)

In other words, Weber sought to use the tools of hermeneutics to understand actors, interaction, and indeed all of human history.[3]

One common misconception about *verstehen* is that it is simply the use of "intuition" by the researcher. Thus many critics see it as a "soft," irrational, subjective research methodology. However, Weber categorically rejected the idea that *verstehen* involved simply intuition, sympathetic participation, or empathy (1903–17/1949). To him, *verstehen* involved doing systematic and rigorous research rather than simply getting a "feeling" for a text or social phenomenon. In other words, for Weber (1921/1968) *verstehen* was a rational procedure of study.

The key question in interpreting Weber's concept of *verstehen* is whether he thought that it was most appropriately applied to the subjective states of individual actors or to the subjective aspects of large-scale units of analysis (for example, culture). We can find aspects of Weber's work that support both alternatives, and there are supporters of both perspectives among Weber's interpreters.

If we look only at Weber's bare position statements, there seems to be overwhelming evidence on the side of the individual-level interpretation of *verstehen* (for example, Weber, 1903–06/1975:125). This interpretation is supported by a number of observers (Burger, 1976; Schutz, 1932/1967; Warriner, 1969).

But a number of people have interpreted *verstehen*, and Weber's statements about it, as a technique aimed at understanding culture. Susan Hekman sees this as the newer interpretation of what Weber meant by focusing on such cultural elements as "intersubjective meanings or socially constituted rules which define the meaning of action within a given society" (1983:46). L. M. Lachman was particularly clear on this: "The plan elements which interest us are not the millions of individual purposes pursued, but the common elements of norms, institutions, and of the general environment in which all these plans have to be carried out" (1971:21). Along the same lines, W. G. Runciman (1972) and Murray Wax (1967) saw *verstehen* as a tool for learning the culture and

---

[3] Hermeneutics has become a major intellectual concern in recent years, especially in the work of Martin Heidegger, Hans-Georg Gadamer, and Jurgen Habermas (Bleicher, 1980). For a strong argument in favor of using hermeneutics today, see Sica (1986), and for an appreciation of Weber's hermeneutics, see Oliver (1983).

the language of a given society. Wax argued not only *for* the large-scale interpretation of *verstehen* but also *against* an individual perspective. Wax used the term *interpersonal intuition* to refer to the individual view. To him, Weber did not intend that we use *verstehen* to understand actors, but rather that we use it to understand the larger culture in which actors exist and which constrains their thoughts and actions.

Finally, some have argued that *verstehen* involves both approaches. P. A. Munch (1975), for example, said that to understand action fully we must (1) identify the sense of the action as intended by the actor and (2) recognize the context in which the action belongs and makes sense.

The multiple interpretations of *verstehen* help us to see why Weber occupies such a central role in sociological theory. The cultural-level interpretation of *verstehen* would be consistent with large-scale theories (for example, structural functionalism), whereas an individual-level view is appropriate for small-scale theories (for example, symbolic interactionism). Munch's compromise position would be acceptable to both sets of theories. Which of these three interpretations is correct? At one level, we can say that it does not really matter. What is important is that there are different interpretations and that they have influenced different theoretical perspectives. On another level, we must come to some conclusion about *verstehen* on the basis of Weber's work. It is in his substantive work, rather than in his programmatic statements about methodology, that we will find the most reliable information on what Weber really meant by *verstehen* and by the other methodological tools that we will encounter. As we will see, Weber's focus on the cultural and social-structural contexts of action leads us to the view that *verstehen* is a tool for macro-level analysis.

Causality

Another aspect of Weber's methodology was his commitment to the study of causality. Weber was inclined to see the study of the causes of social phenomena as being within the domain of history, not sociology. Yet to the degree that history and sociology cannot be clearly separated—and they certainly are not clearly separated in Weber's substantive work—the issue of causality is relevant to sociology. Causality is also important because it is, as we will see, another place in which Weber sought to combine nomothetic and idiographic approaches.

By *causality* Weber (1921/1968) simply meant the probability that an event will be followed or accompanied by another event. It was not, in his view, enough to look for historical constants, repetitions, analogies, and parallels, as many historians are content to do. Instead, the researcher has to look at the reasons for, as well as the meanings of, historical changes (Roth, 1971). Although Weber is most often thought of as having a one-way causal model—in contrast to Marx's dialectical mode of reasoning—in his substantive sociology, he was always attuned to the interrelationships among the economy, society, polity, organization, social stratification, religion, and so forth (Roth, 1968).

Weber was quite clear on the issue of multiple causality in his study of the relationship between Protestantism and the spirit of capitalism. Although he is sometimes interpreted differently, Weber (1904–05/1958) simply argued that the Protestant ethic was *one* of the causal factors in the rise of the modern spirit of capitalism. He labeled as "foolish" the idea that Protestantism was the sole cause. Similarly foolish, in Weber's view, was the idea that capitalism could have arisen "only" as a result of the Protestant Reformation; other factors could have led to the same result. Here is the way Weber made his point:

> We shall as far as possible clarify the manner and the general *direction* in which . . . the religious movements have influenced the development of material culture. Only when this has been determined with reasonable accuracy can the attempt be made to estimate to what extent the historical development of modern culture can be attributed to those *religious forces and to what extent to others.*
>
> (Weber, 1904–05/1958:91–92; italics added)

In *The Protestant Ethic and the Spirit of Capitalism,* as well as in most of the rest of his historical work, Weber was interested in the question of causality, but he did not operate with a simple one-way model; he was always attuned to the interrelationships among a number of social factors. The critical thing to remember about Weber's thinking on causality is his belief that because we can have a special understanding of social life (*verstehen*), the causal knowledge of the social sciences is different from the causal knowledge of the natural sciences. As Weber put it: " 'Meaningfully' interpretable human conduct ('action') is identifiable by reference to 'valuations' and meanings. For this reason, our criteria for *causal* explanation have a unique kind of satisfaction in the 'historical' explanation of such an 'entity' " (1903–06/1975:185). Thus the causal knowledge of the social scientist is different from the causal knowledge of the natural scientist.

Weber's thoughts on causality were intimately related to his efforts to come to grips with the conflict between nomothetic and idiographic knowledge. Those who subscribe to a nomothetic point of view would argue that there is a necessary relationship among social phenomena, whereas the supporters of an idiographic perspective would be inclined to see only random relationships among these entities. As usual, Weber took a middle position, epitomized in his concept of "adequate causality." The notion of *adequate causality* adopts the view that the best we can do in sociology is make probabilistic statements about the relationship between social phenomena; that is, if *x* occurs, then it is *probable* that *y* will occur. The goal is to "estimate the *degree* to which a certain effect is "favored" by certain 'conditions' " (Weber, 1903–17/1949:183).

Ideal Types

The ideal type is one of Weber's best-known contributions to contemporary sociology (Hekman, 1983; McKinney, 1966). As we have seen, Weber believed it was the responsibility of sociologists to develop conceptual tools, which could be used later by historians and sociologists. The most important such conceptual tool was the ideal type.

> An ideal type is formed by the one-sided *accentuation* of one or more points of view and by the synthesis of a great many diffuse, discrete, more or less present and occasionally absent *concrete individual* phenomena, which are arranged according to those one-sidedly emphasized viewpoints into a unified *analytical* construct. . . . In its conceptual purity, this mental construct . . . cannot be found empirically anywhere in reality.
>
> (Weber, 1903–17/1949:90)

In spite of this definition, Weber was not totally consistent in the way he used the ideal type. To get a grasp of what the concept means initially, we will have to overlook some of the inconsistencies. At its most basic level, an *ideal type is a concept* constructed by a social scientist, on the basis of his or her interests and theoretical orientation, to capture the essential features of some social phenomenon.

The most important thing about ideal types is that they are heuristic devices; they are to be useful and helpful in doing empirical research and in understanding the social world. As Lachman said, an ideal type is "essentially a measuring rod" (1971:26). Here is the way Weber put it: "Its function is the comparison with empirical reality in order to establish its divergences or similarities, to describe them with the *most unambiguously intelligible concepts,* and to understand and explain them causally" (1903–17/1949:43). Ideal types are heuristic devices to be used in the study of slices of historical reality. For example, social scientists would construct an ideal-typical bureaucracy on the basis of their immersion in historical data. This ideal type can then be compared to actual bureaucracies. The researcher looks for divergences in the real case from the exaggerated ideal type. Next, the social scientist must look for the causes of the deviations. Some typical reasons for these divergences are:

1 Bureaucrats whose actions are motivated by *misinformation*
2 *Strategic errors,* primarily by the bureaucratic leaders
3 *Logical fallacies* undergirding the actions of leaders and followers
4 Decisions made in the bureaucracy on the basis of *emotion*
5 Any *irrationality in t*he action of bureaucratic leaders and followers

To take another example, an ideal-typical military battle delineates the principal components of such a battle—opposing armies, opposing strategies, materiel at the disposal of each, disputed land ("no-man's" land), supply and support forces, command centers, and leadership qualities. Actual battles may not have all these elements, and that is one thing a researcher wants to know. The basic point is that the elements of any particular military battle may be compared with the elements identified in the ideal type.

The elements of an ideal type (such as the components of the ideal-typical military battle) are not to be thrown together arbitrarily; they are combined on the basis of their compatibility. As Hekman puts it, "Ideal types are not

the product of the whim or fancy of a social scientist, but are logically constructed concepts'' (1983:32).

In Weber's view, the ideal type was to be derived inductively from the real
world of social history. Weber did not believe that it was enough to offer a
carefully defined set of concepts, especially if they were deductively derived
from an abstract theory. The concepts had to be empirically adequate (Roth,
1971). Thus, in order to produce ideal types, researchers had first to immerse
themselves in historical reality and then derive the types from that reality.

In line with Weber's efforts to find a middle ground between nomothetic
and idiographic knowledge, he argued that ideal types should be neither too
general nor too specific. For example, in the case of religion he would reject
ideal types of the history of religion in general, but he would also be critical
of ideal types of very specific phenomena, such as an individual's religious
experience. Rather, ideal types are developed of such intermediate phenomena
as Calvinism, Pietism, Methodism, and Baptism (Weber, 1904–05/1958).

Although ideal types are to be derived from the real world, they are not to
be mirror images of that world. Rather, they are to be one-sided exaggerations
of the essence of what goes on in the real world. In Weber's view, the more
exaggerated the ideal type, the more useful it will be for historical research.

The use of the word *ideal* or *utopia* should not be construed to mean that
the concept being described is in any sense the best of all possible worlds. As
used by Weber, the term meant that the form described in the concept was
rarely, if ever, found in the real world. In fact, Weber argued that the ideal
type need not be positive or correct; it can just as easily be negative or even
morally repugnant (1903–17/1949).

Ideal types should make sense in themselves, the meaning of their components should be compatible, and they should aid us in making sense out
of the real world. Although we have come to think of ideal types as describing
static entities, Weber believed that they could describe either static or dynamic
entities. Thus we can have an ideal type of structure, such as a bureaucracy,
or of a social development, such as bureaucratization.

Ideal types also are not developed once and for all. Because society is constantly changing, and the interests of social scientists are as well, it is necessary
to develop new typologies to fit the changing reality. This is in line with
Weber's view that there can be no timeless concepts in the social sciences
(Roth, 1968).

Although we have presented a relatively unambiguous image of the ideal
type, there are contradictions in the way Weber defined the concept. In addition, in his own substantive work, Weber used the ideal type in ways that
differed from the ways he said it was to be used. As Burger noted, ''The ideal
types presented in *Economy and Society* are a mixture of definitions, classification, and specific hypotheses seemingly too divergent to be reconcilable with
Weber's statements'' (1976:118). Although she disagrees with Burger on
Weber's inconsistency in defining ideal types, Hekman (1983:38–59) also recognizes that Weber offers several varieties of ideal types:

HGSAS - cos.
MOTIVATIONAS

1 *Historical ideal types.* These relate to phenomena found in some particular historical epoch (for example, the modern capitalistic marketplace).
2 *General sociological ideal types.* These relate to phenomena that cut across a number of historical periods and societies (for example, bureaucracy).
3 *Action ideal types.* These are pure types of action based on the motivations of the actor (for example, affectual action).
4 *Structural ideal types.* These are forms taken by the causes and consequences of social action (for example, traditional domination).

Clearly Weber developed an array of varieties of ideal types, and some of the richness in his work stems from their diversity, although common to them all is their mode of construction.

Values   *COMP w/ MARX*

Modern sociological thinking in America on the role of values in the social sciences has been shaped to a large degree by an interpretation, often simplistic and erroneous, of Weber's notion of *value-free* sociology. A common perception of Weber's view is that social scientists should *not* let their personal values influence their scientific research in any way. As we will see, Weber's work on values is far more complicated and should not be reduced to the simplistic notion that values should be kept out of sociology.

Values and Teaching   Weber (1903–17/1949) was most clear about the need for teachers to control their personal values in the classroom. From his point of view, academicians have a perfect right to express their personal values freely in speeches, in the press, and so forth, but the academic lecture hall is different. Weber was opposed to those teachers who preached "their evaluations on ultimate questions 'in the name of science' in governmentally privileged lecture halls in which they are neither controlled, checked by discussion, nor subject to contradiction . . . the lecture hall should be held separate from the arena of public discussion" (1903–17/1949:4). The most important difference between a public speech and an academic lecture lies in the nature of the audience. A crowd watching a public speaker has chosen to be there and can leave at any time. But students, if they want to succeed, have little choice but to listen attentively to their professor's value-laden positions. There is little ambiguity in this aspect of Weber's position on value-freedom. The academician is to express "facts," not personal values, in the classroom. Although teachers may be tempted to insert values because they make a course more interesting, teachers should be wary of employing values, because such values will "weaken the students' taste for sober empirical analysis" (Weber, 1903–17/1949:9). The only question is whether it is realistic to think that professors could eliminate most values from their presentations. Weber could adopt this position because he believed it possible to separate fact and value. However, Marx would disagree, because in his view fact and value were intertwined, dialectically interrelated.

Values shape what we study

Values and Research   Weber's position on the place of values in social research is far more ambiguous. Weber did believe in the ability to separate fact from value, and this view could be extended to the research world: "Investigator and teacher should keep unconditionally separate the establishment of empirical facts . . . and *his* own personal evaluations, i.e., his evaluation of these facts as satisfactory or unsatisfactory" (1903–17/1949:11). He often differentiated between existential knowledge of what is and normative knowledge of what ought to be (Weber, 1903–17/1949). For example, on the founding of the German Sociological Society, he said: "The Association rejects, in principle and definitely, all propaganda for action-oriented ideas from its midst." Instead, the association was pointed in the direction of the study of "what is, why something is the way it is, for what historical and social reasons" (Roth, 1968:5).

However, several facts point in a different direction and show that despite the above evidence, Weber did not operate with the simplistic view that values should be totally eliminated from social research. While, as we will see, Weber perceived a role for values in a specific aspect of the research process, he thought that they should be kept out of the actual collection of research data. By this Weber meant that we should employ the regular procedures of scientific investigation, such as accurate observation and systematic comparison. Values are to be restricted to the time before social research begins. They should shape the selection of what we choose to study. Weber's (1903–17/1949:21) ideas on the role of values prior to social research are captured in his concept of value-relevance. As with many other of Weber's methodological concepts, value-relevance is derived from the work of the German historicist Heinrich Rickert, for whom it involved "a selection of those parts of empirical reality which for human beings embody one or several of those general cultural values which are held by people in the society in which the scientific observers live" (Burger, 1976:36). In historical research, this would mean that the choice of objects to study would be made on the basis of what is considered important in the particular society in which the researchers live. That is, they choose what to study of the past on the basis of the contemporary value system. In his specific case, Weber wrote of value-relevance from the "standpoint of the interests of the modern European" (1903–17/1949:30). For example, bureaucracy was a very important part of the German society of Weber's time, and he chose, as a result, to study that phenomenon (or the lack of it) in various historical settings.

Thus, to Weber, value judgments are not to be completely withdrawn from scientific discourse. Although Weber was opposed to confusing fact and value, he did not believe that values should be excised from the social sciences: "An *attitude of moral indifference* has no connection with *scientific* 'objectivity'" (1903–17/1949:60). He was prepared to admit that values have a certain place, though he warned researchers to be careful about the role of values: "It should be constantly made clear . . . exactly at which point the scientific investigator becomes silent and the evaluating and acting person begins to speak" (Weber,

1903–17/1949:60). When expressing the value positions, sociological researchers must always keep themselves and their audiences aware of those positions.

There is a gap between what Weber said and what he actually did. Weber was not afraid to express a value judgment, even in the midst of the analysis of historical data. For example, he said that the Roman state suffered from a convulsive sickness of its social body. It can be argued that in Weber's actual work values were not only a basic device for selecting subjects to study but also were involved in the acquisition of meaningful knowledge of the social world.

Most American sociologists regard Weber as an exponent of value-free sociology. The truth is that most American sociologists themselves subscribe to the idea of value-freedom, and they find it useful to invoke Weber's name in support of their position. As we have seen, however, Weber's work is studded with values.

One other aspect of Weber's work on values worth noting is his ideas on the role of the social sciences in helping people make choices among various ultimate value positions. Basically, Weber's view is that there is *no way of scientifically choosing* among alternative value positions. Thus social scientists cannot presume to make such choices for people. "The social sciences, which are strictly empirical sciences, are the least fitted to presume to save the individual the difficulty of making a choice" (Weber, 1903–17/1949:19). The social scientist can derive certain factual conclusions from social research, but this research cannot tell people what they "ought" to do. Empirical research can help people choose an adequate means to an end, but it cannot help them choose that end as opposed to other ends. Weber says, "It can never be the task of an empirical science to provide binding norms and ideals from which directions for immediate practical activity can be derived" (1903–17/1949:52).

SUBSTANTIVE SOCIOLOGY

We turn now to Weber's substantive sociology. We will begin, as did Weber in his monumental *Economy and Society*, at the levels of action and interaction, but we will soon encounter the basic anomaly in Weber's work:[4] despite his seeming commitment to a sociology of small-scale processes, his work is primarily at the large-scale levels of the social world.

What Is Sociology?

In discussing what Weber meant by sociology, as well as the inconsistencies between his programmatic statements and his substantive sociology, we should remember that his work on sociology per se came late in his career, long after he had done most of his historical studies. It may well be that the gaps and inconsistencies that appear in his work are traceable to the inherent

---

[4] Many Weberians would disagree with this portrayal of anomaly in Weber's work.

differences between sociology and history and not simply to differences between his programmatic statements and his substantive work.

In articulating his view on sociology, Weber often took a stance against the large-scale evolutionary sociology, the organicism, that was preeminent in the field at the time. For example, Weber said: "I became one [a sociologist] in order to put an end to collectivist notions. In other words, sociology, too, can only be practiced by proceeding from the action of one or more, few or many, individuals, that means, by employing a strictly 'individualist' method" (Roth, 1976:306). Despite his stated adherence to an "individualist" method, Weber was forced to admit that it is impossible to eliminate totally collective ideas from sociology.[5] But even when he admitted the significance of collective concepts, Weber ultimately reduced them to patterns and regularities of individual action: "For the subjective interpretation of action in sociological work these collectivities must be treated as *solely* the resultants and modes of organization of the particular acts of individual persons, since these alone can be treated as agents in a course of subjectively understandable action" (1921/1968:13). At the individual level, Weber was deeply concerned with meaning, and the way in which it was formed. There seems little doubt that Weber believed in, and intended to undertake, a microsociology. But is that, in fact, what he did? Guenther Roth, one of Weber's foremost interpreters, provides us with an unequivocal answer in his description of the overall thrust of *Economy and Society:* "the first strictly *empirical comparison of social structure* and normative order in *world-historical* depth" (1968:xxvii). Mary Fulbrook directly addresses the discontinuity in Weber's work:

> Weber's overt emphasis on the imporance of [individual] meanings and motives in causal explanation of social action does not correspond adequately with the true mode of explanation involved in his comparative-historical studies of the world religions. Rather, the ultimate level of causal explanation in Weber's substantive writings is that of the social-structural conditions under which certain forms of meaning and motivation can achieve historical efficacy.
>
> COll + SUBJECTIVE ⨂   (Fulbrook, 1978:71)

Lars Udehn (1981) has cast light on this problem in interpreting Weber's work by distinguishing between Weber's methodology and his substantive concerns and recognizing that there is a conflict or tension between them. In Udehn's view, Weber uses an "individualist and subjectivist methodology" (1981:131). In terms of the latter, Weber is interested in what individuals do and why they do it (their subjective motives). In the former, Weber is interested in reducing collectivities to the actions of individuals. However, in most of his substantive sociology (as we will see), Weber focuses on large-scale structure (such as bureaucracies, capitalism) and is not focally concerned with what individuals do or why they do it.[6] Such structures are not reduced by Weber to the actions of individuals, and the actions of those in them are

---

[5] In fact, Weber's ideal types *are* collective concepts.
[6] Udehn argues that one exception is Weber's analysis of the behavior of leaders.

determined by the structures, not by their motives. There is little doubt that there is an enormous contradiction in Weber's work, and it will concern us through much of this chapter.

With this as background, we are now ready for Weber's definition of *sociology*: "Sociology . . . is a *science* concerning itself with the *interpretive understanding* of *social action* and thereby with a *causal* explanation of its course and consequences" (1921/1968:4). This definition provides a useful bridge between the preceding section on Weber's methodology and the ensuing discussion of his substantive work. Among the themes discussed earlier that are mentioned or implied in this definition are:

Sociology should be a science.

Sociology should be concerned with causality. (Here, apparently, Weber was combining sociology and history.)

Sociology should utilize interpretive understanding (*verstehen*).

We are now ready for the specific components of Weber's microsociology.

Social Action

Weber's entire sociology, if we accept his words at face value, was based on his conception of social action (S. Turner, 1983). He differentiated between action and purely reactive behavior. The concept of behavior is reserved, then as now (Ritzer, 1975a), to automatic behavior that involves no thought processes. A stimulus is presented and behavior occurs, with little intervening between stimulus and response. Such behavior was not of interest in Weber's sociology. He was concerned with action that clearly involved the intervention of thought processes (and the resulting meaningful action) between the occurrence of a stimulus and the ultimate response. To put it slightly differently, action was said to occur when individuals attached subjective meanings to their action. To Weber, the task of sociological analysis involved "the interpretation of action in terms of its subjective meaning" (1921/1968:8). A good, and more specific, example of Weber's thinking on action is found in his discussion of *economic action,* which he defined as "a *conscious, primary* orientation to economic consideration . . . for what matters is not the objective necessity of making economic provision, but the belief that it is necessary" (1921/1968:64).

In embedding his analysis in mental processes and the resulting meaningful action, Weber (1921/1968) was careful to point out that it is erroneous to regard psychology as the foundation of the sociological interpretation of action. Weber seemed to be making essentially the same point made by Durkheim in discussing at least some nonmaterial social facts. That is, sociologists are interested in mental processes, but this is not the same as psychologists' interest in the mind, personality, and so forth.

Although Weber implied that he had a great concern with mental processes, he actually spent little time on them. Hans Gerth and C. Wright Mills called attention to Weber's lack of concern with mental processes: "Weber sees in the concept of personality a much abused notion referring to a profoundly irrational center of creativity, a center before which analytical inquiry comes to a halt" (1958:55). Schutz (1932/1967) was quite correct when he pointed out that although Weber's work on mental processes is suggestive, it is hardly the basis for a systematic microsociology. But it was the suggestiveness of his work that made him relevant to those who developed the theories of individuals and their behavior—symbolic interactionism, phenomenology, and so forth.

In his action theory, Weber's clear intent was to focus on individuals and patterns and regularities of action and not on the collectivity. "Action in the sense of subjectively understandable orientation of behavior exists only as the behavior of one or more *individual* human beings" (Weber, 1921/1968:13). Weber was prepared to admit that for some purposes, we may have to treat collectivities as individuals, "but for the subjective interpretation of action in sociological work these collectivities must be treated as *solely* the resultants and modes of organization of the particular acts of individual persons, since these alone can be treated as agents in a course of subjectively understandable action" (1921/1968:13). It would seem that Weber could hardly be more explicit: the sociology of action is ultimately concerned with individuals, *not* collectivities.

Weber utilized his ideal-type methodology to clarify the meaning of *action* by identifying four basic types of action. Not only is this typology significant for understanding what Weber meant by action, but it is also, in part, the basis for Weber's concern with larger social structures and institutions. Of greatest importance is Weber's differentiation between the two basic types of rational action. The first is *means-ends rationality*, or action that is "determined by expectations as to the behavior of objects in the environment and of other human beings; these expectations are used as 'conditions' or 'means' for the attainment of the actor's own rationally pursued and calculated ends" (Weber, 1921/1968:24). The second is *value rationality*, or action that is "determined by a conscious belief in the value for its own sake of some ethical, aesthetic, religious, or other form of behavior, independently of its prospects for success" (Weber, 1921/1968:24–25). *Affectual* action (which was of little concern to Weber) is determined by the emotional state of the actor. *Traditional* action (which was of far greater concern to Weber) is determined by the actor's habitual and customary ways of behaving.

It should be noted that although Weber differentiated four ideal typical forms of action, he was well aware that any given action usually involves some combination of all four ideal types of action. In addition, Weber argued that sociologists have a much better chance of understanding action of the more rational variety than they do of understanding action dominated by affect or tradition.

We turn now to Weber's thoughts on social stratification, or his famous ideas on class, status, and party (or power). His analysis of stratification is one of the areas in his work in which Weber does operate, at least at first, as an action theorist.

Class, Status, and Party

One import of this analysis is that Weber refused to reduce stratification to economic factors (or class, in Weber's terms) but saw it as multidimensional. Thus, society is stratified on the bases of economics, status, and power. One implication of this is that people can rank high on one or two of these dimensions of stratification and low on the other (or others). This permits a far more sophisticated analysis of social stratification than is possible when stratification is simply reduced (as it was by some Marxists) to variations in one's economic situation.

Starting with class, Weber adhered to his action orientation by arguing that a class is not a community. Rather, a class is a group of people whose shared situation is a possible, and sometimes frequent, basis for action by the group. Weber contends that a "class situation" exists when three conditions are met:

> (1) A number of people have in common a specific causal component of their life chances, insofar as (2) this component is represented exclusively by economic interests in the possession of goods and opportunities for income, and (3) is represented under the conditions of the commodity or labor markets. This is "class situation."
> (Weber, 1921/1968:927)

The concept of "class" refers to any group of people found in the same class situation. Thus a class is *not* a community but merely a group of people in the same economic, or market, situation.

In contrast to class, status does normally refer to communities; status groups are ordinarily communities, albeit rather amorphous ones. "Status situation" is defined by Weber as "every typical component of the life of men that is determined by a specific, positive or negative, social estimation of honor" (1921/1968:932). As a general rule, status is associated with a style of life. (Status relates to consumption of goods produced, while class relates to economic production.) Those at the top of the status hierarchy have a different lifestyle than do those at the bottom. Thus, while high-status people may have cocktail parties, low-status people may be more likely to have "beer blasts." Those at the top may wear tuxedos to their social occasions, while those at the bottom may wear jeans. In this case, lifestyle, or status, is related to class situation. But class and status are not necessarily linked to one another: "Money and an entrepreneurial position are not in themselves status qualifications, although they may lead to them; and the lack of property is not in itself a status disqualification, although this may be a reason for it" (Weber, 1921/1968:306). There is a complex set of relationships between class and status, and it is made even more complicated when we add the dimension of party.

While classes exist in the economic order and status groups in the social order, parties can be found in the political order. To Weber parties "are always *structures* struggling for domination" (cited in Gerth and Mills, 1958:195; italics added). Thus parties are the most organized elements of Weber's stratification system. Weber thinks of parties very broadly as including not only those that exist in the state but also those that may exist in a social club. Parties usually, but not always, represent class and/or status groups. Whatever they represent, parties are oriented to the attainment of power.

While Weber remained close to his action approach in his ideas on social stratification, these ideas already indicate a movement in the direction of macro-level communities and structures. In most of his other work, Weber focused on such large-scale units of analysis. Not that Weber lost sight of the action; the actor simply moved from being the focus of his concern to being largely a dependent variable determined by a variety of large-scale forces. For example, as we will see, Weber believed that individual Calvinists are impelled to act in various ways by the norms, values, and beliefs of their religion, but his focus was not on the individual but on the collective forces that impel the actor.

Structures of Authority

Weber's sociological interest in the structures of authority was motivated, at least in part, by his political interests. Weber was no political radical; in fact, he was often called the "bourgeois Marx" to reflect the similarities in the intellectual interests of Marx and Weber as well as their very different political orientations. Although Weber was almost as critical of modern capitalism as Marx, he did not advocate revolution. He wanted to change society gradually, not overthrow it. He had little faith in the ability of the masses to create a "better" society. But Weber also saw little hope in the middle classes, which he felt were dominated by shortsighted, petty bureaucrats. Weber was critical of authoritarian political leaders like Bismarck, who he felt left lower-level political leadership severely weakened. Nevertheless, for Weber the hope—if indeed he had any hope—lay with the great political leaders rather than with the masses or the bureaucrats. Along with his faith in political leaders went his unswerving nationalism. He placed the nation above all else: "The vital interests of the nation stand, of course, above democracy and parliamentarianism" (Weber, 1921/1968:1383). Weber preferred democracy as a political form not because he believed in the masses but because it offered maximum dynamism and the best milieu to generate political leaders (Mommsen, 1974). Weber noted that authority structures exist in every social institution, and his political views were related to his analysis of these structures in all settings. Of course, they were most relevant to his views on the polity.

Weber began his analysis of authority structures in a way that was consistent with his assumptions about the nature of action. He defined *domination* as the "probability that certain specific commands (or all commands) will be obeyed by a given group of persons" (Weber, 1921/1968:212). Domination can have a variety of bases, legitimate as well as illegitimate, but what mainly interested Weber were the legitimate forms of domination, or what he called _authority_. What concerned Weber, and what played a central role in much of his sociology, were the three bases on which authority is made legitimate to followers—the rational, traditional, and charismatic bases. In defining these three bases, Weber remained fairly close to his ideas on individual action, but he rapidly moved to the large-scale structures of authority. Authority legitimized on _rational_ grounds rests "on a belief in the legality of enacted rules and the right of those elevated to authority under such rules to issue commands" (Weber, 1921/1968:215). Authority legitimized on _traditional_ grounds is based on "an established belief in the sanctity of immemorial traditions and the legitimacy of those exercising authority under them" (Weber, 1921/1968:215). Finally, authority legitimized by _charisma_[7] rests on the devotion of followers to the exceptional sanctity, heroism, or exemplary character of leaders as well as on the normative order sanctioned by them. All these modes of legitimizing authority clearly imply individual actors, thought processes (beliefs), and actions. But from this point, Weber, in his thinking about authority, did move quite far from an individual action base, as we will see when we discuss the authority structures erected on the basis of these types of legitimacy.

Legal Authority   Legal authority can take a variety of structural forms, but the one that interested Weber most was the _bureaucracy_, which he considered "the purest type of exercise of legal authority" (1921/1968:220).

Ideal-Typical Bureaucracy   Weber depicted bureaucracies in ideal-typical terms. Although he was well aware of their failings, Weber portrayed bureaucracies in a highly positive way:

> From a purely technical point of view, a bureaucracy is capable of attaining the highest degree of efficiency, and is in this sense formally the most rational known means of exercising authority over human beings. It is superior to any other form in precision, in stability, in the stringency of its discipline, and its reliability. It thus makes possible a particularly high degree of calculability of results for the heads of the organization and for those acting in relation to it. It is finally superior both in intensive efficiency and in the scope of its operations and is formally capable of application to all kinds of administrative tasks.
>
> (Weber, 1921/1968:223)

Despite his discussion of the positive characteristics of bureaucracies, here and elsewhere in his work, there is a fundamental ambivalence in his attitude toward them. Although he detailed their advantages, he was well aware of their problems. Weber expressed various reservations about bureaucratic organizations. For example, he was cognizant of the "red tape" that often makes dealing with bureaucracies so trying and so difficult. His major fear,

---

[7] The term _charisma_ is also used in Weber's work in a variety of other ways and contexts; see Miyahara (1983).

however, was that the rationalization that dominates all aspects of bureaucratic life was a threat to individual liberty. As Weber put it:

> No machinery in the world functions so precisely as this apparatus of men and, moreover, so cheaply. . . . Rational calculation . . . reduces every worker to a cog in this bureaucratic machine and, seeing himself in this light, he will merely ask how to transform himself into a somewhat bigger cog. . . . The passion for bureaucratization drives us to despair.
>
> (Weber, 1921/1968:liii)

Weber was appalled by the effects of bureaucratization and, more generally, of the rationalization of the world of which bureaucratization is but one component, but he saw no way out. He described bureaucracies as "escape proof," "practically unshatterable," and among the hardest institutions to destroy once they are established. Along the same lines, he felt that individual bureaucrats could not "squirm out" of the bureaucracy once they were "harnessed" in it. Weber concluded that "the future belongs to bureaucratization" (1921/1968:1401), and time has borne out his prediction.

Weber would say that his depiction of the advantages of bureaucracy is part of his ideal-typical image of the way it operates. The ideal-typical bureaucracy is a purposeful exaggeration of the rational characteristics of bureaucracies. Such an exaggerated model is useful for heuristic purposes and for studies of organizations in the real world, but it is not to be mistaken for a realistic depiction of the way bureaucracies actually operate.

Weber distinguished the ideal-typical bureaucracy from the ideal-typical bureaucrat. He conceived of bureaucracies as structures and of bureaucrats as positions within those structures. He did *not*, as his action orientation might lead us to expect, offer a social psychology of organizations or of the individuals who inhabit those bureaucracies (as modern symbolic interactionists, ethnomethodologists, and phenomenologists might).

The ideal-typical bureaucracy is a type of organization. Its basic units are offices organized in a hierarchical manner with rules, functions, written documents, and means of compulsion. All these are, to varying degrees, large-scale structures that represent the thrust of Weber's thinking. He could, after all, have constructed an ideal-typical bureaucracy that focused on the thoughts and actions of individuals within the bureaucracy. There is a whole school of thought in the study of organizations that focuses precisely on this level rather than on the structures of bureaucracies (see, for example, Blankenship, 1977).

The following are the major characteristics of the ideal-typical bureaucracy:

1 It consists of a continuous organization of official functions (offices) bound by rules.
2 Each office has a specified sphere of competence. The office carries with it a set of obligations to perform various functions, the authority to carry out these functions, and the means of compulsion required to do the job.
3 The offices are organized into a hierarchical system.

4 The offices may carry with them technical qualifications that require that the participants obtain suitable training.
5 The staff that fills these offices does not own the means of production associated with them,[8] staff members are provided with the use of those things that they need to do the job.
6 The incumbent is not allowed to appropriate the position; it always remains part of the organization.
7 Administrative acts, decisions, and rules are formulated and recorded in writing.

A bureaucracy is one of the rational structures that is playing an ever-increasing role in modern society, but one may wonder whether there is any alternative to the bureaucratic structure. Weber's clear and unequivocal answer was that there is no possible alternative: "The needs of mass administration make it today completely indispensable. The choice is only between bureaucracy and dilettantism in the field of administration" (1921/1968:223).

Although we might admit that bureaucracy is an intrinsic part of modern capitalism, we might ask whether a socialist society might be different. Is it possible to create a socialist society without bureaucracies and bureaucrats? Once again, Weber was unequivocal: "When those subject to bureaucratic control seek to escape the influence of existing bureaucratic apparatus, this is normally possible only by creating an organization of their own which is equally subject to the process of bureaucratization" (1921/1968:224). In fact, Weber believed that in the case of socialism we would see an increase, not a decrease, in bureaucratization. If socialism were to achieve a level of efficiency comparable to capitalism, "it would mean a tremendous increase in the importance of professional bureaucrats" (Weber 1921/1968:224). In capitalism, at least the owners are not bureaucrats, but in socialism even the top-level leaders would be bureaucrats. Weber thus believed that even with its problems "capitalism presented the best chances for the preservation of individual freedom and creative leadership in a bureaucratic world" (Mommsen, 1974:xv). We are once again at a key theme in Weber's work: his view that there is really no hope for a better world. Socialists can, in Weber's view, only make things worse by expanding the degree of bureaucratization in society. Weber noted: "Not summer's bloom lies ahead of us, but rather a polar night of icy darkness and hardness, no matter which group may triumph externally now" (cited in Gerth and Mills, 1958:128).

A ray of hope in Weber's work—and it is a small one—is that professionals who stand outside the bureaucratic system can control it to some degree. In this category, Weber included professional politicians, scientists, and even capitalists, as well as the supreme heads of the bureaucracies. For example, Weber said that politicians "must be the countervailing force against bureaucratic

---

[8] Here and elsewhere in his work Weber adopts a Marxian interest in the means of production. This is paralleled by his concern with alienation, not only in the economic sector but throughout social life (science, politics, and so forth).

domination" (1921/1968:1417). His famous essay "Politics as a Vocation" is basically a plea for the development of political leaders with a calling to oppose the rule of bureaucracies and of bureaucrats. Similarly, in "Science as a Vocation" Weber made a plea for professional scientists who can counteract the increasing bureaucratization and rationalization of science. But in the end these appear to be rather feeble hopes. In fact, a good case can be made that these professionals are simply another aspect of the rationalization process and that their development only serves to accelerate that process (Nass, 1986; Ritzer, 1975c; Ritzer and Walczak, 1988).

In Weber's recently translated " 'Churches' and 'Sects' in North America: An Ecclesiastical Socio-Political Sketch" (1906/1985), Colin Loader and Jeffrey Alexander (1985) see a forerunner of Weber's thoughts on the hope provided by an ethic or responsibility in the face of the expansion of bureaucratization. American sects such as the Quakers practice an ethic of responsibility by combining rationality and larger values. Rogers Brubaker defines the *ethic of responsibility* as "the passionate commitment to ultimate values with the dispassionate analysis of alternative means of pursuing them" (1984:108). He contrasts this to the *ethic of conviction,* in which a rational choice of means is foregone and the actor orients "his action to the realization of some absolute value or unconditional demand" (1984:106). The ethic of conviction often involves a withdrawal from the rational world, whereas the ethic of responsibility involves a struggle within that world for greater humanness. The ethic of responsibility provides at least a modicum of hope in the face of the onslaught of rationalization and bureaucratization.

Traditional Authority   In his thinking about traditional authority structures, Weber used his ideal-typical bureaucracy as a methodological tool. His objective was to pinpoint the differences between a traditional authority structure and the ideal-typical bureaucracy.

Whereas legal authority stems from the legitimacy of a rational-legal system, traditional authority is based on a claim by the leaders, and a belief on the part of the followers, that there is virtue in the sanctity of age-old rules and powers. The leader in such a system is not a superior but a personal master. The administrative staff consists not of officials but mainly of personal retainers. In Weber's words, "Personal loyalty, not the official's impersonal duty, determines the relations of the administrative staff to the master" (1921/1968:227). Although the bureaucratic staff owes its allegiance and obedience to enacted rules and to the leader, who acts in their name, the staff of the traditional leader obeys because the leader carries the weight of tradition—he or she has been chosen for that position in the traditional manner.

What interested Weber was the staff of the traditional leader and how it measured up to the ideal-typical bureaucratic staff. He concluded that it was lacking on a number of counts. The traditional staff lacks offices with clearly defined spheres of competence that are subject to impersonal rules. It also does not have a rational ordering of relations of superiority and inferiority; it lacks a clear hierarchy. There is no regular system of appointment and pro-motion on the basis of free contracts. Technical training is not a regular requirement for obtaining a position or an appointment. Appointments do not carry with them fixed salaries paid in money.

Weber used his ideal-type methodology not only to compare traditional to rational-legal authority and to underscore the most salient characteristics of traditional authority but also to analyze historically the different forms of traditional authority. He differenitated between two very early forms of tra-ditional authority. A *gerontocracy* involves rule by elders, whereas *primary patriarchalism* involves leaders who inherit their positions. Both of these forms have a supreme chief but lack an administrative staff. They therefore lack a bureaucracy. A more modern form is *patrimonialism,* which is traditional dom-ination with an administration and a military force that are purely personal instruments of the master. Still more modern is *feudalism,* which limits the discretion of the master through the development of more routinized, even contractual, relationships between leader and subordinate. This, in turn, leads to more stabilized power positions than exist in patrimonialism. All four of these forms may be seen as structural variations of traditional authority, and all of them differ significantly from rational-legal authority.

Weber saw structures of traditional authority, in any form, as barriers to the development of rationality. This is our first encounter with an overriding theme in Weber's work—factors that facilitate or impede the development of (formal) rationality (see below). Over and over we find Weber concerned, as he was here, with the structural factors conducive to rationality in the Western world and the structural and cultural impediments to the develop-ment of a similar rationality throughout the rest of the world. In this specific case, Weber argued that the structures and practices of traditional authority constitute a barrier to the rise of rational economic structures—in particular, capitalism—as well as to various other components of a rational society. Even patrimonialism—a more modern form of traditionalism—while permitting the development of certain forms of "primitive" capitalism, does not allow for the rise of the highly rational type of capitalism characteristic of the modern West.

Charismatic Authority   Charisma is a concept that has come to be used very broadly. The news media and the general public are quick to point to a politician, a movie star, or a rock musician as a charismatic individual. By this they most often mean that the person in question is endowed with extraor-dinary qualities. The concept of charisma plays an important role in the work of Max Weber, but he had a conception of it very different from that held by most laypeople today. Although Weber did not deny that a charismatic leader may have outstanding characteristics, his sense of charisma was more depend-ent on the group of disciples and the way that they *define* the charismatic leader. To put Weber's position bluntly, if the disciples define a leader as charismatic, then he or she is likely to be a charismatic leader irrespective of whether he or she actually possesses any outstanding traits. A charismatic leader, then, can be someone who is quite ordinary. What is crucial is the process by which such a leader is set apart from ordinary people and treated as if endowed with supernatural, superhuman, or at least exceptional powers or qualities that are not accessible to the ordinary person (Miyahara, 1983).

To Weber, charisma was a revolutionary force, one of the most important revolutionary forces in the social world. Whereas traditional authority clearly is inherently conservative, the rise of a charismatic leader may well pose a threat to that system (as well as to a rational-legal system) and lead to a dramatic change in that system. What distinguishes charisma as a revolution-ary force is that it leads to changes in the minds of actors; it causes a "sub-jective or internal reorientation." Such changes may lead to "a radical alteration of the central attitudes and direction of action with a completely new orientation of all attitudes toward different problems of the world" (Weber, 1921/1968:245). Although Weber was here addressing changes in the thoughts and actions of individuals, such changes are clearly reduced to the status of dependent variables. Weber focused on changes in the structure of authority, that is, the rise of charismatic authority. When such a new authority structure emerges, it is likely to change people's thoughts and actions dra-matically.

The other major revolutionary force in Weber's theoretical system, and the one with which he was much more concerned, is (formal) rationality. Whereas charisma is an internal revolutionary force that changes the minds of actors, Weber saw (formal) rationality as an external revolutionary force changing the structures of society first and then ultimately the thoughts and actions of indi-viduals. We will have more to say about rationality as a revolutionary force later, but this closes our discussion of charisma as a revolutionary factor, because Weber had very little to say about it. Weber was interested in the revolutionary character of charisma as well as its structure and the necessity that its basic character be transformed and routinized in order for it to survive as a system of authority.

In his analysis of charisma, Weber began, as he did with traditional author-ity, with the ideal-typical bureaucracy. He sought to determine to what degree the structure of charismatic authority, with its disciples and staff, differs from the bureaucratic system. Compared to that of the ideal-typical bureaucracy, the staff of the charismatic leader is lacking on virtually all counts. The staff members are not technically trained but are chosen instead for their possession of charismatic qualities or, at least, of qualities similar to those possessed by the charismatic leader. The offices they occupy form no clear hierarchy. Their work does not constitute a career, and there are no promotions, clear appoint-ments, or dismissals. The charismatic leader is free to intervene whenever he or she feels that the staff cannot handle a situation. The organization has no formal rules, no established administrative organs, and no precedents to guide new judgments. In these and other ways, Weber found the staff of the charismatic leader to be "greatly inferior" to the staff in a bureaucratic form of organization.

Weber's interest in the organization behind the charismatic leader and the staff that inhabits it led him to the question of what happens to charismatic authority when the leader dies. After all, a charismatic system is inherently fragile; it would seem to be able to survive only as long as the charismatic leader lives. But is it possible for such an organization to live after the leader dies? The answer to this question is of greatest consequence to the staff members of the charismatic leader, for they are likely to live on after the leader dies. They are also likely to have a vested interest in the continued existence of the organization: if the organization ceases to exist, they are out of work. Thus the challenge for the staff is to create a situation in which charisma in some adulterated form persists even after the leader's death. It is a difficult struggle because, for Weber, charisma is by its nature unstable; it exists in its pure form only as long as the charismatic leader lives.

In order to cope with the departure of the charismatic leader, the staff (as well as the followers) may adopt a variety of strategies to create a more lasting organization. The staff may search out a new charismatic leader, but even if the search is successful, the new leader is unlikely to achieve the same aura as his or her predecessor. A set of rules also may be developed that allows the group to identify future charismatic leaders. But such rules rapidly become tradition, and what was charismatic leadership is on the way toward becoming traditional authority. In any case, the nature of leadership is radically changed as the purely personal character of charisma is eliminated. Still another technique is to allow the charismatic leader to designate his or her successor and thereby to transfer charisma symbolically to the next in line. Again it is questionable whether this is ever very successful or whether it can be successful in the long run. Another strategy is having the staff designate a successor and having its choice accepted by the larger community. The staff could also create ritual tests, with the new charismatic leader being the one who successfully undergoes the tests. However, all these efforts are doomed to failure. In the long run, charisma cannot be routinized; it must be transformed into either traditional or rational-legal authority (or into some sort of institutionalized charisma like the Catholic Church).

Indeed, we find a basic theory of history in Weber's work. If successful, charisma almost immediately moves in the direction of routinization. But once routinized, charisma is en route to becoming either traditional or rational-legal authority. Once it achieves one of those states, the stage is set for the cycle to begin all over again. However, despite a general adherence to a cyclical theory, Weber believed that a basic change has occurred in the modern world and that we are more and more likely to see charisma routinized in the direction of rational-legal authority. Furthermore, he saw rational systems of authority as stronger and as increasingly impervious to charismatic movements. The modern, rationalized world may well mean the death of charisma as a significant revolutionary force. Weber contended that rationality—not charisma—is the most irresistible and important revolutionary force in the modern world.

In this section, we have discussed the three types of authority as ideal types, but Weber was well aware that in the real world, any specific form of authority involves a combination of all three. Thus we can think of Franklin D. Roosevelt as a president of the United States who ruled on all three bases. He was elected president in accord with a series of rational-legal principles. By the time he was elected president for the fourth time, a good part of this rule had traditional elements. Finally, many disciples and followers regarded him as a charismatic leader.

Although we have presented the three forms of authority as parallel structures, in the real world there is constant tension and, sometimes, conflict among them. The charismatic leader is a constant threat to the other forms of authority. Once in power, the charismatic leader must address the threat posed by the other two forms. Even if charismatic authority is successfully routinized, there then arises the problem of maintaining its dynamism and its original revolutionary qualities. Then there is the conflict produced by the constant development of rational-legal authority and the threat it poses to the continued existence of the other forms. If Weber was right, however, we might face a future in which the tension among the three forms of authority is eliminated, a world of the uncontested hegemony of the rational-legal system. This is the "iron cage" of a totally rationalized society that Weber feared so much. If such a society were to materialize, the only hope would lie with isolated charismatic individuals who manage somehow to avoid the coercive power of society. But a small number of isolated individuals hardly represents a significant hope in the face of an increasingly powerful bureaucratic machine.

Rationalization

There has been a growing realization in recent years that rationalization lies at the heart of Weber's substantive sociology (Antonio, 1979; Brubaker, 1984; R. Collins, 1980; Eisen, 1978; Kalberg, 1980, 1990; Levine, 1981a; Ritzer, 1983, forthcoming a; Scaff, 1989; Schluchter, 1981; Sica, 1988). However, it is difficult to extract a clear definition of *rationalization* from Weber's work. In fact, he operated with a number of different definitions of the term, and he often failed to specify which definition he was using in a particular discussion (Brubaker, 1984:1). As we saw earlier, Weber did define *rationality*; indeed, he differentiated between two types—means-ends and value rationality. However, these concepts refer to types of *action*. They are the basis of, but not coterminous with, Weber's larger-scale sense of rationalization. Weber is interested in far more than fragmented action orientations; his main concern is with regularities and patterns of action within civilizations, institutions, organizations, strata, classes, and groups. Donald Levine (1981a) argues that Weber is interested in "objectified" rationality; that is, action that is in accord with some

TYPES OF RATIONALITY

process of external systematization. Stephen Kalberg (1980) performs a useful service by identifying four basic types of ("objective") rationality in Weber's work. (Levine offers a very similar differentiation.) These types of rationality were "the basic heuristic tools [Weber] employed to scrutinize the historical fates of rationalization as sociocultural processes" (Kalberg, 1980:1172).

The first type is *practical rationality,* which is defined by Kalberg as "every way of life that views and judges worldly activity in relation to the individual's purely pragmatic and egoistic interests" (1980:1151). People who practice practical rationality accept given realities and merely calculate the most expedient ways of dealing with the difficulties that they present. This type of rationality arose with the severing of the bonds of primitive magic, and it exists trans-civilizationally and trans-historically; that is, it is not restricted to the modern Occident. This type of rationality stands in opposition to anything that threatens to transcend everyday routine. It leads people to distrust all impractical values, either religious or secular-utopian, as well as the theoretical rationality of the intellectuals, the type of rationality to which we now turn.

Theoretical rationality involves a cognitive effort to master reality through increasingly abstract concepts rather than through action. It involves such abstract cognitive processes as logical deduction, induction, attribution of causality, and the like. This type of rationality was accomplished early in history by sorcerers and ritualistic priests and later by philosophers, judges, and scientists. Unlike practical rationality, theoretical rationality leads the actor to transcend daily realities in a quest to understand the world as a meaningful cosmos. Like practical rationality, it is trans-civilizational and trans-historical. The effect of intellectual rationality on action is limited. In that it involves cognitive processes, it need not affect action taken, and it has the potential to introduce new patterns of action only indirectly.

Substantive rationality (like practical rationality, but *not* theoretical rationality) directly orders action into patterns through clusters of values. Substantive rationality involves a choice of means to ends within the context of a system of values. This means that one value system is no more (substantively) rational than another. Thus, this type of rationality also exists trans-civilizationally and trans-historically, wherever consistent value postulates exist. INSTRUMENTAL

Finally, and most important from the author's point of view, is *formal rationality,* which involves means-ends calculation. But whereas in practical rationality this calculation occurs in reference to pragmatic self-interests, in formal rationality it occurs with reference to "universally applied rules, laws, and regulations." As Brubaker puts it, "Common to the rationality of industrial capitalism, formalistic law and bureaucratic administration is its objectified, institutionalized, supra-individual form; in each sphere, rationality is embodied in the social structure and confronts individuals as something external to them" (1984:9). Weber makes this quite clear in the specific case of bureaucratic rationalization:

> Bureaucratic rationalization . . . revolutionizes with *technical means,* in principle, as does every economic reorganization, 'from without': It *first* changes the material

and social orders, and *through* them the people, by changing the conditions of adaptation, and perhaps the opportunities for adaptation, through a rational determination of means and ends.

(Weber, 1921/1968:1116)

Although all the other types of rationality are trans-civilizational and epoch-transcending, formal rationality arose *only* in the West with the coming of industrialization. The universally applied rules, laws, and regulations that characterize formal rationality in the West are found particularly in the economic, legal, and scientific institutions, as well as in the bureaucratic form of domination. Thus, we have already encountered formal rationality in our discussion of rational-legal authority and the bureaucracy.

Although Weber had a complex, multifaceted sense of rationalization, he used it most powerfully and meaningfully in his image of the modern Western world, especially in the capitalistic economy (R. Collins, 1980; Weber, 1927/1981) and bureaucratic organizations (Cohen, 1981:xxxi; Weber, 1921/1968:956–1005), as an iron cage (Mitzman, 1970; Tiryakian, 1981) of formally rational structures. Weber described capitalism and bureaucracies as "two great rationalizing forces" (1921/1968:698).[9] In fact, Weber saw capitalism and bureaucracies as being derived from the same basic source (innerworldly asceticism), involving similarly rational and methodical action, reinforcing one another and in the process furthering the rationalization of the Occident.[10] In Weber's (1921/1968:227, 994) view, the only real rival to the bureaucrat in technical expertise and factual knowledge was the capitalist.

However, if we take Weber at his word, it is difficult to argue that he had an overarching theory of rationalization. He rejected the idea of "general evolutionary sequence" (Weber, 1927/1981:34). He was critical of thinkers like Hegel and Marx, who he felt offered general, teleological theories of society. In his own work, he tended to shy away from studies of, or proclamations about, whole societies. Instead, he tended to focus, in turn, on social structures and institutions such as bureaucracy, stratification, law, the city, religion, the polity, and the economy. Lacking a sense of the whole, he was unlikely to make global generalizations, especially about future directions. Furthermore, the rationalization process that Weber described in one social structure or institution was usually quite different from the rationalization of another structure or institution. As Weber put it, the process of rationalization assumes "unusually varied forms" (1922–23/1958:293; see also Weber, 1921/1958:30; 1904–05/1958:78), and "the history of rationalism shows a development which by no means follows parallel lines in the various departments of life" (1904–05/1958:77; see also Brubaker, 1984:9; Kalberg, 1980:1147).

---

[9] In the 1920 introduction to *The Protestant Ethic and the Spirit of Capitalism,* Weber focused on "a specially trained organization of officials" (bureaucracy) in his discussion of rationalization, but he also mentioned capitalism in the same context as "the most fateful force in our modern life."

[10] Of course, these are not completely distinct because large capitalistic enterprises are one of the places in which we find bureaucracies (Weber, 1922–23/1958:299). On the other hand, Weber also sees the possibility that bureaucracies can stand in opposition to, can impede, capitalism.

This being said, it is clear that Weber does have a deep concern for the overarching effect of the formal rationalization of the economy and bureaucracies on the Western world (Brubaker, 1984). For example, in *Economy and Society*, Weber says:

> This whole process of rationalization in the factory as elsewhere, and especially in the bureaucratic state machine, parallels the centralization of the material implements of organization in the hands of the master. Thus, discipline inexorably takes over ever larger areas as the satisfaction of political and economic needs is increasingly rationalized. This universal phenomenon more and more restricts the importance of charisma and of individually differentiated conduct.
>
> (Weber, 1921/1968:1156)

Formal rationalization will be our main, but certainly not only, concern in this section.

Various efforts have been made to delineate the basic characteristics of formal rationality. In our view, formal rationality may be defined in terms of six basic characteristics (Ritzer, 1983, forthcoming a.) First, formally rational structures and institutions emphasize *calculability*, or those things that can be counted or quantified. Second, there is a focus on *efficiency*, on finding the best means to a given end. Third, there is great concern with ensuring *predictability*, or that things operate in the same way from one time or place to another. Fourth, a formally rational system progressively reduces human technology and ultimately *replaces human technology with nonhuman technology*. Nonhuman technologies (such as computerized systems) are viewed as more calculable, more efficient, and more predictable than human technologies. Fifth, formally rational systems seek to gain *control* over an array of uncertainties, especially the uncertainties posed by human beings who work in, or are served by, them. Finally, rational systems tend to have a series of *irrational consequences* for people involved with them and for the systems themselves, as well as for the larger society (Sica, 1988).

Formal rationality stands in contrast to all the other types of rationality but is especially in conflict with substantive rationality (Brubaker, 1984:4). Kalberg argues that Weber believed that the conflict between these two types of rationality played "a particularly fateful role in the unfolding of rationalization processes in the West" (1980:1157).

In addition to differentiating among the four types of rationality, Kalberg also deals with their capacity to introduce methodical ways of life. Practical rationality lacks this ability because it involves reactions to situations rather than efforts to order them. Theoretical rationality is cognitive and, therefore, has a highly limited ability to suppress practical rationality and seems to be more of an end product than a producer. To Weber, substantive rationality is the *only* type with the "potential to introduce methodical ways of life" (Kalberg, 1980:1165). Thus, in the West, a particular substantive rationality with an emphasis on a methodical way of life—Calvinism—subjugated practical rationality and led to the development of formal rationality.

Weber's fear was that substantive rationality was becoming less significant than the other types of rationality, especially formal rationality, in the West. Thus practitioners of formal rationality, like the bureaucrat and the capitalist, were coming to dominate the West, and one was witnessing a fading away of the type that "embodied Western civilization's highest ideals: the autonomous and free individual whose actions were given continuity by their reference to ultimate values" (Kalberg, 1980:1176).

Although we have emphasized the differences among Weber's four types of rationalization in this section, there are a number of commonalities among them. They all involve mental processes that seek to master reality by banishing particularized perceptions and to order them into comprehensible and meaningful regularities. Thus as we move from institution to institution in the ensuing discussion, we, like Weber, sometimes focus on rationalization in general and, at other times, on the specific types of rationalization.

Economy The most systematic presentation of Weber's thoughts on the rationalization of the economic institution is to be found in his *General Economic History*. Weber's concern is with the development of the rational capitalistic economy in the Occident, which is a specific example of a rational economy defined as a "functional organization oriented to money-prices which originate in the interest-struggles of men in the *market*" (Weber, 1915/1958:331). Although there are the outlines of a general evolutionary trend in *General Economic History*, Weber, as always, is careful to point out that there are various sources of capitalism, alternative routes to it, and a range of results emanating from it. In fact, in the course of rejecting the socialistic theory of evolutionary change, Weber rejects the whole idea of a "general evolutionary sequence" (1927/1981:34).

Weber begins by depicting various irrational and traditional forms such as the household, clan, village, and manorial economies. For example, the lord of the manor in feudalism was described by Weber as being too traditionalistic, "too lacking in initiative to build up a business enterprise in a large scale into which the peasants would have fitted as a labor force" (1927/1981:72). However, by the twelfth and thirteenth centuries in the Occident, feudalism began to break down as the peasants and the land were freed from control by the lord and a money economy was introduced. With this breakdown, the manorial system "showed a strong tendency to develop in a capitalistic direction" (Weber, 1927/1981:79). *FEUD*

At the same time, in the Middle Ages, cities were beginning to develop. Weber focuses on the largely urban development of industry involved in the transformation of raw materials. Especially important to Weber is the development of such industrial production beyond the immediate needs of the house community. Notable here is the rise of free craftsmen in the cities. They developed in the Middle Ages in the Occident because, for one thing, this society had developed greater consumptive needs than any other. In general, there were larger markets, more purchasers, and the peasantry had greater

IND —CRAFTSMAN

SLAVERY

purchasing power. On the other side, forces operated against the major alternative to craftsmen—slaves. Slavery was found to be too unprofitable and too unstable, and it was made increasingly more unstable by the growth of the towns that offered freedom to the slaves.

In the Occident, along with free craftsmen came the development of the guild, defined by Weber as "an organization of craft workers specialized in accordance with the type of occupation . . . [with] internal regulation of work and monopolization against outsiders" (1927/1981:136). Freedom of association was also characteristic of the guilds. But although rational in many senses, guilds also had traditional, anticapitalistic aspects. For example, one master was not supposed to have more capital than another, and this requirement was a barrier to the development of large capitalistic organizations.

As the Middle Ages came to a close, the guilds began to disintegrate. This disintegration was crucial because the traditional guilds stood in the way of technological advance. With the dissolution of the guild system came the rise of the domestic system of production, especially the "putting out" system in the textile industry. In such a system, production was decentralized, with much of it taking place within the homes of the workers. Although domestic systems were found throughout the world, it was only in the Occident that the owners controlled the means of production (for example, tools, raw materials) and provided them to the workers in exchange for the right to dispose of the product. Whereas a fully developed domestic system developed in the West, it was impeded in other parts of the world by such barriers as the clan system (China), the caste system (India), traditionalism, and the lack of free workers.

Next, Weber details the development of the workshop (a central work setting without advanced machinery) and then the emergence of the factory in the fourteenth through sixteenth centuries. In Weber's view, the factory did not arise out of craft work or the domestic system, but alongside them. Similarly, the factory was not called into existence by advances in machinery; the two developments were correlated with each other. The factory was characterized by free labor that performed specialized and coordinated activities, ownership of the means of production by the entrepreneur, the fixed capital of the entrepreneur, and the system of accounting that is indispensable to such capitalizaton. Such a factory was, in Weber's view, a capitalistic organization. In addition to the development of the factory, Weber details the rise of other components of a modern capitalistic economy, such as advanced machinery, transportation systems, money, banking, interest, bookkeeping systems, and so on.

What most clearly defines modern rational capitalistic enterprises for Weber is their calculability, which is best represented in their reliance on modern bookkeeping. Isolated calculable enterprises existed in the past in the Occident as well as in other societies. However, an entire society is considered capitalistic only when the everyday requirements of the population are supplied by

capitalistic methods and enterprises. Such a society is found only in the Occi- _Demand_
dent and there only since the mid-nineteenth century. _from_
   The development of a capitalistic system hinged on a variety of develop- _free L.F._
ments within the economy as well as within the larger society. Within the _DISC W.F._
economy, some of the prerequisites included a free market with large and _M ECono_
steady demand, a money economy, inexpensive and rational technologies, a _TECH-INEX_
4 free labor force, a disciplined labor force, rational capital-accounting tech- _COMMERCIA_
niques, and the commercialization of economic life involving the use of shares,
stocks, and the like. Many of the economic prerequisites were found only in
the Occident. Outside the economy, Weber identified a variety of needed
developments such as a modern state with "professional administration, specialized officialdom, and law based on the concept of citizenship" (1927/ _SPEC-_
1981:313), rational law "made by jurists and rationally interpreted and _OFFICIA_
applied" (1927/1981:313), cities, and modern science and technology. To these _COOM_
Weber adds a factor that will concern us in the next section, "a rational ethic _ADMIN_
for the conduct of life . . . a religious basis for the ordering of life which _LAW_
consistently followed out must lead to explicit rationalism" (1927/1981:313–
314). Like the economic prerequisites, these noneconomic presuppositions _MODERN_
occurred together only in the Occident. The basic point is that a rational econ- _SCIENCE_
omy is dependent upon a variety of noneconomic forces throughout the rest _+TECH._
of society in order to develop.

   Religion   Although we will focus on the rationalization of religion in this
section, Weber spent much time analyzing the degree to which early, more
primitive religions—and religions in much of the world—acted as impediments to the rise of rationality. Weber noted that "the sacred is the uniquely
unalterable" (1921/1968:406). Despite this view, religion in the West did prove
to be alterable; it was amenable to rationalization, and it did play a key role
in the rationalization of other sectors of society (Kalberg, 1990).
   Early religion was composed of a bewildering array of gods, but with
rationalization a clear and coherent set of gods (a pantheon) emerged. Early
religions had household gods, kin-group gods, local political gods, and occupational and vocational gods. We get the clear feeling that Weber did believe
that a cultural force of (theoretical) rationality impelled the emergence of this
set of gods: "*Reason* favored the primacy of universal gods; and every consistent crystallization of a pantheon followed systematic *rational* principles"
(1921/1968:417). A pantheon of gods was not the only aspect of the rationalization of religion discussed by Weber. He also considered the delimitation of
the jurisdiction of gods, monotheism, and the anthropomorphization of gods
as part of this development. Although the pressure for rationalization exists
in many of the world's religions, in areas outside the Western world, the
barriers to rationalization more than counterbalance the pressures for rationalization.
   Although Weber had a cultural conception of rationalization, he did not

view it simply as a force "out there" that impels people to act. He did not have a group-mind concept. In religion, rationalization is tied to concrete groups of people, in particular to priests. Specifically, the professionally trained priesthood is the carrier and the expediter of rationalization. In this, priests stand in contrast to magicians, who support a more irrational religious system. The greater rationality of the priesthood is traceable to several factors. Members go through a systematic training program, whereas the training of magicians is unsystematic. Also, priests are fairly highly specialized, whereas magicians tend to be unspecialized. Finally, priests possess a systematic set of religious concepts, and this, too, sets them apart from magicians. We can say that priests are both the products and the expediters of the process of rationalization.

The priesthood is not the only group that plays a key role in rationalization. Prophets and a laity are also important in the process. Prophets can be distinguished from priests by their personal calling and their emotional preaching. The key role of the prophet is the mobilization of the laity, because there would be no religion without a group of followers. Weber differentiated between two types of prophets, ethical and exemplary. _Ethical prophets_ (Muhammad, Jesus Christ, and the Old Testament Prophets) believe that they have received a commission directly from God and demand obedience from followers as an ethical duty. _Exemplary prophets_ (Buddha is a model) demonstrate to others by personal example the way to religious salvation. In either case, successful prophets are able to attract large numbers of followers, and it is this mass, along with the priests, that forms the heart of religion. Prophets are likely at first to attract a personal following, but it is necessary that that group be transformed into a permanent congregation. Once such a laity has been formed, major strides have been made in the direction of the rationalization of religion.

Prophets play a key initial role, but once a congregation is formed, they are no longer needed. In fact, because they are largely irrational, they represent a barrier to that rationalization of religion. A conflict develops between priests and prophets, but it is a conflict that must be won in the long run by the more rational priesthood. In their conflict, the priests are aided by the rationalization proceeding in the rest of society. As the secular world becomes more and more literate and bureaucratized, the task of educating the masses falls increasingly to the priests, whose literacy gives them a tremendous advantage over the prophets. In addition, while the prophets tend to do the preaching, the priests take over the task of day-to-day pastoral care. Although preaching is important during extraordinary times, pastoral care, or the daily religious cultivation of the laity, is an important instrument in the growing power of the priesthood. It was the church in the Western world that combined a rationalized pastoral character with an ethical religion to form a peculiarly influential and rational form of religion. This rationalized religion proved particularly well suited to winning converts among the urban middle class, and it was there that it played a key role in the rationalization of economic life as well as all other sectors of life.

Law *Law* is defined by Weber not in terms of people's definitions, attitudes, and beliefs but rather as a body of norms (Kronman, 1983:12). Additionally, this body of norms is seen as being external to, and coercive of, individuals and their thoughts and actions. The emphasis is not on how people create law, interpret it, and daily recreate it but on its coercive effect on the individual.

As with his analysis of religion, Weber began his treatment of law with the primitive, which he saw as highly irrational. Primitive law was a rather undifferentiated system of norms. For example, no distinction was made between a civil wrong (a tort) and a crime. Thus cases involving differences over a piece of land and homicide were likely to be handled, and offenders punished, in much the same way. In addition, primitive law tended to lack any official machinery. Vengeance dominated reactions to a crime, and law was generally free from procedural formality or rules. Leaders, especially, were virtually unrestrained in what they could do to followers. From this early irrational period, Weber traced a direct line of development to a formalized legal procedure. And as was usual in Weber's thinking, it is only in the West that a rational, systematic theory of law is held to have developed.

Weber traced several stages in the development of a more rational legal system. An early stage involves charismatic legal revelation through law prophets. Then there is the empirical creation and founding of law by honorary legal officials. Later there is the imposition of law by secular or theocratic powers. Finally, in the most modern case, we have the systematic elaboration of law and professionalized administration of justice by persons who have received their legal training formally and systematically.

In law, as in religion, Weber placed great weight on the process of professionalization: the legal profession is crucial to the rationalization of Western law. There are certainly other factors (for example, the influence of Roman law), but the legal profession was central to his thinking: "Formally elaborated law constituting a complex of maxims consciously applied in decisions has never come into existence without the decisive cooperation of trained specialists" (Weber, 1921/1968:775). Although Weber was aware that there was a series of external pressures—especially from the rationalizing economy—impelling law toward rationalization, his view was that the most important force was the internal factor of the professionalization of the legal profession (1921/1968:776).

Weber differentiated between two types of legal training but saw only one as contributing to the development of rational law. The first is *craft training*, in which apprentices learn from masters, primarily during the actual practice of law. This kind of training produces a formalistic type of law dominated by precedents. The goal is not the creation of a comprehensive, rational system of law but, instead, the production of practically useful precedents for dealing with recurring situations. Because these precedents are tied to specific issues in the real world, a general, rational, and systematic body of law cannot emerge.

In contrast, *academic legal training* laid the groundwork for the rational law of the West. In this system, law is taught in special schools, where the emphasis is placed on legal theory and science—in other words, where legal phenomena are given rational and systematic treatment. The legal concepts produced have the character of abstract norms. Interpretation of these laws occurs in a rigorously formal and logical manner. They are general, in contrast to the specific, precedent-bound laws produced in the case of craft training.

Academic legal training leads to the development of a rational legal system with a number of characteristics, including the following:

1 Every concrete legal decision involves the application of abstract legal propositions to concrete situations.
2 It must be possible in every concrete case to derive the decision logically from abstract legal propositions.
3 Law must tend to be a gapless system of legal propositions or at least be treated as one.
4 The gapless legal system should be applicable to all social actions.

Weber seemed to adopt the view that history has seen law evolve from a cultural system of norms to a more structured system of formal laws. In general, actors are increasingly constrained by a more and more rational legal system. Although this is true, Weber was too good a sociologist to lose sight completely of the independent significance of the actor. For one thing, Weber (1921/1968:754–755) saw actors as crucial in the emergence of, and change in, law. However, the most important aspect of Weber's work in this area—for the purposes of this discussion—is the degree to which law is regarded as part of the general process of rationalization throughout the West.

Polity   The rationalization of the political system is intimately linked to the rationalization of law and, ultimately, to the rationalization of all elements of the social system. For example, Weber argued that the more rational the political structure becomes, the more likely it is to eliminate systematically the irrational elements within the law. A rational polity cannot function with an irrational legal system, and vice versa. Weber did not believe that political leaders follow a conscious policy of rationalizing the law; rather, they are impelled in that direction by the demands of their own increasingly rational means of administration. Once again, Weber took the position that actors are being impelled by structural (the state) and cultural (rationalization) forces.

Weber defined the *polity* as "a community whose social action is aimed at subordinating to orderly domination by the participants a territory and the conduct of the persons within it, through readiness to resort to physical force, including normally force of arms" (1921/1968:901). This type of polity has existed neither everywhere nor always. It does not exist as a separate entity where the task of armed defense against enemies is assigned to the household, the neighborhood association, an economic group, and so forth. Although Weber clearly viewed the polity as a social structure, he was more careful to link his thinking here to his individual action orientations. In his view, modern political associations rest on the prestige bestowed upon them by their members.

As was his usual strategy, Weber went back to the primitive case in order to trace the development of polity. He made it clear that violent social action is primordial. However, the monopolization and rational ordering of legitimate violence did not exist in early societies but evolved over the centuries. Not only is rational control over violence lacking in primitive society, but other basic functions of the modern state either are totally absent or are not ordered in a rational manner. Included here would be functions like legislation, police, justice, administration, and the military. The development of the polity in the West involves the progressive differentiation and elaboration of these functions. But the most important step is their subordination under a single, dominant, rationally ordered state.

The City Weber was also interested in the rise of a distinctively rational city in the West. He defined a *city* as having the following characteristics:

1 It is a relatively closed settlement.
2 It is relatively large.
3 It possesses a marketplace.
4 It has partial political autonomy. —STRUCT.

Although many cities in many societies had these characteristics, Western cities developed a peculiarly rational character with, among other things, a rationally organized marketplace and political structure.

Weber looked at various other societies in order to determine why they did not develop the rational form of the city. He concluded that barriers like the traditional community in China and the caste system in India impeded the rise of such a city. But in the West, a number of rationalizing forces coalesced to create the modern city. For example, the development of a city requires a relatively rational economy. But of course the converse is also true: the development of a rational economy requires the modern city.

Art Forms To give the reader a sense of the breadth of Weber's thinking, we need to say a few words about his work on the rationalization of various art forms. For example, Weber (1921/1958) viewed music in the West as having developed in a peculiarly rational direction. Musical creativity is reduced to routine procedures based on comprehensive principles. Music in the Western world has undergone a "transformation of the process of musical production into a calculable affair operating with known means, effective instruments, and understandable rules" (Weber, 1921/1958:li). Although the process of rationalization engenders tension in all the institutions in which it occurs, that tension is nowhere more noticeable than in music. After all, music is supposed to be an arena of expressive flexibility, but it is being progressively reduced to a rational, and ultimately mathematical, system.

Weber (1904–05/1958) sees a similar development in other art forms. For example, in painting, Weber emphasizes "the rational utilization of lines and spatial perspective—which the Renaissance created for us" (1904–05/1958:15). In architecture, "the rational use of the Gothic vault as a means of distributing pressure and of roofing spaces of all forms, and above all as the constructive principle of great monumental buildings and the foundation of a *style* extending to sculpture and painting, such as that created by our Middle Ages, does not occur elsewhere [in the world]" (Weber, 1904–05/1958:15).

We have now spent a number of pages examining Weber's ideas on rationalization in various aspects of social life. Although nowhere does he explicitly say so, we believe that Weber adopted the view that changes in the cultural level of rationality are leading to changes in the structures as well as in the individual thoughts and actions of the modern world. The rationalization process is not left to float alone above concrete phenomena but is embedded in various social structures and in the thoughts and actions of individuals. To put it slightly differently, the key point is that the cultural system of rationality occupies a position of casual priority in Weber's work. We can illustrate this in still another way by looking at Weber's work on the relationship between religion and economics, more specifically, the relationship between religion and the development, or lack of development, of a capitalist economy.

Religion and the Rise of Capitalism

Weber spent much of his life studying religion—this in spite of, or perhaps because of, his being areligious, or, as he once described himself, "religiously unmusical" (Gerth and Mills, 1958:25). One of his overriding concerns was the relationship among a variety of the world's religions and the development only in the West of a capitalist economic system. It is clear that the vast bulk of this work is done at the structural and cultural levels; the thoughts and actions of Calvinists, Buddhists, Confucians, Jews, Muslims (B. Turner, 1974), and others are held to be affected by changes in social structures and social institutions. Weber was primarily interested in the systems of ideas of the world's religions, in the "spirit" of capitalism, and in rationalization as a modern system of norms and values. He was also very interested in the structures of the world's religions, the various structural components of the societies in which they exist that serve to facilitate or impede rationalization, and the structural aspects of capitalism and the rest of the modern world.

Weber's work on religion and capitalism involved an enormous body of cross-cultural historical research. Freund summarized the complicated interrelationships involved in this research:

1 Economic forces influenced Protestantism.
2 Economic forces influenced religions other than Protestantism (for example, Hinduism, Confucianism, and Taoism).
3 Religious idea systems influence individual thoughts and actions—in particular, economic thoughts and actions.
4 Religious idea systems have been influential throughout the world.
5 Religious idea systems (particularly Protestantism) have had the unique effect in the West of helping to rationalize the economic sector and virtually every other institution.

(Freund, 1968:213)

To this we can add:

6 Religious idea systems in the non-Western world have encountered overwhelming structural barriers to rationalization.

By according the religious factor great importance, Weber appeared to be simultaneously building on and criticizing his image of Marx's work. Weber, like Marx, operated with a complicated model of the interrelationship of primarily large-scale systems: "Weber's sociology is related to Marx's thought in the common attempt to grasp the interrelations of institutional orders making up a social structure: In Weber's work, military and religious, political and juridical institutional systems are functionally related to the economic order in a variety of ways" (Gerth and Mills, 1958:49). In fact, Weber's affinities with Marx are even greater than are often recognized. Although Weber, especially early in his career, gave primacy to religious ideas, he later came to see that material forces, not idea systems, are of central importance (Kalberg, 1985:61). As Weber said, "Not ideas, but material and ideal interests, directly govern men's conduct. Yet very frequently the 'world images' that have been created by 'ideas' have, like switchmen, determined the tracks along which action has been pushed by the dynamic of interest" (Gerth and Mills, 1958:280).

In analyzing the relationship between the world's religions and the economy, Weber (1921/1963) developed a typology of the paths of salvation. Asceticism is the first broad type of religiosity, and it combines an orientation toward action with the commitment of believers to denying themselves the pleasures of the world. Ascetic religions are divided into two subtypes. Otherworldly asceticism involves a set of norms and values that command the followers to work within the secular world but to fight against its temptations. Of greater interest to Weber, because it encompasses Calvinism, was innerworldly asceticism. Such a religion does not reject the world, instead, it actively urges its members to work within the world so that they can find salvation, or at least signs of it. The distinctive goal here is the strict, methodical control of the members' patterns of life, thought, and action. Members are urged to reject everything unethical, esthetic, or dependent on their emotional reactions to the secular world. Innerworldly ascetics are motivated to systematize their own conduct.

Whereas both types of ascetisicm involve some type of action and self-denial, _mysticism_ involves contemplation, emotion, and inaction. Weber sub-divided mysticism in the same way as asceticism. _World-rejecting mysticism_ involves total flight from the world. _Innerworldly mysticism_ leads to contemplative efforts to understand the meaning of the world, but these efforts are doomed to failure, because the world is viewed as being beyond individual comprehension. In any case, both types of mysticism and world-rejecting asceticism can be seen as idea systems that inhibit the development of capitalism and rationality. In contrast, innerworldly asceticism is the system of norms and values that contributed enormously to the development of these phenomena in the West.

The Protestant Ethic and the Spirit of Capitalism   In Max Weber's best-known work, _The Protestant Ethic and the Spririt of Capitalism_ (1904–05/1958), he traced the impact of ascetic Protestantism—primarily Calvinism—on the rise of the spirit of capitalism. This work is but a small part of a larger body of scholarship that traces the relationship between religion and modern capitalism throughout much of the world.

Weber, especially later in his work, made it clear that his most general interest was in the rise of the distinctive rationality of the West. Capitalism, with its rational organization of free labor, its open market, and its rational bookkeeping system, is but one component of that developing system. He directly linked it to the parallel development of rationalized science, law, politics, art, architecture, literature, universities, and the polity.

Weber did not directly link the idea system of the Protestant ethic to the structures of the capitalist system; instead, he was content to link the Protestant ethic to another system of ideas, the "spirit of capitalism." In other words, two systems of ideas are directly linked in this work. Although links of the capitalist economic system to the material world are certainly implied and indicated, they were not Weber's primary concern. Thus, _The Protestant Ethic_ is not about the rise of modern capitalism but is about the origin of a peculiar spirit that eventually made capitalism possible.

Weber began by examining and rejecting alternative explanations of why capitalism arose in the West in the sixteenth and seventeenth centuries. To those who contended that capitalism arose because the material conditions were right at that time, Weber retorted that material conditions were also ripe at other times and capitalism did not arise. Weber also rejected the psychological theory that the development of capitalism was due simply to the acquisitive instinct. In his view, such an instinct always has existed, yet it did not produce capitalism in other situations.

Evidence for Weber's views on the significance of Protestantism was found in an examination of those countries with mixed religious systems. In looking at these countries, he discovered that the leaders of the economic system—business leaders, owners of capital, high-grade skilled labor, and more advanced technically and commercially trained personnel—were all overwhelmingly Protestant. This was taken to mean that Protestantism was a significant cause in the choice of these occupations and, conversely, that other religions (for example, Roman Catholicism) failed to produce idea systems that impelled individuals into these vocations.

In Weber's view, the spirit of capitalism is not defined simply by economic greed; it is in many ways the exact opposite. It is a moral and ethical system, an ethos, that among other things stresses economic success. In fact, it was the turning of profit making into an ethos that was critical in the West. In other societies, the pursuit of profit was seen as an individual act motivated at least in part by greed. Thus it was viewed by many as morally suspect. However, Protestantism succeeded in turning the pursuit of profit into a moral crusade. It was the backing of the moral system that led to the unprecedented expansion of profit seeking and, ultimately, to the capitalist system. On a theoretical level, by stressing that he was dealing with the relationship between one ethos (Protestantism) and another (the spirit of capitalism), Weber was able to keep his analysis primarily at the level of systems of ideas.

The spirit of capitalism can be seen as a normative system that involves a number of interrelated ideas. For example, its goal is to instill an "attitude which seeks profit rationally and systematically" (Weber, 1904–05/1958:64). In addition, it preaches an avoidance of life's pleasures: "Seest thou a man diligent in business? He shall stand before kings" (Weber, 1904–05/1958:53). Also included in the spirit of capitalism are ideas such as "time is money," "be industrious," "be frugal," "be punctual," "be fair," and "earning money is a legitimate end in itself." Above all, there is the idea that it is people's duty ceaselessly to increase their wealth. This takes the spirit of capitalism out of the realm of individual ambition and into the category of ethical imperative. Although Weber admitted that a type of capitalism (for example, adventurer capitalism) existed in China, India, Babylon, and the classical world and during the Middle Ages, it was different from Western capitalism, primarily because it lacked "this particular ethos" (1904–05/1958:52).

Weber was interested not simply in describing this ethical system but also in explaining its derivations. He thought that Protestantism, particularly Calvinism, was crucial to the rise of the spirit of capitalism. Calvinism is no longer necessary to the continuation of that economic system. In fact, in many senses modern capitalism, given its secularity, stands in opposition to Calvinism and to religion in general. Capitalism today has become a real entity that combines norms, values, market, money, and laws. It has become, in Durkheim's terms, a social fact that is external to, and coercive of, the individual. As Weber put it:

> Capitalism is today an immense cosmos into which the individual is born, and which presents itself to him, at least as an individual, as an unalterable order of things in which he must live. It forces the individual, in so far as he is involved in the system of market relationships, to conform to capitalist rules of action.
>
> (Weber, 1904–05/1958:54)

Another crucial point here is that Calvinists did not consciously seek to create a capitalist system. In Weber's view, capitalism was an *unanticipated consequence* of the Protestant ethic. The concept of unanticipated consequences has broad significance in Weber's work, for he believed that what individuals and groups intend by their actions often leads to a set of consequences that are at variance with their intentions. Although Weber did not explain this point, it seems that it is related to his theoretical view that people create social structures but that those structures soon take on a life of their own, over which the creators have little or no control. Because people lack control over them, structures are free to develop in a variety of totally unanticipated directions. Weber's line of thinking led Arthur Mitzman (1970) to argue that Weber created a sociology of reification. Reified social structures are free to move in unanticipated directions, as both Marx and Weber showed in their analyses of capitalism.

Calvinism and the Spirit of Capitalism   Calvinism was the version of Protestantism that interested Weber most. One feature of Calvinism was the idea that only a small number of people are chosen for salvation. In addition, Calvinism entailed the idea of predestination; people were predestined to be either among the saved or among the damned. There was nothing that the individual or the religion as a whole could do to affect that fate. Yet the idea of predestination left people uncertain about whether they were among the saved. To reduce this uncertainty, the Calvinists developed the idea that *signs* could be used as indicators of whether a person was saved. People were urged to work hard, because if they were diligent, they would uncover the signs of salvation, which were to be found in economic success. In sum, the Calvinist was urged to engage in intense, worldly activity and to become a "man of vocation."

However, isolated actions were not enough. Calvinism, as an ethic, required self-control and a systematized style of life that involved an integrated round of activities, particularly business activities. This stood in contrast to the Christian ideal of the Middle Ages, in which individuals simply engaged in isolated acts as the occasion arose in order to atone for particular sins and to increase their chances of salvation. "The God of Calvinism demanded of his believers not single good works, but a life of good works combined into a unified system" (Weber, 1904–05/1958:117). Calvinism produced an ethical system and ultimately a group of people who were nascent capitalists. Calvinism "has the highest ethical appreciation of the sober, middle-class, self-made man" (Weber, 1904–05/1958:163). Weber neatly summarized his own position on Calvinism and its relationship to capitalism as follows:

> The religious valuation of restless, continuous, systematic work in a worldly calling, as the highest means of asceticism, and at the same time the surest and most evident proof of rebirth and genuine faith, must have been the most powerful conceivable lever for the expansion of . . . the spirit of capitalism.
>
> (Weber, 1904–05/1958:172)

In addition to its general link to the spirit of capitalism, Calvinism also had some more specific links. First, as already mentioned, capitalists could ruthlessly pursue their economic interests and feel that such pursuit was not merely self-interest but was, in fact, their ethical duty. This not only permitted unprecedented mercilessness in business but also silenced potential critics, who could not simply reduce these actions to self-interest. Second, Calvinism provided the rising capitalist "with sober, conscientious and unusually industrious workmen who clung to their work as to a life purpose willed by god" (Weber, 1904–05/1958:117). With such a work force, the nascent capitalist could raise the level of exploitation to unprecedented heights. Third, it legitimized an unequal stratification system by giving the capitalist the "comforting assurances that the unequal distribution of the goods of this world was a special dispensation of Divine Providence" (Weber, 1904–05/1958:117).

Weber also had reservations about the capitalist system, as he did about all aspects of the rationalized world. For example, he pointed out that capitalism tends to produce "specialists without spirit, sensualists without heart; this nullity imagines that it has attained a level of civilization never before achieved" (Weber, 1904–05/1958:182).

Although in *The Protestant Ethic* Weber focused on the effect of Calvinism on the spirit of capitalism, he was well aware that social and economic conditions have a reciprocal impact on religion. He chose not to deal with such relationships in this book, but he made it clear that his goal was not to substitute a one-sided spiritualist interpretation for the one-sided materialist explanation that he attributed to Marxists.

If Calvinism was the major fact in the rise of capitalism in the West, then the question arises: Why didn't capitalism arise in other societies? In his effort to answer this question, Weber dealt with spiritual and material barriers to the rise of capitalism. Let us look briefly at Weber's analysis of those barriers in two societies—China and India.

Religion and Capitalism in China   One crucial assumption that allowed Weber to make legitimate the comparison between the West and China is that both had the prerequisites for the development of capitalism. In China, there was a tradition of intense acquisitiveness and unscrupulous competition. There was great industry and an enormous capacity for work in the populace. Powerful guilds existed. The population was expanding. And there was a steady growth in precious metals. With these and other material prerequisites, why didn't capitalism arise in China? As has been pointed out before, Weber's general answer was that social, structural, and religious barriers in China prevented the development of capitalism. This is not to say that capitalism was entirely absent in China. There were moneylenders and purveyors who sought high rates of profit. But a market, as well as various other components of a rational capitalistic system, were absent. In Weber's view, the rudimentary capitalism of China "pointed in a direction opposite to the development of rational economic corporate enterprises" (1916/1964:86).

Structural Barriers Weber listed several structural barriers to the rise of capitalism in China. First, there was the structure of the typical Chinese community. It was held together by rigid kinship bonds in the form of sibs. The sibs were ruled by elders, who made them bastions of traditionalism. The sibs were self-contained entities, and there was little dealing with other sibs. This encouraged small, encapsulated land holdings and a household-based, rather than a market, economy. The extensive partitioning of the land prevented major technological developments, because economies of scale were impossible. Agricultural production remained in the hands of peasants, industrial production in the hands of small-scale artisans. Modern cities, which were to become the centers of Western capitalism, were inhibited in their development because the people retained their allegiance to the sibs. Because of the sibs' autonomy, the central government was never able to govern these units effectively or to mold them into a unified whole.

The structure of the Chinese state was a second barrier to the rise of capitalism. The state was largely patrimonial and governed by tradition, prerogative, and favoritism. In Weber's view, a rational and calculable system of administration and law enforcement, which was necessary for industrial development, did not exist. There were very few formal laws covering commerce, there was no central court, and legal formalism was rejected. This irrational type of administrative structure was a barrier to the rise of capitalism, as Weber made clear: "Capital investment in industry is far too sensitive to such irrational rule and too dependent upon the possibility of calculating the steady and rational operation of the state machinery to emerge within an administration of this type" (1916/1964:103). In addition to its general structure, a number of more specific components of the state acted against the development of capitalism. For example, the officials of the bureaucratic administration had vested material interests that made them oppose capitalism. Officials often bought offices primarily to make a profit, and this kind of orientation did not necessarily make for a high degree of efficiency.

A third structural barrier to the rise of capitalism was the nature of the Chinese language. In Weber's view, it militated against rationality by making systematic thought difficult. It remained largely in the realm of the "pictorial" and the "descriptive." Logical thinking was also inhibited because intellectual thought remained largely in the form of parables, and this hardly was the basis for the development of a cumulative body of knowledge.

Although there were other structural barriers to the rise of capitalism (for example, a country without wars or overseas trade), a key factor was the lack of the required "mentality," the lack of the needed idea system. Weber looked at the two dominant systems of religious ideas in China—Confucianism and Taoism—and the characteristics of both that militated against the development of a spirit of capitalism.

Confucianism A central characteristic of Confucian thinking was its emphasis on a literary education as a prerequisite for office and for social status. To acquire a position in the ruling strata, a person had to be a member of the literati. Movement up the hierarchy was based on a system of ideas that tested literary knowledge, not the technical knowledge needed to conduct the office in question. What was valued and tested was whether the individual's mind was steeped in culture and whether it was characterized by ways of thought suitable to a cultured man. In Weber's terms, Confucianism encouraged "a highly bookish literary education." The literati produced by this system came to see the actual work of administration as beneath them, mere tasks to be delegated to subordinates. Instead, the literati aspired to clever puns, euphemisms, and allusions to classical quotations—a purely literary kind of intellectuality. With this kind of orientation, it is easy to see why the literati were unconcerned with the state of the economy or with economic activities. The world view of the Confucians ultimately grew to be the policy of the state. As a result, the Chinese state came to be only minimally involved in rationally influencing the economy and the rest of society. The Confucians maintained their influence by having the constitution decree that only they could serve as officials, and competitors to Confucians (for example, the bourgeoisie, prophets, and priests) were blocked from serving in the government. In fact, if the emperor dared to deviate from this rule, he was thought to be toying with disaster and his potential downfall.

Many other components of Confucianism militated against capitalism. It was basically an ethic of adjustment to the world and to its order and its conventions. Rather than viewing material success and wealth as a sign of salvation as the Calvinist did, the Confucian simply was led to accept things as they were. In fact, there was no idea of salvation in Confucianism, and this lack of tension between religion and the world also acted to inhibit the rise of capitalism. The snobbish Confucian was urged to reject thrift, because it was something that commoners practiced. It was not regarded as proper for a Confucian gentleman to work, although wealth was prized. Active engagement in a profitable enterprise was regarded as morally dubious and unbecoming to a Confucian's station. The acceptable goal for such a gentleman was a good position, not high profits. The ethic emphasized the abilities of a gentleman rather than the highly specialized skills that could have proved useful to a developing capitalist system. In sum, Weber contended that Confucianism became a relentless canonization of tradition.

Taoism Weber perceived Taoism as a mystical Chinese religion in which the supreme good was deemed to be a psychic state, a state of mind, and not a state of grace to be obtained by conduct in the real world. As a result, Taoists did not operate in a rational way to affect the external world. Taoism was essentially traditional, and one of its basic tenets was "Do not introduce innovations" (Weber, 1916/1964:203). Such an idea system was unlikely to produce any major changes, let alone one as far-reaching as capitalism.

One trait common to Taoism and Confucianism is that neither produced enough tension, or conflict, among the members to motivate them to much innovative action in this world:

> Neither in its official state cult nor in its Taoist aspect could Chinese religiosity produce sufficiently strong motives for a religiously oriented life for the individual such as the Puritan method represents. Both forms of religion lacked even the traces of the Satanic force or evil against which [the] pious Chinese might have struggled for his salvation.
>
> (Weber, 1916/1964:206)

As was true of Confucianism, there was no inherent force in Taoism to impel actors to change the world or, more specificially, to build a capitalist system.

Religion and Capitalism in India   For our purposes, a very brief discussion of Weber's (1916–17/1958) thinking on the relationship between religion and capitalism in India will suffice. The argument, though not its details, parallels the Chinese case. For example, Weber discussed the structural barriers of the caste system (Gellner, 1982:534). Among other things, the caste system erected overwhelming barriers to social mobility, and it tended to regulate even the most minute aspects of people's lives. The idea system of the Brahmans had a number of components. For example, Brahmans were expected to avoid vulgar occupations and to observe elegance in manners and proprieties in conduct. Indifference to the world's mundane affairs was the crowning idea of Brahman religiosity. The Brahmans also emphasized a highly literary kind of education. Although there certainly were important differences between them, the ethos of the Brahmans, like that of Confucians, presented overwhelming barriers to the rise of capitalism.

The Hindu religion posed similar ideational barriers. Its key idea was reincarnation. To the Hindu, a person is born into the caste that he or she deserves by virtue of behavior in a past life. Through faithful adherence to the ritual of caste, the Hindu gains merit for the next life. Hinduism, unlike Calvinism, was traditional in the sense that salvation was to be achieved by faithfully following the rules; innovation, particularly in the economic sphere, could not lead to a higher caste in the next life. Activity in this world was not important, because the world was seen as a transient abode and an impediment to the spiritual quest. In these and other ways, the idea system associated with Hinduism failed to produce the kind of people who could create a capitalist economic system and, more generally, a rationally ordered society.

SUMMARY

Max Weber has had a more powerful positive impact on a wide range of sociological theories than any other sociological theorist. This influence is traceable to the sophistication, complexity, and sometimes even confusion of Weberian theory. Despite its problems, Weber's work represents a remarkable fusion of historical research and sociological theorizing.

We open this chapter with a discussion of the theoretical roots and methodological orientations of Weberian theory. We see that Weber, over the course of his career, moved progressively toward a fusion of history and sociology, that is, toward the development of a historical sociology. One of his most critical methodological concepts is *verstehen*. Although this is often inter-preted as a tool to be used to analyze individual consciousness, in Weber's hands it was more often a scientific tool to analyze structural and institutional constraints on actors. We also discuss other aspects of Weber's methodology, including his propensity to think in terms of causality and to employ ideal types. In addition, we examine his analysis of the relationship between values and sociology.

The heart of Weberian sociology lies in substantive sociology, not in meth-odological statements. Although Weber based his theories on his thoughts about social action and social relationships, his main interest was the large-scale structures and institutions of society. We deal especially with his analysis of the three structures of authority—legal, traditional, and charismatic. In the context of legal authority, we deal with his famous ideal-typical bureaucracy and show how he used that tool to analyze traditional and charismatic author-ity. Of particular interest is Weber's work on charisma. Not only did he have a clear sense of it as a structure of authority, but he was also interested in the processes by which such a structure is produced.

Although his work on social structures—such as authority—is important, it is at the cultural level, in his work on the rationalization of the world, that Weber's most important insights lie. Weber articulated the idea that the world is becoming increasingly dominated by norms and values of rationalization. In this context, we discuss Weber's work on the economy, religion, law, the polity, the city, and art forms. Weber argued that rationalization was sweeping across all these institutions in the West, whereas there were major barriers to this process in the rest of the world.

Weber's thoughts on rationalization and various other issues are illustrated in his work on the relationship between religion and capitalism. At one level, this is a series of studies of the relationship between ideas (religious ideas) and the development of the spirit of capitalism and, ultimately, capitalism itself. At another level, it is a study of how the West developed a distinctively rational religious system (Calvinism) that played a key role in the rise of a rational economic system (capitalism). Weber also studied other societies, in which he found religious systems (for example, Confucianism, Taoism, and Hinduism) that inhibit the growth of a rational economic system. It is this kind of majestic sweep over the history of many sectors of the world that helps give Weberian theory its enduring significance.

CHAPTER **8**

GEORG SIMMEL

PRIMARY CONCERNS
  Dialectical Thinking
INDIVIDUAL CONSCIOUSNESS
SOCIAL INTERACTION ("ASSOCIATION")
  Interaction: Forms and Types
SOCIAL STRUCTURES
OBJECTIVE CULTURE
THE PHILOSOPHY OF MONEY
SECRECY: A CASE STUDY IN SIMMEL'S SOCIOLOGY

*T*HE impact of the ideas of Georg Simmel (1858–1918) on American sociological theory differs markedly from that of the three theorists discussed in
the preceding three chapters of this book. Marx, Durkheim, and Weber,
despite their later significance, had relatively little influence on American theory in the early twentieth century. Simmel was much better known to the
early American sociologists. In recent years, Simmel has been eclipsed by
Marx, Durkheim, and Weber, although he is far more influential today than
Comte or Spencer. His influence is apparent in several specific theories, such
as conflict theory, symbolic interactionism, exchange theory, and network
theory. Moreover, it is possible that we will see an increase in Simmel's impact
on sociological theory (Levine, 1985, 1989) as a result of the growing influence
of one of his most important works, *The Philosophy of Money* (1907/1978).

PRIMARY CONCERNS

While we will focus on Simmel's contributions to sociological theory, it should
be pointed out that he was primarily a philosopher and that most of his
publications dealt with philosophical issues (for example, ethics) and other
philosophers (for example, Kant).

  With the exception of his contribution to the primarily macroscopic conflict
theory (Coser, 1956; Simmel, 1908/1955), Georg Simmel is best known as a
microsociologist who played a significant role in the development of small-
group research (Caplow, 1968), symbolic interactionism, and exchange theory.
All of Simmel's contributions in these areas reflect his belief that sociologists
should primarily study social interaction. Robert Nisbet presents this view of
Simmel's contribution to sociology:

It is the *microsociological* character of Simmel's work that may always give him an edge in timeliness over the other pioneers. He did not disdain the small and the intimate elements of human association, nor did he ever lose sight of the primacy of human beings, of concrete individuals, in his analysis of institutions.

(Nisbet, 1959:480)

David Frisby makes a similar point: "The grounding of sociology in some psychological categories may be one reason why Simmel's sociology has proved attractive not merely to the interactionist but also to social psychology" (1984:57). However, it is often forgotten that Simmel's microsociological work on the forms of interaction is embedded in a broader theory of the relations between individuals and the larger society.

Simmel had a much more complicated and sophisticated theory of social reality than he is commonly given credit for in contemporary American sociology. Tom Bottomore and David Frisby (1978) argue that there are four basic levels of concern in Simmel's work. First are his microscopic assumptions about the psychological components of social life. Second, on a slightly larger scale, is his interest in the sociological components of interpersonal relationships. Third, and most macroscopic, is his work on the structure of, and changes in, the social and cultural "spirit" of his times. Not only did Simmel operate with this image of a three-tiered social reality, but he adopted the principle of *emergence,* the idea that the higher levels emerge out of the lower levels: "Further development replaces the immediacy of interacting forces with the creation of higher supra-individual formations, which appear as independent representatives of these forces and absorb and mediate the relations between individuals" (1907/1978:174). He also said, "If society is to be an autonomous object of an independent science, then it can only be so through the fact that, out of the sum of the individual elements that constitute it, a new entity emerges; otherwise all problems of social science would only be those of individual psychology" (Frisby, 1984:56–57). Overarching these three tiers is a fourth that involves ultimate metaphysical principles of life. These eternal truths affect all of Simmel's work and, as we will see, lead to his image of the future direction of the world.

This concern with multiple levels of social reality is reflected in Simmel's (1950; originally published in 1918) definition of three separable problem "areas" in sociology. The first he described as "pure" sociology. In this area, psychological variables are combined with forms of interaction. Although Simmel clearly assumed that actors have creative mental abilities, he gave little explicit attention to this aspect of social reality. His most microscopic work is with the *forms* that interaction takes as well as with the *types* of people who engage in interaction. The forms include subordination, superordination, exchange, conflict, and sociability. In his work on types, he differentiated between positions in the interactional structure, such as "competitor" and "coquette," and orientations to the world, such as "miser," "spendthrift," "stranger," and "adventurer." At the intermediate level is Simmel's "general"

GEORG SIMMEL: A Biographical Sketch

Georg Simmel was born in the heart of Berlin on March 1, 1858. He studied a wide range of subjects at the University of Berlin. However, his first effort to produce a dissertation was rejected, and one of his professors remarked, "We would do him a great service if we do not encourage him further in this direction" (Frisby, 1984:23). Despite this, Simmel persevered and received his doctorate in philosophy in 1881. He remained at the university in a teaching capacity until 1914, although he occupied a relatively unimportant position as *privatdozent* from 1885 to 1900. In the latter position, Simmel served as an unpaid lecturer whose livelihood was dependent on student fees. Despite his marginality, Simmel did rather well in this position, largely because he was an excellent lecturer and attracted large numbers of (paying) students (Frisby, 1981:17). His style was so popular that even cultured members of Berlin society were drawn to his lectures, which became public events.

Simmel wrote innumerable articles ("The Metropolis and Mental Life") and books (*The Philosophy of Money*). He was well known in German academic circles and even had an international following, especially in the United States, where his work was of great significance in the birth of sociology. Finally, in 1900, Simmel received official recognition, a purely honorary title at the University of Berlin, which did not give him full academic status. Simmel tried to obtain many academic positions, but he failed in spite of the support of such scholars as Max Weber.

One of the reasons for Simmel's failure was that he was a Jew in a nineteenth-century Germany rife with anti-Semitism (Kasler, 1985). Thus, in a report on Simmel written to a

sociology, dealing with the social and cultural products of human history. Here Simmel manifested his larger-scale interests in the group, the structure and history of societies and cultures. Finally, in Simmel's "philosophical" sociology, he dealt with his views on the basic nature, and inevitable fate, of humankind. Throughout this chapter, we will touch on all these levels and sociologies. We will find that although Simmel sometimes separated the different levels and sociologies, he more often integrated them into a broader totality.

Dialectical Thinking

Simmel's way of dealing with the interrelationships among three basic levels of social reality (leaving out his fourth, metaphysical level) gave his sociology a dialectical character reminiscent of Marx's sociology. A dialectical approach, as we saw earlier, is multicausal and multidirectional, integrates fact and value, rejects the idea that there are hard-and-fast dividing lines between social phenomena, focuses on social relations (B. Turner, 1986), looks not only minister of education, Simmel was described as "an Israelite through and through, in his external appearance, in his bearing and in his mode of thought" (Frisby, 1981:25). Another reason was the kind of work that he did. Many of his articles appeared in newspapers and magazines; they were written for a more general audience than simply academic sociologists. In addition, because he did not hold a regular academic appointment, he was forced to earn his living through public lectures. Simmel's audience, both for his writings and his lectures, was more the intellectual public than professional sociologists, and this tended to lead to derisive judgments from fellow professionals. For example, one of his contemporaries damned him because "his influence remained . . . upon the general atmosphere and affected, above all, the higher levels of journalism" (Troeltsch, cited in Frisby, 1981:13). Simmel's personal failures can also be linked to the low esteem that German academicians of the day had for sociology.

In 1914 Simmel finally obtained a regular academic appointment at a minor university (Strasbourg), but he once again felt estranged. On the one hand, he regretted leaving his audience of Berlin intellectuals. Thus his wife wrote to Max Weber's wife: "Georg has taken leave of the auditorium very badly. . . . The students were very affectionate and sympathetic. . . . It was a departure at the full height of life" (Frisby, 1981:29). On the other hand, Simmel did not feel a part of the life of his new university. Thus, he wrote to Mrs. Weber: "There is hardly anything to report from us. We live . . . a cloistered, closed-off, indifferent, desolate external existence. Academic activity is = 0, the people . . . alien and inwardly hostile" (Frisby, 1981:32).

World War I started soon after Simmel's appointment at Strasbourg; lecture halls were turned into military hospitals, and students went off to war. Thus, Simmel remained a marginal figure in German academia until his death in 1918. He never did have a normal academic career. Nevertheless, Simmel attracted a large academic following in his day, and his fame as a scholar has, if anything, grown over the years.

at the present but also at the past and the future, and is deeply concerned with both conflicts and contradictions.

In spite of the similarities between Marx and Simmel in their use of a dialectical approach, there are important differences between them. Of greatest importance is the fact that they focused on very different aspects of the social world and offered very different images of the future of the world. Instead of Marx's revolutionary optimism, Simmel had a view of the future closer to Weber's image of an "iron cage" from which there is no escape (for more on the intellectual relationship between Simmel and Weber, see Scaff, 1989:121–151).

Simmel manifested his commitment to the dialectic in various ways. For one thing, Simmel's sociology was always concerned with relationships, especially interaction (*association*). Overall he was ever attuned to dualisms, conflicts, and contradictions in whatever realm of the social world he happened to be working on. Donald Levine states that this perspective reflects Simmel's belief that *"the world can best be understood in terms of conflicts and contrasts between opposed categories"* (1971:xxxv). Rather than try to deal with this mode of thinking throughout Simmel's work, let us illustrate it from his work on one of his forms of interaction—*fashion.* Simmel used a similar mode of dialectical thinking in most of his essays on social forms and social types, but this discussion of fashion amply illustrates his method of dealing with these phenomena. We will also deal with the dialectic in Simmel's thoughts on subjective-objective culture and the concepts of "more-life" and "more-than-life."

Fashion In one of his typically fascinating and dualistic essays, Simmel (1904/1971) illustrated the contradictions in fashion in a variety of ways. On the one hand, fashion is a form of social relationship that allows those who wish to conform to the demands of the group to do so. On the other hand, fashion also provides the norm from which those who wish to be individualistic can deviate. Fashion involves a historical process as well: at the initial stage, everyone accepts what is fashionable; inevitably individuals deviate from this; and finally, in the process of deviation, they may adopt a whole new view of what is in fashion. Fashion is also dialectical in the sense that the success and spread of any given fashion leads to its eventual failure. That is, the distinctiveness of something leads to its being considered fashionable. However, as large numbers of people come to accept it, it ceases to be distinctive and hence it loses its attractiveness. Still another duality involves the role of the leader of a fashion movement. Such a person leads the group, paradoxically, by *following* the fashion better than anyone else, that is, by adopting it more determinedly. Finally, Simmel argued that not only does following what is in fashion involve dualities but so does the effort on the part of some people to be out of fashion. Unfashionable people view those who follow a fashion as being imitators and themselves as mavericks, but Simmel argued that the latter are simply engaging in an inverse form of imitation. Individuals may avoid what is in fashion because they are afraid that they, like their peers, will lose their individuality, but, in Simmel's view, such a fear is hardly a sign of great personal strength and independence. In sum, Simmel noted that in fashion "all . . . leading antithetical tendencies . . . are represented in one way or another" (1904/1971:317).

Simmel's dialectical thinking can be seen at a more general level as well. As we will see throughout this chapter, he was most interested in the conflicts and contradictions that exist between the individual and the larger social and cultural structures that individuals construct. These structures ultimately come to have a life of their own, over which the individual can exert little or no control.

Individual (Subjective) Culture and Objective Culture People are influenced, and in Simmel's view threatened, by social structures and, more importantly, for Simmel, by their cultural products. Simmel distinguished between individual culture and objective culture. *Objective culture* refers to those things that people produce (art, science, philosophy, and so on). *Individual (subjective) culture* is the capacity of the actor to produce, absorb, and control the elements of objective culture. In an ideal sense, individual culture shapes, and is shaped by, objective culture. The problem is that objective culture comes to have a life of its own. As Simmel put it, "They [the elements of culture] acquire fixed identities, a logic and lawfulness of their own; this new rigidity inevitably places them at a distance from the spiritual dynamic which created them and which makes them independent" (1921/1968:11). The existence of these cultural products creates a contradiction with the actors who created them because it is an example of

> the deep estrangement or animosity which exists between organic and creative processes of the soul and its contents and products: the vibrating, restless life of the creative soul; which develops toward the infinite contrasts with its fixed and ideally unchanging product and its uncanny feedback effect, which arrests and indeed rigidifies this liveliness. Frequently it appears as if creative movement of the soul was dying from its own product.
>
> (Simmel, 1921/1968:42)

As K. Peter Etzkorn said, "In Simmel's dialectic, man is always in danger of being slain by those objects of his own creation which have lost their organic human coefficient" (1968:2).

More-Life and More-Than-Life   Another area of Simmel's thinking, his philosophical sociology, is an even more general manifestation of his dialectical thinking. In discussing the emergence of social and cultural structures, Simmel took a position very similar to some of Marx's ideas. Marx used the concept of the fetishism of commodities to point up the separation between people and their products. For Marx, this separation reached its apex in capitalism, could be overcome only in the future socialist society, and thus was a specific historical phenomenon. But for Simmel this separation is inherent in the nature of human life. In philosophical terms, there is an inherent and inevitable contradiction between "more-life" and "more-than-life" (Oakes, 1984:6; Weingartner, 1959).

The issue of more-life and more-than-life is central in Simmel's essay, "The Transcendent Character of Life" (1918/1971). As the title suggests, and Simmel makes clear, *"Transcendence is immanent in life"* (1918/1971:361). People possess a doubly transcendent capability. First, because of their restless, creative capacities (more-life), people are able to transcend themselves. Second, this transcendent, creative ability makes it possible for people to constantly produce sets of objects that transcend them. The objective existence of these phenomena (more-than-life) comes to stand in irreconcilable opposition to the creative forces (more-life) that produced the objects in the first place. In other words, social life "creates and sets free from itself something that is not life but 'which has its own significance and follows its own law'" (Weingartner, citing Simmel, 1959:53). Life is found in the unity, and the conflict, between the two. As Simmel concludes, "Life finds its essence, its process, in being more-life and more-than-life" (1918/1971:374).

Thus, because of his metaphysical conceptions, Simmel came to an image of the world far closer to Weber's than to Marx's. Simmel, like Weber, saw the world as becoming an iron cage of objective culture from which people have progressively less chance of escape. We will have more to say about a number of these issues in the following sections, which deal with Simmel's thoughts on the major components of social reality.

INDIVIDUAL CONSCIOUSNESS

At the individual level, Simmel focused on forms of association and paid relatively little attention to the issue of individual consciousness, which was rarely dealt with directly in his work. Still, Simmel clearly operated with a sense that human beings possess creative consciousness. As Frisby put it, the bases of social life to Simmel were "conscious individuals or groups of individuals who interact with one another for a variety of motives, purposes, and interests" (1984:61). This interest in creativity is manifest in Simmel's discussion of the diverse forms of interaction, the ability of actors to create social structures, as well as the disastrous effects those structures have on the creativity of individuals.

All of Simmel's discussions of the forms of interaction imply that actors must be consciously oriented to one another. Thus, for example, interaction in a stratified system requires that superordinates and subordinates orient themselves to each other. The interaction would cease and the stratification system collapse if a process of mutual orientation did not exist. The same is true of all other forms of interaction.

Consciousness plays other roles in Simmel's work. For example, although Simmel believed that social (and cultural) structures come to have a life of their own, he realized that people must conceptualize such structures in order for them to have an effect on the people. Simmel stated that society is not simply "out there" but is also " 'my representation'—something dependent on the activity of consciousness" (1908/1959a:339).

Simmel also had a sense of individual conscience and of the fact that the norms and values of society become internalized in individual consciousness. The existence of norms and values both internally and externally

> explains the dual character of the moral command: that on the one hand, it confronts us as an impersonal order to which we simply have to submit, but that, on the other, no external power, but only our most private and internal impulses, imposes it upon us. At any rate, here is one of the cases where the individual, within his own consciousness, repeats the relationships which exist between him, as a total personality, and the group.
>
> (Simmel, 1908/1950a:254)

This very modern conception of internalization is a relatively undeveloped assumption in Simmel's work.

In addition, Simmel had a conception of people's ability to confront themselves mentally, to set themselves apart from their own actions, that is very similar to the views of George Herbert Mead (see Chapter 9) and symbolic interactionists (Simmel, 1918/1971:364; see also Simmel, 1907/1978:64). The actor can take in external stimuli, assess them, try out different courses of action, and then decide what to do. Because of these mental capacities, the actor is not simply enslaved by external forces. But there is a paradox in Simmel's conception of the actor's mental capacities. The mind can keep people from being enslaved by external stimuli, but it also has the capacity to reify social reality, to create the very objects that come to enslave it. As Simmel said, "Our mind has a remarkable ability to think of contents as being independent of the act of thinking" (1907/1978:65). Thus, although their intelligence enables people to avoid being enslaved by the same external stimuli that constrain lower animals, it also creates the structures and institutions that constrain their thoughts and actions.

Although we can find manifestations of Simmel's concern with consciousness in various places in his work, he did very little other than assume its existence. Raymond Aron clearly makes this point: "He [Simmel] must know the laws of behavior . . . of human reaction. But he does not try to discover or to explain what goes on in the mind itself" (1965:5–6).

SOCIAL INTERACTION ("ASSOCIATION")

Georg Simmel is best known in contemporary sociology for his contributions to our understanding of the patterns, or forms, of social interaction. He expressed his interest in this level of social reality in this way:

> We are dealing here with microscopic-molecular processes within human material, so to speak. These processes are the actual occurrences that are concatenated or hypostatized into those macrocosmic, solid units and systems. That people look at one another and are jealous of one another; that they exchange letters or have dinner together; that apart from all tangible interests they strike one another as pleasant or unpleasant; that gratitude for altruistic acts makes for inseparable union; that one asks another to point out a certain street; that people dress and adorn themselves for each other—these are a few casually chosen illustrations from the whole range of relations that play between one person and other. They may be momentary or permanent, conscious or unconscious, ephemeral or of grave consequence, but they incessantly tie men together. At each moment such threads are spun, dropped, taken up again, displaced by others, interwoven with others. These interactions among the atoms of society are accessible only to psychological microscopy.
>
> (Simmel, 1908/1959b:327–328)

Simmel made clear here that one of his primary interests was interaction (association) among conscious actors and that his intent was to look at a wide range of interactions that may seem trivial at some times but crucially important at others. His was not a Durkheimian expression of interest in social facts but a declaration of a smaller-scale focus for sociology.

Because Simmel sometimes took an exaggerated position on the importance of interaction in his sociology, many have lost sight of his insights into the larger-scale aspects of social reality. At times, for example, he equated society with interaction: "Society . . . is only the synthesis or the general term for the totality of these specific interactions. . . . 'Society' is identical with the sum total of these relations" (Simmel, 1907/1978:175). Such statements may be taken as a reaffirmation of his interest in interaction, but, as we will see, in his general and philosophical sociologies, Simmel held a much larger scale conception of society as well as culture.

Interaction: Forms and Types

One of Simmel's dominant concerns was the *form* rather than the *content* of social interaction. This concern stemmed from Simmel's identification with the Kantian tradition in philosophy, in which much is made of the difference between form and content. Simmel's position here, however, was quite simple. From Simmel's point of view, the real world is composed of innumerable events, actions, interactions, and so forth. To cope with this maze of reality (the "contents"), people order it by imposing patterns, or forms, on it. Thus, instead of a bewildering array of specific events, the actor is confronted with a limited number of forms. In Simmel's view, the sociologist's task is to do precisely what the layperson does, that is, impose a limited number of forms on social reality, on interaction in particular, so that it may be better analyzed. This methodology generally involves extracting commonalities that are found in a wide array of specific interactions. For example, the superordination and subordination forms of interaction are found in a wide range of settings, "in the state as well as in a religious community, in a band of conspirators as in an economic association, in art school as in a family" (Simmel, 1908/1959b:317). Donald Levine, one of Simmel's foremost contemporary analysts, describes Simmel's method of doing formal interactional sociology in this way: "His method is to select some bounded, finite phenomenon from the world of flux; to examine the multiplicity of elements which compose it; and to ascertain the cause of their coherence by disclosing its form. Secondarily, he investigates the origins of this form and its structural implications" (1971: xxxi). More specifically, Levine points out that "forms are the patterns exhibited by the associations" of people (1981b:65).[1]

Simmel's interest in the forms of social interaction has been subjected to various criticisms. For example, he has been accused of imposing order where there is none and of producing a series of unrelated studies that in the end really impose no better order on the complexities of social reality than does the layperson. Some of these criticisms are valid only if we focus on Simmel's concern with forms of interaction, his formal sociology, and ignore the other types of sociology he practiced.

---

[1] In the specific case of interaction, contents are the *"drives, purposes and ideas which lead people to associate* with one another" (Levine, 1981b:65).

However, there are a number of ways to defend Simmel's approach to formal sociology. First, it is close to reality, as reflected by the innumerable real-life examples employed by Simmel. Second, it does not impose arbitrary and rigid categories on social reality but tries instead to allow the forms to flow from social reality. Third, Simmel's approach does not employ a general theoretical schema into which all aspects of the social world are forced. He thus avoided the reification of a theoretical schema that plagues a theorist like Talcott Parsons. Finally, formal sociology militates against the poorly conceptualized empiricism that is characteristic of much of sociology. Simmel certainly used empirical "data," but they are subordinated to his effort to impose some order on the bewildering world of social reality.

Social Geometry In Simmel's formal sociology, one sees most clearly his effort to develop a "geometry" of social relations. Two of the geometric coefficients that interested him are numbers and distance (others are position, valence, self-involvement, and symmetry [Levine, 1981b]).

Numbers Simmel's interest in the impact of numbers of people on the quality of interaction can be seen in his discussion of the difference between a dyad and a triad.

Dyad and triad. For Simmel (1950) there was a crucial difference between the *dyad* (two-person group) and the *triad* (three-person group). The addition of a third person causes a radical and fundamental change. Increasing the membership beyond three has nowhere near the same impact as adding a third member. Unlike all other groups, the dyad does not achieve a meaning beyond the two individuals involved. There is no independent group structure in a dyad; there is nothing more to the group than the two separable individuals. Thus, each member of a dyad retains a high level of individuality. The individual is not lowered to the level of the group. This is not the case in the triad. A triad does have the possibility of obtaining a meaning beyond the individuals involved. There is likely to be more to a triad than the individuals involved. It is likely to develop an independent group structure. As a result, there is a greater threat to the individuality of the members. A triad can have a general leveling effect on the members.

With the addition of a third party to the group, a number of new social roles become possible. For example, the third party can take the role of arbitrator or mediator in disputes within the group. Then the third party can use disputes between the other two for his or her own gain or become an object of competition between the other two parties. The third member also can intentionally foster conflict between the other two parties in order to gain superiority (divide and rule). A stratification system and an authority structure then can emerge. The movement from dyad to triad is essential to the development of social structures that can become separate from, and dominant over, individuals. Such a possibility does not exist in a dyad.

The process that is begun in the transition from a dyad to a triad continues as larger and larger groups and, ultimately, societies emerge. In these large social structures, the individual, increasingly separated from the structure of society, grows more and more alone, isolated, and segmented. This results finally in a dialectical relationship between individuals and social structures: "According to Simmel, the socialized individual always remains in a dual relation toward society: he is incorporated within it and yet stands against it. . . . The individual is determined, yet determining; acted upon, yet self-actuating" (Coser, 1965:11). The contradiction here is that "society allows the emergence of individuality and autonomy, but it also impedes it" (Coser, 1965:11).

Group size. At a more general level, there is Simmel's (1908/1871a) ambivalent attitude toward the impact of group *size*. On the one hand, he took the position that the increase in the size of a group or society increases individual freedom. A small group or society is likely to control the individual completely. However, in a larger society, the individual is likely to be involved in a number of groups, each of which controls only a small portion of his or her total personality. In other words, *"Individuality in being and action generally increases to the degree that the social circle encompassing the individual expands"* (Simmel, 1908/1971a:252). However, Simmel took the view that large societies create a set of problems that ultimately threaten individual freedom. For example, he saw the masses as likely to be dominated by one idea, the simplest idea. The physical proximity of a mass makes people suggestible and more likely to follow simplistic ideas, to engage in mindless, emotional actions.

Perhaps most important, in terms of Simmel's interest in forms of interaction, is that increasing size and differentiation tend to loosen the bonds between individuals and leave in their place much more distant, impersonal, and segmental relationships. Paradoxically, the large group that frees the individual simultaneously threatens that individuality. Also paradoxical is Simmel's belief that one way for individuals to cope with the threat of the mass society is to immerse themselves in small groups such as the family.

Distance Another of Simmel's concerns in social geometry was *distance*. Levine offers a good summation of Simmel's views on the role of distance in social relationships: *"The properties of forms and the meanings of things are a function of the relative distances between individuals and other individuals or things."* (1971:xxxiv). This concern with distance is manifest in various places in Simmel's work. We will discuss it in two different contexts—in Simmel's massive *The Philosophy of Money* and in one of his cleverest essays, "The Stranger."

In *The Philosophy of Money* (1907/1978), Simmel enunciated some general principles about value—and about what makes things valuable—that served as the basis for his analysis of money. Because we deal with this work in detail later in this chapter, we discuss this issue only briefly here. The essential point is that the value of something is determined by its distance from the actor. It is not valuable if it is either too close and too easy to obtain or too distant and too difficult to obtain. Objects that are attainable, but only with great effort, are the most valuable.

Distance also plays a central role in Simmel's "The Stranger" (1908/1971b), an essay on a type of actor who is neither too close nor too far. If he (or she) were too close, he would no longer be a stranger, but if he were too far, he would cease to have any contact with the group. The interaction that the stranger engages in with the group members involves a combination of close-ness and distance. The peculiar distance of the stranger from the group allows him to have a series of unusual interaction patterns with the members. For example, the stranger can be more objective in his relationships with the group members. Because he is a stranger, other group members feel more comfort-able expressing confidences to him. In these and other ways, a pattern of coordination and consistent interaction emerges between the stranger and the other group members. The stranger becomes an organic member of the group. But Simmel not only considered the stranger a social type; he considered strangeness a form of social interaction. A degree of strangeness, involving a combination of nearness and remoteness, enters into all social relationships, even the most intimate. Thus we can examine a wide range of specific inter-actions in order to discover the degree of strangeness found in each.

Although geometric dimensions enter a number of Simmel's types and forms, there is much more to them than simply geometry. The types and forms are constructs that Simmel used to gain a greater understanding of a wide range of interaction patterns.

Social Types We have already encountered one of Simmel's types, the stranger; others include the miser, the spendthrift, the adventurer, and the nobleman. To illustrate his mode of thinking in this area, we will focus on one of his types, the poor.

The Poor As is typical of types in Simmel's work, the *poor* were defined in terms of social relationships, as being aided by other people or at least having the right to that aid. Here Simmel quite clearly did not hold the view that *poverty* is defined by a quantity, or rather a lack of quantity, of money.

Although Simmel focused on the poor in terms of characteristic relation-ships and interaction patterns, he also used the occasion of his essay "The Poor" (1908/1971c) to develop a wide range of interesting insights into the poor and poverty. It was characteristic of Simmel to offer a profusion of insights in every essay. Indeed, this is one of his great claims to fame. For example, Simmel argued that a reciprocal set of rights and obligations defines the relationship between the needy and the givers. The needy have the right to receive aid, and this right makes receiving aid less painful. Conversely, the giver has the obligation to give to the needy. Simmel also took the functionalist position that aid to the poor by society helps to support the system. Society requires aid to the poor "so that the poor will not become active and dan-gerous enemies of society, so as to make their reduced energies more pro-ductive, and so as to prevent the degeneration of their progeny" (Simmel, 1908/1971c:154). Thus aid to the poor is for the sake of society, not so much for the poor per se. The state plays a key role here, and, as Simmel saw it, the treatment of the poor grows increasingly impersonal as the mechanism for giving aid becomes more bureaucratized.

Simmel also had a relativistic view of poverty. That is, the poor are not simply those who stand at the bottom of society. From his point of view, poverty is found in *all* social strata. This concept foreshadowed the later sociological concept of *relative deprivation*. If people who are members of the upper classes have less than their peers, then they are likely to feel poor in comparison to them. Therefore, government programs aimed at eradicating poverty can never succeed. Even if those at the bottom are elevated, many people throughout the stratification system will still feel poor in comparison to their peers.

Social Forms As with social types, Simmel looked at a wide range of social forms, including exchange, conflict, prostitution, and sociability. We can illustrate Simmel's (1908/1971d) work on social forms through his discussion of domination, that is, superordination and subordination.

Superordination and Subordination Superordination and subordination have a reciprocal relationship. The leader does not want to determine completely the thoughts and actions of others. Rather, the leader expects the subordinate to react either positively or negatively. Neither this nor any other form of interaction can exist without mutual relationships. Even in the most oppressive form of domination, subordinates have at least some degree of personal freedom.

To most people, superordination involves an effort to eliminate completely the independence of subordinates, but Simmel argued that a social relationship would cease to exist if this were the case.

Simmel asserted that one can be subordinated to an individual, a group, or an objective force. Leadership by a single individual generally leads to a tightly knit group either in support of or in opposition to the leader. Even when opposition arises in such a group, discord can be resolved more easily when the parties stand under the same higher power. Subordination under a plurality can have very uneven effects. On the one hand, the objectivity of rule by a plurality may make for greater unity in the group than the more arbitrary rule of an individual. On the other hand, hostility is likely to be engendered among subordinates if they do not get the personal attention of a leader.

Simmel found subordination under an objective principle to be most offensive, perhaps because human relationships and social interactions are eliminated. People feel they are determined by an impersonal law that they have no ability to affect. Simmel saw subordination to an individual as freer and more spontaneous: "Subordination under a person has an element of freedom and dignity in comparison with which all obedience to laws has something mechanical and passive" (1908/1971d:115). Even worse is subordination to objects (for example, icons), which Simmel found a "humiliatingly harsh and unconditional kind of subordination" (1908/1971d:115). Because the individual is dominated by a thing, "he himself psychologically sinks to the category of mere thing" (Simmel, 1908/1971d:117).

Again, Simmel dealt with a wide range of forms of interaction throughout his work, and this discussion of domination is simply meant to illustrate the kinds of work done by Simmel in this area.

Recently, Guy Oakes (1984) linked Simmel's discussion of forms to his basic problematic, the growing gap between objective and subjective culture. He begins with the position that in "Simmel's view, the discovery of objectivity—the independence of things from the condition of their subjective or psychological genesis—was the greatest achievement in the cultural history of the West" (Oakes, 1984:3). One of the ways that Simmel addresses this objectivity is in his discussion of forms, but although such formalization and objectification are necessary and desirable, they can come to be quite undesirable:

> On the one hand, forms are necessary conditions for the expression and the realization of the energies and interests of life. On the other hand, these forms become increasingly detached and remote from life. When this happens, a conflict develops between the process of life and the configurations in which it is expressed. Ultimately, this conflict threatens to nullify the relationship between life and form, and thus to destroy the conditions under which the process of life can be realized in autonomous structures.
>
> (Oakes, 1984:4)

SOCIAL STRUCTURES

Simmel said relatively little directly about the large-scale structures of society. In fact, at times, given his focus on patterns of interaction, he denied the existence of that level of social reality. A good example of this is found in his effort to define *society*, where he rejected the realist position exemplified by Emile Durkheim that society is a real, material entity. Lewis Coser notes, "He did not see society as a thing or an organism" (1965:5). Simmel was also uncomfortable with the nominalist conception that society is nothing more than a collection of isolated individuals. He adopted an intermediate position, conceiving of society as a set of interactions (Spykman, 1925/1966:88). "*Society* is merely the name for a number of individuals connected by 'interaction'" (Simmel, cited in Coser, 1965:5).

Although Simmel enunciated this interactionist position, in much of his work he operated as a realist, as if society were a real material structure. There is, then, a basic contradiction in Simmel's work on the social-structural level. Simmel noted, "Society transcends the individual and lives its own life which follows its own laws. It, too, confronts the individual with a historical, imperative firmness" (1908/1950a:258). Coser catches the essence of this aspect of Simmel's thought: "The larger superindividual structures—the state, the clan, the family, the city, or the trade union—turn out to be but crystallizations of this interaction, even though they may attain autonomy and permanency and confront the individual as if they were alien powers" (1965:5). Rudolph

Heberle makes essentially the same point: "One can scarcely escape the impression that Simmel views society as an interplay of structural factors, in which the human beings appear as passive objects rather than as live and willing actors" (1965:117).

The resolution of this paradox lies in the difference between Simmel's formal sociology, in which he tended to adhere to an interactionist view of society, and his historical and philosophical sociologies, in which he was much more inclined to see society as an independent, coercive social structure. In the latter sociologies, he saw society as part of the broader process of the development of objective culture, which worried him. Although objective culture is best seen as part of the cultural realm, Simmel included the growth of large-scale social structures as part of this process. That Simmel related the growth of social structures to the spread of objective culture is clear in this statement: "The increasing objectification of our culture, whose phenomena consist more and more of impersonal elements and less and less absorb the subjective totality of the individual . . . also involves sociological structures" (1908/1950b:318). In addition to clarifying the relationship between society and objective culture, this leads to Simmel's thoughts on the cultural level of social reality.

OBJECTIVE CULTURE

One of the main focuses of Simmel's historical and philosophical sociology is the cultural level of social reality, or what he called the "objective culture." In Simmel's view, people produce culture, but because of their ability to reify social reality, the cultural world and the social world come to have lives of their own, lives that come increasingly to dominate the actors who created, and daily re-create, them. "The cultural objects become more and more linked to each other in a self-contained world which has increasingly fewer contacts with the [individual] subjective psyche and its desires and sensibilities" (Coser, 1965:22). Although people always retain the capacity to create and re-create culture, the long-term trend of history is for culture to exert a more and more coercive force on the actor.

> The preponderance of objective over [individual] subjective culture that developed during the nineteenth century . . . this discrepancy seems to widen steadily. Every day and from all sides, the wealth of objective culture increases, but the individual mind can enrich the forms and content of its own development only by distancing itself still further from that culture and developing its own at a much slower pace.
> (Simmel, 1907/1978:449)

In various places in his work, Simmel identified a number of components of the objective culture, for example:

- Tools
- Means of transport

- Products of science
- Technology
- Arts
- Language
- Intellectual sphere
- Conventional wisdom
- Religious dogma
- Philosophical systems
- Legal systems
- Moral codes
- Ideals (for example, the "fatherland")

These and many others constitute the objective cultural level in Simmel's work.

The objective culture grows and expands in various ways. First, its absolute size grows with increasing modernization. This can be seen most obviously in the case of scientific knowledge, which is expanding exponentially, although this is just as true of most other aspects of the cultural realm. Second, the number of different components of the cultural realm also grows. Finally, and perhaps most important, the various elements of the cultural world become more and more intertwined in an ever more powerful, self-contained world that is increasingly beyond the control of the actors (Oakes, 1984:12). Simmel was not only interested in describing the growth of objective culture but also greatly disturbed by it: "Simmel was impressed—if not depressed— by the bewildering number and variety of human products which in the contemporary world surround and unceasingly impinge upon the individual" (Weingartner, 1959:33).

What worried Simmel most was the threat to individual culture posed by the growth of objective culture. Simmel's personal sympathies were with a world dominated by individual culture, but he saw the possibility of such a world as more and more unlikely. It is this that Simmel described as the "tragedy of culture." (We will comment on this in detail in the discussion of *The Philosophy of Money*.) Simmel's specific analysis of the growth of objective culture over individual subjective culture is simply one example of a general principle that dominates all of life: "The total value of something increases to the same extent as the value of its individual parts declines" (1907/1978:199).

We can relate Simmel's general argument about objective culture to his more basic analysis of forms of interaction. In one of his best-known essays, "The Metropolis and Mental Life" (1903/1971), Simmel analyzed the forms of interaction that take place in the modern city. He saw the modern metropolis as the "genuine arena" of the growth of objective culture and the decline of individual culture. It is the scene of the predominance of the money economy, and money, as Simmel often made clear, has a profound effect on the nature of human relationships. The widespread use of money leads to an emphasis on calculability and rationality in all spheres of life. Thus genuine human relationships decline, and social relationships tend to be dominated by a blasé and reserved attitude. Whereas the small town was characterized by greater feeling and emotionality, the modern city is characterized by a shallow intellectuality that matches the calculability needed by a money economy. The city is also the center of the division of labor, and as we have seen, specialization plays a central role in the production of an ever-expanding objective culture, with a corresponding decline in individual culture. The city is a "frightful leveler," in which virtually everyone is reduced to emphasizing unfeeling calculability. It is more and more difficult to maintain individuality in the face of the expansion of objective culture.

It should be pointed out that in his essay on the city (as well as in many other places in his work) Simmel also discussed the liberating effect of this modern development. For example, he emphasized the fact that people are freer in the modern city than in the tight social confines of the small town. We will have more to say about Simmel's thoughts on the liberating impact of modernity at the close of the following section, devoted to Simmel's book *The Philosophy of Money*.

Before we get to that work, it is necessary to indicate that one of the many ironies of Simmel's influence on the development of sociology is that his micro-analytic work is used, but its broader implications are almost totally ignored. Take the example of Simmel's work on exchange relationships. He saw exchange as the "purest and most developed kind" of interaction (Simmel, 1907/1978:82). Although all forms of interaction involve some sacrifice, it occurs most clearly in exchange relationships. Simmel thought of all social exchanges as involving "profit and loss." Such an orientation was crucial to Simmel's microsociological work and specifically to the development of his largely micro-oriented exchange theory. However, the fact is that his thoughts on exchange are also expressed in his broader work on money. To Simmel, money is the purest form of exchange. In contrast to a barter economy, where the cycle ends when one object has been exchanged for another, an economy based on money allows for an endless series of exchanges. This possibility is crucial for Simmel because it provides the basis for the widespread development of social structures and objective culture. Consequently, money as a form of exchange represented for Simmel one of the root causes of the alienation of people in a modern, reified social structure.

In his treatment of the city and exchange, one can see the elegance of Simmel's thinking as he related small-scale sociological forms of exchange to the development of modern society in its totality. Although this link can be found in his specific essays, it is clearest in *The Philosophy of Money*.

THE PHILOSOPHY OF MONEY

The Philosophy of Money (1907/1978) illustrates well the breadth and sophistication of Simmel's thinking. It demonstrates conclusively that Simmel deserves at least as much recognition for his general theory as for his essays on microsociology, many of which can be seen as specific manifestations of his general theory.

Although the title makes it clear that Simmel's focus is money, his interest in that phenomenon is embedded in a set of his broader theoretical and philosophical concerns. For example, as we have already seen, Simmel was interested in the broad issue of value, and money can be seen as simply a specific form of value. At another level, Simmel was interested not in money per se but in its impact on such a wide range of phenomena as the "inner world" of actors and the objective culture as a whole. At still another level, he treated money as a specific phenomenon linked with a variety of other components of life, including "exchange, ownership, greed, extravagance, cynicism, individual freedom, the style of life, culture, the value of the personality, etc." (Kracauer, cited in Bottomore and Frisby, 1978:7). Finally, and most generally, Simmel saw money as a specific component of life capable of helping us to understand the totality of life. As Tom Bottomore and David Frisby put it, Simmel sought no less than to extract "the totality of the spirit of the age from his analysis of money" (1978:7).

The Philosophy of Money has much in common with the work of Karl Marx. Like Marx, Simmel focused on capitalism and the problems created by a money economy. Despite this, the differences are overwhelming. For example, Simmel saw the economic problems of his time as simply a specific manifestation of a more general cultural problem, the alienation of objective from subjective culture. To Marx these problems are specific to capitalism, but to Simmel they are part of a universal tragedy—the increasing powerlessness of the individual in the face of the growth of objective culture. Whereas Marx's analysis is historically specific, Simmel's analysis seeks to extract timeless truths from the flux of human history. As Frisby says, "In his *The Philosophy of Money* . . . [w]hat is missing . . . is a historical sociology of money relationships" (1984:58). This difference in their analyses is related to a crucial political difference between Simmel and Marx. Because Marx saw economic problems as time-bound, the product of capitalist society, he believed that eventually they could be solved. Simmel, however, saw the basic problems as inherent in human life and held out no hope for future improvement. In fact, Simmel believed that socialism, instead of improving the situation, would heighten the kinds of problems discussed in *The Philosophy of Money*. Despite some substantive similarities to Marxian theory, Simmel's thought is far closer to that of Weber and his "iron cage" in terms of his image of both the modern world and its future.

The Philosophy of Money begins with a discussion of the general forms of money and value. Later the discussion moves to the impact of money on the "inner world" of actors and on culture in general. Because the argument is so complex, we can merely highlight it here.

One of Simmel's initial concerns in the work, as we discussed briefly earlier, is the relationship between money and value. In general, he argued that people create value by making objects, separating themselves from them, and then seeking to overcome the "distance, obstacles, difficulties" (Simmel, 1907/ 1978:66). The greater the difficulty of obtaining an object, the greater its value. However, difficulty of attainment has a "lower and an upper limit" (Simmel, 1907/1978:72). The general principle is that the value of things comes from the ability of people to distance themselves properly from objects. Things that are too close, too easily obtained, are not very valuable. Some exertion is needed for something to be considered valuable. Conversely, things that are too far, too difficult, or nearly impossible to obtain are also not very valuable. Things that defy most, if not all, of our efforts to obtain them cease to be valuable to us. Those things that are most valuable are neither too distant nor too close. Among the factors involved in the distance of an object from an actor are the time it takes to obtain it, its scarcity, the difficulties involved in acquiring it, and the need to give up other things in order to acquire it. People try to place themselves at a proper distance from objects, which must be attainable, but not too easily.

In this general context of value, Simmel discussed money. In the economic realm, money serves both to create distance from objects and to provide the means to overcome it. The money value attached to objects in a modern economy places them at a distance from us; we cannot obtain them without money of our own. The difficulty in obtaining the money and therefore the objects makes them valuable to us. At the same time, once we obtain enough money, we are able to overcome the distance between ourselves and the objects. Money thus performs the interesting function of creating distance between people and objects and then providing the means to overcome that distance.

In the process of creating value, money also provides the basis for the development of the market, the modern economy, and ultimately modern (capitalistic) society. Money provides the means whereby these entities acquire a life of their own that is external to, and coercive of, the actor. This stands in contrast to earlier societies in which barter or trade could not lead to the reified world that is the distinctive product of a money economy. Money permits this development in various ways. For example, Simmel argued that money allows for "long-range calculations, large-scale enterprises and long-term credits" (1907/1978:125). Later, Simmel said that "money has . . . developed . . . the most objective practices, the most logical, purely mathematical norms, the absolute freedom from everything personal" (1907/1978:128). He saw this process of reification as but part of the more general process whereby the mind embodies and symbolizes itself in objects. These embodiments, these symbolic structures, become reified and come to exert a controlling force on actors.

Not only does money help to create a reified social world, but it also contributes to the increasing rationalization of that social world (B. Turner, 1986). This is another of the concerns that Simmel shared with Weber. A money economy fosters an emphasis on quantitative rather than qualitative factors. Simmel stated:

It would be easy to multiply the examples that illustrate the growing preponderance of the category of quantity over that of quality, or more precisely the tendency to dissolve quality into quantity, to remove the elements more and more from quality, to grant them only specific forms of motion and to interpret everything that is specifically, individually, and qualitatively determined as the more or less, the bigger or smaller, the wider or narrower, the more or less frequent of those colourless elements and awarenesses that are only accessible to numerical determination—even though this tendency may never absolutely attain its goal by mortal means. . . .

Thus, one of the major tendencies of life—the reduction of quality to quantity—achieves its highest and uniquely perfect representation in money. Here, too, money is the pinnacle of a cultural historical series of developments which unambiguously determines its direction.

(Simmel, 1907/1978:278–280)

Less obviously, money contributes to rationalization by increasing the importance of intellectuality in the modern world (B. Turner, 1986). On the one hand, the development of a money economy presupposes a significant expansion of mental processes. As an example, Simmel pointed to the complicated mental processes that are required by such money transactions as covering bank notes with cash reserves. On the other hand, a money economy contributes to a considerable change in the norms and values of society; it aids in the "fundamental reorientation of culture towards intellectuality" (Simmel, 1907/1978:152). In part because of a money economy, intellect has come to be considered the most valuable of our mental energies.

Simmel saw the significance of the individual declining as money transactions become an increasingly important part of society and as reified structures expand. This is part of his general argument on the decline of individual subjective culture in the face of the expansion of objective culture (the "tragedy of culture"):

The rapid circulation of money induces habits of spending and acquisition; it makes a specific quantity of money psychologically less significant and valuable, while money in general becomes increasingly important because money matters now affect the individual more vitally than they do in a less agitated style of life. We are confronted here with a very common phenomenon; namely, that the total value of something increases to the same extent as the value of its individual parts declines. For example, the size and significance of a social group often becomes greater the less highly the lives and interests of its individual members are valued; the objective culture, the diversity and liveliness of its content attain their highest point through a division of labour that often condemns the individual representative and participant in this culture to a monotonous specialization, narrowness, and stunted growth. The whole becomes more perfect and harmonious, the less the individual is a harmonious being.

(Simmel, 1907/1978:199)

In some senses, it may be difficult to see how money can take on the central role that it does in modern society. On the surface, it appears that money is simply a means to a variety of ends or, in Simmel's words, "the purest form of the tool" (1907/1978:210). However, money has come to be the most extreme example of a means that has become an end in itself:

> Never has an object that owes its value exclusively to its quality as a means, to its convertibility into more definite values, so thoroughly and unreservedly developed into a psychological value absolute, into a completely engrossing final purpose governing our practical consciousness. This ultimate craving for money must increase to the extent that money takes on the quality of a pure means. For this implies that the range of objects made available to money grows continuously, that things submit more and more defencelessly to the power of money, that money itself becomes more and more lacking in quality yet thereby at the same time becomes powerful in relation to the quality of things.
>
> (Simmel, 1907/1978:232)

A society in which money becomes an end in itself, indeed the ultimate end, has a number of negative effects on individuals, two of the most interesting of which are the increase in cynicism and in a blasé attitude. Cynicism is induced when both the highest and lowest aspects of social life are for sale, reduced to a common denominator—money. Thus we can "buy" beauty or truth or intelligence almost as easily as we can buy cornflakes or underarm deodorant. This leveling of everything to a common denominator leads to the cynical attitude that everything has its price, that anything can be bought or sold on the market. A money economy also induces a blasé attitude, "all things as being of an equally dull and grey hue, as not worth getting excited about" (Simmel, 1907/1978:256). The blasé person has lost completely the ability to make value differentiations among the ultimate objects of purchase. Put slightly differently, money is the absolute enemy of esthetics, reducing everything to formlessness, to purely quantitative phenomena.

Another negative effect of a money economy is the increasingly impersonal relations among people. Instead of dealing with individuals with their own personalities, we are increasingly likely to deal solely with positions—the delivery person, the baker, and so forth—regardless of who occupies those positions. In the modern division of labor characteristic of a money economy, we have the paradoxical situation that while we grow more dependent on other positions for our survival, we know less about the people who occupy those positions. The specific individual who fills a given position becomes progressively insignificant. Personalities tend to disappear behind positions that demand only a small part of them. Because so little is demanded of them, many individuals can fill the same position equally well. People thus become interchangeable parts.

Related to this is the impact of the money economy on individual freedom. A money economy leads to an increase in individual enslavement. The individual in the modern world becomes atomized and isolated. No longer embedded within a group, the individual stands alone in the face of an ever-expanding and increasingly coercive objective culture. The individual in the modern world is thus enslaved by a massive objective culture.

Another impact of the money economy is the reduction of all human values to dollar terms, "the tendency to reduce the value of man to a monetary expression" (Simmel, 1907/1978:356). For example, Simmel offers the case in primitive society of atonement for a murder by a money payment. But his best example is the exchange of sex for money. The expansion of prostitution is traceable in part to the growth of the money economy.

Some of Simmel's most interesting insights lie in his thoughts on the impact of money on people's styles of life. For example, a society dominated by a money economy tends to reduce everything to a string of causal connections that can be comprehended intellectually, not emotionally. Related to this is what Simmel called the "calculating character" of life in the modern world. The specific form of intellectuality that is peculiarly suited to a money economy is a mathematical mode of thinking. This, in turn, is related to the tendency to emphasize quantitative rather than qualitative factors in the social world. Simmel concluded that "the lives of many people are absorbed by such evaluating, weighing, calculating, and reducing of qualitative values to quantitatives ones" (1907/1978:444).

The key to Simmel's discussion of money's impact on style of life is in the growth of objective culture at the expense of individual culture. The gap between the two grows larger at an accelerating rate:

> This discrepancy seems to widen steadily. Every day and from all sides, the wealth of objective culture increases, but the individual mind can enrich the forms and contents of its own development only by distancing itself still further from that culture and developing its own at a much slower pace.
>
> (Simmel, 1907/1978:449)

The major cause of this increasing disparity is the increasing division of labor in modern society (Oakes, 1984:19). Increased specialization leads to an improved ability to create the various components of the cultural world. But at the same time, the highly specialized individual loses a sense of the total culture and loses the ability to control it. As objective culture grows, individual culture atrophies. One of the examples of this is that language in its totality has clearly expanded enormously, yet the linguistic abilities of given individuals seem to be declining. Similarly, with the growth of technology and machinery, the abilities of the individual worker and the skills required have declined dramatically. Finally, although there has been an enormous expansion of the intellectual sphere, fewer and fewer individuals seem to deserve the label "intellectual." Highly specialized individuals are confronted with an increasingly closed and interconnected world of products over which they have little or no control. A mechanical world devoid of spirituality comes to dominate individuals, and their lifestyles are affected in various ways. Acts of production come to be meaningless exercises in which individuals do not see their roles in the overall process or in the production of the final product. Relationships among people are highly specialized and impersonal. Consumption becomes little more than a devouring of one meaningless product after another.

The massive expansion of objective culture has had a dramatic effect upon the rhythm of life. In general, the unevenness that was characteristic of earlier epochs has been leveled and replaced in modern society by a much more consistent pattern of living. Examples of this leveling of modern culture abound:

In times past, food consumption was cyclical and often very uncertain. What foods were consumed and when they were available depended on the harvest. Today, with improved methods of preservation and transportation, we can consume virtually any food at any time. Furthermore, the ability to preserve and store huge quantities of food has helped to offset disruptions caused by bad harvests, natural catastrophes, and so forth.

In communication the infrequent and unpredictable mail coach has been replaced by the telegraph, telephone, daily mail service and fax machines, which make communication available at all times.

In an earlier time, night and day gave life a natural rhythm. Now, with artificial lighting, the natural rhythm has been greatly altered. Many activities formerly restricted to daylight hours can now be performed at night as well.

Intellectual stimulation, which was formerly restricted to an occasional conversation or a rare book, is now available at all times because of the ready availability of books and magazines. In this realm, as in all the others, the situation has grown even more pronounced since Simmel's time. With radio, television, video tape recorders, and home computers, the availability and possibilities of intellectual stimulation have grown far beyond anything Simmel could have imagined.

There are positive elements to all this, of course. For example, people have much more freedom because they are less restricted by the natural rhythm of life. In spite of the human gains, problems arise because all these developments are at the level of objective culture and are integral parts of the process by which objective culture grows and further impoverishes individual culture.

In the end, money has come to be the symbol of, and a major factor in, the development of a relativistic mode of existence. Money allows us to reduce the most disparate phenomena to numbers of dollars, and this allows them to be compared to each other. In other words, money allows us to relativize *everything.* Our relativistic way of life stands in contrast to earlier methods of living in which people believed in a number of eternal verities. A money economy destroys such eternal truths. The gains to people in terms of increased freedom from absolute ideas are far outweighed by the costs. The alienation endemic to the expanding objective culture of a modern money economy is a far greater threat to people, in Simmel's eyes, than the evils of absolutism. Perhaps Simmel would not wish us to return to an earlier, simpler time, but he certainly would warn us to be wary of the seductive dangers associated with the growth of a money economy and objective culture in the modern world.

While we have focused most of our attention on the negative effects of the modern money economy, it also has its liberating aspects (Levine, 1981b). First, it allows us to deal with many more people in a much-expanded marketplace. Second, our obligations to one another are highly limited (to specific services or products) rather than all-encompassing. Third, the money economy allows people to find gratifications that were unavailable in earlier economic systems. Fourth, people have greater freedom in such an environment to develop their individuality to a fuller extent. Fifth, people are better able to maintain and protect their subjective center, since they are involved only in very limited relationships. Sixth, the separation of the worker from the means of production, as Simmel points out, allows the individual some freedom from those productive forces. Finally, money helps people grow increasingly free of the constraints of their social groups. For example, in a barter economy people are largely controlled by their groups, but in the modern economic world such constraints are loosened, with the result that people are freer to make their own economic deals. However, while Simmel is careful to point out a variety of liberating effects of the money economy, and modernity in general, in our view the heart of his work lies in his discussion of the problems associated with modernity, especially the "tragedy of culture."

SECRECY: A CASE STUDY IN SIMMEL'S SOCIOLOGY

While *The Philosophy of Money* demonstrates that Simmel has a theoretical scope that rivals that of Marx, Weber, and Durkheim, it remains an atypical example of his work. Thus, in this closing section we return to a more characteristic type of Simmelian scholarship, his work on a specific form of interaction—secrecy. *Secrecy* is defined as the condition in which one person has the intention of hiding something while the other is seeking to reveal that which is being hidden. In this discussion, we are not only interested in outlining Simmel's many insightful ideas on secrecy but also in bringing together under one heading many of the sociological ideas raised through this chapter.

Simmel begins with the basic fact that people must know some things about other people in order to interact with them. For instance, we must know with whom we are dealing (for example, a friend, a relative, a shopkeeper). We may come to know a great deal about other people, but we can never know them absolutely. That is, we can never know all the thoughts, moods, and so on of other people. However, we do form some sort of unitary conception of other people out of the bits and pieces that we know about them; we form a fairly coherent mental picture of the people with whom we interact. Simmel sees a dialectical relationship between interaction (being) and the mental picture we have of others (conceiving): "Our relationships thus develop upon the basis of reciprocal knowledge, and this knowledge upon the basis of actual relations. Both are inextricably interwoven" (1906/1950:309).

In all aspects of our lives we acquire not only truth but also ignorance and error. However, it is in the interaction with other people that ignorance and error acquire a distinctive character. This relates to the inner lives of the people with whom we interact. People, in contrast to any other object of knowledge, have the capacity to *intentionally* reveal the truth about themselves *or* to lie and conceal such information.

The fact is that even if people wanted to reveal all (and they almost always do not), they could not do so because so much information "would drive everybody into the insane asylum" (Simmel, 1906/1950:312). Thus, people must select the things that they report to others. From the point of view of Simmel's concern with quantitative issues, we report only "fragments" of our inner lives to others. Furthermore, we choose which fragments to reveal and which to conceal. Thus, in all interaction, we reveal only a part of ourselves, and which part we opt to show depends on how we select and arrange the fragments we choose to reveal.

This brings us to the *lie,* a form of interaction in which the liar *intentionally* hides the truth from others. In the lie, it is not just that others are left with an erroneous conception but also that the error is traceable to the fact that the liar intended that the others be deceived.

Simmel discusses the lie in terms of social geometry, specifically his ideas on distance. For example, in Simmel's view, we can better accept and come to terms with the lies of those who are distant from us. Thus, we have little difficulty learning that the politicians who habituate Washington, D.C., frequently lie to us. In contrast, "If the persons closest to us lie, life becomes unbearable" (Simmel, 1906/1950:313). The lie of a spouse, lover, or child has a far more devastating impact on us than the lie of a government official whom we know only through the television screen.

More generally, in terms of the issue of distance, it is the case that all everyday communication combines elements known to both parties with facts known to only one or the other. It is the existence of the latter that leads to "distanceness" in all social relationships. Indeed, Simmel argues that social relationships require *both* elements that are known to the interactants and those that are unknown to one party or the other. In other words, even the most intimate relationships require both nearness and distance, reciprocal knowledge and mutual concealment. Thus, secrecy is an integral part of all social relationships, although a relationship may be destroyed if the secret becomes known to the person from whom it was being kept.

Secrecy is linked to the size of society. In small groups, it is difficult to develop secrets; "Everybody is too close to everybody else and his circumstances, and frequency and intimacy of contact involve too many temptations to revelation" (Simmel, 1906/1950:335). Furthermore, in small groups, secrets are not even needed because everyone is much like everyone else. In large groups, in contrast, secrets can more easily develop and are much more needed because there are important differences among people.

On the issue of size, at the most macroscopic level, we should note that secrecy not only is a form of interaction (which, as we have seen, affects many other forms) but also can come to characterize a group in its entirety. Unlike the secret possessed by a single individual, the secret in a *secret society* is shared by all members and determines the reciprocal relations among them. As with the individual case, however, the secret of the secret society cannot be hidden forever. In such a society there is a constant tension caused by the fact that the secret can be uncovered, or revealed, and thus the entire basis for the existence of the secret society can be eliminated.

Simmel examines various forms of social relationships from the point of view of reciprocal knowledge and secrecy. For example, we all are involved in a range of interest groups in which we interact with other people on a very limited basis, and the total personalities of these people are irrelevant to our specific concerns. Thus, in the university the student is concerned with what the professor says and does in the classroom and not in all aspects of the professor's life and personality. Linking this to his ideas on the larger society, Simmel argues that the increasing objectification of culture brings with it more and more limited-interest groups and the kinds of relationships associated with them. Such relationships require less and less of the subjective totality of the individual (individual culture) than do associations in premodern societies.

In the impersonal relationships characteristic of modern objectified society, *confidence*, as a form of interaction, becomes increasingly important. To Simmel "Confidence is intermediate between knowledge and ignorance about a man" (1906/1950:318). In premodern societies people are much more likely to know a great deal about the people they deal with. But in the modern world we do not, and cannot, have a great deal of knowledge about most of the people with whom we have associations. Thus, students do not know a great deal about their professors (and vice versa), but they must have the confidence that their professors will show up at the appointed times and talk about what they are supposed to discuss.

Another form of social relationship is *acquaintanceship*. We know our acquaintances, but we do not have intimate knowledge of them: "One knows of the other only what he is toward the outside, either in the purely social-representative sense, or in the sense of that which he shows us" (Simmel, 1906/1950:320). Thus, there is far more secretiveness among acquaintances than there is among intimates.

Under the heading of "acquaintanceship," Simmel discusses another form of association—*discretion*. We are discrete with our acquaintances, staying "away from the knowledge of all the other does not expressly reveal to us. It does not refer to anything particular which we are not permitted to know, but to a quite general reserve in regard to the total personality" (Simmel,

1906/1950:321). In spite of being discrete, we often come to know more about other people than they reveal to us voluntarily. More specifically, we often come to learn things that others would prefer we do not know. Simmel offers a very Freudian example of how we learn such things: "To the man with the psychologically fine ear, people innumerable times betray their most secret thoughts and qualities, not only *although,* but often *because,* they anxiously try to guard them" (1906/1950:323–324). In fact, Simmel argues that human interaction is dependent on both discretion *and* the fact that we often come to know more than we are supposed to know.

Turning to another form of association, *friendship,* Simmel contradicts the assumption that friendship is based on total intimacy, full reciprocal knowledge. This lack of full intimacy is especially true of friendships in modern, differentiated society: "Modern man, possibly, has too much to hide to sustain a friendship in the ancient sense" (Simmel, 1906/1950:326). Thus, we have a series of differentiated friendships based on such things as common intellectual pursuits, religion, and shared experiences. There is a very limited kind of intimacy in such friendships and thus a good deal of secrecy. However, in spite of these limitations, friendship still involves some intimacy:

> But the relation which is thus restricted and surrounded by discretions, may yet stem from the center of the total personality. It may yet be reached by the sap of the ultimate roots of the personality, even though it feeds only part of the person's periphery. In its idea, it involves the same affective depth and the same readiness for sacrifice, which less differentiated epochs and persons connect only with a common *total* sphere of life, for which reservations and discretion constitute no problem. (Simmel, 1906/1950:326)

Then there is what is usually thought of as the most intimate, least secret form of association—*marriage.* Simmel argues that there is a temptation in marriage to reveal all to the partner, to have no secrets. However, in his view, this would be a mistake. For one thing, all social relationships require "a certain proportion of truth and error," and thus it would be impossible to remove all error from a social relationship (Simmel, 1906/1950:329). More specifically, complete self-revelation (assuming such a thing is even possible) would make a marriage matter-of-fact and remove all possibility of the unexpected. Finally, most of us have limited internal resources, and every revelation reduces the (secret) treasures that we have to offer to others. Only those few with a great storehouse of personal accomplishments can afford numerous revelations to a marriage partner. All others are left denuded (and uninteresting) by excessive self-revelation.

Next, Simmel turns to an analysis of the functions, the positive consequences, of secrecy. Simmel sees the secret as "one of man's greatest achievements . . . the secret produces an immense enlargement of life: numerous contents of life cannot even emerge in the presence of full publicity. The secret offers, so to speak, the possibility of a second world alongside the manifest world" (1906/1950:330). More specifically in terms of its functionality, the secret, especially if it is shared by a number of people, makes for a strong "we feeling" among those who know the secret. High status is also associated with the secret; there is something mysterious about superordinate positions and superior achievements.

Human interaction in general is shaped by secrecy and its logical opposite, *betrayal.* The secret is always accompanied dialectically by the possibility that it can be discovered. Betrayal can come from two sources. Externally, another person can discover our secret, while internally there is always the possibility that we will reveal our secret to others. "The secret puts a barrier between men but, at the same time, it creates the tempting challenge to break through it, by gossip or confession. . . . Out of the counterplay of these two interests, in concealing and revealing, spring nuances and fates of human interaction that permeate it in its entirety" (Simmel, 1906/1950:334).

Simmel links his ideas on the lie to his views on the larger society of the modern world. To Simmel, the modern world is much more dependent on honesty than earlier societies. For example, the modern economy is increasingly a credit economy, and credit is dependent on the fact that people will repay what they promise. For another, in modern science, researchers are dependent on the results of many other studies that they cannot examine in minute detail. Those studies are produced by innumerable other scientists who the researchers are unlikely to know personally. Thus, the modern scientist is dependent on the honesty of all other scientists. Simmel concludes: "Under modern conditions, the lie, therefore, becomes something much more devastating than it was earlier, something which questions the very foundations of our life" (1906/1950:313).

More generally, Simmel connects secrecy to his thoughts on the social structure of modern society. On the one hand, a highly differentiated society permits and requires a high degree of secrecy. On the other hand, and dialectically, the secret serves to intensify such differentiation.

Simmel associates the secret with the modern money economy; money makes possible a level of secrecy that was unattainable previously. First, money's "compressibility" makes it possible to make others rich by simply slipping them checks without anyone else noticing the act. Second, the abstractness and qualityless character of money makes it possible to hide "transactions, acquisitions, and changes in ownership" that could not be hidden if more tangible objects were exchanged (Simmel, 1906/1950:335). Third, money can be invested in very distant things, thereby making the transaction invisible to those in the immediate environment.

Simmel also sees that in the modern world public matters, such as those relating to politics, have tended to lose their secrecy and inaccessibility. In contrast, private affairs are much more secret than they are in premodern societies. Here Simmel ties his thoughts on secrecy to those on the modern city by arguing that "modern life has developed, in the midst of metropolitan crowdedness, a technique for making and keeping private matters secret" (Simmel, 1906/1950:337). Overall, "What is public becomes even more public, and what is private becomes even more private" (Simmel, 1906/1950:337).

Thus, in this section we have seen how Simmel's work on secrecy illustrates many aspects of his theoretical orientation.

SUMMARY

The work of Georg Simmel has been influential in American sociological theory for many years. The focus of this influence seems to be shifting from microsociology to a general sociological theory. Simmel's microsociology is embedded in a broad dialectical theory that interrelates the cultural and individual levels. We identify four basic levels of concern in Simmel's work: psychological, interactional, structural and institutional, and the ultimate metaphysics of life.

Simmel operated with a dialectical orientation, although it is not as well articulated as that of Karl Marx. We illustrate Simmel's dialectical concerns in various ways. We deal with the way they are manifested in forms of interaction—specifically, fashion. Simmel was also interested in the conflicts between the individual and social structures, but his greatest concern was those conflicts that develop between individual culture and objective culture. He perceived a general process whereby objective culture expands and individual culture becomes increasingly impoverished in the face of this development. Simmel saw this conflict, in turn, as part of a broader philosophical conflict between more-life and more-than-life.

The bulk of this chapter is devoted to Simmel's thoughts on each of the four levels of social reality. Although he has many useful assumptions about consciousness, he did comparatively little with them. He had much more to offer on forms of interaction and types of interactants. In this formal sociology, we see Simmel's great interest in social geometry, for example, numbers of people. In this context, we examine Simmel's work on the crucial transition from a dyad to a triad. With the addition of one person, we move from a dyad to a triad and with it the possibility of the development of large-scale structures that can become separate from, and dominant over, individuals. This creates the possibility of conflict and contradiction between the individual and the larger society. In his social geometry, Simmel was also concerned with the issue of distance, as in, for example, his essay on the "stranger," including "strangeness" in social life. Simmel's interest in social types is illustrated in a discussion of the poor, and his thoughts on social forms are illustrated in a discussion of domination, that is, superordination and subordination.

At the macro level, Simmel had comparatively little to say about social structures. In fact, at times he seemed to manifest a disturbing tendency to reduce social structures to little more than interaction patterns. Simmel's real interest at the macro level was objective culture. He was interested in both the expansion of this culture and its destructive effects on individuals. This general concern is manifest in a variety of his specific essays, for example, those on the city and exchange.

In *The Philosophy of Money* Simmel's discussion progressed from money to value to the problems of modern society and, ultimately, to the problems of life in general. Finally, we discussed Simmel's work on secrecy in order to illustrate the full range of his theoretical ideas. The discussion of Simmel's work on money, as well as his ideas on secrecy, demonstrates that he has a far more elegant and sophisticated theoretical orientation than he is usually given credit for by those who are familiar with only his thoughts on micro-level phenomena.

CHAPTER 9

GEORGE HERBERT MEAD

THE PRIORITY OF THE SOCIAL
THE ACT
  Gestures
  Significant Symbols
MENTAL PROCESSES AND THE MIND
SELF
SOCIETY
EVOLUTION
DIALECTICAL THINKING

AS we will see throughout this chapter, the social-psychological theories of George Herbert Mead were shaped by a variety of intellectual sources (Joas, 1985), but of great importance was the influence of psychological behaviorism.[1] Mead defines *behaviorism* in its broadest sense as "simply an approach to the study of the experience of the individual from the point of view of his *conduct*" (1934/1962:2; italics added). (*Conduct* is used here as another word for behavior.) Mead has no trouble with this approach to behaviorism, but he does have difficulty with the way in which behaviorism came to be defined and practiced by the most prominent behaviorist of Mead's day, John B. Watson (Buckley, 1989).

The behaviorism of Mead's time, as practiced by Watson and most others and then applied to humans, had been imported from animal psychology, where it worked quite well. There it was based on the premise that it is impossible through introspection to get at the private, mental experiences (assuming they exist) of lower animals and therefore all that can and should be done is to focus on animal behavior. Rather than seek to adapt behaviorism to the fact that there are obvious mental differences between animals and humans, Watson simply applied the principles of animal behavior to humans. To Watson, people are little more than "organic machines" (Buckley, 1989:x). Given this view of people, and the analogy between humans and animals, Watson rejected the idea of the study of human consciousness by introspection or any other method. As Mead puts it, in colorful fashion, "John B. Watson's attitude was that of the Queen in *Alice in Wonderland*—'Off with their heads!' " (1934/1962:2–3).

In Mead's view, Watson seeks to use behavior (conduct) to explain indi-

---

[1] For a critique of this position, see Natanson (1973b).

vidual experience, without a concern for inner experience, consciousness, and mental imagery. In contrast, Mead believes that even inner experience can be studied from the point of view of the behaviorist, as long as this viewpoint is *not* narrowly conceived. Thus, Mead *is* a behaviorist, albeit what he calls a "social" behaviorist. However, this seemingly slight extension makes an enormous theoretical difference. The symbolic-interactionist theory that emerged, in significant part from Mead's theory, is very different from behaviorist theories (like early exchange theory), and indeed they exist in different sociological paradigms (Ritzer, 1975a; see also the Appendix).[2]

While Mead wants to include what goes on within the mind as part of social behaviorism, he is as opposed as is Watson to the use of introspection to study mental processes. Mead wants to study the mind behavioristically, rather than introspectively:

> The opposition of the behaviorist to *introspection* is justified. It is *not a fruitful* undertaking from the point of view of psychological study. . . . What the behaviorist is occupied with, and what we have to come back to, is the actual reaction itself, and it is only in so far as we can translate the content of introspection over into response that we can get any satisfactory psychological doctrine.
>
> (Mead, 1934/1962:105; italics added)

Instead of studying the mind introspectively, Mead focuses on the *act* or, if other people are involved, the *social* act. Acts are behaviors defined in part in terms of the behaviorists' notions of stimulus and response. That is, some external stimulus causes the person to respond with an act. Mead's extension here is to argue that "part of the act lies within the organism and only comes to expression later; it is that side of behavior which I think Watson has passed over" (1934/1962:6). Mead does not ignore the inner experience of the individual because that inner experience is *part,* indeed a crucial part, of the act (we will have much more to say about the act shortly). It is in this sense that Mead contends that "the existence as such of mind or consciousness, in some sense or other, must be admitted" (1934/1962:10). Mead is aware that the mind cannot be reduced solely to behaviors, but he argues that it is possible to explain it in behavioral terms without denying its existence.

Mead defines the mind in *functional* rather than idealist terms. That is, the mind is viewed in terms of what it does, the role it plays in the act, rather than as some transcendental, subjective phenomenon. The mind is a part, the key part, of the central nervous system, and Mead seeks to extend the analysis of the act, especially the social act, to what transpires in the central nervous system: "What I am insisting upon is that the patterns which one finds in the central nervous system are patterns of action—not of contemplation" (1934/ 1962:26). Furthermore, what goes on in the central nervous system is not really

---

[2] However, there are those (for example, Lewis and Smith, 1980) who argue that this difference has more to do with the way Mead's work was interpreted by his successors, especially Herbert Blumer, than with Mead's theories themselves (see also McPhail and Rexroat, 1979).

separable from the act; it is an integral part of the act. Thus, Mead does not want to think of the mind in subjective terms but rather as something which is part of an objective process.

Another important intellectual input into Mead's thinking was *pragmatism*; indeed, Mead was one of the key figures in the development of pragmatic philosophy (others were John Dewey and Charles Peirce) (Lewis and Smith, 1980). Mead (1938/1972) regarded pragmatism as a "natural American outgrowth." Pragmatism reflected the triumph of science and the scientific method within American society and their extension into the study of the social world (J. Baldwin, 1986). Instead of being contemplative and otherworldly, as were previous philosophical systems, pragmatism adopted a focus on this world, on empirical reality. Pragmatists believe in the superiority of scientific data over philosophical dogma and all other types of knowledge. As John Baldwin summarizes, "Science is superior to trial-and-error learning, introspection, a priori logic, religious dogma, idealism, speculative philosophy, and all other nonempirical sources of knowledge" (1986:16). Science is seen as the optimum means not only for obtaining knowledge but also for analyzing and solving social problems. Scientific theories, as well as ideas in general, are to be tested using the full array of scientific procedures. The ideas that survive are those that are likely to provide knowledge that is useful and solves problems. Pragmatists reject the idea that there are such things as absolute truths. Rather, following the scientific model, they regard all ideas as provisional and subject to change in light of future research.

Pragmatism also involves a series of ideas that relate more directly to Mead's sociological theory (Charon, 1989). First, to pragmatists, truth and reality do not exist "out there" in the real world; they are "actively created as we act in and toward the world" (Hewitt, 1984:8; see also Shalin, 1986). Second, people remember the past and base their knowledge of the world on what has proved useful to them. They are likely to alter what no longer "works." Third, people define the social and physical "objects" that they encounter in the world according to their use for them. Finally, if we want to understand actors, we must base our understanding on what they actually do in the world. Given these viewpoints, we can understand John Baldwin's contention that pragmatism is "rooted in a 'rough and ready' American ethic developed by the settlers who had faced the challenges of new frontiers and dealt with the practical problems of taming a new land" (1986:22). In sum, pragmatism is a "pragmatic" philosophy in several senses, including the fact that it adopts the scientists' focus on the here and now as well as scientific methods, it is concerned with what people actually do, and it is interested in generating practical ideas that can help us cope with society's problems.

Lewis and Smith (1980) differentiate between two strands of pragmatism— *nominalist pragmatism* (associated with John Dewey and William James) and *philosophical realism* (associated with Mead). The nominalist position is that although societal phenomena exist, they do not exist independently of people and do not have a determining effect upon individual consciousness and behavior (in contrast to Durkheim's social facts and the reified worlds of Marx, Weber, and Simmel). More positively, this view "conceives of the individuals themselves as existentially free agents who accept, reject, modify, or otherwise 'define' the community's norms, roles, beliefs, and so forth, according to their own personal interests and plans of the moment" (Lewis and Smith, 1980:24). In contrast, to social realists the emphasis is on society and how it constitutes and controls individual mental processes. Rather than being free agents, actors and their cognitions and behaviors are controlled by the larger community.[3]

Given this distinction, Lewis and Smith conclude that Mead's work fits better into the realist camp. There is much of merit in this position, and it will inform some of the ensuing discussion (especially on the priority Mead accords to the social). However, to classify Mead as a realist would be to include him in the same category as Durkheim, and this is unacceptable because there are clearly important differences between their theories. In fact, Mead's theory cannot be forced into either of these categories. There are elements of *both* nominalism and realism in Mead's thinking. To put it more concretely, in most of Mead's work, social processes and consciousness mutually inform one another and cannot be clearly distinguished. In other words, there is a dialectic between realism and nominalism in Mead's work.

This brings us to another important source of Mead's thinking—the philosophy of Hegel, especially his dialectical approach. We have already encountered the dialectic, especially in Chapter 5, on Marx, and many of the ideas expressed there apply to Mead's thinking. We will return to this issue later in the chapter because, as we will see, dialectical thinking makes it almost impossible to separate Mead's many theoretical ideas; they are dialectically related to one another. However, adopting the strategy followed by Mead himself, we will differentiate among various concepts for the sake of clarity of discussion. Bear in mind (and occasionally the reader will be reminded) through each of the specific discussions that there is a dialectical interrelationship among the various concepts.

THE PRIORITY OF THE SOCIAL

In his review of Mead's best-known work, *Mind, Self and Society*, Ellsworth Faris argued that "not mind and then society; but society first and then minds arising with that society . . . would probably have been [Mead's] preference" (cited in Miller, 1982a:2). Faris's inversion of the title of this book reflects the widely acknowledged fact, recognized by Mead himself, that society, or more broadly the social, is accorded priority in Mead's analysis.

In Mead's view, traditional social psychology began with the psychology of the individual in an effort to explain social experience; in contrast, Mead always gives priority to the social world in understanding social experience. Mead explains his focus in this way:

---

[3] For a criticism of this distinction, see Miller (1982b, 1985).

GEORGE HERBERT MEAD: A Biographical Sketch

Most of the important theorists discussed throughout this book achieved their greatest recognition in their lifetimes for their published work. George Herbert Mead, however, was at least as important, at least during his lifetime, for his teaching as for his writing. His words had a powerful impact on many people who were to become important sociologists in the twentieth century. As one of his students said, "Conversation was his best medium; writing was a poor second" (T. V. Smith, 1931:369). Let us have another of his students, himself a well-known sociologist—Leonard Cottrell—describe what Mead was like as a teacher:

For me, the course with Professor Mead was a unique and un-forgettable experience. . . . Professor Mead was a large, amiable-looking man who wore a magnificent mustache and a Vandyke beard. He characteristically had a benign, rather shy smile matched with a twinkle in his eyes as if he were enjoying a secret joke he was playing on the audience. . . .

As he lectured—always without notes—Professor Mead would manipulate the piece of chalk and watch it intently. . . . When he made a particularly subtle point in his lecture he would glance up and throw a shy, almost apologetic smile over our heads—never looking directly at anyone. His lecture flowed and we soon learned that questions or comments from the class were not welcome. Indeed, when someone was bold enough to raise a question there was a murmur of disapproval from the students. They objected to any interruption of the golden flow. . . .

His expectations of students were modest. He never gave exams. The main task for each of us students was to write as learned a paper as one could. These Professor Mead read with great care, and what he thought of your paper was your grade in the course. One might suppose that students would read materials for the paper rather than attend his lectures but that was not the case. Students always came. They couldn't get enough of Mead.

(Cottrell, 1980:49–50)

Over the years, many of Mead's sociological ideas came to be published, especially in *Mind, Self and Society.* This book and others of Mead's works have had a powerful influence on contemporary sociology.

Born in South Hadley, Massachusetts, on February 27, 1863, Mead was trained mainly in philosophy and its application to social psychology. He received a bachelor's degree from Oberlin College (where his father was a professor) in 1883, and after a few years as a secondary-school teacher, surveyor for railroad companies, and private tutor, Mead began graduate study at Harvard in 1887. After a few years of study at Harvard, as well as at the Universities of Leipzig and Berlin, Mead was offered an instructorship at the University of Michigan in 1891. It is interesting to note that Mead *never* received any graduate degrees. In 1894, at the invitation of John Dewey, he moved to the University of Chicago and remained there for the rest of his life. In addition to his teaching and his scholarly activities, Mead was active politically, especially in the reform movement in Chicago (Joas, 1985).

George Herbert Mead died on April 26, 1931.

We are not, in social psychology, building up the behavior of the social group in terms of the behavior of separate individuals composing it; rather, we are *starting out with a given social whole* of complex group activity, into which we analyze (as elements) the behavior of each of the separate individuals composing it. . . . We attempt, that is, to explain the conduct of the social group, rather than to account for the organized conduct of the social group in terms of the conduct of the separate individuals belonging to it. For social psychology, the *whole* (*society*) *is prior to the part* (*the individual*), not the part to the whole; and the part is explained in terms of the whole, not the whole in terms of the part or parts.

(Mead, 1934/1962:7; italics added)

To Mead, the social whole precedes the individual mind both logically and temporally. A thinking, self-conscious individual is, as we will see later, logically impossible in Mead's theory without a prior social group. The social group comes first, and it leads to the development of self-conscious mental states.

THE ACT

Mead considers the act to be the most "primitive unit" in his theory (1982:27). It is not in itself an emergent phenomenon but is rather the base of all emergence. In other words, the act is the base from which all other aspects of Mead's analysis emerge. In analyzing the act, Mead comes closest to the behaviorist's approach and focuses on stimulus and response. However, even here the stimulus does not elicit an automatic, unthinking response from the human actor. As Mead says, "We conceive of the stimulus as an occasion or opportunity for the act, not as a compulsion or a mandate" (1982:28).

Mead (1938/1972) identified four basic and interrelated stages in the act; the four stages represent an organic whole (in other words, they are dialectically interrelated). Both lower animals and humans act, and Mead is interested in the similarities, and especially the differences, between the two. The first stage is that of the *impulse*, which involves an "immediate sensuous stimulation" and the actor's reaction to the stimulation, the need to do something about it. Hunger is a good example of an impulse. The actor (both nonhuman and human) may respond immediately and unthinkingly to the impulse, but more likely the human actor will think about the appropriate response (for example, eat now or later). In thinking about a response, the person will consider not only the immediate situation but also past experiences and anticipated future results of the act.

We have focused above on an impulse, hunger, that can be traced to the individual, but such impulses also involve the environment. Hunger may come from an inner state of the actor or may be elicited by the presence of food in the environment, or, most likely, it may arise from some combination of the two. Furthermore, the hungry person must find a way of satisfying the impulse in an environment in which food may not be immediately available or plentiful. This impulse, like all others, may be related to a problem in the environment (that is, the lack of immediately available food), a problem that must be overcome by the actor. Indeed, while an impulse like hunger may come largely from the individual (although even here hunger can be induced by an external stimulus, and there are also social definitions of when it is appropriate to be hungry), it is usually related to the existence of a problem in the environment (for example, the lack of food). To take another example, the approach of a dangerous wild animal may be an impulse to a person to act. Overall, the impulse, like all other elements of Mead's theory, involves both the actor and the environment.

The second stage of the act is *perception,* in which the actor searches for, and reacts to, stimuli that relate to the impulse, in this case hunger as well as the various means available to satisfy it. People have the capacity to sense or perceive stimuli through hearing, smell, taste, and so on. Perception involves both incoming stimuli as well as the mental images they create. People do not simply respond immediately to external stimuli but rather think about, and assess, them through mental imagery. People are not simply subject to external stimulation; they also actively select characteristics of a stimulus and choose among sets of stimuli. That is, a stimulus may have several dimensions, and the actor is able to select among them. Furthermore, people are usually confronted with many different stimuli, and they have the capacity to choose which to attend to and which to ignore. Mead refuses to separate people from the objects that they perceive. It is the act of perceiving an object that makes it an object to a person; perception and object cannot be separated from (are dialectically related to) one another.

Third is the stage of *manipulation.* Once the impulse has been manifest and the object has been perceived, the next step is manipulating the object or, more generally, taking action with regard to it. In addition to their mental advantages, people have another advantage over lower animals. People have hands (with opposable thumbs) that allow them to manipulate objects far more subtly than can lower animals. The manipulation phase constitutes, for Mead, an important temporary pause in the process so that a response is not manifest immediately. A hungry human being sees a mushroom, but before eating it, he or she is likely to pick it up first, examine it, and perhaps check in a guidebook to see whether that particular variety is edible. The lower animal, on the other hand, is likely to eat the mushroom without handling and examining it (and certainly without reading about it). The pause afforded by handling the object allows humans to contemplate various responses. In thinking about whether to eat the mushroom, both the past and the future are involved. People may think about past experiences in which they ate certain mushrooms that made them ill, and they may think about the future sickness, or even death, that might accompany eating a poisonous mushroom. The manipulation of the mushroom becomes a kind of experimental method in which the actor mentally tries out various hypotheses about what would happen if the mushroom is consumed.

On the basis of these deliberations, the actor may decide to eat the mushroom (or not), and this constitutes the last phase of the act, *consummation,* or more generally the taking of action which satisfies the original impulse. Both humans and lower animals may consume the mushroom, but the human is less likely to eat a bad mushroom because of his or her ability to manipulate the mushroom and to think (and read) about the implications of eating it. The lower animal must rely on a trial-and-error method, and this is a less efficient technique than the capacity of humans to think through their actions. Trial and error in this situation is quite dangerous; as a result, it seems likely that lower animals are more prone to die from consuming poison mushrooms than are humans.

While, for ease of discussion, the four stages of the act have been separated from one another in sequential order, the fact is that Mead sees a dialectical relationship among the four stages. John Baldwin expresses this idea in the following way: "Although the four parts of the act sometimes *appear* to be linked in linear order, they actually interpenetrate to form one organic process: Facets of each part are present at all times from the beginning of the act to the end, such that each part affects the other" (1986:55–56). Thus, the later stages of the act may lead to the emergence of earlier stages. For example, the manipulation of food may lead the individual to the impulse of hunger and the perception that one is hungry and that food is available to satisfy the need.

Gestures

While the act involves only one person, the *social act* involves two or more persons. The *gesture* is in Mead's view the basic mechanism in the social act and in the social process more generally. As he defines them, "Gestures are movements of the first organism which act as specific stimuli calling forth the (socially) appropriate responses of the second organism" (Mead, 1934/1962:14; see also Mead, 1959:187). Both lower animals and humans are capable of gestures in the sense that the action of one individual mindlessly and automatically elicits a reaction by another individual. The following is Mead's famous example of a dog fight in terms of gestures:

> The act of each dog becomes the stimulus to the other dog for his response. . . . The very fact that the dog is ready to attack another becomes a stimulus to the other dog to change his own position or his own attitude. He has no sooner done this than the change of attitude in the second dog in turn causes the first dog to change his attitude.
>
> (Mead, 1934/1962:42–43)

Mead labels what is taking place in this situation a "conversation of gestures." One dog's gesture automatically elicits a gesture from the second; there are no thought processes taking place on the part of the dogs.

Humans sometimes engage in mindless conversations of gestures. Mead gives as examples many of the actions and reactions that take place in boxing and fencing matches, where one combatant adjusts "instinctively" to the actions of the second. Mead labels such unconscious actions "nonsignificant" gestures; what distinguishes humans is their ability to employ "significant" gestures, or those that require thought on the part of the actor before a reaction takes place.

The vocal gesture is particularly important in the development of significant gestures. However, not all vocal gestures are significant. The bark of one dog to another is not significant; even some human vocal gestures (for example, a mindless grunt) may not be significant. However, it is the development of vocal gestures, especially in the form of language, which is the most important factor in making possible the distinctive development of human life: "The specialization of the human animal within this field of the gesture has been responsible, ultimately, for the origin and growth of present human society and knowledge, with all the control over nature and over the human environment which science makes possible" (Mead, 1934/1962:14).

The above development is related to a distinctive characteristic of the vocal gesture. When we make a physical gesture, such as a facial grimace, we cannot see what we ourselves are doing (unless we happen to be looking in the mirror). On the other hand, when we utter a vocal gesture, we hear ourselves just as others do. One result of this is that the vocal gesture can affect the speaker in much the same way that it affects the listeners. Another is that we are far better able to stop ourselves in vocal gestures than we are able to do in physical gestures. In other words, we have far better control over vocal gestures than physical ones. This ability to control oneself and one's reactions is critical, as we will see, to the other distinctive capabilities of humans. More generally, "It has been the vocal gesture that has preeminently provided the medium of social organization in human society" (Mead, 1959:188).

Significant Symbols

A significant symbol is a kind of gesture, one of which only humans are capable. Gestures become *significant symbols* when they arouse in the individual making them the same kind of response (it need not be identical) as they are supposed to elicit from those to whom the gestures are addressed. Only when we have significant symbols can we truly have communication; communication in the full sense of the term is not possible among ants, bees, and so on. Physical gestures can be significant symbols, but as we have seen, they are not ideally suited to this because people cannot easily see or hear their own physical gestures. Thus, it is vocal utterances that are most likely to become significant symbols, although not all vocalizations are such symbols. The set of vocal gestures that are most likely to become significant symbols is *language:* "a symbol which answers to a meaning in that experience of the first individual and which also calls out the meaning in the second individual. Where the gesture reaches that situation it has become what we call 'language.' It is now a significant symbol and it signifies a certain meaning" (Mead, 1934/1962:46). In a conversation of gestures, only the gestures themselves are communicated. However, with language the gestures as well as their meanings are communicated.

One of the things that language, or significant symbols more generally, does is call out the same response in the individual as it does in others. The word *dog* or *cat* elicits the same mental image in the person uttering the word as it does in those to whom it is addressed. Another effect of language is that it stimulates the person speaking as it does others. The person yelling "fire" in a crowded theater is at least as motivated to leave the theater as are those to whom the shout is addressed. Thus, significant symbols allow people to be the stimulators of their own actions.

Adopting his pragmatist orientation, Mead also looks at the "functions" of gestures, in general, and significant symbols, in particular. The function of the gesture "is to make adjustment possible among the individuals implicated in any given social act with reference to the object or objects with which that act is concerned" (Mead, 1934/1962:46). Thus, an involuntary facial grimace may be made in order to prevent a child from going too close to the edge of a precipice and thereby prevent him or her from being in a potentially danger-ous situation. While the nonsignificant gesture works, the

> significant symbol affords far greater facilities for such adjustment and readjustment than does the nonsignificant gesture, because it calls out in the individual making it the same attitude toward it . . . and enables him to adjust his subsequent behavior to theirs in the light of that attitude. In short, the conscious or significant conver-sation of gestures is a much more adequate and effective mechanism of mutual adjustment within the social act . . . than is the unconscious or nonsignificant con-versation of gestures.
>
> (Mead, 1934/1962:46)

From a pragmatic point of view, a significant symbol works better in the social world than a nonsignificant gesture. In other words, in communicating our displeasure to others, an angry verbal rebuke works far better than contorted body language. The individual manifesting displeasure is not usually con-scious of body language and therefore is unlikely to be able to consciously adjust later actions in light of how the other person reacts to the body lan-guage. On the other hand, a speaker is conscious of uttering an angry rebuke and reacts to it in much the same way (and at about the same time) as the person to whom it is aimed reacts. Thus, the speaker can think about how the other person might react and can prepare his or her reaction to that reaction.

Of crucial importance in Mead's theory is another function of significant symbols, and that is that they make the mind, mental processes, and so on possible. It is only through significant symbols, especially language, that human *thinking* is possible (lower animals cannot think, in Mead's terms). Mead defines *thinking* as "simply an internalized or implicit conversation of the individual with himself by means of such gestures" (1934/1962:47). Even more strongly, Mead argues: "Thinking is the same as talking to other people" (1982:155). In other words, thinking involves talking to oneself. Thus, we can see clearly here how Mead defines thinking in behaviorist terms. Conversa-tions involve behavior (talking), and that behavior also occurs within the indi-vidual; when it does, thinking is taking place. This is not a mentalistic definition of thinking; it is decidedly behavioristic.

Significant symbols also make possible *symbolic interaction*.[4] That is, people can interact with one another not just through gestures but also through significant symbols. This, of course, makes a world of difference and makes possible much more complex interaction patterns and forms of social organization than would be possible through gestures alone.

The significant symbol obviously plays a central role in Mead's thinking. In fact, Miller accords the significant symbol *the* central role in Mead's theory: "Mead's most profound insight consists in understanding that the significant symbol, the language symbol, consists of a gesture whose meaning is had by both the one who makes the gesture and the other to whom it is addressed. He spent most of his intellectual life unraveling the implications of this insight" (1982a:10–11).

MENTAL PROCESSES AND THE MIND

Mead uses a number of similar-sounding concepts when discussing mental *processes*, and it is important to sort them out. Before we do, the point should be made that Mead is always inclined to think in terms of processes rather than structures or contents. In fact, Mead is often labeled a "process philosopher" (Cronk, 1987; Miller, 1982a).

One term that sounds like it belongs under the heading of "mental processes" but actually does not in Mead's thinking is *intelligence*.[5] Mead defines *intelligence* most broadly as the mutual adjustment of the acts of organisms. By this definition, lower animals clearly have "intelligence" because in a conversation of gestures they adapt to one another. Similarly, humans can adapt to one another through the use of nonsignificant symbols (for example, involuntary grimaces). However, what distinguishes humans is that they can also exhibit intelligence, or mutual adaptation, through the use of significant symbols. Thus, a bloodhound has intelligence, but the intelligence of the detective is distinguished from that of the bloodhound by the capacity to use significant symbols.

Mead argues that animals have "unreasoning intelligence." In contrast, humans have "reason," which Mead defines in a characteristically behavioristic manner: "When you are reasoning you are indicating to yourself the characters that call out certain responses—and that is all you are doing" (1934/1962:93). In other words, individuals are carrying on conversations with themselves.

What is crucial to the reflective intelligence of humans is their ability to temporarily inhibit action, to delay their reactions to a stimulus (Mead, 1959:84). In the case of lower animals, a stimulus leads immediately and inevitably to a reaction; lower animals lack the capacity to temporarily inhibit their

---

[4] This is the label that was ultimately affixed (by Herbert Blumer) to the sociological theory derived, in significant part, from Mead's ideas.
[5] Although, as we will see later, Mead uses this term inconsistently; it is sometimes used to include mental processes.

reactions. As Mead puts it, "Delayed reaction is necessary to intelligent[6] con-duct. The organization, implicit testing, and final selection . . . would be impossible if his overt responses or reactions could not in such situations be delayed" (1934/1962:99). There are three components here. First, humans, because of their ability to delay reactions, are able to organize in their own minds the array of possible responses to a situation. Humans possess in their minds the alternative ways of completing a social act in which they are involved. Second, people are able to test out mentally, again through an inter-nal conversation with themselves, the various courses of action. In contrast, lower animals lack this capacity and therefore must try out reactions in the real world in trial-and-error fashion. The ability to try out responses mentally, as we saw in the case of the poison mushroom, is much more effective than the trial-and-error method. There is no social cost involved in mentally trying out a poorly adapted response. However, when a lower animal actually uses such a response in the real world (for example, when a dog approaches a poisonous snake), the results can be costly, even disastrous. Finally, humans are able to pick out one stimulus among a set of stimuli rather than simply reacting to the first or strongest stimulus. In addition, humans can select among a range of alternative actions, whereas lower animals simply act. As Mead says:

> It is the entrance of the alternative possibilities of future response into the deter-mination of present conduct in any given environmental situation, and their oper-ation, through the mechanism of the central nervous system, as part of the factors or conditions determining present behavior, which *decisively* contrasts intelligent conduct or behavior with reflex, instinctive, and habitual conduct or behavior-delayed reaction with immediate reaction.
>
> (Mead, 1934/1962:98; italics added)

The ability to choose among a range of actions makes it probable that the choices of humans are likely to be better adapted to the situation than the immediate and mindless reactions of lower animals. As Mead contends, "Intelligence is largely a matter of selectivity" (1934/1962:99).

Mead also discusses *consciousness,* which he sees as having two distinguish-able meanings (1938/1972:75). The first is that to which the actor alone has access, that which is entirely subjective. Mead is less interested in this sense of consciousness than in the second, which basically involves reflective intelli-gence. Thus, Mead is less interested in the way in which we experience imme-diate pain or pleasure than he is in the way in which we think about the social world.

Consciousness is to be explained or accounted for within the social process. That is, in contrast to most analysts, Mead believes that consciousness is *not* lodged in the brain: "Consciousness is functional not substantive; and in either

---

[6] Here is one place where Mead is using *intelligence* in a different sense than the way he employed it in the above discussion.

of the main senses of the term it must be located in the objective world rather than in the brain—it belongs to, or is a characteristic of, the environment in which we find ourselves. What is located, what does take place, in the brain, however, is the physiological process whereby we lose and regain consciousness" (1934/1962:112).

In a similar manner, Mead refuses to position *mental images* in the brain but sees them as social phenomena:

> What we term 'mental images' . . . can exist in their relation to the organism without being lodged in a substantial consciousness. The mental image is a memory image. Such images which, as symbols, play so large a part in thinking, belong to the environment. The passage we read is made up from memory images, and the people we see about us we see very largely by the help of memory images. . . . We can proceed with *a behavioristic treatment* without having the difficulties in which Watson found himself in dealing with mental images.
>
> (Mead, 1934/1962:332; italics added)

Meaning is yet another related concept that Mead addresses behavioristically. Characteristically, Mead rejects the idea that meaning lies in consciousness: "Awareness or consciousness is not necessary to the presence of meaning in the process of social experience" (1934/1962:77). Similarly, Mead rejects the idea that meaning is a "psychical" phenomenon or an "idea." Rather, *meaning* lies squarely within the social act: "Meaning arises and lies within the field of the relation between the gesture of a given human organism and the subsequent behavior of this organism as indicated to another human organism by that gesture. If that gesture does so indicate to another organism the subsequent (or resultant) behavior of the given organism, then it has meaning" (Mead, 1934/1962:75–76). It is the adjustive response of the second organism that gives meaning to the gesture of the first organism. The meaning of a gesture can be seen as the "ability to predict the behavior that is likely to occur next" (J. Baldwin, 1986:72).

While meaning is to be found in behavior, it becomes conscious when meaning is associated with symbols. However, while meaning can become conscious among humans, it is present in the social act *prior* to the emergence of consciousness and the awareness of meaning. Thus, in these terms, lower animals (and humans) can engage in meaningful behavior even though they are not aware of the meaning.

Like consciousness, the *mind*, which is defined by Mead as a process and not a thing, as an inner conversation with one's self, is not found within the individual; it is not intracranial but is a social phenomenon. It arises and develops within the social process and is an integral part of that process. Thus, the social process precedes the mind; it is not, as many believe, a product of the mind. Thus, the mind, too, is defined functionally rather than substantively. Given these similarities to ideas like consciousness, is there anything distinctive about the mind? We have already seen that humans have the peculiar capacity to call out in themselves the response they are seeking to elicit from others. A distinctive characteristic of the mind is the ability of the individual "to call out in himself not simply a single response of the other but the response, so to speak, of the community as a whole. That is what gives to an individual what we term 'mind.' To do anything now means a certain organized response; and if one has in himself that response, he has what we term 'mind' " (Mead, 1934/1962:267). Thus, the mind can be distinguished from other like-sounding concepts in Mead's work by its ability to respond to the overall community and put forth an organized response.

Mead also looks at the mind in another, pragmatic way. That is, the mind involves thought processes oriented toward problem solving. The real world is rife with problems, and it is the function of the mind to try to solve those problems and permit people to operate more effectively in the world.

SELF

Much of Mead's thinking in general, and especially on the mind, involves his ideas on the critically important concept of the "self." Up to this point we have avoided this concept, but it is now necessary to discuss it in order to get a fuller flavor of Mead's thinking.

The *self* is basically the ability to take oneself as an object; the self has the peculiar ability to be both subject and object. As is true of all Mead's major concepts, the self presupposes a social process: communication among humans. Lower animals do not have selves, nor do human infants at birth. The self arises with development and through social activity and social relationships. To Mead, it is impossible to imagine a self arising in the absence of social experiences. However, once a self has developed, it is possible for it to continue to exist without social contact. Thus, Robinson Crusoe developed a self while he was in civilization, and he continued to have it when he was living alone on what he thought for a while was a deserted island. In other words, he continued to have the ability to take himself as an object. Once it is developed, people usually, but not always, manifest a self. For example, the self is not involved in habitual actions or in immediate physiological experiences of pleasure or pain.

The self is dialectically related to the mind (we will have more to say shortly about the dialectic in Mead's thought). That is, on the one hand, Mead argues that the body is not a self and becomes a self only when a mind has developed. On the other hand, the self, and its reflexiveness, is essential to the development of the mind. Of course, it is impossible to separate mind and self, because the self is a mental process. However, even though we may think of it as a mental process, the self—like all other mental processes in Mead's theoretical system—is a social process. In his discussion of the self, as we saw above in regard to all other mental phenomena, Mead resists the idea of lodging it in consciousness and instead embeds it in social experience and social processes. In this way, Mead seeks to give a behavioristic sense of the self: "But it is where one does respond to that which he addresses to another and where that response of his own becomes a part of his conduct, where he not only hears himself but responds to himself, talks and replies to himself as truly as the other person replies to him, that we have *behavior* in which the individuals become objects to themselves" (1934/1962:139; italics added). The self, then, is simply another aspect of the overall social process of which the individual is a part.

The general mechanism for the development of the self is reflexivity, or the ability to put ourselves unconsciously into others' places and to act as they act. As a result of this, people are able to examine themselves as others would examine them. As Mead says:

> It is by means of reflexiveness—the turning-back of the experience of the individual upon himself—that the whole social process is thus brought into the experience of the individuals involved in it; it is by such means, which enable the individual to take the attitude of the other toward himself, that the individual is able consciously to adjust himself to that process, and to modify the resultant process in any given social act in terms of his adjustment to it.
>
> (Mead, 1934/1962:134)

The self also allows people to take part in their conversations with others. That is, one is aware of what one is saying and as a result is able to monitor what is being said and to determine what is going to be said next.

In order to have selves, individuals must be able to get "outside themselves" so that they can evaluate themselves, so that they can become objects to themselves. To do this, people basically put themselves in the same experiential field as they put everyone else. The fact is that everyone is an important part of that experiential situation, and people must take themselves into account if they are to be able to act rationally in a given situation. Having done this, they seek to examine themselves impersonally, objectively and without emotion.

However, people cannot experience themselves directly. They can do so only indirectly by putting themselves in the position of others and viewing themselves from that standpoint. People can do this either by putting themselves in the position of other particular individuals or by looking at themselves from the viewpoint of the social group as a whole. As Mead puts it, most generally, "It is only by taking the roles of others that we have been able to come back to ourselves" (1959:184–185). We will have more to say shortly about this important distinction between putting ourselves in the place of a specific individual or putting ourselves in the position of a collectivity.

Mead is very interested in the genesis of the self. He sees the conversation of gestures as the background for the self, but it does not involve a self, since in such a conversation the people are not taking themselves as objects. Mead traces the genesis of the self through two stages in childhood development. The first is the *play stage*, and it is during this stage that children learn to take the attitude of particular others to themselves. While lower animals also play, only human beings "play at being someone else" (Aboulafia, 1986:9). Mead gives the example of a child playing (American) "Indian": "This means that the child has a certain set of stimuli which call out in itself the responses they would call out in others, and which answer to an Indian" (1934/1962:150). As a result of such play, the child learns to become both subject and object and begins to become able to build a self. However, it is a limited self because the child is only capable of taking the role of distinct and separate others. Children may play at being "mommy" and "daddy" and in the process develop the ability to evaluate themselves as their parents, and other specific individuals, do. However, they lack a more general and organized sense of themselves.

It is the next stage, the *game stage,* that is required if the person is to develop a self in the full sense of the term. While in the play stage the child takes the role of discrete others, in the game stage the child must take the role of everyone else involved in the game. Furthermore, these different roles must have a definite relationship to one another. In illustrating the game stage, Mead gives his famous example of a baseball (or, as he calls it, "ball nine") game:

> But in a game where a number of individuals are involved, then the child taking one role must be ready to take the role of everyone else. If he gets in a ball nine he must have the responses of each position involved in his own position. He must know what everyone else is going to do in order to carry out his own play. He has to take all of these roles. They do not all have to be present in consciousness at the same time, but at some moments he has to have three or four individuals present in his own attitude, such as the one who is going to throw the ball, the one who is going to catch it, and so on. These responses must be, in some degree, present in his own make-up. In the game, then, there is a set of responses of such others so organized that the attitude of one calls out the appropriate attitudes of the other.
>
> (Mead, 1934/1962:151)

In the play stage, children are not organized wholes because they play at a series of discrete roles. As a result, in Mead's view they lack definite personalities. However, in the game stage,[7] such organization begins and a definite personality starts to emerge. Children begin to become able to function in organized groups and, most importantly, to determine what they will do within a specific group.

The game stage yields one of Mead's (1959:87) best-known concepts, the *generalized other.* The generalized other is the attitude of the entire community or, in the example of the baseball game, the attitude of the entire team. The ability to take the role of the generalized other is essential to the self: "Only in so far as he takes the attitudes of the organized social group to which he belongs toward the organized, co-operative social activity or set of such activities in which that group is engaged, does he develop a complete self" (Mead, 1934/1962:155). It is also crucial that people be able to evaluate themselves from the point of view of the generalized other and not merely from the viewpoint of discrete others. Taking the role of the generalized other, rather

---

[7] While Mead discusses games, it is clear, as Aboulafia (1986:198) points out, that he means any system of organized responses (for example, the family).

than that of discrete others, allows for the possibility of abstract thinking and objectivity (Mead, 1959:190). Here is the way Mead describes the full development of the self:

> So the self reaches its full development by organizing these individual attitudes of others into the organized social or group attitudes, and by thus becoming an individual reflection of the general systematic pattern of social or group behavior in which it and others are involved—a pattern which enters as a whole into the individual's experience in terms of these organized group attitudes which, through the mechanism of the central nervous system, he takes toward himself, just as he takes the individual attitudes of others.
>
> (Mead, 1934/1962:158)

In other words, to have a self, one must be a member of a community and be directed by the attitudes common to the community. While play requires only pieces of selves, the game requires a coherent self.

Not only is taking the role of the generalized other essential to the self, but it is also crucial for the development of organized group activities. A group requires that individuals direct their activities in accord with the attitudes of the generalized other. The generalized other also represents Mead's familiar propensity to give priority to the social, since it is through the generalized other that the group influences the behavior of individuals.

Mead also looks at the self from a pragmatic point of view. At the individual level, the self allows the individual to be a more efficient member of the larger society. Because of the self, people are more likely to do what is expected of them in a given situation. Since people often try to live up to group expectations, they are more likely to avoid the inefficiencies that come from failing to do what the group expects. Furthermore, the self allows for greater coordination in society as a whole. Because individuals can be counted on to do what is expected of them, the group can operate more effectively.

The preceding, as well as the overall discussion of the self, might lead us to believe that Mead's actors are little more than conformists and that there is little individuality, since everyone is busy conforming to the expectations of the generalized other. But Mead is clear that each self is different from all others. Selves share a common structure, but each self receives unique biographical articulation. In addition, it is clear that there is not simply one grand generalized other but that there are many generalized others in society, because there are many groups in society. People, therefore, have multiple generalized others and, as a result, multiple selves. Each person's unique set of selves makes him or her different from everyone else. Furthermore, people need not accept the community as it is; they can reform things and seek to make them better. We are able to change the community because of our capacity to think. But Mead is forced to put this issue of individual creativity in familiar, behavioristic terms: "The only way in which we can react against the disapproval of the entire community is by setting up a higher sort of community which in a certain sense out-votes the one we find . . . he may stand out by himself over against it. But to do that he has to comprehend the voices of the past and of the future. That is the only way the self can get a voice which is more than the voice of the community" (1934/1962:167–168). In other words, to stand up to the generalized other, the individual must construct a still larger generalized other, composed not only from the present but also from the past and the future, and then respond to it.

Mead identifies two aspects, or phases, of the self, which he labels the "I" and the "me." As Mead puts it, "The self is essentially a social process going on with these two distinguishable phases" (1934/1962:178). It is important to bear in mind that the "I" and "me" are processes within the larger process of the self; they are not "things." The "I" is the immediate response of an individual to others. It is the incalculable, unpredictable, and creative aspect of the self. People do not know in advance what the action of the "I" will be: "But what that response will be he does not know and nobody else knows. Perhaps he will make a brilliant play or an error. The response to that situation as it appears in his immediate experience is uncertain" (Mead, 1934/1962:175). We are never totally aware of the "I," and through it we surprise ourselves with our actions. We know the "I" only after the act has been carried out. Thus, we know the "I" only in our memories. Mead lays great stress on the "I" for four reasons. First, it is a key source of novelty in the social process. Second, Mead believes that it is in the "I" that our most important values are located. Third, the "I" constitutes something that we all seek—the realization of the self. It is the "I" that permits us to develop a "definite personality." Finally, Mead sees an evolutionary process in history in which people in primitive societies are dominated more by "me" while in modern societies there is a greater component of "I."

The "I" gives Mead's theoretical system some much-needed dynamism and creativity. Without it, Mead's actors would be totally dominated by external and internal controls. With it, Mead is able to deal with the changes brought about not only by the great figures in history (for example, Einstein) but also by individuals on a day-to-day basis. It is the "I" that makes these changes possible. Since every personality is a mix of "I" and "me," the great historical figures are seen as having a larger proportion of "I" than most others. But in day-to-day situations, anyone's "I" may assert itself and lead to change in the social situation. Uniqueness is also brought into Mead's system through the biographical articulation of each individual's "I" and "me." That is, the specific exigencies of each person's life give him or her a unique mix of "I" and "me."

The "I" reacts against the "me," which is the "organized set of attitudes of others which one himself assumes" (Mead, 1934/1962:175). In other words, the "me" is the adoption of the "generalized other." In contrast to the "I," people are conscious of the "me"; the "me" involves conscious responsibility. As Mead says, "The 'me' is a conventional, habitual individual" (1934/1962:197). Conformists are dominated by "me," although everyone—whatever his or her degree of conformity—has, and must have, substantial "me." It is through the "me" that society dominates the individual. Indeed, Mead defines the idea of *social control* as the dominance of the expression of the "me" over the expression of the "I." Later in *Mind, Self and Society*, Mead elaborates on his ideas on social control:

> Social control, as operating in terms of self-criticism, exerts itself so intimately and extensively over individual behavior or conduct, serving to integrate the individual and his actions with reference to the organized social process of experience and behavior in which he is implicated. . . . Social control over individual behavior or conduct operates by virtue of the social origin and basis of such [self-] criticism. That is to say, self-criticism is essentially social criticism, and behavior controlled socially. Hence social control, so far from tending to crush out the human individual or to obliterate his self-conscious individuality, is, on the contrary, actually constitutive of and inextricably associated with that individuality.
>
> (Mead, 1934/1962:255)

Mead also looks at the "I" and "me" in pragmatic terms. The "me" allows the individual to live comfortably in the social world, while the "I" makes the change of society possible. Society gets enough conformity to allow it to function, and it gets a steady infusion of new developments to prevent it from stagnating. The "I" and the "me" are thus part of the whole social process and allow both individuals and society to function more effectively.

SOCIETY

At the most general level, Mead uses the term *society* to mean the ongoing social process that precedes both the mind and the self. Given its importance in shaping the mind and self, society is clearly of central importance to Mead. At another level, society to Mead represents the organized set of responses that are taken over by the individual in the form of the "me." Thus, in this sense individuals carry society around with them, and it is this that allows them, through self-criticism, to control themselves. Mead also, as we will see, deals with the evolution of society. But Mead has relatively little to say explicitly about society, in spite of its centrality in his theoretical system. His most important contributions lie in his thoughts on mind and self. Even John Baldwin, who sees a much more societal (macro) component in Mead's thinking, is forced to admit: "The macro components of Mead's theoretical system are not as well developed as the micro" (1986:123).

At a more specific societal level Mead does have a number of things to say about social *institutions*. Mead broadly defines an *institution* as the "common response in the community" or "the life habits of the community" (1934/1962:261, 264; see also Mead, 1936:376). More specifically, he says that "the whole community acts toward the individual under certain circumstances in an identical way . . . there is an identical response on the part of the whole community under these conditions. We call that the formation of the institution" (Mead, 1934/1962:167). We carry this organized set of attitudes around with us, and they serve to control our actions, largely through the "me."

Education is the process by which the common habits of the community (the institution) are "internalized" in the actor. This is an essential process, since, in Mead's view, people neither have selves nor are genuine members of the community until they can respond to themselves as the larger community does. To do so, people must have internalized the common attitudes of the community.

But again Mead is careful to point out that institutions need not destroy individuality or stifle creativity. Mead recognizes that there are "oppressive, stereotyped, and ultra-conservative social institutions—like the church—which by their more or less rigid and inflexible unprogressiveness crush or blot out individuality" (1934/1962:262). However, he is quick to add: "There is no necessary or inevitable reason why social institutions should be oppressive or rigidly conservative, or why they should not rather be, as many are, flexible and progressive, fostering individuality rather than discouraging it" (Mead, 1934/1962:262). To Mead, institutions should define what people ought to do only in a very broad and general sense and should allow plenty of room for individuality and creativity. Mead here demonstrates a very modern conception of social institutions as both constraining individuals *and* enabling them to be creative individuals (see Giddens, 1984).

What Mead lacks in his analysis of society in general, and institutions in particular,[8] is a true macro sense of them in the way that theorists like Comte, Spencer, Marx, Weber, and Durkheim dealt with this level of analysis. This is true in spite of the fact that Mead does have a notion of *emergence* in the sense that the whole is seen as more than the sum of its parts. More specifically, "Emergence involves a reorganization, but the reorganization brings in something that was not there before. The first time oxygen and hydrogen come together, water appears. Now water is a combination of hydrogen and oxygen, but water was not there before in the separate elements" (Mead, 1934/1962:198). However, Mead is much more prone to apply the idea of emergence to consciousness than to apply it to the larger society. That is, mind and self are seen as emergent from the social process. Moreover, Mead is inclined to use the term *emergence* merely to mean the coming into existence of something new or novel (Miller, 1973:41).

EVOLUTION

We have already encountered a bit of Mead's thinking on the evolutionary process in the movement from primitive societies dominated by "me" to modern societies dominated by "I." Influenced by bioevolutionists Charles Darwin and Jean Baptiste Lamarck, as well as Hegel, Mead sees humans, like all other organisms, as evolving in the direction of greater adaptation to their environ-

---

[8] There are at least two places where Mead offers a more macro sense of society. At one point he defines *social institutions* as "organized forms of group or social activity" (Mead, 1934/1962:261). Earlier, in an argument reminiscent of Comte, he offers a view of the family as the fundamental unit within society and as the base of such larger units as the clan and state.

ment as well as increased ability to exercise control over the environment. Mead looks at the evolutionary process in pragmatic terms: "Evolution is the process of meeting and solving problems" (1936:143). As a result, Mead does not see evolution as a single, uniform process but as a diverse set of ways of solving problems. Evolution will take different forms depending on local conditions, but all these forms *are* shaped by their adaptation to those conditions.

The evolution of human society has progressed far beyond that of other organisms and has still greater potential in the future. Humans, unlike lower animals, have the ability to alter their inorganic environment. Humans, of course, have this capacity because of their self-consciousness. Self-consciousness allows people to alter their environment, make progressive social changes in the social world, and develop their personalities so that they can keep pace with the changes they are making in society. In Mead's view, "The realization of the self in the intelligent performance of a social function remains the higher stage [in evolution] in the case of nations as of individuals" (1934/1962:317). While Mead sees considerable evolution among humans, he also makes it clear that there is a long way to go before the evolutionary process is anywhere near complete.

Mead sees science as a crucial product of the evolutionary process. To Mead, science is the surest kind of knowledge that we possess (Moore, 1936). In pragmatic terms, science simply involves problem-solving activity. But the problem-solving activity is distinctive in that it formally adopts a research attitude involving, among other things, the development of hypotheses to be tested (and a rejection of all dogma), the use of observational methods to find something novel or unanticipated, and the search for uniformities, rules, and laws. However, even if new laws are discovered, they never become dogma, and the scientist is always prepared to revise or drop a law when new, contradictory data become available. Scientists continue to use given hypotheses as long as they work, and they are willing to drop them when they no longer fit the facts. Scientists also do not look toward some vague, distant goal and then plot a course to it. Rather, scientists focus on problems in the current system and on what can be done to solve those problems. The test of a scientific solution is whether it enables the system to work better than it did in the past.

To Mead, science simply does more quickly and efficiently what people in general have done throughout the evolutionary process. That is, while in normal evolution solutions to problems emerge gradually over very long periods of time, in the modern world "we solve the problem directly by what we call the 'scientific method'" (Mead, 1936:365). Mead details several steps in the experimental method of science—the presence of a problem, the statement of a problem in terms of how it can be solved, the formation of hypotheses, the mental testing of hypotheses, and finally the experimental or observational testing of hypotheses. But Mead then goes on to say that these are "merely the elaboration of the simple processes of everyday inference by which we meet our constantly recurring difficulties" (1938/1972:83).

The evolution of science is related to the overall evolution of human mind. Here is the way Mead relates many of the ideas outlined earlier on mental processes to evolution:

> When we reach the human form with its capacity for indicating what is important in a situation, through the process of analysis; when we get to the position in which a mind can arise in the individual form, that is, where the individual can come back upon himself and stimulate himself just as he stimulates others; where the individual can call out in himself the attitudes of the whole group; where he can acquire the knowledge that belongs to the whole community; where he can respond as the whole community responds under certain conditions when they direct this organized intelligence toward particular ends; then we have this process which provides solutions for problems working in a self-conscious way. In it we have the *evolution* of the human mind which makes use directly of the sort of intelligence which has been developed in the whole process of *evolution.*
>
> (Mead, 1936:366; italics added)

Clearly, a mind with the above characteristics is capable of science, and science, in turn, is a formal expression of those distinctive human capabilities. Mead leaves no doubt about his position: "After all, the scientist is simply making a technique out of human intelligence" (1936:373).

Mead also relates his ideas on the evolution of science to the need for society to maintain order but still be able to change and progress. In his view, science offers a method by which society can change, but in an orderly fashion. This is also linked to Mead's social reformism, in which ideas derived from scientific study can be used to expedite the evolutionary process and ameliorate problems in society.

DIALECTICAL THINKING

As we indicated at the outset of this chapter, while Mead's concepts are discussed separately, it is clear that they are dialectically related to one another (Cronk, 1987:3). Mead's dialectical approach may be traced to a number of philosophical sources, especially the work of Hegel, and it is similar in at least some respects to Marx's dialectic.

At the most general level, one cannot clearly separate the concepts, especially mind, self, and society, that have been discussed throughout this chapter. They are intimately related to each other, and all are aspects or phases of the social process, most broadly defined. Ferguson also makes this point: "These concepts are related dialectically, for intrinsic to each factor is its relationship to the other factors. The act of defining any one of them demands an examination of its relationship to others" (1980:26). Let us look at the major elements of the dialectic and the way in which they are manifest in Mead's work.

First, the dialectician refuses to look at the world in one-way, causal terms. There are many places in Mead's work where he looks at the reciprocal relationships among social phenomena. For example, the self is seen as arising out of society, and selves then contribute to the development of a more elaborately organized society and to the increased differentiation, evolution, and organization of society (Mead, 1934/1962:164, see also 180, 196). For another example, as was pointed out above, the four stages of the act need not occur in sequence, and each later stage may act back on earlier stages.

Second, the dialectician refuses to separate fact and value, and although Mead's work is not nearly as value-laden as Marx's, Mead is not averse to making value judgments such as the one mentioned earlier involving his aversion to the Church as a constraining social institution.

Third, the dialectician does not see hard-and-fast dividing lines among social phenomena, and this is clear throughout Mead's work in his unwillingness to clearly separate mind, self, and society. This view is quite explicit in a discussion of selves in which Mead argues: "Selves can only exist in definite relationships to other selves. No *hard-and-fast* line can be drawn between our own selves and the selves of others, since our own selves exist and enter as such into our experience only in so far as the selves of others exist and enter as such into our experience also. The individual possesses a self only in relation to the selves of the other members of his social group" (1934/1962:164; italics added; see also Mead, 1907/1964:81, 1982:73).

Fourth, dialectical thinkers take a relational view to the world. Ferguson discusses, most generally, "the relational character of Mead's analysis" (1980:66). Again this is clear throughout Mead's thinking on mind, self, and society, but it is manifest in his thinking on the relationship between the "I" and the "me," which require one another in order to exist: "There would not be an 'I' in the sense in which we use the term if there were not a 'me'; there would not be a 'me' without a response in the form of this 'I'" (1934/1962:182). Ferguson contends that the "I" and "me" "are dialectically related in such a way that each can only be defined in terms of the other" (1980:33). Similarly, Natanson discusses "the 'I'-'me' dialectic" (1973b:60). More generally, Berger and Luckmann argue that Mead offered a "theory of the dialectic between society and the individual" (1967:194).

Fifth, dialectical thinkers are interested not only in the present but also in its relationship to both the past and the future. This interest in past, present, and future is manifest most generally in Mead's thinking on social evolution. Mead takes the position that the past and the future are to be found in the present: "The functional boundaries of the present are those of its undertaking—of what we are doing. The pasts and the futures indicated by such activity belong to the present. They arise out of it and are criticized and tested by it" (1959:88). Again, to give a more specific example, Mead looks at intelligence[9] in this way: "Intelligence is essentially the ability to solve the problems of *present* behavior in terms of its possible *future* consequences as implicated

[9] Here is another instance in which Mead is using the term *intelligence* differently from the way it was defined initially in this chapter.

on the basis of *past* experience—the ability, that is, to solve the problems of *present* behavior in the light of, or by reference to, both the *past* and *future;* it involves both memory and foresight" (1934/1962:100; italics added).

Sixth, the dialectician does not have a deterministic view of the future. While Mead (like Marx) does have an ideal state toward which he sees society evolving (to Mead it is a world of free, open, and perfect communication), he does not see it as inevitable that we will reach that state. What people, either the great figures in history or people on a daily basis, do matters and will determine how far we will progress toward the evolutionary ideal.

The seventh element of the dialectic is a concern for conflict and contradiction. This, too, can be found in Mead's work, but it is not nearly as pronounced as in Marx's theories. There are important conflicts and contradictions in Mead's work, such as between the "I" and the "me" as well as between the need to conform to society and the need to be innovative and change society. Cronk (1987) sees a model of interaction between consensus and conflict in Mead's work, with the interaction leading to resolutions and new forms of consensus. There are even, in Mead's work, ideas of the negation of the present through revolutionary activities. However, these conflicts and contradictions do not seem to be as crucially important as they are in Marx's work. Furthermore, while Marx sees the resolution of conflicts in new syntheses, the logic of Mead's work leads us to assume that there must be a continuation of a healthy conflict between "I" and "me," self and society, conformity and change.

Thus, all the elements of the dialectic can be applied to Mead's work. Although it is not often recognized, Mead *was* a dialectical thinker, and an understanding of this fact greatly enhances our ability to comprehend his work.

SUMMARY

George Herbert Mead developed his sociological theory out of the confluence of a number of intellectual inputs, the most important of which was behaviorism. Basically, Mead accepted the behavioristic approach and its focus on conduct but sought to extend it to a concern for mental processes. He was also a creator of, and influenced by, pragmatism. Pragmatism gave Mead a powerful faith in science and, more generally, in conduct motivated by reflective intelligence. It, like behaviorism, led Mead to focus on what people actually "do" in the social world. He was also strongly influenced by Hegel, and this is manifest in a number of places (for example, his focus on evolution), especially in his dialectical approach to the social world.

Substantively, Mead's theory accorded primacy and priority to the social world. That is, it is out of the social world that consciousness, the mind, the self, and so on emerge. The most basic unit in his social theory is the act, which includes four dialectically related stages—impulse, perception, manipulation, and consummation. Even in his thoughts on the act Mead does not emphasize external stimuli (as a behaviorist would); rather, he holds that a stimulus is an opportunity, not a compulsion, to act. A *social* act involves two or more persons, and the basic mechanism of the social act is the gesture. While lower animals and humans are capable of having a conversation of gestures, only humans can communicate the conscious meaning of their gestures.

Humans are peculiarly able to create vocal gestures, and this leads to the distinctive human ability to develop and use significant symbols. Significant symbols lead to the development of language and the distinctive capacity of humans to communicate, in the full sense of the term, with one another. Significant symbols also make possible thinking as well as symbolic interaction.

Mead looks at an array of mental processes as part of the larger social process; such mental processes include reflective intelligence, consciousness, mental images, meaning, and, most generally, the mind. Humans have the distinctive capacity to carry on an inner conversation with themselves. All the mental processes are not, in Mead's view, lodged in the brain but rather in the social process.

The self is the ability to take oneself as an object. Again, the self arises within the social process. The general mechanism of the self is the ability of people to put themselves in the place of others and to act as others act and to see themselves as others see them. Mead traces the genesis of the self through the play and game stages of childhood. Especially important in the latter stage is the emergence of the generalized other. The ability to see oneself from the viewpoint of the community is essential to the emergence of the self as well as of organized group activities. The self also has two phases—the "I," which is the unpredictable and creative aspect of the self, and the "me," which is the organized set of attitudes of others assumed by the actor. Social control is manifest through the "me," while the "I" is the source of innovation in society.

Mead has relatively little to say about society, which is most generally seen by him as the ongoing social processes that precede mind and self. Mead largely lacks a macro sense of society. Institutions are defined as little more than collective habits. Mead does have a strong sense of evolution, especially of reflective intelligence as well as of science, the latter being merely a concrete and formalized manifestation of that intelligence. Finally, Mead manifests dialectical thinking throughout his theoretical system.

Mead's theory is not as broad as most of the other theorists examined in this book. Nevertheless, it continues to be influential in contemporary symbolic interactionism, social psychology, and sociology more generally. New work continues to emerge in sociology (as well as in philosophy) building upon Mead's theories (for example, R. Collins, 1989b). Mead's work still attracts new theorists both in the United States and in the rest of the world (for example, Habermas, 1984). This is the case in spite of a number of notable weaknesses in his theory. The greatest weakness, one that has been mentioned several times in this chapter, is that he has little to offer to our understanding of the macro-societal level. Other weaknesses include some vague and fuzzy concepts; an inconsistent definition of concepts (especially intelligence); the difficulty in clearly differentiating one of his concepts from the others; his lack of concern, in spite of his focus on the micro level, for emotional and unconscious aspects of human conduct; and the fact that about the only source of social change in his theoretical system appears to be the individual, especially through the "I." In spite of these and other weaknesses, Mead offers a powerful and important theory that is likely to be influential in sociology for many years to come.

ALFRED SCHUTZ

*O*F all the theorists discussed in this book, it is the inclusion of Alfred Schutz that is the most controversial. Schutz is not often included in the pantheon of classical sociological theorists because his work has only recently come to be widely influential in sociology, especially in the contemporary theories of phenomenological sociology and ethnomethodology. However, because of its recently expanding influence, as well as the fact that it offers a profound, wide-ranging, and distinctive perspective, Schutzian theory warrants full-chapter treatment in this text on classical sociological theory. It is thought of as *classical* theory because of its nature and scope as well as the time of its development. Schutz's most important theoretical statement, *The Phenomenology of the Social World* (1932/1967), was published in the 1930s—the same decade that witnessed the publication of such other now-classical theoretical works as Mead's *Mind, Self and Society* and Parsons's *The Structure of Social Action*.

INTERPRETATIONS OF SCHUTZ'S WORK

We can divide traditional interpretations of Schutz's work into several camps. First, ethnomethodologists and phenomenologists saw in Schutz the source of their interest in the way actors create or construct social reality. Among the ethnomethodologists, for example, Hugh Mehan and Houston Wood argued that the focus of their approach was on the way actors "create situations and rules, and so at once create themselves and their social realities" (1975:115). They went on to say that "ethnomethodologists adopted this research program from Schutz" (Mehan and Wood, 1975:115). Monica Morris, in her book on creative sociology, came to a similar conclusion: "For Schutz, the subject matter of sociology is the manner in which human beings constitute, or create, the world of everyday life" (1977:15). These commentators as well as many others generally have seen Schutz as focusing on the way actors create social reality, and they have lauded him for this micro orientation.

Other commentators have taken a similar view of the substance of his work but have come to very different conclusions about it. A good example is Robert Bierstedt, who criticized Schutz for his focus on the way actors construct social reality and his corresponding lack of concern with the reality of the larger structures of society:

> The phenomenological reduction . . . has consequences of a . . . rather serious kind for sociology. . . . Society itself, as an objective phenomenon, tends to disappear in the realm of the intersubjective. That is, society itself . . . comes to be a creation of the mind in intersubjectivity and something that is wholly exhausted in the commonplace affairs of daily living.
>
> (Bierstedt, 1963:91)

Thus Bierstedt criticized Schutz for precisely the same thing for which Mehan and Wood, Morris, and others praised him.

Although these two camps came to very different conclusions about Schutz's work, they did at least agree on its micro focus. A third school of thought, however, views Schutz in an almost diametrically opposite way, as a cultural determinist. For example, Robert Gorman (1975a, 1975b, 1977) suggested that, contrary to the interpretations of the ethnomethodological and sociological establishments, Schutz emphasized the constraints imposed on the actor by society. Actors do not freely choose beliefs or courses of action, nor do they freely construct a sense of social reality. Rather, as members of society, they are free only to obey.

> Socially determined action patterns are adhered to by free actors. Each actor bases his action on his stock of knowledge at hand, and this knowledge consists of these socially determined action patterns. Each of us chooses, for himself, to act as these patterns prescribe, even though they have been imposed from outside.
>
> (Gorman, 1975a:11)

Gorman concluded that for Schutz "social behavior is apparently caused by factors independent of the subject [actor]" (1977:71).

As we review Schutz's theory, we will see that the most legitimate perspective involves a combination of the first and third views of his work. That is, Schutz's actors do create social reality but that creation takes place in, and is constrained by, socially determined action patterns (Thomason, 1982). We will also see that the second position, articulated by Bierstedt, is erroneous and ignores the constraining reality of culture and society in Schutz's theory.

ALFRED SCHUTZ: A Biographical Sketch

Alfred Schutz was not widely known during his lifetime, and only in recent years has his work attracted the attention of large numbers of sociologists. Although his obscurity was in part a result of his intellectual orientation—his then highly unusual interest in phenomenology—a more important cause was his very unusual career as a sociologist.

Born in Vienna, Austria, in 1899, Schutz received his academic training at the University of Vienna (Wagner, 1983). Soon after completing his law examination, he embarked on a lifelong career in banking. Although rewarding economically, banking did not satisfy his need for deeper meaning in his life. Schutz found that meaning in his work on phenomenological sociology. He was not an academician in the 1920s, but many of his friends were, and he participated in a number of informal lecture and discussion circles (Prendergast, 1986). Schutz was drawn to Weberian theory, especially Weber's work on action and the ideal type. Although impressed with Weber's work, Schutz sought to overcome its weaknesses by integrating ideas from the philosophers Edmund Husserl and Henri Bergson. According to Christopher Prendergast (1986), Schutz was motivated to provide the Austrian School of Economics with a scientific, subjective theory of action. These influences led to the publication by Schutz in 1932 of what was to become a very important book in sociology, *The Phenomenology of the Social World*. It was not translated into English until 1967, so that a wide appreciation of Schutz's work in the United States was delayed thirty-five years.

As World War II approached, Schutz emigrated, with an intervening period in Paris, to the United States, where for many years he divided his time between serving as legal counsel to a number of banks and writing about and teaching phenomenological sociology. Simultaneously with his work in banking, Schutz began teaching courses in 1943 at the New School for Social Research in New York City. As Richard Grathoff points out, the result was

THE IDEAS OF EDMUND HUSSERL

Before turning to the theories of Alfred Schutz, we need to deal with the ideas of his most important intellectual predecessor, the philosopher Edmund Husserl. While other thinkers (for example, Henri Bergson and Max Weber) had a strong impact on Schutz, the influence of Husserl stands above that of all the others.

Husserl's highly complicated philosophy is not easily translated into sociological concepts; indeed, a good portion of it is not directly relevant to sociology (Srubar, 1984). We discuss here a few of his ideas that proved useful to Alfred Schutz, as well as other phenomenological sociologists.

In general, Husserl believed that people view the world as a highly ordered place; actors are always engaged in the active and highly complex process of ordering the world. However, people are unaware that they are patterning the world; hence they do not question the process by which this is accomthat "the social theorist for whom scientific thought and everyday life defined two rather distinct and separate realms of experience upheld a similar division in his personal life" (1978:112). Not until 1956 did Schutz give up his dual career and concentrate entirely on teaching and writing phenomenological sociology. Because of his interest in phenomenology, his dual career, and his teaching at the then avant-garde New School, Schultz remained on the periphery of sociology during his lifetime. Nevertheless, Schutz's work and his influence on students (for example, Peter Berger, Thomas Luckmann, Harold Garfinkel) moved him to the center of sociological theory.

Another factor in Schutz's marginal position in sociological theory was that his theory seemed highly abstract and irrelevant to the mundane social world. Although Schutz did separate theory from reality, he did not feel that his work was irrelevant to the world in which he lived. To put it in terms of his phenomenology, he saw a relationship between the everyday construction of reality and the pregiven historical and cultural world. To think otherwise is to think that the man who fled National Socialism (Nazism) regarded his academic work as irrelevant. The following quotation from one of his letters indicates that although Schutz was not optimistic, he was not prepared to accept the irrelevance of his theorizing and, more generally, the social construction of reality to the world as a whole:

> You are still optimist enough to believe that phenomenology may save itself among the ruins of this world—as the *philosophica aera perennis?* I do not believe so. More likely the African natives must prepare themselves for the ideas of national socialism. This shall not prevent us from dying the way we have lived; and we must try, therefore, to build . . . order into *our* world, which we must find lacking in—our *world.* The whole conflict is hidden in this shift of emphasis.
>
> (Schutz, cited in Grathoff, 1978:130)

In short, although the ability of people to affect the larger society is restricted by such phenomena as Nazism, they must continue to strive to build a social and cultural reality that is *not* beyond their reach and control.

Alfred Schutz died in 1959.

---

plished. Actors see the social world as naturally ordered, not structured by them. Unlike people in the everyday world, phenomenologists are acutely aware that patterning is taking place, and that ordering process becomes for them an important subject of phenomenological investigation (Freeman, 1980).

Husserl's scientific phenomenology involves a commitment to penetrate the various layers constructed by actors in the social world in order to get to the essential structure of consciousness, the transcendental ego. Schutz defines the *transcendental ego* as "the universe of our conscious life, the stream of thought in its integrity, with all its activities and with all its cogitations and experiences" (1973:105).

The idea of the transcendental ego reflects Husserl's interest in the basic and invariant properties of human consciousness. As Schutz says, "According to Husserl, phenomenology aims to be an eidetical science, dealing not with existence but with essence" (1973:113), especially the essence of consciousness—the transcendental ego.

Although he is often misinterpreted on this point, Husserl did not have a mentalistic, metaphysical conception of consciousness. For him, consciousness is not a thing or a place but a process. Consciousness is found not in the head of the actor but in the relationship between the actor and objects in the world. Husserl expressed this in the idea of *intentionality*. For him, consciousness is always consciousness of something, some object. Consciousness is found in this relationship; consciousness is not interior to the actor. Heap and Roth argue, simply, that "consciousness *is* intentional" (1973:355). Furthermore, meaning does not inhere in objects but in the relationship of actors to objects. This conception of consciousness as a process that gives meaning to objects is at the heart of Husserl's phenomenology and is the starting point for Schutzian theory.

Another key to Husserl's work was his orientation to the *scientific* study of the basic structures of consciousness. Husserl sought to develop "philosophy as a rigorous science" (Kockelmans, 1967b:26). However, to Husserl science did not mean empiricism and statistical analysis of empirical data. In fact, he feared that such a science would reject consciousness as an object of scientific scrutiny and that consciousness would be found either to be too metaphysical or to have been turned into something physical.

What Husserl did mean by science was a philosophy that was methodologically rigorous, systematic, and critical. In using science in this way, Husserl believed that phenomenologists ultimately could arrive at absolutely valid knowledge of the basic structures of actors' "lived experience" (especially that which is conscious). This orientation to science has had two effects on later phenomenologists, including Alfred Schutz. First, phenomenologists continue to eschew the tools of modern social-science research (although they do research; see Psathas, 1989)—standardized methods, high-powered statistics, and computerized results. They prefer, as did Husserl, attention to, and description of, all social phenomena, as *experienced* by human beings, including social situations, events, activities, interaction, and social objects. Second, phenomenologists continue to oppose vague, "soft" intuitionism. In other words, they are opposed to "subjectivism" that is not concerned with discovering the basic structures of phenomena as experienced by people. Philosophizing about consciousness is a rigorous and systematic enterprise.

Husserl conceived of actors' natural standpoint, or their "natural attitude," as the major obstacle to the scientific discovery of phenomenological processes. Because of actors' natural attitude, conscious ordering processes are hidden to them. These processes will remain hidden to phenomenologists unless they are able to overcome their own natural attitudes. Phenomenologists must be able to accomplish the very difficult task of "disconnecting," or "setting aside," ("bracketing") the natural attitude so that they will be able to get at the most basic aspects of consciousness involved in the ordering of the world (Freeman, 1980). In Husserl's view, the natural attitude is a source of bias and distortion to the phenomenologist.

Once the natural attitude is set aside, or "bracketed," the phenomenologist can begin to examine the invariant properties of consciousness that govern all people. Here is the way Schutz describes Husserl's orientation on this issue:

> The phenomenologist does not deny the existence of the outer world, but for his analytical purpose he makes up his mind to suspend belief in its existence—that is, to refrain intentionally and systematically from all judgments related directly or indirectly to the existence of the outer world. . . . Husserl called this procedure "putting the world in brackets" or "performing the phenomenological reduction" . . . [to] go beyond the natural attitude of man living within the world he accepts, be it reality or mere appearance . . . to disclose the pure field of consciousness.
>
> (Schutz, 1973:104)

The phenomenologist also must set aside the incidental experiences of life that tend to dominate consciousness. Husserl's ultimate objective was to get at the pure form of consciousness, stripped of all empirical content.

Ilja Srubar (1984) argues that Husserl not only did a rigorous philosophy of consciousness but also laid the groundwork for a phenomenological sociology. That is, Husserl found it necessary to extend his work to the world of interpersonal relations, the "life-world." Thus Husserl's work helps point to the position that "phenomenology must become a science of the life world" (Srubar, 1984:70). However, Schutz concluded that "the least satisfactory part of [Husserl's] analysis is that dealing with sociality and social groups" (1975:38). As a result, while Husserl's work largely turned inward to the transcendental ego, Schutz's work turned outward to intersubjectivity, the social world, and the life-world. Here is the way Wagner explained the task confronting Schutz:

> The phenomenological method, by definition, serves the exploration of the solitary consciousness. It can procure access to the social realm of human experience only if it offers a solution for what Husserl called the problem of intersubjectivity. A viable theory of intersubjectivity, in turn, would be the strongest, albeit indirect, support for the sociology of understanding that phenomenology could supply. . . . Schutz placed the whole problem on the level of mundanity, that of everyday life. Here, he was confident, a phenomenological-psychological bridge between ego and alter could be found.
>
> (Wagner, 1983:43)

We will have much more to say about intersubjectivity and the life-world later, but before we do, we need to discuss Schutz's ideas on science and typifications.

SCIENCE AND THE SOCIAL WORLD

As was true of Husserl, Schutz sees phenomenology as a rigorous science. He explicitly counters many of the critics of phenomenology by arguing that it is *not* based on "a kind of uncontrollable intuition or metaphysical revelation" (Schutz, 1973:101). Also in accord with Husserl, Schutz sees science as a theoretical and conceptual endeavor. The science of sociology, from Schutz's point of view, is not merely about describing the social world but involves the construction of rigorous conceptual and theoretical models of that world. As Schutz put it:

> We should certainly be surprised if we found a cartographer in mapping a town restricting himself to collecting information from natives. Nevertheless, social scientists frequently choose this strange method. They forget that their scientific work is done on a level of [theoretical] interpretation and understanding different from the naive attitudes of orientation and interpretation peculiar to people in daily life.
> (Schutz, 1976:67)

We gain considerable insight into Schutz's views on science when we understand that he considers science to be one of a multitude of "realities." To Schutz there are a number of different realities, including the worlds of dreams, art, religion, and the insane. The *paramount reality*, however, is the intersubjective world of everyday life (the life-world) because it is "the archetype of our experience of reality. All the other provinces of meaning may be considered as its modifications" (Schutz, 1973:xlii). As we will see, Schutz is focally concerned in his phenomenological sociology with the life-world, but our interest here is with its relationship to another reality, that of science.

There are several key differences between the life-world and the world of science, especially social science. First, the common-sense actor in the life-world is oriented toward dealing pragmatically with the mundane problems of everyday life. The social scientist, in contrast, is "aloof," a "disinterested observer" who is not pragmatically involved in the life-world of the actors being studied and their mundane problems. Second, the stock of knowledge of the common-sense actor is derived from the everyday world, whereas the scientist works with the stock of knowledge that belongs to the body of science. The social scientist exists in a world of problems stated, solutions suggested, methods worked out, and results obtained by other social scientists. Third, in their theorizing, as we have already discussed, social scientists must detach themselves from (must "bracket") their own biographical situations in the life-world and operate in that province of meaning labeled "the world of science." Common-sense actors, in contrast, are enmeshed in their biographical situations and operate in the life-world. These three differences not only help us define the world of science, but furthermore the social scientist who fulfills these criteria can be seen as having attained the scientific attitude needed to study the life-world. To have the proper scientific attitude, social scientists must be detached from (that is, have a nonpragmatic interest in) the life-world of those they are studying, enmeshed in the world of science, and must bracket their own biographical situation within the life-world.

While the world of everyday life is populated by people who act sensibly or reasonably, scientists must create a model of that world which is composed of people who act rationally. In the everyday world people act *sensibly*, that is, their actions are in accord with socially approved rules for dealing with typical problems using typical means to achieve typical ends. People may also act *reasonably* in making "judicious" choices of means to ends, even if they merely follow traditional or habitual patterns. While people may act sensibly or reasonably in the everyday world, it is only in the theoretical models cre-ated by social scientists that they act *rationally* in the full sense of the term, possessing "clear and distinct insight into the ends, the means, and the sec-ondary results" (Schutz, 1973:28). (Here Schutz is using rationality in the same way that Weber used means-ends rationality.) Schutz makes it quite clear that rationality is a theoretical construct in his work: "Thus, the concept of ration-ality in the strict sense already defined does not refer to actions within the common-sense experience of everyday life in the social world; it is the expres-sion for a *particular* type of construct of certain *specific* models of the social world made by the social scientist for certain methodological purposes" (1973:42). Action in everyday life is, at best, only partly rational. People who act sensibly or reasonably are rational only to some degree; they are far from fully rational. Thus, it is the task of the social scientist to construct rational theoretical models of the largely less-than-fully-rational everyday social world. This is premised on the belief that the social scientist can, indeed must, use rational models to analyze the less-than-rational behavior that is found in the life-world. (Again, this is similar to Weber and his development and use of ideal types.)

But the everyday social world is "meaningful" to the actors in it, and the social scientist is confronted with the problem of constructing fully rational systems of knowledge of the subjective-meaning structures of everyday life. Schutz found himself in the paradoxical position of attempting to develop a subjective sociology in the tradition of Max Weber while also meeting the demands of a rigorous conception of science. As Schutz put the question (the answer to which lies at the heart of his theoretical system): "How is it, then, possible to grasp by a system of objective knowledge subjective meaning struc-tures?" (1973:35). Schutz's response is that "it is possible to construct a model of a sector of the social world consisting of typical human interaction and to analyze this typical interaction pattern as to the meaning it might have for the personal types of actors" (1973:36).

The ability to accomplish this is based on the fact that both in the world of everyday life and in science we rely on constructs (ideal types) in order to interpret reality and grasp the part of reality that is relevant to us. The con-structs that we use in the life-world are first-order constructs ("typifications"; see below), and the social scientist develops second-order constructs on the basis of these first-order constructs. It is this building of scientific constructs on everyday constructs that makes an objective, rational science of subjectivity possible. However, to meet the demands of science, the meaning of the world from the actor's perspective must be captured in abstraction from its unique and unpredictable expression within immediate reality. Schutz is not con-cerned with specific, unique actors but with typical actors and typical actions. All observers in the life-world develop constructs that allow them to under-stand what is going on there, but the ability to understand the life-world is increased in science because the (scientific) observer systematically creates much more abstract and standardized constructs with which to understand everyday life.

The key to Schutz's scientific approach is the construction of these second-order constructs or, in more conventional sociological terms, ideal types of social actors and social action. (Good examples are set forth in Schutz's essays on the "stranger" and the "homecomer.") This involves the theoretical replacement of human beings in the life-world with puppets (or as Schutz often calls them, "homunculi") created by the social scientist. The scientific model of the life-world is "not peopled with human beings in their full humanity, but with puppets, with *types;* they are constructed as though they could perform working actions and reactions" (Schutz, 1973:255). Schutz thinks in terms of types of people as well as types of courses of action that actors might take.

Social scientists restrict the puppets' consciousness to what is necessary to perform the typical course of action relevant to the scientific problem under consideration. The puppets are not able to selectively perceive objects in their environment that may be relevant for the solution of problems at hand. They exist in situations created not by them but by the social scientist. The puppets do not choose, nor do they have knowledge outside of the typical knowledge granted them by the social scientist. The following is one of Schutz's most complete articulations of the nature of the social scientist's puppets:

> A merely specious consciousness is imputed to them by the scientist, which is constructed in such a way that its presupposed stock of knowledge at hand (including the ascribed set of invariant motives) would make actions originating from it subjectively understandable, provided that these actions were performed by real actors within the social world. But the puppet and his artificial consciousness is not subjected to the ontological conditions of human beings. The homunculus was not born, he does not grow old, and he will not die. He has no hopes and fears; he does not know anxiety as the chief motive of all of his deeds. He is not free in the sense that his acting could transgress the limits his creator, the social scientist, has predetermined. He cannot, therefore, have other conflicts of interest and motives than those the social scientist has imputed to him. He cannot err, if to err is not his typical destiny. He cannot choose, except among the alternatives the social scientist has put before him as standing to his choice . . . the homunculus, placed into a social relationship is involved therein in his totality. He is nothing else but the originator of his typical function because the artificial consciousness imputed to him contains merely those elements which are necessary to make such functions subjectively meaningful.
>
> (Schutz, 1973:41)

Thus, through the construction of ideal-typical actors and actions, the social scientist develops the tools needed to analyze the social world.

The construction of these puppets (or ideal types, more generally) is not an arbitrary process. To adequately reflect the subjective reality of the life-world and the demands of a rigorous science, ideal types must meet the following criteria:

1 *Postulate of relevance:* Following Weber, Schutz asserted that the topic being investigated in the social world should determine what is to be studied and how it is to be approached. In other words, what the social scientist does must be relevant to the topic being investigated in the life-world.

2 *Postulate of adequacy:* According to this principle, ideal types should be constructed by the social scientist so that the typifications of the actors' behavior in the life-world would make sense to the actors themselves as well as to their contemporaries.

3 *Postulate of logical consistency:* Types must be constructed with a high degree of consistency, clarity, and distinctness and must be compatible with the principles of formal logic. Fulfillment of this postulate "warrants the objective validity of the thought objects constructed by the social scientist" (Schutz, 1973:43).

4 *Postulate of compatibility:* The types constructed by the social scientist must be compatible with the extant body of scientific knowledge or must demonstrate why at least part of this body of knowledge is inadequate.

5 *Postulate of subjective interpretation:* The scientific types, as well as the more general model of the social world, must be based on, and be compatible with, the subjective meaning that action has for real actors in the world of everyday life.

In Schutz's view, the social scientist who adheres to these five postulates will create types and models that meet the need to be true both to the subjective meaning of actors in the life-world and to the demands of a rigorous science.

TYPIFICATIONS AND RECIPES

In the preceding section we discussed Schutz's use of ideal types (second-order constructs) to analyze the social world scientifically. However, as we have already mentioned, it is also the case that people develop and use *typifications* (first-order constructs) in the social world. In any given situation in the world of everyday life an action is determined "by means of a type constituted in earlier experiences" (Schutz and Luckmann, 1973:229). Typifications ignore individual, unique features and focus on only generic and homogeneous characteristics.

While we routinely typify others, it is also possible for people to engage in self-typification: "Man typifies to a certain extent his own situation within the social world and the various relations he has to his fellow-men and cultural objects" (Schutz, 1976:233).

Typification takes many forms. When we label something (for example, a man, a dog), we are engaging in typification. More generally, any time we are using language, we are typifying; indeed Schutz calls language "the typifying medium *par excellence*" (1973:75). Language can be thought of as a "treasure house" of typologies that we use to make sense of the social world.

The linking of typifications to language makes it clear that typifications exist in the larger society and that people acquire and store typifications throughout the socialization process, indeed throughout their lives. The typologies that we use are largely socially derived and socially approved. They have stood the test of time and have come to be institutionalized as traditional and habitual tools for dealing with social life. While the individual may create some typifications, most of them are preconstituted and derived from the larger society.

Schutz sometimes talks of *recipes* when he discusses typifications, and he often uses the terms synonymously. Recipes, like typifications, "serve as techniques for understanding or at least controlling aspects of . . . experience" (Natanson, 1973a:xxix). Recipes, however, tend to deal with situations, while typifications refer more to people. People use recipes to handle the myriad routine situations that they encounter each day. Thus, when someone greets us with the recipe "How are you?" we respond with the recipe "Fine, and you?" Continuing the cooking analogy, Schutz argues that we function with "cook-book knowledge . . . recipes . . . to deal with the routine matters of daily life. . . . Most of our daily activities from rising to going to bed are of this kind. They are performed by following recipes reduced to cultural habits of unquestioned platitudes" (1976:73–74). Even when we encounter unusual or problematic situations, we first try to use our recipes. Only when it is abundantly clear that our recipes won't work do we abandon them and seek to create, to work out mentally, new ways of dealing with situations.

Schutz and Luckmann (1973:231) outline conditions under which situations become problematic and people must create new ways of dealing with them (new recipes or typifications). If there is no recipe available to handle a novel situation, or if a recipe does not allow one to handle the situation it is supposed to deal with, a new one must be created. In other words, when the stock of knowledge currently available is inadequate, the person must add to it by creating new recipes (or typifications).

Because of the recurrent existence of problematic situations, people cannot rely totally on recipes and typifications. They must be adaptive enough to deal with unforeseen circumstances. People need "practical intelligence" in order to deal with unpredictable situations by assessing alternative courses of action and devising new ways of handling situations.

INTERSUBJECTIVITY

Most broadly, Schutz's phenomenological sociology focuses on intersubjectivity not only because intersubjectivity was largely ignored by Husserl but also because Schutz believed it to be taken for granted and unexplored by any other science. The study of intersubjectivity seeks to answer questions such as these: How do we know other minds? Other selves? How is a reciprocity of perspectives possible? How is mutual understanding and communication possible?

An intersubjective world is not a private world; it is common to all. It exists "because we live in it as men among other men, bound to them through common influence and work, understanding others and being understood by them" (Schutz, 1973:10). Intersubjectivity exists in the "vivid present" in which we speak and listen to each other. We share the same time and space with others. "This simultaneity is the essence of intersubjectivity, for it means that *I grasp the subjectivity of the alter ego at the same time as I live in my own stream of consciousness. . . .* And this grasp in simultaneity of the other as well as his reciprocal grasp of me makes possible *our* being in the world together" (Natanson, 1973: xxxii–xxxiii; italics added).

The italicized portion of the last quotation gets to the essence of Schutz's thinking on intersubjectivity. Schutz was not interested in the physical interaction of people but in the way they grasp each other's consciousness, the manner in which they relate to one another intersubjectively.

Schutz also uses the idea of intersubjectivity in a broader sense to mean anything that is social. He argues that knowledge is intersubjective (or social) in three senses. First, there is a *reciprocity of perspectives* in which we assume that other people exist and objects are known or knowable by all. In spite of this reciprocity of perspectives, it is clear that the same object may mean somewhat different things to different people. This difficulty is overcome in the social world by the existence of two "idealizations." The idealization of the *interchangeability of standpoints* assumes that if we stood in the place of others, we would see things as they do. The idealization of the *congruency of the system of relevance* assumes that we can ignore our differences and that objects are defined sufficiently alike to allow us to proceed on a practical basis as if the definitions were identical. (Schutz calls these two idealizations the "general thesis of reciprocal perspectives.")

The second sense in which knowledge is intersubjective (or social) is in the *social origin of knowledge.* While individuals create a very small part of their own knowledge, most of it exists in shared stocks of knowledge and is acquired through social interaction with parents, teachers, and peers.

Third, knowledge is intersubjective in that there is a *social distribution of knowledge.* That is, the knowledge people possess varies according to their position in the social structure. In our common-sense thinking we take into account the fact that the stock of actual knowledge varies from individual to individual according to their social positions.

Thus, while Husserl identified the transcendental ego as his primary focus, Schutz turned phenomenology outward to a concern for the intersubjective, social world. (While this is an important difference, we should not lose sight of the fact that both thinkers focused on subjectivity, Husserl within the realm of consciousness and Schutz in the social world.)

THE LIFE-WORLD

The *life-world* (or *Lebenswelt*) is Schutz's term (derived from Husserl) for the world in which intersubjectivity takes place. We have encountered this idea previously, especially in the effort to contrast the life-world with the world of science. It is now necessary to discuss the life-world more systematically.

Schutz uses many terms to communicate his sense of this world, including "common-sense world," "world of everyday life," "everyday working world," "mundane reality," "the paramount reality of common-sense life," and so on (Natanson, 1973:xxv). It is in this world that people operate in the "natural attitude," that is, they take the world for granted and do not doubt its reality or existence until a problematic situation arises.

Schutz defines six basic characteristics of the life-world. First, it is characterized by a special tension of consciousness, which Schutz labels "wide-awakeness" (1973:213), in which the actor gives "full attention to life and its requirements." In contrast, in the dream world, for example, the actor would not be wide awake. Second, the actor suspends doubt in the existence of this world. Again by way of contrast, in the world of social science the scientist does doubt the life-world, and it is this doubting that permits him or her to analyze it scientifically. Third, it is in the life-world that people engage in working; that is, they engage in "action in the outer world, based upon a project and characterized by the intention to bring about the projected state of affairs by bodily movement" (Schutz, 1973:212). It is work that lies at the heart of the life-world:

> The core region of the life-world is the world of working. . . . Specifically, it is a sphere of activities directed upon objects, animals, and persons "within our actual reach." Typically, operations in it follow "tested recipes of action": it is "my world of routine activities." . . . Such working is planful physical acting upon tangible objects in order to shape and use them for tangible purposes.
>
> (Wagner, 1983:290)

In contrast, in the fantasy world people do not work in this sense of the term. Fourth, there is a specific form of experiencing one's self in which the working self is experienced as the total self. In social science, the working self of the scientist is not experienced as a total self, since the scientist's work is only a part of his or her life. Fifth, the life-world is characterized by a specific form of sociality involving the "common intersubjective world of communication and social action" (Schutz, 1973:230). Obviously, the worlds of dreams and fantasies are not intersubjective worlds. Finally, in the life-world there is a specific time perspective that involves the intersection of the person's own flow of time and the flow of time in the larger society. By contrast, in dreams or fantasies the person's flow of time is usually out of touch with the flow of time in the larger society. That is, one may fantasize, for example, about life in the Middle Ages while one is living in the twentieth century.

While Schutz writes often as if there is only one life-world, the fact is that each of us has our own life-world, although there are many common elements in all of them. Thus others belong to our life-world and we belong to the life-worlds of many others.

The life-world is an intersubjective world, but it is one which existed long before our birth; it was created by our predecessors. It (particularly typifications and recipes, but also social institutions and so on) is given to us to experience and to interpret. Thus in experiencing the life-world, we are experiencing an obdurate world that constrains what we do. However, we are not simply dominated by the preexisting structure of the life-world:

> We have to dominate it and we have to change it in order to realize the purposes which we pursue within it among our fellow-men . . . these objects offer resistance to our acts which we have either to overcome or to which we have to yield . . . a pragmatic motive governs our natural attitude toward the world of everyday life. World, in this sense, is something that we have to modify by our actions or that modifies our actions.
>
> (Schutz, 1973:209)

It is here that we begin to get a sense of Schutz's thinking as dialectical, with actors and structures mutually affecting one another. Wagner takes such a dialectical position when he argues that Schutz's ideas on the life-world blend individual experience "not only with those of social interaction and therefore with the life worlds of others but also with the socially pregiven interpretive schemes and prescriptions [typifications and recipes] for practical conduct" (1983:289).

This dialectic is even clearer in Schutz's thinking about the cultural world. On the one hand, it is clear that the cultural world was created by people in the past as well as in the present since it "originates in and has been instituted by human actions, our own and our fellow-men's, contemporaries and predecessors. All cultural objects—tools, symbols, language systems, works of art, social institutions, etc.—point back by their very origin and meaning to the activities of human subjects" (Schutz, 1973:329). On the other hand, this cultural world is external and coercive of actors: "I find myself in my everyday life within a world not of my own making . . . I was born into a preorganized social world which will survive me, a world shared from the outset with fellow-men who are organized in groups" (Schutz, 1973:329).

In his analysis of the life-world, Schutz was mainly concerned with the shared social stock of knowledge that leads to more or less habitual action. We have already discussed *knowledge of typifications and recipes,* which is a major component of the stock of knowledge. Schutz views such knowledge as the most variable element in our stock of knowledge because in a problematic situation we are able to come up with innovative ways of handling the situation. Less likely to become problematic are the other two aspects of our stock of knowledge. *Knowledge of skills* (for example, how to walk) is the most basic form of knowledge in that it rarely becomes problematic (an exception in the case of walking would be temporary paralysis) and thus is accorded a high degree of certainty. *Useful knowledge* (for example, driving a car or playing the piano) is a definite solution to a situation that was once problematic. Useful knowledge is more problematic (for example, needing to think about one's driving in an emergency situation) than knowledge of skills, but it is not as likely to become problematic as recipes and typifications.

Private Components of Knowledge

Schutz also was aware that all the elements of the cultural realm can and often do vary from individual to individual because personal experience differs. The stock of knowledge is "biographically articulated":

> That means that I "know" more or less adequately that it is the "result" of prior situations. And further, I "know" that this, my situation, is in that respect absolutely "unique." Indeed, the stock of knowledge, through which I determine the present situation, has its "unique" biographical articulation. This refers not only to the content, the "meaning" of all the prior experiences sedimented in it, in situations. It refers also to the intensity, ... duration, and sequence of these experiences. This circumstance is of singular importance, since it really constitutes the individual stock of knowledge.
>
> (Schutz and Luckmann, 1973:111–112)

Thus, according to Schutz, the stock of knowledge always has a private component. However, even this unique and private component of the stock of knowledge is not solely of the actor's own making: "It must be stressed . . . that sequence, experiential depth and nearness, and even the duration of experiences and the acquisition of knowledge, are socially objectivated and determined. In other words, there are social categories of biographical articulation" (Schutz and Luckmann, 1973:113).

Because of their source in individual biography, private stocks of knowledge are not part of the life-world. Because they are biographical in nature, Schutz did not feel that the unique and private components of knowledge are amenable to scientific study. They are, in Schutz's view, nonetheless important components of the everyday life of actual actors.

REALMS OF THE SOCIAL WORLD

Schutz identified four distinct realms of social reality. Each is an abstraction of the social world and is distinguished by its degree of immediacy (the degree to which situations are within reach of the actor) and determinability (the degree to which they can be controlled by the actor). The four realms are *umwelt,* the realm of directly experienced social reality; *mitwelt,* the realm of indirectly experienced social reality; *folgewelt,* the realm of successors; and *vorwelt,* the realm of predecessors. The realms of successors and predecessors (*folgewelt* and *vorwelt*) were of peripheral interest to Schutz. However, we shall deal with them briefly because the contrast between them illustrates some of the characteristics of Schutz's major focus—the *umwelt* and the *mitwelt.*

Folgewelt and *Vorwelt*

The future (*folgewelt*) is a purely residual category in Schutz's work (in contrast to Marx's, for example, where it plays a crucial role in his dialectic). It is a totally free and completely indeterminant world. It can be anticipated by the social scientist only in a very general way and cannot be depicted in any great detail. One could not place great stock in the ideal types and models of the future constructed by the social scientist. Thus, there is little that Schutz's phenomenological science has to offer to the conventional scientist seeking to understand or predict the future.[1]

The past (*vorwelt*), on the other hand, is somewhat more amenable to analysis by the social scientist. The action of those who lived in the past is totally determined; there is no element of freedom, because the causes of their actions, the actions themselves, and their outcomes have already occurred. Despite its determinacy, the study of predecessors presents difficulties for a subjective sociology. It is difficult to interpret the actions of people who lived in an earlier time because we would probably have to use contemporary categories of thought in the historical glance back rather than the categories that prevailed at the time. The interpretation of contemporaries is likely to be more accurate because sociologists share interpretive categories with those whose action they seek to understand. Thus, although a subjective sociology of the past is possible, the probability of misinterpretation is great.

The essential point here is that the objective for Schutz was to develop a sociology based on the interpretations of the social world made by the actors being studied. It is difficult to know the interpretations of predecessors and impossible to understand those of successors. However, it is possible to understand contemporaries (*mitwelt*) and the interpretations of those with whom we are in immediate face-to-face contact (*umwelt*).

Umwelt and We Relations

The *umwelt* involves what Schutz calls "consociates," or people involved in face-to-face relationships with one another. Thus, the idea of the *umwelt* is "equally applicable to an intimate talk between friends and the co-presence of strangers in a railroad car" (Schutz, 1973:16). Being in face-to-face contact is all that is required to be considered part of the *umwelt*. There is a unique character and intensity in the *umwelt*:

> Each partner participates in the on rolling life of the other, can grasp in a vivid present the other's thoughts as they are built up step by step. They may thus share one another's anticipations of the future as plans, or hopes or anxieties. In brief, consociates are mutually involved in one another's biography; they are growing older together; they live, as we may call it, in a pure we-relationship.
>
> (Schutz, 1973:16–17)

---

[1] We can study what contemporaries *expect* of the future, but we cannot study the future itself.

We relations are defined by a relatively high degree of intimacy, which is determined by the extent to which the actors are acquainted with one another's personal biographies. The pure we relation is a face-to-face relationship "in which the partners are aware of each other and sympathetically participate in each other's lives for however short a time" (Schutz, 1932/1967:164). The we relation encompasses the consciousness of the participants as well as the patterns of action and interaction that characterize face-to-face interaction. The we relation is characterized by a "thou orientation," which "is the universal form in which the other is experienced 'in person'" (Schutz and Luckmann, 1973:62). In other words, we relations are highly personal and immediate.

The immediacy of interaction has two implications for social relations. First, in a we relation, unlike in a they relation, there are abundant indicators of the other's subjective experience. Immediacy allows each actor to enter into the consciousness of the other. Second, when entering any social relation, an individual has only typical knowledge of the other. However, in the continuing process of a face-to-face interaction, typifications of the other are tested, revised, reenacted, and modified. That is, interaction with others necessarily modifies typologies.

Schutz not only offered a number of insights into we relations per se but also linked these relationships to cultural phenomena in the real world. For example, in we relations actors learn the typifications that allow them to survive socially. People not only learn recipes in we relations but use them there as well—trying them out, altering them when they prove ineffective or inappropriate.

Schutz was aware that there is considerable give-and-take among actors in we relations. People try out different courses of action on other people. They may quickly abandon those that elicit hostile reactions and continue to use those that are accepted. People also may find themselves in situations where recipes do not work at all, and they must create appropriate and workable sets of actions. In other words, in we relations people constantly adjust their actions with regard to those with whom they interact.

People also adjust their conceptions of others. They enter a given relationship with certain assumptions about what the other actors are thinking. In general, people assume that the thinking of others is of the same order as their own. Sometimes this is confirmed by what they find, but in other circumstances the facial expressions, the movements, the words, and the actions of others are inconsistent with people's sense of what others are thinking. People then must revise their view of others' thought processes and then adjust their responses on the basis of this new image of what others are thinking. This is an indirect process, because people cannot actually know what others are thinking. Thus they may tentatively change their actions in the hope that this will elicit responses consistent with what they now think is going on in others' minds. People may be forced to revise their conception of others' thought processes and their actions a number of times before they are able to understand why others are acting in a particular way. It is even conceivable that in some instances people cannot make an adequate number of adjustments, with the result that they are likely to flee the particular interaction, completely confused. In such a case, they may seek more comfortable situations where familiar recipes can be applied.

Even within we relations in everyday life most action is guided by recipes. People do not *usually* reflect on what they do or on what others do. However, when they encounter problems, inappropriate thoughts and actions, they must abandon their recipes and reflect on what is going on to create an appropriate response. This is psychologically costly, because people prefer to act and inter-act in accord with recipes.

Because of the freedom of actors within it, the *umwelt* is clearly difficult to deal with from a scientific point of view. In the *umwelt* people and their actions are often not typified. However, people in the *umwelt* do employ typifications of other people and their courses of action. The result is that the social scientist can, albeit with some difficulty, construct typifications of the *umwelt*. In other words, rational models of this often nonrational world can be constructed, and these models can be used to better understand life in the *umwelt*. At the minimum, they can be used to assess differences between the rational models and the way people actually behave. In this, Schutz (1976:81) is using typifi-cations in much the same way that Weber used his ideal types.

Before we turn to the *mitwelt*, it should be pointed out that it is in the *umwelt* that the typifications used in daily life (first-order constructs) are created. Thus, to Schutz, the *umwelt* is the crucial source of first-order constructs (in contrast to the second-order constructs used in the social sciences), and it is an important, albeit difficult, arena of scientific study. While it is difficult to analyze the *umwelt* scientifically, it is far easier to study the *mitwelt* in this manner. However, although it may be easier to study the *mitwelt*, such study is not likely to be as rewarding as a study of the *umwelt* because of the latter's key role in the creation of typifications and its central role in the social lives of people in the life-world.

Mitwelt and They Relations

The *mitwelt* is that aspect of the social world in which people deal only with types of people or with larger social structures rather than with actual actors. People do fill these types and these structures, but in this world of "contem-poraries," these people are not experienced directly. Because actors are dealing with types rather than with actual people, their knowledge of people is not subject to constant revision on the basis of face-to-face interaction. This rela-tively constant knowledge of general types of subjective experience can be studied scientifically and can shed light on the general process by which peo-ple deal with the social world. A number of specific examples of the *mitwelt* will be discussed below.

While in the *umwelt* people coexist in the same time and space, in the *mitwelt* spatial distances make it impossible to interact on a face-to-face basis.

If the spatial situation changes and the people draw closer to each other, then face-to-face interaction becomes possible, but if it occurs, we have returned to the *umwelt*. People who were once in my *umwelt* may draw away from me and ultimately, because of spatial distances, become part of the *mitwelt*. Thus, there is a gradual transition from *umwelt* to *mitwelt* as people grow apart from one another. Here is the way Schutz describes this gradual transition:

> Now we are face-to-face, saying good-bye, shaking hands; now he is walking away. Now he calls back to me; now I see him waving to me; now he has disappeared around the corner. It is impossible to say at which precise moment the face-to-face situation ended and my partner became a mere contemporary of whom I have knowledge (he has, probably, arrived home) but no direct experience.
>
> (Schutz, 1976:37)

Similarly, there are no clear dividing lines among the various levels of the *mitwelt* discussed below.

The *mitwelt* is a stratified world with levels arranged by degree of anonymity. The more anonymous the level, the more people's relationships are amenable to scientific study. Some of the major levels within the *mitwelt*, beginning with the least anonymous, are:

1 Those whom actors encountered face-to-face in the past and could meet again. Actors are likely to have fairly current knowledge of them because they have been met before and could be met again. Although there is a relatively low level of anonymity here, such a relationship does not involve ongoing face-to-face interaction. If these people were to be met personally at a later date, this relationship would become part of the *umwelt* and no longer be part of the *mitwelt*.

2 Those once encountered not by us but by people with whom we deal. Because this level is based on second-hand knowledge of others, it involves more anonymity than the level of relationships with people we have encountered in the past. If we were ever to meet people at this level, the relationship would become part of the *umwelt*.

3 Those whom we are on the way to meet. As long as we have not yet met them, we relate to them as types, but once we actually meet them, the situation again becomes part of the *umwelt*.

4 Those whom we know not as concrete individuals but simply as positions and roles. For example, we know that there are people who sort our mail or process our checks, but although we have attitudes about them as types, we never encounter them personally.

5 Collectivities whose function we may know without knowing any of the individuals who exist within them. For example, we know about the Senate, but few people actually know any of the individuals in it, although we do have the possibility of meeting those people.

6 Collectivities that are so anonymous that we have little chance of ever

encountering people in them. For most people, the Mafia would be an example of such a collectivity.

7 Objective structures of meaning that have been created by contemporaries with whom actors do not have and have not had face-to-face interaction. The rules of English grammar would be an example of such a structure of meaning.

8 Physical artifacts that have been produced by a person we have not met and whom we are not likely to meet. For example, people would have a highly anonymous relationship with a museum painting.

As we move further into the *mitwelt* relationships, they become more impersonal and anonymous. People do not have face-to-face interaction with others and thus cannot know what goes on in others' minds. Their knowledge is therefore restricted to "general types of subjective experience" (Schutz, 1932/ 1967:181).

They relations, which are found in the *mitwelt*, are characterized by interaction with impersonal contemporaries (for example, the unseen postal employee who sorts our mail) rather than consociates (for example, a personal friend). In they relations, the thoughts and actions of people are dominated by anonymous typifications.

In the "pure" they relation, the typical schemes of knowledge used to define other actors are not available for modification. Because we do not interact with actual people but with impersonal contemporaries, information that varies from our typifications is not provided to us. In other words, new experiences are not constituted in they relations. Cultural typifications determine action, and they cannot be altered by the thoughts and actions of actors in a they relationship. Thus, whereas we relations are subject to negotiation, they relations are not.

In spite of the distinction between we and they relations, the typifications used in they relations have their historical roots in we relations: "The first and originally objective solution of a problem was still largely dependent on the subjective relevance awareness of the individual" (Schutz and Luckmann, 1973:225). However, these solutions ultimately become more typified and anonymous—in short, more and more a part of the cultural realm.

CONSCIOUSNESS

While Husserl had focused on consciousness, especially the universal structures of consciousness, Schutz turned away from consciousness and toward the direction of intersubjectivity, the life-world, and we and they relations. Thus consciousness is not of focal concern to Schutz; rather, it constitutes the point of departure for his science of intersubjectivity.

Schutz believed that in the everyday world, as long as things are running smoothly in accord with recipes, consciousness is relatively unimportant and actors pay little attention to what is going on in their minds as well as in the minds of others. Similarly, Schutz (1932/1967:190) believed that in the science of phenomenological sociology one could ignore individual consciousness. In fact, because Schutz found the mind impervious to scientific study, and because he wanted to focus on intersubjectivity, he admitted in his own work that he was going to abandon the traditional phenomenological focus on mental processes (1932/1967:97). We thus have the seemingly paradoxical situation of a sociologist who is the field's most famous phenomenologist abandoning the approach for which phenomenology is best known. However, the paradox is resolved when we realize that Schutz does carry on the traditional phenomenological concern with subjectivity. Instead of focusing on individual subjectivity (as Husserl did), Schutz focuses, as we have seen throughout this chapter, on intersubjectivity.

Despite Schutz's avowed focus on intersubjectivity, he offered many insights into consciousness. In fact, Schutz argued that the base of all his sociological concerns lay in the "processes of meaning establishment and understanding occurring within individuals, processes of interpretation of the behavior of other people and processes of self-interpretation" (1932/1967:11).

The philosophical basis of Schutz's image of the social world, albeit a basis that is, for him, not amenable to scientific study, is deep consciousness (*durée*), in which is found the process of meaning establishment, understanding, interpretation, and self-interpretation. A phenomenological sociology must be based on "the way meaning is constituted in the individual experience of the solitary Ego. In so doing we shall track meaning to its very point of origin in the inner time consciousness in the duration of the ego as it lives through its experience" (Schutz, 1932/1967:13). This is the domain that was of central concern to Schutz's philosophical predecessors, Henri Bergson and Edmund Husserl. They were interested in philosophizing about what went on in the mind, but a central question to Schutz was how to turn this interest into a scientific sociological concern.

Schutz was drawn to the work of Max Weber, particularly that part of Weber's work concerned with social action, because it reflected, he thought, both an interest in consciousness and a concern for a scientific sociology. As we saw in Chapter 7, the interest in individual action was only a minor and secondary concern for Weber, who was more concerned with the impact of social structures on action than with the bases of action in consciousness. According to Prendergast, Schutz had "no apparent interest in Weber's theory of bureaucracy, sociology of religion, political sociology, or general economic history" (1986:15). Schutz, therefore, was concerned with only a small and peripheral portion of Weber's sociology. But even in that, Weber was a less-than-satisfying model for Schutz but not for the reasons implied above. To Schutz, the problem with Weber's work was that there were inadequacies in his conception of consciousness. Weber failed to distinguish among types of meanings, and he failed to distinguish meanings from motives. In clarifying what Weber failed to do, Schutz told us much about his own conception of consciousness.

Meanings and Motives

Schutz argued that we must distinguish meanings from motives. In the process, he differentiated between two subtypes of both meanings and motives. Although he did not always succeed in keeping them neatly separated, for Schutz *meanings* concern how actors determine what aspects of the social world are important to them, whereas *motives* involve the reasons that actors do what they do. One type of meaning is the *subjective* meaning context. That is, through our own independent mental construction of reality, we define certain components of reality as meaningful. However, although this process is important in the everyday life-world, Schutz did not see it as amenable to scientific study because it is too idiosyncratic.

Of concern to scientific sociology is the second type of meaning, the *objective* meaning context, the sets of meanings that exist in the culture as a whole and that are the shared possession of the collectivity of actors. In that these sets of meanings are shared rather than idiosyncratic, they are as accessible to sociologists as to anyone else. In that they have an objective existence, they can be studied scientifically by the sociologist, and they were one of Schutz's main concerns. Schutz was critical of Weber for failing to differentiate between subjective and objective meaning and for failing to make it clear that objective meaning contexts can be most easily scrutinized in scientific sociology.

Schutz also differentiated between two types of motives—"in-order-to" and "because" motives. Both involve reasons for an individual's actions, but only because motives are accessible to both the person acting and the sociologist. *In-order-to motives* are the reasons that an actor undertakes certain actions; actions are undertaken to bring about some future objective or occurrence. They only exist when action is taking place. In-order-to motives are "subjective." They are part of deep consciousness, the ongoing stream of consciousness, and as such are inaccessible to both the actor and the scientific observer. In-order-to motives can be grasped only retrospectively by the actor, after the action is completed and the objective is (or is not) achieved. Sociology is little concerned with in-order-to motives because they are difficult to study scientifically. But sociology can study *because motives,* or retrospective glances at the past factors (for example, personal background, individual psyche, environment) that caused individuals to behave as they did. Since because motives are "objective," they can be studied retrospectively using scientific methods. Since the actions have already occurred, the reasons for them are accessible to both the actor and the social scientist. However, neither other actors nor social scientists can know others' motives, even because motives, fully. Both actors and scientists must be satisfied with being able to deal with typical motives.

In spite of their greater accessibility to the social scientist, Schutz was little more inclined to study because motives than in-order-to motives. They represented a Husserlian return to a concern for consciousness, while Schutz, as we have seen many times, was interested in moving on to the intersubjective world. However, Schutz believed that all social interaction was founded on a reciprocity of motives: "[T]he actor's in-order-to motives will become because-motives of his partner and vice versa" (1976:23).

Schutz embeds his most basic sociological concepts in consciousness. *Action*, for example, is "conduct self-consciously projected by the actor" (Natanson, 1973:xxxiv), "conduct devised by the actor in advance" (Schutz, 1973:19). More explicitly, Natanson argues: "The crucial feature of action in every case is its purposive and projective character. Action has its source in the *consciousness* of the actor" (1973:xxxiv; italics added). *Social action* is "action which involves the attitudes and actions of others and is oriented to them in its course" (Schutz, 1976:13).

One other point should be made about Schutz's thoughts on consciousness. Schutz sees within consciousness a fundamental human anxiety that lies at the base of his intersubjective world:

> I know that I shall die and I fear to die. This basic experience we suggest calling the *fundamental anxiety*. It is the primordial anticipation from which all the others originate. From the fundamental anxiety spring the many interrelated systems of hopes and fears, of wants and satisfactions, of chances and risks which incite man within the natural attitude to attempt the mastery of the world; to overcome obstacles, to draft projects and to realize them.
>
> (Schutz, 1973:228)

INTERPRETING SCHUTZIAN THEORY

In many ways, Schutzian theory is more difficult to interpret than the work of any other major theorist discussed thusfar in this book. First, Schutz (along, perhaps, with Mead) is probably the most single-mindedly abstract theorist whom we have encountered. Others have been much more deeply involved in the empirical world. Weber, for example, offered us his theory embedded in a great deal of historical detail. Marx moved back and forth between theoretical abstraction and the real-world evils of capitalism. Even Parsons, whom we encounter in the next chapter and who was a highly abstract thinker, touched base now and again with the real world. As close as Schutz (1976) ever came to the real world were his abstract essays on such social types as the stranger and the homecomer.

Second, Schutz's theory is embedded in a philosophical tradition that is foreign to sociology and translates only with great difficulty into sociological terms. James Heap and Phillip Roth (1973) argue that it is highly questionable whether Husserl's phenomenology, which is one of the main roots of Schutzian theory, can be translated into sociology. We can characterize Schutz's work as an effort to do just that. The success of Schutz's efforts is illustrated by the popularity of theories derived from his work—particularly phenomenological sociology and ethnomethodology. Nevertheless, his roots in phenomenological philosophy make it difficult for us to adequately grasp his sociology.

This brings us back to the debate with which we began this chapter. First, some commentators praise Schutz for his micro focus on how actors create the social world. Others criticize him for this. Still others see Schutz as having a large-scale, cultural focus. The view developed in this chapter constitutes a rejection of the second position and an integration of the first and third positions. That is, Schutz was dialectically concerned with how actors create the social world and with the impact on actors of the large-scale social and cultural world that they create. While he shares this dialectic with many classical theorists, what distinguishes Schutz's approach is that it is purely and exclusively subjective.

SUMMARY

Alfred Schutz took the phenomenological philosophy of Edmund Husserl, which was aimed inward toward an understanding of the transcendental ego, and turned it outward toward a concern for intersubjectivity, the life-world, and the social world.

The key to understanding Schutz's approach is a comprehension of his sense of science. Science was one of a number of worlds examined by Schutz—others included the worlds of dreams, fantasies, insanity, and especially the "paramount reality" of the everyday world. In contrast to people in the everyday world, scientists are not pragmatically involved in the everyday world of the subjects they study or, while they are doing science, their own everyday world. Rather, they are involved in the world of science and rely on its stock of knowledge rather than on the stock of knowledge associated with life in the everyday world.

While in the everyday world people may behave sensibly or reasonably, it is only in the theoretical models of the social scientist that they can behave in a fully rational manner. The rational models and (second-order) constructs of the social scientists (that is, the "ideal types") are based upon the first-order constructs that people must use to function in their daily lives. The social scientists' analyses result in constructed ideal types of fully rational actors (puppets, or "homunculi") and their courses of action. The construction of these ideal types must meet the demands of a rigorous science. It is this type of theorizing, says Schutz, that makes an objective rational science of subjectivity possible.

Implied in much of the above is the centrality of typifications to both social scientists and people in the everyday world. Typifications are usually socially derived and socially approved and allow people to function on a daily basis. It is only in problematic situations that people (reluctantly) abandon their typifications (and recipes) and create new ways of dealing with the social world.

As mentioned above, Schutz was focally concerned with intersubjectivity, or the way in which people grasp the consciousness of others while they live within their own streams of consciousness. Much of Schutz's work focuses on the life-world, or the world of everyday life. This is an intersubjective world in which people both create social reality and are constrained by the preexisting social and cultural structures created by their predecessors. While much of the life-world is shared, there are also private (biographically articulated) aspects of that world.

There are four realms of the social world—the future (*folgewelt*); the past (*vorwelt*); the present world of consociates, with whom we have face-to-face contact (*umwelt*); and the present world of contemporaries whom we know only as types (*mitwelt*). First-order constructs are created in the *umwelt*, while the social scientists' second-order constructs can be most easily applied to the *mitwelt*, although they are most importantly applied to the *umwelt*. Intimate we relations are found in the *umwelt*, and typified they relations characterize the *mitwelt*.

While Schutz had turned away from consciousness, he did offer insights into it, especially in his thoughts on meaning and motives.

While there is controversy over whether Schutz offers a micro or a macro theory, the view in this chapter is that his theory is concerned with the dialectical relationship between the way people construct social reality and the already present, obdurate cultural reality that others have constructed and are continuing to construct. People are influenced by these realities, but they are also capable of "making sense" of, interpreting, and even reconstructing the cultural world.

TALCOTT PARSONS

WE come now to the last, and most contemporary, of the classical theorists to be discussed in this book, Talcott Parsons (1902–1979). Although Parsons died only a little more than a decade ago, it is appropriate to discuss his work in this book for two major reasons. For one thing, it was Parsons, in *The Structure of Social Action* (1937), who brought European classical theory, especially the work of Weber and Durkheim, to the attention of American sociology (Camic, 1989). For another, Parsons created his own distinctive "grand" (or classical) theory. Parsons's theory rivals in scope and grandeur the other classical theories discussed in the preceding chapters of this book.

Parsons was undoubtedly the most important American sociological theorist. His written work was widely cited and used by sociologists. Even more important, he shaped the structure of a large portion of American sociological theory, as well as sociology in general, from his position as professor at Harvard University. Many of the most important American theorists were his students, and they went on to endow their own departments, and their own students, with Parsonsian-style theory. Among the many theorists who worked with Parsons at Harvard were Robert Merton, Kingsley Davis, Robin Williams, Wilbert Moore, Marion Levy, and Neil Smelser.

TALCOTT PARSONS: A Biographical Sketch

Talcott Parsons was born in 1902 in Colorado Springs, Colorado. He came from a religious and intellectual background; his father was a Congregational minister, a professor, and ultimately president of a small college. Parsons got an undergraduate degree from Amherst College in 1924 and set out to do graduate work at the London School of Economics. In the next year, he moved on to Heidelberg, Germany. Max Weber had spent a large portion of his career at Heidelberg, and although he had died five years before Parsons arrived, Weber's influence survived and his widow continued to hold meetings in her home, meetings that Parsons attended. Parsons was greatly affected by Weber's work and ultimately wrote his doctoral thesis at Heidelberg dealing, in part, with Weber's ideas.

Parsons became an instructor at Harvard in 1927, and although he switched departments several times, Parsons remained at Harvard until his death in 1979. His career progress was not rapid; he did not obtain a tenured position until 1939. Two years previously, he had published *The Structure of Social Action,* a book that not only introduced major sociological theorists like Weber to large numbers of sociologists but also laid the groundwork for Parsons's own developing theory.

After that, Parsons made rapid academic progress. He was made chairman of the Harvard sociology department in 1944 and two years later set up and chaired the innovative Department of Social Relations, which included not only sociologists but a variety of other social scientists. By 1949, he had been elected president of the American Sociological Association. In the 1950s and into the 1960s, with the publication of such books as *The Social System* (1951), Parsons became the dominant figure in American sociology.

However, by the late 1960s, Parsons came under attack from the emerging radical wing of American sociology. Parsons was seen as being a political conservative, and his theory was seen as highly conservative and little more than an elaborate categorization scheme. But in the 1980s, there was a resurgence in interest in Parsonian theory not only in the United States but around the world (Buxton, 1985; Sciulli and Gerstein, 1985). Holton and Turner (1986:13) have perhaps gone the farthest, arguing that "Parsons' work . . . represents a more powerful contribution to sociological theory than that of Marx, Weber, Durkheim

PARSONS'S INTEGRATIVE EFFORTS

Of all the sociological theorists discussed in this book, Parsons was the most explicit in his intention to develop an integrated approach to sociological theory (see the Appendix). There are a number of manifestations of this. First, Parsons founded the Department of Social Relations at Harvard University with the intention of unifying the various social sciences. Included in his integrative goal were such fields as clinical psychology, behavioral psychology, anthropology, and sociology. Second, in his own theorizing Parsons developed a clear sense of levels of social analysis, best exemplified in his notion of four action systems—behavioral organism, personality, social system, and or any of their contemporary followers." Furthermore, Parsons's ideas are influencing not only conservative thinkers but neo-Marxian theorists as well.

Upon his death, a number of his former students, themselves sociologists of considerable note, reflected on Parsonsian theory as well as on the man behind the theory. In their musings, these sociologists offered some interesting insights into Parsons and his work. The few glimpses of Parsons reproduced here do not add up to a coherent picture, but they do offer some provocative glimpses of the man and his work.

Robert Merton was one of his students when Parsons was just beginning his teaching career at Harvard. Merton, who became a noted theorist in his own right, makes it clear that graduate students did not come to Harvard in those years to study with Parsons but rather with Pitirim Sorokin, the senior member of the department, who was to become Parsons's archenemy:

> Of the very first generation of graduate students coming to Harvard . . . precisely none came to study with Talcott. They could scarcely have done so for the simplest of reasons: in 1931, he had no public identity whatever as a sociologist.
> Although we students came to study with the renowned Sorokin, a subset of us stayed to work with the unknown Parsons.
>
> (Merton, 1980:69)

Merton's reflections on Parsons's first course in theory are interesting, too, especially because the material provided the basis for one of the most influential theory books in history:

> Long before Talcott Parsons became one of the Grand Old Men of world sociology, he was for an early few of us its Grand Young Man. This began with his first course in theory. . . . [It] would provide him with the core of his masterwork, *The Structure of Social Action* which . . . did not appear in print until five years after its first oral publication.
>
> (Merton, 1980:69–70)

Although all would not share Merton's positive evaluation of Parsons, they would acknowledge the following:

> The death of Talcott Parsons marks the end of an era in sociology. When [a new era] does begin . . . it will surely be fortified by the great tradition of sociological thought which he has left to us.
>
> (Merton, 1980:71)

cultural system. Finally, Parsons argued in one of his most important works, *The Social System*, that the integration of levels of social analysis is of central importance in the social world:

> This *integration* of a set of common value patterns with the internalized need-disposition structure of the constituent personalities is the core phenomenon of the dynamics of social systems. That the stability of any social system except the most evanescent interaction process is dependent on a degree of such integration may be said to be the *fundamental dynamic theorem of sociology*.
>
> (Parsons, 1951:42; italics added)

Elsewhere Parsons made a similar point when he argued that the key issue to him was "the problem of theoretical formulation of the relations between the *social system* and the *personality* of the individual" (1970a:1; italics added).

This integrative goal, which runs through a large portion of Parsons's work, is to be lauded and indeed has been applauded by some; however, others (for example, Alexander, 1978; Menzies, 1977) came to see it as "muddled" and "confused." These critics argued that Parsons began *The Structure of Social Action* as a micro-oriented action theorist but that even before he finished that work, and progressively as the years passed, he moved more and more in the direction of a macro-oriented structural-functional theory. Some confusion is seen in Parsons's work as a result of his inability to give up older theoretical positions or to integrate them adequately with newer ones. As early as the preface to the second edition of *The Structure of Social Action,* Parsons spoke of his shift

> from the analysis of the structure of social action as such to the structural-functional analysis of social systems. They are, of course, in the last analysis, systems of social action. But the structure of such systems is, in the newer version, treated not directly in action terms, but as "institutionalized patterns."
>
> (Parsons, 1949:D)

One view (Menzies, 1977), shared by this author, is that a basic problem of Parsons's work stems from his never having completed the shift from action theory to structural functionalism, with the result that the two theories are interrelated in a muddled fashion throughout his work. It is not that the integration of action theory and structural functionalism is impossible or undesirable; rather, it is that Parsons never did reconcile them adequately. They often stand side by side in his work rather than being intertwined.

Parsons's frequent use of two different definitions of many key concepts reflects the continuing duality of his theoretical orientation. For example, Ken Menzies (1977) said that in defining *deviance,* Parsons used both a structural-functional approach, emphasizing the larger system's failure to socialize the actor adequately, and an action-theory approach, defining it as a "motivated tendency for an actor to behave in contravention of one or more institutionalized normative patterns" (Parsons, 1951:250).

In part, Parsons's integrative work is muddled because he never reconciled his Weberian action theory (as he interpreted Weber) with his Durkheimian structural functionalism. It is this, along with other factors we will discuss as we proceed, that mars, but does not destroy, Parsons's theoretical approach.[1]

GENERAL PRINCIPLES

A starting point for getting at the substance of Parsons's theoretical orientation is the general principles behind his theory building (Devereux, 1961). Parsons

---

[1] As will be seen throughout this chapter, the author tends to adopt an admiring, but critical, stance toward Parsons's work. For an even more positive analysis, see Richard Münch (1981, 1982).

set as his goal the constructon of an adequate general theory, a grand theory[2] that was to be analytical, systematic, complete, and elegant. First, such a theory must, from his point of view, be an action theory in which "the central mechanism must always be some notion of actors orienting themselves to situations, with various sorts of goals, values, and normative standards, and behaving accordingly" (Devereux, 1961:19). Second, such a theory must be based on the principle of *voluntarism*, that is, an actor's "choice among alternative values and courses of action must remain at least potentially free" (Devereux, 1961:20). Third, such cultural phenomena as ideas, ideals, goals, and norms must be considered causally relevant factors. Fourth, Parsons adopted the idea of *emergence*—the notion that higher-order systems emerge out of lower-order systems. Such higher-order systems, he felt, must not be able to be inferred from, or explained in terms of, component parts. Finally, the emergent systems must never become wholly detached from their component parts. We will have numerous occasions in this chapter to question how well Parsons actually carried through on these principles in the course of his theoretical work. Although Parsons moved away from this base as his career progressed, the principles are those upon which he built his entire theory.

Philosophical and Theoretical Roots

The source of these ideas on theory can be found in Parsons's 1937 analysis of the roots of modern sociology. Here, and in other works, Parsons always gave the impression that he felt the whole of recent intellectual history was converging in him and his work. He analyzed and criticized utilitarianism and classical economics for dealing with isolated individuals, for assuming individual rationality, and for holding the view that social order came either from the pursuit of individual self-interest or from externally imposed sanctions. Parsons believed that we need to analyze nonrational as well as rational action and that we need to look toward institutionalized common values for the source of social order. He attacked positivism for its view of the world as a closed, deterministic system leaving no room for such critical notions as mind, consciousness, values, ends, and norms. Finally, Parsons lauded idealism for accepting the very ideas rejected by positivism, but he rejected the view that all the social world could be explained by such cultural factors.

The bulk of *The Structure of Social Action* is devoted to a discussion of Alfred Marshall, Vilfredo Pareto, Emile Durkheim, and Max Weber, who developed ideas that were converging on what Parsons called the "voluntaristic theory of action." Parsons's work on these four thinkers is largely a summary of their work, and there is little that is new in it. However, it has been criticized

---

[2] Ironically, Parsons praised Durkheim for *not* doing grand theory, for doing what many critics felt Parsons never did, that is, integrating theory and reality: "Durkheim was a scientific theorist in the best sense of one who never theorized 'in the air,' never indulged in 'idle speculation' but was always seeking the solution of crucially important empirical problems" (1937:302).

severely for being highly biased and deceptive. What is significant is that Parsons used their work to derive a number of ideas that proved crucial to him, including the nonrational, action, voluntarism, norms, and values. Basically Parsons was saying that these thinkers had freed themselves from their theoretical roots (such as utilitarianism, positivism) and by so doing provided *him* with the tools *he* needed to construct a voluntaristic theory of action.

Action Theory

As a result of these influences and interpretations, Parsons's early work is heavily oriented to action theory. Not too many years ago, a book on sociological theory would have devoted a great deal of attention to action theorists (MacIver, 1931, 1942; Parsons, 1937; Znaniecki, 1934). Today, however, interest in action theory has faded, although some recent work (Coleman, 1986; Sciulli, 1986) has helped resuscitate it to some degree.

Action theory had its origin in Max Weber's work on social action (see Chapter 7). Although Weber embedded his work in assumptions on actors and action, his real interest was in the cultural and structural constraints on them. Instead of focusing on this aspect of Weber's work, action theory operated at the level of individual thought and action. This is clear from Roscoe Hinkle's summary of the tenets of action theory:

1 Men's social activities arise from their consciousnesses of themselves (as subjects) and of others and the external situations (as objects).
2 As subjects, men act to achieve their (subjective) intentions, purposes, aims, ends, objectives, or goals.
3 They use appropriate means, techniques, procedures, methods, and instruments.
4 Their courses of action are limited by unmodifiable conditions or circumstances.
5 Exercising will or judgment, they choose, assess, and evaluate what they will do, are doing, and have done.
6 Standards, rules, or moral principles are invoked in arriving at decisions.
7 Any study of social relationships requires the researcher to use subjective investigative techniques such as *"verstehen,"* imaginative or sympathetic reconstruction, or vicarious experience.

(Hinkle, 1963:706–707)

There is some evidence that such a micro-level action approach was anticipated by pre-World War I sociologists such as Lester Ward, E. A. Ross, Franklin Giddings, Albion Small, and Charles H. Cooley, although their link to modern action theory is tenuous. Most of these early sociologists were preoccupied with the large-scale question of societal evolution. They discussed an active, creative view of the individual but tended to give society coercive power over the individual.

The exception to this tendency was Cooley. Although he accepted some of the tenets of his contemporaries, and their interest in evolution, "what became ultimately significant in social life [were] subjective consciousness and personal feelings, sentiments, ideas, or ideals in terms of which men initiate and terminate their actions toward one another" (Hinkle, 1963:709).

Sociologists who worked between the end of World War I and the Depression exhibited far more connection with later action theory. Among the more important of these sociologists were Robert Park, Ellsworth Faris, W. I. Thomas, George Herbert Mead, and Talcott Parsons. Parsons was the major inheritor of the Weberian orientation, and his use of action theory in his early work gave that approach its widest audience.

Parsons's Action Theory   Parsons was eager to differentiate action theory from behaviorism. In fact, he chose the term *action* because it had a different connotation from that of *behavior*. *Behavior* implies mechanical response to stimuli, whereas *action* implies an active, creative, "mental" process. Parsons was careful to differentiate action theory from behaviorism: "A theory which, like behaviorism, insists on treating human beings in terms which exclude his subjective aspect, is not a theory of action" (1937:77–78).

Three concepts lie at the heart of Parsons's action theory—the unit act, voluntarism, and *verstehen*. The most basic phenomenon in Parsons's action theory is what he called the *unit act,* which he defined in terms of four components. First, it implies the existence of an *actor.* Second, the unit act involves an *end,* or a future state toward which action is oriented. Third, the action takes place in a *situation* that involves two elements: things the actor cannot control *(conditions)* and those over which the actor can exert control *(means).* Finally, *norms* and *values* serve to shape the actor's choice of means to ends (Parsons, 1937). Parsons said that there is "no such thing as action except as effort to conform to norms" (1937:76–77). Already in the unit act we see the integrative concerns that were to dominate Parsons throughout his life. Although he began with an interest in actors and their actions, he implied an interest in consciousness in terms of the voluntary choice of means to ends. But that choice is not free, which implies an interest on Parsons's part in the social structures that constrain action. Cultural entities such as norms and values play a key role here, as they do throughout Parsons's work. Intimately related to the unit act is Parsons's concept of voluntarism. *Voluntarism* pertains to actors who are seen as making choices in social situations (Procter, 1978). This is not to say that the actors are totally free in those choices; voluntarism is not equivalent to "free will." Nevertheless, the concept of voluntarism clearly implies a mind, consciousness, and individuals making decisions. Finally, there is the concept of *verstehen,* or the need to analyze action from the subjective perspective.

The Turn Away from Action Theory

In our view, while Parsons never abandoned the idea of individual choice constrained by external forces, he did abandon the focus on consciousness and action implied strongly in *The Structure of Social Action.* This is reflected in the degree to which Parsons backed off from three central concepts in his early work—the unit act, voluntarism, and *verstehen* (which he interpreted as a method largely oriented to the study of consciousness and action).

The unit act lies at the very core of the theoretical contribution of *The Structure of Social Action*, but it progressively disappears as Parsons's theories developed. In *The Social System* (1951) the unit act is cited only three times in a book that runs close to 600 pages. When it is cited, the impression is that Parsons simply used it to legitimize his earlier work and that it has no relevance to the project at hand. In *The Social System*, Parsons perfunctorily remarked that the unit act is still the basic unit, but

> for most purposes of the more macroscopic analysis of social systems . . . it is convenient to make use of a higher order unit than the act, namely the status-role. . . . It is the structure of the *relations* between the actors as involved in the interactive process which is essentially the structure of the social system. . . . It is the *participation* of an actor in a patterned interactive relationship which is for many purposes the most significant unit of the social system.
>
> (Parsons, 1951:25)

The unit act and the status-role are very different phenomena, as far as we are concerned. The unit act refers to actors and action while *status-role* refers to positions within a structure of interaction. In his later work Parsons developed the concept of need-disposition as the most significant unit at the personality level, and value orientations occupy the same position in the cultural system. As we will see later, *need-dispositions* are biological needs shaped by external forces, and *value orientations* are internalized cultural standards. The issue here is whether these three new concepts have "emerged" from the unit act or whether they are entirely new concepts. Only the value orientation is traceable directly to the unit act and Parsons's thinking in 1937. Status-role and need-disposition are entirely new, arising out of Parsons's later thought. In his preface to the second edition of *The Structure of Social Action* (1949), Parsons admitted that in the 1937 edition he did not include two critical influences—those of Sigmund Freud on the psychological side and those of anthropologists such as Franz Boas. It is from these sources that Parsons's concepts of need-disposition and status-role undoubtedly came. Clearly, we do not need the unit act to understand the three later concepts. Furthermore, Parsons did not need (or use) the unit act to analyze the social, cultural, and personality systems. As he became, in turn, a structural functionalist, a functionalist, and an evolutionist, the unit act became increasingly extraneous. In his basic work on evolution, *Societies* (1966), the unit act disappears completely.

John F. Scott (1963) is the strongest proponent of the idea that Parsons abandoned voluntarism after 1937 as part of a general abandonment of small-scale sociology. Jonathan Turner and Leonard Beeghley (1973; see also R. Münch, 1982) argued for continuity in Parsons's thinking contending that he never abandoned the voluntaristic thesis. Scott's error, they said, was equating voluntarism with free will. Parsons never argued for a free-will position;

instead, he always believed that individual choice is circumscribed by norms, values, ideas, situations, and so forth. While Turner and Beeghley are correct in their interpretation of voluntarism, the fact is that Parsons turned away from individual choice and came to focus instead on norms, values, and the rest of the more macro-level phenomena.

Finally, there is the disappearance of *verstehen* from Parsons's theory. As Parsons put it: "Contrary to the point of view held by the author in *The Structure of Social Action*, it now appears that this postulate [the subjective point of view] is not essential to the frame of reference of action in its most elementary form" (1951:543). Thus *verstehen* followed the unit act and voluntarism into Parsonsian oblivion. In fact, the subjective perspective had to go when Parsons deserted the unit act and voluntarism. It was because he was looking at a voluntaristic unit act that Parsons needed a subjective methodology. According to Scott, it was the influence of behaviorism that helped to move Parsons away from *verstehen*. Finally, a sociologist need not use *verstehen* in order to study need-dispositions, status-roles, or value orientations, concepts that characterized the next phase of Parsons's work and which we discuss in the following section.

Need-Dispositions   In work published in the early 1950s, Parsons's interest in the individual level took a new turn. Parsons moved from the unit act, voluntarism, and *verstehen* to need-dispositions and the orientations of actors to situations. There is a concern with consciousness here, albeit a constrained one, one devoid of virtually all creativity. Actors are depicted as being driven by need-dispositions to seek the optimization of gratification; that is, they are impelled by innate needs that are shaped and molded by external forces into dispositions. Within this context Parsons dealt with the motivational and value orientations of actors.

Motivational Orientations   Actors use the framework of motivational orientations to analyze social phenomena that are of interest to them. Of major concern is the degree to which the phenomena represent actual or potential satisfaction of their need-dispositions. This process involves three dimensions. For one thing, actors must analyze the situation *cognitively*. That is, they must:

1 Locate social phenomena (individuals, collectivities, physical culture objects).
2 Differentiate them from other social phenomena.
3 Relate them to general classes of objects.
4 Determine the social phenomenon's properties.
5 Determine the social phenomenon's actual or potential functions.

Simultaneoulsy, the actors must assess the *cathectic* significance of the social phenomenon: they must decide how much affect, or emotion, to invest in each phenomenon they perceive. That determination is influenced by the degree to which a phenomenon is likely to gratify or deprive actors in terms of their need-dispositions. Then actors go through an *evaluative* process in which they determine how to allocate their energies in order to optimize gratification and minimize deprivation.

This discussion of motivational orientation relates to consciousness to some extent. However, it is not the conscious process but the norms and values that shape this process that were of prime significance to Parsons.

Value Orientations   It is in the context of norms and values that Parsons dealt with value orientations, or the cultural standards for judging solutions to each of the three motivational issues discussed above. Through the social-ization process, actors internalize these standards, which become aspects of the actors' orientations and commit them to the observance of certain norms, standards, and criteria of selection whenever they must make *choices*. Parsons described three value orientations that parallel the three modes of motiva-tional orientation.

First, the actors acquire a set of *cognitive* standards. Among other things, these standards help the actors decide whether the data they are receiving are important, whether their observations are useful, and the relative importance of various situations and problems. In other words, cognitive standards han-dle informational problems associated with a motivational decision. Then there are *appreciative* standards that allow actors to assess the appropriateness and the consistency of the amount of cathectic energy they have invested in various social phenomena. These are the social rules that help us determine whether a given social entity will satisfy our need-dispositions. Finally, there are *moral* standards that permit actors to assess the consequences of their actions for the integrity of and interrelationship between the personality and social systems. Overall, the existence of these three sets of standards in Par-sons's work, and the sense that they guide (to a large extent even determine) actors' choices, leads us to doubt that Parsons retained very much of a sense of voluntarism.

Types of Action   Parsons used the three modes of motivational and value orientation to develop four basic types of action. *Intellectual action* involves cognitive motivational interests and cognitive value standards; *expressive action* combines cathectic interests and appreciative standards; and *moral action* involves evaluative interests and moral standards. *Instrumental action,* the fourth type, is more complex. It involves future goals determined by cathectic interests and appreciative standards and means to those goals determined by cognitive standards.[3]

Although Parsons was willing to offer us a static typology of action, there is in fact very little sense of dynamic individual action in his work. He based his model of a social system on the interaction of ego and alter ego, but he had very little to say about this, using it only as a base on which to build his large-scale sense of the social system. This lack of action in Parsons, even when

---

[3] As a matter of fact, this is a good definition of Weber's "value-rational action."

he was supposedly an action theorist, led William F. Whyte to argue that "in the world of Talcott Parsons, actors are constantly orienting themselves to situations and very rarely, if ever, acting" (1961:255).

Pattern Variables

Returning to Parsons's work on action and consciousness, we encounter the famous, or infamous, pattern variables, which reflect Parsons's overwhelming penchant for parallelisms and conceptual neatness. At the most basic level, the *pattern variables* are a conceptual set of five dichotomous choices of action that actors must make in every situation. At this level they are tools for analyzing conscious processes. The pattern variables are universal choices an actor must make before a situation will have determinate meaning; they address the fundamental problem of orienting oneself to a situation (Parsons, 1951:60). The pattern variables are:

1 *Affectivity—affective neutrality:* The attitudinal problem of how we feel toward a social phenomenon; how much emotion, affect, to invest in it. For example, should physicians develop emotional ties to patients or should physicians keep patients at a distance?

2 *Specificity—diffuseness:* The attitudinal problem of whether to orient ourselves to part or all of the social phenomenon. Should patients accept advice from physicians on all kinds of problems or only on those within the physicians' area of expertise?

3 *Universalism—particularism:* The problem of how to categorize social phenomena. Are we to judge them in terms of general standards that apply universally to all such entities, or are we to use more specific, more emotional standards in such judgments? For example, we are likely to judge potential physicians with universal standards, but we are likely to assess our own children with more particular standards.

4 *Ascription—achievement:* The problem of whether we characterize social phenomena by what they are endowed with or by what they acquire. Are people born with the ability to become physicians, or are such abilities learned?

5 *Self—collectivity:* The dilemma of whether we should pursue our own private interests or those shared with other members of the collectivity. Is the physicians' desire to earn a good living incompatible with their stated goal of helping humankind?

Parsons went on to use the pattern variables to analyze other aspects of his theoretical system. They can be used to differentiate habits of choice within the personality system. Or they can be used to examine the different role expectations within the social system. Finally, they can be used to differentiate among the various normative patterns in the cultural system. This tendency to use the same conceptual scheme at different levels of social analysis gives

Parsons's work an orderly feel, but it also created problems for him. There is no obvious reason why the same concepts should fit such diverse levels. As Alfred Baldwin said: "The problem of integrating motives within the person bears only a slight resemblance to that of integrating people in society" (1961:185). In general, there is no persuasive reason to believe that all systems, no matter what their level of complexity, have the same set of dilemmas.

AGIL

As has been pointed out on several occasions, over the course of his career Parsons moved from action theory to structural functionalism. We will encounter some of Parsons's thoughts on structures and systems shortly, but first we will discuss some of his ideas on functionalism. A *function* is "a complex of activities directed towards meeting a need or needs of the system" (Rocher, 1975:40). Using this definition, Parsons believed that there are four functional imperatives that are necessary for (characteristic of) all systems— (A) adaptation, (G) goal attainment, (I) integration, and (L) latency, or pattern maintenance (AGIL). In order to survive, a system must perform these four functions:

1 *Adaptation:* A system must cope with external situational exigencies. It must adapt to its environment and adapt the environment to its needs.
2 *Goal attainment:* A system must define and achieve its primary goals.
3 *Integration:* A system must regulate the interrelationship of its component parts. It also must manage the relationship among the other three functional imperatives (A, G, L).
4 *Latency (pattern maintenance):* A system must furnish, maintain, and renew both the motivation of individuals and the cultural patterns that create and sustain the motivation.

As with the pattern variables, Parsons designed the AGIL scheme to be used at *all* levels in his theoretical system. As Chandler Morse noted:

> The four functional imperatives, or problems, operate at both a micro-analytic and a macro-analytic level in the Parsonsian model. At the micro-level they purport to specify the phases through which *individual actors* in a small action system and the action system as a whole must progress during an action cycle. At the macro-level the imperatives provide a means of (a) allocating roles analytically among four functional subsystems of any given system, and of (b) sorting out the input-output flows among those sub-systems.
>
> (Morse, 1961:116)

We will illustrate how Parsons uses the AGIL system in the discussion below on the four action systems; later, we will show how he applies it to society.

At their most general level, the four functional imperatives are linked to the four action systems (discussed in detail shortly). The *biological organism* is the action system that handles the adaptation function by adjusting to and

L

Cultural System	Social System
Behavioral Organism	Personality System

A

I

G

FIGURE 11.1 Structure of the General Action System

transforming the external world. The *personality system* performs the goal-attainment function by defining system goals and mobilizing resources to attain them. The *social system* copes with the integration function by controlling its component parts. Finally, the *cultural system* performs the latency function by providing actors with the norms and values that motivate them for action. Figure 11.1 summarizes the structure of the action system in terms of the AGIL schema:

Consistency in Parsonsian Theory: Integration and Order

We have been stressing some of the changes in Parsonsian theory but have, if anything, understated them, since Parsonsian theory takes many other twists and turns. For example, in his later work Parsons came to think of his approach not so much as action, structural functional, or functional but as cybernetic. His concern was with communication among action systems as well as control of lower-order systems by higher-order ones. In spite of all these dramatic changes, there were consistent elements in Parsonsian theory. Parsons himself, while he came to admit certain shifts, emphasized his "essential continuity over the forty-year period since *The Structure of Social Action*" (1977a:2).

One of Parsons's most important concerns from the beginning was the question of order in society (Burger, 1977b). Given a modern, complex society, the question arises of how a "war of all against all," rampant social conflict, is avoided. Throughout his career, Parsons argued that power is not the force that prevents such social warfare. In his view, power is not a sound means of maintaining order in society. Although exercises of power may work in the short run, in the long run they are only likely to bring about more disorder. The use of power evokes negative reactions that lead to further disintegration in society. Furthermore, constant vigilance is required in order for the exercise of power to work. It is difficult, time-consuming, and expensive to maintain order in society on the basis of power. In short, power is an inadequate and inefficient method of maintaining order in society. This antipower position was a consistent theme of Parsons from his earliest works.

Another consistent idea of Parsons was his alternative solution to the problem of order. To Parsons, the ideal way for a society to maintain order is to develop a cultural system that emphasizes cooperation and then have that set of ideas internalized in the actors through socialization. This relates to Parsons's fundamental theorem, which involves the integration of "common value patterns" (culture) and "need-dispositions" (personality). To put this somewhat crudely, order in society is best maintained when people are put in the position of constraining themselves. Because people carry common value patterns around in their heads, they are able to determine for themselves if they are out of line and are able to realign themselves with the cultural value system. Ideally, no external power source is needed to maintain order in society; that society governs best that governs least. Of course, in some instances power is necessary, but these should be few and far between. If the authorities are forced to use power too often, then a society is in deep trouble, perhaps even in danger of disintegration.

This issue of order, power, and integration was an essential theme of Parsons throughout his career. At the end of *The Structure of Social Action* (1937) he considered the solution of the power question to be in value integration. The integration of values and need-dispositions lies at the heart of *The Social System* (1951) and is central to many of his books and essays after that time. For example, in a well-known essay on organizations, Parsons argued that his "main point of reference for analyzing the [organization] . . . is its value pattern" (1960:20). Although he did discuss power, his primary interest was in cultural dimensions that provide organizational integration. Thus while most people conceive of organizations as arenas of power and power struggles, Parsons emphasized the values that held organizations together. This kind of thinking over the years earned Parsons the title of "consensus" theorist. We will have occasion to return to this theme in the next section.

THE ACTION SYSTEM

We are now ready to discuss the overall shape of Parsons's action system, which is, in many ways, a system of levels of social analysis (see the Appendix). Figure 11.2 is an outline of the major levels of Parsons's schema.

It is obvious that Parsons had a clear notion of "levels" of social analysis

FIGURE 11.2   Parsons's Action Schema

High information
(controls)

Hierarchy of
conditioning
factors

High energy
(conditions)

1. Environment of action:
   ultimate reality
2. Cultural system
3. Social system
4. Personality system
5. Behavioral organism
6. Environment of action:
   physical-organic environment

High information
(controls)

Hierarchy of
controlling
factors

High energy
(conditions)

as well as their interrelationship. The hierarchical arrangement is clear, and the levels are integrated in Parsons's system in two ways. First, each of the lower levels provides the conditions, the energy, needed for the higher levels. Second, the higher levels control those below them in the hierarchy.

In terms of the environments of the action system, the lowest level, the physical and organic environment, involves the nonsymbolic aspects of the human body, its anatomy and physiology. The highest level, ultimate reality, has, as Jackson Toby suggests, "a metaphysical flavor," but Toby also argues that Parsons "is not referring to the supernatural so much as to the universal tendency for societies to address symbolically the uncertainties, concerns, and tragedies of human existence that challenge the meaningfulness of social organization" (1977:3).

The heart of Parsons's work is found in his four action systems. In discussing these systems and their interrelationships, Parsons moved away from his earlier action theory and in the direction of structural functionalism (this move is also clear in the earlier discussion of AGIL). In the assumptions that Parsons made regarding his action systems, we encounter once again the problem of order that was his overwhelming concern from the beginning and that has become a major source of criticism of his work (Schwanenberg, 1971). The Hobbesian problem of order—what prevents a social war of all against all— was not answered to Parsons's (1937) satisfaction by the earlier philosophers. Parsons found his answer to the problem of order in structural functionalism, which operates with the following set of assumptions:

1 Systems have the property of order and interdependence of parts.
2 Systems tend toward self-maintaining order, or equilibrium.
3 The systems may be static or involved in an ordered process of change.
4 The nature of one part of the system has an impact on the form that the other parts could take.
5 Systems maintain boundaries with their environments.
6 Allocation and integration are two fundamental processes necessary for a given state of equilibrium of a system.
7 Systems tend toward self-maintenance involving the maintenance of boundaries and of the relationships of parts to the whole, control of environmental variations, and control of tendencies to change the system from within.

These assumptions led Parsons to make the analysis of the *ordered* structure of society his first priority. In so doing, he did little with the issue of social change, at least until later in his career:

> We feel that it is uneconomical to describe changes in systems of variables before the variables themselves have been isolated and described; therefore, we have chosen to begin by studying particular combinations of variables and to move toward description of how these combinations change when a firm foundation for such has been laid.
>
> (Parsons and Shils, 1951:6)

Parsons was so heavily criticized for his static orientation that he devoted more and more attention to change; in fact, as we will see, he eventually focused on the evolution of societies. However, in the view of most observers, even his work on social change tended to be highly static and structured.

In reading about the four action systems, the reader should keep in mind that they do not exist in the real world but are, rather, analytical tools for analyzing the real world.

Social System

Parsons's conception of the social system begins at the micro-level with interaction between ego and alter ego, defined as the most elementary form of the social system. He spent little time analyzing this level, although he did argue that features of this interaction system are present in the more complex forms taken by the social system. Parsons defined a social system thus:

> A social system consists in a plurality of individual actors *interacting* with each other in a situation which has at least a physical or environmental aspect, actors who are motivated in terms of a tendency to the "optimization of gratification" and whose relation to their situations, including each other, is defined and mediated in terms of a system of culturally structured and shared symbols.
>
> (Parsons, 1951:5–6)

This definition seeks to define a social system in terms of many of the key concepts in Parsons's work—actors, interaction, environment, optimization of gratification, and culture.

Despite his commitment to viewing the social system as a system of interaction, Parsons did not take interaction as his fundamental unit in the study of the social system. Rather, he used the *status-role* complex as a basic unit of the system. As mentioned earlier, this is neither an aspect of actors nor an aspect of interaction but rather a *structural* component of the social system. *Status* refers to a structural position within the social system, and *role* is what the actor does in such a position, seen in the context of its functional significance for the larger system. The actor is viewed not in terms of thoughts and actions but instead (at least in terms of position in the social system) as nothing more than a bundle of statuses and roles.

In his analysis of the social system, Parsons was interested primarily in its structural components. In addition to his concern with the status-role, Parsons (1966:11) was interested in such large-scale components of social systems as collectivities, norms, and values. In his analysis of the social system, however, Parsons was not simply a structuralist but also a functionalist. He thus delineated a number of the functional prerequisites of a social system. First, social systems must be structured so that they operate compatibly with other systems. Second, to survive, the social system must have the requisite support from other systems. Third, the system must meet a significant proportion of the needs of its actors. Fourth, the system must elicit adequate participation from its members. Fifth, it must have at least a minimum of control over potentially disruptive behavior. Sixth, if conflict becomes sufficiently disruptive, it must be controlled. Finally, a social system requires a language in order to survive.

It is clear in Parsons's discussion of the functional prerequisites of the social system that his focus was large-scale systems and their relationship to one another. Even when he talked about actors, it was from the point of view of the system. Also, the discussion reflects Parsons's concern with the maintenance of order within the social system.

However, Parsons did not completely ignore the issue of the relationship between actors and social structures in his discussion of the social system. In fact, as we saw earlier, he called the integration of value patterns and need-dispositions "the fundamental dynamic theorem of sociology" (Parsons, 1951:42). Given his central concern with the social system, of key importance in this integration are the processes of internalization and socialization. That is, Parsons was interested in the ways that the norms and values of a system are transferred to the actors within the system. In a successful socialization process these norms and values are internalized; that is, they become part of the actors' "consciences." As a result, in pursuing their own interests, the actors are in fact serving the interests of the system as a whole. As Parsons put it, "The combination of value-orientation patterns which is acquired [by the actor in socialization] *must in a very important degree be a function of the fundamental role structure and dominant values of the social system*" (1951:227).

In general, Parsons assumed that actors usually are passive recipients in the socialization process.[4] Children learn not only how to act but also the norms and values, the morality, of society. Socialization is conceptualized as a conservative process in which need-dispositions (which are themselves largely molded by society) bind children to the social system, and it provides the means by which the need-dispositions can be satisfied. There is little or no room for creativity; the need for gratification ties children to the system as it exists. Parsons sees socialization as a lifelong experience. Because the norms and values inculcated in childhood tend to be very general, they do not prepare children for the various specific situations that they encounter in adulthood. Thus socialization must be supplemented throughout the life cycle with a series of more specific socializing experiences. Despite this need later in life, the norms and values learned in childhood tend to be stable and, with a little gent e reinforcement, tend to remain in force throughout life.

Despite the conformity induced by lifelong socialization, there is a wide range of individual variation in the system. The question is: Why is this normally not a major problem for the social system, given its need for order? For one thing, a number of social control mechanisms can be employed to induce conformity. However, as far as Parsons was concerned, social control is strictly

---

[4] This is a controversial interpretation of Parsons's work with which many disagree. François Bourricaud, for example, talks of "the dialectics of socialization" (1981:108) in Parsons's work and not of passive recipients of socialization.

a second line of defense. A system runs best when social control is used only sparingly. For another thing, the system must be able to tolerate some variation, some deviance. A flexible social system is stronger than a brittle one that accepts no deviation. Finally, the social system should provide a wide range of role opportunities that allow different personalities to express themselves without threatening the integrity of the system.

Socialization and social control are the main mechanisms that allow the social system to maintain its equilibrium. Modest amounts of individuality and deviance are accommodated, but more extreme forms must be met by reequilibrating mechanisms. Thus social order is built into the structure of Parsons's social system:

> Without deliberate planning on anyone's part there have developed in our type of social system, and correspondingly in others, mechanisms which, within limits, are capable of forestalling and reversing the deep-lying tendencies for deviance to get into the vicious circle phase which puts it beyond the control of ordinary approval-disapproval and reward-punishment sanctions.
>
> (Parsons, 1951:319)

Again, Parsons's main interest was the system as a whole rather than the actor in the system—how the system controls the actor, not how the actor creates and maintains the system. This reflects Parsons's commitment on this issue to a structural-functional orientation.

Although the idea of a social system encompasses all types of collectivities, one specific and particularly important social system is *society*, "a relatively self-sufficient collectivity the members of which are able to satisfy all their individual and collective needs and to live entirely within its framework" (Rocher, 1975:60). As a structural functionalist, Parsons distinguished among four structures, or subsystems, in society in terms of the functions (AGIL) they perform (see Figure 11.3). The *economy* is the subsystem that performs the function for society of adapting to the environment through labor, production, allocation. Through such work, the economy adapts the environment to society's needs, and it helps society adapt to these external realities. The *polity* (or political system) performs the function of goal attainment by pursuing societal objectives and mobilizing actors and resources to that end. The *fiduciary system* (for example, in the schools, the family) handles the latency function by transmitting culture (norms and values) to actors and allowing it to be internalized by them. Finally, the integration function is performed by the *societal com-*

L | | | I   FIGURE 11.3   Society, Its Subsystems,
and the Functional Imperatives

Fiduciary System	Societal Community
Economy	Polity

A _____ G

munity (for example, the law), which coordinates the various components of society (Parsons and Platt, 1973).

As important as the structures of the social system were to Parsons, the cultural system was more important. In fact, as we saw earlier, the cultural system stood at the top of his action system, and Parsons (1966) labeled himself a "cultural determinist."

Cultural System

Parsons conceived of culture as the major force binding the various elements of the social world or, in his terms, the action system. It mediates interaction among actors and integrates the personality and the social systems. Culture has the peculiar capacity to become, at least in part, a component of the other systems. Thus in the social system culture is embodied in norms and values, and in the personality system it is internalized by the actor. But the cultural system is not simply a part of other systems; it also has a separate existence in the form of the social stock of knowledge, symbols, and ideas. These aspects of the cultural system are available to the social and personality systems, but they do not become part of them (Morse, 1961:105, Parsons and Shils, 1951:6).

Parsons defined the cultural system, as he did his other systems, in terms of its relationship to the other action systems. Thus *culture* is seen as a patterned, ordered system of symbols that are objects of orientation to actors, internalized aspects of the personality system, and institutionalized patterns (Parsons, 1990) in the social system. Because it is largely symbolic and subjective, culture is readily transmitted from one system to another. This allows it to move from one social system to another through diffusion and from one personality system to another through learning and socialization. However, the symbolic (subjective) character of culture also gives it another characteristic, the ability to control Parsons's other action systems. This is one of the reasons that Parsons came to view himself as a cultural determinist.

Again establishing parallelism and orderliness in his thinking, Parsons argued that the cultural system has three components that parallel the three modes of motivational orientation discussed earlier. The *cognitive* motivational orientation is paralleled in culture by systems of beliefs and idea systems that represent guidelines to the solution of motivational problems. The *cathectic* motivational orientation has its parallel in culture in systems of expressive symbols, means of expressing a cathectic attachment to a social object. Finally, the *evaluative* motivational orientation is paralleled by similar cultural guidelines—systems of value orientations. (Each component can be subdivided in precisely the same way. Thus, for example, as discussed earlier, the system of value orientations can be broken down into cognitive, appreciative, and moral standards.) Parsons came to the conclusion that the moral standards are "the superordinate integrative techniques of a system of action" (Parsons and Shils, 1951:170). This conclusion reflects the crucial idea in Parsons's theory—that the cultural system is preeminent. But if culture is preeminent, Parsons's integrative work is questionable, for any kind of determinism is suspect from the point of view of an integrated sociology. (For a more integrated conception of Parsons's work, see Camic, 1990.) This problem is exacerbated when we look at the personality system and see how weakly it is developed in Parsons's work.

Personality System

The personality system is controlled not only by the cultural system but also by the social system. Parsons's early conception of consciousness and action, in terms of his work on the unit act, voluntarism, and so forth, was reviewed earlier and found wanting. Parsons seemed to be aware of the charge that he had given up his earlier emphasis on voluntarism, and he sought to salvage his position by according some independence to the personality system:

> My view will be that, while the main content of the structure of the personality is derived from social systems and culture through socialization, the personality becomes an independent system through its relations to its own organism and through the uniqueness of its own life experience; it is not a mere epiphenomenon.
> (Parsons, 1970a:82)

We get the feeling here that Parsons is protesting too much. If the personality system is not an epiphenomenon, it is certainly reduced to secondary or dependent status in his theoretical system.

The *personality* is defined as the organized system of orientation and motivation of action of the individual actor. The basic component of the personality is the need-disposition, a concept we discussed earlier but which now needs further explication. Parsons and Shils defined *need-dispositions* as the "most significant units of motivation of action" (1951:113). They differentiated need-dispositions from drives, which are innate tendencies—"physiological energy that makes action possible" (Parsons and Shils, 1951:111). In other words, drives are better seen as part of the biological organism. Need-dispositions are then defined as "these same tendencies when they are not innate but acquired through the process of action itself" (Parsons and Shils, 1951:111). In other words, need-dispositions are drives that are shaped by the social setting.

Need-dispositions impel actors to accept or reject objects presented in the environment or to seek out new objects if the ones that are available do not adequately satisfy need-dispositions. Parsons differentiated among three basic types of need-dispositions. The first type impels actors to seek love, approval, and so forth, from their social relationships. The second type includes internalized values that lead actors to observe various cultural standards. Finally, there are the role expectations that lead actors to give and get appropriate responses.

This gives a very passive image of actors. They seem to be either impelled by drives, dominated by the culture, or, more usually, shaped by a combination of drives and culture (that is, by need-dispositions). A passive personality system is clearly a weak link in an integrated theory, and Parsons seemed to be aware of it. On various occasions, he tried to endow the personality with some creativity. For example, he said: "We do not mean . . . to imply that a person's values are entirely 'internalized culture' or mere adherence to rules and laws. The person makes creative modifications as he internalizes culture; but the novel aspect is not the cultural aspect" (Parsons and Shils, 1951:72). Despite claims such as these, the dominant impression that emerges from Parsons's work is one of a passive personality system.

Parsons's emphasis on need-dispositions creates other problems. Because it leaves out so many other important aspects of personality, his system becomes a largely impoverished one. Alfred Baldwin, a psychologist, makes precisely this point:

> It seems fair to say that Parsons fails in his theory to provide the personality with a reasonable set of properties or mechanisms aside from need-dispositions, and gets himself into trouble by not endowing the personality with enough characteristics and enough different kinds of mechanisms for it to be able to function.
>
> (Baldwin, 1961:186)

Baldwin makes another telling point about Parsons's personality system, arguing that even when Parsons analyzed the personality system, he was really not focally interested in it: "Even when he is writing chapters on personality structure, Parsons spends many more pages talking about social systems than he does about personality" (1961:180). This is reflected in the various ways that Parsons linked the personality to the social system. First, actors must learn to see themselves in a way that fits with the place they occupy in society (Parsons and Shils, 1951:147). Second, role expectations are attached to each of the roles occupied by individual actors. Then there is the learning of self-discipline, internalization of value orientations, identification, and so forth. All these forces point toward the integration of the personality system with the social system, which Parsons emphasized. However, he also pointed out the possible malintegration, which is a problem for the system that needs to be overcome.

Another aspect of Parsons's work reflects the passivity of the personality system. This is his interest in internalization as the personality system's side of the socialization process. Parsons (1970a:2) derived this interest from Durkheim's work on internalization as well as from Freud's work, primarily that on the superego. In emphasizing internalization and the superego, Parsons once again manifested his conception of the personality system as passive and externally controlled.

Although Parsons was willing to talk about the subjective aspects of personality in his early work, he progressively abandoned that perspective. In so doing, he limited the insights into the personality system he could offer. Parsons at one point stated clearly that he was shifting his attention away from the internal meanings that the actions of people may have: "The organization of observational data in terms of the theory of action is quite possible and fruitful in modified behavioristic terms, and such formulation avoids many of the difficult questions of introspection or empathy" (Parsons and Shils, 1951: 64).

Behavioral Organism

Though he included the behavioral organism as one of the four action systems, Parsons had very little to say about it. It is included because it is the source of energy for the rest of the systems. Although it is based on genetic constitution, its organization is affected by the processes of conditioning and learning that occur during the individual's life.[5] The biological organism is clearly a residual system in Parsons's work, but at the minimum Parsons is to be lauded for including it as a part of his sociology, if for no other reason than that he anticipated the current interest in sociobiology among at least a few sociologists.

CHANGE AND DYNAMISM IN PARSONSIAN THEORY

Evolutionary Theory

Parsons's work with such conceptual tools as the pattern variables, the functional imperatives, and the four action systems led to the accusation that he offered a structural theory that was unable to deal with social change. Parsons had long been sensitive to this charge, arguing that although a study of change was necessary, it must be preceded by a study of structure. But by the 1960s he could resist the charges no longer and made another major shift in his work, this time to the study of social change,[6] particularly the study of social evolution. By Parsons's (1977b:50) own testimony that interest was first stimulated by a seminar on social evolution held in 1963.

Parsons's (1966) general orientation to the study of social change was shaped by biology. To deal with this process, Parsons developed what he called "a paradigm of evolutionary change."

The first component of that paradigm is the process of *differentiation*. Parsons assumed that any society is composed of a series of subsystems that differ in terms of both their *structure* and their *functional* significance for the larger society. As society evolves, new subsystems are differentiated. This is not enough, however; they also must be more adaptive than earlier subsystems. This led Parsons to the essential aspect of his evolutionary paradigm, the idea of *adaptive upgrading*. Parsons described this process:

---

[5] Because of this social element, in his later work Parsons dropped the word *organism* and labeled this the "behavioral system" (1975:104).

[6] To be fair, Parsons had done some earlier work on social change, but it did not become a paramount concern, and his contributions were minimal, until the 1960s (see Parsons, 1942, 1947; see also Alexander, 1981; Baum and Lechner, 1981).

> If differentiation is to yield a balanced, more evolved system, each newly differ-
> entiated substructure . . . must have increased adaptive capacity for performing its
> *primary* function, as compared to the performance of *that* function in the previous,
> more diffuse structure. . . . We may call this process the *adaptive upgrading* aspect
> of the evolutionary change cycle.
>
> (Parsons, 1966:22)

This is a highly positive model of social change. It assumes that as society evolves, it grows generally better able to cope with its problems. In contrast, in Marxian theory social change leads to the eventual destruction of capitalist society. For this reason, among others, Parsons is often thought of as a very conservative sociological theorist. In addition, while he did deal with change, he tended to focus on the positive aspects of social change in the modern world rather than modernity's dark side.

Next, Parsons argued that the process of differentiation leads to a new set of problems of *integration* for society. As subsystems proliferate, the society is confronted with new problems in coordinating the operations of these units.

A society undergoing evolution must move from a system of ascription to one of achievement. A wider array of skills and abilities is needed to handle the more diffuse subsystems. The generalized abilities of people must be freed from their ascriptive bonds so that they can be utilized by society. Most generally, this means that groups formerly excluded from contributing to the system must be freed for inclusion as full members of the society.

Finally, the *value* system of the society as a whole must undergo change as social structures and functions grow increasingly differentiated. However, since the new system is more diverse, it is harder for the value system to encompass it. Thus a more differentiated society requires a value system that is "couched at a higher level of generality in order to legitimize the wider variety of goals and functions of its subunits" (Parsons, 1966:23). However, this process of generalization of values often does not proceed smoothly as it meets resistance from groups committed to their own narrow value systems.

Evolution proceeds through a variety of cycles, but no general process affects all societies equally. Some societies may foster evolution, whereas others may "be so beset with internal conflicts or other handicaps" that they impede the process of evolution, or they may even "deteriorate" (Parsons, 1966:23). What most interested Parsons were those societies in which developmental "breakthroughs" occur, since he believed that once they occur, the process of evolution would follow his general evolutionary model.

Although Parsons conceived of evolution as occurring in stages, he was careful to avoid a unilinear evolutionary theory: "We do not conceive societal evolution to be either a continuous or a simple linear process, but we can distinguish between broad levels of advancement without overlooking the considerable variability found in each" (1966:26). Making it clear that he was simplifying matters, Parsons distinguished three broad evolutionary stages— primitive, intermediate, and modern. Characteristically, he differentiated among these stages primarily on the basis of cultural dimensions. The crucial development in the transition from primitive to intermediate is the development of language, primarily written language. The key development in the shift from intermediate to modern is "the institutionalized codes of normative order," or law (Parsons, 1966:26).

Parsons next proceeded to analyze a series of specific societies in the context of the evolution from primitive to modern society. One particular point is worth underscoring here: Parsons turned to evolutionary theory, at least in part, because he was accused of being unable to deal with social change. However, his analysis of evolution is *not* in terms of process; rather, it is an attempt to "order structural types and relate them sequentially" (Parsons, 1966:111). This is comparative *structural* analysis, not really a study of the processes of social change. Thus, even when he was supposed to be looking at change, Parsons remained committed to the study of structures and functions.

Generalized Media of Interchange

One of the ways in which Parsons introduces some dynamism, some fluidity (Alexander, 1983:115) into his theoretical system is through his ideas on the generalized media of interchange within and among the four action systems (especially within the social system) discussed above. The model for the generalized media of interchange is money, which operates as such a medium within the economy. But instead of focusing on material phenomena such as money, Parsons focuses on *symbolic* media of exchange. Even when Parsons does discuss money as a medium of interchange within the social system, he focuses on its symbolic rather than its material qualities. In addition to money, and more clearly symbolic, are other generalized media of interchange—political power, influence, and value commitments. Parsons makes it quite clear why he is focusing on symbolic media of interchange: "The introduction of a theory of media into the kind of structural perspective I have in mind goes far, it seems to me, to refute the frequent allegations that this type of structural analysis is inherently plagued with a static bias, which makes it impossible to do justice to dynamic problems" (1975:98–99).

Symbolic media of interchange have the capacity, like money, to be created and to circulate in the larger society. Thus, within the social system, those in the political system are able to create political power. More importantly, they can expend that power, thereby allowing it to circulate freely in, and have influence over, the social system. Through such an expenditure of power, leaders presumably strengthen the political system as well as the society as a whole. More generally, it is the generalized media that circulate between the four action systems and within the structures of each of those systems. It is their existence and movement that gives dynamism to Parsons's largely structural analyses.

As Alexander (1983:115) points out, generalized media of interchange lend dynamism to Parsons's theory in another sense. They allow for the existence of "media entrepreneurs" (for example, politicians) who do not simply accept the system of exchange as it is. That is, they can be creative and resourceful and in this way alter not only the quantity of the generalized media but also the manner and direction in which the media flow.

SUMMARY

In a few short years Talcott Parsons went from being the dominant figure in sociological theory to being, in some quarters, nearly a theoretical outcast. Neither extreme status is deserved. Parsons's theoretical system always had serious weaknesses, but it is certainly not without major significance.

To his credit, Parsons articulated early in his work an interest in integrating the diverse levels of social analysis, and he maintained that interest, despite basic changes in his theoretical system, throughout his life. Most basically, Parsons was interested in integrating the social and personality systems. Despite such a laudable goal, his work has been marred by some basic confusions, specifically the uncomfortable mix of action theory and structural functionalism. On the basis of his analyses of the people whom he considered to be the major thinkers in the history of sociology, Parsons initially articulated what seemed to be a micro orientation in his action theory. This is particularly clear in his emphasis on the unit act and voluntarism in his early work. However, over the years the unit act and voluntarism tended to disappear from Parsons's theory, as did action theory. In its place, there evolved a structural-functional theory in which actors were seen not as acting in a voluntaristic manner but as primarily constrained by social structures and culture. In the 1940s and 1950s Parsons developed new concepts such as need-dispositions, motivational orientations, and value orientations. They all reflected Parsons's increasing tendency to see actors as constrained by external structures rather than as voluntaristic actors. Other well-known Parsonsian concepts were developed in this period, including the pattern variables and later the AGIL system. Through these changes Parsons retained a lifelong interest in order and a preference for cultural rather than power solutions to the problem of order.

The heart of Parsons's theory lies in his sense of the major levels of social analysis, especially the four action systems. Although Parsons is probably best known for his work on the social system, the most important level in his theory is the cultural system. It stands at the pinnacle of the four action systems (the others are the social, personality, and behavioral organism systems) and exercises control over them. Although the other levels are not completely controlled by the cultural system, Parsons described himself as a "cultural determinist." Parsons retained an interest in the actor in his later work, but he talked of the personality system, not voluntaristic actors. The problem here is that Parsons tended to see the personality system as determined by the systems that stand above it, the social system and, particularly, the cultural system.

In his later work, Parsons sought to give his perspective more of a change orientation. This is reflected in his work on the evolution of societies. However, despite an apparent focus on change, Parsons's ideas on evolution remained more structural and functional than change-oriented. Also in his later work, Parsons sought to give his approach more dynamism through his ideas on the generalized media of interchange.

APPENDIX

SOCIOLOGICAL METATHEORIZING AND A METATHEORETICAL SCHEMA FOR ANALYZING SOCIOLOGICAL THEORY

*I*n Chapter 2 we saw that one of the most recent developments in sociological theory is the boom in interest in sociological metatheorizing. While theorists take the social world as their subject matter, metatheorists engage in *the systematic study of the underlying structure of sociological theory.* Among our goals in this Appendix is a look at the explosion of interest in metatheorizing in sociology and the basic parameters of this approach.

An analysis of such a recent development would be out of place in this book on classical sociological theory (although, as we will see, many of the classical theorists did metatheoretical work) were it not for the fact that the entire structure of this book rests on a specific set of metatheoretical perspectives developed by the author (Ritzer, 1975a, 1981a). Because the primary objective of the text has been to present classical sociological theory, it was decided to make this organizing schema as unobtrusive as possible. Thus, all chapters, as well as the book as a whole, can be read without knowledge of the organizing schema that undergirds them. However, some students may be interested in that schema, either early in their reading of the book or after they have finished it. Thus, another objective of this Appendix is to present the metatheoretical ideas that inform the text, but before we can do that, we need to present an overview of metatheorizing in sociology.

METATHEORIZING IN SOCIOLOGY

We start by making it clear that sociologists are not the only ones to do meta-analysis, that is, to reflexively study their own discipline. Others who do such work include philosophers (Radnitzky, 1973), psychologists (Gergen, 1973, 1986; Schmidt et al., 1984), political scientists (Connolly, 1973), a number of other social scientists (various essays in Fiske and Shweder, 1986), and historians (White, 1973). Some of their efforts are quite similar to at least some types of meta-analysis in sociology, while others differ considerably from the types of work done in sociology. The key point is that the study of one's own discipline is not the exclusive province of the sociologist.

Beyond the fact that meta-analysis is found in other fields, it is also the case that various kinds of sociologists, not just metatheorists, do such analysis. We can group the various types of meta-analysis in sociology under the heading "metasociology," which we can define as the reflexive study of the underlying structure of sociology in general, as well as of its various components—substantive areas (for example, Hall's [1983] overview of occupational sociology), concepts (Rubenstein's [1986] analysis of the concept of "structure"), methods (*metamethods;* for example, Brewer and Hunter's [1988] and Noblit and Hare's [1988] efforts to synthesize sociological methods), data (*meta-data-analysis;*[1] for example, Fendrich, 1984; Hunter, Schmidt, and Jackson, 1982; Polit and Falbo, 1987; Wolf, 1986) and theories. It is the latter, *metatheorizing,* that will concern us in this Appendix.

What distinguishes work in this area is not so much the process of metatheorizing (or systematically studying theories, which all metatheorists share) but rather the nature of the end products. There are three varieties of metatheorizing, largely defined by differences in their end products (Ritzer, 1990d, 1991). The first type, *metatheorizing as a means of attaining a deeper understanding of theory* (M_U), involves the study of theory in order to produce a better, more profound understanding of extant theory (Ritzer, 1988).[2] M_U is concerned, more specifically, with the study of theories, theorists, and communities of theorists, as well as the larger intellectual and social contexts of theories and theorists. The second type, *metatheorizing as a prelude to theory development* (M_P), entails the study of extant theory in order to produce new sociological theory. (It is this second type of metatheorizing in which the classical theorists were

---

[1] I have labeled this (somewhat awkwardly) "meta-data-analysis" in order to differentiate it from the more generic meta-analysis. In meta-data-analysis the goal is to seek ways of cumulating research results across research studies. In his introduction to Wolf's *Meta-Analysis,* Niemi defines *meta-analysis* as "the application of statistical procedures to collections of empirical findings from individual studies for the purpose of integrating, synthesizing, and making sense of them" (Wolf, 1986:5).

[2] While in my earlier work (Ritzer, 1987, 1988) I tended to equate this type with all of metatheorizing, I now see it as only one of three major types. I also prefer now to discuss metatheorizing as the generic process rather than metatheory, which is, as we shall see, only one of three possible end products of metatheorizing.

most likely to engage.) There is also a third type, *metatheorizing as a source of perspectives that overarch sociological theory* (M_O), in which the study of theory is oriented toward the goal of producing a perspective, one could say *a* metatheory, that overarches some part or all of sociological theory. (As we will see, it is this type of metatheorizing that provided the framework used in constructing this book.) Given these definitions, let us examine each type of metatheorizing in greater detail.

The first type of metatheorizing, M_U, is composed of four basic subtypes, all of which involve the formal or informal study of sociological theory to attain a deeper understanding of it. The first subtype focuses on intellectual or cognitive issues that are internal to sociology. Included here are attempts to identify major cognitive paradigms (Ritzer, 1975a, 1975b; see also the discussion below) and "schools of thought" (Sorokin, 1928), more dynamic views of the underlying structure of sociological theory (Harvey, 1982, 1987; Wiley, 1979) and the development of general metatheoretical tools with which to analyze existing sociological theories and to develop new theories (Alexander et al., 1987; Edel, 1959; Gouldner, 1970; Ritzer, 1989, 1990a; Wiley, 1988). The second subtype (internal-social) also looks within sociology, but it focuses on social rather than cognitive factors. The main approach here emphasizes the communal aspects of various sociological theories and includes efforts to identify the major "schools" in the history of sociology (Bulmer, 1984, 1985; Tiryakian, 1979, 1986), the more formal, network approach to the study of the ties among groups of sociologists (Mullins, 1973, 1983), as well as studies of theorists themselves that examine their institutional affiliations, their career patterns, their positions within the field of sociology, and so on (Gouldner, 1970). The third variant (external-intellectual) turns to other academic disciplines for ideas, tools, concepts, and theories that can be used in the analysis of sociological theory (for example, Brown, 1987, 1990). Finally, the external-social approach shifts to a more macro-level to look at the larger society (national setting, sociocultural setting, etc.) and the nature of its impact on sociological theorizing (for example, Vidich and Lyman, 1985).

Most metatheorizing in sociology is not M_U; rather, it is the second type, metatheorizing as a prelude to the development of sociological theory (M_P). Most important classical (and contemporary) theorists developed their theories, at least in part, on the basis of a careful study of, and reaction to, the work of other theorists. Among the most important examples are Marx's theory of capitalism (see Chapter 5), developed out of a systematic engagement with Hegelian philosophy as well as other ideas such as political economy and utopian socialism; Parsons's action theory (see Chapter 11), developed out of a systematic study of the work of Durkheim, Weber, Pareto, and Marshall; Alexander's (1982–83) multidimensional, neofunctional theory, based on a detailed study of the work of Marx, Weber, Durkheim, and Parsons; and Habermas's (1987) communication theory, based on his examination of the work of various critical theorists as well as that of Marx, Weber, Parsons, Mead, and Durkheim. Since this is a book on classical theory, let us look in more detail at M_P as it was practiced by two classical theorists discussed in this book—Marx and Parsons.

In *Economic and Philosophic Manuscripts of 1844*, Marx (1932/1964) develops his theoretical perspective on the basis of a detailed and careful analysis and critique of the works of political economists like Adam Smith, Jean-Baptiste Say, David Ricardo, and James Mill; philosophers like G. W. F. Hegel, the Young Hegelians (for example, Bruno Bauer), and Ludwig Feuerbach; utopian socialists like Etienne Cabet, Robert Owen, Charles Fourier, and Pierre Proudhon; and a variety of other major and minor intellectual schools and figures. It seems safe to say that in almost its entirety the *Manuscripts of 1844* is a metatheoretical treatise in which Marx develops his own ideas out of an engagement with a variety of idea systems.

What of Marx's other works? Are they more empirical? Less metatheoretical? In his preface to *The German Ideology* (Marx and Engels, 1845–46/1970), C. J. Arthur describes that work as comprised mainly of "detailed line by line polemics against the writings of some of their [Marx and Engels's] contemporaries" (1970:1). In fact, Marx himself describes *The German Ideology* as an effort "to set forth together our conception as opposed to the ideological one of German philosophy, in fact to settle accounts with our former philosophical conscience. The intention was carried out in the form of a critique of post-Hegelian philosophy" (1859/1970:22). *The Holy Family* (Marx and Engels, 1845/1956) is, above all, an extended critique of Bruno Bauer, the Young Hegelians, and their propensity toward speculative "critical criticism."[3] In their foreword, Marx and Engels make it clear that this kind of metatheoretical work is a prelude to their coming theorizing: "We therefore give this polemic as a preliminary to the independent works in which we . . . shall present our positive view" (1845/1956:16). In the *Grundrisse* Marx (1857–58/1974) chooses as his metatheoretical antagonists the political economist David Ricardo and the French socialist Pierre Proudhon (Nicolaus, 1974). Throughout the *Grundrisse* Marx is struggling to solve an array of theoretical problems, in part through a critique of the theories and theorists mentioned above and in part through an application of ideas derived from Hegel. In describing the introduction to the *Grundrisse,* Nicolaus says that it "reflects in its every line the struggle of Marx against Hegel, Ricardo and Proudhon. From it, Marx carried off the most important objective of all, namely the basic principles of writing history dialectically" (1974:42). *A Contribution to the Critique of Political Economy* (Marx, 1859–1970) is, as the title suggests, an effort to build a distinctive economic approach on the basis of a critique of the works of the political economists.

Even *Capital* (1867/1967)—which is admittedly one of Marx's most empirical works, since he deals more directly with the reality of the capitalist work world through the use of government statistics and reports—is informed by Marx's earlier metatheoretical work and contains some metatheorizing of its

---

[3] In fact, the book is subtitled *Against Bruno Bauer and Co.*

own. In fact, the subtitle, *A Critique of Political Economy*, makes the metatheoretical roots absolutely clear. However, Marx is freer in *Capital* to be much
more "positive," that is, to construct his own distinctive theoretical orientation. This freedom is traceable, in part, to his having done much of the metatheoretical groundwork in earlier works. Furthermore, most of the new
metatheoretical work is relegated to the so-called fourth volume of *Capital*,
published under the title *Theories of Surplus Value* (Marx, 1862–63/1963, 1862–
63/1968). *Theories* is composed of many extracts from the work of the major
political economists (for example, Smith, Ricardo) as well as critical analyses
of them by Marx. In sum, it is safe to say that Marx was, largely, a meta-
theorist, perhaps the *most* metatheoretical of all classical sociological theorists.

Talcott Parsons's *The Structure of Social Action* (1937) may be the purest
example (except, perhaps, for the work of the neo-Parsonian, Jeffrey Alexander) of M_P. Most of *The Structure of Social Action* is devoted to a serious study
of the work of Alfred Marshall, Vilfredo Pareto, Emile Durkheim, and Max
Weber.[4] And Parsons uses that metatheoretical work to begin to lay out his
own action theory. The roots of Parsons's work lie not in the empirical world
but in what, in his view, were the convergent ideas of the theorists mentioned
above.

In fact, Parsons was explicit about his M_P approach. He sees *The Structure
of Social Action* as an "*empirical* monograph" and states that the phenomena
under scrutiny "happen to be the theories that certain writers have held about
other phenomena . . . the theories that have been discussed [are] just as much
a question of fact as any other, to be verified by the same method, that of
observation. The facts in this case have reference to the published works of
these writers" (1949:697). But Parsons is not content simply to analyze extant
theories; his study "has also done some explicit theorizing on its own
account" (1949:697). In the preface to the second edition of *The Structure of
Social Action* Parsons makes a similar point in reflecting on the work over a
decade after its publication: "This was a convenient vehicle for the clarification
of problems and concepts, of implications and interrelations. It was a means
of taking stock of the theoretical resources at our disposal. . . . The clarification gained from this stocktaking has opened up possibilities for further theoretical development of sufficient scope so that its impetus is as yet by no
means exhausted" (1949:B).

Only two years after the publication of the second edition of *The Structure
of Social Action*, Parsons and Shils (with the assistance of Olds) make the
metatheoretical roots of the revised theory of action perfectly clear. In *Toward
a General Theory of Action* (1951) they state in the very first footnote, which
follows the first four words of text:

> The present exposition of the theory of action represents in one major respect a
> revision and extension of the position stated in Parsons, *The Structure of Social Action*

---

[4] It also involves studies of a variety of philosophical traditions—for example, utilitarianism,
positivism, empiricism.

> . . . particularly in the light of psychoanalytic theory, of developments in behavior psychology, and of developments in the anthropological analysis of culture.
>
> (Parsons and Shils, 1951:53)

Between the 1937 publication of *The Structure of Social Action* and the early 1950s' works on the theory of action, Parsons amended and changed his theoretical orientation. It *may* be that those changes were the result of changes in the social world, but it is *certainly* the case that Parsons's theoretical ideas changed as he metatheoretically engaged the ideas of a variety of theorists over the years, including the psychiatrist Sigmund Freud,[5] the anthropologist Franz Boas,[6] the behaviorist Edward Tolman, and so on. Above all, Parsons elaborated his theory on the basis of a metatheoretical reanalysis of his own work as well as of the criticisms of that work. Thus, for example, late in his life Parsons (1966, 1971) shifted to evolutionary theory on the basis of his own analysis of the shortcomings of his earlier work as pointed out by the critics.[7] Parsons makes this clear in one of his earlier works on change:

> I should address myself to the problem of social change. I am very happy to do this, both because of the intrinsic importance of the subject and because its place in my own work has been the subject of considerable concern, even controversy. Furthermore, I have been devoting more explicit attention to this field recently than before, and some of the things I have to say are, I think, new.
>
> (Parsons, 1961:219)

While we have singled out Marx and Parsons for detailed discussion, the fact is that virtually all classical (and contemporary) theorists were metatheorists, and, more specifically, they practiced M$_P$.

There are a number of examples of the third type of metatheorizing, M$_O$. They include Wallace's (1988) "disciplinary matrix," Ritzer's (1979, 1981a) "integrated sociological paradigm" (see below), Furfey's (1953/1965) positivistic metasociology, Gross's (1961) "neodialectical" metasociology, Alexander's (1982) "general theoretical logic for sociology" and Lehman's (1988) presuppositions and models of the state (derived from Alexander).

Wallace's and Ritzer's works fit best into the category of M$_O$ because their transcendent perspectives are derived from a careful study of sociological theory. In contrast, the works of Furfey and Gross posit their overarching orientations as preceding and informing sociological theory. Finally, the works of Alexander and Lehman represent mixed types. Their adoption of a multi-

---

[5] In fact, in the preface to the second edition of *The Structure of Social Action*, Parsons discusses the need to do a "full-dress analysis of Freud's theoretical development seen in the context of the 'theory of social action' " (1949).

[6] However, Parsons does not see Boas as being "of comparable *theoretical* stature" to Freud, Durkheim, or the other major thinkers analyzed by him (1949).

[7] In terms of his metatheoretical work, I have not even mentioned Parsons's forays into M$_U$ in his frequent essays on the general state of sociological theory, such as "The Prospects of Sociological Theory" (1954a) and "The Present Position and Prospects of Systematic Theory in Sociology" (1954b). Also worth mentioning is Parsons's role as the initial editor of the original *American Sociologist*, which was founded as a major outlet for metasociological work.

disciplinary approach precedes the study of theory, while their focus on action and order is derived more from an M_O approach. In spite of these differences, all six works produce overarching theoretical perspectives.

The three varieties of metatheory are ideal types. In actual cases there is often considerable overlap in the objectives of metatheoretical works. Nevertheless, those who do one type of metatheorizing tend to be less interested in achieving the objectives of the other two types. Of course, there are sociologists who at one time or another have done all three types of metatheorizing. For example, Alexander (1982–1983) creates overarching perspectives (M_O) in the first volume of *Theoretical Logic in Sociology*, uses them in the next three volumes to achieve a better understanding (M_U) of the classic theorists, and more recently has sought to help create neofunctionalism (M_P) as a theoretical successor to structural functionalism (Alexander, 1985b; Alexander and Colomy, 1990).

The Gains From Metatheorizing

Metatheorizing provides three absolutely essential aids to sociological theory. First, M_U offers systematic methods of understanding, evaluating, criticizing, and improving extant theories. Second, M_P is one of several important bases for creating new theory. Third, through M_O, theorists (as well as practitioners and researchers) are provided with useful overarching theoretical perspectives. Let us look at each of the three functions in turn.

It is the distinctive responsibility of metatheorizing (M_U) to deepen the level of understanding of all sociological theories. While many sociologists read theory, often very casually, metatheorists systematically study theory and do detailed (often comparative) studies of an array of sociological theories. Metatheorists have at their disposal an arsenal of tools that allows them to uncover many things about sociological theory that would not be visible to the more casual student of theory. Beyond facilitating deeper comprehension of theory, systematic metatheorizing allows them to more adequately evaluate and critically analyze extant theories. Finally, and perhaps most importantly, metatheorists are better able to uncover ways of improving specific theories as well as theory in general.

The use of M_U tools allow metatheorists to uncover interesting, important, and sometimes surprising things about theories and theorists. For example, M_U tools used in comparative analyses show that sociological theory has moved through four major periods over the last four decades (Ritzer, forthcoming b). The paradigm concept allows us to describe the 1960s as multiparadigmatic, with theoretical divisions and conflicts among and within paradigms (Ritzer, 1975a, 1975b). The micro-macro distinction pointed to both the rise of microsociological theories in the 1970s (Ritzer, 1985) and the theoretical efforts at micro-macro synthesis in the 1980s (Ritzer, 1990a). The latter observations have led to the identification of the emergence of a much wider array of synthetic efforts as we enter the 1990s (Ritzer, 1990b).

These analyses, taken together, do *not* constitute a history of recent sociological theory, but they do represent a metatheoretical analysis of that history. They are not offered as an alternative to a history of sociological theory. Indeed, the combination of metatheoretical and more straightforward historical analyses would greatly increase our level of understanding of theory.

Not only does M_U improve the understanding of sociological theory, but it allows metatheorists to systematically evaluate and criticize theories. For example, the micro-macro conceptualization used in a critical examination (Ritzer, 1985) of Randall Collins's (1981a, 1981b) work on interaction ritual chains indicated that the work erred on the side of micro reductionism. Collins's (1988) later work has tried to rectify this imbalance by giving greater importance to macro phenomena.

M_U analyses not only permit metatheorists to better understand and evaluate theories but also can directly help to improve sociological theories. For example, the metatheoretical analysis of the current movement toward theoretical syntheses suggests that sociological theory would be enhanced if *some* supporters of virtually all sociological theories were to move away from narrow adherence to a specific theory or level of analysis. (However, this is not meant to imply that all theorists should move toward synthesis. There is utility in narrower theoretical perspectives.) The model might be, for example, structural functionalism, which is being enhanced as thinkers (Alexander, 1985b; Alexander and Colomy, 1990) seek to integrate insights from a range of other theoretical perspectives (for example, conflict theory, ethnomethodology). At the same time, the traditional focus of structural functionalism on macro-level phenomena (social structure, culture) is being extended to include greater interest in micro-level phenomena. This two-pronged extension is transforming structural functionalism into neofunctionalism and greatly enhancing its scope and power. Out of this development we may see either the triumph of a more integrative neofunctionalism or a bifurcation in which structural functionalism remains committed to a macro-level focus and neofunctionalism becomes a distinctive, integrative perspective. Similar kinds of things are occurring at the frontiers of many other theoretical perspectives (for example, symbolic interactionism [Fine, 1990]).

The second major contribution of metatheorizing is the creation of new theory. While this is the distinctive goal of M_P, theory creation also results from M_U. The dividing line between an enhanced theory and a new theory is often quite indistinct. For example, we have argued that Alexander, in part through M_U analysis, has embarked on an effort to enhance structural functionalism. However, there are those (for example, Turner and Maryanski, 1988) who see so many differences between traditional structural functionalism and neofunctionalism that the latter might be considered a new theory.

It is also the case that M_O works can lead to the creation of new theory. Such overarching perspectives as positivism, antipositivism, and postpositivism have helped generate a wide range of theories over the years. Theories like structural functionalism and exchange theory have clear roots in positivism, while many varieties of neo-Marxian theory and phenomenology are more rooted in antipositivistic overarching perspectives. Postpositivism may be seen at the base of postmodernism, poststructuralism, and perhaps even neofunctionalism.

New theory creation is *the* function of M_P. Methatheoretical reflection on the work of other theorists has been, continues to be, and should be an important source of new theory. One of the most important functions of metatheorizing, especially M_P, for the discipline of sociology is the production of a steady and continuing supply of new theory.

The third major function of metatheorizing is the production of overarching theoretical perspectives. While this is the distinctive role of M_O, it is possible for M_U and M_P to function in similar ways. For example, M_U work (Ritzer, 1975a) on the paradigmatic structure of sociology led to the generation of a transcendent orientation, the integrated sociological paradigm (Ritzer, 1981a). M_O, however, is specifically directed toward the generation of overarching perspectives. In an era characterized by a focus on narrow syntheses of theories and levels of analysis (as desirable as such work is), it is important that at least some sociologists produce such transcendent perspectives (see Antonio, 1990; Kellner, 1990). These overarching perspectives are essential in preventing us from losing sight of the field's parameters.

The Critics of Metatheorizing

Until the mid-1980s, the most visible aspects of metatheorizing may have been the criticisms, often quite severe, that were leveled at it (R. Collins, 1986; Skocpol, 1986; J. Turner, 1985a, 1986; for a review and analysis of these critiques, see Ritzer, 1988). This a rare event in academic history—the appearance of highly visible and influential critiques *before* the overt emergence of the field being attacked. What this meant, of course, is that the field, at least in an inchoate state, actually was there all the time. Much metatheoretical work had been done under a wide range of other headings—"sociology of sociology," "sociology of science," "sociology of knowledge," "history of sociology"— and, most notably, as an integral part of sociological theory. In fact, most of the criticisms have been made by closet metatheoreticians (for example, R. Collins, Skocpol, J. Turner) who may not have had a clear conception of what they were criticizing. Let us look at the three major critiques of sociological metatheorizing.

Jonathan Turner is critical of metatheory largely on pragmatic grounds because, in his view, it "often gets bogged down in weighty philosophical matters and immobilizes theory building . . . meta-theory often stymies as much as stimulates theoretical activity because it embroils theorists in inherently unresolvable and always debatable controversies" (1986:10; see also J. Turner 1985a). Later, Turner describes metatheory as "interesting but counterproductive" and contends that those who propound it "never get around to developing theory" (1986:26).

In a review of a book (Alford and Friedland, 1985) on political sociology, Theda Skocpol (1986) makes it clear that in her view what is good and useful in that subfield is substantive theory and research. She describes the Alford and Friedland work, pejoratively, as "five hundred pages of nothing but metatheory" (Skocpol, 1986:10). She attacks the authors for "pigeonholing" the work of political sociologists, for arguing for the need for an integrated theory that draws from every pigeonhole but never specifies what it is about, for arguing that different types of approaches fit best at different levels of analysis, and for ignoring the fact that the best work in political sociology has dealt with the interrelations among such levels. She hopes that Alford and Friedland will return to substantive work in political sociology, but in the meantime "may the good lord protect other political sociologists from wandering into the dead end of metatheory" (Skocpol, 1986:11–12). The use of the phrase "dead end" in this sentence, as well as in the title of her review, implies clearly that Skocpol sees *no* productive role for metatheory within sociology.

Perhaps the most interesting critique of metatheory comes from Randall Collins (1986). At first, Collins associates metatheory with mindless antipositivism. However, he quickly moves to a much broader critique:

> It is not surprising to me that metatheory does not go anywhere; it is basically a reflexive specialty, capable about making comments on other fields but dependent on intellectual life elsewhere that it can formalize and ideologize . . or critique. That is why so much of the intellectual work of today consists of commentaries on works of the past rather than constructions that are creative in their own right.
>
> (R. Collins, 1986:1343)

In spite of his critique of metatheory, Collins proceeds to do what he condemns: he undertakes a metatheoretical analysis of a variety of works of the (recent) past.

Rather than having the desired effect of retarding the development of metatheorizing in sociology, critiques like those above have had the opposite effect, galvanizing metatheorists and leading to a flowering of metatheoretical work.

The Current Explosion of Interest in Metatheorizing

By the idea of a boom in metatheorizing we simply mean that there is a great increase in the quantity of work that is *explicitly* and *self-consciously* metatheoretical. The most objective evidence comes from a study by Fuhrman and Snizek (1990) of publications over the last decade which indicates strong and growing interest in metatheorizing in sociology. A very large number of the references in their paper are to recently published, or soon-to-be-published, works. Many other metatheoretical works have appeared in the brief time since that study was completed (for example, Berger, Wagner, and Zelditch, 1989; J. Turner, 1989a). This growth is notable in the journal *Sociological Theory*, which has devoted increasing space to essays that are explicitly metatheoretical (for example, Fararo, 1989; Levine, 1989; Ritzer, 1988). In addition, a number of recent (and forthcoming books) have also been overtly metatheoretical (Fiske and Shweder, 1986; Osterberg, 1988; Ritzer, 1991; J. Turner, 1989b) and many, perhaps even most, other books in sociological theory are implicitly metatheoretical. In March 1990, *Sociological Forum* devoted a special mini-issue to metatheorizing in sociology (Ritzer, 1990c), and in 1992 Sage will publish a book devoted to studies in metatheorizing (Ritzer, forthcoming c). Beyond this is a whole, and seemingly expanding, range of works that have dealt with more specific metatheoretical issues such as the micro-macro linkage (Alexander et al., 1987; R. Collins, 1981a, 1981b, 1988; Ritzer, 1990a), the relationship between agency and structure (Archer, 1982, 1988; Bernstein, 1971; Giddens, 1984), and levels of social analysis (Ritzer, 1989; Wiley, 1988, 1989). Although it is possible that all this represents a peak in metatheorizing in sociology, there are many reasons to believe that it more likely represents the takeoff point for a wide variety, and an increasing number, of explicitly metatheoretical works in sociology.

Given this overview, it is now time to turn to the specific metatheoretical approach that undergirds this book. As will become clear, it involves a combination of M_U and M_O. We begin with a brief review of the work of Thomas Kuhn, and then we examine my (M_U) analysis of sociology's multiple paradigms. Finally, we review the metatheoretical tool—the integrated sociological paradigm (M_O)—that is the source of the levels of analysis used to analyze sociological theories throughout this book.

THE IDEAS OF THOMAS KUHN

In 1962 the philosopher of science Thomas Kuhn published a rather slim volume entitled *The Structure of Scientific Revolutions*. Because this work grew out of philosophy, it appeared fated to a marginal status within sociology. This seemed especially likely because it focused on the hard sciences (physics, for example) and had little directly to say about the social sciences. However, the theses of the book proved extremely interesting to people in a wide range of fields (for example, Hollinger, 1980, in history; Searle, 1972, in linguistics; Stanfield, 1974, in economics), and to none was it more important than to sociologists. In 1970 Robert Friedrichs published the first important work from a Kuhnian perspective, *A Sociology of Sociology*. Since then there has been a steady stream of work from this perspective (Eckberg and Hill, 1979; Effrat, 1972; Eisenstadt and Curelaru, 1976; Falk and Zhao, 1989, 1990; Friedrichs, 1972a; Greisman, 1986; Lodahl and Gordon, 1972; Phillips, 1973, 1975; Quadagno, 1979; Ritzer, 1975a, 1975b, 1981b; Rosenberg, 1989; Snizek, 1976; Snizek et al., 1979). There is little doubt that Kuhnian theory is an important variety of M_U, but what exactly is Kuhn's approach?

One of Kuhn's goals in *The Structure of Scientific Revolutions* was to challenge commonly held assumptions about the way in which science changes. In the view of most laypeople and many scientists, science advances in a cumulative manner, with each advance building inexorably on all that preceded it. Science has achieved its present state through slow and steady increments of knowledge. It will advance to even greater heights in the future. This conception of science was enunciated by the physicist Sir Isaac Newton, who said, "If I have seen further, it is because I stood on the shoulders of giants." But Kuhn regarded this conception of cumulative scientific development as a myth and sought to debunk it.

Kuhn acknowledged that accumulation plays some role in the advance of science, but the truly major changes come about as a result of revolutions. Kuhn offered a theory of how major changes in science occur. He saw a science at any given time as dominated by a specific *paradigm* (defined for the moment as a fundamental image of the science's subject matter). *Normal science* is a period of accumulation of knowledge in which scientists work to expand the reigning paradigm. Such scientific work inevitably spawns *anomalies,* or findings that cannot be explained by the reigning paradigm. A *crisis* stage occurs if these anomalies mount, and this crisis may ultimately end in a scientific revolution. The reigning paradigm is overthrown as a new one takes its place at the center of the science. A new dominant paradigm is born, and the stage is set for the cycle to repeat itself. Kuhn's theory can be depicted diagrammatically:

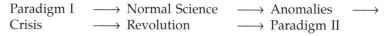

Paradigm I $\longrightarrow$ Normal Science $\longrightarrow$ Anomalies $\longrightarrow$
Crisis $\longrightarrow$ Revolution $\longrightarrow$ Paradigm II

It is during periods of revolution that the truly great changes in science take place. This view clearly places Kuhn at odds with most conceptions of scientific development.

The key concept in Kuhn's approach, as well as in this Appendix, is the paradigm. Unfortunately, Kuhn is vague on what he means by a paradigm. According to Margaret Masterman (1970), he used it in at least twenty-one different ways. But we will employ a definition of *paradigm* that we feel is true to the sense and spirit of his early work.

A paradigm serves to differentiate one scientific community from another. It can be used to differentiate physics from chemistry or sociology from psychology. These fields have different paradigms. It can also be used to differentiate between different historical stages in the development of a science. The paradigm that dominated physics in the nineteenth century is different from the one that dominated it in the early twentieth century. There is a third usage of the paradigm concept, and it is the one that is most useful to us here. Paradigms can differentiate among cognitive groupings *within* the same science. Contemporary psychoanalysis, for example, is differentiated into Freudian, Jungian, and Horneyian paradigms (among others)—that is, there are *multiple paradigms* in psychoanalysis—and the same is true of sociology and of most other fields.

We can now offer a definition of *paradigm* that we feel is true to the sense of Kuhn's original work:

A paradigm is a fundamental image of the subject matter within a science. It serves to define what should be studied, what questions should be asked, how they should be asked, and what rules should be followed in interpreting the answers obtained. The paradigm is the broadest unit of consensus within a science and serves to differentiate one scientific community (*or subcommunity*) from another. It subsumes, defines, and interrelates the exemplars, *theories* [italics added], and methods and instruments that exist within it.

(Ritzer, 1975a:7)

With this definition we can begin to see the relationship between paradigms and theories. *Theories are only part of larger paradigms.* To put it another way, a paradigm may encompass two or more *theories,* as well as different *images* of the subject matter, *methods* (and instruments), and *exemplars* (specific pieces of scientific work that stand as a model for all of those who follow). An objective of this Appendix will be to identify the basic paradigms in sociology.

SOCIOLOGY: A MULTIPLE-PARADIGM SCIENCE

The idea that sociology is a multiple-paradigm science has received some empirical support (Lodahl and Gordon, 1972), but most of the analyses of the paradigmatic status of sociology have been conceptual.

In the earliest systematic application of Kuhnian ideas to sociology, Robert Friedrichs (1970) presented two different images of the paradigmatic status of sociology, but both affirmed the idea that sociology was a multiple-paradigm science. At one level, Friedrichs argued that despite greater consensus in the past, sociology is split largely between a *system* paradigm (emphasizing societal integration and consensus) and a *conflict* paradigm (emphasizing societal disintegration and coercion), with a wide array of other perspectives as potential paradigms. These paradigms are based on the fundamental images of the subject matter of sociology, but Friedrichs thinks of them as being of secondary importance to two other paradigms that focus on sociologists' images of themselves as scientific agents. These are the *prophetic* and the *priestly* paradigms. Whereas prophetic sociologists perceive themselves as agents of social change, priestly sociologists conceive of themselves as "value-free" scientists. The crucial point for our purposes is that, whether Friedrichs looks at images of the subject matter or images of the sociologists themselves, he concludes that sociology is a multiple-paradigm science.

Andrew Effrat (1972) clearly aligned himself with those who see sociology as a multiple-paradigm science, although he mistook more specific theories for paradigms. Effrat ended up with a cumbersome list of paradigms, including Marxian, Freudian, Durkheimian, Weberian, phenomenological, ethnomethodological, symbolic interactionist, and exchange theory. As we will see, all these are best viewed as theoretical components of sociology's multiple paradigms, but Effrat was on the right track in his multiparadigmatic image of sociology.

S. N. Eisenstadt and M. Curelaru (1976) differentiated among discrete, closed-system, and open-system paradigms. They framed their paradigms in terms of the historical development of the field. The earliest is the *discrete paradigm,* in which the focus was on separate concrete entities such as ecological properties, size of groups, or racial and psychological characteristics. Given this image of the world as a set of isolated units, those who operated within this paradigm had difficulty dealing with such relational issues as emergence, innovation, and creativity. This early and primitive paradigm left only a small mark on the development of sociology and persists today in only isolated domains. It was replaced, historically, by the *closed-system model,* whose supporters saw society as composed of separate but interrelated elements. Those who operated within this paradigm tended to see one element as dominant over the others. In Eisenstadt and Curelaru's view (but not this author's), Marx was operating within this paradigm with his emphasis on the economic sector. This paradigm was replaced, in turn, by the *open-system model,* which focuses on the "internal systemic dynamics, interconnections, and continuous feedback processes among the components of the social order" (Eisenstadt and Curelaru, 1976:92). Although the evolution of these paradigms follows "no simple, natural, chronological trend," and there is "considerable temporal and operative overlapping of the several approaches," there is in Eisenstadt and Curelaru's view a long-term trend toward the open-system paradigm.

Charles Lemert argued that rather than being composed of multiple paradigms, sociology is unified in its *homocentrism,* "the peculiarly nineteenth-century idea which holds that *man* is the measure of all things" (1979:13). Although it is true that sociology is person-centered, it is questionable whether this is really evidence that sociology is unified. One equally plausible conclusion is that there are multiple paradigms in sociology and that the sources of their differences are their varied interpretations *of* humankind. In the author's view, the ideas of homocentrism and multiple paradigms are not mutually exclusive.

Lemert concluded that in spite of their homocentrism, there are important paradigmatic differences among the various modes of sociological discourse. He differentiated among them on a linguistic basis. The first is *lexical sociology,* which is primarily technical in orientation. Second is *semantical sociology,* which focuses on the interpretation of meaning that only people (not animals) are capable of producing. Finally, there is *syntactical sociology,* which is much more political in its orientation to sociology. Thus, for Lemert, there *are* multiple paradigms, at least in contemporary sociology.

Major Sociological Paradigms

Although all the preceding perspectives have some degree of utility, it is my own earlier work on the paradigmatic status of sociology (Ritzer, 1975a, 1975b, 1980) that provides the basis for the metatheoretical perspective that has guided the analysis of classical sociological theory throughout this book. Like most of those discussed above, I conceive of sociology as a multiple-paradigm science. In my view, there are *three* paradigms that dominate sociology, with several others having the potential to achieve paradigmatic status. I label the three paradigms the *social-facts, social-definition,* and *social-behavior* paradigms. Each paradigm is analyzed in terms of the four components of a paradigm outlined in the definition discussed earlier.

The Social-Facts Paradigm

1 *Exemplar:* The model for social factists is the work of Emile Durkheim, particularly *The Rules of Sociological Method* and *Suicide.*
2 *Image of the subject matter:* Social factists focus on what Durkheim termed social facts, or large-scale social structures and institutions. Those who subscribe to the social-facts paradigm focus not only on these phenomena but on their effect on individual thought and action.
3 *Methods:* Social factists are more likely than those who subscribe to the other paradigms to use the interview-questionnaire[8] and historical-comparative methods.
4 *Theories:* The social-facts paradigm encompasses a number of theoretical perspectives. *Structural-functional* theorists tend to see social facts as neatly interrelated and order as maintained by general consensus. *Conflict* theorists tend to emphasize disorder among social facts as well as the notion that order is maintained by coercive forces in society. Although structural functionalism and conflict theory are the dominant theories in this paradigm, there are others, including *systems* theory.

The Social-Definition Paradigm

1 *Exemplar:* To social definitionists, the unifying model is Max Weber's work on social action.
2 *Image of the subject matter:* Weber's work helped lead to an interest among social definitionists in the way actors define their social situations and the effect of these definitions on ensuing action and interaction.
3 *Methods:* Social definitionists, although they are most likely to use the interview-questionnaire method, are more likely to use the observation method than those in any other paradigm. In other words, observation is the distinctive methodology of social definitionists.
4 *Theories:* There are a wide number of theories that can be included within social definitionism: *action theory, symbolic interactionism, phenomenology, ethnomethodology,* and *existentialism.*

The Social-Behavior Paradigm

1 *Exemplar:* The model for sociologists who accept the social-behavior paradigm is the work of the psychologist B. F. Skinner.

---

[8] William Snizek (1976) has shown that the interview-questionnaire is dominant in *all* paradigms.

2 *Image of the subject matter:* The subject matter of sociology to social behaviorists is the unthinking *behavior* of individuals. Of particular interest are the rewards that elicit desirable behaviors and the punishments that inhibit undesirable behaviors.

3 *Methods:* The distinctive method of social behaviorism is the experiment.

4 *Theories:* Two theoretical approaches in sociology can be included under the heading "social behaviorism." The first is *behavioral sociology,* which is very close to pure psychological behaviorism, and the second, and much more important, is *exchange theory.*[9]

TOWARD A MORE INTEGRATED SOCIOLOGICAL PARADIGM

In addition to detailing the nature of sociology's multiple paradigms, I also sought in my earlier work to make the case for more paradigmatic integration in sociology. Although there is reason for extant paradigms to continue to exist, there is also a need for a more integrated paradigm. Extant paradigms tend to be one-sided, focusing on specific levels of social analysis while paying little or no attention to the others. This is reflected in the social factists' concern with macro structures; the social definitionists' concern with action, interaction, and the social construction of reality; and the social behaviorists' concern with behavior. It is this kind of one-sidedness that has led to what I perceive to be a growing interest in a more integrated approach among a wide range of sociologists (Ritzer, forthcoming b). (This is but part of what I see as a growing interest in integration within and even among many social sciences; see especially Mitroff and Kilmann, 1978.) For example, Robert Merton, representing social factism, saw it and social definitionism as mutually enriching, as "opposed to one another in about the same sense as ham is opposed to eggs: they are perceptively different but mutually enriching" (1975:30). Among social definitionists, Hugh Mehan and Houston Wood argue that one theoretical component of social definitionism (ethnomethodology) accepts at least one basic tenet of social factism, "the reality of an external and constraining world" (1975:180). Among social behaviorists, Arthur Staats (1976) seeks to integrate creative mental processes (a key element of social definitionism) with traditional behaviorism. Calls for a more integrated paradigm are clearly important, but what is necessary is an effort to delineate what such a paradigm might look like.

The key to an integrated paradigm is the notion of *levels* of social analysis (Ritzer, 1979, 1981a). As the reader is well aware, *the social world is not really divided into levels.* In fact, social reality is best viewed as an enormous variety of social phenomena that are involved in continuing interaction and change. Individuals, groups, families, bureaucracies, the polity, and numerous other highly diverse social phenomena represent the bewildering array of phenom-

---

[9] Analyses of Ritzer's paradigm schema include Eckberg and Hill (1979), Friedheim (1979), Harper, Sylvester, and Walczak (1980), Snizek (1976), and Staats (1976).

ena that make up the social world. It is extremely difficult to get a handle on such a large number of wide-ranging and mutually interpenetrating social phenomena. Some sort of conceptual schema is clearly needed, and sociologists have developed a number of such schema in an effort to deal with the social world. The idea of levels of social analysis employed here should be seen as but one of a large number of such schema that can be, and have been, used for purposes of dealing with the complexities of the social world.

Levels of Social Analysis: A Review of the Literature

Although the idea of levels is implicit in much of sociology, it has received relatively little explicit attention. In concentrating on levels here, we are doing little more than making explicit what has been implicit in sociology.

The close of this Appendix will offer a conceptualization of the major levels of social analysis. To understand adequately that conceptualization, some preliminary differentiations must be made. As will be seen, two continua of social reality are useful in developing the major levels of the social world. The first is the *microscopic-macroscopic* continuum. Thinking of the social world as being made up of a series of entities ranging from those large in scale to those small in scale is relatively easy, because it is so familiar. Most people in their day-to-day lives conceive of the social world in these terms. In the academic world, a number of thinkers have worked with a micro-macro continuum (including Alexander et al., 1987; Blalock and Wilken, 1979; Bosserman, 1968; Edel, 1959; Gurvitch, 1964; Johnson, 1981; Korenbaum, 1964; Ritzer, 1990a; Wagner, 1964). For laypeople and academics alike, the continuum is based on the simple idea that social phenomena vary greatly in size. At the macro end of the continuum are such large-scale social phenomena as groups of societies (for example, the capitalist and socialist world systems), societies, and cultures. At the micro end are individual actors and their thoughts and actions. In between are a wide range of groups, collectivities, social classes, and organizations. We have little difficulty recognizing these distinctions and thinking of the world in micro-macro terms. There are no clear dividing lines between the micro social units and the macro units. Instead, there is a continuum ranging from the micro to the macro ends.

The second continuum is the *objective-subjective* dimension of social analysis. At each end of the micro-macro continuum we can differentiate between objective and subjective components. At the micro, or individual, level, there are the subjective mental processes of an actor and the objective patterns of action and interaction in which he or she engages. *Subjective* here refers to something that occurs solely in the realm of ideas, whereas *objective* relates to real, material events. This same differentiation is also found at the macro end of the continuum. A society is made up of both objective structures, such as governments, bureaucracies, and laws, and subjective phenomena, such as norms and values. The objective-subjective continuum is more complicated than the micro-macro continuum, and it is even, as we will see, more complicated than is implied in this introduction. To try to clarify matters and to work toward greater complexity, let us look at a concrete example as well as at the work of a number of sociologists on the objective-subjective continuum.

Consider the purchase of a new automobile. At the micro-subjective level, we would focus on the attitudes and orientations of the individual buyer that influence the kind of car to be purchased. But—and this is the key distinction between the micro-subjective and micro-objective levels of analysis—the buyer may desire (subjective state) a sports car and actually buy (objective act) an economy compact. Some sociologists are interested in subjective mental states, others in objective acts. In many cases it is useful and important to understand the interplay between these two micro levels.

The macro level also has subjective and objective dimensions. For many years most Americans shared a set of preferences for larger and ever more powerful cars. This was a subjective set of attitudes shared by a large number of people. Then a series of objective changes at the societal level had an impact on these shared attitudes. OPEC was formed, oil deliveries to the United States were curtailed, and the government played a more active role in oil-related matters. These and other macro-structural changes led to changes in the shared preferences of large numbers of people. Almost overnight many people came to prize small, fuel-efficient automobiles. This change, in turn, led to a massive alteration in the structure of the American automobile companies. Also affected were the thoughts and actions of many individual Americans. Thus, the purchase of a car, as well as most other mundane and extraordinary activities, involves the complex interaction of the micro-macro and objective-subjective components of social life.

Now let us turn to the work of several sociologists on the objective-subjective continuum. As we saw in Chapters 1 and 5, an important influence on Karl Marx was German idealism, particularly the work of G. W. F. Hegel. The Hegelian dialectic was a subjective process taking place within the realm of ideas. Although affected by this view, Marx and, before him, the Young Hegelians, were dissatisfied with the dialectic because it was not rooted in the objective, material world. Marx, building on the work of Ludwig Feuerbach and others, sought to extend the dialectic to the material world. On the one hand, this meant that he was concerned with real, sentient actors rather than idea systems. On the other hand, he came to focus on the objective structures of capitalist society, primarily the economic structure. Marx became increasingly interested in the real material structures of capitalism and the contradictions that exist among and within them. This is not to say that Marx lost sight of subjective ideas; in fact, notions of false and class consciousness play a key role in his work. It is the materialism-idealism split, as manifest in the work of Marx and others, that is one of the major philosophical roots of the objective-subjective continuum in modern sociology.

We can also find this continuum, although in a different form, in the work of Emile Durkheim (Chapter 6). In his classic work on methodology, Durkheim differentiated between material (objective) and nonmaterial (subjective) social facts. In *Suicide,* Durkheim said, "The social fact is sometimes materialized as to become an element of the external world" (1897/1951:313). He discussed architecture and law as two examples of material (objective) social facts. However, most of Durkheim's work emphasizes nonmaterial (subjective) social facts:

> Of course it is true that not all social consciousness achieves such externalization and materialization. Not all aesthetic spirit of a nation is embodied in the works it inspires; not all morality is formulated in clear precepts. The greater part is diffused. There is a large collective life which is at liberty; all sorts of currents come, go, circulate everywhere, cross and mingle in a thousand different ways, and just because they are constantly mobile are never crystallized in an objective form. Today a breath of sadness and discouragement descends on society: tomorrow, one of joyous confidence will uplift all hearts.
>
> (Durkheim, 1897/1951:315)

These social currents do not have material existence; they can exist only within the consciousness of individuals and between them. In *Suicide,* Durkheim concentrated on examples of this kind of social fact. He related differences in suicide rates to differences in social currents. For example, where there are strong currents of anomie (normlessness), we find high rates of anomic suicide. Social currents such as anomie, egoism, and altruism clearly do not have a material existence, although they may have a material effect by causing differences in suicide rates. Instead, they are intersubjective phenomena that can exist only in the consciousness of people.

Peter Blau (1960) has been in the forefront of those employing an objective-subjective continuum. His differentiation between institutions (subjective entities) and social structures (objective entities) is of this genre. He defined *subjective institutions* as "the common values and norms embodied in a culture or subculture" (Blau, 1960:178). Conversely, there are *social structures* that are "the networks of social relations in which processes of social interaction become organized and through which social positions of individuals and subgroups become differentiated" (Blau, 1960:178).

It can be argued that the objective-subjective continuum plays a crucial role in the thought of people like Marx, Durkheim, Blau, and many others. But there is a rather interesting problem in their use of the continuum: they employ it almost exclusively at the macroscopic level. However, it also can be applied at the microscopic level. Before giving an example of this, we need to underscore the point that we must deal not only with the microscopic-macroscopic and objective-subjective continua *but also with the interaction between them.*

One example of the use of the objective-subjective continuum at the microscopic level is an empirical study by Mary and Robert Jackman (1973) of what they called "objective and subjective social status." Their micro-subjective concern was "the individual's perception of his own position in the status hierarchy" (Jackman and Jackman, 1973:569). Micro subjectivity in this study involved the feelings, the perceptions, and the mental aspects of the actors' positions in the stratification system. These are related to various components of the micro-objective realm that include the actor's socioeconomic status, social contacts, amount of capital owned, ethnic group membership, or status as a breadwinner or a union member. Instead of dealing with actors' feelings, these dimensions involve the more objective characteristics of the individuals—the patterns of action and interaction in which they actually engage.

At a more general level, the microscopic aspect of the objective-subjective continuum is manifest in both the social-definition and social-behavior paradigms, as well as in the differences between them. Although both tend to focus on the micro-objective patterns of action and interaction, they split on the micro-subjective dimension. All the theoretical components of the social-definition paradigm (for example, symbolic interactionism, ethnomethodology, and phenomenology) share an interest in micro-subjectivity—the feelings and thoughts of actors. However, the social behaviorists reject the idea that it is necessary to study the micro-subjective components of social life. This is exemplified by B. F. Skinner's (1971) attack on what he called the idea of "autonomous man." To Skinner, we imply that people are autonomous when we attribute to them such ideas as feeling, minding, freedom, and dignity. People are held to possess some sort of inner core from which their actions emanate. They are able to initiate, originate, and create because of this inner core of micro-subjectivity. To Skinner, the idea that people have an inner, autonomous core is a mystical, metaphysical position of the kind that must be eliminated from the social sciences: "Autonomous man serves to explain only the things we are not yet able to explain in other ways. His existence depends on our ignorance, and he naturally loses status as we come to know more about behavior" (1971:12). Although we need to reject this kind of political diatribe, the key point is this: the microscopic level has *both* a subjective and an objective dimension.

Levels of Social Analysis: A Model

The most important thinker on the issue of levels of social analysis was the French sociologist Georges Gurvitch. While he did not use the same terms, Gurvitch (1964) had a sense of *both* micro-macro and objective-subjective continua. Even more important, he had a profound sense of how these two continua are related. To his credit, he also steadfastly refused to treat the two continua and their interrelationships as static tools but used them to underscore the dynamic quality of social life. But Gurvitch has one major difficulty: his analytical schema is extremely complex and cumbersome. The social world is very complicated, and in order to get a handle on it, we need relatively simple models.

The simple model we are seeking is formed out of the intersection of the two continua of levels of social reality discussed in the last several pages. The first, the microscopic-macroscopic continuum, can be depicted as in Figure A.1.

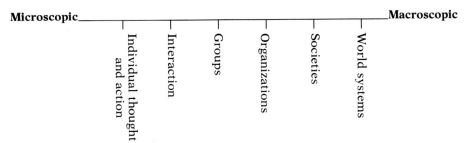

FIGURE A.1   The Microscopic-Macroscopic Continuum, with Identification of Some Key Points on the Continuum

The objective-subjective continuum presents greater problems, yet it is no less important than the micro-macro continuum. In general, an objective social phenomenon has a real, material existence. We can think of the following, among others, as objective social phenomena; actors, action, interaction, bureaucratic structures, law, and the state apparatus. It is possible to see, touch, or chart all these objective phenomena. However, there are social phenomena that exist *solely* in the realm of ideas; they have no material existence. These are sociological phenomena such as mental processes, the social construction of reality (Berger and Luckmann, 1967), norms, values, and many elements of culture. The problem with the objective-subjective continuum is that there are many phenomena in the middle that have *both* objective and subjective elements. The family, for example, has a real material existence as well as a series of subjective mutual understandings, norms, and values. Similarly, the polity is composed of objective laws and bureaucratic structures as well as subjective political norms and values. In fact, it is probably true that the vast majority are mixed types of social phenomena representing some combination of objective and subjective elements. Thus it is best to think of the objective-subjective continuum as two polar types with a series of variously mixed types in the middle. Some of these types may have more objective than subjective characteristics, while others may have the reverse combination. Figure A.2 shows the objective-subjective continuum.

Although these continua are interesting in themselves, the interrelationship of the two continua concerns us here. Figure A.3 is a schematic representation of the intersection of these two continua and the four major levels of social analysis derived from it.

The contention here is that an integrated sociological paradigm must deal with the four basic levels of social analysis identified in the figure and their interrelationships (for similar models, see Alexander, 1985a; Wiley, 1988). It must deal with macroscopic objective entities like bureaucracy, macro-subjective realities like values, micro-objective phenomena like patterns of interaction, and micro-subjective facts like the process of reality construction. We must remember that in the real world, all these gradually blend into the others as part of the larger social continuum, but we have made some artificial and

Objective ─── **Subjective**

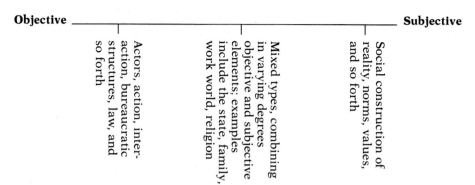

Actors, action, inter-action, bureaucratic structures, law, and so forth

Mixed types, combining in varying degrees objective and subjective elements; examples include the state, family, work world, religion

Social construction of reality, norms, values, and so forth

FIGURE A.2   The Objective-Subjective Continuum, with Identification of Some Mixed Types

rather arbitrary differentiations in order to be able to deal with social reality. These four levels of social analysis are posited for heuristic purposes and are not meant to be accurate depictions of the social world. An obvious question is how these four levels relate to the three paradigms discussed earlier as well as to the integrated paradigm. Figure A.4 relates the four levels to the three paradigms.

The social-facts paradigm focuses primarily on the macro-objective and macro-subjective levels. The social-definition paradigm is largely concerned with the micro-subjective world and that part of the micro-objective world that depends on mental processes (action). The social-behavior paradigm deals with that part of the micro-objective world that does not involve the minding process (behavior). Whereas the three extant paradigms cut across the levels of social reality horizontally, an integrated paradigm cuts across vertically. This depiction makes it clear why the integrated paradigm does not supersede the others. Although each of the three existing paradigms deals with a given

FIGURE A.3   Major Levels of Social Analysis

MACROSCOPIC

I. Macro-objective	II. Macro-subjective
Examples—society, law, bureaucracy, architecture, technology, and language	Examples—culture, norms, and values

OBJECTIVE ─── SUBJECTIVE

III. Micro-objective	IV. Micro-subjective
Examples—patterns of behavior, action, and interaction	Examples—the various facets of the social construction of reality

MICROSCOPIC

LEVELS OF SOCIAL ANALYSIS	SOCIOLOGICAL PARADIGMS	
Macro-subjective Macro-objective	Social Facts	Integrated Sociological Paradigm
Micro-subjective Micro-objective	Social Definition	
	Social Behavior	

FIGURE A.4   Levels of Social Analysis and the Major Sociological Paradigms

level or levels in great detail, the integrated paradigm deals with all levels but does not examine any given level in anything like the degree of intensity of the other paradigms. Thus the choice of a paradigm depends on the kind of question being asked. Not all sociological issues require an integrated approach, but it is certain that at least some do.

What has been outlined in the preceding pages is a model for the image of the subject matter of an integrated sociological paradigm. This sketch will need to be detailed more sharply in future years. But that is another task (see Ritzer, 1981a). The goal of this discussion is not the development of a new sociological paradigm but the delineation of an overarching metatheoretical schema (M_O) that allows us to analyze sociological theory in a coherent fashion. The model developed in Figure A.3 forms the basis for this analysis.

The work of the various classical theorists is analyzed using the four levels of social analysis depicted in Figure A.3. This figure provides us with a metatheoretical tool that can be used in the comparative analysis of sociological theorists. It enables us to analyze the concerns of a theorist and how they relate to the concerns of every other sociological theorist.

One thing to be avoided at all costs is the simple identification of a theorist with specific levels of social analysis. Although it is true, given the preceding description of the current paradigmatic status of sociology, that sociological theorists who adhere to a given paradigm tend to focus on a given level or levels of social analysis, it often does them an injustice simply to equate the breadth of their work with one or more levels. For example, Karl Marx is often thought of as focusing on macro-objective structures—in particular, on the economic structures of capitalism. But the use of the multiple levels of social analysis schema allows us to see that Marx had rich insights regarding all levels of social reality and their interrelationships. Similarly, symbolic interactionism is generally considered a perspective that deals with micro subjectivity and micro objectivity, but it is not devoid of insights into the macroscopic levels of social analysis (Maines, 1977).

It is also important for the reader to remember that the use of levels of social analysis to analyze the work of a theorist tends to break up the wholeness, the integrity, and the internal consistency of the work. Although the levels are useful for understanding a theory and comparing it to others, one must take pains to deal with the interrelationship among levels and with the theoretical totality of the work of an individual.

In sum, the metatheoretical schema outlined in Figure A.3, the development of which was traced in this Appendix, provides the basis for the analysis of the various sociological theorists discussed in this book.

REFERENCES

Abbott, Andrew
1988   *The System of Professions: An Essay on the Division of Labor.* Chicago:
            University of Chicago Press.

Aboulafia, Mitchell
1986   *The Mediating Self: Mead, Sartre, and Self-Determination.* New Haven: Yale
            University Press.

Abrams, Philip
1968   *The Origins of British Sociology: 1834–1914.* Chicago: University of
            Chicago Press.
1982   *Historical Sociology.* Ithaca, N.Y.: Cornell University Press.

Abrams, Philip, Deem, Rosemary, Finch, Janet, and Rock, Paul
1981   *Practice and Progress: British Sociology 1950–1980.* London: Allen and
            Unwin.

Alexander, Jeffrey
1978   "Formal and Substantive Voluntarism in the Work of Talcott Parsons:
            A Theoretical and Ideological Reinterpretation." *American Sociological
            Review* 43:177–198.
1981   "Revolution, Reaction, and Reform: The Change Theory of Parsons's
            Middle Period." *Sociological Inquiry* 51:267–280.
1982   *Theoretical Logic in Sociology.* Vol. 1, *Positivism, Presuppositions, and
            Current Controversies.* Berkeley: University of California Press.
1982–1983   *Theoretical Logic in Sociology.* 4 vols. Berkeley: University of California
            Press.
1983   *Theoretical Logic in Sociology.* Vol. 4, *The Modern Reconstruction of Classical
            Thought: Talcott Parsons.* Berkeley: University of California Press.
1984   "The Parsons Revival in German Sociology." In R. Collins (ed.),
            Sociological Theory—1984. San Francisco: Jossey-Bass: 394–412.
1985a   "The 'Individualist Dilemma' in Phenomenology and Interactionism."
            In S. N. Eisenstadt and H. J. Helle (eds.), *Macro-Sociological Theory.* Vol.
            1. London: Sage: 25–57.
1987   "Action and Its Environments." In J. Alexander et al. (eds.), *The Micro-
            Macro Link.* Berkeley: University of California Press: 289–318.

Alexander, Jeffrey (ed.)
1985b   *Neofunctionalism.* Beverly Hills, Calif.: Sage.
1988   *Durkheimian Sociology: Cultural Studies.* Cambridge: Cambridge
            University Press.

Alexander, Jeffrey, and Colomy, Paul
1985   "Toward Neo-Functionalism." *Sociological Theory* 3:11–23.
1990   "Neofunctionalism: Reconstructing a Theoretical Tradition." In G.
            Ritzer (ed.), *Frontiers of Social Theory: The New Syntheses.* New York:
            Columbia University Press: 33–67.

Alexander, Jeffrey, Giesen, Bernard, Munch, Richard, and Smelser, Neil J. (eds.)
1987   *The Micro-Macro Link.* Berkeley: University of California Press.
Alford, Robert R., and Friedland, Roger
1985   *Powers of Theory: Capitalism, the State, and Democracy.* Cambridge: Cambridge University Press.
Alt, John
1985–1986   "Reclaiming C. Wright Mills." *Telos* 66:6–43.
Althusser, Louis
1969   *For Marx.* Harmondsworth, Eng.: Penguin.
Amsterdamska, Olga
1985   "Institutions and Schools of Thought." *American Journal of Sociology* 91: 332–358.
Andreski, Stanislav
1971   *Herbert Spencer: Structure, Function and Evolution.* New York: Scribner's.
Antonio, Robert J.
1979   "Domination and Production in Bureaucracy." *American Sociological Review* 44:895–912.
1985   "Values, History and Science: The Metatheoretic Foundations of the Weber-Marx Dialogues." In R. J. Antonio and R. M. Glassman (eds.), *A Weber-Marx Dialogue.* Lawrence: University Press of Kansas: 20–43.
1990   "The Decline of the Grand Narrative of Emancipatory Modernity: Crisis or Renewal in Neo-Marxian Theory?" In G. Ritzer (ed.), *Frontiers of Social Theory: The New Syntheses.* New York: Columbia University Press: 88–116.
Antonio, Robert J., and Glassman, Ronald M. (eds.)
1985   *A Weber-Marx Dialogue.* Lawrence: University Press of Kansas.
Antonio, Robert, and Kellner, Douglas
forthcoming "Metatheorizing Historical Rupture: Classical Theory and Modernity." In G. Ritzer (ed.), *Metatheorizing.* Beverly Hills, Calif.: Sage.
Archer, Margaret S.
1982   "Morphogenesis versus Structuration: On Combining Structure and Action." *British Journal of Sociology* 33:455–483.
1988   *Culture and Agency: The Place of Culture in Social Theory.* Cambridge: Cambridge University Press.
Aron, Raymond
1965   *Main Currents in Sociological Thought,* Vol. 1. New York: Basic Books.
Arthur, C. J.
1970   "Editor's Introduction." In K. Marx and F. Engels, *The German Ideology.* Part 1. New York: International Publishers: 4–34.
Avineri, Shlomo
1968   *The Social and Political Thought of Karl Marx.* London: Cambridge University Press.
Bailey, Kenneth
1990   *Social Entropy Theory.* Albany: State University of New York Press.
Baldwin, Alfred
1961   "The Parsonian Theory of Personality." In M. Black (ed.), *The Social Theories of Talcott Parsons.* Englewood Cliffs, N.J.: Prentice-Hall: 153–190.

Baldwin, John
1986   *George Herbert Mead: A Unifying Theory for Sociology*. Newbury Park,
             Calif.: Sage.
Ball, Richard A.
1979   "The Dialectical Method: Its Application to Social Theory." *Social Forces*
             57:785–798.
Banner, Lois
1984   *Women in Modern America: A Brief History*. New York: Harcourt Brace
             Jovanovich.
Baran, Paul, and Sweezy, Paul M.
1966   *Monopoly Capital: An Essay on the American Economic and Social Order*.
             New York: Monthly Review Press.
Barbalet, J. M.
1983   *Marx's Construction of Social Theory*. London: Routledge and Kegan Paul.
Baudrillard, Jean
1983   *Simulations*. New York: Semiotext(e).
Baum, Rainer C., and Lechner, Frank J.
1981   "National Socialism: Toward an Action-Theoretical Perspective."
             Sociological Inquiry 51:281–308.
Bauman, Zygmunt
1976   *Towards a Critical Sociology: An Essay on Commonsense and Emancipation*.
             London: Routledge and Kegan Paul.
Bender, Frederick (ed.)
1970   *Karl Marx: The Essential Writings*. New York: Harper.
Benjamin, Jessica
1988   *The Bonds of Love: Psychoanalysis, Feminism, and the Problem of
             Domination*. New York: Pantheon.
Berger, Joseph, Wagner, David G., and Zelditch, Morris
1989   "Theory Growth, Social Processes and Metatheory." In J. Turner (ed.),
             Theory Building in Sociology: Assessing Theoretical Cumulation. Newbury
             Park, Calif.: Sage: 19–42.
Berger, Peter, and Luckmann, Thomas
1967   *The Social Construction of Reality*. Garden City, N.Y.: Anchor.
Berki, R. N.
1983   *Insight and Vision: The Problem of Communism in Marx's Thought*.
             London: J. M. Dent and Sons.
Berlin, Isaiah
1954   *Historical Inevitability*. London: Oxford University Press.
Bernstein, Richard J.
1971   *Praxis and Action: Contemporary Philosophies of Human Activity*.
             Philadelphia: University of Pennsylvania Press.
Besnard, Philippe (ed.)
1983a   *The Sociological Domain*. Cambridge: Cambridge University Press.
Besnard, Philippe
1983b   "The 'Année Sociologique' Team." In P. Besnard (ed.), *The Sociological
             Domain*. Cambridge: Cambridge University Press: 11–39.
Bierstedt, Robert
1963   "The Common Sense World of Alfred Schutz." *Social Research* 30:116–
             121.

1981 *American Sociological Theory: A Critical History.* New York: Academic Press.

Blalock, Hubert, and Wilken, Paul

1979 *Intergroup Processes: A Micro-Macro Perspective.* New York: Free Press.

Blankenship, Ralph L. (ed.)

1977 *Colleagues in Organization: The Social Construction of Professional Work.* New York: Wiley.

Blau, Peter

1960 "Structural Effects." *American Sociological Review* 25:178–193.

1964 *Exchange and Power in Social Life.* New York: Wiley.

Bleicher, Josef

1980 *Contemporary Hermeneutics: Hermeneutics as Method, Philosophy and Critique.* London: Routledge and Kegan Paul.

Bookman, Ann, and Morgen, Sandra (eds.)

1988 *Women and the Politics of Empowerment.* Philadelphia: Temple University Press.

Bosserman, Phillip

1968 *Dialectical Sociology: An Analysis of the Sociology of Georges Gurvitch.* Boston: Porter Sargent.

Bottomore, Tom

1984 *The Frankfurt School.* Chichester, Eng.: Ellis Horwood.

Bottomore, Tom, and Frisby, David (eds.)

1978 Introduction to the translation of Georg Simmel, *The Philosophy of Money* (orig. 1907). London: Routledge and Kegan Paul: 1–49.

Bourdieu, Pierre

1977 *Outline of a Theory of Practice.* London: Cambridge University Press.

Bourricaud, François

1981 *The Sociology of Talcott Parsons.* Chicago: University of Chicago Press.

Bowles, Samuel, and Gintis, Herbert

1986 *Democracy and Capitalism: Property, Community, and the Contradictions of Modern Social Thought.* New York: Basic Books.

Bramson, Leon

1961 *The Political Context of Sociology.* Princeton: Princeton University Press.

Braverman, Harry

1974 *Labor and Monopoly Capital: The Degradation of Work in the Twentieth Century.* New York: Monthly Review Press.

Breault, K. D.

1986 "Suicide in America: A Test of Durkheim's Theory of Religion, 1933–1980." *American Journal of Sociology* 92:628–656.

Brewer, John, and Hunter, Albert

1989 *Multimethod Research: A Synthesis of Styles.* Newbury Park, Calif.: Sage.

Brown, Richard H.

1987 *Society as Text: Essays on Rhetoric, Reason and Reality.* Chicago: University of Chicago Press.

1990 "Social Science and the Poetics of Public Truth." *Sociological Forum* 5:55–74.

Brubaker, Rogers

1984 *The Limits of Rationality: An Essay on the Social and Moral Thought of Max Weber.* London: George Allen and Unwin.

Bryant, Christopher G. A.
1985   *Positivism in Social Theory and Research.* New York: St. Martin's.
Buckley, Kerry W.
1989   *Mechanical Man: John Broadus Watson and the Beginnings of Behaviorism.*
            New York: Guilford Press.
Buckley, Walter
1967   *Sociology and Modern Systems Theory.* Englewood Cliffs, N.J.: Prentice-
            Hall.
Bulmer, Martin
1984   *The Chicago School of Sociology: Institutionalization, Diversity, and the Rise
            of Sociological Research.* Chicago: University of Chicago Press.
1985   "The Chicago School of Sociology: What Made It a 'School'?" *The
            History of Sociology: An International Review* 5:62–77.
Burawoy, Michael
1979   *Manufacturing Consent: Changes in the Labor Process under Monopoly
            Capitalism.* Chicago: University of Chicago Press.
Burger, Thomas
1976   *Max Weber's Theory of Concept Formation: History, Laws and Ideal Types.*
            Durham, N.C.: Duke University Press.
1977a   "Max Weber's Interpretive Sociology, the Understanding of Actions and
            Motives, and a Weberian View of Man." *Sociological Inquiry* 47:127–132.
1977b   "Talcott Parsons, the Problem of Order in Society, and the Program of
            an Analytical Sociology." *American Journal of Sociology* 83:320–334.
Burns, Tom R.
1986   "Actors, Transactions, and Social Structure: An Introduction to Social
            Rule System Theory." In U. Himmelstrand (ed.), *Sociology: The
            Aftermath of Crisis.* London: Sage: 8–37.
Burns, Tom R., and Flam, Helena
1986   *The Shaping of Social Organization: Social Rule System Theory with
            Applications.* Beverly Hills, Calif.: Sage.
Burt, Ronald
1982   *Toward a Structural Theory of Action: Network Models of Social Structure.*
            New York: Academic Press.
Buttel, Frederick H. (ed.)
1990   "Symposium: Evolution and Social Change." *Sociological Forum* 5:153–
            212.
Buxton, William
1985   *Talcott Parsons and the Capitalist Nation-State: Political Sociology as a
            Strategic Vocation.* Toronto: University of Toronto Press.
Camic, Charles
1987   "The Making of a Model: A Historical Reinterpretation of the Early
            Parsons." *American Sociological Review* 52:421–439.
1989   "Structure after 50 Years: The Anatomy of a Charter." *American Journal
            of Sociology* 95:38–107.
1990   "An Historical Prologue." *American Journal of Sociology* 55:313–319.
Caplow, Theodore
1968   *Two Against One: Coalition in Triads.* Englewood Cliffs, N.J.: Prentice-
            Hall.

Carden, Maren Lockwood
1974   *The New Feminist Movement*. New York: Russell Sage
            Foundation.
Carver, Terrell
1983   *Marx and Engels: The Intellectual Relationship*. Bloomington: Indiana
            University Press.
Carveth, Donald
1982   "Sociology and Psychoanalysis: The Hobbesian Problem Revisited."
            Canadian Journal of Sociology 7:201–229.
Catlin, George E. G.
1964   "Introduction." In E. Durkheim, *The Rules of Sociological Method*. New
            York: Free Press: xi–xxxvi.
Chafetz, Janet Saltzman
1984   *Sex and Advantage*. Totowa, N.J.: Rowman and Allanheld.
Chafetz, Janet Saltzman, and Dworkin, Anthony Gary
1986   *Female Revolt: Women's Movements in World and Historical Perspectives*.
            Totowa, N.J.: Rowman and Allanheld.
Charon, Joel
1989   *Symbolic Interaction: An Introduction, an Interpretation, an Integration*. 3rd
            ed. Englewood Cliffs, N.J.: Prentice-Hall.
Chitnis, Anand C.
1976   *The Scottish Enlightenment: A Social History*. Totowa, N.J.: Rowman and
            Littlefield.
Chodorow, Nancy
1978   *The Reproduction of Mothering: Psychoanalysis and the Sociology of Gender*.
            Berkeley: University of California Press.
Clark, Priscilla P., and Clark, Terry Nichols
1982   "The Structural Sources of French Structuralism." In I. Rossi (ed.),
            Structural Sociology. New York: Columbia University Press:
            22–46.
Cohen, G. A.
1978   *Karl Marx's Theory of History: A Defence*. Princeton, N.J.: Princeton
            University Press.
Cohen, Ira
1981   "Introduction to the Transaction Edition." In M. Weber, *General
            Economic History*. New Brunswick, N.J.: Transaction: xv–lxxxiii.
Cohen, Jere, Hazelrigg, Lawrence, and Pope, Whitney
1975   "DeParsonizing Weber: A Critique of Parsons' Interpretation of Weber's
            Sociology." *American Sociological Review* 40:229–241.
Coleman, James
1968   Review of H. Garfinkel, *Studies in Ethnomethodology*. *American
            Sociological Review* 33:126–130.
1971   "Community Disorganization and Conflict." In R. Merton and R.
            Nisbet (eds.), *Contemporary Social Problems*. 3rd ed. New York: Harcourt
            Brace Jovanovich: 657–708.
1986   "Social Theory, Social Research, and a Theory of Action." *American
            Journal of Sociology* 91:1309–1335.
1990   *Foundations of Social Theory*. Cambridge: Belknap Press of Harvard
            University Press.

Colfax, J. David, and Roach, Jack L.
1971   *Radical Sociology.* New York: Basic Books.
Collins, F. Howard
1889   *An Epitome of the Synthetic Philosophy.* London and Edinburgh: Williams
            and Norgate.
Collins, Patricia Hill
1990   *Black Feminist Thought: Knowledge, Consciousness and Empowerment.*
            Boston: Unwin Hyman.
Collins, Randall
1975   *Conflict Sociology: Toward an Explanatory Science.* New York: Academic
            Press.
1980   "Weber's Last Theory of Capitalism: A Systematization." *American
            Sociological Review* 45:925–942.
1981a   "On the Microfoundations of Macrosociology." *American Journal of
            Sociology* 86:984–1014.
1981b   "Micro-Translation as Theory-Building Strategy." In K. Knorr-Cetina
            and A. Cicourel (eds.), *Advances in Social Theory and Methodology.* New
            York: Methuen: 81–108.
1981c   "Introduction." In R. Collins (ed.), *Sociology since Midcentury: Essays in
            Theory Cumulation.* New York: Academic Press: 1–9.
1985   *Weberian Sociological Theory.* Cambridge: Cambridge University Press.
1986   "Is 1980s Sociology in the Doldrums?" *American Journal of Sociology*
            91:1336–1355.
1987a   "Interaction Ritual Chains, Power and Property: The Micro-Macro
            Connection as an Empirically Based Theoretical Problem." In J.
            Alexander et al. (eds.), *The Micro-Macro Link.* Berkeley: University of
            California Press: 193–206.
1987b   "A Micro-Macro Theory of Intellectual Creativity: The Case of German
            Idealistic Philosophy." *Sociological Theory* 5:47–69.
1988a   "The Micro Contribution to Macro Sociology." *Sociological Theory* 6:242–
            253.
1988b   "The Durkheimian Tradition in Conflict Sociology." In J. Alexander
            (ed.), *Durkheimian Sociology: Cultural Studies.* Cambridge: Cambridge
            University Press: 107–128.
1989a   "Sociology: Proscience or Antiscience?" *American Sociological Review*
            54:124–139.
1989b   "Toward a Neo-Meadian Sociology of Mind." *Symbolic Interaction* 12:1–
            32.
1990   "Conflict Theory and the Advance of Macro-Historical Sociology." In
            G. Ritzer (ed.), *Frontiers of Social Theory: The New Syntheses.* New York:
            Columbia University Press: 68–87.
Colomy, Paul
1986   "Recent Developments in the Functionalist Approach to Change."
            Sociological Focus 19:139–158.
1990   "Introduction: The Neofunctionalist Movement." In P. Colomy (ed.),
            Neofunctionalist Sociology. Brookfield, Vt.: Edward Elgar Publishing: xi–
            xli.

Comte, Auguste
1830–1842/   *The Positive Philosophy of August Comte*. New York: Calvin
1855   Blanchard.
1851/1957   *A General View of Positivism*. New York: R. Speller.
1851/1968   *System of Positive Polity*, Vol. 1. New York: Burt Franklin.
1852/1968   *System of Positive Polity*, Vol. 2. New York: Burt Franklin.
1853/1968   *System of Positive Polity*, Vol. 3. New York: Burt Franklin.
1854/1968   *System of Positive Polity*, Vol. 4. New York: Burt Franklin.
1891/1973   *The Catechism of Positive Religion*. Clifton, N.J.: A. M. Kelley, Publishers.

Connolly, William E.
1973   "Theoretical Self-Consciousness." *Polity* 6:5–35.

Cook, Judith, and Fonow, Mary Margaret
1986   "Knowledge and Women's Interests: Issues of Epistemology and
        Methodology in Feminist Sociological Research." *Sociological Inquiry* 56:
        2–29.

Cook, Karen S. (ed.)
1987a   *Social Exchange Theory*. Beverly Hills, Calif.: Sage.
1987b   "Emerson's Contributions to Social Exchange Theory." In Karen S.
        Cook (ed.), *Social Exchange Theory*. Beverly Hills, Calif.: Sage: 209–222.

Cook, Karen, O'Brien, Jodi, and Kollock, Peter
1990   "Exchange Theory: A Blueprint for Structure and Process." In G. Ritzer
        (ed.), *Frontiers of Social Theory: The New Syntheses*. New York: Columbia
        University Press: 158–181.

Coser, Lewis
1956   *The Functions of Social Conflict*. New York: Free Press.
1975a   Presidential Address: "Two Methods in Search of a Substance."
        American Sociological Review 40:691–700.
1975b   "Structure and Conflict." In P. Blau (ed.), *Approaches to the Study of
        Social Structure*. New York: Free Press: 210–219.
1977   *Masters of Sociological Thought*. 2nd ed. New York: Harcourt Brace
        Jovanovich.

Coser, Lewis (ed.)
1965   *Georg Simmel*. Englewood Cliffs, N.J.: Prentice-Hall.

Cottrell, Jr., Leonard S.
1980   "George Herbert Mead: The Legacy of Social Behaviorism." In R. K.
        Merton and M. W. Riley (eds.), *Sociological Traditions from Generation to
        Generation: Glimpses of the American Experience*. Norwood, N.J.: Ablex.:
        45–65.

Craib, Ian
1976   *Existentialism and Sociology: A Study of Jean-Paul Sartre*. Cambridge:
        Cambridge University Press.

Cronk, George
1987   *The Philosophical Anthropology of George Herbert Mead*. New York: Peter
        Lang.

Crozier, Michel, and Friedberg, Erhard
1980   *Actors and Systems: The Politics of Collective Action*. Chicago: University
        of Chicago Press.

Curtis, Bruce
1981   *William Graham Sumner*. Boston: Twayne.

Dahrendorf, Ralf
1959   *Class and Class Conflict in Industrial Society.* Stanford: Stanford
            University Press.
Daniels, Arlene Kaplan
1988   *Invisible Careers: Women Civic Leaders from the Volunteer World.* Chicago:
            University of Chicago Press.
Dawe, Alan
1978   "Theories of Social Action." In T. Bottomore and R. Nisbet (eds.), *A
            History of Sociological Analysis.* New York: Basic Books: 362–417.
Deckard, Barbara Sinclair
1979   *The Women's Movement: Political, Socioeconomic and Psychological Issues.*
            New York: Harper & Row.
Densmore, Dana
1973   "Independence from the Sexual Revolution." In A. Koedt et al. (eds.),
            Radical Feminism. New York: Quadrangle: 107–118.
Devereux, Edward C.
1961   "Parsons's Sociological Theory." In M. Black (ed.), *The Social Theories of
            Talcott Parsons.* Englewood Cliffs, N.J.: Prentice-Hall: 1–63.
Ditton, Jason (ed.)
1980   *The View from Goffman.* New York: St. Martin's.
Donovan, Josephine
1985   *Feminist Theory: The Intellectual Traditions of American Feminism.* New
            York: Ungar.
Douglas, Jack
1967   *The Social Meanings of Suicide.* Princeton, N.J.: Princeton University
            Press.
Douglas, Jack, and Johnson, John
1977   "Introduction." In J. Douglas et al. (eds.), *Existential Sociology.*
            Cambridge: Cambridge University Press: vii–xv.
Durkheim, Emile
1893/1960   *Montesquieu and Rousseau: Forerunners of Sociology.* Ann Arbor:
            University of Michigan Press.
1893/1964   *The Division of Labor in Society.* New York: Free Press.
1895/1964   *The Rules of Sociological Method.* New York: Free Press.
1897/1951   *Suicide.* New York: Free Press.
1900/1973   "Sociology in France in the Nineteenth Century." In R. Bellah (ed.),
            Emile Durkheim: On Morality and Society. Chicago: University of Chicago
            Press: 3–32.
1912/1965   *The Elementary Forms of Religious Life.* New York: Free Press.
1913–1914/ *Pragmatism and Sociology.* Cambridge: Cambridge University Press.
1983
1914/1973   "The Dualism of Human Nature and Its Social Condition." In R. Bellah
            (ed.), *Emile Durkheim.* Chicago: University of Chicago Press: 149–163.
1922/1956   *Education and Sociology.* New York: Free Press.
1928/1962   *Socialism.* New York: Collier Books.
1957   *Professional Ethics and Civil Morals.* London: Routledge and Kegan Paul.
1973   *Moral Education: A Study in the Theory and Application of the Sociology of
            Education.* New York: Free Press.
Durkheim, Emile, and Mauss, Marcel
1903/1963   *Primitive Classification.* Chicago: University of Chicago Press.

Eckberg, Douglas Lee, and Hill, Lester
1979   "The Paradigm Concept and Sociology: A Critical Review." *American Sociological Review* 44:925–937.
Edel, Abraham
1959   "The Concept of Levels in Social Theory." In L. Gross (ed.), *Symposium on Sociological Theory*. Evanston, Ill.: Row Peterson: 167–195.
Effrat, Andrew
1972   "Power to the Paradigms: An Editorial Introduction." *Sociological Inquiry* 42:3–33.
Eisen, Arnold
1978   "The Meanings and Confusions of Weberian 'Rationality.' " *British Journal of Sociology* 29:57–70.
Eisenstadt, S. N., with Curelaru, M.
1976   *The Form of Sociology: Paradigms and Crises*. New York: Wiley.
Elster, Jon
1982   "Marxism, Functionalism and Game Theory: The Case for Methodological Individualism." *Theory and Society* 11:453–482.
1985   *Making Sense of Marx*. Cambridge: Cambridge University Press.
Emerson, Richard M.
1972a   "Exchange Theory, Part I: A Psychological Basis for Social Exchange." In J. Berger, M. Zelditch, Jr., and B. Anderson (eds.), *Sociological Theories in Progress*, vol. 2. Boston: Houghton-Mifflin: 38–57.
1972b   "Exchange Theory, Part II: Exchange Relations and Networks." In J. Berger et al. (eds.), *Sociological Theories in Progress*, vol. 2. Boston: Houghton-Mifflin: 58–87.
1981   "Social Exchange Theory." In M. Rosenberg and R. H. Turner (eds.), *Social Psychology: Sociological Perspectives*. New York: Basic Books: 30–65.
Engels, Friedrich
1884/1970   *The Origins of the Family, Private Property and the State*. New York: International.
1890/1972   "Letter to Joseph Bloch." In R. C. Tucker (ed.), *The Marx-Engels Reader*. New York: Norton: 640–642.
Etzkorn, K. Peter (ed.)
1968   *Georg Simmel: The Conflict in Modern Culture and Other Essays*. New York: Teachers College Press, Columbia University.
Evans, Sara
1980   *Personal Politics: The Roots of the Women's Liberation Movement in the Civil Rights Movement and the New Left*. New York: Vintage.
Faghirzadeh, Saleh
1982   *Sociology of Sociology: In Search of . . . Ibn-Khaldum's Sociology Then and Now*. Teheran: Soroush Press.
Faia, Michael A.
1986   *Dynamic Functionalism: Strategy and Tactics*. Cambridge: Cambridge University Press.
Falk, William, and Zhao, Shanyang
1989   "Paradigms, Theories and Methods in Contemporary Rural Sociology: A Partial Replication." *Rural Sociology* 54:587–600.
1990   "Paradigms, Theories and Methods Revisited: We Respond to Our Critics." *Rural Sociology* 55:112–122.

Fararo, Thomas J.
1989   "The Spirit of Unification in Sociological Theory." *Sociological Theory*
            7:175–190.

Fararo, Thomas J., and Skvoretz, John
1986   "E-State Structuralism: A Theoretical Method." *American Sociological
            Review* 51:591–602.

Faris, R. E. L.
1970   *Chicago Sociology: 1920–1932*. Chicago: University of Chicago Press.

Farnham, C. (ed.)
1987   *The Impact of Feminist Research on the Academy*. Bloomington: Indiana
            University Press.

Faught, Jim
1980   "Presuppositions of the Chicago School in the Work of Everett
            Hughes." *American Sociologist* 15:72–82.

Fendrich, Michael
1984   "Wives' Employment and Husbands' Distress: A Meta-analysis and a
            Replication." *Journal of Marriage and the Family* 46:871–879.

Fenton, Steve
1984   *Durkheim and Modern Sociology*. Cambridge: Cambridge University
            Press.

Ferguson, Kathy E.
1980   *Self, Society and Womankind: The Dialectic of Liberation*. Westport, Conn.:
            Greenwood Press.

Fine, Gary
1990   "Symbolic Interactionism in the Post-Blumerian Age." In G. Ritzer (ed.),
            Frontiers of Social Theory: The New Syntheses. New York: Columbia
            University Press: 117–157.

Fine, William F.
1979   *Progressive Evolutionism and American Sociology, 1890–1920*. UMI
            Research Press (*n.p.*).

Fischer, Norman
1984   "Hegelian Marxism and Ethics." *Canadian Journal of Political and Social
            Theory* 8:112–138.

Fiske, Donald W., and Shweder, Richard A. (eds.)
1986   *Metatheory in Social Science: Pluralisms and Subjectivities*. Chicago:
            University of Chicago Press.

Fontana, Andrea
1980   "Toward a Complex Universe: Existential Sociology." In J. D. Douglas
            et al. (eds.), *Introduction to the Sociologies of Everyday Life*. Boston: Allyn
            and Bacon: 155–181.

1984   "Introduction: Existential Sociology and the Self." In J. Kotarba and A.
            Fontana (eds.), *The Existential Self in Society*. Chicago: University of
            Chicago Press: 3–17.

Frank, André Gunder
1966/1974   "Functionalism and Dialectics." In R. S. Denisoff, O. Callahan, and
            M. H. Levine (eds.), *Theories and Paradigms in Contemporary Sociology*.
            Itasca, Ill.: Peacock: 342–352.

Frank, R. I.
1976   Translator's introduction to Max Weber, *The Agrarian Sociology of Ancient Civilizations*. London: NLB: 7–33.

Freeman, C. Robert
1980   "Phenomenological Sociology and Ethnomethodology." In J. D. Douglas et al. (eds.), *Introduction to the Sociologies of Everyday Life*. Boston: Allyn and Bacon: 113–154.

Freund, Julian
1968   *The Sociology of Max Weber*. New York: Vintage.

Friedheim, Elizabeth
1979   "An Empirical Comparison of Ritzer's Paradigms and Similar Metatheories: A Research Note." *Social Forces* 58:59–66.

Friedman, Debra, and Hechter, Michael
1988   "The Contribution of Rational Choice Theory to Macrosociological Research." *Sociological Theory* 6:201–218.
1990   "The Comparative Advantages of Rational Choice Theory." In G. Ritzer (ed.), *Frontiers of Social Theory: The New Syntheses*. New York: Columbia University Press: 214–229.

Friedrichs, Robert
1970   *A Sociology of Sociology*. New York: Free Press.
1972a   "Dialectical Sociology: Toward a Resolution of Current 'Crises' in Western Sociology." *British Journal of Sociology* 13:263–274.
1972b   "Dialectical Sociology: An Exemplar for the 1970's." *Social Forces* 50:447–455.

Frisby, David
1981   *Sociological Impressionism: A Reassessment of Georg Simmel's Social Theory*. London: Heinemann.
1984   *Georg Simmel*. Chichester, Eng.: Ellis Horwood.

Fuhrman, Ellsworth R.
1980   *The Sociology of Knowledge in America: 1883–1915*. Charlottesville: University Press of Virginia.

Fuhrman, Ellsworth R., and Snizek, William
1990   "Neither Proscience nor Antiscience: Metasociology as Dialogue." *Sociological Forum* 5:17–31.

Fulbrook, Mary
1978   "Max Weber's 'Interpretive Sociology.' " *British Journal of Sociology* 29:71–82.

Furfey, Paul
1953/1965   *The Scope and Method of Sociology: A Metasociological Treatise*. New York: Cooper Square Publishers.

Gandy, D. Ross
1979   *Marx and History: From Primitive Society to the Communist Future*. Austin: University of Texas Press.

Garfinkel, Harold
1967   *Studies in Ethnomethodology*. Englewood Cliffs, N.J.: Prentice-Hall.

Garland, Anne Witte
1988   *Women Activists: Challenging the Abuse of Power*. New York: Feminist Press.

Gellner, David
1982   "Max Weber, Capitalism and the Religion of India." *Sociology* 16:526–543.
Gergen, Kenneth J.
1973   "Social Psychology as History." *Journal of Personality and Social
            Psychology* 26:309–320.
1986   "Correspondence versus Autonomy in the Language of Understanding
            Human Action." In D. W. Fiske and R. A. Shweder (eds.), *Metatheory in
            Social Science: Pluralisms and Subjectivities.* Chicago: University of
            Chicago Press: 136–162.
Gerth, Hans, and Mills, C. Wright
1953   *Character and Social Structure.* New York: Harcourt, Brace and World.
Gerth, Hans, and Mills, C. Wright (eds.)
1958   *From Max Weber.* New York: Oxford University Press.
Giddens, Anthony
1972   "Introduction: Durkheim's Writings in Sociology and Social
            Philosophy." In A. Giddens (ed.), *Emile Durkheim: Selected Writings.*
            Cambridge: Cambridge University Press: 1–50.
1979   *Central Problems in Social Theory: Action, Structure and Contradiction in
            Social Analysis.* Berkeley: University of California Press.
1982   *Profiles and Critiques in Social Theory.* Berkeley: University of California
            Press.
1984   *The Constitution of Society: Outline of the Theory of Structuration.* Berkeley:
            University of California Press.
Giddings, Paula
1984   *When and Where I Enter: The Impact of Black Women on Race and Sex in
            America.* New York: William Morrow.
Goffman, Erving
1959   *Presentation of Self in Everyday Life.* Garden City, N.Y.: Anchor.
Gorman, Robert A.
1975a   "Alfred Schutz: An Exposition and Critique." *British Journal of Sociology*
            26:1–19.
1975b   "The Phenomenological 'Humanization' of Social Science: A Critique."
            British Journal of Sociology 26:389–405.
1977   *The Dual Vision: Alfred Schutz and the Myth of Phenomenological Social
            Science.* London: Routledge and Kegan Paul.
Gould, Carol
1978   *Marx's Social Ontology: Individuality and Community in Marx's Theory of
            Social Reality.* Cambridge: MIT Press.
Gouldner, Alvin
1959/1967   "Reciprocity and Autonomy in Functional Theory." In N. Demerath
            and R. Peterson (eds.), *System, Change and Conflict.* New York: Free
            Press: 141–169.
1970   *The Coming Crisis of Western Sociology.* New York: Basic Books.
Grathoff, Richard (ed.)
1978   *The Theory of Social Action: The Correspondence of Alfred Schutz and Talcott
            Parsons.* Bloomington: Indiana University Press.
Greisman, Harvey C.
1986   "The Paradigm That Failed." In R. C. Monk (ed.), *Structures of Knowing.*
            Lanham, Md.: University Press of America: 273–291.

Greisman, Harvey C., and Ritzer, George
1981   "Max Weber, Critical Theory and the Administered World." *Qualitative Sociology* 4:34–55.

Gross, Llewellyn
1961   "Preface to a Metatheoretical Framework for Sociology." *American Journal of Sociology* 67:125–136.

Gurney, Patrick J.
1981   "Historical Origins of Ideological Denial: The Case of Marx in American Sociology." *American Sociologist* 16:196–201.

Gurvitch, Georges
1964   *The Spectrum of Social Time.* Dordrecht, Neth.: D. Reidel.

Haas, Jack, and Shaffir, William
1982   "Taking on the Role of Doctor: A Dramaturgical Analysis of Professionalization." *Symbolic Interaction* 5:187–203.

Habermas, Jurgen
1984   *The Theory of Communicative Action.* Vol. 1, *Reason and the Rationalization of Society.* Boston: Beacon Press.
1987   *The Theory of Communicative Action.* Vol. 2, *Lifeworld and System: A Critique of Functionalist Reason.* Boston: Beacon Press.

Haines, Valerie
1988   "Is Spencer's Theory an Evolutionary Theory?" *American Journal of Sociology* 93:1200–1223.

Halfpenny, Peter
1982   *Positivism and Sociology: Explaining Social Life.* London: George Allen and Unwin.

Hall, Richard
1983   "Theoretical Trends in the Sociology of Occupations." *Sociological Quarterly* 24:5–23.

Harper, Diane Blake, Sylvester, Joan, and Walczak, David
1980   "An Empirical Comparison of Ritzer's Paradigms and Similar Metatheories: Comment on Friedheim." *Social Forces* 59:513–517.

Hartsock, Nancy
1983   *Money, Sex and Power: Towards a Feminist Historical Materialism.* New York: Longman.

Harvey, David
1989   *The Condition of Postmodernity: An Enquiry into the Origins of Cultural Change.* Oxford: Basil Blackwell.

Harvey, Lee
1982   "The Use and Abuse of Kuhnian Paradigms in the Sociology of Knowledge." *British Journal of Sociology* 16:85–101.
1987   "The Nature of 'Schools' in the Sociology of Knowledge: The Case of the 'Chicago School.' " *Sociological Review* 35:245–278.

Hawthorn, Geoffrey
1976   *Enlightenment and Despair.* Cambridge: Cambridge University Press.

Hayim, Gila
1980   *The Existential Sociology of Jean-Paul Sartre.* Amherst: University of Massachusetts Press.

Heap, James L., and Roth, Phillip A.
1973   "On Phenomenological Sociology." *American Sociological Review* 38:354–367.
Heberle, Rudolph
1965   "Simmel's Methods." In L. Coser (ed.), *Georg Simmel*. Englewood Cliffs, N.J.: Prentice-Hall: 116–121.
Hechter, Michael
1983a   "Introduction." In M. Hechter (ed.), *The Microfoundations of Macrosociology*. Philadelphia: Temple University Press: 3–15.
1983b   "A Theory of Group Solidarity." In M. Hechter (ed.), *The Microfoundations of Macrosociology*. Philadelphia: Temple University Press: 16–57.
1987   *Principles of Group Solidarity*. Berkeley: University of California Press.
Hegel, G. W. F.
1807/1967   *The Phenomenology of Mind*. New York: Harper Colophon.
1821/1967   *The Philosophy of Right*. Oxford: Clarendon Press.
Heilbron, Johan
1990   "Auguste Comte and Epistemology." *Sociological Theory* 8:153–162.
Hekman, Susan
1983   *Weber, the Ideal Type, and Contemporary Social Theory*. Notre Dame, Ind.: University of Notre Dame Press.
Heller, Agnes
1976   *The Theory of Need in Marx*. New York: St. Martin's.
Heritage, John
1984   *Garfinkel and Ethnomethodology*. Cambridge: Polity Press.
Hewitt, John P.
1984   *Self and Society: A Symbolic Interactionist Social Psychology*. 3rd ed. Boston: Allyn and Bacon.
Heyl, John D., and Heyl, Barbara S.
1976   "The Sumner-Porter Controversy at Yale: Pre-Paradigmatic Sociology and Institutional Crisis." *Sociological Inquiry* 46:41–49.
Hilbert, Richard A.
1986   "Anomie and Moral Regulation of Reality: The Durkheimian Tradition in Modern Relief." *Sociological Theory* 4:1–19.
Himes, Joseph
1966   "The Functions of Racial Conflict." *Social Forces* 45:1–10.
Hinkle, Roscoe
1963   "Antecedents of the Action Orientation in American Sociology before 1935." *American Sociological Review* 28:705–715.
1980   *Founding Theory of American Sociology: 1881–1915*. London: Routledge and Kegan Paul.
Hinkle, Roscoe, and Hinkle, Gisela
1954   *The Development of American Sociology*. New York: Random House.
Hofstadter, Richard
1959   *Social Darwinism in American Thought*. New York: Braziller.
Hollinger, David
1980   "T. S. Kuhn's Theory of Science and Its Implications for History." In G. Gutting (ed.), *Paradigms and Revolutions*. Notre Dame, Ind.: Notre Dame University Press: 195–222.

Holton, Robert J., and Turner, Bryan S.
1986   "Reading Talcott Parsons: Introductory Remarks." In R. J. Holton and
            B. S. Turner (eds.), *Talcott Parsons on Economy and Society*. London:
            Routledge and Kegan Paul: 1–24.

Homans, George C.
1958   "Social Behavior as Exchange." *American Journal of Sociology* 63:597–606.
1961   *Social Behavior: Its Elementary Forms*. New York: Harcourt, Brace and
            World.
1962   *Sentiments and Activities*. New York: Free Press.
1969   "The Sociological Relevance of Behaviorism." In R. Burgess and D.
            Bushell (eds.), *Behavioral Sociology*. New York: Columbia University
            Press: 1–24.
1984   *Coming to My Senses: The Autobiography of a Sociologist*. New Brunswick,
            N.J.: Transaction Books.

Hook, Sidney
1965   "Pareto's Sociological System." In J. H. Meisel (ed.), *Pareto and Mosca*.
            Englewood Cliffs, N.J.: Prentice-Hall: 57–61.

Horowitz, Irving L.
1962/1967   "Consensus, Conflict, and Cooperation." In N. Demerath and R.
            Peterson (eds.), *System, Change and Conflict*. New York: Free Press: 265–
            279.
1983   *C. Wright Mills: An American Utopian*. New York: Free Press.

Huaco, George
1986   "Ideology and General Theory: The Case of Sociological
            Functionalism." *Comparative Studies in Society and History* 28:34–54.

Hunter, J. E., Schmidt, F. L., and Jackson, G. B.
1982   *Meta-analysis: Cumulating Research Findings across Studies*. Beverly Hills,
            Calif.: Sage.

Israel, Joachim
1971   *Alienation: From Marx to Modern Sociology*. Boston: Allyn and Bacon.

Jackman, Mary R., and Jackman, Robert W.
1973   "An Interpretation of the Relation between Objective and Subjective
            Social Status." *American Sociological Review* 38:569–582.

Jameson, Fredric
1984   "Postmodernism, or the Cultural Logic of Late Capitalism." *New Left
            Review* 146:53–93.

Jay, Martin
1973   *The Dialectical Imagination*. Boston: Little, Brown.
1984   *Marxism and Totality: The Adventures of a Concept from Lukacs to
            Habermas*. Berkeley: University of California Press.
1986   *Permanent Exiles: Essays on the Intellectual Migration from Germany to
            America*. New York: Columbia University Press.

Joas, Hans
1985   *G. H. Mead: A Contemporary Re-examination of His Thought*. Cambridge:
            MIT Press.

Johnson, Doyle Paul
1981   *Sociological Theory: Classical Founders and Contemporary Perspectives*. New
            York: Wiley.

Jones, Greta
1980   *Social Darwinism and English Thought: The Interaction between Biological and Social Theory.* Atlantic Highlands, N.J.: Humanities Press.

Jones, Robert Alun
1986   "Durkheim, Frazer, and Smith: The Role of Analogies and Exemplars in the Development of Durkheim's Sociology of Religion." *American Journal of Sociology* 92:596–627.

Kalberg, Stephen
1980   "Max Weber's Types of Rationality: Cornerstones for the Analysis of Rationalization Processes in History." *American Journal of Sociology* 85:1145–1179.
1985   "The Role of Ideal Interests in Max Weber's Comparative Historical Sociology." In R. J. Antonio and R. M. Glassman (eds.), *A Weber-Marx Dialogue.* Lawrence: University Press of Kansas: 46–67.
1990   "The Rationalization of Action in Max Weber's Sociology of Religion." *Sociological Theory* 8:58–84.

Kandal, Terry R.
1988   *The Woman Question in Classical Sociological Theory.* Miami: Florida International University Press.

Kanter, Rosabeth Moss
1977   *Men and Women of the Corporation.* New York: Basic Books.

Karady, Victor
1983   "The Durkheimians in Academe: A Reconsideration." In P. Besnard (ed.), *The Sociological Domain.* Cambridge: Cambridge University Press: 71–89.

Kasler, Dirk
1985   "Jewishness as a Central Formation-Milieu of Early German Sociology." *History of Sociology: An International Review* 6:69–86.

Kellner, Douglas
1988   "Postmodernism as Social Theory: Some Challenges and Problems." *Theory, Culture and Society* 5:239–269.
1990a   "The Postmodern Turn: Positions, Problems, and Prospects." In G. Ritzer (ed.), *Frontiers of Social Theory: The New Syntheses.* New York: Columbia University Press: 255–286.
1990c   *Television and the Crisis of Democracy.* Boulder: Westview Press.

Kellner, Douglas (ed.)
1990b   *Postmodernism: Jameson: Critique.* Washington, D.C.: Maisonneuve Press.

Kent, Raymond A.
1981   *A History of British Empirical Sociology.* Aldershot, Hants, Eng.: Gower.

Kitahara, Michio
1986   "Commodore Perry and the Japanese: A Study in the Dramaturgy of Power." *Symbolic Interaction* 9:53–65.

Knorr-Cetina, Karin
1981   "Introduction: The Micro-Sociological Challenge to Macro-Sociology: Towards a Reconstruction of Social Theory and Methodology." In K. Knorr-Cetina and A. Cicourel (eds.), *Advances in Social Theory and Methodology.* New York: Methuen: 1–47.

Kockelmans, Joseph J.
1967a   *Phenomenology: The Philosophy of Edmund Husserl and Its Interpretations.*
             Garden City, N.Y.: Anchor.
1967b   "Some Fundamental Themes of Husserl's Phenomenology." In J. J.
             Kockelmans (ed.), *Phenomenology: The Philosophy of Edmund Husserl and
             Its Interpretations.* Garden City, N.Y.: Anchor: 24–36.
Kohn, Melvin L.
1976   "Occupational Structure and Alienation." *American Journal of Sociology*
             82:111–127.
Kolb, William L.
1944   "A Critical Evaluation of Mead's 'I' and 'Me' Concepts." *Social Forces*
             22:291–296.
Korenbaum, Myrtle
1964   Translator's preface to Georges Gurvitch. *The Spectrum of Social Time.*
             Dordrecht, Neth.: D. Reidel: ix–xxvi.
Kotarba, Joseph A., and Fontana, Andrea (eds.)
1984   *The Existential Self in Society.* Chicago: University of Chicago Press.
Kronman, Anthony
1983   *Max Weber.* Stanford: Stanford University Press.
Kuhn, Thomas
1962   *The Structure of Scientific Revolutions.* Chicago: University of Chicago
             Press.
1970   *The Structure of Scientific Revolutions.* 2nd ed. Chicago: University of
             Chicago Press.
Kurzweil, Edith
1980   *The Age of Structuralism: Lévi-Strauss to Foucault.* New York: Columbia
             University Press.
1987   "Psychoanalysis as the Macro-Micro Link." In J. Alexander et al. (eds.),
             The Micro-Macro Link. Berkeley: University of California Press: 237–254.
Lachman, L. M.
1971   *The Legacy of Max Weber.* Berkeley, Calif.: Glendessary Press.
Laclau, Ernesto and Mouffe, Chantal
1985   *Hegemony and Socialist Strategy: Towards a Radical Democratic Politics.*
             London: Verso.
Layder, Derek
1985   "Power, Structure and Agency." *Journal for the Theory of Social Behaviour*
             15:131–149.
Lefebvre, Henri
1968   *The Sociology of Marx.* New York: Vintage.
Lehman, Edward W.
1988   "The Theory of the State versus the State of Theory." *American
             Sociological Review* 53:807–823.
Lemert, Charles
1979   *Sociology and the Twilight of Man: Homocentrism and Discourse in
             Sociological Theory.* Carbondale: Southern Illinois University Press.
1990   "The Uses of French Structuralisms in Sociology." In G. Ritzer (ed.),
             Frontiers of Social Theory: The New Syntheses. New York: Columbia
             University Press: 230–254.
1991   "Sociological Metatheory and Its Cultured Despisers." In G. Ritzer

(ed.), *Metatheorizing*. Beverly Hills, Calif.: Sage.

Lemert, Charles (ed.)
1981   *French Sociology: Rupture and Renewal since 1968.* New York: Columbia University Press.

Lengermann, Patricia Madoo
1979   "The Founding of the *American Sociological Review.*" *American Sociological Review* 44:185–198.

Lengermann, Patricia M., and Niebrugge-Brantley, Jill
1990   "Feminist Sociological Theory: The Near-Future Prospects." In G. Ritzer (ed.), *Frontiers of Social Theory: The New Syntheses.* New York: Columbia University Press: 316–344.

Lengermann, Patricia Madoo, and Wallace, Ruth A.
1985   *Gender in America: Social Control and Social Change.* Englewood Cliffs, N.J.: Prentice-Hall.

Lenzer, Gertrud (ed.)
1975   *Auguste Comte and Positivism: The Essential Writings.* Magnolia, Mass.: Peter Smith.

Levine, Donald
1971   "Introduction." In D. Levine (ed.), *Georg Simmel: Individuality and Social Forms.* Chicago: University of Chicago Press: ix–xiv.
1981a   "Rationality and Freedom: Weber and Beyond." *Sociological Inquiry* 51: 5–25.
1981b   "Sociology's Quest for the Classics: The Case of Simmel." In B. Rhea (ed.), *The Future of the Sociological Classics.* London: George Allen and Unwin: 60–80.
1985   "Ambivalent Encounters: Disavowals of Simmel by Durkheim, Weber, Lukacs, Park and Parsons." In D. Levine (ed.), *The Flight from Ambiquity: Essays in Social and Cultural Theory.* Chicago: University of Chicago Press: 89–141.
1989   "Simmel as a Resource for Sociological Metatheory." *Sociological Theory* 7:161–174.

Levine, Donald, Carter, Ellwood B., and Gorman, Eleanor Miller
1976a   "Simmel's Influence on American Sociology—I." *American Journal of Sociology* 81:813–845.
1976b   "Simmel's Influence on American Sociology—II." *American Journal of Sociology* 81:1112–1132.

Levy-Bruhl, Lucien
1903/1973   *The Philosophy of Auguste Comte.* Clifton, N.J.: A. M. Kelley, Publishers.

Lewis, J. David, and Smith, Richard L.
1980   *American Sociology and Pragmatism: Mead, Chicago Sociology, and Symbolic Interaction.* Chicago: University of Chicago Press.

Lilienfeld, Robert
1978   *The Rise of Systems Theory: An Ideological Analysis.* New York: Wiley-Interscience.

Liska, Allen E.
1990   "The Significance of Aggregate Dependent Variables and Contextual Independent Variables for Linking Macro and Micro Theories." *Social Psychology Quarterly* 53:292–301.

Loader, Colin, and Alexander, Jeffrey C.
1985   "Max Weber on Churches and Sects in North America: An Alternative
            Path toward Rationalization." *Sociological Theory* 3:1–6.
Lockwood, David
1956   "Some Remarks on *The Social System*." *British Journal of Sociology* 7:134–
            146.
Lodahl, Janice B., and Gordon, Gerald
1972   "The Structure of Scientific Fields and the Functioning of University
            Graduate Departments." *American Sociological Review* 37:57–72.
Lodge, Peter
1986   "Connections: W. I. Thomas, European Social Thought and American
            Sociology." In R. C. Monk (ed.), *Structures of Knowing*. Lanham, Md.:
            University Press of America: 135–160.
Lukács, Georg
1922/1968   *History and Class Consciousness*. Cambridge: MIT Press.
Lukes, Steven
1972   *Emile Durkheim: His Life and Work*. New York: Harper & Row.
1977   "Power and Structure." In S. Lukes, *Essays in Social Theory*. London:
            Macmillan: 3–29.
Luxenberg, Stan
1985   *Roadside Empires: How the Chains Franchised America*. New York: Viking.
Lyman, Stanford, and Scott, Marvin
1970   *A Sociology of the Absurd*. New York: Appleton-Century-Crofts.
Lyotard, Jean-Francois
1984   *The Postmodern Condition: A Report on Knowledge*. Minneapolis:
            University of Minnesota Press.
MacCrae, Donald G.
1974   *Max Weber*. Harmondsworth, Eng.: Penguin.
MacIver, Robert
1931   *Society: Its Structure and Changes*. New York: Ray Long and Richard R.
            Smith.
1942   *Social Causation*. Boston: Ginn.
MacKinnon, Catherine
1979   *Sexual Harassment of Working Women*. New Haven: Yale University Press.
Maines, David R.
1977   "Social Organization and Social Structure in Symbolic Interactionist
            Thought." In A. Inkeles, J. Coleman, and N. Smelser (eds.), *Annual
            Review of Sociology*, Vol. 3. Palo Alto, Calif.: Annual Reviews: 259–285.
Mann, Michael
1986   *The Sources of Social Power*, Vol. 1. New York: Cambridge University
            Press.
Manning, Peter
1973   "Existential Sociology." *The Sociological Quarterly* 14:200–225.
Manuel, Frank E.
1962   *The Prophets of Paris*. Cambridge: Harvard University Press.
Marx, Karl
1842/1977   "Communism and the *Augsburger Allegemeine Zeitung*." In D. McLellan
            (ed.), *Karl Marx: Selected Writings*. New York: Oxford University Press:
            20.

1847/1963   *The Poverty of Philosophy.* New York: International Publishers.
1852/1963   *The Eighteenth Brumaire of Louis Bonaparte.* New York: International
            Publishers.
1857–1858/ *Pre-Capitalist Economic Foundations,* Eric J. Hobsbawm (ed.). New
1964   York: International Publishers.
1857–1858/ *The Grundrisse: Foundations of the Critique of Political Economy.* New
1974   York: Random House.
1859/1970   *A Contribution to the Critique of Political Economy.* New York:
            International Publishers.
1862–1863/ *Theories of Surplus Value,* Part 1. Moscow: Progress Publishers.
1963
1862–1863/ *Theories of Surplus Value,* Part 2. Moscow: Progress Publishers.
1968
1867/1967   *Capital: A Critique of Political Economy,* Vol. 1. New York: International
            Publishers.
1932/1964   *The Economic and Philosophic Manuscripts of 1844,* Dirk J. Struik (ed.).
            New York: International Publishers.

Marx, Karl, and Engels, Friedrich
1845/1956   *The Holy Family.* Moscow: Foreign Language Publishing House.
1845–1846/ *The German Ideology,* Part 1, C. J. Arthur (ed.). New York:
1970   International Publishers.
1848/1948   *Manifesto of the Communist Party.* New York: International Publishers.

Masterman, Margaret
1970   "The Nature of a Paradigm." In I. Lakatos and A. Musgrove (eds.),
            Criticism and the Growth of Knowledge. Cambridge: Cambridge University
            Press: 59–89.

Matthews, Fred H.
1977   *Quest for an American Sociology: Robert E. Park and the Chicago School.*
            Montreal: McGill University Press.

Mazlish, Bruce
1984   *The Meaning of Karl Marx.* New York: Oxford University Press.

McKinney, John C.
1966   *Constructive Typology and Social Theory.* New York: Appleton-Century-
            Crofts.

McLellan, David
1973   *Karl Marx: His Life and Thought.* New York: Harper Colophon.

McLellan, David (ed.)
1971   *The Thought of Karl Marx.* New York: Harper Torchbooks.

McMurty, John
1978   *The Structure of Marx's World-View.* Princeton: Princeton University
            Press.

McPhail, Clark, and Rexroat, Cynthia
1979   "Mead vs. Blumer." *American Sociological Review* 44:449–467.

Mead, George H.
1907/1964   "Concerning Animal Perception." In A. J. Reck (ed.), *Selected Writings.*
            Indianapolis: Bobbs-Merrill.
1934/1962   *Mind, Self and Society: From the Standpoint of a Social Behaviorist.* Chicago:
            University of Chicago Press.

1936   *Movements of Thought in the Nineteenth Century.* Chicago: University of Chicago Press.
1938/1972   *The Philosophy of the Act.* Chicago: University of Chicago Press.
1959   *The Philosophy of the Present.* LaSalle, Ill.: Open Court Publishing.
1982   *The Individual and the Social Self: Unpublished Work of George Herbert Mead.* Chicago: University of Chicago Press.

Mehan, Hugh, and Wood, Houston
1975   *The Reality of Ethnomethodology.* New York: Wiley.

Menzies, Ken
1977   *Talcott Parsons and the Social Image of Man.* London: Routledge and Kegan Paul.

Merton, Robert K.
1949/1968   "Manifest and Latent Functions." In R. Merton, *Social Theory and Social Structure.* New York: Free Press: 73–138.
1968   *Social Theory and Social Structure.* New York: Free Press.
1975   "Structural Analysis in Sociology." In P. Blau (ed.), *Approaches to the Study of Social Structure.* New York: Free Press: 21–52.
1980   "Remembering the Young Talcott Parsons." *American Sociologist* 15:68–71.

Mészáros, István
1970   *Marx's Theory of Alienation.* New York: Harper Torchbooks.

Mill, John Stuart
1961   *Auguste Comte and Positivism.* Ann Arbor: University of Michigan Press.

Miller, David
1973   *George Herbert Mead: Self, Language and the World.* Austin: University of Texas Press.
1982a   "Introduction." In G. H. Mead, *The Individual and the Social Self: Unpublished Work of George Herbert Mead.* Chicago: University of Chicago Press: 1–26.
1982b   Review of J. D. Lewis and R. L. Smith, *American Sociology and Pragmatism. Journal of the History of Sociology* 4:108–114.
1985   "Concerning J. David Lewis' Response to My Review of *American Sociology and Pragmatism.*" *Journal of the History of Sociology* 5:131–133.

Mills, C. Wright
1951   *White Collar.* New York: Oxford University Press.
1956   *The Power Elite.* New York: Oxford University Press.
1959   *The Sociological Imagination.* New York: Oxford University Press.
1960   *Listen Yankee: The Revolution in Cuba.* New York: McGraw-Hill.
1962   *The Marxists.* New York: Dell.

Mitroff, Ian
1974   "Norms and Counter-Norms in a Select Group of the Apollo Moon Scientists: A Case Study of the Ambivalence of Scientists." *American Sociological Review* 39:579–595.

Mitroff, Ian, and Kilmann, Ralph
1978   *Methodological Approaches to Social Science.* San Francisco: Jossey-Bass.

Mitzman, Arthur
1970   *The Iron Cage.* New York: Universal Library.

Miyahara, Kojiro
1983   "Charisma: From Weber to Contemporary Sociology." *Sociological Inquiry* 55:368–388.
Mommsen, Wolfgang J.
1974   *The Age of Bureaucracy.* New York: Harper & Row.
Moore, Merritt H.
1936   "Introduction." In G. H. Mead, *Movements of Thought in the Nineteenth Century.* Chicago: University of Chicago Press: xi–xxxvii.
Morgan, Robin (ed.)
1970   *Sisterhood Is Powerful: An Anthology of Writings from the Women's Liberation Movement.* New York: Vintage.
Morris, Monica B.
1977   *Excursion into Creative Sociology.* New York: Columbia University Press.
Morse, Chandler
1961   "The Functional Imperatives." In M. Black (ed.), *The Social Theories of Talcott Parsons.* Englewood Cliffs, N.J.: Prentice-Hall: 100–152.
Mueller-Vollmer, Kurt
1985   "Language, Mind and Artifact: An Outline of Hermeneutic Theory since the Enlightenment." In K. Mueller-Vollmer (ed.), *The Hermeneutics Reader.* New York: Continuum: 1–53.
Mullins, Nicholas
1973   *Theories and Theory Groups in Contemporary American Sociology.* New York: Harper & Row.
1983   "Theories and Theory Groups Revisited." In R. Collins (ed.), *Sociological Theory—1983.* San Francisco: Jossey-Bass: 319–337.
Munch, P. A.
1975   " 'Sense' and 'Intention' in Max Weber's Theory of Action." *Sociological Inquiry* 45:59–65.
Münch, Richard
1981   "Talcott Parsons and the Theory of Action. I. The Structure of the Kantian Core." *American Journal of Sociology* 86:709–739.
1982   "Talcott Parsons and the Theory of Action. II. The Continuity of the Development." *American Journal of Sociology* 87:771–826.
1987   "The Interpenetration of Microinteraction and Macrostructures in a Complex and Contingent Institutional Order." In J. Alexander et al. (eds.), *The Micro-Macro Link.* Berkeley: University of California Press: 319–336.
Nass, Clifford I.
1986   "Bureaucracy, Technical Expertise, and Professionals: A Weberian Approach." *Sociological Theory* 4:61–70.
Natanson, Maurice
1973a   "Introduction." In A. Schutz, *Collected Papers I: The Problem of Social Reality.* The Hague: Martinus Nijhoff: xxv–xlvii.
1973b   *The Social Dynamics of George H. Mead.* The Hague: Martinus Nijhoff.
Nicolaus, Martin
1974   "Foreword." In K. Marx, *The Grundrisse.* New York: Random House: 7–63.
Nisbet, Robert
1959   "Comment." *American Sociological Review* 24:479–481.

1967   *The Sociological Tradition.* New York: Basic Books.

1974   *The Sociology of Emile Durkheim.* New York: Oxford University Press.

Noblit, George W., and Hare, R. Dwight

1988   *Meta-Ethnography: Synthesizing Qualitative Studies.* Newbury Park, Calif.: Sage.

Oakes, Guy (ed.)

1984   *Georg Simmel on Women, Sexuality and Love.* New Haven: Yale University Press.

Oliver, Ivan

1983   "The 'Old' and the 'New' Hermeneutic in Sociological Theory." *British Journal of Sociology* 34:519–553.

Ollman, Bertell

1976   *Alienation.* 2nd ed. Cambridge: Cambridge University Press.

O'Neill, William L.

1971   *A History of Feminism in America.* Chicago: Quadrangle Books.

Osterberg, Dag

1988   *Metasociology: An Inquiry into the Origins and Validity of Social Thought.* Oslo, Norway: Norwegian University Press.

Pareto, Vilfredo

1935   *A Treatise on General Sociology.* 4 vols. New York: Dover.

Park, Robert E.

1927/1973 "Life History." *American Journal of Sociology* 79:251–260.

Parsons, Talcott

1934–1935 "The Place of Ultimate Values in Sociological Theory." *International Journal of Ethics* 45:282–316.

1937   *The Structure of Social Action.* New York: McGraw-Hill.

1942   "Some Sociological Aspects of the Fascist Movements." *Social Forces* 21:138–147.

1947   "Certain Primary Sources and Patterns of Aggression in the Social Structure of the Western World." *Psychiatry* 10:167–181.

1949   *The Structure of Social Action.* 2nd ed. New York: McGraw-Hill.

1951   *The Social System.* Glencoe, Ill.: Free Press.

1954a   "The Prospects of Sociological Theory." In T. Parsons, *Essays in Sociological Theory.* New York: Free Press: 348–369.

1954b   "The Present Position and Prospects of Systematic Theory in Sociology." In T. Parsons, *Essays in Sociological Theory.* New York: Free Press: 212–237.

1960   "A Sociological Approach to the Theory of Organizations." In T. Parsons (ed.), *Structure and Process in Modern Societies.* New York: Free Press: 16–58.

1961   "Some Considerations on the Theory of Social Change." *Rural Sociology* 26:219–239.

1966   *Societies.* Englewood Cliffs, N.J.: Prentice-Hall.

1970a   *Social Structure and Personality.* New York: Free Press.

1970b   "On Building Social System Theory: A Personal History." *Daedalus* 99:826–881.

1971   *The System of Modern Societies.* Englewood Cliffs, N.J.: Prentice-Hall.

1975   "Social Structure and the Symbolic Media of Interchange." In P. Blau (ed.), *Approaches to the Study of Social Structure*. New York: Free Press: 94–100.

1977a   "General Introduction." In T. Parsons (ed.), *Social Systems and the Evolution of Action Theory*. New York: Free Press: 1–13.

1977b   "On Building Social System Theory: A Personal History." In T. Parsons (ed.), *Social Systems and the Evolution of Action Theory*. New York: Free Press: 22–76.

Parsons, Talcott, and Platt, Gerald

1973   *The American University*. Cambridge: Harvard University Press.

Parsons, Talcott, and Shils, Edward A. (eds.)

1951   *Toward a General Theory of Action*. Cambridge: Harvard University Press.

Peel, J. D. Y.

1971   *Herbert Spencer: The Evolution of a Sociologist*. New York: Basic Books.

Perrin, Robert

1976   "Herbert Spencer's Four Theories of Social Evolution." *American Journal of Sociology* 81:1339–1359.

Phillips, Derek

1973   "Paradigms, Falsifications and Sociology." *Acta Sociologica* 16:13–31.

1975   "Paradigms and Incommensurability." *Theory and Society* 2:37–62.

Polit, Denise F., and Falbo, Toni

1987   "Only Children and Personality Development: A Quantitative Review." *Journal of Marriage and the Family* 49:309–325.

Pope, Whitney

1973   "Classic on Classic: Parsons' Interpretation of Durkheim." *American Sociological Review* 38:399–415.

1975   "Durkheim as Functionalist." *Sociological Quarterly* 16:361–379.

1976   *Durkheim's Suicide: A Classic Analyzed*. Chicago: University of Chicago Press.

Pope, Whitney, and Cohen, Jere

1978   "On R. Stephen Warner's 'Toward a Redefinition of Action Theory: Paying the Cognitive Element Its Due.' " *American Journal of Sociology* 83:1359–1367.

Pope, Whitney, Cohen, Jere, and Hazelrigg, Lawrence E.

1975   "On the Divergence of Weber and Durkheim: A Critique of Parsons' Convergence Thesis." *American Sociological Review* 40:417–427.

Pope, Whitney, and Johnson, Barclay D.

1983   "Inside Organic Solidarity." *American Sociological Review* 48:681–692.

Powers, Charles H.

1986   *Vilfredo Pareto*. Newbury Park, Calif.: Sage.

Prendergast, Christopher

1986   "Alfred Schutz and the Austrian School of Economics." *American Journal of Sociology* 92:1–26.

Procter, Ian

1978   "Parsons's Early Voluntarism." *Sociological Inquiry* 48:37–48.

Puner, Helen Walker

1947   *Freud: His Life and His Mind*. New York: Dell.

Quadagno, Jill S.

1979   "Paradigms in Evolutionary Theory: The Sociobiological Model of Natural Selection." *American Sociological Review* 44:100–109.

Radnitzky, Gerard
1973   *Contemporary Schools of Metascience.* Chicago: Henry Regnery.
Rattansi, Ali
1982   *Marx and the Division of Labour.* London: Macmillan.
Rhoades, Lawrence J.
1981   *A History of the American Sociological Association.* Washington, D.C.:
            American Sociological Association.
Rich, Adrienne
1976   *Of Woman Born: Motherhood as Experience and Institution.* New York:
            Bantam.
Ritzer, George
1975a   *Sociology: A Multiple Paradigm Science.* Boston: Allyn and Bacon.
1975b   "Sociology: A Multiple Paradigm Science." *American Sociologist* 19:156–
            167.
1975c   "Professionalization, Bureaucratization and Rationalization: The Views
            of Max Weber." *Social Forces* 53:627–634.
1977   *Working: Conflict and Change.* 2nd ed. Englewood Cliffs, N.J.: Prentice-
            Hall.
1979   "Toward an Integrated Sociological Paradigm." In W. Snizek et al.
            (eds.), *Contemporary Issues in Theory and Research.* Westport, Conn.:
            Greenwood Press: 25–46.
1980   *Sociology: A Multiple Paradigm Science.* Rev. ed. Boston: Allyn and Bacon.
1981a   *Toward an Integrated Sociological Paradigm: The Search for an Exemplar and
            an Image of the Subject Matter.* Boston: Allyn and Bacon.
1981b   "Paradigm Analysis in Sociology: Clarifying the Issues." *American
            Sociological Review* 46:245–248.
1983   "The McDonaldization of Society." *Journal of American Culture* 6:100–
            107.
1985   "The Rise of Micro-Sociological Theory." *Sociological Theory* 3:88–98.
1987   "The Current State of Metatheory." *Sociological Perspectives: The Theory
            Section Newsletter* 10:1–6.
1988   "Sociological Metatheory: Defending a Subfield by Delineating Its
            Parameters." *Sociological Theory* 6:187–200.
1989   "Of Levels and 'Intellectual Amnesia.'" *Sociological Theory* 7:226–229.
1990a   "Micro-Macro Linkage in Sociological Theory: Applying a
            Metatheoretical Tool." In G. Ritzer (ed.), *Frontiers of Social Theory: The
            New Syntheses.* New York: Columbia University Press: 347–370.
1990b   "The Current Status of Sociological Theory: The New Syntheses." In G.
            Ritzer (ed.), *Frontiers of Social Theory: The New Syntheses.* New York:
            Columbia University Press: 1–30.
1990d   "Metatheorizing in Sociology." *Sociological Forum* 5:3–15.
1991   *Metatheorizing in Sociology.* Lexington, Mass.: Lexington Books.
forthcom-   *Big Mac Attack: The McDonaldization of Society.* New York: Lexington
ing a   Books.
forthcom-   "The Recent History and the Emerging Reality of American
ing b   Sociological Theory: A Metatheoretical Interpretation." *Sociological
            Forum.*

Ritzer, George (ed.)
1990c   "Symposium: Metatheory: Its Uses and Abuses in Contemporary
             Sociology." *Sociological Forum* 5:1–74.

forthcom-
ing c   *Metatheorizing*. Newbury Park, Calif.: Sage.

Ritzer, George, and Bell, Richard
1981   "Emile Durkheim: Exemplar for an Integrated Sociological Paradigm?"
             Social Forces 59:966–995.

Ritzer, George, and Walczak, David
1986   *Working: Conflict and Change*. 3rd ed. Englewood Cliffs, N.J.: Prentice-
             Hall.

1988   "Rationalization and the Deprofessionalization of Physicians." *Social
             Forces* 67:1–22.

Rocher, Guy
1975   *Talcott Parsons and American Sociology*. New York: Barnes and Noble.

Rock, Paul
1979   *The Making of Symbolic Interactionism*. Totowa, N.J.: Rowman and
             Littlefield.

Roemer, John E.
1982   "Methodological Individualism and Deductive Marxism." *Theory and
             Society* 11:513–520.

1986   *Analytical Marxism*. Cambridge: Cambridge University Press.

Rosenberg, Morris
1989   "Self-Concept Research: A Historical Review." *Social Forces* 68:34–44.

Rossi, Alice
1974   *The Feminist Papers: From Adams to de Beauvoir*. New York: Bantam.

Roth, Guenther
1968   "Introduction." In G. Roth and C. Wittich (eds.), *Max Weber, Economy
             and Society*. 3 vols. Totowa, N.J.: Bedminster Press: xxvii–civ.

1971   "Sociological Typology and Historical Explanations." In G. Roth and R.
             Bendix (eds.), *Scholarship and Partisanship: Essays on Max Weber*.
             Berkeley: University of California Press: 109–128.

1976   "History and Sociology in the Work of Max Weber." *British Journal of
             Sociology* 27:306–318.

Rubinstein, David
1986   "The Concept of Structure in Sociology." In M. L. Wardell and S. P.
             Turner (eds.), *Sociological Theory in Transition*. Boston: Allen and Unwin:
             80–94.

Runciman, W. G.
1972   *A Critique of Max Weber's Philosophy of Social Science*. London:
             Cambridge University Press.

Ryan, Mary
1990   *Women in Public: From Barriers to Ballots 1825–1880*. Baltimore: Johns
             Hopkins University Press.

Ryan, William
1971   *Blaming the Victim*. New York: Pantheon.

Salomon, A.
1945   "German Sociology." In G. Gurvitch and W. F. Moore (eds.), *Twentieth Century Sociology*. New York: Philosophical Library: 586–614.
Sanday, Peggy Reeves
1990   *Fraternity Gang Rape: Sex, Brotherhood and Privilege on Campus*. New York: New York University Press.
Scaff, Lawrence
1989   *Fleeing the Iron Cage: Culture, Politics, and Modernity in the Thought of Max Weber*. Berkeley: University of California Press.
Schluchter, Wolfgang
1981   *The Rise of Western Rationalism: Max Weber's Developmental History*. Berkeley: University of California Press.
Schmidt, Neal, Gooding, Richard Z., Noe, Raymond A., and Kirsch, Michael
1984   "Meta-analyses of Validity Studies Published between 1964 and 1982 and the Investigation of Study Characteristics." *Personnel Psychology* 37:407–422.
Schneider, Louis
1967   *The Scottish Moralists: On Human Nature and Society*. Chicago: University of Chicago Press.
1971   "Dialectic in Sociology." *American Sociological Review* 36:667–678.
Schroeter, Gerd
1985   "Dialogue, Debate, or Dissent? The Difficulties of Assessing Max Weber's Relation to Marx." In R. J. Antonio and R. M. Glassman (eds.), *A Weber-Marx Dialogue*. Lawrence: University Press of Kansas: 2–19.
Schutz, Alfred
1932/1967   *The Phenomenology of the Social World*. Evanston, Ill.: Northwestern University Press.
1973   *Collected Papers I: The Problem of Social Reality*. The Hague: Martinus Nijhoff.
1975   *Collected Papers III: Studies in Phenomenological Philosophy*. The Hague: Martinus Nijhoff.
1976   *Collected Papers II: Studies in Social Theory*. The Hague: Martinus Nijhoff.
Schutz, Alfred, and Luckmann, Thomas
1973   *The Structure of the Life World*. Evanston, Ill.: Northwestern University Press.
Schwanenberg, Enno
1971   "The Two Problems of Order in Parsons' Theory: An Analysis from Within." *Social Forces* 49:569–581.
Schwendinger, Julia, and Schwendinger, Herman
1974   *Sociologists of the Chair*. New York: Basic Books.
Scimecca, Joseph
1977   *The Sociological Theory of C. Wright Mills*. Port Washington, N.Y.: Kennikat Press.
Sciulli, David
1986   "Voluntaristic Action as a Distinct Concept: Theoretical Foundations of Societal Constitutionalism." *American Sociological Review* 51:743–766.
Sciulli, David, and Gerstein, Dean
1985   "Social Theory and Talcott Parsons in the 1980s." *Annual Review of Sociology* 11:369–387.

Scott, John Finley
1963   "The Changing Foundations of the Parsonian Action Schema."
            American Sociological Review 28:716–735.
Scully, Diana
1980   *Men Who Control Health: The Miseducation of Obstetrician-Gynecologists.*
            Boston: Houghton Mifflin.
1990   *Understanding Sexual Violence: A Study of Convicted Rapists.* Boston:
            Unwin Hyman.
Searle, John
1972   "Chomsky's Revolution in Linguistics." *The New York Review of Books*
            18:16–24.
Seidman, Steven
1983   *Liberalism and the Origins of European Social Theory.* Berkeley: University
            of California Press.
Selvin, Hanan C.
1958   "Durkheim's *Suicide* and Problems of Empirical Research." *American
            Journal of Sociology* 63:607–619.
Shalin, Dmitri
1986   "Pragmatism and Social Interactionism." *American Sociological Review* 51:
            9–29.
Sharrock, Wes, and Anderson, Bob
1986   *The Ethnomethodologists.* Chichester, Eng.: Ellis Horwood.
Shreve, Anita
1989   *Women Together, Women Alone: The Legacy of the Consciousness Raising
            Movement.* New York: Viking.
Shweder, Richard A., and Fiske, Donald W.
1986   "Introduction: Uneasy Social Science." In D. W. Fiske and R. A.
            Shweder (eds.), *Metatheory in Social Science.* Chicago: University of
            Chicago Press: 1–18.
Sica, Alan
1986   "Hermeneutics and Axiology: The Ethical Content of Interpretation." In
            M. L. Wardell and S. P. Turner (eds.), *Sociological Theory in Transition.*
            Boston: Allen and Unwin: 142–157.
1988   *Weber, Irrationality and Social Order.* Berkeley: University of California
            Press.
Simmel, Georg
1903/1971   "The Metropolis and Mental Life." In D. Levine (ed.), *Georg Simmel.*
            Chicago: University of Chicago Press: 324–339.
1904/1971   "Fashion." In D. Levine (ed.), *Georg Simmel.* Chicago: University of
            Chicago Press: 294–323.
1906/1950   "The Secret and the Secret Society." In K. Wolff (ed. and trans.), *The
            Sociology of Georg Simmel.* New York: Free Press: 307–376.
1907/1978   *The Philosophy of Money,* Tom Bottomore and David Frisby (eds. and
            trans.). London: Routledge and Kegan Paul.
1908/1950a "Subordination under a Principle." In K. Wolff (ed. and trans.), *The
            Sociology of Georg Simmel.* New York: Free Press: 250–267.
1908/1950b "Types of Social Relationships by Degrees of Reciprocal Knowledge of
            the Participants." In Kurt Wolff (ed. and trans.), *The Sociology of Georg
            Simmel.* New York: Free Press: 317–329.

1908/1955   *Conflict and the Web of Group Affiliations.* New York: Free Press.
1908/1959a   "How Is Society Possible?" In K. Wolff (ed.), *Essays in Sociology, Philosophy and Aesthetics.* New York: Harper Torchbooks: 337–356.
1908/1959b   "The Problem of Sociology." In K. Wolff (ed.), *Essays in Sociology, Philosophy and Aesthetics.* New York: Harper Torchbooks: 310–336.
1908/1971a   "Group Expansions and the Development of Individuality." In D. Levine (ed.), *Georg Simmel.* Chicago: University of Chicago Press: 251–293.
1908/1971b   "The Stranger." In D. Levine (ed.), *Georg Simmel.* Chicago: University of Chicago Press: 143–149.
1908/1971c   "The Poor." In D. Levine (ed.), *Georg Simmel.* Chicago: University of Chicago Press: 150–178.
1908/1971d   "Domination." In D. Levine (ed.), *Georg Simmel.* Chicago: University of Chicago Press: 96–120.
1918/1971   "The Transcendent Character of Life." In D. Levine (ed.), *Georg Simmel.* Chicago: University of Chicago Press: 353–374.
1921/1968   "The Conflict in Modern Culture." In K. P. Etzkorn (ed.), *Georg Simmel.* New York: Teachers College Press, Columbia University: 11–25.
1950   *The Sociology of Georg Simmel,* Kurt Wolff (ed. and trans.). New York: Free Press.
1984   *On Women, Sexuality and Love,* Guy Oakes (trans.). New Haven: Yale University Press.
Skinner, B. F.
1971   *Beyond Freedom and Dignity.* New York: Knopf.
Skocpol, Theda
1979   *States and Social Revolutions.* Cambridge: Cambridge University Press.
1986   "The Dead End of Metatheory." *Contemporary Sociology* 16:10–12.
Smelser, Neil
1987   "Depth Psychology and the Social Order." In J. Alexander et al. (eds.), *The Micro-Macro Link.* Berkeley: University of California Press: 267–286.
1988   "Sociological Theory: Looking Forward." *Perspectives: The Theory Section Newsletter* 11:1–3.
Smith, Dorothy
1974   "Women's Perspective as a Radical Critique of Sociology." *Sociological Inquiry* 44:7–13.
1975   "An Analysis of Ideological Structures and How Women Are Excluded: Consideration for Academic Women." *Canadian Review of Sociology and Anthropology* 12:353–369.
1978   "A Peculiar Eclipsing: Women's Exclusion from Man's Culture." *Women's Studies International Quarterly* 1:281–295.
1979   "A Sociology for Women." In J. A. Sherman and E. T. Beck (eds.), *The Prism of Sex: Essays in the Sociology of Knowledge.* Madison: University of Wisconsin Press.
1987   *The Everyday World as Problematic: A Feminist Sociology.* Boston: Northeastern University Press.
1990   *The Conceptual Practices of Power: A Feminist Sociology of Knowledge.* Boston: Northeastern University Press.
Smith, Norman Erik
1979   "William Graham Sumner as an Anti-Social Darwinist." *Pacific Sociological Review* 22:332–347.

Smith, T. V.
1931   "The Social Philosophy of George Herbert Mead." *American Journal of
             Sociology* 37:368–385.

Snitow, Ann, Stansell, Christine, and Thompson, Sharon
1983   *Powers of Desire: The Politics of Sexuality.* New York: Monthly Review
             Press.

Snizek, William E.
1976   "An Empirical Assessment of 'Sociology: A Multiple Paradigm
             Science.'" *American Sociologist* 11:217–219.

Snizek, William E., Fuhrman, Ellsworth R., and Miller, Michael K. (eds.)
1979   *Contemporary Issues in Theory and Research.* Westport, Conn.: Greenwood
             Press.

Snow, David, Zurcher, Louis A., and Peters, Robert
1986   "Victory Celebrations as Theatre: A Dramaturgical Approach to Crowd
             Behavior." *Symbolic Interaction* 8:21–42.

Sorokin, Pitirim
1928   *Contemporary Scoiological Theories.* New York: Harper.
1937–1941   *Social and Cultural Dynamics.* 4 vols. New York: American Book.
1956   *Fads and Foibles in Modern Sociology and Related Sciences.* Chicago:
             Regnery.
1963   *A Long Journey: The Autobiography of Pitirim Sorokin.* New Haven:
             College and University Press.

Spencer, Herbert
1850/1954   *Social Statics.* New York: Robert Schalkenbach Foundation.
1864/1883/ *Reasons for Dissenting from the Philosophy of M. Comte and Other
1968   Essays.* Berkeley, Calif.: Glendessary Press.
1873/1961   *The Study of Sociology.* Ann Arbor: University of Michigan Press.
1883   *Recent Discussions in Science, Philosophy and Morals.* New York:
             Appleton.
1892/1965   *The Man versus the State.* Caldwell, Idaho: Caxton.
1897/1978   *The Principles of Ethics.* 2 vols. Indianapolis: Liberty Classics.
1902/1958   *First Principles.* New York: DeWitt Revolving Fund.
1904a   *An Autobiography,* Vol. 1. New York: Appleton.
1904b   *An Autobiography,* Vol. 2. New York: Appleton.
1908a   *The Principles of Sociology,* Vol. 1. New York: Appleton.
1908b   *The Principles of Sociology,* Vol. 2. New York: Appleton.
1908c   *The Principles of Sociology,* Vol. 3. New York: Appleton.

Spender, Dale
1982   *Women of Ideas (And What Men Have Done to Them).* London: Routledge
             and Kegan Paul.

Spender, Dale (ed.)
1983   *Feminist Theorists: Three Centuries of Key Women Thinkers.* New York:
             Random House.

Spykman, Nicholas
1925/1966   *Social Theory of Georg Simmel.* Chicago: Aldine.

Srubar, Ilja
1984   "On the Origin of 'Phenomenological' Sociology." In K. H. Wolff (ed.),
             Alfred Schutz: Appraisals and Developments. Dordrecht, Neth.: Martinus
             Nijhoff: 57–83.

Staats, Arthur W.
1976   "Skinnerian Behaviorism: Social Behaviorism or Radical Behaviorism?"
          American Sociologist 11:59–60.
Stacey, Judith, and Thorne, Barrie
1985   "The Missing Feminist Revolution in Sociology." *Social Problems* 32:301–
          316.
Standley, Arline R.
1981   *Auguste Comte*. Boston: Twayne.
Stanfield, Ron
1974   "Kuhnian Scientific Revolutions and the Keynesian Revolution." *Journal
          of Economic Issues* 8:97–109.
Swartz, David
1990   "The Reflexive Sociologies of Pierre Bourdieu and Alvin Gouldner and
          Metatheorizing in Sociology." Paper presented at meetings of the
          American Sociological Association, Washington, D.C., August.
Swedberg, Richard (ed.)
1990   *Economics and Sociology: Redefining Their Boundaries: Conversations with
          Economists and Sociologists*. Princeton: Princeton University Press.
Symbolic Interaction
1988   Special issue on Herbert Blumer's legacy. 11:1–160.
Szacki, Jerzy
1979   *History of Sociological Thought*. Westport, Conn.: Greenwood Press.
Takla, Tendzin, and Pope, Whitney
1985   "The Force Imagery in Durkheim: The Integration of Theory,
          Metatheory and Method." *Sociological Theory* 3:74–88.
Terkel, Studs
1974   *Working*. New York: Pantheon.
Thomas, William I., and Thomas, Dorothy S.
1928   *The Child in America: Behavior Problems and Programs*. New York: Knopf.
Thomason, Burke C.
1982   *Making Sense of Reification: Alfred Schutz and Constructionist Theory*.
          Atlantic Highlands, N.J.: Humanities Press.
Thompson, Kenneth
1975   *Auguste Comte: The Foundation of Sociology*. New York: Halstead Press.
Tilman, Rick
1984   *C. Wright Mills: A Native Radical and His American Intellectual Roots*.
          University Park: Pennsylvania State University Press.
Tiryakian, Edward A.
1965   "Existential Phenomenology and the Sociological Tradition." *American
          Sociological Review* 30:674–688.
1979   "The Significance of Schools in the Development of Sociology." In W.
          Snizek, E. Fuhrman, and M. Miller (eds.), *Contemporary Issues in Theory
          and Research*. Westport, Conn.: Greenwood Press: 211–233.
1981   "The Sociological Import of Metaphor." *Sociological Inquiry* 51:27–33.
1986   "Hegemonic Schools and the Development of Sociology: Rethinking the
          History of the Discipline." In R. C. Monk (ed.), *Structures of Knowing*.
          Lanham, Md.: University Press of America: 417–441.
forthcoming "Pathways to Metatheory: Rethinking the Presuppositions of

Macrosociology." In G. Ritzer (ed.), *Metatheorizing*. Beverly Hills, Calif.: Sage.

Toby, Jackson
1977   "Parsons' Theory of Societal Evolution." In T. Parsons, *The Evolution of Societies*. Englewood Cliffs, N.J.: Prentice-Hall: 1–23.

Touraine, Alain
1977   *The Self-Production of Society*. Chicago: University of Chicago Press.

Tucker, Robert C. (ed.)
1970   *The Marx-Engels Reader*. New York: Norton.

Turner, Bryan S.
1974   *Weber and Islam: A Critical Study*. London: Routledge and Kegan Paul.
1981   *For Weber: Essays in the Sociology of Fate*. Boston: Routledge and Kegan Paul.
1986   "Simmel, Rationalization and the Sociology of Money." *Sociological Review* 34:93–114.

Turner, Jonathan
1973   "From Utopia to Where? A Strategy for Reformulating the Dahrendorf Conflict Model." *Social Forces* 52:236–244.
1985a   "In Defense of Positivism." *Sociological Theory* 3:24–30.
1985b   *Herbert Spencer: A Renewed Appreciation*. Beverly Hills, Calif.: Sage.
1986   *The Structure of Sociological Theory*. 4th ed. Homewood, Ill.: Dorsey Press.
1989a   "Introduction: Can Sociology Be a Cumulative Science?" in J. Turner (ed.), *Theory Building in Sociology: Assessing Theoretical Cumulation*. Newbury Park, Calif.: Sage: 8–18.
1990a   "The Past, Present, and Future of Theory in American Sociology." In G. Ritzer (ed.), *Frontiers of Social Theory: The New Syntheses*. New York: Columbia University Press: 371–391.
1990b   "The Misuse and Use of Metatheory." *Sociological Forum* 5:37–53.
1991   *The Structure of Sociological Theory*. 5th ed. Belmont, Calif.: Wadsworth.

Turner, Jonathan (ed.)
1989b   *Theory Building in Sociology: Assessing Theoretical Cumulation*. Newbury Park, Calif.: Sage.

Turner, Jonathan, and Beeghley, Leonard
1974   "Current Folklore in the Criticisms of Parsonsian Action Theory." *Sociological Inquiry* 44:47–63.

Turner, Jonathan, and Maryanski, A. Z.
1988   "Is 'Neofunctionalism' Really Functional?" *Sociological Theory* 6:110–121.

Turner, Stephen
1983   "Weber on Action." *American Sociological Review* 48:506–519.

Udehn, Lars
1981   "The Conflict between Methodology and Rationalization in the Work of Max Weber." *Acta Sociologica* 24:131–147.

van den Berghe, Pierre
1963   "Dialectic and Functionalism: Toward Reconciliation." *American Sociological Review* 28:695–705.

Venable, Vernon
1945   *Human Nature: The Marxian View*. New York: Knopf.

Vetter, Betty M., Baber, Eleanor, and Jensen-Fisher, Susan
1982   *Professional Women and Minorities: A Manpower Resource Service.*
            Washington, D.C.: Scientific Manpower Commission.
Vidich, Arthur J., and Lyman, Stanford M.
1985   *American Sociology: Worldly Rejections of Religion and Their Directions.*
            New Haven: Yale University Press.
Wagner, Helmut
1964   "Displacement of Scope: A Problem of the Relationship between Small
            Scale and Large Scale Sociological Theories." *American Journal of
            Sociology* 69:571–584.
1983   *Alfred Schutz: An Intellectual Biography.* Chicago: University of Chicago
            Press.
Wallace, Ruth A. (ed.)
1989   *Feminism and Sociological Theory.* Newbury Park, Calif.: Sage.
Wallace, Walter
1988   "Toward a Disciplinary Matrix in Sociology." In N. Smelser (ed.),
            Handbook of Sociology. Newbury Park, Calif.: Sage: 23–76.
Wallerstein, Immanuel
1974   *The Modern World-System: Capitalist Agriculture and the Origins of the
            European World Economy in the 16th Century.* New York: Academic
            Press.
1980   *The Modern World-System II: Mercantilism and the Consolidation of the
            European World-Economy, 1600–1750.* New York: Academic Press.
1986   "Marxisms as Utopias: Evolving Ideologies." *American Journal of
            Sociology* 91:1295–1308.
1989   *The Modern World-System III: The Second Era of Great Expansion of the
            Capitalist World-Economy, 1730–1840s.* San Diego: Academic Press.
Wallimann, Isidor
1981   *Estrangement: Marx's Conception of Human Nature and the Division of
            Labor.* Westport, Conn.: Greenwood Press.
Wallwork, Ernest
1972   *Durkheim: Morality and Milieu.* Cambridge: Harvard University Press.
Warriner, Charles
1969   "Social Action, Behavior and Verstehen." *Sociological Quarterly* 10:501–
            511.
Warsh, David
1990   "Modern Thinkers Merge Sociology, Economics to Explain Today's
            World." *Washington Post* Aug. 15: D3.
Wartenberg, Thomas E.
1982   " 'Species-Being' and 'Human Nature' in Marx." *Human Studies* 5:77–95.
Wax, Murray
1967   "On Misunderstanding Verstehen: A Reply to Abel." *Sociology and
            Social Research* 51:323–333.
Weber, Marianne
1975   *Max Weber: A Biography,* Harry Zohn (ed. and trans.). New York: Wiley.
Weber, Max
1896–1906/ *The Agrarian Sociology of Ancient Civilizations.* London: NLB.
1976

1903–1906/ 1973	*Roscher and Knies: The Logical Problems of Historical Economics.* New York: Free Press.
1903–1917/ 1949	*The Methodology of the Social Sciences,* Edward Shils and Henry Finch (eds.). New York: Free Press.
1904–1905/ 1958	*The Protestant Ethic and the Spirit of Capitalism.* New York: Scribner's.
1906/1985	" 'Churches' and 'Sects' in North America: An Ecclesiastical Socio-Political Sketch." *Sociological Theory* 3:7–13.
1915/1958	"Religious Rejections of the World and Their Directions." In H. H. Gerth and C. W. Mills (eds.), *From Max Weber: Essays in Sociology.* New York: Oxford University Press: 323–359.
1916/1964	*The Religion of China: Confucianism and Taoism.* New York: Macmillan.
1916–1917/ 1958	*The Religion of India: The Sociology of Hinduism and Buddhism.* Glencoe, Ill.: Free Press.
1921/1958	*The Rational and Social Foundations of Music.* Carbondale: Southern Illinois University Press.
1921/1963	*The Sociology of Religion.* Boston: Beacon Press.
1921/1968	*Economy and Society.* 3 vols. Totowa, N.J.: Bedminster Press.
1922–1923	"The Social Psychology of the World Religions." In H. H. Gerth and C. W. Mills (eds.), *From Max Weber: Essays in Sociology.* New York: Oxford University Press: 267–301.
1927/1981	*General Economic History.* New Brunswick, N.J.: Transaction Books.

Weingartner, Rudolph H.

1959	"Form and Content in Simmel's Philosophy of Life." In K. Wolff (ed.), *Essays on Sociology, Philosophy and Aesthetics.* New York: Harper Torchbooks: 33–60.

White, Hayden

1973	*The Historical Imagination in Nineteenth-Century Europe.* Baltimore: Johns Hopkins University Press.

Whitehead, Alfred North

1917/1974	*The Organization of Thought, Educational and Scientific.* Westport, Conn.: Greenwood Press.

Whyte, William F.

1961	"Parsons' Theory Applied to Organizations." In M. Black (ed.), *The Social Theories of Talcott Parsons.* Englewood Cliffs, N.J.: Prentice-Hall: 250–267.

Wiley, Norbert

1979	"The Rise and Fall of Dominating Theories in American Sociology." In W. Snizek, E. Fuhrman, and M. Miller (eds.), *Contemporary Issues in Theory and Research.* Westport, Conn.: Greenwood Press: 47–79.
1986	"Early American Sociology and *The Polish Peasant.*" *Sociological Theory* 4:20–40.
1988	"The Micro-Macro Problem in Social Theory." *Sociological Theory* 6:254–261.
1989	"Response to Ritzer." *Sociological Theory* 7:230–231.

Williams, Robin

1980a	"Talcott Parsons: The Stereotypes and the Reality." *American Sociologist* 15:64–66.
1980b	"Pitirim Sorokin: Master Sociologist and Prophet." In R. Merton and

M. W. Riley (eds.), *Sociological Traditions from Generation to Generation*. Norwood, N.J.: Ablex: 93–107.

Wilner, Patricia
1985   "The Main Drift of Sociology between 1936 and 1982." *History of Sociology: An International Review* 5:1–20.

Wiltshire, David
1978   *The Social and Political Thought of Herbert Spencer*. London: Oxford University Press.

Wolf, Frederic M.
1986   *Meta-Analysis: Quantitative Methods for Research Synthesis*. Beverly Hills, Calif.: Sage University Papers.

Worsley, Peter
1982   *Marx and Marxism*. Chichester, Eng.: Ellis Horwood.

Wright, Erik Olin
1985   *Classes*. London: Verso.
1987   "Toward a Post-Marxist Radical Social Theory." *Contemporary Sociology* 16:748–753.

Wright, Erik Olin, and Martin, Bill
1987   "The Transformation of the American Class Structure, 1960–1980." *American Journal of Sociology* 93:1–29.

Yeatman, Anna
1987   "Women, Domestic Life and Sociology." In C. Pateman and E. Gross (eds.), *Feminist Challenges: Social and Political Challenges*. Boston: Northeastern University Press: 157–172.

Zeitlin, Irving M.
1981   *Ideology and the Development of Sociological Theory*. 2nd ed. Englewood Cliffs, N.J.: Prentice-Hall.
1990   *Ideology and the Development of Sociological Theory*. 4th ed. Englewood Cliffs, N.J.: Prentice-Hall.

Znaniecki, Florian
1934   *Method of Sociology*. New York: Farrar and Rhinehart.

Zurcher, Louis A.
1985   "The War Game: Organization Scripting and the Expression of Emotion." *Symbolic Interaction* 8:191–206.

NAME INDEX

427

SUBJECT INDEX